Frontiers in Sociology and Social Research

Volume 2

Series editor
John DeLamater
Department of Sociology, University of Wisconsin, Madison, USA

Frontiers of Sociology and Sociological Research publishes a series of edited volumes that will focus on new directions in (sub)specialties of sociology as these are reflected in novel theoretical paradigms, innovative methodologies, and contemporary substantive findings that exemplify and anticipate trends in these fields. The volumes will parallel and complement the volumes in the *Handbooks of the Sociology and Social Research* series. *Frontiers of Sociology and Sociological Research* series begins where the *Handbooks* leave off by looking to the future. The series is predicated on the observation that any field of knowledge in contemporary times is a dynamic, rapidly changing body of perspectives and understanding that continuously builds upon the foundation of extant scholarship.

More information about this series at http://www.springer.com/series/8690

Duane F. Alwin · Diane H. Felmlee
Derek A. Kreager
Editors

Social Networks and the Life Course

Integrating the Development of Human Lives and Social Relational Networks

Springer

Editors
Duane F. Alwin
Department of Sociology and Criminology
Pennsylvania State University
University Park, PA, USA

Diane H. Felmlee
Department of Sociology and Criminology
Pennsylvania State University
University Park, PA, USA

Derek A. Kreager
Department of Sociology and Criminology
Pennsylvania State University
University Park, PA, USA

Frontiers in Sociology and Social Research
ISBN 978-3-030-10072-8 ISBN 978-3-319-71544-5 (eBook)
https://doi.org/10.1007/978-3-319-71544-5

Printed on acid-free paper

This Springer imprint is published by the registered company Springer International Publishing AG part of Springer Nature.
The registered company address is: Gewerbestrasse 11, 6330 Cham, Switzerland

We dedicate this book to those whose lives we are linked and whose support made it possible

Foreword

When I was in graduate school at the University of Minnesota many years ago, two then junior scholars – a sociologist and a statistician, Joe Galaskiewicz and Stanley Wasserman – initiated what seemed to me a most exciting and productive working group on social networks (they continued collaborating; see Wasserman and Galaskiewicz 1994). In this working group, I learned about the measurement of such concepts as network density and network centrality, even as I was simultaneously being heavily influenced by Glen Elder's seminal work on the life course, *Children of the Great Depression* (1974). I was drawn to what seemed to be two important strands of social research, but I never thought about putting the two – network and life-course framings – together. Rather, I felt I had to choose one over the other in order to define my own field of specialization. Picking up Glen Elder at the airport when he came to Minnesota, and talking to him while getting lost on the way to Reuben Hill's house, served to seal my identity as a (gendered) life-course scholar – a small biographical example of linked lives.

In hindsight and after reading *Social Networks and the Life Course*, it is readily apparent that social network and life-course theoretical and empirical approaches address relationships in overlapping ways. Both focus on the importance of social context. Both delineate descriptive patterns of and heterogeneity in social relations, as well as their antecedents, mechanisms, and consequences. Both often move back and forth across levels of analysis. Both are frequently dynamic in presuming, if not empirically examining, continuities and changes over time. Both capture disparities, what Tilly (1998) called *durable inequalities*. But prior to this book, with a few key exceptions (e.g., Cornwell et al. 2008; Cornwell and Schafer 2016), both remained remarkably isolated from one another.

That is what makes *Social Networks and the Life Course* pathbreaking. It is not simply a compilation of conference papers; rather, it breaks new ground by demonstrating how concepts and methodologies from these two fields can be integrated in ways that advance both social theory and social research.

Social relations are the stuff of social networks, to be sure, but they have also been the *mechanisms* for understanding individual lives, beginning as early as Thomas and Znaniecki (1918–1920), a hundred years ago as a way of capturing social change, and further fleshed out by Elder's advances in life-course inquiry spanning two centuries (e.g., Elder 1974; Elder and George 2016).

Fruitful collaborations, concepts, methods, and propositions could well be the resulting impacts of such integration (c.f. Alwin 2012). In his 25th anniversary edition of *Children of the Great Depression* (Elder 1999), Elder identifies four key principles, all of which can inform the integration of network and life-course perspectives.

The first principle is "The life course of individuals is embedded in and shaped by the historical times and events they experiences over their lifetime" (Elder 1999:304). The network/life-course synergy exemplified in *Social Networks and the Life Course* is coming at a time when disruptions in institutions, technologies, and lives are commonplace, reminiscent of the period when *The Polish Peasant* was written (Thomas and Znaniecki 1918–1920). Change may indeed be constant in societies, social relationships, and biographies, but the *pace* of disruption accelerates at certain times and places. I would argue this is just such a moment in history and that studies of social relations need grounding in this whirlwind of multilayered and multilevel transformations.

Elder's second principle is "The developmental impact of a succession of life transitions or events is contingent on when they occur in a person's life" (Elder 1999: 306). Time and age are fundamental to life-course analysis (Settersten and Mayer 1997); social relations change with changing roles, risks, and resources of individuals as they age (biographical and social time). "Linked lives" and "network ties" are isomorphic, but not quite the same. The concept of "linked lives" in life-course research often invokes the idea of "linked lives through time," while "network ties" typically refers to "network ties at one point in time." But *when* in the life course? Timing matters. It shapes contexts, mechanisms, and meanings, as well as the pathways and processes of relating to one another.

The third principle is "Lives are lived interdependently and social-historical influences are expressed through this network of shared relationships" (Elder 1999: 307). This life-course principle is explicitly about shared relationships occurring in the contexts of history – wars and economic downturns to be sure, but also changing technologies, demographies, organizations, cultures, and social policies (*historical* and *social* time). Witness, for example, the impact on virtually all relationships of the introduction and widespread adoption of the smartphone, which is only 10 years old.

Elder's fourth life-course principle is "Individuals construct their own life course through the choices and actions they take within the opportunities and constraints of history and social circumstances" (Elder 1999: 308). The ebb and flow of social relationships are both personally *and* socially constructed. It is important to remember that the so-called conventional life course of schooling, work and family, and then retirement is itself socially constructed. Scholars like me are arguing for nascent life-course stages, *emergent (or early) adulthood* and *encore adulthood* (Arnett 2004, 2010; Moen 2016; Mortimer and Moen 2016; Settersten and Ray 2010) with corresponding shifts in opportunities and constraints around entering, remaining in, or exiting relationships and roles, as well as the risks, costs, and rewards of doing so. The social organization of education, labor markets, occupations, neighborhoods, consumption, and health care perpetuate differential access to and quality of information, medical treatments, the latest technologies, "good" jobs (e.g., Kalleberg 2011), and other resources, along with different lifestyle behaviors (such as smoking, exercise, sleeping, and diet/eating habits).

The chapters in *Social Networks and the Life Course* make a compelling case for new ways of collecting data to capture social relations from several vantage points, not just through surveys of individuals. What is required are *group-level data* on couples, parents and children, neighbors, work teams, managers and their direct reports, medical practitioners and patients, care recipients, and care providers. *And* we need to capture these group-level data at different ages and stages of a more varied and disparate twenty-first-century life course. Data are also required on the simultaneously shifting and intransigent *structural contexts* of relationships, the frequently outmoded policies and practices at odds with the driving forces of disruption touching every aspect of the lives and networks of individuals.

Finally, in-depth, *qualitative studies* as well as *creative survey questions* are needed to get to the *meanings* of social ties: Are they voluntary or involuntary? Are they supportive, stressful, or some of each? And why are some people entering or remaining in certain types of social relationships, while others (or the same people at different points in their biographies) are exiting or avoiding them altogether? This gets to the selection issue of agency (Hitlin and Elder 2007a, b: Hitlin and Kwon 2016). What relations are "optional" as it were, and which ones seem thrust upon us? These are only a few suggestive examples of the rich and varied agenda *Social Networks and the Life Course* invokes.

Department of Sociology
University of Minnesota
Minneapolis, MN, USA

Phyllis Moen

References

Alwin, D. F. (2012). Integrating varieties of life course concepts. *Journals of Gerontology, Series B: Psychological Sciences and Social Sciences, 60*(Special Issue II), 7–14.

Arnett, J. J. (2004). *Emerging adulthood: The winding road from late teens through the twenties*. New York: Oxford University Press.

Arnett, J. J. (2010). *Adolescence and emerging adulthood: A cultural approach* (4th ed.). Upper Saddle River: Prentice Hall.

Cornwell, B., & Schafer, M. (2016). Social networks in later life. In L. K. George & K. F. Ferraro (Eds.), *Handbook of aging and the social sciences* (Eighth ed., pp. 181–201). Waltham: Academic Press.

Cornwell, B., Laumann, E. O., & Philip Schumm, L. (2008). The social connectedness of older adults: A national profile. *American Sociological Review, 73*, 185–203.

Elder, G. H., Jr. (1974). *Children of the great depression: Social change in life experience*. Chicago: University of Chicago Press.

Elder, G. H., Jr. (1999). *Children of the great depression: Social change in life experience* (25th anniversary ed.). Boulder: Westview Press.

Elder, G. H., Jr., & George, L. K. (2016). Age, cohorts, and the life course. In M. J. Shanahan, J. T. Mortimer, & M. K. Johnson (Eds.), *Handbook of the life course* (Vol. II, pp. 59–86). New York: Springer International Publishing.

Hitlin, S., & Elder, G. H., Jr. (2007a). Agency: An empirical model of an abstract concept. *Advances in Life Course Research* 11: 33-67.

Hitlin, S., & Elder, G. H., Jr. (2007b). Understanding 'Agency': Clarifying a curiously abstract concept. *Sociological Theory, 25*(2), 170–191.

Hitlin, S., & Kwon, H. W. (2016). Agency across the life course. In M. J. Shanahan, J. T. Mortimer, & M. K. Johnson (Eds.), *Handbook of the life course* (Vol. II, pp. 431–449). New York: Springer International Publishing.

Kalleberg, A. L. (2011). *Good jobs, bad jobs: The rise of polarized and precarious employment systems in the United States, 1970s–2000s*. New York: Russell Sage Foundation.

Moen, P. (2016). *Encore adulthood: Boomers on the edge of risk, renewal, and purpose*. New York: Oxford University Press.

Mortimer, J. T., & Moen, P. (2016). The changing social construction of age and the life course: Precarious identity and enactment of 'Early' and 'Encore' stages of adulthood. In M. J. Shanahan, J. T. Mortimer, & M. K. Johnson (Eds.), *Handbook of the life course* (Vol. II, pp. 111–129). New York: Springer International Publishing.

Settersten, R. A., Jr., & Mayer, K. U. (1997). The measurement of age, age structuring the life course. *Annual Review of Sociology, 23*, 233–261.

Settersten, R. A., Jr., & Ray, B. (2010). *Not quite adults: Why 20-somethings are choosing a slower path to adulthood, and why It's good for everyone*. New York: Random House.

Thomas, W. I., & Znaniecki, F. (1918/1920). *The polish peasant in Europe and America volumes I and II*. New York: Dover Publications.

Tilly, C. (1998). *Durable inequality*. Berkeley: University of California Press.

Wasserman, S., & Galaskiewicz, J. (Eds.). (1994). *Advances in social network analysis: Research in the social and behavioral sciences*. Thousand Oaks: Sage.

Preface

This book is based on papers initially presented at a conference held in University Park, Pennsylvania, on May 1–2, 2015, sponsored by the Center for Life Course and Longitudinal Studies (C2LS). The latter organization, formed in collaboration between the College of the Liberal Arts and the Department of Sociology and Criminology, was established to foster the development of research and scholarship at Penn State University in the study of the life course. The focus of the conference, titled "Together Through Time: Social Networks and the Life Course," was to develop a set of presentations that would serve as the basis of thought and discussion regarding the potential of life-course theories, in combination with innovative social network approaches and methodology, to advance the development of knowledge at the intersection of the two subfields. The organization of the conference was implemented through a committee made up of faculty from the Department of Sociology and Criminology, made up of Duane Alwin, Diane Felmlee, Michelle Frisco, Derek Kreager, and Jeremy Staff. The "Together Through Time" conference was held over a two-day period at the Penn Stater Conference Center in University Park, Pa, with over 20 nationally representative participants present to discuss the life-course concept of "linked lives" and its connection to the field of social networks. As noted, the overarching objective of the conference was to encourage discussion regarding the intersections between the life-course perspective, its concept of "linked lives," and the field of social networks, as well as the incorporation of other network concepts into life-course discourse. Based on the success of the conference, we actively commissioned a set of papers that promised to provide further theoretical, methodological, and substantive developments in the overlap between life-course studies and social network analyses, and these papers form the basis for this book's chapters. These papers collectively focus explicitly on life-course perspectives on social networks, as well as social network perspectives on the life course. As a result, we believe there is much to be gained for both life course and network research in the publication of the chapters of this volume. Last but not least, we wish to acknowledge the assistance of Judy Bowes, C2LS staff member, for her assistance in implementing the goals of the "Together Through Time" conference and Kerri Weitzel for her help in tracking the papers for this volume. Finally, this book and the project on which it is based owes an enormous debt to Susan Welch, Dean of the College of the Liberal Arts, Pennsylvania State University, and Associate Dean Eric Silver, whose financial support of the C2LS made all of this work possible.

State College, PA, USA
June 2017

Duane F. Alwin
Diane H. Felmlee
Derek A. Kreager

Contents

Contributors

Duane F. Alwin Department of Sociology and Criminology, Pennsylvania State University, University Park, PA, USA

Paul R. Amato Department of Sociology, Pennsylvania State University, State College, PA, USA

Vern L. Bengtson School of Social Work, University of Southern California, Los Angeles, CA, USA

Martin Bouchard School of Criminology, Simon Fraser University, Burnaby, Canada

Ronald S. Burt University of Chicago Booth School of Business, Chicago, IL, USA

Deborah Carr Department of Sociology, Boston University, Boston, MA, USA

Jacob E. Cheadle Department of Sociology, University of Nebraska, Lincoln, NE, USA

Benjamin Cornwell Department of Sociology, Cornell University, Ithaca, NY, USA

Robert Crosnoe Department of Sociology, University of Texas, Austin, TX, USA

George De Leon Department of Psychiatry, New York University, New York, NY, USA

Jennifer L. Doty Division of General Pediatrics and Adolescent Health, Department of Pediatrics, University of Minnesota, Minneapolis, MN, USA

Andrea Vest Ettekal Department of Recreation, Park and Tourism Sciences, Texas A&M University, College Station, TX, USA

Robert Faris Department of Sociology, University of California at Davis, Davis, CA, USA

Mark Feinberg Bennett Pierce Prevention Research Center, Pennsylvania State University, State College, PA, USA

Diane H. Felmlee Department of Sociology and Criminology, Pennsylvania State University, University Park, PA, USA

Claude S. Fischer Department of Sociology, University of California, Berkeley, CA, USA

Scott D. Gest Department of Human Development and Family Studies, Pennsylvania State University, State College, PA, USA

Megan Gilligan Department of Human Development and Family Studies, Iowa State University, Ames, IA, USA

Spencer L. James School of Family Life, Brigham Young University, Provo, UT, USA

Derek A. Kreager Department of Sociology and Criminology, Pennsylvania State University, University Park, PA, USA

Edward O. Laumann Department of Sociology, University of Chicago, Chicago, IL, USA

Keunbok Lee Department of Sociology, University of California, Berkeley, CA, USA

Peter V. Marsden Department of Sociology, Harvard University, Cambridge, MA, USA

Cassie McMillan Department of Sociology and Criminology, Pennsylvania State University, University Park, PA, USA

Phyllis Moen Department of Sociology, University of Minnesota, Minneapolis, MN, USA

Jeylan T. Mortimer Department of Sociology, University of Minnesota, Minneapolis, MN, USA

Shira Offer Department of Sociology and Anthropology, Bar Ilan University, Ramat Gan, Israel

Julie Skalamera Olson Department of Sociology, University of Texas, Austin, TX, USA

D. Wayne Osgood Department of Sociology and Criminology, Pennsylvania State University, University Park, PA, USA

Siyun Peng Department of Sociology, Purdue University, West Lafayette, IN, USA

Paulina Inara Rodis Department of Sociology and Criminology, Pennsylvania State University, University Park, PA, USA

Michael J. Rosenfeld Department of Sociology, Stanford University, Stanford, CA, USA

Kelly L. Rulison Department of Public Health Education, University of North Carolina at Greensboro, Greensboro, NC, USA

Marissa Rurka Department of Sociology, Purdue University, West Lafayette, IN, USA

David R. Schaefer Department of Sociology, University of California, Irvine, CA, USA

Markus H. Schafer Department of Sociology, University of Toronto, Toronto, ON, Canada

Richard A. Settersten Jr. College of Public Health and Health Sciences, Oregon State University, Corvallis, OR, USA

Kyler J. Sherman-Wilkins Department of Sociology and Criminology, Pennsylvania State University, University Park, PA, USA

Merril Silverstein Department of Sociology, Syracuse University, Syracuse, NY, USA

Sandra D. Simpkins School of Education, University of California, Irvine, CA, USA

Michaela Soyer Department of Sociology, Hunter College, New York, NY, USA

J. Jill Suitor Department of Sociology, Purdue University, West Lafayette, IN, USA

Jason R. Thomas Department of Sociology and Criminology, Pennsylvania State University, University Park, PA, USA

Yoosik Youm Department of Sociology, Yonsei University, Seoul, South Korea

Jacob T. N. Young School of Criminology and Criminal Justice, Arizona State University, Tempe, AZ, USA

Gary Zajac Department of Sociology and Criminology, Pennsylvania State University, University Park, PA, USA

Part I
Theoretical Perspectives on Social Networks and the Life Course

Chapter 1
Together Through Time – Social Networks and the Life Course

Duane F. Alwin, Diane H. Felmlee, and Derek A. Kreager

Introduction

The life course perspective has made important contributions to many substantive disciplines in recent decades. Indeed, the increase in life course thinking has been remarkable in its abundance and diversity, and in recent years the key principles in this work have drawn the attention of numerous scholars from several different disciplines. These observations are supported by a review of literature published in the recent edition of the *Handbook of the Life Course*, which drew upon the Thomson/Reuters *Web of Science* database of publications (Shanahan et al. 2016, pp. 2–3). The authors provided trend lines for publications using the concept of life course for three fields: sociology, psychology and epidemiology since the early 1990s, making a persuasive case for the proliferation of the term "life course" in research over the past 2–3 decades, especially in the field of epidemiology. Their data revealed very little publication activity prior to 1990, and through 1998 the activity was not substantial, but from then on, the number of publications using the "life course" topic, title or theme increased exponentially. So pervasive has the life course concept become in the social and behavioral sciences in recent years that it was recently adopted by the World Health Organization as its conceptual approach to understanding the determinants of health in older age (Beard et al. 2015, p. 7).

Applications of the life course concept can be seen across a wide range of disciplines and sub-disciplines, from the social sciences (economics, anthropology, sociology and political science), to the epidemiological and clinical sciences (psychology, epidemiology and the health sciences). It has been usefully applied across diverse fields, including the study of child health and development (e.g., Case et al. 2002; Braveman and Barclay 2009), health and aging (e.g., Ferraro 2011; Moen and

D. F. Alwin (✉) · D. H. Felmlee · D. A. Kreager
Department of Sociology and Criminology, Pennsylvania State University,
University Park, PA, USA
e-mail: dfa2@psu.edu

D. F. Alwin et al. (eds.), *Social Networks and the Life Course*, Frontiers in Sociology and Social Research 2, https://doi.org/10.1007/978-3-319-71544-5_1

Spencer 2006; Herd et al. 2011), health disparities across the life span (e.g., Alwin and Wray 2005; Wadsworth and Kuh 2016; Ferraro 2016), demography (e.g., Rindfus 1991; Willekens 1999), criminology (e.g., Laub and Sampson 2003; Sampson and Laub 1996; Wakefield and Apel 2016), family (e.g., Pavalko and Elder 1990; Amato and Keith 1991; Hofferth and Goldscheider 2016), education (e.g., Entwistle et al. 2003; Pallas 2003; Crosnoe and Benner 2016), public health (Halfon and Hochstein 2002; Halfon et al. 2014; Berkman et al. 2011), and epidemiology (Ben-Shlomo and Kuh 2002; Kuh and Ben-Shlomo 2004, 1997). Only recently have life course researchers begun to integrate social network concepts with the study of life course dynamics (see Cornwell and Silverstein 2015; Cornwell and Schafer 2016).

These trends in the use of the "life course" concept mentioned above raise questions about the potential for growth in understanding the dynamics of human lives and the ways in which we may increase our knowledge about the connections between social networks and the life course. The life course perspective assumes that people's lives are uniquely shaped by the timing and sequencing of life events (both intended and unintended), and that lives are embedded in historical contexts, institutional structures and social networks. A key component of the life course perspective is that individual lives are linked both intra-generationally and inter-generationally, and distinctive birth cohort experiences are considered to reflect many of these exogenous influences (Ryder 1965; Alwin and McCammon 2003, 2007). Such social network phenomena are captured within the life course perspective via the concept of "linked lives," which emphasizes the fact that lives are lived interdependently, within and between generations (Elder 1994). The life course framework further assumes that early life events and exposures contribute in meaningful ways to later life outcomes, and that events and transitions occurring in the life course of one individual often entail transitions for other people as well. Various strands of individual life trajectories, (such as schooling, work, military service, marriage, family, criminal histories, wealth and health) are interconnected to one another, and to the life trajectories of persons within the interpersonal contexts and micro-level settings inhabited by multiple people, hence, the concept of "linked lives" (Elder et al. 2003; Elder and O'Rand 1996; Elder and Shanahan 2006).

Our intention in this chapter is both to reinforce the broad appeal of the life course concept and life course perspectives for the study of human behavior, but also to suggest how the integration of ideas about the life course and the understanding of social networks can further the study of both. Our purpose in this chapter is to present the overarching framework within which the understanding of social networks can improve the understanding of the life course, and *vice versa*. Individuals are often the primary focus of sociologists and others, and yet individual lives are linked to one another. People inhabit a multi-layered environment, a set of uniquely nested structures, like a set of Russian Matryoshka dolls. In short, lives are lived interdependently. People inhabit what are called N + 2 systems—dyads, triads, tetrads, and larger interpersonal structures (Bronfenbrenner 1979, p. 47; Felmlee and Faris 2013). At the same time, a large portion of contemporary research on the life course relies on data and methods for studying individuals singly (Belli et al. 2009; Freedman et al. 1988), which rarely includes information on the environments they inhabit and their social networks. Social network analysis has developed into its own field, existing at the intersection of several different disciplines, and there is an important opportunity to capitalize on the developments in the field of social networks and apply these results to the study of lives (see Cornwell and Silverstein 2015). Cross-fertilization among fields, or even sub-disciplines often provides the means by which knowledge is advanced, and we see a significant increase in research that integrates life course theory and social network concepts.

At the same time, most social network studies focus on *social structure*, that is, the relationships among people in a particular group as represented by their social ties and how they produce structures of relationships. Students of social networks do not always incorporate data on individual characteristics and those of their network ties; similarly, studies of individuals typically do not include the characteristics of other persons who are in their social networks. Yet, the topics that social and behavioral scientists study, e.g., marriage, friendship, kinship, caregiving, work, organizational memberships, and neighborhood ties are all relevant to outcomes for individuals, and increasingly, sociological studies are focusing on the social network ties, or the social structures, that bind individuals together over their lives (see, e.g., Cornwell and Silverstein 2015; Cornwell and Schafer 2016; Morgan 1988; Adams 1987; Alwin et al. 1991; Wrzus et al. 2013). Still, greater integration of social network science and sociology is needed, and innovative methodological approaches (especially with respect to gathering data) are necessary to advance knowledge about the interplay of human development and social structures as mediated by social environments and cultural norms. It would be invaluable if sociological theory and methodology were to draw more upon the mathematical and other contributions of social network science (graph theory, visualization tools, block modeling, etc.) with applications to the study of people's lives examined longitudinally (Alwin et al. 2016; Alwin et al. 2006).

Within life course studies, the concept of "linked lives" appears to be less developed than other aspects of the life course perspective, at least as compared to the concepts of life transitions, trajectories, and historical change (see Deborah Carr's chapter in the present volume). Moreover, the concept of linked lives may be operationalized relatively narrowly as the connections between children and their parents, for instance, but not likely to extend to include the potentially powerful school network in which those children are located, for much of the waking hours. A social network perspective, therefore, stretches the concept of "linked lives" to include far-ranging sets of ties, such as those of the school, the neighborhood, friendships, an extended kin network, the workplace, or the institutional setting. A number of sophisticated methodological advances within the social network field are useful for life course perspectives, such as the focus on network centrality, cliques or sub-clusters, weak ties, brokerage, as well as recent exponential random graph models (ERGM).

The field of social networks also could benefit from a more serious consideration of life course concepts and research problems. Social network research often focuses narrowly on specific, methodological innovations and often fails to integrate theoretically with broader sociological approaches. It would be useful if network specialists were to further develop the ways in which their approach overlaps with general, sociological theory; the life course perspective, with its emphasis on "linked lives," appears to be a particularly useful sociological perspective for such a task. Life course theory offers novel avenues of investigation for network researchers. Its dynamic focus on social change, for instance, highlights the notions that the linked lives of networks will seldom remain stable over time and that historical events shape social ties, as well. The life course focus on turning points, furthermore, points to potential stages in time when people's networks are apt to change abruptly, such as when young people exit school.

The Life Course

The life course concept emerged in sociology more than 50 years ago, beginning with Leonard Cain's chapter on "life course and social structure" published in the 1964 *Handbook of Modern Sociology* (Cain 1964). He defined the life course as "those successive statuses individuals are called upon to occupy in various cultures and walks of life as a result of aging" (p. 278). It was not a new idea, as the age-graded nature of stages of human life has been recognized for millenia. For example, Cain noted the writings of Solon, the Athenian poet and lawmaker born in the seventh century, B.C., who suggested a 10-stage life course of 7 years each, beginning with "the boy as the unripe man," and ending with "the time to depart on the ebb-tide of Death" (Cain 1964, p. 277). There are other examples (e.g. Erikson's "Eight Ages of Man," 1950).

Contemporary uses of the life course concept are in many ways more refined and complex. In order to reduce some potential confusion, we distinguish between the *life course* and the *life course perspective(s)*. The former—the life course—consists of a complex set of *interlocking trajectories*, or *pathways*, across the entire life span of an individual (from conception to death). These *pathways* occur within several domains, (e.g., region and nation, gender, race, residence, household, family, schooling, work, health (physical, mental, diet and nutrition), economic conditions, etc.) that are marked by sequences of *events*, *transitions* and *exposures* (ETXs) across (and within) the biologically- and socially-defined life stages (or phases) that comprise the human life span, *embryo*, *infancy*, *childhood,adolescence*, *adulthood*, etc. These sequences and transitions are socially defined and institutionalized (Kohli 1988, 2007). Traversing the *life stages* and moving between them, while experiencing unique sets of ETXs at every stage essentially defines an individual's life course, theoretically producing differential outcomes (Clausen 1986).

On the other hand, *life course perspectives* are disciplinary or sub-disciplinary *lenses* on the life course (as defined above), focusing on people's lives with a particular interest in either one phase of life (e.g., adolescence, or older age) or the connection between two or more phases (e.g., the transition to adulthood, e.g. Hogan 1981; Hogan and Astone 1986; McLeod and Almazan 2003), or the transition to old age (e.g., Ferraro 2001), and/or outcomes within one particular domain

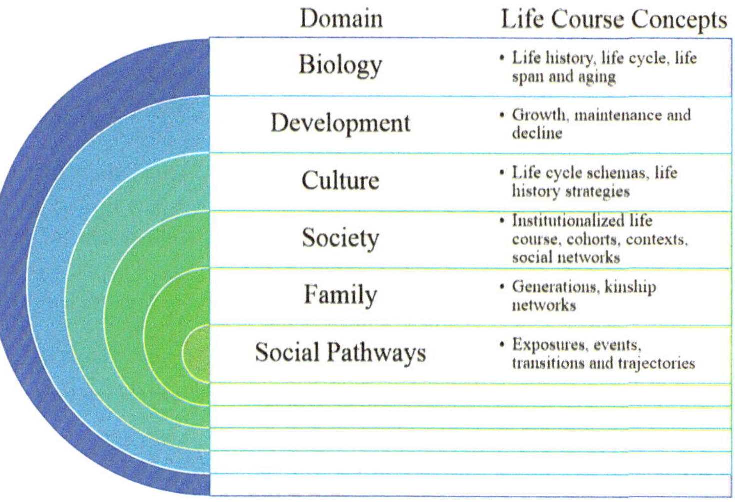

Fig. 1.1 Domains of relevance and key life course concepts

(e.g., health, or education, etc.) (e.g., Ferraro 2016). These elements may combine in such a way that the particular sub-discipline may focus on one set of outcomes during a particular life phase (e.g., chronic disease in adulthood). It is important to emphasize, however, that there is *more than one life course perspective*, each attending to different aspects of the individual's life course. For example, there is a sociological perspective on the life course (e.g., Elder 1994), an epidemiological perspective (e.g. Kuh et al. 2003; Kuh and the New Dynamics of Aging 2007), and so on. In general, life course analysis focuses on the nature and determinants of particular transitions, their timing, their links to events and exposures in earlier life stages, and their consequences for outcomes of human development, for example, health, well-being and mortality in adulthood (e.g., Blackwell et al. 2001; Case et al. 2002; Haas 2007, 2008; Hayward and Gorman 2004; Montez and Hayward 2011; Schafer et al. 2011).

The life course perspectives of today transcend the original notions of age-graded life stages (see Cain 1964). There are several recognizable and distinct life course perspectives and/or paradigms that motivate the study of human lives across many different fields. Each approach relies on its own concepts, which are often mistakenly applied inter-changeably across fields, but each makes a distinctive contribution that deserves notice in mapping this domain (Elder 2000; Alwin 2012). Life course research has made major inroads in understanding the connections between lives, time, and place, and how to handle these complexities in theory and research. Conceptually, these areas are roughly nested within one another, and extend from the species level (which establishes certain fixed parameters) down to the level of the individual life course (where lower-level concepts are nested within the one above). These substantive domains and associated life course concepts are shown in Fig. 1.1. This scheme emphasizes the biological roots of relevant domains (see

Finch and Kirkwood 2000; Olshansky et al. 2002), life history perspectives (Charnov 1993; Roff 1992; Stearns 1992; Carey 2003, 2009; Lee 2003), as well as the cultural and societal contributions to understanding how lives develop (Ellis et al. 2009; Kaplan et al. 2000; Kaplan and Robson 2002; Hogan 2000; Alwin 2015; Sewell 1992), and life-span developmental perspectives (Baltes 1987, 1997; Baltes and Baltes 1980; Baltes et al. 1999; Featherman 1983; Staudinger et al. 1995; Alwin and Wray 2005). Ultimately, the relevant domains include aspects of social networks that are based in society, the family, and individual trajectories. By nesting these concepts across levels of discourse and disciplines, as in Fig. 1.1, we can achieve a much more integrated framework that amplifies meaning and creates a holistic interpretation of lives within a multidisciplinary context (Alwin 2012). Because of space limitations, we do not expand upon the distinctiveness of each of these several different approaches to the study of the life course, as they are thoroughly discussed elsewhere (see Alwin 2012, 2016).

Social Networks

A social network perspective points to the interconnections among actors as a key component of social interaction, with a primary focus on the relational aspects of social processes. Network data then differs from individual surveys typical to social sciences in that there is an equal emphasis on individual attributes and the ties that connect individuals into a web of social relations. The science of networks, similar to the study of the life course, represents a multidisciplinary field that extends to multiple domains, including the social sciences, as well as the physical and biological sciences, computer science and engineering, and in some instances, the humanities.

Not unlike the life course paradigm, social network research also has experienced remarkable growth in recent years. Scholarship in the field demonstrated consistent increases over the past couple of decades, a trend noted consistently across multiple literature searches. For example, in a search of three databases, including Sociological Abstracts, Medline Advanced, and PsychINFO, Otte and Rousseau (2002) detected a largely linear growth in yearly publications on the topic of social networks over approximately a 25-year period from 1974 until 1999. A recent examination of Scopus and PsychINFO continued to document a noteworthy expansion in social network publications, with accelerated growth over the last decade (Felmlee and Sinclair, in press). In 1985, for instance, there were 628 new publications on "social networks"; there were close to three times as many in 2005 (1761), and in 2015 a search on the same topic yielded a total of 9324 novel publications, representing over 12 times as many as 10 years earlier.

Historical Roots of Network Analysis

The roots of modern network models began with the work of Jacob Moreno (1934) and Helen Jennings (1943). Early work focused on the use of sociometric analysis in conjunction with psychotherapy and psychodrama. Barnes (1954) is normally credited with the first use of the term "social network" to refer to a set of social relationships. Divergences occurred in students of networks who studied them from an "ego centric" versus a "socio centric" point of view, that is, taking the perspective of individual actors versus a "social structure" that characterizes the group of network ties. There are several comprehensive reviews of the topic of social networks that follow its development. Freeman (2004) traces the history of the development of social network analysis. Wasserman and Galaskiewicz (1994) discuss a range of substantive applications. Marsden (1990) reviews the literature on the measurement of social networks. Wasserman and Faust (1994) discuss the analytic methods.

The social network perspective shares several common characteristics with those of the life course and dovetails nicely with that approach to social life. Both have conceptual and theoretical elements and implications, for example, but each represents more of a guiding approach to scholarship than a pure theory, per se. In addition, each approach takes a fundamentally social perspective on human behavior, embedding individual actors within a larger social sphere. Both point to interconnectedness among actors as a key to understanding social life, building on the concept of a "network of ties" within the social network tradition and the life course concept of "linked lives."

At the same time, the two approaches contrast in a number of ways. Perhaps the most major point of departure between the two traditions is that the social network approach represents not only a set of theoretical concepts and principles, but it also brings with it a distinct set of methodological procedures to examine social interaction. Network analysis involves a series of unique concepts and an array of methodological tools designed to investigate and incorporate the lack of independence among actors in an extended set of social ties. In addition, the social network perspective generally takes a narrower focus on social interaction than does that of the life course. It points to the interconnectedness of actors, as does aspects of the life course approach, but the social network approach deems this relational nature of interaction as preeminent. Relational ties represent the focus of investigation. Research on the life course might attend to "linked lives," in some cases, but often focuses instead on other concepts such as those of trajectories, turning points, and historical changes. On the other hand, social networks encompass a more extensive notion of actors. Actors in the life course tradition tend to be individuals, whereas those in social networks often consist of a range of alternative entities, such as larger collections of people, including small groups, schools, organizations, and nation states. Social network actors also may entail objects of social value, including books purchased on Amazon, tweets on the social media website, Twitter, and central topics in political discussions.

Principles of a Social Network Perspective

A social network perspective emphasizes that interconnections among sets of actors need to be considered in order to better understand social processes. This approach differs from that of a more individualistic or dyadic viewpoint, because these interconnections consist of actors one step away and reach out to those connected at farther distances, that is, extended ties. Note, too, that two genres of network data exist—egocentric networks and global, or sociocentric, networks. *Ego networks*, or personal networks, are made up of a set of actors, "egos," and the ties that emanate from that set. *Global networks*, on the other hand, contain information regarding all the possible ties between a set of actors and global networks tend to be more extensive than ego networks; ego networks typically do not contain data on the ties between the various egos. The chapters in this book represent both types of network data.

According to several network scholars (e.g., Wasserman and Faust 1994; Wellman 1998), a number of propositions comprise a social network perspective. Several key principles include: (1) The relationships, or sets of ties, among actors serve as the focal point of theoretical and empirical analysis. (2) The behavior of one actor is interdependent with that of actors to whom they are connected. (3) Elements of the structure of the broader network influence actors' behavior. (4) Networks act as conduits for the spread of resources, support, information, rumors, social norms, and other types of positive and negative interchanges among actors. These principles serve as the foundation for much of social network research, pointing to the central relational and structural elements of the network perspective. These network concepts have been useful in life course research focusing on network transitions in older age, e.g., the bridging potential of social networks (Cornwell 2009a, b).

Social Network Concepts and Theories

A number of key concepts characterize a social network approach to scholarship, and we briefly describe several of these. *Degree* refers to the number of *edges*, or ties, that connect one network *node*, or actor, to another in a symmetric, or undirected network graph. In a *directed* network or graph, nodes possess both an indegree and outdegree, where *indegree* measures the number of ties leading towards a node, and *outdegree* is the number of edges that originate with a node and lead outwards. *Network density* measures the overall level of connectedness in a graph, and in a binary network it represents the proportion of all edges that are present, out of all possible edges.

Network centrality represents one of the focal concepts for social network research and has stimulated a considerable amount of scholarship in the field. *Centrality* identifies actors who are the most prominent, influential, or the most connected to others in the network. Numerous measures of actor, network centrality exist (Freeman 1979), and here we focus on three key measures—degree centrality, closeness, and betweenness. *Degree centrality* is the simplest, and it enumerates the number of others to whom each actor is linked. *Closeness centrality* depends upon the shortest path, or *geodesic*, between all other actors, with those who are at shorter distances from others having the highest level of closeness. Actor *betweenness centrality* measures the number of times in which a node occurs as a bridge along the geodesic connecting other nodes (Freeman 1979). Each of these centrality measures taps into a different conceptualization of node prominence, or importance. Network centrality relates significantly to numerous positive and negative outcomes, including job perceptions (e.g., Ibarra and Andrews 1993), performance of individuals and groups (Sparrowe et al. 2001), adolescent drinking (Kreager et al. 2011), school victimization (e.g., Felmlee and Faris 2016), and student satisfaction and performance (e.g., Baldwin et al. 1997).

A focus on network centrality emphasizes strong interconnections in a graph. Granovetter (1973), however, argues that it is the weak ties, rather than those that are strong, that play a crucial role in social networks, where w*eak ties* refer to *network bridges* that provide a link between otherwise disconnected nodes. Because strong ties, such as family and friendship connections, tend to possess similar types of information, novel forms of communication and influence are apt to originate from contacts that are weak and distant (e.g., Ellison et al. 2007; Kreager and Haynie 2011).

Burt's (1992) theory of *structural holes* extends the notion of weak connections to a focus on the actors that serve as bridges, or gatekeepers, in a work organization. A *structural hole* refers to a gap between people in an ego network, and it is individuals that bridge these holes that occupy advantageous positions in firms. Such brokers can transfer or gate keep useful information between groups, or combine information in innovative ways. *Structural constraint*, on the other hand, measures the degree to which a manager's connections are located within a single group of interconnected colleagues, that is, they possess no ability to broker structural holes. The degree to which managers were social brokers in a firm corresponded directly to their level of wages, valued ideas, performance evaluations, and the likelihood of promotion (Burt 2004).

These various network concepts and theories can be combined with a life course perspective in intriguing ways. The notion of "linked lives" can be extended, for example, to note that certain connected lives are more central and influential than others, and that the locus of centrality no doubt shifts considerably over the life course. In addition, people's lives can be influenced by their ties to third parties, not only by direct family and friends, and that such extended ties are worthy of attention. Links between individuals also likely vary in strength, and perhaps surprisingly, it may be their weak, rather than strong, ties that substantially shape life transitions and trajectories over time. Furthermore, having many, deeply interconnected, linked lives may constrain, rather than enhance, peoples' opportunities and innovativeness as they progress through life's stages.

This should not be interpreted to mean that life course researchers have ignored social network concepts. There have been several applications of social network concepts in the study of life course and aging. Due to the importance of social network change in older age, gerontological research has been interested in the extent to which network structure and composition differences in older age impact upon the individual in suboptimal ways (see Ferraro 2001), contributing to the long standing interest of social gerontologists in phenomena relating to health, family, community and other domains in which it offers a fruitful set of avenues for research (Cornwell and Silverstein 2015). There has been considerable research on the social integration of older adults, suggesting that with age there is a decline in access to social support, community involvement and network connectedness (see Alwin et al. 1985; Morgan 1988; Cornwell 2011a, 2012; Cornwell et al. 2008). These results are consistent with other findings, which suggest that both core and peripheral networks decline with age, although some more recent results suggest that family networks are stable in size from adolescence through old age (Wrzus et al. 2013). These results have stimulated more dialogue between social network researchers and social gerontologists, and has focused on older adults' bridging prospects, and while age is unrelated to bridging, some of the phenomena that accompany old age reduce bridging potential. Individual's cognitive and physical health play an important role in social network bridging, making it less likely for those of poorer health to span structural holes (Cornwell 2009a, b). This work raises important questions about the relational advantages that women and men have in older age, contradicting to some extent the traditional stereotypes about women having more close-knit kin-centered networks than men (Cornwell 2011b).

At the same time, the life course perspective nudges social network research in a number of critical directions, one of which is to attend to variation over time. Although recent network methodological advances, and the availability of longitudinal network data sets, enable the study of changing networks, the bulk of work in the field has focused on network structure at one point in time. Furthermore, life transitions, such as shifts between levels of schooling, transitions in and out of marriage, and geographic mobility, often portend considerable fluctuations in one's social network. Life transitions, thus, are also network transitions (Roberts and Dunbar 2015). Moreover, social life is not only embedded within a distinctive social network, according to the life course approach, it is located within a particular cultural and historical framework that, too, fundamentally shapes personal outcomes.

Organization of This Volume

The volume is organized into nine parts, extending from theoretical perspectives to practical applications of social networks and life course perspectives to prevention and social amelioration. The volume begins with theoretical perspectives—life course perspectives on social networks and social network perspectives on the life course. Lives do not exist independently, because they are linked and relationships are formed, developed and are dissolved in the context of those linkages or social networks. In Chap. 2 and 3, writing from the point of view of life course researchers, Richard Settersten and Deborah Carr review the issues that social relations and social networks pose to life course researchers. Settersten's chapter addresses the question of the effects of social relationships on life course transitions and trajectories. His discussion takes a unique approach, in that the tendency in the life course literature is to view this set of issues from the standpoint of life course events and pathways affecting the nature of social ties. By focusing on the reasons social relationships matter for life course events and transitions, Settersten reverses the typical linkage to consider ways in which human lives are constructed socially and "permeate and punctuate" the life course.

Deborah Carr's chapter focuses on the ways in which the concept of "linked lives" has been operationalized in research. A great deal of research on health and chronic disease by epidemiologists, sociologists, psychologists and others has relied on life course concepts. This chapter provides an overview of several integrative themes that have developed within the sociological perspective on the life course: (a) lives are embedded in and shaped by historical context; (b) the meaning and impact of a life transition is contingent on when it occurs; (c) individuals construct their own lives through their choices and actions, yet within the constraints of historical and social circumstances, and (d) lives are "linked" through social relationships – the theme that is most focal to this volume. Her chapter reviews developments in data collection and analytic methods that involve dyadic, family-level and network data, and focuses specifically on one core substantive area—the impact of marriage and marital transitions on health and well-being—that has employed social network concepts in the study of lives.

Social Network Perspectives on the Life Course

The foregoing contributions are complemented by two chapters that take another view, namely the ways in which life course concepts can be used to study network characteristics of individuals. In Part II, there are two chapters written from the perspective of social network specialists employing life course concepts. The chapter by Ronald Burt addresses how the life courses of individuals working within the leadership of organizational units can be understood to interact with participation in organizational activities. The focus of his chapter is anchored on the well-known phenomenon of *network advantage*, and explores how a life-course perspective enriches what is known about this phenomenon. His disquisition builds upon his concept of *structural holes* and the bridging potential of social networks by incorporating ideas of life cycle (or age) into the study of the returns to network advantage with groups of managers. His results show that the benefits of network advantage are age contingent, and his discussion of these ideas leads to a number of interesting questions for future research.

Peter Marsden's chapter on life course events and network composition takes the orientation of looking at how life course events produce outcomes that measure social relationships. This chapter examines social survey data with respect to several, life-course transitions of adults in the general, U.S. population. It proposes that life course events influence individuals' social networks and examines patterns between events and networks using both cross-sectional and longitudinal data from the General Social Survey. The main argument is that changes in the life course affect social networks through a process of creating new opportunities for network interaction and eliminating others. Results suggest that various life course stages and events help to shape network composition and the types of activities involving social networks. Marital status, entry into the paid labor force, and residential mobility, for example, are all associated with network outcomes. Modest gender differences support the argument that the life course experiences of men and women differ, especially concerning family-related events, such as marriage. These findings are borne out by the chapters in Part V (see below).

Marriage and Family Networks

The section of marriage and family networks – Part III – that we propose as a critical part of Together Through Time contains three chapters dealing with essential considerations in conceptualizing how the most fundamental social networks, namely networks connected to marriage and family, affect the individual. The chapter by Shira Offer and Claude Fischer takes advantage of data from the first wave of Fischer's UCNets project, a longitudinal study of personal networks. The study investigates the variability in the availability, accessibility, and mobilization of close kin. The focus of this paper is on the relationships of "close kin" (relationships with parents and their adult children). In many ways the paper is about social support, and is unique in its focus on what are essentially "lifelong connections."

By focusing on just one narrow slice of kinship ties that may involve lifelong connections, the paper by Paul Amato and Spencer James examines the changes in spousal relationships over the marital life course. This chapter addresses an important topic, given that a large proportion of the population is married at any given time. Their analysis of changes in marital happiness is innovative and nicely framed for the volume. The pattern that is documented by which a number of marriages are able to maintain and secure satisfying and rewarding bonds over an extended period of time is indeed surprising, notable, and likely to stimulate further research. The results also have noteworthy ramifications for theories of marital quality and functioning.

Childhood and Adolescent Social Networks

Following the chapters on marriage, in Part IV we turn to the periods of the life course where many social relationships are formed, namely childhood and adolescence. The chapter by Diane Felmlee and colleagues addresses two key questions about adolescent friendship networks: first, what is the nature of change in youth friendship networks, specifically in the nature of popularity and centrality, over a period of 6 years? And second, what changes in social network dimensions (e.g. centrality) are linked to transitions in the institutionalized life course, specifically, the transition from elementary to middle school, as well as leaving middle school to attend high school? This is a very unique set of issues, presented by network specialists interested in the life course. This chapter describes the results from the Promoting School-Community Partnerships to Enhance Resilience (PROSPER) study, which contains a unique set of measures within the context of a powerful study design—data from some 13,200 students who attended middle and/or high schools within one of 28 small public school districts participating in the study. Following a detailed analysis of network characteristics, the authors conclude that the friendship structure of young people often shifts during the years from middle to high school, resulting in substantial, detrimental effects on social networks, particularly network centrality.

Complementing this chapter on the origins of friendship networks in adolescence is the related chapter by Robert Faris and Diane Felmlee, which focuses on an important set of issues regarding adolescent friendship networks, specifically: how much do friendship networks change over significant periods of time, and what are the consequences of stability vs. change for outcomes of interest? This chapter fits perfectly with several other central themes of the proposed volume, as it addresses key questions related to social networks and time for one critical life stage, the period of adolescence. They find that most adolescents experience high rates of turnover in their friendships, with nearly one-third changing their friendship ties every 6 months. They conclude that maintaining high quality friendship ties and letting go of problematic ones is one of the key challenges for adolescents, and this observation is reinforced by their central finding that friendship consistency is critical for the investment in future life goals.

The final paper in this section by Rob Crosnoe and colleagues suggests that social networks at school and relationships at home both contribute to the well-being of adolescents. The authors examine the correlations between adolescents' parental warmth (i.e., "Most of the time your mother [father] is warm and loving toward you."), fitting in at school, and sociometric nominations (indegree and outdegree). They posited that problems at home will transfer to problems at school, either due to socioemotional or neurological deficits. Using data from Add Health saturated schools (i.e., those where network data were collected in Waves 1 and 2), they first predicted feelings of fitting in at school and found that, net of the lagged outcome variable, adolescents who reported less parental warmth reported lower perceptions of school integration. With SIENA analyses of networks in two large schools, they found no associations between negative parent relationships and friendship formation. They conclude that relationships with parents were not consistently implicated in peer dynamics at school, but, when relationships in the home and school were connected, they often pointed to social risks for adolescents with problems at home.

Gender and Social Networks

We have included three chapters that address issues of gender, which all point to the acknowledged premise that the life course is gendered and should be understood as such. Using a large and highly unique study of married and cohabiting couples, Michael Rosenfeld's "Who wants the breakup?" focuses on the question of gender differentials in who initiated a divorce or breakup. Using a sophisticated set of analytic tools, he finds that most divorces were wanted by the wife, whereas for most non-marital heterosexual couples, a breakup was gender neutral. Further analyses involving "competing risks" suggest that power differentials between men and women with regard to education and income do not account for women's preference for a divorce. Findings show, too, that there is a gender gap in marital satisfaction that remains constant over the adult age distribution, and that it has remained relatively stable over the period from 1973 to 2014. Rosenfeld concludes that the findings are consistent with the argument that marriage is a "gender factory," in which traditional gender roles are reproduced.

Markus Schafer's chapter looks at the linkages between a key life course event that occurs in older age, namely driving cessation, and its implications for social network ties. He finds that the processes involved interact with gender. With respect to social networks, the paper focuses on network size, added ties over time, and the bridging potential of social networks. The paper extends the existing literature by focusing specifically on aspects of social networks that tie into themes of autonomy and empowerment in later life. Driving cessation (DC) is an important issue in older age, and especially so in a "car dependent" society. There is a literature on DC in gerontology; but for the most part it is not studied within a life course framework, nor using longitudinal data. While understanding the link between DC and social networks is critical, the paper makes the important observation, as others have, that life course transitions occur in a gendered context; men and women experience life differently, with distinct life trajectories, and these may occur at different ages. The gendered life course is directly applicable to DC transitions in later life, given that driving may have different meaning and role implications for men and women, e.g. women are more likely to be passengers than drivers. Few population-based studies have examined these processes, and Schafer's relies on data from the National Social Life, Health, and Aging Project (NSHAP) to address these issues. Little research has given attention to the different psychological and social implications of DC for men and women, and Schafer's chapter suggests that engagement in social networks may provide a key mediating link to well-being in future research, due to the fact that social networks are key to providing rides (for medical appointments, recreational performances, church, etc.) among other kinds of social support.

Jill Suitor and her colleagues touch on two subthemes of the volume—social support and inter-generational relations. Building on the time-worn observation that social support and psychological well-being are interconnected, they argue there are "costs of caring," a theme developed in the early feminist literature on the family (e.g. in the early work of Jessie Bernard [1972], and in the 1980s by Nel Noddings [1984]). The paper is also linked to the literature, developed in earlier decades, on "role overload" and "role conflict," in which role enactment is conceived of in terms of both its costs and benefits. And, while role burdens of this sort have been studied in inter-generational relationships, the present research focuses on the potential consequences of enacting multiple roles within the same social status, that is, with the same role partner. The authors find that there is an association between performing a multitude of roles for one's mother and depressive symptoms.

Race and the Life Course

Part VI contains two chapters on race and the life course. Duane Alwin and his colleagues investigate the potential linkage between race/ethnicity and social networks within the framework of the "racialized life course." They point out that recent theorizing about present-day racial inequalities minimizes the importance of racial animus, and instead points to major differences among racial/ethnic groups in structural barriers and their access to key social networks. These accounts emphasize family and neighborhood social networks—processes that are historically tied to slavery and the subsequent de-jure period of Jim Crow segregation. Employing the recent work of Daria Roithmayr (2014), they suggest that racial inequalities reflect the "locked in" nature of historically-based institutional racism, according to this argument, not the racist attitudes of protagonists in the contemporary social system. These views are compatible with other theorizing in the social science of race, wherein it is argued that even after centuries of change, associational ties (including marital relationships) of African-Americans in the post-slavery era, are in many ways reproductive of the social connections of institutionalized structures that impoverished them centuries earlier, especially African-American men (Patterson 1998). Using this as a strong theoretical basis for their investigation, they take as problematic differences among racial-ethnic groups in their social networks and associational ties (see McPherson et al. 2001). Using data from the GSS, they examine black-white differences in social network ties in addition to aspects of social participation, and social connections generally. They develop a theoretical discussion of how these network integration measures are tied to the life course. Their results reinforce Patterson (1998) conclusions that in the GSS network data African-Americans register significantly smaller social "core discussion" networks, they have fewer kin in those networks, and (if married) are less likely to include their spouse in their network. The results of their analysis go further in suggesting some of the key black-white differences, not only in the extent of network contacts, but with respect to social participation more generally. While blacks may not have large social networks, they are more likely to activate those they have, resulting in higher social participation levels than whites.

The chapter in Part VI by David Schaefer and his colleagues focuses on racial/ethnic friendship segregation among adolescents. Extracurricular activities (ECAs) within high schools offer the capacity to bring diverse adolescents together and promote friendships that reduce outgroup prejudices. Despite their promise, only a few researchers have tested the effects of ECAs on racial/ethnic friendship segregation. Using data from 108 schools in the National Longitudinal Study of Adolescent Health (AddHealth), they consider two prominent theories that offer insight into the processes by which ECAs might affect intergroup friendship—focus theory contends that activities attract relatively homogenous subsets of the student body, thereby promoting friendship homophily (e.g., racial friendship segregation), whereas intergroup contact theory suggests ECAs can decrease homophily by offering opportunities for familiarization and engagement with peers who are dissimilar. In this chapter, they examine these seemingly contradictory processes and explain how, in fact, they can occur in tandem. At the macro level, ECAs can promote homophily by homogenizing the pool of available friends, whereas at the micro level, ECAs can decrease the relative salience of attributes such as race/ethnicity during friend selection. With a few notable exceptions, ECAs did not predict preferences for homophily, but ECAs did predict the frequency of cross-group friendships, and thus, may provide many of the desired benefits of integration despite not producing short-term changes in friendship preferences.

Tracking Social Networks Through Time

One idea that emerged from many of the papers in this volume is that the nature of social connections varies across the life span, and that life course events tend to concentrate at different life stages. Part VII, explicating a fundamental theme of the book, focuses on the issue of tracking social networks through time. Benjamin Cornwell and Edward Laumann consider older age, examining the question of how social networks are shaped by the experience of the death or other loss of a close network member. Using data on egocentric networks from the National Social Life, Health, and Aging Project (NSHAP) (see Cornwell et al. 2009), covering the period 2005/6 to 2010/11, they find that the loss of confidants due to any cause more than doubles the likelihood that a confidant will be added to one's network. This effect is apparent especially if it involves confidant mortality. Network recruitment in old age is a topic of interest to specialists in aging and gerontology, and this chapter provides a basis for further research into this topic.

The chapter by Yoosik Youm and his colleagues explicitly addresses the question of the changing nature of network composition over the life span, from early adulthood through older age. They approach this topic in a novel way and present a very clever application of latent class models to available measures of network ties using the GSS 2002 network module data. Their chapter develops a latent class model for seven indicators of social network ties, and uses the latent classes of this model to overlay (or cross-classify with) several age groups in order to infer the nature of changes in social network composition over the life span, from early to late adulthood. The key idea behind this paper is that the nature of social connections, or network composition, varies across the life span. Life course events tend to concentrate at different life stages, resulting in an inevitable change in the composition of networks. The content of the paper fits well with the themes of this volume, and one of the few papers that truly focuses on the nature of changes in social networks over a lifetime, and it does so without longitudinal data, but relies simply on a one-off study of social networks. They also take the analysis further by analyzing how various types of network classes are related to a criterion variable, happiness; and how this relationship differs by life stage/age group. Finally, an important part of this paper is its focus on happiness as a criterion to assess the predictive validity of the several "types" of network composition, as assessed in this study. Their goal in this regard is to use personal network composition to relate to overall happiness, and to use the features of "types" of network composition to reason about their effects on happiness.

Inter-generational Social Networks

The two chapters in Part VIII focus on inter-generational social networks. The chapter by Jennifer Doty and Jeylan Mortimer use data from the longitudinal Minnesota Youth Development Study to examine trajectories of levels of closeness from a child towards a mother during adolescence to adulthood (ages 15–36/38). Based on a growth mixture model latent trajectory, they identify three key trajectories of patterns of change in mother-child closeness: high/dynamic, average/decreased, and low/increased. Those in the average/decreased trajectory and those in the low-increased trajectory experienced significantly greater depressed mood than did those in the high/dynamic trajectory. The individuals in the average/decreased trajectory also reported lower self-esteem than those who were classified in the high/dynamic trajectory. Neither past levels of depression or self-esteem, nor negative life events, accounted for the trajectory effects.

The second paper in Part VIII by Merril Silverstein and Vern L. Bengtson investigates the extent to which the family as an institution provides cross-generational continuity. Silverstein and Bengtson focus on religion, arguing that family differences in religion resist social change, and thus, religiosity tends to run in families. The authors frame the intergenerational transmission of religiosity within the context of profound changes in the religious makeup of contemporary society and the changes reflected therein, and argue that religiosity is a trait deeply embedded within families and transmitted across generations. Using longitudinal data from the Longitudinal Study of Generations, a four decade study of multi-generational families, the authors estimate a three-level hierarchical linear model, in which level-1 grandchild-specific variables predict grandchildren's religiosity within parent and within grandparent units; level-2 expresses effects on parental religiosity; and level-3 predicts grandparent's religiosity. This is a good example of how multilevel models can be applied to inter-generational data, especially when children are clustered within parents, and parents within grandparents. In addition, they include an interaction for parental marital history, which augments the model, and again, this is a nice application of multilevel interaction effects. The authors note that grandparents have been little considered in social science research on intergenerational transmission of beliefs and attitudes, and their results attest to the fact that this could be a promising avenue for inter-generational research.

The Potential of Social Networks as Mechanisms for Prevention

Part IX contains two papers that explore the potential of social networks as mechanisms for prevention and social amelioration. Derek Kreager and his colleagues point out the life course transitions commonly found related to criminal desistance, including marriage, military service, parenthood, and steady employment, have proven difficult to translate into policy or miss the most at-risk population in need of change. However, the control capacity of prison provides a unique context for introducing positive peer influence for behavioral change. They discuss how therapeutic community substance abuse treatment programs (within prison settings) rely on peer influence mechanisms to alter inmates' substance use trajectories. Dynamic social network data and methods provide tools for testing the peer influence mechanisms thought to underlie the treatment program and understand how it can become a turning point in addicts' substance use trajectories. The following chapter by Rulison and her colleagues makes a similar case about the potential role of social network analyses for the implementation of substance use and delinquency prevention programs in secondary schools. They argue that a consideration of the dynamic peer contexts of school-based friendship networks helps policy-makers understand how interventions diffuse through the social system. From a life course perspective, a network approach prioritizes between-person interdependence and peer influence to understand how an intervention can create a turning point in adolescents' behavioral trajectories.

Conclusions

There is much to be gained for both life course and social network research to investigate areas where the two fields intersect—a focus on how social relationships matter for the development of lives and how events and transitions in life shape the nature of one's social relationships. The chapters in this volume will be of interest to researchers who study social networks, the life course, or both. This is a large audience, and the appeal is clear—life course researchers are looking for guidance from social networks experts about how to include network concepts and measures in new research, and social network researchers desire a greater understanding of life course concepts and processes in order to more realistically apply their ideas to sociological and behavioral problems. The typical life course researcher has very little understanding of social network concepts and mathematical tools for understanding relational characteristics, and how to best model their effects. There is substantial knowledge to be gained by life course researchers from social network approaches in order to move beyond the universal observation that lives are lived interdependently. This volume can help introduce life course researchers to the theories, concepts, and methods used by social network analysts. At the same time, we envision there is a subset of network analysts who will view the life course framework as a useful paradigm within which to study social structure and transitions of social networks. Moreover, this volume introduces substantive topics in the life course perspective where social network methodologists may apply their mathematical techniques. Both bodies of researchers are the targets of the present volume, as this will hopefully speak to the cross-disciplinary aspirations of the afore-mentioned scholars.

References

Adams, R. G. (1987). Patterns of network change: A longitudinal study of friendships of elderly women. *The Gerontologist, 27*, 222–227.

Alwin, D. F. (2012). Integrating varieties of life course concepts. *Journals of Gerontology, Series B: Psychological Sciences and Social Sciences, 60*(Special Issue II), 7–14.

Alwin, D. F. (2015). *Constructing lives and de-constructing the life course*. Keynote Address. International Symposium on the Life Course. University of Galway. Ireland.

Alwin, D. F. (2016). It takes more than one to tango: Life course epidemiology and related approaches. *International Journal of Epidemiology, 45*(4), 988–993. https://doi.org/10.1093/ije/dyw108.

Alwin, D. F., & McCammon, R. J. (2003). Generations, cohorts and social change. In J. T. Mortimer & M. Shanahan (Eds.), *Handbook of the life course* (pp. 23–49). New York: Kluwer Academic/Plenum Publishers.

Alwin, D. F., & McCammon, R. J. (2007). Rethinking generations. *Research in Human Development, 4*, 219–237.

Alwin, D. F., & Wray, L. A. (2005). A life-span developmental perspective on social status and health. *Journals of Gerontology, Series B: Psychological Sciences and Social Sciences, 60*(Special Issue II), 7–14.

Alwin, D. F., Converse, P. E., & Martin, S. S. (1985). Living arrangements and social integration. *Journal of Marriage and Family, 47*, 319–334.
Alwin, D. F., Cohen, R. L., & Newcomb, T. M. (1991). *Political attitudes over the life span: The Bennington women after fifty years*. Madison: University of Wisconsin Press.
Alwin, D. F., Hofer, S. M., & McCammon, R. J. (2006). Modeling the effects of time: Integrating demographic and developmental perspectives. In R. H. Binstock & L. K. George (Eds.), *Handbook of aging and the social sciences* (6th ed., pp. 20–38). New York: Academic.
Alwin, D. F., Thomas, J. R., & Wray, L. A. (2016). Cognitive development and the life course: Growth, stability and decline. In M. Shanahan, J. Mortimer, & M. K. Johnson (Eds.), *Handbook of the life course* (Vol. 2, pp. 451–488). Cham: Springer International Publishing.
Amato, P. R., & Keith, B. (1991). Parental divorce and adult well-being: A meta analysis. *Journal of Marriage and Family, 53*, 43–58.
Baldwin, T. T., Bedell, M., & Johnson, J. J. (1997). Social networks in a team-based MBA program: Effects on student satisfaction and performance. *Academy of Management Journal, 40*, 1369–1397.
Baltes, P. B. (1987). Theoretical propositions of life-span developmental psychology: On the dynamics between growth and decline. *Developmental Psychology, 23*, 611–626.
Baltes, P. B. (1997). On the incomplete architecture of human ontogeny: Selection, optimization and compensation as the foundation of developmental theory. *American Psychologist, 52*, 366–380.
Baltes, P. B., & Baltes, M. (1980). Plasticity and variability in psychological aging: Methodological and theoretical issues. In G. E. Gurski (Ed.), *Determining the effects of aging on the central nervous system* (pp. 41–66). Berlin: Schering.
Baltes, P. B., Staudinger, U. M., & Lindenberger, U. (1999). Lifespan psychology: Theory and application to intellectual functioning. *Annual review of psychology, 50*, 471–507. Palo Alto: Annual Reviews Inc.
Barnes, J. S. (1954). Class and committees in a Norwegian Island Parish. *Human Relatiolns, 7*, 39–58.
Beard, J. R., Officer, A., & Cassels, A. (Eds.). (2015). *World report on ageing and health*. Geneva: World Health Organization.
Belli, R. F., Stafford, F. P., & Alwin, D. F. (Eds.). (2009). *Calendar and time diary methods in life course research*. Thousand Oaks: Sage Publications.
Ben-Shlomo, Y., & Kuh, D. (2002). A life course approach to chronic disease epidemiology: Conceptual models, empirical challenges and interdisciplinary perspectives. *International Journal of Epidemiology, 31*, 285–293.
Berkman, L. F., Ertel, K. A., & Glymour, M. M. (2011). In R. H. Binstock, L. K. George (Eds.), *Handbook of aging and the social sciences* (pp. 337–352). New York: Academic.
Blackwell, D., Hayward, M. D., & Crimmins, E. M. (2001). Does childhood health affect chronic morbidity in later life? *Social Science and Medicine, 52*, 1269–1284.
Braveman, P., & Barclay, C. (2009). Health disparities beginning in childhood: A life course perspective. *Pediatrics, 124*, S163–S175.
Bronfenbrenner, U. (1979). *The ecology of human development—Experiments by nature and design*. Cambridge, MA: Harvard University Press.
Burt, R. S. (1992). *Structural holes: The social structure of competition*. Cambridge, MA: Harvard University Press.
Burt, R. (2004). Structural holes and good ideas. *American Journal of Sociology, 110*, 349–399.
Cain, L. D. (1964). Life course and social structure. In R. E. L. Faris (Ed.), *Handbook of modern sociology* (pp. 272–309). Chicago: Rand McNally.
Carey, J. R. (2003). The life span: A conceptual overview. In J. R. Carey, & S. Tuliapurkar (Eds.). *Population Development and Review, 29*, S1–S18.
Carey, J. R. (2009). *Longevity—The biology and demography of life span*. Princeton: Princeton University Press.
Case, A., Lubotsky, D., & Paxson, C. (2002). Economic status and health in childhood: The origins of the gradient. *American Economic Review, 92*, 1308–1334.

Charnov, E. (1993). *Life history invariants*. Oxford: Oxford University Press.
Clausen, J. A. (1986). *The life course—A sociological perspective*. New York: Prentice-Hall.
Cornwell, B. (2009a). Network bridging potential in later life: Life course experiences and social network position. *Journal of Aging and Health, 21*, 129–154.
Cornwell, B. (2009b). Good health and the bridging of structural holes. *Social Networks, 31*, 92–103.
Cornwell, B. (2011a). Age trends in daily social contact patterns. *Research on Aging, 33*, 598–631.
Cornwell, B. (2011b). Independence through social networks: A comparison of older men's and women's bridging potential. *Journals of Gerontology: Social Sciences, 66B*, 782–794.
Cornwell, B. (2012). Spousal network overlap as a basis for spousal support. *Journal of Marriage and Family, 74*, 229–238.
Cornwell, B., & Schafer, M. (2016). Social networks in later life. In L. K. George & K. F. Ferraro (Eds.), *Handbook of aging and the social sciences* (8th ed., pp. 181–201). Waltham: Academic.
Cornwell, B., & Silverstein, M. (2015). The social network approach in Gerontological research. *Journal of Gerontology Series B: Psychological and Social Sciences, 70*, 87–90.
Cornwell, B., Laumann, E. O., & Philip Schumm, L. (2008). The social connectedness of older adults: A national profile. *American Sociological Review, 73*, 185–203.
Cornwell, B., Laumann, E. O., Philip Schumm, L., & Graber, J. (2009). Social networks in the NSHAP study: Rationale, measurement, and preliminary findings. *Journals of Gerontology: Social Sciences, 64B*(S1), 47–55.
Crosnoe, R., & Benner, A. D. (2016). Educational pathways. In M. J. Shanahan, J. T. Mortimer, & M. K. Johnson (Eds.), *Handbook of the Life Course* (Vol. 2, pp. 179–200). Cham: Springer International Publishing.
Elder, G. H., Jr. (1994). Time, human agency, and social change: Perspectives on the life course. *Social Psychology Quarterly, 57*, 4–15.
Elder, G. H., Jr. (2000). The life course. In E. F. Borgatta & R. J. V. Montgomery (Eds.), *Encyclopedia of sociology* (Vol. 3, 2nd ed., pp. 1614–1622). New York: Macmillan Reference USA.
Elder, G. H., Jr., & O'Rand, A. M. (1996). Adult lives in a changing society. In K. S. Cook, G. A. Fine, & J. S. House (Eds.), *Sociological perspectives on social psychology* (pp. 452–475). Boston: Allyn and Bacon.
Elder, G. H., Jr., & Shanahan, M. J. (2006). The life course and human development. In W. Damon & R. M. Lerner (Eds.), *Handbook of child psychology. 6th edition. Volume 1: Theoretical models of human development* (pp. 665–715). New York: Wiley.
Elder, G. H., Jr., Johnson, M. K., & Crosnoe, R. (2003). The emergence and development of life course theory. In J. T. Mortimer & M. J. Shanahan (Eds.), *Handbook of the life course* (pp. 3 19). New York: Kluwer Academic/Plenum Publishers.
Ellis, B. C., Figueredo, A. J., Brumbach, B. H., & Schlomer, G. L. (2009). Fundamental dimensions of environmental risk. *Human Nature, 20*, 204–268.
Ellison, N. B., Steinfield, C., & Lampe, C. (2007). The benefits of Facebook "friends:" Social capital and college students' use of online social network sites. *Journal of Computer-Mediated Communication, 12*, 1143–1168.
Entwistle, D., Alexander, K. L., & Olson, L. S. (2003). The first-grade transition in life course perspective. In J. T. Mortimer & M. J. Shanahan (Eds.), *Handbook of the life course* (pp. 229–250). New York: Kluwer Academic/Plenum Publishers.
Erikson, E. H. (1950). *Childhood and society*. New York: W.W. Norton & Company.
Featherman, D. L. (1983). Life-span perspectives in social science research. In P. B. Baltes & O. G. Brim Jr. (Eds.), *Life-span development and behavior* (Vol. 5, pp. 1–57). New York: Academic.
Felmlee, D., & Colleen Sinclair, H. (In Press). Social networks and personal relationships. In A. Vangelisti & D. Perlman (Eds.), *The Cambridge handbook of personal relationships* (2nd ed.). London: Cambridge University Press.
Felmlee, D., & Faris, R. (2013). Interaction in social networks. In J. Delamater & A. Ward (Eds.), *Handbook of social psychology* (2nd ed., pp. 389–409). New York: Springer.
Felmlee, D., & Faris, R. (2016). Toxic ties: Networks of friendship, dating, and cyber victimization. *Social Psychology Quarterly, 79*, 243–262.

Ferraro, K. F. (2001). Aging and role transitions. In R. H. Binstock & L. K. George (Eds.), *Handbook of aging and the social sciences* (5th ed., pp. 313–330). New York: Academic.
Ferraro, K. F. (2011). Health and aging: Early origins, persistent inequalities. In R. A. Settersten Jr. & J. L. Angel (Eds.), *Handbook of sociology of aging* (pp. 465–475). NewYork: Springer.
Ferraro, K. F. (2016). Life course lens on aging and health. In M. J. Shanahan, J. T. Mortimer, & M. K. Johnson (Eds.), *Handbook of the life course* (Vol. 2, pp. 389–406). Cham: Springer International Publishing.
Finch, C. E., & Kirkwood, T. B. L. (2000). *Chance, development and aging*. Oxford: Oxford University Press.
Freedman, D., Thornton, A., Camburn, D., Alwin, D. F., & Young-DeMarco, L. (1988). The life history calendar: A technique for collecting retrospective data. In C. C. Clogg (Ed.), *Sociological methodology* (pp. 37–68). Washington, DC: American Sociological Association.
Freeman, L. C. (1979). Centrality in social networks I: Conceptual clarification. *Social Networks, 1*, 215–239.
Freeman, L. C. (2004). *The development of social network analysis: A study in the sociology of science*. Vancouver: Empirical Press.
Granovetter, M. S. (1973). The strength of weak ties. *American Journal of Sociology, 78*, 1360–1380.
Haas, S. A. (2007). The long-term effects of poor childhood health: An assessment and application of retrospective reports. *Demography, 44*(1), 113–135.
Haas, S. A. (2008). Trajectories of functional health: The 'long arm' of childhood health and socioeconomic factors. *Social Science and Medicine, 66*(4), 849–861.
Halfon, N., & Hochstein, M. (2002). Life course health development: An integrated framework for developing health, policy and research. *The Milbank Quarterly, 80*, 433–479.
Halfon, N., Larson, K., Lu, M., Tullis, E., & Russ, S. (2014). Lifecourse health development: Past, present and future. *Maternal and Child Health Journal, 18*, 344–365.
Hayward, M. D., & Gorman, B. K. (2004). The long arm of childhood: The influence of early-life social conditions on men's mortality. *Demography, 41*, 87–107.
Herd, P., Robert, S. A., & House, J. S. (2011). Health disparities among older adults: Life course influences and policy solutions. In R. H. Binstock & L. K. George (Eds.), *Handbook of aging and the social sciences* (pp. 121–134). New York: Academic.
Hofferth, S., & Goldscheider, F. (2016). Family heterogeneity over the life course. In M. J. Shanahan, J. T. Mortimer, & M. K. Johnson (Eds.), *Handbook of the life course* (Vol. 2, pp. 161–178). Cham: Springer International Publishing.
Hogan, D. P. (1981). *Transitions and social change: The early lives of American men*. New York: Academic.
Hogan, D. P. (2000). Life cycle. In E. F. Borgatta & R. J. V. Montgomery (Eds.), *Encyclopedia of sociology* (2nd ed., pp. 1623–1627). New York: Macmillan.
Hogan, D. P., & Astone, N. M. (1986). The transition to adulthood. *Annual Review of Sociology, 12*, 109–130.
Ibarra, H., & Andrews, S. B. (1993). Power, social influence, and sense making: Effects of network centrality and proximity on employee perceptions. *Administrative Science Quarterly, 38*, 277–303.
Jennings, H. H. (1943). *Leadership and isolation*. New York: Longmans, Green.
Kaplan, H. S., & Robson, A. J. (2002). The emergence of humans: The coevolution of intelligence and longevity with intergenerational transfers. *Proceedings of the National Academy of Sciences USA, 99*, 10221–10226.
Kaplan, H. S., Hill, K., Lancaster, J. B., & Hurtado, A. M. (2000). A theory of human life history evolution: Diet, intelligence, and longevity. *Evolutionary Anthropology, 9*, 156–185.
Kohli, M. (1988). Ageing as a challenge for sociological theory. *Ageing and Society, 8*, 367–394.
Kohli, M. (2007). The institutionalization of the life course: Looking back to look ahead. *Research in Human Development, 4*, 253–271.
Kreager, D. A., & Haynie, D. L. (2011). Dangerous liaisons? Dating and drinking diffusion in adolescent peer networks. *American Sociological Review, 76*(5), 737–763.

Kreager, D. A., Rulison, K., & Moody, J. (2011). Delinquency and the structure of adolescent peer groups. *Criminology, 49*(1), 95–127.
Kuh, D., & Ben-Shlomo, Y. (2004). *A life course approach to chronic disease epidemiology* (2nd ed.). Oxford: Oxford University Press. [1st edition, 1997].
Kuh, D., & the New Dynamics of Ageing Preparatory Network. (2007). A life course approach to healthy aging, frailty, and capability. *Journal of Gerontology: Medical Sciences, 62A*, 717–721.
Kuh, D., Ben-Shlomo, Y., John, L., Hallqvist, J., & Power, C. (2003). Life course epidemiology. *Journal of Epidemiology and Community Health, 57*, 778–783.
Laub, J. H., & Sampson, R. J. (2003). *Shared beginnings, divergent lives: Delinquent boys to age 70*. Cambridge, MA: Harvard University Press.
Lee, R. D. (2003). Rethinking the evolutionary theory of aging: Transfers, not births, shape senescence in social species. *Proceedings of the National Academic of Sciences, 100*, 9637–9642.
Marsden, P. V. (1990). Network data and measurement. *Annual Review of Sociology, 16*, 435–463.
McLeod, J. D., & Almazan, E. P. (2003). Connections between childhood and adulthood. In J. T. Mortimer & M. Shanahan (Eds.), *Handbook of the life course* (pp. 391–411). New York: Kluwer Academic/Plenum Publishers.
McPherson, M., Smith-Lovin, L., & Cook, J. M. (2001). Birds of a feather: Homophily in social networks. *Annual Review of Sociology, 27*(1), 415–444.
Moen, P., & Spencer, D. (2006). Converging divergences in age, gender, health, and well-being: Strategic selection in the Third Age. In R. A. Binstock & L. K. George (Eds.), *Handbook of aging and the social sciences* (6th ed., pp. 127–144). New York: Academic Press.
Montez, J. K., & Hayward, M. D. (2011). Early life conditions and later life mortality. In R. G. Rogers & E. M. Crimmings (Eds.), *International handbook of adult mortality* (pp. 187–206). Dordrecht: Springer.
Moreno, J. L. (1934). *Who shall survive?* Washington, DC: Nervous and Mental Disease Publishing.
Morgan, D. L. (1988). Age differences in social network participation. *Journal of Gerontology: Social Sciences, 43*, S129–S137.
Olshansky, S. J., Carnes, B. A., & Brody, J. (2002). A biodemographic interpretation of life span. *Population and Development Review, 28*, 501–513.
Otte, E., & Rousseau, R. (2002). Social network analysis: A powerful strategy, also for the information sciences. *Journal of Information Sciences, 28*, 441–453.
Pallas, A. M. (2003). Educational transitions, trajectories and pathways (pp. 165–184). In J. T. Mortimer & M. Shanahan (Eds.), *Handbook of the life course* (pp. 23–49). New York: Kluwer Academic/Plenum Publishers.
Patterson, O. (1998). *Rituals of blood: Consequences of slavery in two American centuries*. New York: Basic Civitas.
Pavalko, E. K., & Elder, G. H., Jr. (1990). World War II and divorce: A life course perspective. *American Journal of Sociology, 95*, 1213–1234.
Rindfus, R. R. (1991). The young adult years: Diversity, structural change, and fertility. *Demography, 28*, 493–512.
Roberts, S. B. G., & Dunbar, R. I. M. (2015). Managing relationship decay: Network, gender and contextual effects. *Human Nature, 26*(4), 426–450.
Roff, D. (1992). *The evolution of life histories: Theory and analysis*. New York: Chapman and Hall.
Roithmayr, D. (2014). *Reproducing racism: How everyday choices lock in white advantage*. New York: New York University Press.
Ryder, N. B. (1965). The cohort as a concept in the study of social change. *American Sociological Review, 30*, 843–861.
Sampson, R. J., & Laub, J. H. (1996). Socioeconomic achievement in the life course of disadvantaged men: Military service as a turning point, circa 1940–1965. *American Sociological Review, 61*, 347–367.
Schafer, M. H., Ferraro, K. F., & Mustillo, S. A. (2011). Children of misfortune: Early adversity and cumulative inequality in perceived life trajectories. *American Journal of Sociology, 116*, 1053–1091.
Sewell, W. H., Jr. (1992). A theory of structure: Duality, agency, and transformation. *American Journal of Sociology, 98*, 1–29.

Shanahan, M. J., Mortimer, J. T., & Johnson, M. K. (2016). Introduction: Life course studies – Trends, challenges, and future directions. In Shanahan et al. (Eds.), *Handbook of the life course* (Vol. 2, pp. 1–23). Cham: Springer International Publishing.

Sparrowe, R. T., Liden, R. C., Wayne, S. J., & Kraimer, M. L. (2001). Social networks and the performance of individuals and groups. *Academy of Management Journal, 44*, 316–325.

Staudinger, U. M., Marsiske, M., & Baltes, P. B. (1995). Resilience and reserve capacity in later adulthood: Potentials and limits of development across the life span. In D. Cicchetti & C. Cohen (Eds.), *Developmental psychopathology.: Vol. 2: Risk, disorder, and adaptation* (pp. 801–847). New York: Wiley.

Stearns, S. (1992). *The evolution of life histories*. Oxford: Oxford University Press.

Wadsworth, M. E. J., & Kuh, D. (2016). Epidemiological perspectives on the life course. In M. J. Shanahan, J. T. Mortimer, & M. K. Johnson (Eds.), *Handbook of the life course* (Vol. 2, pp. 639–659). Cham: Springer International Publishing.

Wakefield, S., & Apel, R. (2016). Criminal justice and the life course. In M. J. Shanahan, J. T. Mortimer, & M. K. Johnson (Eds.), *Handbook of the life course* (Vol. 2, pp. 301–319). Cham: Springer International Publishing.

Wasserman, S., & Faust, K. (1994). *Social network analysis: Methods and applications*. New York: Cambridge University Press.

Wasserman, S., & Galaskiewicz, J. (Eds.). (1994). *Advances in social network analysis: Research in the social and behavioral sciences*. Thousand Oaks: Sage.

Wellman. (1998). Structural analysis: From method and metaphor to theory and substance. In B. Wellman & S. D. Berkowitz (Eds.), *Social structures: A network approach* (pp. 19–61). Cambridge: Cambridge University Press.

Willekens, F. J. (1999). The life course: Models and analysis. In L. J. G. van Wissen & P. A. Dykstra (Eds.), *Population issues: An interdisciplinary focus* (pp. 23–51). New York: Kluwer Academic/Plenum Publishers.

Wrzus, C., Hänel, M., Wagner, J., & Neyer, F. J. (2013). Social network changes and life events across the life span: A meta-analysis. *Psychological Bulletin, 139*, 53–80.

Duane F. Alwin is the inaugural holder of the Tracy Winfree and Ted H. McCourtney Professorship in Sociology and Demography at Pennsylvania State University, where he directs the Center for Life Course and Longitudinal Studies. He is also Emeritus Research Professor at the Survey Research Center, Institute for Social Research and Emeritus Professor of Sociology, University of Michigan, Ann Arbor, where he was affiliated for 23 years. His main areas of specialization include research methods, social stratification, social psychology, family and the life course.

Diane H. Felmlee is Professor of Sociology and Demography at Pennsylvania State University and Research Associate in the Population Research Institute. Her interests lie at the intersection of social networks and life course studies, pursuing research on aggression and friendship networks, cyberbullying, and gender inequalities.

Derek A. Kreager is Professor of Sociology, Criminology, and Demography at Pennsylvania State University, Research Associate in the Population Research Institute, and Director of the Justice Center for Research. His research focuses on social networks and criminal/delinquent behavior, including the connection between the experiences of incarceration and community re-entry.

Chapter 2
Nine Ways That Social Relationships Matter for the Life Course

Richard A. Settersten Jr.

Human life is social. Indeed, an individual's life course is hardly their own because it is so enmeshed with other people. A key tenet of a life course perspective – 'linked lives,' first put forward by Glen Elder in 1994 as one of its four 'paradigmatic principles' – reflects these interdependencies by underscoring the fact that an individual's life affects and is affected by others (see also Carr, Chap. 3, this volume).

And yet, analytically, much research on the life course is focused on individuals and operates as if individuals exist in isolation of others. As outlined in Chap. 1, the 'life course' is typically conceptualized as a set of interlocking trajectories that span the life *of an individual* – through domains such as family, education, and work, and marked by particular events, transitions, and other exposures. But those 'individual' trajectories are intimately interwoven with other people, and most 'personal' experiences are actually *interpersonal* (Hagestad and Settersten 2017). One could even argue that there is no such thing as an 'individual' life course.

To say that lives are 'linked' does not reveal how they are linked, for how long, for what purposes, or with what consequences. In this chapter, I briefly sketch nine ways that social relationships matter for the life course. It is my hope to offer some fruitful ideas to not only advance theory and research on the *social* aspects of the life course, but to offer bridges between the study of the life course and the study of social networks, as this book aims to do.

R. A. Settersten Jr. (✉)
College of Public Health and Health Sciences, Oregon State University, Corvallis, OR, USA
e-mail: richard.settersten@oregonstate.edu

D. F. Alwin et al. (eds.), *Social Networks and the Life Course*, Frontiers in Sociology and Social Research 2, https://doi.org/10.1007/978-3-319-71544-5_2

Relationships Permeate and Punctuate the Life Course

We are literally born to other people and, until the moment we die, our lives are stories of 'we' and 'us,' entangled with others. The most intimate of these are family relationships – parents and children (see also Offer and Fischer, Chap. 6; Doty and Mortimer, Chap. 18), spouses and partners (see also Amato and James, Chap. 7; Rosenfeld, Chap. 11), and grandparents (see also Silverstein and Bengtson, Chap. 19).

Chief among life's major turning points are changes in relationship statuses – forming a partnership or marriage, becoming a parent, getting divorced, being widowed. Even the statuses of 'single' and 'childless' signal times when people are without or not yet in relationships that are culturally or statistically normative. The departure of children from home and the death of parents also trigger movement into new life phases. Ultimately, all major milestones in life occur alongside others, or result from contributions or actions of others – whether graduating from high school, pursuing higher education, leaving home, being promoted or demoted, experiencing unemployment, or retiring.

Some transitions even require actions on the part of other people before we, in turn, move into a new status – what has been called 'counterpoint transitions' (Riley et al. 1988) or 'countertransitions' (Hagestad 1981) throughout the family matrix. Marriages and partnerships create 'in-law' relationships; divorces and separations create 'ex' relationships. Parenting prompts transitions into grandparenthood or great-grandparenthood, and turns sisters and brothers into aunts and uncles. Many other life transitions – changes in employment or schools, in residence, or in faith or political party – require us, and the people attached to us, to form new relationships and be incorporated into new networks.

We mark the passage of time through relationships. Anniversaries reflect the duration of time since a relationship's beginning, or of time since its end, and involve social celebrations or acknowledgments. But the passage of time is also marked through relationships in smaller ways – how long it has been since we had that argument or took that trip; or in the life transitions of others – how long it has been since a daughter graduated or son married. Additionally, relationships have their *own* turning points, as they reach new states that are qualitatively different – when, for better or worse, we are no longer what we once were and there may be no going back. For example, some couples and families may emerge from difficult periods with stronger and deeper relationships, while others may end up with more fragile or severed relationships – say, in the case of infidelity or the death of a child or sibling.

Other People Are Sources of Life Course Decisions and Expectations

If a relationship is central to our lives, we have probably worked hard to maintain it and have been significantly affected by it. There is a 'we' that ultimately drives the organization of *our* lives – plural. The most intimate of relationships, especially a spouse or partner, demand that lives are 'in synch' so that they might unfold *together* as smoothly as possible. Big decisions are generally made jointly, not singly: where to live, learn, and work; whether or when to marry or parent; how many children to have, and how to space them; how much to work when children are young; how to manage care of parents when they are old. These and other decisions are often carefully negotiated, and supported or compromised, within the context of multiple relationships, especially couple relationships.

When individuals' lives are 'out of synch,' friction must be resolved if relationships are to be sustained and healthy. Couples may separate in the face of new desires or goals related to education, work, or leisure; or due to romantic entanglements with others. Couples may experience crisis amid the departure of children or the arrival of a retirement. The care needs of a parent or child may strain or make it necessary to release other obligations or meaningful activities. The demands of family or work responsibilities may undermine the quality of a marriage.

Other people can regulate relationships, attempting to hasten or prevent them. Parents, for example, may try to influence the relationships of their children – and their children's life chances – through the neighborhoods and schools they choose, the teachers their children are assigned, the families they befriend, and the friendships and activities they encourage children to take up or release. As children grow older, parents may persuade or dissuade children from dating or marrying particular people, and even attempt to influence the number and timing of grandchildren. Of course, the reverse is also true: Children may try to influence the relationships of parents, especially amid marital strife, divorce, or the new relationships a parent might form thereafter.

We are generally unaware of how long a relationship will last, and we probably misjudge its durability and permanence. After all, 'until death do us part' continues to be repeated in marital vows, even though the likelihood of divorce is high. In high-longevity contexts, or in cultures like the United States where it is difficult to discuss finitude, individuals seem likely to overestimate the length of life or inadequately prepare for its end. Nonetheless, our ages and those of others may prompt us to think in more conscious ways of how much time might be left. The declining health of aging parents, for example, may lead children, who are themselves middle-aged or older, to an awareness that their visits are numbered. Couples also imagine their own ends: Who will go first? How will the survivor manage? Children, too, wonder these things about their parents: If mom dies before dad, or dad before mom, how will each fare without the other? What care needs might result and how will those needs be met? Would one be more likely to remarry than the other? Similarly, parents of adolescents may be acutely aware that time with children *as children* is quickly diminishing. In each of the situations, the anticipation of the future, and of limited time left, may prompt people to change their behavior now.

When a relationship is understood to be time-bound, its duration may affect how much effort or emotion is put into it – whether we give it our all while we have it, or hold back knowing that it will leave us. For example, a short-term relocation may lead a worker and her co-workers to not invest deeply in each other. Encounters with life threatening illnesses may leave people acutely aware that their relationship is running out of time, that time gotten is a kind of 'grace time,' or that death may take it away before they are ready.

Inheritance is an interesting case for demonstrating how projected time left might enter a relationship. Parents may demand things of children in connection to an inheritance, even specifying conditions in a will, in an effort to control their children before or after they die. Similarly, the possibility of inheritance may lead children to do things they might not otherwise do for fear of losing these resources. The likelihood of inheritance may also depend on relationship 'chains,' as the death of one person versus another in a couple may completely alter the flow and priority of resources across families and generations, dramatically improving or reducing one's life circumstances. These resources may be especially threatened when there are remarriages and stepchildren.

How much time is left in one relationship may also alter what is done in another relationship. For example, couples may move more quickly into marriage or parenthood so that a parent or grandparent can be part of the process and experience these roles. The needs of a dying parent may in turn require a caregiver to be less responsive to the needs of spouses and children, with the understanding that time in these other relationships can be reclaimed later. Promises made to loved ones on their deathbeds also often involve caring and looking out for others.

Relationships Help Judge Progress in Life

Human beings understand their experiences in relation to a variety of other people. We judge ourselves relative to our age peers, such as when we feel surpassed by those who have completed degrees, secured jobs, found partners, or become parents. These kinds of comparisons are inevitable among close friends and siblings. But these judgments also occur among peers in social institutions (such as graduation classes in schools or hiring classes in workplaces), and with respect to perceptions of larger cohort patterns (e.g., "Compared to most people my age, I ...").

We evaluate ourselves relative to parents, who are natural personal and historical anchors. For example, in evaluating my life, I cannot help but remember what my parents were like when they were my age. I use my father, especially, as a yardstick for measuring my aging. As I near the onset ages of my parents' illness episodes or diagnoses, I sense that I, too, am entering a period of increased vulnerability.

We judge ourselves relative to how old we are or will be when we experience something in a relationship – as when a man becomes a father, or a woman a mother, at an early or late age; or how old a woman or man might be upon divorce or widowhood, or upon a child's entry into kindergarten or graduation from high school or college. We may also judge ourselves in terms of relationship duration – for example, in feeling shame or embarrassment if a marital relationship is short-lived, or in taking pride in one that is long-lived.

We also evaluate ourselves in terms of how others attached to us are doing. For example, parents judge their own success on the basis of children's outcomes (e.g., grades in school, colleges attended, degrees achieved, professions entered, partners married). Recently, my mother said, "At this age, I don't worry about myself, I worry about everyone else. I just want all of you kids to get along and be happy!" Just as parents evaluate their success on the basis of the achievements of their children, children are judged on the basis of the perceived success of their parents. Cultural markers of social status – where a child lives or goes to school, or the degrees, occupations, and financial resources of parents – affect how kids see and sort themselves, and are seen and sorted by others, into peer groups and cliques.

Relationships Are Drivers of Ambition, Persistence, and Achievement

Relationships can help us think and live in new ways, offering support or an example for doing or being things we might not otherwise attempt. For example, a high school teacher might encourage a non-college bound student to college, or a college professor might inspire a student to pursue a graduate degree. First-generation college students sometimes speak of striving in college because their parents did not have the opportunity to go or dropped out; they say that they are doing it *for* their parents. A highly accomplished scientist I know often recalls a professor who called her "stupid" and said she would never amount to anything; 50 years after receiving her Ph.D., his voice is still in the back of her head, propelling her forward. Parents might coach each other or strategize with other parents in an effort to become better mothers or fathers. Social movements and front-line activists can also forge new models of life, and new civil rights and legal protections, for groups of people who have been marginalized or invisible, such as African-Americans, women, LGBT people, and immigrants.

Relationships can reveal what we do not want to do or be. For example, couples talk about the marital and parenting styles of their parents, and about what they do not want to reproduce. High school students from working-class families may aspire to college in an effort to have middle-class jobs and greater career options. Students in Ph.D. or M.D. programs might drop out after witnessing their mentors' professional lives and struggles to balance work and family.

Relationships Are Sources of Stability and Disruption, Protection and Risk

Relationships have both light and dark sides. At the end of the day, and of life, relationships are often the most important sources of personal meaning; but they can also drain life of its meaning. Relationships keep us 'grounded' and 'anchored'; but they also curtail freedom, create disruption and unpredictability, and even lead us to relinquish life goals and plans. Relationships are essential to human welfare because of the many types of support they provide; but they can also put us at risk and place our welfare in jeopardy. Particular relationships connect individuals to larger social networks, which are gateways to opportunity and resources; but they can also block opportunities and deplete resources. Indeed, interpersonal processes – such as tracking in schools and workplaces, assigning negative or positive social labels to individuals and groups, or discriminating in explicit or subtle ways – are key mechanisms for the accumulation of advantage and disadvantage across the life course, and for the transmission of inequality across generations (Dannefer 2003).

Many relationships are chosen, but some of the most central are not. We are born into complex, multigenerational family structures which, for most of us, comprise the longest-running relationships we will ever have. We not only have no control over our families of origin, but we often do not ask for the experiences we have as family members make decisions about where to live, when to move, and whether and when to divorce or remarry.

Relationships Are Conditioned by Local Environments …

To a great extent, the relationships we form stem from local environments. Children's friendships are based in the neighborhoods, and therefore schools, that parents choose from the options they have. As adults, too, relationships are most often formed in the colleges, workplaces, churches, and communities we seek or find ourselves.

These settings not only offer possibilities of both supportive and destructive relationships, they also regulate relationships – especially when relationships are hierarchical, such as between teachers and students, or between supervisors and workers. The policies and practices of schools or workplaces may determine which types of relationships are permissible, or monitor how they are experienced – such as boundaries related to sex and intimacy, the abuse of power, or separation of professional and private life. Legal rights and obligations concerning dependency also come to mind, whether in accessing children or children's information at school or in making decisions for spouses or parents as part of medical directives in healthcare institutions.

The social composition of a locale – in terms of age, sex, race and ethnicity, education, or income – determines the kinds of people with whom we come into contact and potentially form relationships. A good example is the 'marriage market' and 'pool of eligibles' in a city or region, such as unmarried men with good jobs, or being one of a few old men among many old women in a community or senior environment. The strongest job opportunities through university career centers are often local or regional; the decision about where to attend college may therefore channel the subsequent life course by sending graduates into nearby markets as they secure housing, find mates, and form families.

… and Relationships Are Conditioned by Distal Environments

In contemplating the significance of social relationships in the life course, it is natural to focus on the most intimate of relationships and on immediate and known networks in proximal environments. But distal environments are also powerful, but more often invisible, in conditioning the availability and nature of relationships: history and social change, demography, and social policies.

Relationships must be understood within the context of their historical times. In the last half century alone, the life course has been radically transformed by dramatic changes in family formation, gender roles, access to higher education, the nature of work, and civil rights, among other things. The digital world has also brought new modes of finding and maintaining relationships, both locally and at great distance. Some of these changes are about relationships – such as co-residence with parents, increasing rates of cohabitation or divorce, or legal recognition of LGBT couples and families. Other changes, such as women's greater educational attainment and labor force participation, or men's more precarious work or greater investments in fathering, mean that relationships are being navigated or revised in turn. And as Glen Elder's long line of research has shown, beginning with *Children of the Great Depression* (1974), the family is the sphere through which the effects of macro-level changes, like economic recessions or depressions, are mediated – and experienced and given meaning by its members.

When a society experiences rapid change, existing social systems are strained – including relationships. A key question is how individuals create, maintain, or terminate relationships amid the uncertainty of their social environments. For example, in the last decade, many people around the globe have experienced upheaval in political and economic systems, or war and violence, which have serious implications for relationships. Widespread patterns of migration and immigration affect families as they are united or separated by long distances. The abuse of women and children around the world, too, fractures human relationships. On one hand, climates of uncertainty may breed more temporary, instrumental, and self-interested relationships and create inauthentic attachments, loyalties, and commitments. On the other hand, these climates may also bring and bind people together in deep ways.

Revolutionary demographic changes in mortality and morbidity have altered the very terms of life, illness, and death. For example, the longevity of individual lives has made relationships long-lived too. People experience each other at new ages and in new life periods for which there are not always clear scripts for how relationships are supposed to look or feel – as young adult children with middle-aged parents, as middle-aged children with old parents, or as old children with very old parents. Family relationships carry the potential to be significant and positive because there are fewer relationships in which to invest, they are of longer duration, and they exist across many generations – thereby creating conditions that might strengthen the stability of family relationships and deepen attachment. New parenting styles and investments in relationships with children and grandchildren have also reinforced intergenerational connections.

And yet, it is possible that family relationships in these demographic conditions may become *less* important, active, and intense, or may result in "long-term lousy relationships," to use Vern Bengtson's (2001) phrase. Because the presence of ties can be counted on for many decades, individuals may *disinvest* in relationships at certain times under the assumption that they be activated as needed, making them more sporadic. When relationships go awry, individuals may (mistakenly) assume that there is still time for the relationship to come back or be fixed. High levels of divorce may also offset some of the potential relationship gains that come with greater longevity. One could even argue that longevity has made it more likely that marriages will eventually sour.

Finally, social policies also condition the kinds of relationships that are or are not legally recognized or protected (e.g., gay and lesbian couples and families, unmarried heterosexual partners, widows or widowers), ensured (e.g., state laws that require children to care for aging parents, or grandparents to care for the children of teen mothers), monitored (e.g., custody, visitation, alimony), or credited (e.g., rules related to duration of marriage, who counts as a dependent).

Relationships Are Core to Human Identities

As George Herbert Mead (1934), and John Dewey (1916) before him, argued, the self is not 'ready-made' but arises out of social experience and action. We have multiple selves that stem from multiple relationships—even, it could be argued, as many selves as people we know. Indeed, many of life's big themes relate to the aggregates of people to whom we are connected: nations, regions, states, cities or towns, and neighborhoods; or social categories like gender, race and ethnicity. These "people like me" shape how we see ourselves. As identities are formed and reshaped over time, individuals wrestle with similarities and differences between themselves and these peoples. Similarities can be points of pride, and differences can be points of struggle and crisis. These connections determine the people with whom individuals associate, the aspirations they set, and the people they reject or disregard.

Much of one's sense of self, however, is connected to genes inherited and/or socialization received from parents: personality traits and characteristics, values and attitudes, health symptoms or conditions, demeanor and physical appearance. We see our parents in ourselves, and ourselves in our children. These dynamics may lead children to consciously embrace or attempt to transcend certain things in themselves that were transmitted from parents, or to lead parents to consciously attempt to transmit, or prevent the transmission of, things about them to their children.

In my own case, I am the spitting image of my father. I literally see *him* when I look in the mirror! Two decades ahead of me, his aging is a window into mine. How I see myself is not only about how he sees me, but how I see him – a twist on Charles Horton Cooley's (1902) 'looking glass self.' One of my earliest memories is of sitting on his lap as a young child and, from across my grandmother's kitchen table, having relatives comment on how much I look like him. This has been a common occurrence in my life, and it has reinforced the fact that I am 'Richard's son.' I am also a 'Jr.,' so my formal name literally signals that I am his son. The common practice of namesakes symbolically connects descendants to past generations and honors special others who came before.

The language and presentation of kinship nicely illustrates how central these relationships are to identity. Just as I am a 'Richard and Diann's son,' I am known and define myself as a brother, partner, father, uncle, nephew, cousin, and an 'in-law' to a long list of particular people. I was also once a grandson and great-grandson to generations that have now passed. Particularly as a result of divorce ('ex-'), remarriage ('step-'), and unmarried relationships, there are not always easy ways to explain or label how we are related to others – as Matilda White Riley (Riley and Riley 1996) noted long before the complexity and diversity we know today.

All of these relationships have origin stories: of how people found each other or were put together, of what they mean to each other. Think, for example, of the tales couples tell about when they first met or saw one another. There is power in telling and retelling the story, in embellishing or refining it, and in how each partner has their own variation of it. The experience is shared, the stories are often a little different, but what counts is that it is the story of *us*.

As relationships start and unfold, they are subject to social rituals and reinforcements. They are recognized, or perhaps renewed, through commitments and ceremonies. In the classic anthropological account, Arnold van Gennep (1908) described *rites de passage* associated with major life transitions. These rites involve a process of 'ceasings and becomings' that involve an individual's separation from an earlier status and an initiation into, and eventually the full incorporation of, a new status. A key feature of these rites of passage is that they are communal. When these thresholds are crossed, it is not just that individuals think of themselves differently; it is that others think of them differently too. Marriages and childbirth are good examples of rites of passage that create new statuses through the linking of lives. Of course, relationships can also be socially contested or negatively sanctioned – especially those that are deemed to be non-normative, such as those that cross social boundaries related to age, race, gender, and social class.

Just as there can be rites of passage that mark entry into social roles, there can be rites that mark *exits* from social roles – what Zena Smith Blau (1973) called *rites of separation*. These changes also affect social relationships. Legally, divorce is an obvious example of a formal rite of separation. It is meant to *unlink* lives. While these relationships may be severed or regulated legally, they generally do not vanish socially. The 'ex' label will live on in the identity of the people who were once attached, even long after the relationship is dissolved. There is much to be learned about the dissolution of relationships by choice or by circumstance – and the messy business of managing endings and unlinking lives. Some of our biggest points of embarrassment, shame, and regret are in how poorly we managed relationship conflicts and endings in family, work, school, and community environments.

New life phases and transitions can significantly alter social networks and reference groups (see also Burt, Chap. 4; Mardsen, Chap. 5), separating us from people and groups who were once important and incorporating new ones. For example, long-term couple friends may back away from a new widow or widower, who may have to recruit new members into the social network (see also Cornwell and Laumann, Chap. 16). Individuals with life-threatening illnesses at an early age may feel disconnected from the lifestyles and preoccupations of their age peers. Staying single when friends are marrying, or getting married before others do, may put individuals in different social networks. Upwardly mobile individuals feel caught between the social worlds from which they came and the social worlds they are joining.

Similarly, transitions can reinforce or alter ideas about what a good relationship is. For example, individuals who become seriously ill may find that, out of concern, some central relationships are deepened and some peripheral relationships move to the center, while discomfort may move others to the periphery. Individuals who are divorced may likewise find themselves estranged from people to whom they once felt very close. Experiences like these can teach difficult lessons about the impermanence of relationships and the tenuousness of their quality.

Perhaps the most poignant example of the significance of social relationships to identity is the obituary, which is at its core a story of lives both tightly and loosely bound together – of fellow travelers in time, of relationships left behind, and of accomplishments that rested on collaboration with or support from others. Wakes, too, are communal experiences that involve shared stories that affirm the life and the loss.

When we lose longstanding relationships, especially through death, we lose people who are the 'library of our lives' (Neugarten 1995) and cannot be replaced. These people are no longer present to corroborate our existence or memories, and their losses are felt acutely. This kind of identity loss occurs with the death of parents or older family members, as we are pushed up the family ladder and, once at the top, become orphans in time.

Relationships Are Essential to Human Experience and Emotion

Long ago, William James (1920) said that the "deepest principle in human nature is the craving to be appreciated" – a craving that is satisfied by others. In fact, most core human experiences and emotions have social roots in that they stem from or occur in interaction with others: Love, attachment, attraction, jealousy, revenge, shame, forgiveness, loneliness, purpose, mattering, longing, belonging, joy, sorrow, suffering.

Social relationships also play into one of the most cherished cultural values in the United States: independence. This value is to a great extent discrepant with the reality that *inter*dependence, not independence, is the key hallmark of human life – as this essay has repeatedly demonstrated. Despite this fact, a U-shaped curve of dependence is nonetheless implicit in family conversations, public and political discourse, and research in human development: the first decade and a half of life is assumed to be a period of complete dependence on others; followed by a period of increasing independence early into the third decade, at which point individuals are assumed to be completely independent until old age, when failing health may make it necessary to depend on others. Even then, the need to rely on care from others is sometimes described as 'burden' because being in a state of dependence violates a cultural value. For this reason, the prospect of young adult children living with parents, and of old parents living with children, can prompt shame or embarrassment.

It is an illusion to believe that those who are no longer young but not yet old are completely independent. Adult life is composed of many decades that are heavily constrained by social relationships, in which one's own welfare is inextricably dependent on the choices, behaviors, and resources of others, and in which the welfare of others is inextricably dependent on one's own choices, behaviors, and resources. This is especially apparent in family life. It is also especially apparent in the United States, where the government and the public place a high premium on personal responsibility and self-reliance. The irony is that the relatively limited supports of 'liberal market' welfare states, such as the United States, do not promote independence as much as they result in greater *inter*dependence among people (Hagestad and Dykstra 2016; Settersten 2007). That is, individuals and their families must shoulder responsibility for and rely on each other to solve problems that arise as they navigate markets for education, jobs, partners, or care using whatever knowledge and resources they have acquired or can access.

Conclusion

I have sketched nine ways that social relationships matter for the life course:

1. Relationships permeate and punctuate the life course
2. Other people are sources of life course decisions and expectations
3. Relationships help judge progress in life
4. Relationships are drivers of ambition, persistence, and achievement
5. Relationships are sources of stability and disruption, protection and risk
6. Relationships are conditioned by local environments
7. Relationships are conditioned by distal environments
8. Relationships are core to human identities
9. Relationships are essential to human experience and emotion

There are surely others. But these nine underscore the fact that the life course is a *social* entity: it is significantly driven by relationships with shared histories and identities, relationships formed and dissolved in social settings and institutions. The 'individual' life course is a misnomer in that it is experienced and co-constructed with other people – over 35 years ago, Bertaux (1981) emphasized the significance of "co-biographers"; Plath (1980) called them "consociates"; Kahn and Antonucci (1980) spoke of "convoys." Advances in theories and methods are needed to better reflect the inherently *social* nature of the life course, probing the full spectrum of social relationships from dyads to cohorts, and the full complement of social forces that affect them (see also Dannefer et al. 2016; Levy and Bühlmann 2016; Settersten 2017). Where couples are concerned, deVries and colleagues' (2017) 'relationship timeline method' offers an important strategy for studying shared experiences in relational contexts.

Many examples raised in this chapter have illustrated that there is a great need to bring *time* into relationships. Relationships have histories of their own – beginnings, middles, and ends that can be described 'objectively' as well as in the mind (Settersten 2015). There is much to learn about what brings and keeps people together, how they create and navigate a shared life course, and how they adapt to changing needs and circumstances.

Many examples also reveal the need to enter the realms of meaning and intersubjectivity, and of motivation, goal setting, and decision-making, to get deeper into the lived experience of relationships. So, too, is there a need to look underneath the major life course events that are the focus of research and social accounting (e.g., residential, educational, occupational, and family statuses) and instead toward the everyday interactions and emotions on which these events are based. Researchers too often mark the life course with big moments, but these big moments are built upon minutes, hours, days, weeks, and years of social experiences in the many settings of daily life.

Finally, the study of the life course is in need of a more dedicated examination of chance encounters. Social science is predicated on the idea that there are patterns to human life that can be understood, predicted, and intervened into if necessary or desired. And yet, in looking back on life, we are so often conscious of the role of chance encounters – that there were key junctures where, if we had not been connected to a particular person or group, or had not had a particular opportunity, or had not made a particular decision, pathways through life would have been dramatically different. We would not have had *this* spouse, or *these* children, friends, and mentors, or be in *this* community, workplace, or job.

From my vantage point, the study of human development and the life course is *under-socialized*. Individuals are too often studied as if they exist in isolation of others, and available methods further fracture whole people into tiny variables and control away the complexity of the social world. Theories and research do not adequately capture the richness of human social relationships, and the deep reality of human attachment and connection, whether in daily life or over decades.

The coupling of a life course perspective and a social networks perspective offers a powerful window into linked lives that neither perspective can gain on its own (for strategies, see Kreager, Felmlee, and Alwin, Chap. 22). A life course perspective can reveal the kinds of dynamics I have offered in this chapter. But the contributions of a social network perspective are similarly unique because it emphasizes network structure and the individual's position within it – and concepts such as social network size, composition and 'internal wiring,' density, centrality, and 'bridging' positions that close the gap between people who would otherwise not be connected (for applications in gerontology, see Cornwell et al. 2015, and in Cornwell and Shafer 2016). Dually combined, these two perspectives can provide a more rigorous understanding of linked lives.

Acknowledgment Seeds for some of the material developed here were planted in Settersten (2015), which is cited below and was published by Taylor & Francis.

References

Bengtson, V. (2001). Beyond the nuclear family: The increasing importance of multigenerational bonds. *Journal of Marriage and Family, 63*, 1–16.

Bertaux, D. (Ed.). (1981). *Biography and society: The life history approach in the social sciences*. Beverly Hills: Sage.

Blau, Z. S. (1973). *Old age in a changing society*. New York: Franklin Watts.

Cooley, C. H. (1902). *Human nature and the social order*. New York: Charles Scriber's Sons.

Cornwell, B., & Shafer, M. (2016). Social networks in later life. In L. K. George & K. Ferraro (Eds.), *Handbook of aging and the social sciences* (8th ed., pp. 181–201). San Diego: Academic.

Cornwell, B., Marcum, C., & Silverstein, M. (2015). The social network approach in gerontological research. *Journals of Gerontology: Social Sciences, 70B*, 87–90. https://doi.org/10.1093/geronb/gbu157.

Dannefer, D. (2003). Cumulative advantage/disadvantage and the life course: Cross-fertilizing age and social science theory. *Journal of Gerontology: Social Sciences, 58B*, S327–S337.

Dannefer, D., Kelley-Moore, J., & Huang, W. (2016). Opening the social: Sociological imagination in life course studies. In M. J. Shanahan et al. (Eds.), *Handbook of the life course, volume II* (pp. 87–110). New York: Springer.

de Vries, B., LeBlanc, A. L., Alston-Stepnitz, E., Stephenson, R., & Woodyatt, C. R. (2017). The relationship timeline: A method for the study of shared life experiences in relational contexts. *Advances in Life Course Research, 32*, 55–64. https://doi.org/10.1016/j.alcr.2016.07.002.

Dewey, J. (1916). *Democracy and education*. New York: Macmillan.

Elder, G. H., Jr. (1974). *Children of the great depression: Social change in life experience*. Chicago: University of Chicago Press.

Elder, G. H., Jr. (1994). Time, agency, and social change. *Social Psychology Quarterly, 57*, 4–15.

Hagestad, G. O. (1981). Problems and promises in the social psychology of intergenerational relations. In R. W. Fogel, E. Hattfield, S. B. Kiesler, & E. Shanas (Eds.), *Aging, stability, and change in the family* (pp. 11–47). New York: Academic.

Hagestad, G. O., & Dykstra, P. (2016). Structuration of the life course: Some neglected aspects. In M. J. Shanahan et al. (Eds.), *Handbook of the life course, volume II* (pp. 131–157). New York: Springer.

Hagestad, G. O., & Settersten, R. A., Jr. (2017). Aging: It's interpersonal! Reflections from two life course migrants. *The Gerontologist, 57*, 136–144. https://doi.org/10.1093/geront/gnw117.

James, W. (1920). *The letters of William James: Volume 2*. Boston: The Atlantic Monthly Press.

Kahn, R., & Antonucci, T. (1980). Convoys over the life course: Attachment, roles, and social support. In P. B. Baltes & O. Brim (Eds.), *Life-span development and behavior* (Vol. 3, pp. 254–283). New York: Academic.

Levy, R., & Bühlmann, F. (2016). Towards a socio-cultural framework for life course analysis. *Advances in Life Course Research, 30*, 30–42. https://doi.org/10.1016/j.alcr.2016.03.005.

Mead, G. H. (1934). *Mind and society*. Chicago: University of Chicago Press.

Neugarten, B. L. (1995). The costs of survivorship. *Center on Aging Newsletter, 11*. Evanston: Buehler Center on Aging, Northwestern University.
Plath, D. W. (1980). Contours of consociation: Lessons from a Japanese narrative. In P. B. Baltes & O. G. Brim Jr. (Eds.), *Life-span development and behavior* (Vol. 3, pp. 287–305). New York: Academic.
Riley, M. W., & Riley, J. W., Jr. (1996). Generational relations: A future perspective. In T. K. Hareven (Ed.), *Aging and generational relations over the life course* (pp. 526–532). New York: Walter de Gruyter.
Riley, M. W., Foner, A., & Waring, J. (1988). Sociology of age. In N. Smelser (Ed.), *Handbook of sociology* (pp. 243–290). Newbury Park: Sage.
Settersten, R. A., Jr. (2007). Passages to adulthood: Linking demographic change and human development. *European Journal of Population, 23*, 251–272. https://doi.org/10.1007/s10680.007.9132-8.
Settersten, R. A., Jr. (2015). Relationships in time and the life course: The significance of linked lives. *Research in Human Development, 12*(3–4), 217–223. https://doi.org/10.1080/15427609.2015.1071944.
Settersten, R. A., Jr. (2017). Some things I have learned about aging by studying the life course. *Innovation in Aging, 1*(2). Advance Access, 1 Sep. https://doi.org/10.1093/geroni/igx014.
van Gennep, A. (1908/1960). The rites of passage (M. B. Vizedom & S. T. Kimball, Trans.). Chicago: University of Chicago Press.

Richard A. Settersten Jr. is Professor of Human Development and Family Sciences, and Endowed Director of the Hallie Ford Center for Healthy Children and Families, at Oregon State University. He is a specialist in life-course studies, often focused on the first and last few decades of adulthood, but always with an eye toward understanding the whole of human life.

Chapter 3
The Linked Lives Principle in Life Course Studies: Classic Approaches and Contemporary Advances

Deborah Carr

Social relationships are essential to our emotional, social, physical, and economic well-being at every stage of the life course (House et al. 1988). National surveys consistently show that more than 95 percent of persons in the United States rate their families as "very" or "extremely" important to them, and more than three-quarters rate their friendships as such (Moore 2003). Yet even our most personal and intimate relationships are powerfully shaped by social structures, including historical and cultural contexts, and the social institutions in which we are embedded. That social contexts shape human relationships is a core theme of sociological perspectives on the life course (Elder 1994, 2000). This framework rests on four foundational concepts: historical context; personal timing; agency versus structure; and social relationships (i.e., linked lives). The latter theme is essential to the study of contemporary research on social networks, which uses state of the art methods to understand the complex role that social ties play in shaping attitudes, behaviors, health, and well-being over the life course.

In this chapter, I provide an overview of four integrative themes widely used by sociologists working in the life course tradition, and offer examples of classic and contemporary studies exemplifying these themes. Second, I describe recent developments in data collection and analytic methods that enable researchers to more effectively study linked lives over the life course, with particular attention to the use of dyadic, family-level, and network data. Third, I focus on one core substantive area in linked lives research – the impact of marriage and marital transitions on health and well-being – to illustrate how our understanding of linked lives is

D. Carr (✉)
Department of Sociology, Boston University,
100 Cummington Mall, Boston 02215, MA, USA
e-mail: carrds@rutgers.edu

D. F. Alwin et al. (eds.), *Social Networks and the Life Course*, Frontiers in Sociology and Social Research 2, https://doi.org/10.1007/978-3-319-71544-5_3

advanced by adopting dyadic and family-level perspectives. I conclude by showing how attention to linked lives can redirect and challenge conventional wisdom regarding social relationships and health.

Sociological Perspectives on the Life Course: An Overview

Life course sociologists have developed sophisticated theoretical frameworks for examining human lives and the social contexts and relationships that shape these lives (Alwin 2012; Elder 1994). Sociological perspectives on the life course share commonalities with yet diverge in significant ways from psychological models of the life span, which generally conceptualize human development as a function of biological and genetic influences and behavioral adaptation (see Mayer 2003, for review). Sociological approaches to the life course, by contrast, emphasize the influence of social institutions, structures, and public policies on individual lives (Kohli 2007).

Sociologists have adopted a variety of conceptual frames for studying the life course, although Elder's articulation of the life course paradigm is arguably the most influential and widely cited (Alwin 2012). Conceptually, four key assumptions guide this research: (a) lives are embedded in and shaped by historical context; (b) the meaning and impact of a life transition is contingent on when it occurs; (c) individuals construct their own lives through their choices and actions, yet within the constraints of historical and social circumstances, and (d) lives are "linked" through social relationships – the theme that is most central to this volume.

Life course scholars also rely on rigorous research methods and data sources – including national censuses, sample surveys, in-depth interviews, and historical records – to document continuity and change in human lives. Because a key question of life course research is "how do historical time and place shape lives?" researchers often compare data obtained at different points in time, from different birth cohorts, and from different national and cultural contexts. Researchers also rely heavily on longitudinal data, or data obtained from the same person at multiple points in time, so they can track continuity, change, and maturation within a single life. Until relatively recently, however, most studies conducted in the life course tradition relied on data from a single reporter – even when researchers were focused on inherently social phenomena, such as the individual's personal relationships and integration within social networks. This single individual would report on persons belonging to their social networks, or would rate the quality of relationships with family members and friends, yet studies rarely if ever incorporated data directly from those other actors. Much of this chapter will focus on the ways that methodological, data collection, and theoretical advances have enabled life course researchers to truly capture linked lives and social networks in their work. Before delving more fully into these important advances, I provide a brief synopsis and historical overview of the core themes, concepts, and methods of the life course paradigm (Elder 2000).

Historical Time and Place

The life course of individuals is embedded in and shaped by the historical times and places they inhabit. Socioeconomic prospects and trajectories including the choice of one's occupation (Signer and Saldana 2001), the financial wherewithal to purchase a home (U.S. Census Bureau 2015), and whether one's schooling is interrupted by war or a financial crisis are shaped by macroeconomic and political factors (Elder 1994). Social relationship structures and processes also are shaped by sociocultural norms and historical contexts. For example, when and whether to marry and have children (Manning et al. 2014); the social acceptability of divorce, cohabitation, life-long singlehood, and same-sex relations (Baunach 2012; Thornton and Young-Demarco 2001); the balance of power and division of household labor among spouses (Cunningham 2007); and cultural expectations for providing care to aging relatives have changed dramatically over the 20th and 21st centuries (Brody et al. 1983).

The notion that human lives are shaped by social and historical context dates back to the writings of C. Wright Mills. In *The Sociological Imagination*, Mills (1959) asserted that to understand human social life, scholars must consider both one's "biography" and "history." Mills observed that "the sociological imagination enables its possessor to understand the larger historical scene in terms of its meaning for the inner life and external career of a variety of individuals" (Mills 1959: 7).

The impact of history on individual lives is most evident during periods of rapid social change. Adjacent birth cohorts may experience very different historical contexts during their formative years, which lead to a generational divergence in values, beliefs, and life chances (Mannheim 1928/1952). For example, during the latter half of the twentieth century, women's social roles changed dramatically, as educational and occupational opportunities expanded in the wake of the Women's Movement. White middle-class women who were stay-at-home mothers in the 1950s witnessed their Baby Boom and Generation X cohort daughters grow up to have successful professional careers that historically were considered men's domain. Although mothers and daughters share many similarities, including genetic background, ethnicity, religion, and (often) social class, historical changes created a seismic divide in the life choices made by these two generations of women (Carr 2004a). Theoretical writings underscore the importance and complexity of generations for understanding the life course. Alwin and McCammon (2007) clarify that "generation" encompasses three related yet distinct concepts: (1) position in family lineages (e.g., mothers and daughters); (2) birth cohort (e.g., Greatest Generation versus Baby Boom cohort); and (3) an indicator of historical participation (e.g., exposure to flourishing versus restricted opportunities for women).

The impact of history on life course trajectories varies based on one's age when a major historical trend unfolds. Young people who were in elementary school when the internet explosion occurred can't remember life before e-mail, and prefer to maintain social ties with terse text messages. Older adults, by contrast, prefer the more personal connection conveyed with a telephone call or face-to-face visit (Smith 2011; Teo et al. 2015). The effects of specific historical events also vary based on one's age when the event occurred. Elder (1974) showed that World War II affected soldiers differently, based on their age during the war years. Young enlistees had no family or work responsibilities when they shipped off to Japan or Europe, whereas older soldiers were leaving behind jobs and marriages when they headed overseas. While the young soldiers returned home to new opportunities in work, family, and education (due in part to the educational benefits provided by the G.I. Bill), the older soldiers often came home to find their marriages were strained, or their former jobs were no longer available (MacLean and Elder 2007).

Place also affects how individual lives unfold. Place can be defined as broadly as one's nation, or as narrowly as one's neighborhood or city block. Nation-level characteristics, such as the level of economic development can profoundly influence its citizens' attitudes, values, gender roles, childbearing behavior, educational opportunities, health, and even personality (Inkeles and Levinson 1969). One's local social context also matters. Neighborhood characteristics like the social cohesiveness and integration of a city block and or the level of instability, poverty, and crime in one's neighborhood can affect residents' educational prospects, physical and mental health, occupational opportunities, and life span (Sampson et al. 2002). Social networks are tightly tied to place as well; both classic (Cantor 1975) and contemporary (Clarke et al. 2014) research shows that older adults' mobility, health, social integration, and capacity to access instrumental and expressive support is linked to characteristics of the neighborhoods in which they live. Although geography and history are hardly destiny they do play essential roles in shaping one's social networks, interpersonal relations, and life trajectories.

Timing in Lives

The developmental impact of a personal transition or historical event is contingent on when it occurs in a person's life. For example, marrying at age 17 may mean that a young person is especially likely to drop out of high school, divorce, have many children, and hold a poorly paying job that does not require a high school diploma. By contrast, persons who marry for the first time at age 35 likely have already completed their education, perhaps earning a graduate degree, and having spent many years in the paid work force prior to marrying. Yet marrying at age 35 may mean that one will have only one or two children, given that the likelihood of conceiving a child declines steadily for women after age 35 (e.g., Bumpass 1990). Family size and generation length, in turn, can affect socioemotional aspects of intergenerational and sibling relations (Seltzer and Bianchi 2013).

These examples illustrate the importance of social timing which refers to the ways that age shapes whether, when, how, and to what end one experiences important social roles and transitions between roles (George 1993). The timing of life transitions reflects a broad range of biological, social, and political forces. For example, the age at which a woman can physically bear children is contingent upon the biological transition to menarche. Social norms also provide guidelines for the culturally appropriate time for making transitions. Life course sociologist Bernice Neugarten (Neugarten et al. 1965) observed that people are expected to comply with a "social clock." This refers to "age norms and age expectations [that] operate as prods and brakes upon behavior, in some instances hastening behavior and in some instances delaying it" (Neugarten et al. 1965: 710).

Neugarten and colleagues conducted surveys showing that Americans generally agree that there is a "right" age to marry, start a job, and set up one's own home (Settersten and Hägestad 1996). Norms dictating the "right" age for life transitions change over historical time, however. For example, marrying at age 19 and having one's first child at 20 was normal and even desirable for women in the late 1950s. By contrast, few college students in the twenty-first century would endorse marrying at such a young age (Settersten and Hägestad 1996). "Mistimed" transitions – or transitions that occur earlier or later than one's peers may create psychological stress, personal challenges, and social disapproval. For example, Carlson (2012) found that persons who married for the first time at an age much younger or older than they desired went on to experience poorer emotional health than those marrying at the normative age.

Cultural norms informally prescribe the timing of life course transitions, yet public policies mandate the timing of many important transitions (Leisering 2003). Although state laws vary in the U.S., the law typically dictates that children must stay in school until age 16, and cannot marry until age18 unless they obtain parental permission. Likewise, the age at which one can vote, drive, drink legally, serve in the military, retire with full Social Security benefits, or become President of the United States is dictated by federal or state law (Kohli 2007). Laws, like social norms, also change over historical time. While children labored on farms and in factories in past centuries, child labor was banned in the United States by the Fair Labor Act of 1938, and strict rules now mandate the age at which children can work for pay (Moehling 1999).

Life course scholars recognize that legal, biological, and social time tables may be out of sync with one another; these asynchronies may cause difficulties as individuals negotiate their life choices and relationships. For instance, boys and girls may be physically able to bear a child at age 13, yet they may not be emotionally prepared to enter the role of parent. Public polices encourage (and in some cases, mandate) workers to retire at age 65, although most older employees are healthy, cognitively sharp and willing to remain in the work force for another decade (Leisering 2003). Thus, the life course paradigm reveals the importance of both personal and historical time.

Importance of Agency and Constraint

Individuals construct their own life course through their choices and actions, within the opportunities and constraints of historical and social circumstances. Sociological perspectives on the life course emphasize that life chances are a function of both personal agency and structural constraint. Individuals select social roles and opportunities that are consistent with their own personal preferences, traits, resources, and even genetic predispositions (e.g., Landecker and Panofsky 2013; Scarr and McCartney 1983) – yet freedom of choice is not distributed evenly throughout the population. Persons with fewer economic resources have fewer opportunities to seek out and pursue desirable options, while characteristics such as age, race, gender, physical ability status, sexual orientation and religion may create obstacles for some individuals – at least at certain points in history.

John Clausen's (1993) classic book *American Lives* provides a compelling example of the ways that agency and structure influence life course trajectories. Clausen tracked a cohort of men and women who were born in the early twentieth century, and followed them for more than 60 years. A cluster of traits he labeled "planful competence" increased one's chances of successful careers, stable marriages, rewarding interpersonal relationships, and good health more than five decades after the adolescents had graduated from high school. Planful competence encompasses self-confidence, intellectual investment, and dependability. These attributes, in turn, are associated with superior academic performance in school, well-developed plans for post-secondary schooling, and focus when selecting one's career. Planful competence encompasses one's own ambition, aspirations for the future, and conscientiousness in pursuing one's goals. Yet these traits are shaped by structural constraints. Children from more advantaged social and economic backgrounds were more likely than their less well-off peers to enjoy high levels of competence (Clausen 1993). In sum, human lives are shaped by the complex interplay between individual-level preferences, traits and aptitudes and macrolevel economic, political, and social structures (Elder 1994).

Linked Lives

The life course theme of linked lives is most germane to and unifies the chapters in this edited volume. This integrative theme proposes that lives are experienced interdependently in the context of social networks, and social and historical influences are expressed through this network of shared relationships. The linked lives principle specifies the ways that one's life is embedded in a large network of social relationships – with parents, children, siblings, friends, coworkers, in-laws, romantic partners, and others. The notion that social relationships matter dates back to Émile Durkheim's (1951: 1897) classic writings on social integration in *Suicide*. Durkheim found that persons with tight-knit social networks had lower rates of suicide than those with weaker social ties. Married persons had lower suicide rates than the unmarried, Catholics fared better than Protestants, and parents revealed lower suicide rates than childless persons. Since the publication of Durkheim's work, social scientists have continued to explore why and how social relationships affect the life course.

The concept of linked lives also refers to the ways that generations are linked to one another (Alwin 2012). A focal area of life course research is intergenerational transmission; parents pass on their values, attitudes, and socioeconomic and intellectual resources to their offspring (Furstenberg et al. 1987; Sewell and Hauser 1975). Although classic studies of socialization revealed how children became like their parents, researchers also have focused on identifying why and how children turn out differently from their parents – highlighting many other social relationships and social contexts that a child experiences (Glass et al. 1986). For example, James Coleman's (1961) *Adolescent Society* shows how high schools students socialize their peers to hold values that are in opposition to the values held by their parents, while the Bennington College study (Alwin et al. 1991) traced the process through which young women, largely from politically conservative families, became more politically liberal after studying at Bennington. These attitudinal shifts were most pronounced among women who established close social ties to older students and faculty members who strongly endorsed liberal ideals.

Life course sociologists also recognize that life domains are linked. Even within a single individual, work and family choices affect one another; working full-time may preclude one from being a stay-at-home parent, or intensive parenting demands may prevent one from working as many hours as one would like (Bianchi and Milkie 2010). Likewise, economic standing and physical health are mutually influential; poverty exposes people to health risks such as poor nutrition and limited access to care, yet poor health compromises one's ability to work full-time (Goldman 1994). Moreover, life course influences can occur both cross-person and cross-domain. A spouse's work strain may affect one's own psychological health (Hammer et al. 1997), while a parent's job loss may affect a child's health and educational attainment (Levine 2011).

The emerging subfield of life course epidemiology provides a powerful example of cross-generation, cross-domain linkages. In general, this work delineates how social and economic characteristics of one's parents may have long-term influences on an offspring's physical and emotional health (Wadsworth and Kuh 2016). Longitudinal studies consistently show that socioeconomic disadvantage during childhood is associated with higher rates of functional limitation at midlife and more rapid declines in physical function at older ages (Haas 2008); heightened risk of mid- and later-life diseases including cancer (Morton et al. 2012), heart attack (O'Rand and Hamil-Luker 2005), and hypertension (Stein et al. 2010); and ultimately earlier death (Hayward and Gorman 2004).

Linked Lives over the Life Course: Methodological Advances

Sociological research on the life course is distinguished by its conceptual richness, with deep attention to continuity and change, agency and structure, macro- and micro-social intersections, biography and history, a focus on complex intersections across life domains, and recognition of the importance of dyadic, family-level, school, neighborhood, and workplace relationships for individual-level experiences. Methodologically, however, most life course research has focused on a single individual as its unit of analysis – until recently. Even in studies of social relationships and health, relationships traditionally were assessed by asking only one person – such as one spouse, one parent, or one child – to appraise the levels of love, support, strain, influence, instrumental and expressive support, and financial resources exchanged. As Carr and Springer (2010: 755) observed, "one of the most ironic limitations of studies on 'families' and health is that most studies focus on one individual within the larger family network. This limitation is due, in part, to traditional models of data collection where one person answers survey questions on his or her own union, parental status, relationship quality, and own health as well as the health of one's spouse or a randomly selected child." As elaborated below, this single-reporter approach offers an incomplete and potentially misleading portrayal of both the nature of one's relationships and the implications of these relationships for health and well-being. However, over the past two decades social science data and analytic techniques have expanded dramatically, offering tools to better explore the complexities of linked lives.

Data Resources

Multi-generation, multi-reporter data resources have flourished in recent years (Institute of Medicine 2014; National Research Council 2013, 2014). In the U.S., these new data resources or expansions to long-standing data sets span the life course, focusing primarily on *childhood and adolescence* (National Longitudinal Study of Adolescent Health [Add Health]); *adulthood* (Midlife Development in the United States [MIDUS]), *later life* (Changing Lives of Older Couples [CLOC]; Disability and Use of Time [DUST]; Health and Retirement Study [HRS]; National Social Life, Health and Aging Project [NSHAP]); or *extended observation periods spanning several life course stages* (Longitudinal Study of Generations [LSOG]; National Longitudinal Studies of Youth [NLSY]; Panel Study of Income Dynamics [PSID]; Wisconsin Longitudinal Study [WLS]). An important exception to these longitudinal data resources is the General Social Survey [GSS], a repeated cross-sectional survey started in 1972, which uses a name generator method to obtain egocentric network data on respondents. A brief summary of selected data resources is presented in Appendix A. This list is not intended to be inclusive, but rather highlights widely used population-based data sets for studying social networks and their influence on health over the life course, including several data sets featured in other chapters in this volume.

In general, these data resources can be grouped into four main categories: (a) husband and wife reports (e.g., CLOC, DUST, HRS, NSHAP, WLS); (b) sibling and/or twin reports (MIDUS, WLS); (c) intergenerational studies, typically with reports from parents and children, although some extend to as many as four generations (LSOG, NLSY, PSID); and (d) data sets which enable linkages between the focal respondent and social network members, such as high school classmates or friends (Add Health, WLS). These data sets typically obtain parallel interviews from two persons, such as husbands and wives, and also ask respondents to provide their own assessments of partner traits such as health and personality. Others ask study participants to name network members, enabling researchers to link an individual's response with the survey responses of his or her named friends and classmates, provided that those persons are in the study's sample.

Data from multiple reporters in one's interpersonal networks enable researchers to explore a range of innovative questions, as the empirical chapters in this edited volume reveal. Substantive advances fostered by these data resources include assessments of concordance and discrepancy in the reports made by network members as well as the implications of such (mis)matches in perceptions for health and well-being (e.g., Carr and Boerner 2009 [CLOC]); investigations of cross-over and "contagion" effects (e.g., Carr et al. 2014a, b, 2015 [DUST]; Larson and Almeida 1999); explorations of within-family differences in parent transfers to and treatment of children (e.g., Behrman and Rosenzweig 2004 [PSID]; Davey et al. 2009 [MIDUS]); similarities and differences in the consequences of early social and economic resources for sibling outcomes (e.g., Hauser et al. 1999[WLS]); the impact of social network members' attitudes and health behaviors on one's own health and well-being (e.g., Cohen-Cole and Fletcher 2008 [Add Health]; Falba and Sindelar 2008 [HRS]); and factors linked with changes in the composition and nature of one's social ties over the life course (e.g., Cornwell et al. 2014 [NSHAP]). The sections below provide further detail on how these relational data resources, used with appropriate analytic tools, have expanded our understanding of the ways social relationships shape physical and emotional health over the life course.

Dyadic Data Analytic Techniques

One of the most important advances in the study of linked lives is the development of dyadic data analysis techniques. These methods enable researchers to use data from multiple reporters, such as husbands' and wives' reports of marital quality, to estimate how much each person's outcome is associated with both own (i.e., actor) and partner characteristics. The most widely used statistical approach is actor-partner interdependence models (APIM; Cook and Kenny 2005). These models are increasingly widely used because they enable researchers to simultaneously estimate the effect of a person's own variable (i.e., "actor effect") and the effect of the same variable provided from the partner (i.e., "partner" effect) on some outcome measure. For instance, in a study examining the impact of one partner's health on the other partner's psychological well-being, a researcher would not only want to examine whether a wife's psychological well-being is affected by her husband's physical health (i.e., partner effect) but would simultaneously explore whether the wife's own physical health affects her own psychological well-being, given well-documented correlations between husbands' and wives' health due to factors like shared social environment and (un)healthy lifestyle (Kenny, Kashy and Cook 2006).

Social Network Methods

The design, collection, and use of social networks data to understand life course processes will be elaborated in subsequent chapters. I provide a brief summary here, to show how these techniques enable researchers to rigorously examine the role of linked lives in shaping health over the life course. A social network is a collection of relationships – referred to as "edges" – connecting individuals, or aggregations of individuals (e.g., schools or workplaces) – called "nodes." Contemporary social network research has been informed by life course scholarship, with researchers using sophisticated data to show how social ties shift as one ages. For example, a recent analysis of NSHAP data traced changes in the social networks of older adults over a five-year period, and found that 80 percent added at least one person to their social circle and more than half acquired new confidantes with whom they could share their private thoughts and feelings (Cornwell and Laumann 2015). Surprisingly, a higher proportion of NSHAP participants reported a net gain (38 percent) versus a net loss (27 percent) in the size of their social networks. This longitudinal research challenges earlier cross-sectional studies showing that the mean number of ties reported by retirement age persons was lower than persons of working age, and that persons in their upper 70s had fewer ties than those in slightly younger age groups (Morgan 1988).

Methodological advances including the use of Exponential Random Graph Models (ERGMs) and Stochastic Actor-Based Models (SABMS) such as SIENA enable researchers to model dynamic aspects of networks over time, and to document links between micro-level processes and macro-level outcomes (Snijders et al. 2006; Snijders et al. 2010). Researchers can then explore how multiple aspects of these relationships affect individual-level outcomes over the life course. For example, Cornwell and Laumann (2015) found that older adults who added new confidantes to their social circles went on to show improvements in physical health, physical and cognitive functioning, and psychological well-being, whereas those whose social networks constricted experienced a slight decline in physical (but not emotional) health.

Network data on younger adults allow researchers to explore questions of peer influence in more sophisticated ways than ever before. For example, the Add Health, a study of adolescents and young adults in the United States, allowed participants to name up to five female and five male friends at the baseline interview. These data have been widely used to examine prospectively how young adults' health, health behaviors, and sexual activity are shaped by the behaviors of their friends, romantic partners, friends-of-friends, and friends-of-romantic partners. Analyses of these data also show that the strength of peer influences is conditional upon a particular peer's place in the social network – such as how popular he or she is, or how tightly-knit or diffuse the social network is. For instance, Kreager and Haynie (2011) examined 449 dating couples in the Add Health and found that one's romantic partner connected the teenager to new peer contexts that, in turn, triggered changes in drinking behavior. By using network data and APIM models, they could document the unique effects of a romantic partner's drinking, friends' drinking, and friend-of-partner's drinking on teen's own future binge drinking and drinking frequency. Surprisingly, they found that friends-of-partners' drinking had stronger effects than own friends' drinking. This study powerfully shows how methodological advances are enabling researchers to specify precisely how social network members can have complex and often surprising effects on youth as they make the transition to adulthood.

Contemporary Linked Lives Research: Have We Learned Anything New About Marriage and Health?

Research dating back to Durkheim (1951: 1897) shows that married persons enjoy better health than their unmarried counterparts. Empirical studies in the United States, Europe, and most wealthy nations consistently document protective effects of marriage on health outcomes including disability, morbidity, mortality, and self-assessed mental and physical health. By contrast, never married persons and persons whose marriages ended either via divorce or widowhood have poorer physical and mental health than their married counterparts (see Carr et al. 2014b for review). Yet researchers have recently documented that marriage is not uniformly protective; rather, the "marriage benefit" is limited to those who enjoy supportive, high quality unions (Proulx et al. 2007). For example, mounting research suggests that unmarried persons report better mental health than married persons in unhappy or high-conflict marriages (Williams 2003).

High quality marriage is protective because it provides emotional support that enhances mental health, and instrumental support that may directly bolster physical health or buffer against the health-depleting effects of stress (Carr and Pudrovska 2015). Happily married persons also enjoy more satisfying sexual relations, which provide physical and emotional health benefits (Waite et al. 2015). High quality marriages are considered a particularly effective source of social control (Umberson

1992). Spouses who love and care for one another will encourage the adoption of healthy behaviors and the loss of unhealthy ones. Husbands and wives may encourage each other to eat nutritious meals, take their daily medications, eschew or limit their smoking and alcohol consumption, and exercise together. By contrast, persons in poor quality marriages exhibit poor eating habits, erratic sleep patterns, and higher rates of smoking, alcohol use, and nonmedical use of prescription medications (Miller et al. 2013).

Yet much of what we know about marriage and health is based on only one partner's self-reported behaviors and marital assessments, raising questions about the processes through which marital dynamics affect health (Carr and Springer 2010). Further, most studies of marriage and health fail to consider that spouses are embedded in extended social networks, such that relationships with children, friends, and other relatives may condition the associations among marriage and health. The following sections briefly highlight contemporary studies using innovative data and methods to challenge taken-for-granted assumptions about marriage and health, thus advancing our understanding of linked lives over the life course.

Marital Quality and Well-Being: His, Hers, and Ours?

An implicit assumption underlying most research on marital quality and well-being is that one partner's perception of the marriage provides an accurate snapshot of the couple's life together. However, mounting research spanning multiple data sets including the CLOC, DUST, and HRS shows that spouses' marital quality appraisals are modestly correlated (r = 0.30 to 0.50), even in long-married couples (Bulanda 2011; Carr and Boerner 2009; Carr et al. 2014a, b, 2016). Thus, researchers are increasingly interested in exploring whether the well-documented association between marital quality and well-being (e.g., Proulx et al. 2007; Robles et al. 2014) differs based on whether one's own or one's partner's appraisals are considered, and whether the effects of marital quality are amplified when both spouses offer similar appraisals. These analyses are motivated by the recognition that marital quality is a fluid, dynamic, and mutually constructed component of a relationship. For example, if one partner is dissatisfied with the marriage, he or she could act negatively toward the spouse by criticizing or withdrawing affection. Conversely, happily married persons may be motivated to provide support and encouragement to their partner, thereby enhancing their partner's health and happiness. Thus, one partner's marital (dis)satisfaction may be linked to the well-being of the other, even independent of their own appraisal (Carr et al. 2014a, b).

Recent studies using dyadic data and APIM methods find strong evidence of both actor and partner effects, occasionally revealing counterintuitive results. For example, Choi et al. (2016) examined changes in marital quality and health among couples in the HRS and found that increases in positive aspects of marriage, such as feeling loved and supported by one's partner, led to declines in disability and functional limitations of the other partner. Yet very different patterns result when researchers explore linkages between marital quality and emotional, rather than physical health. In an analysis of couple-level data from the DUST, Carr et al. (2016) found that when wives report high levels of marital support, their husbands report higher levels of frustration, perhaps because the help they received undermines their feelings of autonomy or competence.

Other studies find that one spouse's marital quality appraisal may buffer or amplify the effects of the other's appraisal. Birditt et al. (2015) tracked married couples in the HRS and found that negative relationship quality predicted increases in both husband's and wife's blood pressure when *both* members of the couple reported strained relations. Carr and colleagues (2014a, b) found evidence of amplification for men only; in an analysis of dyadic data in the DUST, the effect of men's marital quality appraisals on his own life satisfaction is contingent on his wife's marital appraisals. A man who views his marriage very unfavorably may still enjoy relatively high levels of life satisfaction if his wife views the marriage favorably. A happily married woman may be highly motivated to provide care and practical support to her spouse, such that even an unhappily married man may receive practical benefits that enhance his overall well-being. Women also tend to engage partners in marital issues, whether a happily married woman praising positive aspects, or an unhappily married woman criticizing her husband. Men tend to take a more passive approach, where their feelings toward the marriage may not be conveyed to their spouse and thus may not compound their wives' marital dissatisfaction to affect her overall well-being. These complexities would not have been detected in studies using only one spouse's appraisal of the relationship.

Marriage and Health: Whose Health Behaviors Matter?

Marriage is considered protective for health because spouses, especially wives, exert social control over one another's health behaviors (Umberson 1992). An underlying assumption is that spouses encourage healthy behaviors and dissuade unhealthy ones. The "marriage as social control" perspective has been challenged and extended in recent years by dyadic studies examining the health behaviors of both spouses. In general, this work shows that a spouse with an unhealthy lifestyle may increase unhealthy behaviors in their partner, thus undermining the protective effects of marriage on health (Meyler et al. 2007).

For example, Falba and Sindelar (2008) analyzed multiwave dyadic data from the HRS and found that one spouse's changes in smoking, drinking, exercising, cholesterol screening, and obtaining a flu shot triggered comparable changes in the other partner's behaviors; these strong patterns persisted even when sociodemographic and shared environment factors were controlled. Further challenging the assumption that marriage is uniformly protective, Margolis and Wright (2016) found that being married to a smoker was more deleterious to one's well-being than not being married at all. Using multiwave data from the HRS, they found that persons married to smokers and those whose spouses had quit but then relapsed back into smoking were less likely than their unpartnered counterparts to quit smoking and adhere to smoking cessation themselves. By contrast, partners of non-smokers or quitters fared better than their unmarried counterparts with respect to their own health behaviors, revealing that individuals may be "better alone than with a smoker" (Margolis and Wright 2016).

Another nuanced study explored the extent to which health behaviors change following transitions in and out of marriage, uncovering the complex ways that marital status, gender, and a partner's health behavior shape one's own health behaviors. Analyzing multiwave data from the HRS, Reczek et al. (2016) found that spouses' drinking converges over the course of a marriage, albeit in different ways for men and women. Wives' heavy alcohol use is associated with decreases in husbands' alcohol use, whereas husbands' heavy drinking is associated with increases in wives' heavy drinking (Reczek et al. 2016). Taken together, these studies suggest that being married does not necessarily promote healthy behaviors; rather, spouses may also adopt one another's (un)healthy behaviors, underscoring the complex influence of linked lives on marriage.

Beyond the Dyad: The Role of Other Linked Lives in Marriage and Health Research

Even the most interdependent married couple maintains relationships with friends, siblings, parents, and children, and these relationships may shape both the nature of one's marriage and the ways that marriage and marital dissolution affect health and well-being.

Mounting research suggests that marriage and marital transitions are linked with other social relationships in complex ways (see Wrzus et al. 2013 for review). For example, conventional wisdom would suggest that friendships heighten the protective effects of marriage, where more support is generally better for individuals. However, one recent analysis of network data from the NSHAP suggests otherwise. Cornwell and Laumann (2011) explore how social integration beyond the marital dyad affects one particular health outcome: men's risk of erectile dysfunction (ED). Paradoxically, they find that one presumably positive aspect of the marital relationship, the couple's level of social integration, actually threatens men's sexual health. Wives who talk frequently to her husband's confidants pose a threat to the husband's sense of masculinity and consequently, his risk of ED.

Emerging research underscores the importance of social networks as both a resource and liability as one experiences marital transitions. Although transitions like widowhood and divorce historically were considered stressful events with uniformly deleterious consequences, more recent work suggests that marital transitions may trigger changes in one's other social relations, and these changes, in turn may buffer against or exacerbate the distressing consequences of marital dissolution. For instance, Kaljimn (Kalmijn 2012) analyzed 12 years of data from the Swiss Household Panel (SHP) and found that friendship ties tend to grow weaker and less important when one marries, yet those ties re-emerge as an important source of support and integration after a divorce or spousal loss, especially for women.

Non-marital social ties also moderate the effects of marital status changes on health and well-being, revealing that some ties are more protective than others. Bookwala et al. (2014) tracked marital histories of participants in the WLS, and examined whether the health-related consequences of divorce and widowhood were moderated by one's other social ties. The effect of widowhood on depressive symptoms, sick days and poor self-rated health was buffered for those who had a friend confidante, yet having a confidante in the family provided no benefit. These findings challenge the assumption that social support is uniformly protective, instead revealing that particular social ties confer benefits in particular social circumstances, whereas other ties may provide no help or even undermine one's adaptation to stress (Rook 1984).

Mounting research on marital transitions also explicitly recognizes that these transitions are embedded in and shaped by one's larger social networks. For example, studies generally show that upon the death of a spouse, older adults grow increasingly dependent on and close with their adult children (Ha et al. 2006), yet recent studies have found that these patterns are conditional upon the quality of the late marriage. Analyzing multiwave data from the CLOC, Carr and Boerner (2013a, b) found that bereaved spouses who had enjoyed high levels of marital warmth went on to receive higher levels of support from children post-loss, whereas those with strained marriages subsequently received less emotional support from and were less dependent on their children; these effects persisted net of the bereaved person's personality and depressive symptoms.

Similarly, a bereaved spouse's pursuit of new romantic relationships is powerfully shaped by their larger social networks. In general, widowers are more likely than widows to both seek out and establish new romantic relationships (Carr 2004b), however these patterns vary based on one's ties with children and friends. Older widowers with high levels of social support from friends are less likely than their counterparts with weaker social ties to seek out new romantic relationships, suggesting that friendships may be a substitute for at least some of the benefits of marriage in later life (Carr 2004b). By contrast, widowers who have strained relationships with their children are more likely to seek out and pursue new romantic relationships, perhaps to meet emotional and social needs that are not fulfilled by their immediate family (Carr and Boerner 2013a, b). Taken together, contemporary research reveals that marital relationships are deeply embedded in and mutually influenced by one's larger network of familial and friendship ties. Common assumptions regarding the health-enhancing benefits of marriage (especially high-quality marriages) and the distressing effects of marital dissolution have been contested and expanded by recent studies drawing on dyadic- and family-level data over the life course.

Conclusion

This chapter has described the importance of sociological perspectives on the life course for understanding human connections and their consequences for health and well-being. Our knowledge of the complex ways that relationships shape health has been advanced in the past two decades, due in part to investments in multi-generation, multi-reporter longitudinal data sets and the development of analytic tools that enable researchers to move beyond the individual as the unit of analysis, and explore the intricate and often surprising ways that social ties within and beyond the family shape individual lives. Contemporary research reveals that two individuals in a single relationship may experience that relationship very differently, with perceptions often shaped by cohort-specific gendered dynamics and expectations (e.g., Carr et al. 2014a, b; 2016). The perceptions of both partners, however, may have multiplicative effects on the health and well-being of one or more partner, where the harmful effects of strain are amplified when both partners offer negative appraisals of the relationship (e.g., Birditt et al. 2015) or buffered when only one rates the relationship as problematic. Experiences within a marital dyad also are intricately linked to one's other social ties, with children, friends and other relatives. As such, transitions out of marriage – historically considered a uniformly distressing event – may be less difficult for those with high levels of support (Bookwala et al. 2014), whereas transitions into new romantic relationships are more or less desirable depending on the level of support or strain experienced in one's other social ties (Carr 2004b; Carr and Boerner 2013a, b).

Despite these advances and challenges to what we know about relationships and health, the study of linked lives and their implications for health and well-being is still in its nascent stages. Future generations of researchers face the challenge of adopting a broader and more expansive view of what constitutes meaningful social ties. Emerging family structures and processes over the past five decades include: non-marital cohabitation; non-coresidential romantic partnerships (i.e., living apart together [LATs]); same-sex marital and non-marital unions; higher order marriages; presence of step-parents, step-children and step-siblings in families; enduring social and economic ties with former spouses and partners; and "skip-generation" families (i.e., grandparent-grandchild households where middle generation is absent). Each of these social ties, in turn, is embedded in their own networks of neighbors, coworkers, friendships, social networking site (SNS) ties, and so on. As such, researchers will need to cast a wider net in conceptualizing and measuring social relationships, and in theorizing the ways that these diverse relationships – permanent versus fleeting, "real" versus virtual, coresidential versus physically distant, collegial versus conflicted, legally recognized versus socially recognized – will shape social, emotional, physical and economic well-being over the life course.

Appendix A: Selected Resources for Investigating Link Lives over the Life Course: Dyadic, Multigenerational, and Network Data Sets

Data set	Study summary	Respondents	Example publications	Website
Changing Lives of Older Couples (CLOC)	Prospective study of spousal bereavement in later life.	1545 married persons at baseline (including 423 spousal dyads); 250 of whom become bereaved.	Carr et al. 2001; Carr and Boerner 2009	http://cloc.isr.umich.edu/
Disability and Use of Time (DUST)	Daily diary and survey study of married couples ages 60 + .	DUST sampled more than 500 older couples in the 2009 PSID.	Carr et al. 2014a, 2016	http://psidonline.isr.umich.edu/DUST/dust09_UserGuide.pdf
General Social Survey	Biannual repeated cross-section started in 1972. Egocentric network data in selected years.	Persons ages 18–99, with sample size averaging around 3000.	Smith, McPherson, and Smith-Lovin 2014;	http://gss.norc.org/
Health and Retirement Study (HRS)	Multiwave study of older adults started in 1992, with attention to finances and health.	Persons born 1931–41 and their spouses.	Birditt et al. 2015; Falba and Sindelar 2008	http://hrsonline.isr.umich.edu/
Longitudinal Study of Generations (LSOG)	Multiwave survey of four generations, focused on values and affiliation.	300 four-generation families in southern California.	Bengtson et al. 2002.	http://www.icpsr.umich.edu/icpsrweb/ICPSR/studies/22100
Midlife Development in the United States (MIDUS)	Psychosocial and biological factors in health, among adults born 1920–75 interviewed at three waves since 1995.	More than 3000 adults, 950 of their siblings, and nearly 1000 twin pairs.	Davey et al. 2009; Schnittker 2008	http://midus.wisc.edu/

(continued)

Data set	Study summary	Respondents	Example publications	Website
National Longitudinal Study of Adolescent Health (Add Health)	A large nationally representative sample of 7th to 12th graders during the 1994 and 1995 school year, tracked across multiple waves.	More than 90,000 interviews with children, parents, administrators, and data linkage to peers and romantic partners	Kreager and Haynie 2011	http://www.cpc.unc.edu/projects/addhealth
National Longitudinal Studies of Youth (1979, 1997)	A multi-cohort study of the transition to adulthood, and the children of primary respondents.	Nearly 13,000 persons age 14–22, in 1979 and their children.	Gillespie and Treas, 2015; Kim 2014;	http://www.bls.gov/nls/
National Social Life, Health, and Aging Project (NSHAP)	A three-wave survey of adults born 1920–47 and their spouses, focused on biosocial factors in health and aging.	More than 3000 interviewed at baseline, with spouse/partner interviews at subsequent waves.	Cornwell et al. 2014; Waite et al. 2015	http://www.norc.org/Research/Projects/Pages/national-social-life-health-and-aging-project.aspx
Panel Study of Income Dynamics (PSID)	The original 1968 sample included 18,000 individuals in 5000 families. All children of original sample tracked over time.	Nearly 70,000 people have participated in the PSID, and as many four generations are represented.	Behrman and Rosenzweig 2004	http://psidonline.isr.umich.edu/
Wisconsin Longitudinal Study (WLS)	Multiwave study tracking a random 1/3 sample of all high school seniors in Wisconsin in 1957.	10,317 high school graduates, a randomly selected sibling, and spouse. Data linkage to high school friends.	Carr 2004a, Hauser, Sheridan and Warren 1999	http://www.ssc.wisc.edu/wlsresearch/

References

Alwin, D. F. (2012). Integrating varieties of life course concepts. *Journals of Gerontology, Series B: Psychological Sciences and Social Sciences 60* (Special Issue II), 7–14.

Alwin, D. F., Cohen, R. L., & Newcomb, T. M. (1991). *Political attitudes over the life span: The Bennington women after fifty years*. Madison: University of Wisconsin Press.

Alwin, D. F., & McCammon, R. J. (2007). Rethinking generations. *Research in Human Development, 4*, 219–237.

Baunach, D. M. (2012). Changing same-sex marriage attitudes in America from 1988 through 2010. *Public Opinion Quarterly, 76*, 364–378.

Bengtson, V. L., Biblarz, T. J., & Roberts, R. E. (2002). *How families still matter: A longitudinal study of youth in two generations*. New York: Cambridge University Press.

Behrman, J. R., & Rosenzweig, M. R. (2004). Parental allocations to children: New evidence on bequest differences among siblings. *Review of Economics and Statistics, 86*, 637–640.

Bianchi, S. M., & Milkie, M. A. (2010). Work and family research in the first decade of the 21st century. *Journal of Marriage and Family, 72*, 705–725.

Birditt, K. S., Newton, N. J., Cranford, J. A., & Ryan, L. H. (2015). Stress and negative relationship quality among older couples: Implications for blood pressure. *Journals of Gerontology: Social Sciences*. Advanced Access.

Bookwala, J., Marshall, K. I., & Manning, S. W. (2014). Who needs a friend? Marital status transitions and physical health outcomes in later life. *Health Psychology, 33*, 505–515.

Brody, E. M., Johnsen, P. T., Fulcomer, M. C., & Lang, A. M. (1983). Women's changing roles and help to elderly parents: Attitudes of three generations of women. *Journal of Gerontology, 38*, 597–607.

Bulanda, J. R. (2011). Gender, marital power, and marital quality in later life. *Journal of Women & Aging, 23*, 2–22.

Bumpass, L. L. (1990). What's happening to the family? Interactions between demographic and institutional change. *Demography, 27*, 483–498.

Cantor, M. H. (1975). Life space and the social support system of the Inner City elderly of New York. *The Gerontologist, 15*, 23–27.

Carlson, D. L. (2012). Deviations from desired age at marriage: Mental health differences across marital status. *Journal of Marriage and Family, 74*, 743–758.

Carr, D. (2004a). 'My daughter has a career – I just raised babies': Women's intergenerational social comparisons. *Social Psychology Quarterly, 67*, 132–154.

Carr, D. (2004b). The desire to date and remarry among older widows and widowers. *Journal of Marriage and Family, 66*, 1051–1068.

Carr, D., & Boerner, K. (2009). Do spousal discrepancies in marital quality assessments affect psychological adjustment to widowhood? *Journal of Marriage and Family, 71*, 495–509.

Carr, D., & Boerner, K. (2013a). The impact of spousal loss on parent-child relations in later life: Are effects contingent upon the quality of the late marriage? *Family Science, 4*, 37–49.

Carr, D., & Boerner, K. (2013b). Dating after late-life spousal loss: Does it compromise relationships with adult children? *Journal of Aging Studies, 27*, 487–498.

Carr, D., House, J. S., Wortman, C., Nesse, R., & Kessler, R. C. (2001). Psychological adjustment to sudden and anticipated spousal loss among older widowed persons. *The Journals of Gerontology Series B: Psychological Sciences and Social Sciences, 56*(4), S237–S248.

Carr, D., Cornman, J. C., & Freedman, V. A. (2015). Marital quality and negative experienced well-being: An assessment of actor and partner effects among older married persons. *The Journals of Gerontology. Series B, Psychological Sciences and Social Sciences, 71*(1), 177–187.

Carr, D., Cornman, J. C., & Freedman, V. A. (2016). Does marital quality protect against distress? Marital quality and momentary negative mood in later life. *Journal of Gerontology: Social Sciences, 71*, 177–187.

Carr, D., Freedman, V. A., Cornman, J. C., & Schwarz, N. (2014a). Happy marriage, happy life? Marital quality and subjective well-being in later life. *Journal of Marriage and Family, 76*, 930–948.
Carr, D., & Pudrovska, T. (2015). Marital quality and health. In J. Wright (Ed.), *International Encyclopedia of social and behavioral sciences* (2nd ed., pp. 512–517). New York: Elsevier.
Carr, D., & Springer, K. (2010). Advances in families and Health Research in the 21st century. *Journal of Marriage and Family, 72*, 744–762. Decade in Review Special Issue.
Carr, D., Springer, K., & Williams, K. (2014b). Health and families. In J. Treas, J. Scott, & M. Richards (Eds.), *Wiley-Blackwell Companion to the sociology of families* (pp. 255–276). New York: Wiley.
Choi, H., Yorgason, J. B., & Johnson, D. R. (2016). Marital quality and health in middle and later adulthood: Dyadic associations. *Journals of Gerontology: Social Sciences, 71*, 154–164.
Clarke, P., Morenoff, J., Debbink, M., Golberstein, E., Elliott, M. R., & Lantz, P. M. (2014). Cumulative exposure to neighborhood context consequences for health transitions over the adult life course. *Research on Aging, 36*, 115–142.
Clausen, J. (1993). *American lives: Looking back at the children of the great depression*. New York: Free Press.
Cohen-Cole, E., & Fletcher, J. M. (2008). Is obesity contagious? Social networks versus environmental factors in the obesity epidemic. *Journal of Health Economics, 27*, 1382–1387.
Coleman, J. S. (1961). *Adolescent society: The social life of teenagers and its impact on education*. New York: Free Press.
Cook, W. L., & Kenny, D. A. (2005). The actor–partner interdependence model: A model of bidirectional effects in developmental studies. *International Journal of Behavioral Development, 29*, 101–109.
Cornwell, B., & Laumann, E. O. (2011). Network position and sexual dysfunction: Implications of partner Betweenness for men. *American Journal of Sociology, 117*, 172–208.
Cornwell, B., & Laumann, E. O. (2015). The health benefits of network growth: New evidence from a National Survey of older adults. *Social Science & Medicine, 125*, 94–106.
Cornwell, B., Philip Schumm, L., Laumann, E. O., Kim, J., & Kim, Y.-J. (2014). Assessment of social network change in a National Longitudinal Survey. *Journals of Gerontology: Social Sciences, 69*(Suppl. 2), S75–S82.
Cunningham, M. (2007). Influences of Women's employment on the gendered division of household labor over the life course evidence from a 31-year panel study. *Journal of Family Issues, 28*, 422–444.
Davey, A., Tucker, C. J., Fingerman, K., & Savla, J. (2009). Within-family variability in representations of past relationships with parents. *Journals of Gerontology: Psychological Sciences, 64B*, 125–136.
Durkheim, É. (1951). *Suicide*. Glencoe, IL: The Free Press. (Original work published 1897).
Elder, G. H., Jr. (1974). *Children of the great depression: Social change in life experience*. Chicago: University of Chicago Press.
Elder, G. H., Jr. (1994). Time, human agency, and social change: Perspectives on the life course. *Social Psychology Quarterly, 57*, 4–15.
Elder, G. H., Jr. (2000). The life course. In E. F. Borgatta & R. J. V. Montgomery (Eds.), *Encyclopedia of sociology* (2nd ed., pp. 1614–1622). New York: Macmillan Reference USA.
Falba, T. A., & Sindelar, J. L. (2008). Spousal concordance in health behavior change. *Health Services Research, 43*, 96–116.
Furstenberg, F. F., Jr., Brooks-Gunn, J., & Philip Morgan, S. (1987). *Adolescent mothers in later life*. New York: Cambridge University Press.
George, L. K. (1993). Sociological perspectives on life transitions. *Annual Review of Sociology, 19*, 353–373.
Gillespie, B. J., & Treas, J. (2015). *Adolescent intergenerational cohesiveness and young adult proximity to mothers*. Advance Access: Journal of Family Issues.

Glass, J., Bengtson, V. L., & Dunham, C. C. (1986). Attitude similarity in three-generation families: Socialization, status inheritance, or reciprocal influence? *American Sociological Review, 51*, 685–698.

Goldman, N. (1994). Social factors and health: The causation-selection issue revisited. *Proceedings of the National Academy of Sciences, 91*, 1251–1255.

Ha, J.-H., Carr, D., Utz, R., & Nesse, R. (2006). Older adults' perceptions of intergenerational support after widowhood: How do men and women differ? *Journal of Family Issues, 27*, 3–30.

Haas, S. A. (2008). Trajectories of functional health: The 'long arm' of childhood health and socioeconomic factors. *Social Science and Medicine, 66*, 849–861.

Hammer, L. B., Allen, E., & Grigsby, T. D. (1997). Work–family conflict in dual-earner couples: Within-individual and crossover effects of work and family. *Journal of Vocational Behavior, 50*, 185–203.

Hauser, R. M., Sheridan, J. T., & Warren, J. R. (1999). Socioeconomic achievements of siblings in the life course new findings from the Wisconsin longitudinal study. *Research on Aging, 21*, 338–378.

Hayward, M. D., & Gorman, B. K. (2004). The long arm of childhood: The influence of early-life social conditions on men's mortality. *Demography, 41*, 87–107.

House, J. S., Landis, K. R., & Umberson, D. (1988). Social relationships and health. *Science, 241*, 540–545.

Inkeles, A., & Levinson, D. (1969). National character: The study of modal personality and sociocultural systems. In G. Lindzey & E. Aronson (Eds.), *The handbook of social psychology* (2nd ed., pp. 418–507). Reading: Addison-Wesley.

Institute of Medicine and National Research Council. (2014). *Investing in the health and well-being of young adults*. Washington, DC: The National Academies Press.

Kalmijn, M. (2012). Longitudinal analyses of the effects of age, marriage, and parenthood on social contacts and support. *Advances in Life Course Research, 17*, 177–190.

Kenny, D. A., Kashy, D. A., & Cook, W. L. (2006). Dyadic data analysis. In *New York*. Guilford: Press.

Kim, K. (2014). Intergenerational transmission of age at first birth in the United States: Evidence from multiple surveys. *Population Research and Policy Review, 33*, 649–671.

Kohli, M. (2007). The institutionalization of the life course: Looking back to look ahead. *Research in Human Development, 4*, 253–271.

Kreager, D. A., & Haynie, D. L. (2011). Dangerous liaisons? Dating and drinking diffusion in adolescent peer networks. *American Sociological Review, 76*, 737–763.

Landecker, H., & Panofsky, A. (2013). From social structure to gene regulation, and back: A critical introduction to environmental epigenetics for sociology. *Annual Review of Sociology, 39*, 333–357.

Larson, R. W., & Almeida, D. M. (1999). Emotional transmission in the daily lives of families: A new paradigm for studying family process. *Journal of Marriage and Family, 61*, 5–20.

Leisering, L. (2003). Government and the Life Course. In J. T. Mortimer & M. J. Shanahan (Eds.), *Handbook of the life course* (pp. 205–225). New York: Kluwer.

Levine, P. B. (2011). How does parental unemployment affect children's educational performance? In G. J. Duncan & R. J. Murnane (Eds.), *Whither opportunity: Rising inequality, schools, and children's life chances* (pp. 31–358). New York: Russell Sage Foundation.

MacLean, A., & Elder, G. H., Jr. (2007). Military service in the life course. *Annual Review of Sociology, 33*, 175–196.

Mannheim, K. (1928). The problem of generations. In *Essays on the sociology of knowledge* (pp. 276–322). London: Routledge & Keagan Paul.

Manning, W. D., Brown, S. L., & Payne, K. K. (2014). Two decades of stability and change in age at first union formation. *Journal of Marriage and Family, 76*, 247–260.

Margolis, R., & Wright, L. (2016). Better off alone than with a smoker: The influence of partner's smoking behavior in later life. *Journals of Gerontology: Social Sciences, 71*(40), 687–697.

Mayer, K. U. (2003). The Sociology of the Life Course and Life Span Psychology: Diverging or Converging Pathways? In M. Staudinger Ursula & U. Lindenberger (Eds.), *Understanding Human Development: Dialogues with Lifespan Psychology* (p. 463). New York: Kluwer Academic.

Meyler, D., Stimpson, J. P., & Kristen Peek, M. (2007). Health concordance within couples: A systematic review. *Social Science & Medicine, 64*, 2297–2310.

Mills, C. W. (1959). *The sociological imagination*. New York: Oxford University Press.

Miller, R. B., Hollist, C. S., Olsen, J., & Law, D. (2013). Marital quality and health over 20 years: A growth curve analysis. *Journal of Marriage and Family, 75*, 667–680.

Moehling, C. M. (1999). State child labor Laws and the decline of child labor. *Explorations in Economic History, 36*, 72–106.

Moore, D. W. (2003). *Family, health most important aspects of life.*. Washington, DC: Gallup (January 3, 2003). http://www.gallup.com/poll/7504/Family-Health-Most-Important-Aspects-Life.aspx?g_source=mn2-books. Accessed 8 Mar 2016.

Morgan, D. L. (1988). Age differences in social network participation. *Journal of Gerontology, 43*, S129–S137.

Morton, P. M., Schafer, M. H., & Ferraro, K. F. (2012). Does childhood misfortune increase cancer risk in adulthood? *Journal of Aging and Health, 24*(6), 1–37.

National Research Council. (2013). New Directions in the Sociology of Aging. In L. J. Waite & T. J. Plewes (Eds.), *Panel on New Directions in Social Demography, Social Epidemiology, and the Sociology of Aging, Committee on Population, Division of Behavioral and Social Sciences and Education*. Washington, DC: The National Academies Press.

National Research Council. (2014). Civic engagement and social cohesion: Measuring dimensions of social capital to inform policy. In K. Prewitt, C. D. Mackie, & H. Habermann (Eds.), *Panel on Measuring Social and Civic Engagement and Social Cohesion in Surveys. Committee on National Statistics. Division of Behavioral and Social Sciences and Education*. Washington, DC: The National Academies Press.

Neugarten, B. L., Moore, J. W., & Lowe, J. C. (1965). Age norms, age constraints, and adult socialization. *American Journal of Sociology, 70*, 710–717.

O'Rand, A. M., & Hamil-Luker, J. (2005). d. *Journal of Gerontology: Social Science, 60B*(Special Issue II), 117–124.

Proulx, C. M., Helms, H. M., & Buehler, C. (2007). Marital quality and personal well-being: A meta-analysis. *Journal of Marriage and Family, 69*, 576–593.

Reczek, C., Pudrovska, T., Carr, D., & Umberson, D. (2016). Men's and women's alcohol trajectories across the gendered marital biography. *Journal of Health & Social Behavior, 57*(1), 77–96.

Robles, T. F., Slatcher, R. B., Trombello, J. M., & McGinn, M. M. (2014). Marital quality and health: A meta-analytic review. *Psychological Bulletin, 140*, 140–187.

Rook, K. S. (1984). The negative side of social interaction: Impact on psychological well-being. *Journal of Personality and Social Psychology, 46*, 1097–1108.

Sampson, R. J., Morenoff, J. D., & Gannon-Rowley, T. (2002). Assessing neighborhood effects: Social processes and new directions in research. *Annual Review of Sociology, 28*, 443–478.

Scarr, S., & McCartney, K. (1983). How people make their own environments: A theory of genotype-environment effects. *Child Development, 54*, 424–435.

Schnittker, J. (2008). Happiness and success: Genes, families, and the psychological effects of socioeconomic position and social support. *American Journal of Sociology, 114*, S233–S259.

Seltzer, J. A., & Bianchi, S. M. (2013). Demographic change and parent-child relationships in adulthood. *Annual Review of Sociology, 39*, 275–290.

Settersten, R. A., & Hägestad, G. O. (1996). What's the latest? Cultural age deadlines for family transitions. *The Gerontologist, 36*, 178–188.

Sewell, W. H., & Hauser, R. M. (1975). *Education, occupation, and earnings: Achievements in the early career*. New York: Academic Press.

Signer, B., & Saldana, D. (2001). Educational and career aspirations of high school students and race, gender, class differences. *Race, Gender, & Class, 8*, 22–34.

Smith, A. (2011). *Americans and text messaging*. Washington, DC: Pew Research Center.
Smith, J. A., McPherson, M., & Smith-Lovin, L. (2014). Social distance in the United States: Sex, race, religion, age, and education homophily among confidants, 1985 to 2004. *American Sociological Review, 79*(3), 432–456.
Snijders, T. A. B., Van de Bunt, G. G., & Steglich, C. E. G. (2010). Introduction to stochastic actor-based models for network dynamics. *Social Networks, 32*, 44–60.
Snijders, T. A. B., Pattison, P., Robins, G., & Handcock, M. (2006). New specifications for exponential random graph models. *Sociological Methodology, 36*(1), 99–153.
Stein Dan, J., Kate, S., Haro Abad Josep, M., Sergio, A.-G., Jordi, A., Matthias, A., Koen, D., de Giovanni, G., Noboru, I., José, P.-V., Viviane, K., Carmen, L., Johan, O., Kessler, R. C., & Michael, V. K. (2010). Early childhood adversity and later hypertension: Data from the world mental health survey. *Annals of Clinical Psychiatry., 22*(1), 19–28.
Teo, A. R., Choi, H. J., Andrea, S. B., Valenstein, M., Newsom, J. T., Dobscha, S. K., & Zivin, K. (2015). Does mode of contact with different types of social relationships predict depression in older adults? Evidence from a nationally representative survey. *Journal of the American Geriatrics Society, 63*, 2014–2022.
Thornton, A., & Young-DeMarco, L. (2001). Four decades of trends in attitudes toward family issues in the United States: The 1960s through the 1990s. *Journal of Marriage and Family, 63*, 1009–1037.
Umberson, D. (1992). Gender, marital status and the social control of health behavior. *Social Science & Medicine, 34*, 907–917.
U.S. Census Bureau. (2015). *Residential vacancies and homeownership in the second quarter 2015*. http://www.census.gov/housing/hvs/files/qtr215/currenthvspress.pdf
Wadsworth, M. E. J., & Kuh, D. (2016). Epidemiological perspectives on the life course. In M. J. Shanahan, J. T. Mortimer, & M. K. Johnson (Eds.), *Handbook of the life course* (Vol. 2, pp. 639–659). Cham: Springer.
Waite, L. J., Iveniuk, J., Laumann, E. O., & McClintock, M. K. (2015). Sexuality in older couples: Individual and dyadic characteristics. *Archives of Sexual Behavior*. Advance Access.
Williams, K. (2003). Has the future of marriage arrived ? A contemporary examination of gender, marriage, and psychological well-being. *Journal of Health and Social Behavior, 44*(4), 470–487.
Wrzus, C., Hänel, M., Wagner, J., & Neyer, F. J. (2013). Social network changes and life events across the life span: A meta-analysis. *Psychological Bulletin, 139*, 53–80.

Deborah Carr was until recently the professor and chair of the Department of Sociology at Rutgers University, where she was also the (interim) director of the Institute for Health, Health Care Policy & Aging Research. She is now a professor of sociology at Boston University. Her research and teaching interests include the sociology of the life course, aging, social psychology, and gender.

Part II
Social Network Perspectives on the Life Course

Chapter 4
Life Course and Network Advantage: Peak Periods, Turning Points, and Transition Ages

Ronald S. Burt

This is an exploration of the interface between two areas of research, social networks and the life course. There are alternative strategies for such exploration. I prefer a strategy of anchoring on a phenomenon known well on one side and exploring how current understanding is enriched by viewing the phenomenon from the other side. Such a strategy ignores much of the interface, but ideas discussed are more likely to be incorporated into future research because they are concretely relevant to something well known. Given my past research, I anchor on the well-known phenomenon of network advantage, and then explore how a life-course perspective enriches what we know about the phenomenon.

Empirical research over the last two decades shows that achievement is associated with large, open social networks. The division of labor makes information homogeneous, tacit, and therefore sticky within clusters of densely connected people doing similar work such that clusters disconnect, buffered from one another by structural holes between the clusters. Two people who have no connection with one another are more likely than connected people to operate in different clusters, working with different ideas and practices. The more disconnected the contacts are in a person's network, the more likely the network spans structural holes. These people (call them network brokers, connectors, hubs, or entrepreneurs), have

I am grateful to the University of Chicago Booth School of Business and the MaxPo research Center in Paris for financial support during the work reported here. I am also grateful to Joe Galaskiewicz and Ezra Zuckerman for early comments, to Thomas Burt for editorial comments, and for incorporated comments in workshops at the University of Arizona, the Centre de Recherché en Economie et Statistique, Michigan State University, Pennsylvania State University, the SciencesPo Center for the Sociology of Organizations, and Washington University in St. Louis. Allison Asher provided voluminous editorial comments, and the three book editors offered substantive comments to clarify and broaden the discussion.

R. S. Burt (✉)
University of Chicago Booth School of Business, Chicago, IL, USA
e-mail: ron.burt@chicagobooth.edu

D. F. Alwin et al. (eds.), *Social Networks and the Life Course*, Frontiers in Sociology and Social Research 2, https://doi.org/10.1007/978-3-319-71544-5_4

information diversity, timing, and arbitrage advantages over people with densely-connected networks: Network brokers are more familiar with the diversity of surrounding opinion and behavior, so they are more likely to detect new productive combinations of previously segregated information, more likely to identify alternative sets of people who would be interested in the new combinations, and more capable of framing their proposals to appeal to target audiences. Thus, a structural hole is a potentially valuable context for action, brokerage is the action of coordinating across the hole with bridge connections between people on opposite sides of the hole, and brokers are the people who build the bridges.

Accordingly, network brokers are rewarded socially and materially for their work decoding and encoding information: people with access to structural holes are paid more than peers, receive more positive evaluations and recognition, get promoted more quickly to senior positions, and are more likely to be recognized as leaders (see Burt 2005; Burt et al. 2013, for review of the argument and evidence).

Age is typically treated as a control variable in estimating the returns to network advantage. The achievements associated with bridging structural holes become more likely as a person ages — compensation increases, people are more likely to hold senior positions in their organization, and older people in more senior positions are more likely to be recognized as leaders.

However, merely including age in a model that predicts achievement ignores variation in the network effect across a person's life. Trust and cooperation are central to network advantage, and both qualities vary with a person's age relative to others' in the demography of a population (Pfeffer 1983; McCain et al. 1983; Wagner et al. 1984; Zenger and Lawrence 1989; Reagans and Zuckerman 2001), and vary more generally over life-course events and transitions (Elder 1975, 1994, 2014; Alwin 2012). It is therefore reasonable to expect the network association with achievement to vary with age such that people at certain ages enjoy more advantage, or better returns to advantage.

This chapter is about that possibility. I ask three questions: Are there certain peak periods in a manager's life when network advantage is more valuable? How are those peak periods visible as transitions in the networks providing advantage? To what extent is the achievement associated with network advantage contingent on peak periods? My summary conclusion is that network models of advantage do not need to be re-defined to take peak periods into account, however, organization-specific norms about age and aging are a factor to bear in mind when predicting achievement within a specific organization.

Data

The six organizations from which I will draw evidence are listed in Table 4.1. The constituent people hold senior positions in their organizations, and range from just below direct reports to the CEO, down to people in middle management. Network and manager data are indicated in Table 4.1, along with publications in which the

Table 4.1 Six management study populations

Organization	Age contingency	N	Network	Performance	Controls
Computer Manufacturer (Burt 1992:115ff., 2010:195ff.)	Old Valued	170	General discussion (9 generators)	Relatively early promotion	Job rank, function, BU, geography
HR in a Commercial Bank (Burt 2010:80–85)	Old Valued	283	General discussion (11 generators)	Relative compensation	Job rank, function, age, BU, gender, geography, job evaluations
Financial Services	Old Devalued	654	Frequent and substantive work discussion (also 360 & email data)	Relative compensation	Job rank, function, age, BU, gender, geography
Supply Chain in Electronics (Burt 2004, 2007, 2010:72–78)	Old Devalued	455	Frequent and substantive work discussion	Relative compensation	Job rank, function, age, BU, education, gender, geography
Investment Bank (Burt, 2007, 2010:85–93)	Old and Young Devalued	531	Frequent and substantive work discussion (from 360 data)	Relative compensation	Job rank, function, age, BU, gender, Geography, peer evaluations
Software Engineering in Electronics	Old and Young Devalued	113	Frequent and substantive work discussion	Relative compensation	Job rank, function, BU, education, gender, geography

Note: These are the six organizations from which managers are drawn for study in this chapter. Publications with data description are listed. Variables in the unpublished study populations are operationalized as they are in the published work

data have been described, often with a sociogram of the population network. The network data vary in richness — from populations surveyed online with a single name generator eliciting "frequent and substantive contacts" to populations surveyed with a printed instrument eliciting contacts for several kinds of relations (the online and printed name generators are listed in Burt 2010:284–286). For the purposes of this chapter, I focus on the structure of the network around each manager relative to others in the same organization. I have not published a report on the software-engineering organization, but I have the same network and manager data described in the published reports on the supply-chain organization. Also, I have not published a report on the financial-services organization shown in the second row of Table 4.1, but the network data were obtained with the same instrument used in the supply-chain organization (augmented with 360 and email data).

I do not offer these six organizations as representative of all organizations, but the six are sufficient to illustrate the three patterns of age contingency to be reported in this chapter. I selected two organizations to illustrate each pattern, to ensure my results occur in more than one organization. I am confident that the results to be reported exist and represent the organizations I studied for this chapter, but other results could exist in organizations beyond the ones I studied.[1]

Figure 4.1 shows the usual achievement association with network advantage in the six Table 4.1 study populations. The horizontal axis (Network Constraint) distinguishes people by the extent to which their social networks provide no access to structural holes (Burt 1992:Chap. 3; Burt 2005:Chap. 1; Burt et al. 2013:531–534). As illustrated by the sociograms at the bottom of Fig. 4.1, constraint is high to the right in the graph on people with small, closed networks (no access to structural holes). To the left in the graph, constraint is low on people with large, open networks (access to many structural holes).

The vertical axis (Z-Score Residual Performance) is a measure of achievement relative to peers. Within each organization, each study-person's achievement (fourth column in Table 4.1) was predicted by various individual differences (right-most column in Table 4.1) known from previous analysis to be associated with achievement. Job rank is not held constant because I use it later in the analysis, explicitly holding it constant when estimating network effects. The studentized residual from achievement predicted by individual differences is the performance measure on the vertical axis in Fig. 4.1. It is a z-score measure of individual achievement relative to peers in the same organization, same function, business unit, geography, and so on, through demographic characteristics significant in the individual's organization.

Averages are plotted in Fig. 4.1 to keep the graph simple. (Effects will be tested with the individual-level data.) To compute averages, people were assigned to one of twenty 5-unit intervals of network constraint between zero and 100: 0 to 4.99, 5 to 9.99, and so on. The data plotted in Fig. 4.1 are average achievement scores on the vertical axis and average network constraint scores on the horizontal axis for people within each 5-unit interval in each pair of organizations illustrating the three age-contingency patterns to be discussed. Fifty-five averages are plotted in Fig. 4.1 (20 for each of the three patterns, with five averages missing when there are no managers in an interval of constraint).

Figure 4.1 shows a familiar nonlinear, downward sloping association in which network brokers (to the left in the graph) enjoy achievement higher on average than the achievements of people embedded in a single, dense cluster (to the right in the

[1]Beyond the organizations in Table 4.1, I studied another four for this chapter. Three are organizations for which I have not published reports. All four showed the "Old Valued" pattern reported below for two of the organizations in Table 4.1 (for both of which I have published reports). For this exploratory analysis, I did not require six examples of one pattern, so I only present results on the two organizations for which published reports are available.

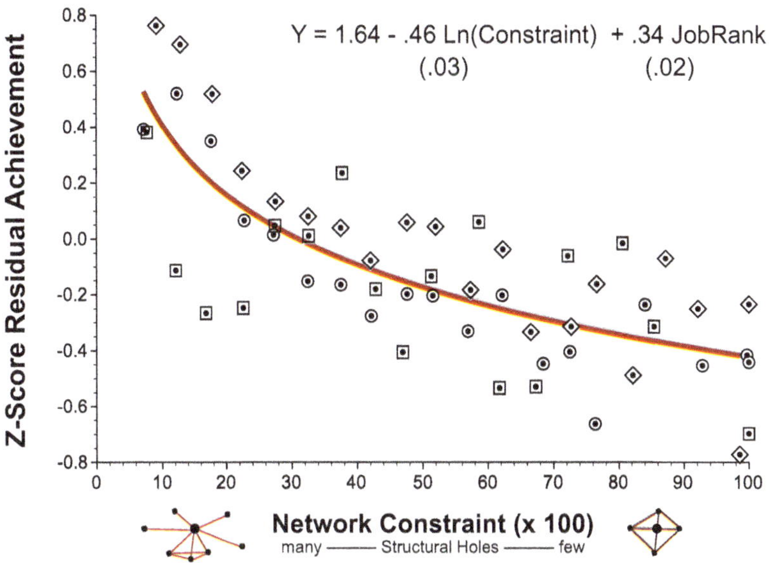

Fig. 4.1 Network advantage and access to structural holes
Note: Symbols in the graph are average scores across 2206 senior people in the six Table 4.1 firms, within five-unit categories on the horizontal axis. Vertical axis is manager achievement measured by z-score annual compensation, evaluation, or promotion adjusted for associated manager differences on control variables in Table 4.1. Job rank is not held constant. Looking ahead to Fig. 4.3, the negative association between achievement and network constraint occurs in all three categories of organizations: symbol ◉ indicates averages for the managers in organizations where returns to brokerage increase with age ($r_{xy} = -.84$ across averages in graph). Symbol ◘ indicates averages where returns decrease with age ($r_{xy} = -.92$), and ◆ indicates averages where returns increase and decrease ($r_{xy} = -.52$). Regression equation in the graph is estimated with controls for job rank and firm fixed-effects (respectively 18.21 t-test and 70.36 $F_{2,2136}$ F-test, $P < .001$; standard errors in parentheses beneath coefficients).

graph; cf., Burt 2005:37, 69; 2012:547; Burt et al. 2013:535). More specifically, achievement has a strong, negative association with log network constraint (−14.50 t-test, $P < 0.001$), with fixed effects for the six organizations and a control for manager job rank (with 1 as the highest rank in a population, one less for each rank lower). And the nonlinear, downward sloping association is apparent in organizations illustrating each of the three patterns to be discussed (note to Fig. 4.1). Other popular measures of access to structural holes are network betweenness (a count of the structural holes to which ego has exclusive access) and effective size (a count of ego's nonredundant contacts, i.e., the clusters to which ego is connected). Both measures reveal the same strong achievement-network associations as in Fig. 4.1 (e.g., Burt 2015), but I rely on the network constraint metric in this chapter.

Peak Periods

The achievement expected with network advantage depends on social standing. Access to structural holes is a competitive advantage in detecting and developing good ideas, but implementation requires that the broker be accepted as a source of the good idea (or the broker needs to find someone whose endorsement creates that acceptance). Job rank can provide the social standing necessary to be accepted, as can high network status within the informal organization, or reputation with the people with whom one has worked.

Age too can bestow social standing. In organizations where grey hair is treated as a signal of credibility, a person without grey hair can be considered too young to propose a significant idea. Elsewhere, a person can be considered too old — people from that generation do not understand current practices. Let the "peak period" in an organization be an age interval during which age is a competitive advantage. People of an age within their organization's peak period, relative to people of ages outside the peak period, are a more attractive source of ideas and suggestions such that they enjoy higher returns to network advantage. If the achievement-network association in Fig. 4.1 is uniform across managers of different ages in an organization, then there is no peak period, which means ideas and suggestions are accepted from managers regardless of their age.

Figure 4.2 shows that the association is not uniform across age. Rather, there is an inverted-U age-contingency pattern that peaks in middle age. The graph at the top of Fig. 4.2 shows that access to structural holes increases with age for the young, to a maximum among people in their late 30s and early 40s, then decreases with advancing age. Average network constraint scores are plotted for people in each age category on the horizontal axis. Average network constraint is lowest for middle-age people, specifically people in their late 30s and early 40s. In the late 40s, and continuing thereafter, people have increasingly closed networks, providing decreasing access to structural holes. The graph at the bottom of Fig. 4.2 shows that the network association with achievement increases from nothing for young managers, to a maximum among people in their 40s to early 50s, then decreasing with age back to nothing again. The data plotted are t-tests for the achievement association with log network constraint when the equation in Fig. 4.1 is estimated within each age category on the horizontal axis. Again, the maximum achievement-network association occurs during middle age, during a manager's 40s to early 50s. This is not an artifact of young people holding less senior job ranks. Differences in job rank are held constant in the graph at the bottom of Fig. 4.2.

I know of no research on the inverted-U pattern in Fig. 4.2, but the pattern is not inconsistent with McDonald and Elder's (2006) study of the ages during which social capital is an advantage in job search. McDonald & Elder do not have network data. They use the National Longitudinal Survey of Youth (NLSY) to compare jobs obtained through formal channels to the jobs obtained through a contact or without searching for the job. Relying on a "formal channel" is taken to indicate a person who does not have a network advantage in the job search. McDonald and Elder

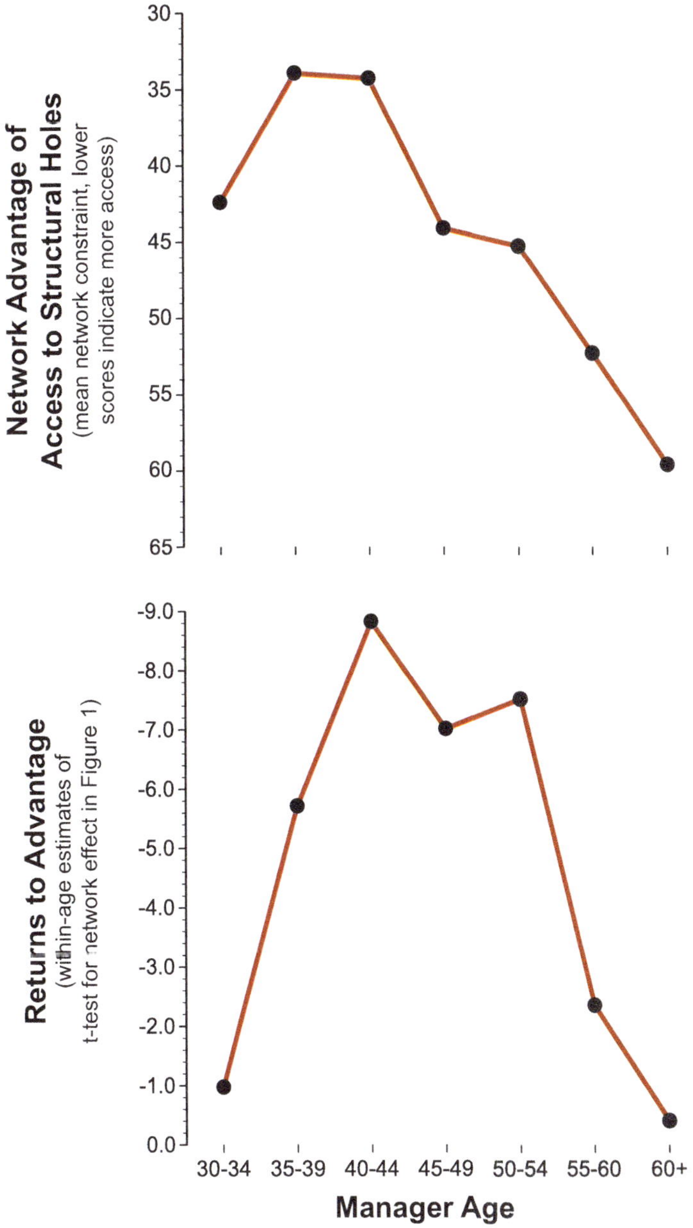

Fig. 4.2 Network advantage by manager age

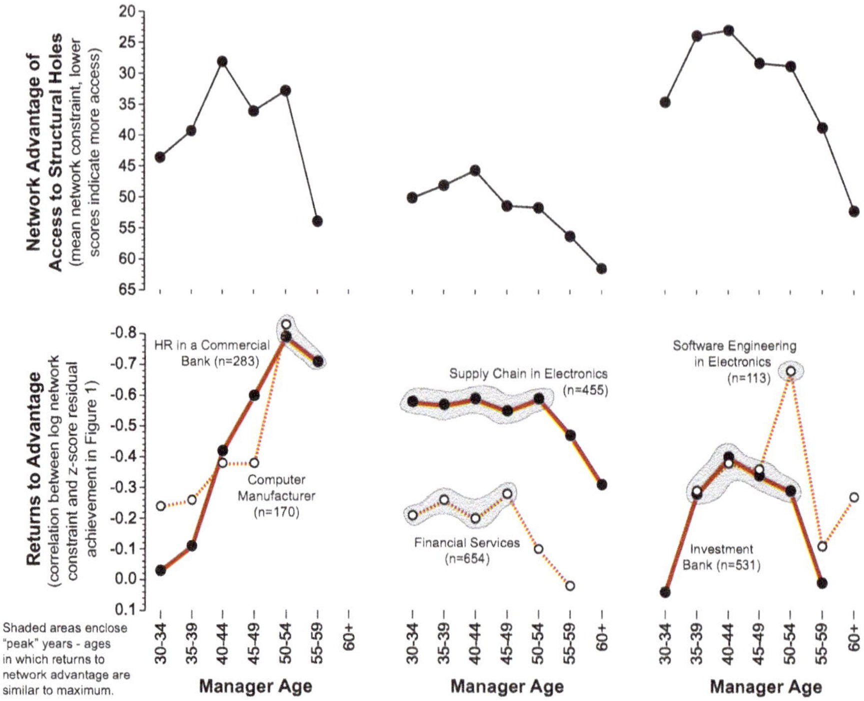

Fig. 4.3 Three patterns of age contingency
(**a**) Old Valued (returns increase with age), (**b**) Old Devalued (returns decrease with age), (**c**) Old and Young Devalued (returns increase & decrease)

(2006:541) find the strongest difference during middle age, specifically for men in their 30s, and conclude: "during the middle of the work career, (1) people with the best social capital resources are more likely to get their new jobs without searching than through a formal job search, and (2) non-searchers receive better jobs on average than formal job seekers." Relative to the data available to McDonald & Elder, the data in Fig. 4.2 are more clearly tied to personal achievement and network advantage, but as concluded by McDonald & Elder, the graph shows a peak association in middle age, which begins in a person's 30s, and continues here, past the ages available to McDonald & Elder, into a person's early 50s.

Digging past the aggregate pattern in Fig. 4.2, age contingency within the individual organizations has one of three patterns displayed in Fig. 4.3. The organization-specific patterns are in some aspects similar to the aggregate pattern. As in the Fig. 4.2 aggregate, middle-age managers consistently have the most access to structural holes within their organization (graphs at the top of Fig. 4.3). Also as in the aggregate, the achievement association with network advantage is single-peaked within each organization. There is a single period of maximum association in each organization. And the inverted U can be seen in two of the organizations. The graph to the lower right in Fig. 4.3 shows achievement strongly associated with network advantage during middle age in two of the organizations, after a youth has gained sufficient experience to be credible, and before the experience of elderly managers is deemed no longer relevant to current operations.

In contrast to the aggregate, middle-age managers are not the primary beneficiaries of network advantage in the other four organizations. In the "Old Devalued" pattern (Fig. 4.3b), the youngest managers also enjoy a strong association between achievement and network advantage. Only the elderly are excluded from network-associated achievement. The network association with achievement remains strong into a manager's 50s, after which the association weakens with increasing age.

The third pattern is most different from the aggregate. The "Old Valued" pattern (Fig. 4.3a) shows achievement more associated with network advantage for middle-age managers than it is for the youngest managers, but the strongest association occurs among the oldest managers. The association increases as a manager ages. This pattern looks suspiciously like an artifact of job rank since older managers are more likely to hold senior job rank, and network advantage is more beneficial for people in more senior job ranks, where work is more complex, crafted by the individual, and subject to collaboration from peers (e.g., Burt 1997; 2005:156–162). The pattern is robust to job rank, however, in that the regression model in the first column of Table 4.2 shows that the Fig. 4.3c pattern of increasing association between achievement and network advantage exists after individual differences in job rank are held constant.

Models in Table 4.2 estimate the achievement-network association for managers in an organization's peak period, and an adjustment for managers of ages outside the peak period. Fig. 4.1 displays across organizations the negative association between achievement and closed networks. Within each organization, I distinguish a peak period of maximum achievement association with network advantage. Peak periods are indicated in Fig. 4.3 by the shaded area along each line in the graphs at the bottom of the figure.[2] For example, the regression model in the first column of Table 4.2 shows achievement higher for managers in more senior job ranks (10.3 t-test, $P < 0.001$), and strongly associated with network advantage during the peak period of ages 50 and older (−8.0 t-test for the weaker achievements of manag-

[2] For each organization, I operationalized peak period as follows: Locate the maximum point on a returns-to-brokerage curve in the lower half of Fig 4.3. Test for the difference between the maximum achievement-network association, and the association in the adjacent age category. If the difference is negligible, add the adjacent age category to the peak period. Now test for difference from the association in the next adjacent age category. When the difference is statistically significant, stop. For example, the maximum achievement-network association occurs for the HR managers age 50 to 54. The −0.79 beta plotted in Fig. 4.3 for HR managers in the 50–54 age category is negligibly different from the −0.71 beta for HR managers age 55–59 (0.89 t-test, $P \sim 0.38$), so the peak period is extended to age 59. There are no older HR managers, so 59 is the upper end of the peak period in the HR organization. In the other direction, the −0.79 beta for HR managers age 50–54 is significantly higher than the −0.60 beta for HR managers age 45–49 (2.66 t-test, $P < 0.01$), so the peak period begins at age 50. The HR peak period of ages 50 through 59 is enclosed in grey shading in the lower-left graph in Fig. 4.3.

Table 4.2 Estimates of the Cost to Being of an Age Outside the Peak Period in an Organization

	Returns to network increase with age (Fig. 4.3a)		Returns to network decrease with age (Fig. 4.3b)		Returns to network increase and decrease (Fig. 4.3c)	
Job rank	.29 (10.3)	.28 (10.3)	.34 (12.4)	.33 (9.9)	.52 (9.6)	.51 (9.5)
Log network constraint	−1.08 (−8.0)	−1.08 (−4.4)	−.54 (−11.0)	−.64 (−6.9)	−.41 (−7.1)	−.46 (−7.8)
Years away from peak	.02 (2.9)		−.01 (−1.1)		−.02 (−1.0)	
Interaction years away and Log network constraint	.06 (5.9)		.02 (1.1)		.01 (0.4)	
Not peak		−2.24 (2.5)		−.70 (−1.6)		−1.34 (−3.7)
Interaction not peak and log network constraint		.74 (3.0)		.18 (2.9)		.35 (3.1)
R^2	.35	.31	.22	.24	.23	.25
N	453	453	1109	1109	582	582

Note: These are ordinary least squares estimates predicting achievement (Fig. 4.1) from network constraint within each of the three age-contingency patterns (Fig. 4.3), with firm fixed-effects and a control for job rank (routine t-tests in parentheses). "Job Rank" is 1 for the highest rank in a population, one integer less for each lower rank. "Years Away" is number of years between a person's age and the closest peak age. "Not Peak" is a dummy variable equal to 1 if a person's age is outside the peak years for her organization. Interactions are defined for log constraint measured as the deviation from mean log constraint in the study population. Coefficients in the second row measure achievement association with log network constraint during an organization's peak period. Coefficients in the fourth and sixth rows show adjustments to the association for ages outside the peak period

ers more constrained by lack of access to structural holes). For each year separating a manager's age from the peak ages in his organization, the achievement association with network constraint becomes weaker and weaker (5.9 t-test for the weakening negative association with network constraint, $P < 0.001$).[3]

[3] The strategy used here to test for significant differences between managers within versus outside an organization's peak period is the strategy used to test for network discrimination more generally (Burt 1992:Chp. 4; 2010:Chp. 7). Using the dummy variable models in Table 4.2, I tested for significant differences in the returns to network advantage for men versus women, for whites versus nonwhites, and for managers formerly employed by a suspect company (e.g., the electronics supply chain organization recently acquired one of the company's close rivals giving rise to rumors that managers formerly employed by the rival were second-choice for promotion). None of the differences are statistically significant. There is evidence of network discrimination in the computer equipment organization: Women and men in the lowest sampled job rank receive significantly lower returns to network advantage, which is why I exclude them from this chapter (170 senior men in the first row of Table 4.1 are from the complete sample of 284 senior men, junior men, and women at all ranks, Burt 1992:Chp. 4; 1998). In this chapter, I want to test for age discrimination

Beyond documenting the statistical significance of the distinction between peak and non-peak ages, the results in Table 4.2 is to show that peak period is a qualitative distinction more than a quantitative one. There are two models in Table 4.2 for each pattern of age contingency. The first model tests for slope adjustment outside the peak period according to a manager's age in years away from his organization's peak period. The model in column one of the table is an example. An HR manager age 55 is zero years away from the peak period for the HR organization. An HR manager age 49 is 1 year below peak period. An HR manager 40 years of age is 10 years below peak period. The slope adjustment for years-away-from-peak in an "Old Valued" organization is statistically significant (5.9 t-test), showing that the achievement-network association for managers in these organizations gets stronger as a manager gets closer in age to the peak period for his organization. In contrast, slope adjustments for years away from the peak period are negligible for the other four organizations — the ones in which old managers are devalued (1.1 t-test) and the ones in which old and young are devalued (0.4 t-test).

The second models in Table 4.2 make a qualitative distinction between in and out of the peak period. For example, the model in the second column of Table 4.2, shows achievement strongly associated with job rank, as in the first column, but averages all managers outside the peak period to estimate two associations between achievement and network constraint: one for managers inside the peak period (second row) and another for managers outside the peak period (second row minus sixth row adjustment). Each pattern of age dependency shows a significantly positive adjustment for managers outside their organization's peak period, indicating a significantly weaker achievement-network association for managers outside the peak period — in organizations where old is valued (3.0 t-test), in organizations where old is devalued (2.9 t-test), and in organizations where both old and young are devalued (3.1 t-test). In short, the slope adjustment for non-peak managers is defined less by their years away from the peak period than by whether or not they are outside the peak period. What matters for network advantage is not how much a manager differs from his organization's privileged age. The distinction significant for network advantage is whether or not the manager is of privileged age within the organization.

Turning Points and Transition Ages

Given a peak period in a manager's organization, aging into and out of the peak period are turning points in the manager's career in the sense of marking a transition in social behavior between what was and what will be (e.g., Elder 1985; Abbott 1997). Brokering connections across structural holes was perhaps tolerated before

free of discrimination in other forms. One could argue that my study populations have been "cleaned" of discrimination, but that would create a bias against finding evidence age discrimination. The results in Table 4.2 and Fig. 4.3 make it clear that the managers differentiate colleagues by age.

entering the peak period. Now it is expected, praised, and rewarded. I expect aging into the peak period to be marked by celebratory rituals involving achievement awards, mentoring duties, and leadership responsibilities. At the other end of the peak period, exit can be expected to have its own rituals easing the transition out of leadership responsibilities (e.g., Gusfield 1957, on "easing off" processes and the "neutrality of rules;" Goffman 1952, on "cooling the mark out").

I do not have event data to describe conditions when managers enter or leave their organization's peak period, but in three of the Table 4.1 organizations I know the age of colleagues cited as contacts. Those age data are sufficient to draw some inferences about how entering or leaving a peak period is associated with change in the manager's network. The three organizations are marked by bold lines in the graphs at the bottom of Fig. 4.3 (the HR organization, the supply-chain organization, and the investment bank). Each of the three organizations clearly shows its "Old Valued," "Old Devalued," or "Old and Young Devalued" peak period.

Age Homophily

Citation data for the three organizations are aggregated in Table 4.3. Citations are treated as symmetric. A citation between ages 40 and 42 is simultaneously a citation between ages 42 and 40. Each cell of the symmetric table contains two entries: the actual frequency of citations between row and column, and the frequency expected if age were independent of citations (in parentheses). For example, there are 356 citations connecting managers age 30–34 with colleagues age 30–34. Given the number of citations involving managers in that age group, there would be less than half that number if citations were made independent of age (140.5 in parentheses is computed as 1018 times 1018 divided by the total number of citations, 7376).

Table 4.3 shows two patterns. Homophily is one of the patterns. Managers tend to cite colleagues their own age. This familiar homophily preference is evident in that the observed frequencies in the diagonal cells are larger than the expected frequencies in parentheses if citations were made independent of age (McPherson et al. 2001, especially pages 424–425 on age homophily). For example the observed citations between people within the 30–34 age category are more than twice what would be expected under independence (356/140.5, or 2.53). In contrast, citations between managers age 30–34 with managers age 50–54 occur less than half as often as would be expected under independence (47/113.2, or 0.42). On average, the observed frequencies in the diagonal cells of Table 4.3 are more than twice what would be expected under independence (2.23 average ratio of observed to expected within the seven diagonal cells). The citation frequency between people in adjacent age categories is a little less than half of what would be expected (1.83 average ratio), and the citation frequency between people more than a category apart in age is about three quarters what would be expected under independence (0.78 average ratio).

Table 4.3 Interaction within and between ages

	30–34	35–39	40–44	45–49	50–54	55–59	60+	Total
30–34	356 (140.5)							1018
35–39	263 (145.8)	583 (430.0)						1781
40–44	243 (280.9)	527 (491.4)	661 (561.4)					2035
45–49	101 (175.3)	263 (306.7)	322 (350.4)	281 (218.7)				1270
50–54	47 (113.2)	110 (198.0)	193 (226.2)	188 (141.2)	178 (91.2)			820
55–59	7 (47.5)	33 (83.1)	72 (94.9)	80 (59.2)	76 (38.2)	57 (16.0)		344
60+	1 (14.9)	2 (26.1)	17 (29.8)	35 (18.6)	28 (12.0)	19 (5.0)	6 (1.6)	108
Total	1018	1781	2035	1270	820	344	108	7376

Note: These are citations between managers and colleagues summed across the three bold-line organizations in Fig. 4.3 (HR, Supply Chain, and Investment Bank). For example, there are 356 citations connecting people age 30–34 with colleagues age 30–34. The frequency expected if citations were independent of age is given in parentheses

Transition Age

The other pattern in Table 4.3 is an age transition during the mid-40s. For the first three age categories in the Table (30–34, 35–39, and 40–44), citations are concentrated within one's own age group and the adjacent age group. In contrast, managers age 45–49 are more likely than expected to cite anyone older than themselves, and they are unlikely to cite colleagues who are younger. Managers in the older age categories (50–54, 55–59, 60+) are more likely than expected to cite managers 45 years or older, and less likely than expected to cite colleagues younger than 45. There is a transition in the mid 40s: citations are more likely than expected between people on either side of the transition and less likely than expected between people on opposite sides of the transition.

Age 45 seems to be a critical year. Before age 45, relations are with people similar to my age. After age 45, relations are with people my age and older, excluding people younger than age 45.

But the category boundaries in Table 4.3 are arbitrary, merely a convenience for aggregating data. I want to look past the arbitrary category boundaries, to see specific ages at which transitions occur. Is age 45 in fact a turning point for managers?

The network concept of structural equivalence is useful here. Two ages i and j are structurally equivalent, and so fall within the same social category of age, to the

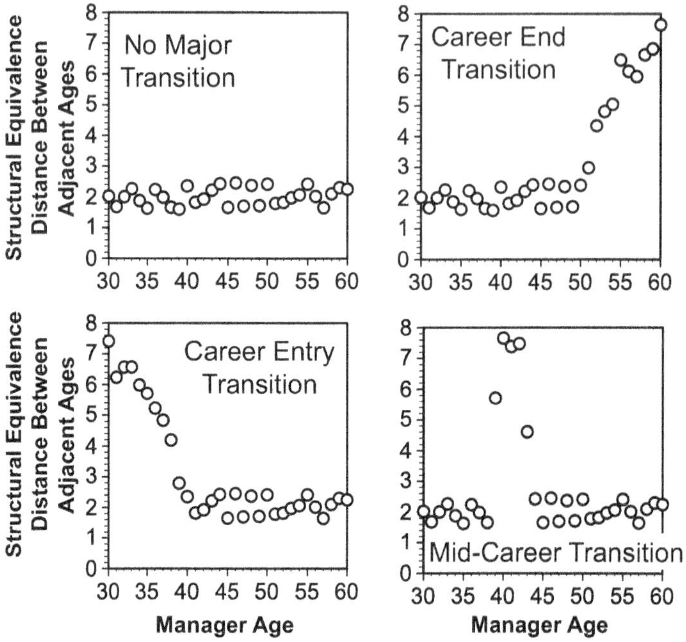

Fig. 4.4 Detecting transition ages
Structural equivalence distance between years i and j is the square root of the sum across columns k of: $[f_{ik}/E(f_{ik}) - f_{jk}/E(f_{jk})]^2$ where f_{ik} is the frequency of citations connecting managers age i with colleagues of age k, and $E(f_{ik})$ is the frequency expected if citations from age i were independent of colleague age.

extent that people of ages i and j connect similarly with people of other ages (Burt 1991). Imagine that the seven rows in Table 4.3 were expanded to one row for each age between 30 and 60. Two ages would be structurally equivalent to the extent that people of either age have similar connections with colleagues of each other age. Such structural equivalence is often measured by a Euclidean distance (equation in Fig. 4.4), and distances between adjacent ages can be plotted as illustrated in Fig. 4.4 to detect age transitions in network behavior. Age transitions are marked by a spike up in the distance between adjacent years, which indicates that the pattern of citations between ages this year are unusually different from the patterns in adjacent years. For example, the upper-right graph in Fig. 4.4 shows an age transition at the end of a manager's career. The ages of colleagues cited by older managers become increasingly distinct from the ages of colleagues cited by younger managers. Transition could occur as a manager rises to managerial rank (lower-left graph), or as a person makes a transition in mid-life (lower-right graph, as illustrated for the mid-40s managers in Table 4.3). Or there might be no age transitions in a study population, which would show up as each year about equi-distant from adjacent years (upper-left graph in Fig. 4.4).

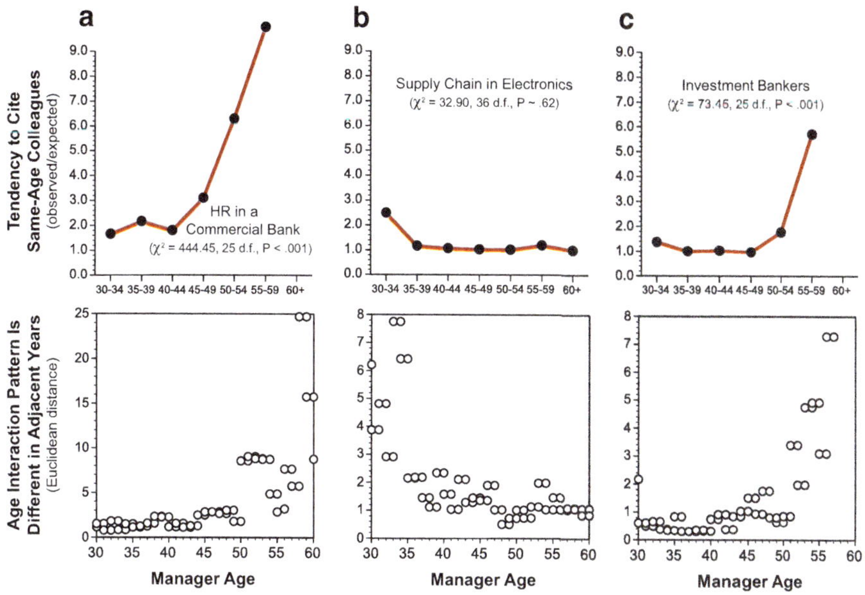

Fig. 4.5 Age transitions in the observed careers
(**a**) Old Valued, (**b**) Old Devalued, (**c**) Old and Young Devalued
Note: In the top panel, the vertical axis is the citation frequency observed in the diagonal cells of Table 4.2 for each of the bold-line organizations in Fig. 4.3 (HR, Supply Chain, and Investment Bank), divided by the frequency expected if citations were independent of manager and colleague age. Chi-square statistics describe the extent to which citations are independent of age across the whole table, but the primary deviations happen down the diagonal and adjacent cells. Excluding citations to the manager's supervisor does not change the relative magnitudes of the chi-square statistics. Managers in the supply chain organization are older than in the other two organizations, so there are observations in all seven age categories, creating 36 degrees of freedom versus 25 in the other two organizatons. If the supply-chain chi-square statistic is computed just for the six age categories observed in the other two organizations, citations are more independent of manager and colleague age ($\chi^2 = 17.77$, 25 d.f., P ~ .85). In the bottom panel, vertical axis is the Euclidean distance at each age to the age interaction pattern in the previous and subsequent year, as illustrated in Fig. 4.4.

Transition Ages Not Coincident with Peak Periods

For the three study organizations, Fig. 4.5 shows age transitions at the beginning and end of manager careers, not at the beginning or end of peak periods. The graphs at the top in Fig. 4.5 show the ages at which managers in each organization are most likely to cite colleagues their own age. The graphs at the bottom in Fig. 4.5 show Euclidean distances between adjacent ages within each organization.

Figure 4.5a shows an age transition corresponding to the peak period for network advantage in the organization. The peak period is age 50 and above. The age distances show a transition beginning around age 50 (lower-left graph in Fig. 4.5), and that age transition is to networks composed of other old managers (upper-left in Fig. 4.5).

Figure 4.5b shows an age transition that has no overlap with the peak period. The age transition occurs as young people rise to managerial rank (lower-middle graph in Fig. 4.5). There is a slight tendency for the higher homophily in youthful networks to be replaced with contacts of more varied age (upper-middle graph in Fig. 4.5). That does not correspond to the peak period in this organization. Youth is within the peak period. It is the older managers who do not benefit from network advantage. There is neither age transition, nor increased homophily, evident in the networks of the older managers.

Figure 4.5c also shows an age transition that does not map onto the peak period. The age transition is again at the end of the career (lower-right graph in Fig. 4.5) and involves increasing homophily as older managers limit their citations to other older managers (upper-right graph in Fig. 4.5). The age transition for older managers corresponds to the lack of achievement associated with network advantage for older managers in this organization. However, there is neither age transition nor increased homophily evident in the networks of the young managers, and they too lie outside the peak period for network advantage in this organization.

Conclusions

Age clearly matters for network advantage. People of an age within their organization's peak period, relative to people of ages outside the peak period, are a more attractive source of ideas and suggestions such that they enjoy higher returns to network advantage. Middle-age is peak period in the aggregate (Fig. 4.2), but individual organizations display one of three distinct single-peaked patterns of age contingency (Fig. 4.3): There is an "Old Valued" pattern in which the peak period is at the end of the career: achievement becomes increasingly linked to network advantage as a person ages. There is an "Old Devalued" pattern in which the peak period spans the beginning and middle of the career: network advantage is consistently valuable until a person reaches their 50s, after which achievement is decreasingly associated with network advantage. Finally, there is an "Old and Young Devalued" pattern in which the peak period is during middle age: network advantage is most valuable for middle-age managers, offering little value to young or old managers.

Implications for Management Careers

An immediate implication is that "acting one's age" is organization-specific guidance for managers at the beginning or end of their careers. Brokering connections across structural holes provides advantage for middle-age managers in all of the study organizations, but in certain organizations managers in their early 30s are not rewarded for such behavior (Fig. 4.3a, c), while in other organizations they are

(Fig. 4.3b). Managers in their 50s and older are handsomely rewarded for brokerage in some organizations (Fig. 4.3a), while in others they are not (Fig. 4.3b, c). Beyond showing that people of certain ages are likely to fail when they try to broker in certain organizations, the implications are a call to action: there are opportunity costs for a manager of peak age who does not try to benefit from network brokerage. Action delayed past peak age can be too late as much as action before peak age can be premature.

Broader implications for strategic job hopping could be inferred from the results (Bidwell and Briscoe 2010): Begin the career in an organization in which the young benefit from network advantage ("Old Devalued" organization), then switch mid-career to an organization in which the middle-aged benefit ("Old and Young Devalued"), then finish in an organization that celebrates the most experienced managers ("Old Valued").

Here is a quick caution against such inference: the presented results show that returns to network advantage are age contingent. The results do not explain why advantage is age contingent. The cross-sectional data in Fig. 4.6 describing age contingency do not distinguish manager age, from cohort, from period effects. The text is written in terms of age effects. People of an age within their organization's peak period benefit more from network advantage. With more contextual information, the results could have been discussed in terms of period effects if peak ages reflect the kind of work being done when the network data were gathered. Or, the results could have been discussed in terms of cohort effects. For example, there was an internal labor market for managers in the computer manufacturer in Fig. 4.3a that displays an "Old Valued" pattern. People joined the firm early and stayed in the firm for the rest of their working lives — not everyone, but most people. The oldest managers in the company are not just old; they are founding employees who grew up together as the organization prospered. They are respected as members of the initial cohort of employees who built the organization. A new hire of comparable age should not expect to enjoy the same respect.

Implications for Network Models of Advantage

The significant differences between peak and non-peak managers in Fig. 4.3 and Table 4.2 mean that organization-specific norms about age are a factor to bear in mind when predicting achievement within a specific organization. Nevertheless, I conclude that network models of advantage (which is to say, the usual measures of network betweeness, constraint, or nonredundant contacts) need not be re-defined to incorporate peak periods.

My primary reason is that the difference in returns to network advantage for peak versus non-peak managers is a difference in magnitude, not form. Consider Fig. 4.6, which is the same as the evidence graph in Fig. 4.1, but with managers of an age within the peak period (bold line and solid dots) here distinguished from managers of a non-peak age (dashed line and hollow dots). The dashed line in Fig. 4.6 is lower

Job rank	18.44	18.38
Network Constraint	-14.92	-14.78
NonPeak, All		
Level	-4.60	
Slope	4.63	
NonPeak, Old Valued		
Level		-1.51
Slope		2.99
NonPeak, Old Devalued		
Level		-4.39
Slope		4.19
R^2	.23	.24

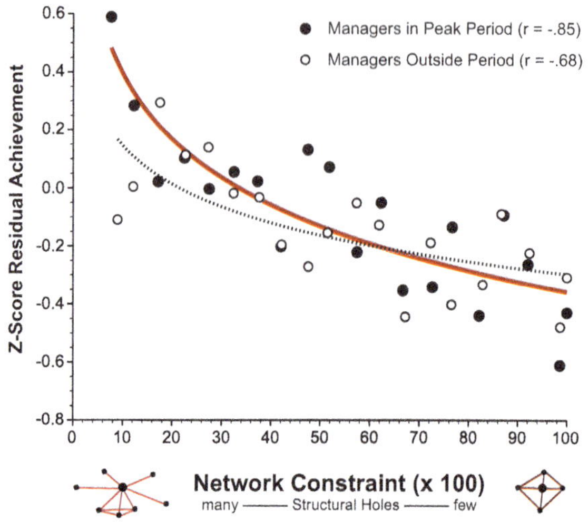

Fig. 4.6 Network advantage during peak and not-peak ages
The graph displays associations between achievement and network constraint for managers at peak ages in their organization versus managers outside the peak ages. The graph is constructed in the same way as the graph in Fig. 4.1. Correlations are computed from data in the graph. The table to the left contains t-tests for regression models predicting, for 2144 individuals, the vertical axis in the graph using a person's job rank and log network constraint, with firm fixed-effects and level and slope adjustments for managers outside the peak age in their organization (first for everyone outside peak age, then separating non-peak in the two Fig. 4.3 organizations in which old is valued from non-peak in the four organizations in which old is devalued).

than the bold line, and the slope adjustments for non-peak managers are statistically significant in the Fig. 4.6 table. However, achievement has the same downward-sloping, nonlinear association with network constraint for peak and non-peak managers, and there is a strong correlation between achievement and network constraint for managers outside their organization's peak period (−0.68). The correlation is stronger for managers of an age within their organization's peak period (−0.85), but the achievement-network correlation is strong for managers both in and outside the peak period.

More, the peak period in an organization seems less a phenomenon grounded in a person's network than it is a phenomenon grounded in the broader social norms and culture around the person. Consider three points: First, number of years away from an organization's peak period matters less for achievement than whether or not a manager is within the peak period (Table 4.2). In other words, the peak period in an organization seems to be a qualitative state of eligibility, a sequence of ages distinguished by the prevailing social norms in an organization. Second, if peak periods were grounded in the networks around individual managers, then a manager's network should change upon entry and exit from a peak period. In contrast, transition ages in manager networks do not map onto people entering and leaving the peak period (Fig. 4.5). The results in Fig. 4.5 do not rule out the possibility that entry and exit are coincident with other significant events in the manager's career or personal life more generally, events not observable in the network data analyzed here. Such explanation would be attractive for the middle-age contingency displayed in Fig. 4.2. The peak period begins in a person's late 30s. Academics are being evaluated for tenure. Professional service people are being evaluated for promotion to partner. More generally, it is an age of social activity and transition in American lives: work colleagues and friends beyond work are often cited as key personal contacts, and children start to replace parents as key family contacts (Burt 1991: Figs. 4.2, 4.3, Table 4.1). The peak period ends in a person's mid-50s, which is an age in American lives when colleagues are much less often cited as key personal contacts, and parents have all but disappeared as key family contacts (Burt 1991). A plausible life-course-events story could be told with respect to Fig. 4.2, however, my third point is that Fig. 4.3 shows peak periods beginning and ending at diverse ages, for people going through very different life events. There is of course variation between individuals such that the over-50 managers in the Fig. 4.3a organizations are probably more involved with colleagues than the over-50 managers in the Figs. 4.3b, c organizations within which managers over-50 are not rewarded for brokerage. Regardless, the peak periods in Fig. 4.3 occur at such different ages in different organizations that life-course events experienced by individuals in the peak period seem an unlikely explanation for peak periods.

More Broadly

Organizational demography is a promising lens on peak periods. Following Pfeffer (1983), organizational demography reasons from volume and variation in employee cohorts. For example, McCain et al. (1983) provide an organizational demography perspective on faculty turnover in university departments (cf. Wagner et al. 1984, on top managers leaving their organization). Early retirements by full professors, and resignations by full and assistant professors, are more likely from departments in which there is an unusually large age cohort, or a gap between age cohorts — as occurs when a department is being renovated, or grown anew, or when a breakthrough occurs so people of a certain age are especially attractive hires. Multiple people hired at the same time constitute an age cohort. People in the same cohort are brought together by their mutual experiences, which facilitates and strengthens their relations with one another. To the extent that the cohort is large, it can become a "dominant age cohort" constituting a cohesive lump in the age distribution of employees, creating distance between cohort employees and employees outside the cohort — and that is the kernel from which a peak period in the organization can develop. Reasoning from the above two empirical papers by Pfeffer and his colleagues, for example, executive and faculty turnover should be higher among people outside their organization's peak period than it is for people within the peak period.

And organization demography is implicitly a source of dynamics. The peak periods and patterns of age contingency in Fig. 4.3 are characteristic of the study organizations when they were observed, by which time all six were well established. The software organization was founded in the 1980s, the computer manufacturer in the 1950s, the electronics supply chain organization in the 1920s, the financial services organization and investment bank just before World War I, and the commercial bank before the Civil War. Ongoing business and social processes can be expected to preserve the status quo, and therefore an organization's current peak period. However, none of the six study organizations was observed over time, and organization cultures change as a function of new people entering, ongoing events and networks that integrate certain employees while segregating others, and the departure of previous employees (Harrison and Carroll 2006). As an element of organization culture, the peak periods observed in Fig. 4.3 could shift or disappear as a function of new cohorts, events, and the exit of old cohorts. In sum, peak periods exist, but when and where they exist remains an interesting empirical question.

References

Abbott, A. ([1997] 2001). On the concept of turning point. In A. Abbott (Ed.), *Time matters* (pp. 240–260). Chicago: University of Chicago Press.
Alwin, D. F. (2012). Integrating varieties of life course concepts. *Journal of Gerontology, 67*, 206–220.
Bidwell, M., & Briscoe, F. (2010). The dynamics of interorganizational careers. *Organization Science, 21*, 1034–1053.
Burt, R. S. (1991). Measuring age as a structural concept. *Social Networks, 13*, 1–34.
Burt, R. S. (1992). *Structural Holes*. Cambridge, MA: Harvard University Press.
Burt, R. S. (1997). The contingent value of social capital. *Administrative Science Quarterly, 42*, 339–365.
Burt, R. S. (1998). The gender of social capital. *Rationality and Society, 10*, 5–46.
Burt, R. S. (2004). Structural holes and good ideas. *American Journal of Sociology, 110*, 349–399.
Burt, R. S. (2005). *Brokerage and Closure*. Oxford: Oxford University Press.
Burt, R. S. (2007). Secondhand brokerage: evidence on the importance of local structure for managers, bankers, and analysts. *Academy of Management Journal, 50*, 119–149.
Burt, R. S. (2010). *Neighbor networks*. Oxford: Oxford University Press.
Burt, R. S. (2012). Network-related personality and the agency question: Multirole evidence from a virtual world. *American Journal of Sociology, 118*, 543–591.
Burt, R. S. (2015). Reinforced structural holes. *Social Networks, 43*, 149–161.
Burt, R. S., Kilduff, M., & Tasselli, S. (2013). Social network analysis, through a focus on network advantage. *Annual Review of Psychology, 64*, 527–547.
Elder, G. H., Jr. (1975). Age differentiation and the life course. *Annual Review of Sociology, 1*, 165–190.
Elder, G. H., Jr. (1985). Perspectives on the life course. In G. H. Elder Jr. (Ed.), *Life course dynamics* (pp. 23–49). Ithaca: Cornell University Press.
Elder, G. H., Jr. (1994). Time, human agency, and social change: Perspectives on the life course. *Social Psychology Quarterly, 57*, 4–15.
Elder, G. H., Jr. (2014). Studying lives in changing times: A life-course journey. In R. M. Lerner, A. C. Petersen, R. K. Silbereisen, & J. Brooks-Gunn (Eds.), *The developmental science of adolescence* (pp. 134–149). New York: Psychology Press.
Goffman, E. (1952). On cooling the mark out. *Psychiatry, 15*, 451–463.

Gusfield, J. R. (1957). The problem of generations in an organizational structure. *Social Forces, 35*, 323–330.
Harrison, J. R., & Carroll, G. R. (2006). *Culture and demography in organizations*. Princeton: Princeton University Press.
McCain, B. E., O'Reilly, C., & Jeffrey Pfeffer, J. (1983). The effects of departmental demography on turnover: The case of a university. *Academy of Management Journal, 26*, 626–641.
McDonald, S., & Elder, G. H., Jr. (2006). When does social capital matter? Non-searching for jobs across the life course. *Social Forces, 85*, 531–549.
McPherson, M., Smith-Lovin, L., & Cook, J. M. (2001). Birds of a feather: Homophily in social networks. *Annual Review of Sociology, 27*, 415–444.
Pfeffer, J. (1983). Organizational demography. *Research in Organizational Behavior, 5*, 299–357.
Reagans, R. E., & Zuckerman, E. W. (2001). Networks, diversity, and performance: The social capital of corporate R&D units. *Organization Science, 12*, 502–517.
Ronald S. Burt, (1997) The Contingent Value of Social Capital. Administrative Science Quarterly 42 (2):339
Wagner, W. G., Pfeffer, J., & O'Reilly, C. A. I. I. I. (1984). Organizational demography and turnover in top-management group. *Administrative Science Quarterly, 29*, 74–92.
Zenger, T. R., & Lawrence, B. S. (1989). Organizational demography: The differential effects of age and tenure distributions on technical communication. *Academy of Management Journal, 32*, 353–376.

Ronald S. Burt is the Hobart W. Williams Professor of Sociology and Strategy, Booth School of Business, University of Chicago. A pioneer in the conceptual and methodological development of network science, he studies the ways that social networks create competitive advantage in careers, organizations, and markets.

Chapter 5
Life Course Events and Network Composition

Peter V. Marsden

The life course paradigm (Elder 1985; Elder 1994; Elder 1995; Marshall and Mueller 2003) focuses attention on individual life trajectories composed of interrelated transitions into and out of states such as marriage or employment. It examines the manner in which lives unfold in connection with the intersecting social rhythms of multiple careers (in domains including, e.g., intimate relationships, childbearing and childrearing, and work), constraints and opportunities associated with institutional structures and historical events, and the parallel lives of other persons. The paradigm has a clear affinity with the study of social networks: life course transitions often imply the formation of new relationships or the dissolution of previously-existing ones. Indeed, the perspective's foundational principle of "linked lives" (Elder 1995: p. 112) emphasizes the interdependencies among the life histories of persons connected by ties of kinship (especially), friendship, and other bonds.

The literature on social networks likewise alludes to ideas involving the life course when developing accounts for variations between the social networks of individuals (e.g. Marsden 1987), and in particular when theorizing about network change (e.g. Wellman et al. 1997); the connection is only sometimes made explicit (e.g. Bidart and Lavenu 2005; Kalmijn 2003). The occurrence of a major life event

Author's Note: A first rendition of the ideas here was presented at the May, 2015 conference "Together Through Time" held at Penn State University. Subsequently they were discussed at colloquia held in CIS Summer Seminars on Sociological and Political Research at the Real Colegio Complutense (August, 2015 and 2016), the Forschungskolloquium Mikrosoziologie at the Institut für Soziologie, Universität Bremen (November, 2015), and the Department of Sociology at the University of North Carolina at Chapel Hill (March, 2016). I appreciate the helpful comments I received from participants in all of these sessions, and from the editors of this volume.

P. V. Marsden (✉)
Department of Sociology, Harvard University, Cambridge, MA, USA
e-mail: pvm@wjh.harvard.edu

D. F. Alwin et al. (eds.), *Social Networks and the Life Course*, Frontiers in Sociology and Social Research 2, https://doi.org/10.1007/978-3-319-71544-5_5

such as marriage, parenthood, employment or retirement, however, is readily seen as an occasion that may alter opportunities to form or continue social ties, closer and more distal alike.

The premise of this volume is that making more direct connections between the bodies of research on the life course and on social networks will be mutually profitable. This chapter, rooted in social network studies, contributes to that enterprise by examining general-population social survey data on the life course positions and social networks of U.S. adults. Emphasizing a conceptualization of the life course as a set of transitions (Alwin 2012), it examines the manner in which life course events shape networks. After reviewing findings of some prior studies that link these phenomena, it proposes opportunity-based network theories (e.g. Blau 1977)—Feld's (1981) focus theory in particular—as a basis for understanding how life course transitions may shape the size and composition of individual social networks. It then examines General Social Survey data on how network size, network composition, and network activity vary across life course states. In keeping with a prominent emphasis in life course theory (Moen 2001), it considers the prospect that particular transitions hold different consequences for men and women.

Background

A number of prior studies consider the interplay between the life course and network development. Many of these examine cross-sectional differences in network structure and composition across life course states or stages; less commonly, they use longitudinal designs that measure both life course change and network turnover. We review some of the theoretical arguments and findings of this research here: a recurrent theme is the idea that a life course event such as marriage, divorce, or retirement can put the continuation of existing relationships at risk, while at the same time providing opportunities to initiate new ones.

A classic work on social support networks (Kahn and Antonucci 1980) made a close and overt connection between the life course and social networks. Its central concept was the "convoy," defined as "a structure within which social support is given and received"—that is, a set of family, friends, and others who provide social support to a focal individual (Kahn and Antonucci 1980: pp. 253, 267). A convoy is, in essence, a personal or egocentric network (Crossley et al. 2015) composed of those "alters" involved in supportive transactions with a focal actor or "ego". Kahn and Antonucci invoked role theory to link the life course to change in convoys, arguing that life events involve the acquisition of new roles and/or the shedding of previously-held ones; the changes in expectations associated with roles imply changes in role-dependent affiliations with others. Their argument suggested that a convoy's most central members—typically linked to the ego via strong, "multiplex" relationships comprised of multiple strands associated with different roles—remain relatively stable across transitions, and that network size tends to decline with the gradual exit from roles in later life.

Subsequent research finds that closer ties indeed are more durable (Degenne and Lebeaux 2005; Morgan et al. 1997; Wellman et al. 1997). While Antonucci and Akiyama (1987) found no differences in network size by age in their sample of adults over age 50, a later study of a similar sample (Cornwell et al. 2008) did find networks to be smaller among older people; Fischer (1982), Marsden (1987) and Kalmijn (2012) report inverse associations between network size and age for adult samples spanning a broader age range.

Longitudinal studies sometimes examine several transitions. In their panel study of young adults, Bidart and Lavenu (2005) found a steady dropoff in contacts with nonkin during the transition to adulthood; relatively large networks during the "teenage sociability" period usually became smaller as subjects left school, entered the labor market, and formed steady partnerships. Mollenhorst, Volker and Flap (2014) linked divorce and the death of a spouse or partner to the dissolution of previously-existing relationships; widowhood was also associated with forming new relationships in new settings, however.

Other studies of changes in social networks over the life course focus on particular changes in life course states. An early study of adult men (Stueve and Gerson 1977) found marriage and parenthood to be associated with a shift in the sources of "best friends"; friendships drawn from work, neighborhood, and association settings tended to supplant those rooted in school and childhood experience. Wellman et al. (1997) likewise reported that entry into marriage was linked to substantial turnover in networks over a decade.

Hurlbert and Acock (1990) examined differences in confiding networks by marital status, finding that the networks of both married and widowed persons tend to be composed of higher proportions of family members than are those of single, divorced, or separated persons. Kalmijn (2003) examined the "dyadic withdrawal" hypothesis holding that marriage and cohabitation are associated with a general decline in network size and a concomitant rise in the interpenetration of the networks of spouses/partners. He found that the number of friends reported fell as subjects entered into partnerships and raised children; as well, the dissolution of a partnership via divorce was linked to a decline in friendships. Part of the latter may reflect the tendency toward increased jointness in spousal networks over the course of a marriage, which rendered friendships within them vulnerable to disruption in the aftermath of divorce. Sarkisian and Gerstel (2016) reported that rates of socializing and of support exchanges with parents and siblings alike were highest among never-married people and lowest for the currently married, while those of ever-married persons[1] lay in between.

An early study on the transition to parenthood by Hammer, Gutwirth and Phillips (1982) found that it reconfigured social networks in several ways: by increasing the emphasis on kin rather than nonkin relationships, and by reducing the frequency of contact with those in the network. It reported no general difference in network size between parents and non-parents, though, and called attention to "child-linked contacts" as by-products of day care or participation in other child-related activities

[1] i.e. those who are separated, divorced, or widowed.

such as parent-teacher organizations, scouting, or athletic activities (see also Chua et al. 2016; Small 2009). McCannell (1988) studied a convenience sample of women over time, from mid-pregnancy to one year post-partum. She observed a notable decline in overall network size, but no reduction in the number of persons providing several specific types of social support. Moore (1990) reported that confiding networks were slightly smaller among adults with children at home.

Transitions in the domain of work and employment too have been examined. As noted, Bidart and Lavenu (2005) reported that nonkin contacts fell upon labor market entry. Fischer (1982) found that employed persons had more contacts with nonkin, but Moore (1990) reported no difference in confiding network size between full-time or part-time workers and other adults—including both the unemployed and those outside the labor market. In the study of older U.S. adults by Cornwell et al. (2008), confiding network size was higher among retired persons than those who remained active in the labor market.

Moen (2001) wrote about the gendering of the life course, observing that men and women of a given age may be differently situated within the life course, and further that the consequences flowing from a given life course position may differ for women and men. Examining associations between life course and social network phenomena separately for women and men is therefore common. Many such studies find fewer gender-related interactions than they anticipate; those differences that do appear often reflect a disparate influence of parenthood on the networks of women and men. Fischer and Oliker (1983) found that during early parenthood, women have fewer relationships with nonkin than do men; after children have left the home, however, women maintain more such relationships. Moore (1990) reported that employment was associated with fewer kin ties among women, but not among men. Munch, McPherson and Smith-Lovin (1997) focused on parenthood, finding confiding networks to be smallest among women—but not men—when the youngest child in a household was aged 3 or 4. Chua et al. (2016) found no overall difference in network size or span between women and men, but attributed differences in the types of contacts maintained to varying life course experiences.

This selective and undoubtedly incomplete survey of related research nonetheless provides ample warrant for anticipating that the size and composition of social networks varies across life course states, and moreover for expecting certain changes in social networks to follow adult life course transitions. In the next section, we suggest one route through which this connection arguably operates: life course transitions entail entry into and exit from social foci or settings, which in turn expand or limit opportunities for network formation.

Supply-Side Theories of Social Structure

Among the foundational axioms of Blau's (1977) theory of social structure is that "rates of social association depend on opportunities for social contact" (Blau and Schwartz 1984: p. 29). It calls attention to the potentially available associates found in any arena in which social ties might be formed; I have elsewhere (Marsden 1990) termed it a supply-side theory of social structure, contrasting it with demand-side theories that stress individual choices and preferences. The number and composition of the others found in a social setting constrains the scale and types of the networks and relationships that can form within it. Several other opportunity-related theories of social networks, including Fischer's (1977) choice/constraint theory and Verbrugge's (1977) distinction between "meeting and mating," draw similar contrasts.

We place special emphasis here on an opportunity-related concept developed by Feld (1981), termed a "focus of activity." Feld (p. 1016) defines a focus as "a social, psychological, legal or physical entity around which joint activities are organized," observing that a variety of settings—including persons, places, and groups, among others—may serve as foci (p. 1018). The foci of principal interest here are groups such as families or workplaces. Feld argues that foci serve to channel and organize social relations: "[t]hey may actively bring people together or passively constrain them to interact" (p. 1018), so that two persons jointly situated within a focus are more apt to interact with one another than are two who have no arena in common.

Foci can enable—or even require—the development or elaboration of social relationships. Feld observes that foci vary from one another (1981: p. 1019) in at least two crucial respects. First, they differ in size; people involved in a large focus are apt to encounter more meeting opportunities than are those in a smaller one. McPherson and Smith-Lovin (1982), for example, note that while men and women—on average—belong to the same number of voluntary organizations, men tend to be involved in larger groups linked with economic institutions, while otherwise-comparable women tend to participate in smaller groups concerned with domestic and community affairs (see also Chua 2013). They reason that these differences imply that the potential contacts men are prone to encounter in associations are more varied and valuable than those that women tend to meet.

Second, while all foci promote associations among those affiliated with them, the extent to which they do so differs considerably. At one extreme are "total institutions" (Goffman 1961)—such as prisons or nursing homes—that organize most or all aspects of a person's life. At the other pole lie more discretionary settings, such as voluntary associations, in which participation is both less obligatory and much more episodic. The more time and attention that a focus requires of participants, the greater the constraint it poses on their opportunities to form and sustain social ties.

The focus concept is key for linking the life course and social networks because major life course transitions usually involve entry into new foci of activity, withdrawal from old ones, or changes in levels of commitment to foci in which one is already embedded. The formation of a romantic partnership creates a new focus—often an intense and demanding one—and secondarily links someone to the family and friendship networks of the partner or spouse; divorce or separation have the reverse consequences. The presence of children intensifies family commitments—particularly during childrearing—ordinarily entailing affiliations and obligations that extend throughout one's life. Entering the labor force implies affiliation with one or more workplaces, and can draw someone into related organizations such as professional associations or trade unions; these constraints likely bear more strongly on those who have committed larger segments of their lives to work, e.g. full-time rather than part-time workers, or those who take on management responsibilities (Jonczyk et al. 2016). Events such as unemployment or retirement often sever such connections.

By the logic of Feld's theory, life course events that alter the configuration of foci in which someone's activities are situated will tend to expand or limit the pools and types of potential associates to whom one is exposed, and thereby the relationships that actually form. Variations in the size of the foci within which people participate imply variations in network size, while differences in the types of foci in which one is engaged, and the intensity of engagement within them, may shape network composition.

Our emphasis on shifts in foci as sources of network change has some resonance with Kahn and Antonucci's (1980) arguments about the acquisition and shedding of roles as a source of network change. Roles certainly hold implications for relationships, and life course transitions surely involve entry into and exit from roles, or expansion/contraction in the degree of commitment to roles. Because Feld's focus concept highlights variations in the size and composition of the sets of potential alters with whom one can associate while in different life course states, it has particular appeal as a device for understanding how life course transitions may prompt network change.

As noted, much prior work (e.g. Moen 2001; Munch et al. 1997; Kalmijn 2003) offers grounds for anticipating that the consequences of life course transitions may not be the same for men and women, given that women often assume the role of "kin keeper" (Moore 1990). In particular, the presence of (young) children may channel mothers and fathers into very different social worlds, which in turn could imply different changes in networks. Most analyses undertaken in this chapter therefore consider the possibility of gender differences.

Before presenting those analyses, I enter one disclaimer. The perspective adopted here posits that life course phenomena are explanatory variables that lead to differences and changes in network phenomena. The life course and social networks, however, likely have a bidirectional relationship, such that features of social networks might also prompt life course change. Lois (2016), for example, suggests that people with "family-centered" rather than "family-remote" networks are more apt to become parents; Balbo and Barban (2014) find that childbearing by friends is associated with a greater likelihood of entering parenthood. Bernardi and Klärner (2014) present an overview of such research, suggesting that four network mechanisms (learning, pressure, contagion and support) underlie such effects. It is certainly possible that individuals, at least to some extent, alter their networks in anticipation of upcoming life course changes. It seems unlikely that all such consequences will be foreseen, however, or that individuals will be aware in advance of all of the new potential associates they later encounter in connection with a life course transition.

Data and Measures

The analyses that follow draw on data assembled by the General Social Survey (GSS) project, a continuing survey of U.S. adults stressing over-time replication of social indicators. The GSS began in 1972 and has been conducted every year or two since then. It uses a repeated cross-sectional design: each round draws a new sample of Americans aged 18 and over, and measures numerous sociodemographic variables—including important life course states—together with many behaviors and attitudes. The study regularly includes topical modules on subjects of current social science interest, including social networks. See Marsden and Smith (2012) for an overview of the GSS's basic study design and content, and http://www.gss.norc.org/ for many more details and access to GSS data.

Analyses of network composition presented below draw on egocentric network data obtained in topical modules administered in 1985 and 1987.[2] Cross-sectional analyses of network activity use measures of socializing that appeared in the 28 GSSs conducted between 1974 and 2014; data from those studies are combined here. The network activity analyses also examine GSS panel data assembled between 2006 and 2014. Respondents to the 2006, 2008, and 2010 GSSs were subsequently reinterviewed 2 and 4 years later, yielding three-wave panels covering 2006–2010, 2008–2012, and 2010–2014; we pool these to examine linkages between life course transitions and changes in socializing.

Network Measures

The 1985 GSS obtained the first egocentric network data representative of a national population. It focused on "core" or "confiding" networks (Marsden 1987) consisting of those other persons (or "alters") with whom a GSS respondent had spoken about "important matters" during the recent past. Those deemed to be part of a respondent's network were elicited using the following "name generator" (Burt 1984) question:

> From time to time, most people discuss important matters with other people. Looking back over the last six months, who are the people with whom you discussed matters important to you? Just tell me their first names or initials.

Subjects who initially provided less than five names were probed once for additional names. The 1987 GSS used the identical name-generating question, but probed only when fewer than three names were given at first. In both years, the number of names given ranged from 0 to 6 or more; as shown in panel B of Table 5.1,

[2] The 2004 GSS also included name generator data parallel to those collected in 1985. Because serious questions have been raised regarding anomalies in those data (Fischer 2009; Paik and Sanchagrin 2013), however, we do not study them here.

Table 5.1 Descriptive statistics for network indicators and explanatory measures

A. Explanatory measures (percentages or means)				
	1985	1987	2006–2010	1974–2014
Marital status				
Currently married	64.7%	54.9%	54.7%	60.5%
Ever-married	17.6%	26.2%	19.4%	18.3%
Never-married	17.7%	18.9%	25.9%	21.2%
# children in household				
<6 years old	0.27	0.22	0.21	0.24
6–12 years old	0.28	0.28	0.24	0.30
13–17 years old	0.26	0.25	0.20	0.25
Employment status				
Employed full-time	49.2%	52.1%	49.2%	50.2%
Employed part-time	11.4%	11.4%	11.5%	11.2%
Retired	11.9%	13.6%	13.8%	11.7%
Other	27.5%	22.9%	25.5%	26.9%
Residence				
City	29.6%	33.0%	36.5%	35.4%
Environs of city	48.8%	45.1%	48.2%	45.3%
Not in or near city	21.6%	21.8%	15.3%	19.2%
Age (years)	44.5	45.4	45.8	44.4
Education (years)	12.4	12.5	13.4	12.8
Race				
White	86.8%	83.4%	74.5%	82.2%
Black	10.0%	13.0%	13.3%	12.2%
Nonwhite, nonblack	3.2%	3.6%	12.2%	5.6%
Sex (female)	53.0%	56.2%	54.5%	54.6%
(N [range])	(1527–1534)	(1809–1819)	(4707–4744)	(34,574–34,690)
B. Network composition indicators				
Role relationship		1985		1987
Relative		52.2%		56.3%
Neighbor		9.4%		11.1%
Coworker		18.2%		15.9%
Mean network size		3.0		2.5
(N [alters])		(4482)		(4169)
(N [respondents])		(1531)		(1800)
C. Mean levels of network activity (socializing)				
Type of socializing		2006–2010	1974–2014	
Relatives		4.7	4.6	
Friends outside neighborhood		4.1	4.1	
Neighbors		3.4	3.5	
Bars or taverns		2.4	2.4	
(N [range])		(4739–4743)	(34,587–34,636)	

Note: Figures are weighted by number of adults in household, to adjust for oversampling of black respondents in 1982 and 1987, and for two-phase sampling beginning in 2004

2006–2010 and 1974–2014 figures are for respondents who made at least one valid response to items about socializing

the mean network size was about 3 in 1985 (Marsden 1987) and modestly smaller (2.5) in 1987—likely due to the lower threshold used for probing.

After naming alters, respondents were asked to describe each of them in several ways. Network composition was assessed by way of a question about the role relations that connect the respondent to an alter. We consider whether the subject deemed the alter to be any one of five types of kin, a neighbor, or a coworker.[3] Relatives comprised more than half of those cited in both 1985 and 1987 (Table 5.1, panel B); about a tenth were labeled as neighbors and a sixth as coworkers.

The analyses of network activity rely on this measure of informal socializing:

Would you use this card and tell me which which answer comes closest to how often you do the following things?

A. Spend a social evening with relatives
B. Spend a social evening with friends who live outside the neighborhood
C. Spend a social evening with someone who lives in your neighborhood
D. Go to a bar or tavern

Responses ranged from "never" (scored 1 here) to "almost every day" (scored 7). Socializing with relatives is most common: on average it occurs several times a month (panel C, Table 5.1). A typical respondent spends an evening with friends about once a month, and one with neighbors less often. Nearly half of respondents "never" visit a bar or tavern; an average respondent does so once to several times per year.

Life Course Measures

We focus here principally on transitions involving the family and the labor force. Within the family, we distinguish currently, ever-, and never-married persons, and also examine differences in networks associated with the presence of children in different age brackets (0–5, 6–12, and 13–17) in the respondent's household. For labor force involvement, we compare respondents who are employed full-time, employed part-time, in retirement, and in some other work status (e.g. unemployment, keeping house, education). Additionally, we consider the ways in which mobility across residential settings may be linked to network composition,

---

[3]The wording of the role relation question is: "Here is a list of some of the ways in which people are connected to each other. Some people can be connected to you in more than one way. For example, a man could be your brother and he may belong to your church and be your lawyer. When I read you a name, please tell me all the ways that person is connected to you. How is (NAME) connected to you?" Answer options included spouse, parent, sibling, child, other family, co-worker, member of group, neighbor, friend, advisor, and "other." Respondents could select more than one answer for each alter; after their initial answer, interviewers probed once for additional connections.

contrasting persons who live in cities, in suburbs or unincorporated areas surrounding cities, and in towns or smaller areas. Descriptive statistics for these predictors are shown in panel A of Table 5.1.

Controls

All regression analyses control for four additional sociodemographic background measures—age, education, race, and sex. The alter-specific analyses of network composition also take account of the ordinal position in which the respondent named an alter; because closer alters tend to be named earlier (Burt 1986), this distinguishes alters by tie strength to some extent. As such, it contrasts those who are more central in a respondent's network—and hence apt to remain stable (Kahn and Antonucci 1980)—and those with whom someone has weaker, more role-dependent relationships that are apt to turn over more rapidly. To assess conjectures that life course differences in networks are gendered, we examined interactions involving sex and the life course measures discussed.

Network Size and Life Course States

One of Alwin's (2012) life course concepts stresses age-graded regularities in social phenomena, so we begin with a brief examination of cross-sectional differences in the size of confiding networks by age and life course states, relying on the 1985 and 1987 egocentric data. Table 5.2 presents data on average network size by selected explanatory variables.

In accord with prior findings (e.g. Fischer 1982; Marsden 1987; Cornwell et al. 2008), Table 5.2 indicates that networks tend to be smaller among older persons. In the 1985 data, average network size falls steadily from a mean of 3.4 among those under age 30 to one of just over 2 among those aged 70 and above. Age differences are somewhat more modest in the 1987 data.[4] Formerly married people have somewhat smaller networks than do the currently or (especially) never-married; employed respondents tend to have slightly more confidants than do retired persons (particularly) or those in other labor force statuses. For both the 1985 and 1987 data, the largest confiding networks are found among those living in suburban or exurban settings and the smallest ones among rural residents, while those of urban dwellers are close to the average size. No notable association of network size with the presence of children in the household is evident.

[4] Qualitatively similar, but even less pronounced, age differences are found in name generator data about "good friends" collected in the 1988 and 1998 GSSs. Because these studies did not obtain information on network composition, we do not examine them further here.

Table 5.2 Mean confiding network size, by life course states and sociodemographic background

	1985	1987
Age		
Under 30	3.4	2.8
30–39	3.3	2.7
40–49	3.1	2.8
50–59	2.9	2.7
60–69	2.8	2.4
70 and above	2.1	2.2
Marital status		
Currently married	3.0	2.7
Ever-married	2.7	2.5
Never-married	3.3	2.7
Labor force status		
Employed full-time	3.2	2.7
Employed part-time	3.4	2.8
Retired	2.4	2.2
Other	2.9	2.6
Residence		
City	2.9	2.6
Environs of city	3.3	2.8
Rural	2.7	2.4
Education		
0–11 years	2.2	2.1
12 years	2.9	2.6
13 or more years	3.7	3.0
Race		
White	3.1	2.7
Black	2.2	2.3
Nonwhite, nonblack	3.0	2.6
Sex		
Male	3.0	2.6
Female	3.1	2.7
All	3.0	2.6
(N [range])	(1526–1532)	(1802–1808)

Note: Figures are weighted by number of adults in household and (in 1987) to adjust for oversampling of black respondents

Among the sociodemographic variables considered here, differences by education appear largest. In the 1985 data, those completing 11 or fewer years of education cite just over two confidants on average, while those who attended at least one year of college name nearly four. Black respondents cite notably fewer alters than do those who are either white or nonwhite/nonblack. Table 5.2 indicates that men and women tend to have networks of roughly the same size, on average.

These life course and sociodemographic indicators are correlated with one another, of course. In regression analyses (not displayed) that enter all of them as predictors, education differences emerge as the largest and most consistent, together with the difference between black and nonblack respondents. In the 1985 data, age differences in network size remain statistically significant after adjusting for other explanatory variables; they do not in the 1987 data, however.

Cross-Sectional Differences in Network Composition by Life Course States

To examine differences in network composition, we asked whether persons in different life course states are more or less apt to cite alters drawn from three foci: the family, the residential neighborhood, and the workplace. Table 5.3 presents estimates for logistic regression analyses in which the life course and control variables predict binary indicators of whether a respondent described a given alter as a relative, neighbor, or coworker; alters are nested within respondents.

Opportunity-based theories anticipate that those whose lives are more deeply embedded within families will rely more on relatives as confidants. The findings for marital status are in keeping with this logic. Citation of relatives is substantially more likely among currently-married people; the odds that a given alter is described as a relative are more than three times higher among married than never-married respondents, in both 1985 and 1987. Formerly married (separated, widowed, or divorced) people are somewhat more apt to cite relatives than are those who have never married.

Table 5.3 does not, however, suggest that living in households having many children enhances the likelihood of citing family members as confiding contacts, with the exception of one significant coefficient (for 1987) indicating that those with more pre-teenage children tend to name relatives. Nor are relatives cited more often by those who have larger numbers of siblings.

Employment, however, is inversely linked to naming family members. The odds that an alter is a family member are more than 25% lower for the full-time employed than for those outside the labor force. Part-time employment also is negatively associated with naming family members, significantly so in the 1987 confiding data. These findings could well reflect competition among foci, as work-related activities come to consume more of someone's time and energy.

Turning to the control variables, we see that women consistently name family members as confidants more often than men do, in keeping with Moore's (1990) prior findings based on the 1985 data. Respondents with more education are less

Table 5.3 Network composition and life course states (logistic regression coefficients)

	Whether respondent cited alter as a…					
	Relative		Neighbor		Coworker	
Explanatory variable	1985	1987	1985	1987	1985	1987
Marital status[a]						
Now married	**1.22** (0.16)	**1.17** (0.17)	−0.11 (0.30)	−0.34 (0.33)	0.20 (0.20)	0.30 (0.22)
Ever-married	**0.35** (0.17)	0.17 (0.18)	−0.04 (0.32)	−0.01 (0.39)	−0.11 (0.24)	−0.20 (0.26)
# children in household						
Age 0–5	−0.05 (0.08)	0.10 (0.09)	0.21 (0.12)	−0.20 (0.16)	−0.00 (0.12)	0.00 (0.12)
Age 6–12	−0.14 (0.08)	**0.13** (0.07)	0.21 (0.15)	0.22 (0.14)	−0.06 (0.12)	0.03 (0.09)
Age 13–17	−0.06 (0.08)	0.03 (0.08)	**0.34** (0.15)	0.13 (0.13)	0.01 (0.12)	0.14 (0.10)
# siblings	0.02 (0.01)	0.01 (0.02)	−0.02 (0.02)	0.02 (0.03)	0.03 (0.03)	0.00 (0.02)
Labor force status[a]						
Full-time	**−0.32** (0.15)	**−0.35** (0.14)	**−0.64** (0.22)	**−0.66** (0.24)	**1.62** (0.21)	**1.35** (0.20)
Part-time	−0.06 (0.16)	**−0.44** (0.16)	0.15 (0.27)	0.01 (0.28)	**1.43** (0.26)	**1.08** (0.27)
Retired	0.19 (0.21)	0.07 (0.21)	0.32 (0.30)	−0.29 (0.41)	−0.41 (0.44)	−0.02 (0.30)
Residence[a]						
City	−0.34 (0.21)	−0.08 (0.17)	−0.38 (0.27)	0.13 (0.37)	0.15 (0.23)	−0.06 (0.27)
Environs of city	−0.14 (0.22)	−0.29 (0.16)	−0.54 (0.29)	0.08 (0.37)	−0.05 (0.22)	−0.07 (0.25)
Age	**−0.09** (0.02)	−0.02 (0.03)	−0.20 (0.04)	−0.01 (0.04)	**0.18** (0.04)	0.02 (0.03)
Age²/100	**0.09** (0.02)	0.01 (0.02)	0.02 (0.03)	0.02 (0.03)	**−0.22** (0.04)	−0.01 (0.03)
Education	**−0.07** (0.02)	**−0.04** (0.02)	0.00 (0.03)	−0.07 (0.04)	0.03 (0.03)	**0.13** (0.03)
Race[a]						
Black	−0.30 (0.24)	**−0.29** (0.13)	0.44 (0.33)	−0.48 (0.27)	−0.23 (0.37)	**−0.79** (0.22)
Nonblack, nonwhite	−0.53 (0.28)	**−0.51** (0.24)	−0.65 (0.48)	0.09 (0.91)	−0.12 (0.38)	−0.26 (0.42)
Sex (female)	**0.36** (0.11)	**0.26** (0.10)	0.35 (0.21)	−0.20 (0.22)	**−0.41** (0.15)	**−0.56** (0.17)
Citation order	**−0.15** (0.04)	**−0.53** (0.05)	0.01 (0.05)	**0.34** (0.07)	0.07 (0.04)	**0.16** (0.06)

(continued)

Table 5.3 (continued)

	Whether respondent cited alter as a...					
	Relative		Neighbor		Coworker	
Explanatory variable	1985	1987	1985	1987	1985	1987
Rho	**0.26** (0.03)	**0.31** (0.03)	**0.49** (0.03)	**0.56** (0.04)	**0.39** (0.03)	**0.42** (0.04)
(N)						
(Respondents)	(1383)	(1687)	(1383)	(1687)	(1383)	(1687)
(Alters)	(4437)	(4142)	(4437)	(4142)	(4437)	(4142)

Note: Robust standard errors (clustered within GSS sampling areas) are given in parentheses. **Bold** coefficients have associated p values of 0.05 or less

[a]Reference categories for categorical variables are: (marital status) never-married; (labor force status) other, including students, homemakers, etc.; (residence) town or rural area; (race) white

likely to name family members, while white respondents appear more likely to do so than nonwhites. In both years, earlier-cited alters tend to be relatives, suggesting that respondents tend to have closer, more multiplex relationships with kin.

Few of the factors considered are predictive of whether an alter is a neighbor. The only consistent finding here is that full-time employed people are less likely to cite neighbors; the odds that a full-time worker does so are about half as large as those for someone not in the labor force. In the 1987 data, neighbors tend to be among the later-cited (and hence less close) alters.

Both full- and part-time workers are much more likely to cite coworkers than non-employed people are; the odds of doing so grow by factors of between 3 and 5. Work consumes more attention from employed persons, of course, and they also have ready access to coworkers. Controlling for employment status, women are less likely to cite coworkers than men are, and blacks appear somewhat less apt than whites to do so. Later-cited alters are modestly more likely to be coworkers, as is to be expected for these role-dependent relationships.

In both years, substantial intraclass correlations (rho) are present for all three types of alters. These indicate that—after adjusting for all predictors considered—respondents vary in the extent to which they are embedded in particular foci of activity. If one alter is (or is not) a relative, others also tend to be (or not to be). Such clustering appears especially pronounced for citation of neighbors.

Gender Differences

To examine possible gender differences in how life course states and confiding are linked, interactions of sex with marital status, the numbers of children in the household, employment status, and residence were estimated. Few systematic sex differences in associations of life course states with network composition were evident. The most consistent patterns involved differences in the citation of coworkers: employment—both full- and part-time—is more strongly linked to naming work colleagues among women than among men (see Moore 1990). This suggests, perhaps, that the states of membership and non-membership in the labor force are more sharply differentiated experiences for women than for men. Less pronounced was a finding that having more teenagers in the household is more negatively associated with citing coworkers among women, perhaps indicating a gender difference in how work-family conflicts are experienced; it is the only statistically significant interaction involving children. Beyond these, the estimates for 1985 (but not those for 1987) suggest that employment and non-rural residence may be negatively linked to citing relatives among women, but not men. Overall, however, inspection of these interactions leaves an impression of similarity rather than difference in the way that life course states predict network composition for men and women.

Network Activity and the Life Course: Cross-Sectional Differences

We next examine differences across life course states in the frequency of informal socializing. Socializing may involve less intense network contacts than does than confiding about important matters, likely a mixture of stronger and weaker relationships. We begin by examining cross-sectional associations using the pooled 1974–2014 GSSs. For analyses focused on time trends in socializing over most of this period, see Marsden and Srivastava (2012).

Opportunity-oriented theories of network formation would anticipate that events marking family formation, including marriage and the arrival of children, would intensify one's involvement in family-related foci and hence tend to increase the frequency of socializing with relatives while decreasing non-familial social activity. Some results of regression analyses presented in Table 5.4 are in accord with this, most notably the finding that married and formerly-married people socialize with relatives more often. Also of interest here is that those with more pre-school age children in the household tend to see more of their relatives. The reverse holds, however, for those having more children over 5 years of age; this is associated with small decreases in the frequency with which relatives are seen, perhaps reflecting engagement in school- and community-based activities involving children of these ages.

The negative associations between marriage and the presence of children with the other forms of socializing measured in the GSS (spending social evenings with friends and neighbors, and visiting bars and taverns) also align with expectations

Table 5.4 Socializing levels and life course states (regression coefficients), 1974–2014 GSSs

	Frequency of social evenings with…			
Explanatory variable	Relatives	Friends	Neighbors	Visit bar or tavern
Marital status[a]				
Now married	**0.15** (0.03)	**−0.44** (0.03)	**−0.49** (0.04)	**−0.71** (0.03)
Ever-married	**0.11** (0.04)	**−0.14** (0.03)	**−0.20** (0.04)	**−0.17** (0.03)
# children in household				
Age 0–5	**0.05** (0.02)	**−0.18** (0.02)	**−0.05** (0.02)	**−0.19** (0.02)
Age 6–12	**−0.07** (0.02)	**−0.13** (0.01)	−0.01 (0.02)	**−0.11** (0.01)
Age 13–17	**−0.06** (0.02)	**−0.07** (0.02)	**−0.04** (0.02)	**−0.06** (0.02)
Labor force status[a]				
Full-time	0.02 (0.02)	0.02 (0.02)	**−0.43** (0.03)	**0.18** (0.03)
Part-time	−0.00 (0.03)	**0.13** (0.03)	**−0.15** (0.04)	**0.12** (0.03)
Retired	0.06 (0.04)	**0.21** (0.04)	0.08 (0.05)	**0.12** (0.03)
Residence[a]				
City	**−0.25** (0.04)	**0.19** (0.03)	**−0.37** (0.04)	**0.17** (0.05)
Environs of city	**−0.14** (0.04)	**0.16** (0.03)	**−0.34** (0.04)	**0.11** (0.06)
Age	**−0.01** (0.00)	**−0.03** (0.00)	**−0.01** (0.00)	
Age ≤ 23				**0.30** (0.02)
Age > 23				**−0.04** (0.00)
Education	**−0.04** (0.00)	**0.06** (0.00)	**0.03** (0.00)	**0.04** (0.00)
Race[a]				
Black	**0.25** (0.03)	**−0.11** (0.03)	**0.10** (0.04)	**−0.38** (0.03)
Nonblack, nonwhite	0.01 (0.06)	**−0.20** (0.04)	**−0.13** (0.05)	**−0.49** (0.05)
Sex (female)	**0.26** (0.01)	**−0.03** (0.02)	**−0.23** (0.03)	**−0.57** (0.02)
Year	**0.01** (0.00)	**−0.00** (0.00)	**−0.01** (0.00)	**−0.01** (0.00)
R^2	0.03	0.14	0.04	0.21
(N)	(34,235)	(34,219)	(34,208)	(34,187)

Note: Robust standard errors (clustered within GSS sampling areas) are given in parentheses (standard errors of 0.00 reflect rounding). **Bold** coefficients have associated p values of 0.05 or less
[a]Reference categories for categorical variables are: (marital status) never-married; (labor force status) other, including students, homemakers, etc.; (residence) town or rural area; (race) white

based on focus theory. Differences between currently- and never-married people are most notable here, but the presence of children of any age is inversely, though weakly, associated with non-familial socializing.

Differences in socializing related to labor force status are comparatively modest. The full-time employed are less apt to spend evenings with neighbors and more likely to visit bars and taverns than are those outside the labor force; socializing with friends is most common among part-time employees and retired persons. These findings likely reflect the availability of time together with involvement in

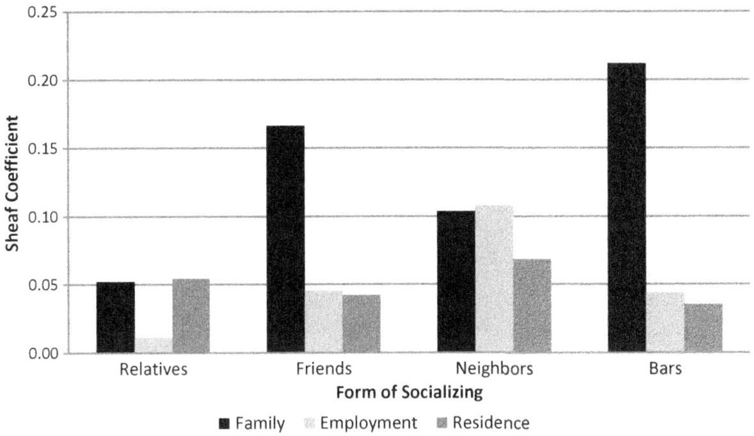

Fig. 5.1 Sheaf coefficients summarizing strength of associations of family-related, employment, and residential factors with socializing, based on Table 5.4

activities that are either competitive or synergistic with workplace demands. Employment status is unrelated to socializing with relatives.

Differences by residential setting mirror those reported by Marsden and Srivastava (2012): respondents living in more urbanized places tend to socialize more with friends outside their neighborhoods than do rural dwellers, and are also more apt to visit bars and taverns, while those living in towns or rural areas are more likely to socialize with relatives and neighbors. These differences can be attributed to variations in both the availability of the different types of associates and the varying ecologies of these residential settings: urban settings make a diversity of potential friends readily accessible, thereby facilitating "chosen" relationships (Fischer 1982), while rural ones facilitate contact with neighbors.

Figure 5.1 displays standardized sheaf (or multiple-partial) regression coefficients (Heise 1972; Whitt 1986) that summarize the relative magnitudes of the differences in socializing in Table 5.4 that are related to family-related factors (both marital status and children in the household), employment status, and residential setting. Overall, family status appears to have the most pervasive associations with socializing, particularly with friends and in bars/taverns. In this sense, family may be the most constraining focus of the three. Relatively speaking, employment status appears most consequential for neighboring, while residence is most important for socializing with relatives and neighbors.

We remark briefly on some findings for the control variables in Table 5.4. Women are significantly more likely to socialize with relatives than are men, and less apt to be engaged in the other types of informal contact, again consistent with Moore's (1990) image of "kin-keeping." Socializing of all types grows less frequent with

Table 5.5 Gender differences in associations between socializing levels and life course states (regression coefficients conditional on gender), 1974–2014 GSSs

	Frequency of social evenings with…							
Explanatory variable	Relatives		Friends		Neighbors		Visit bar or tavern	
	Men	Women	Men	Women	Men	Women	Men	Women
Marital status[a]								
Now married	**0.22**	**0.10**	**−0.51**	**−0.38**	**−0.57**	**−0.40**		
Ever-married	−0.02	**0.18**			**−0.30**	**−0.13**	−0.05	**−0.24**
# children in household								
Age 0–5					−0.00	**−0.09**		
Age 6–12								
Age 13–17	−0.03	**−0.09**						
Labor force status[a]								
Full-time					**−0.33**	**−0.50**		
Part-time					−0.02	**−0.20**		
Retired								
Residence[a]								
City								
Environs of city			**0.10**	**0.20**				
(N)	(34,235)		(34, 219)		(34,208)		(34,187)	

Note: **Bold** conditional associations have associated p values of 0.05 or less. All pairs of coefficients displayed differ significantly from each other ($p < 0.05$)

[a]Reference categories for categorical variables are: (marital status) never-married; (labor force status) other, including students, homemakers, etc.; (residence) town or rural area

age.[5] Those with more years of education are less likely to socialize with relatives, but more likely to see those outside the family. The 40-year span covered by the data saw slight rises in familial socializing, and slight declines in the non-familial forms.

Gender Differences

To assess the prospect that socializing varies with life course states in different ways for men and women, we estimated interactions of gender with marital status, the presence of children, employment status, and residence. The large sample available for the cross-sectional socializing analyses allows detection of more such differences than for confiding. Most gender differences found had to do with family-related life course states, particularly marital status. Table 5.5 presents all pairs of conditional regression coefficients that differ significantly between men and women.

[5]An exception is that visiting bars and taverns rises sharply with age until age 23, represented here using a spline function. The peak age of visiting bars is just above the legal age for alcohol consumption in the United States. For more detailed examination of age patterns in socializing, see Marsden and Srivastava (2012).

The way in which socializing varies with marital status differs by gender. Being married is more strongly linked to frequent contact with relatives among men than among women, though both see their relatives more than the never-married do. Formerly-married women, however, remain more likely than their never-married counterparts to socialize with relatives, while formerly married men do not. Both of these findings suggest that women maintain a more enduring connection to family than do men.

Outside of the family, the negative association between being currently married and seeing friends is somewhat stronger among men than among women. Similarly, the tendency for both currently- and ever-married people to socialize less with neighbors is significantly larger among men. Together with the difference in socializing with relatives already mentioned, these results indicate that marriage realigns the social lives of men more than it does those of women. Currently married men and women alike are much less apt to visit bars and taverns than are the never married (Table 5.4); formerly-married women remain unlikely to do so, however, while formerly-married men do not differ from otherwise comparable never-married ones.

A few gender differences in links between children and socializing were found, though many others proved to be insignificant. Those that were identified are consistent with the idea that children may impact the social lives of women more strongly than those of men. Women with teenage children in their household are somewhat less likely to see their relatives frequently, while no such difference is evident for men. The presence of very young children has no association with neighboring among men, but women in households with children under 6 tend to socialize less often with neighbors.

For the most part, socializing does not vary with employment status in notably different ways for men and women. An exception that resonates somewhat with the above findings about confiding has to do with seeing neighbors: both full- and part-time employment is more strongly linked to less neighboring among women than among comparable men. The difference in socializing with friends between women who live in suburban or exurban places and those in rural ones is also larger than that found among men.

These findings lend some credence to assertions that life course phenomena hold different implications for the social networks of women and men. As such arguments anticipate, the most consistent findings revolve around family-linked events, especially marriage. It is worth noting that most gender differences found here are of modest magnitude, and hence can be detected only with abundant data, but those differences that were isolated are of considerable substantive interest.

Transitions and Changes in Network Activity

To further probe the links between the life course and socializing, we turn to longitudinal analyses of the GSS panel data. Some respondents changed life course states (e.g., became married or entered retirement) during the 2 years that elapsed between

Table 5.6 Fixed effect estimates for socializing levels (regression coefficients), GSS panel data, 2006–2014

	Frequency of social evenings with…			
Explanatory variable	Relatives	Friends	Neighbors	Visit bar or tavern
Marital status[a]				
Now married	0.01 (0.09)	**−0.43** (0.11)	−0.10 (0.15)	**−0.28** (0.11)
Ever-married	0.12 (0.14)	−0.14 (0.14)	0.14 (0.19)	−0.11 (0.13)
# children in household				
Age 0–5	0.06 (0.04)	−0.04 (0.04)	**−0.13** (0.06)	−0.06 (0.04)
Age 6–12	0.05 (0.04)	0.00 (0.04)	−0.03 (0.05)	**−0.07** (0.03)
Age 13–17	−0.06 (0.04)	−0.07 (0.04)	−0.06 (0.06)	−0.04 (0.03)
Labor force status[a]				
Full-time	**−0.21** (0.06)	0.01 (0.05)	**−0.19** (0.08)	**0.13** (0.06)
Part-time	**−0.15** (0.07)	**0.12** (0.06)	0.07 (0.10)	0.06 (0.06)
Retired	0.03 (0.08)	−0.01 (0.04)	0.07 (0.05)	0.02 (0.05)
Residence[a]				
City	−0.10 (0.14)	**0.15** (0.15)	**−0.37** (0.20)	0.06 (0.11)
Environs of city	−0.16 (0.15)	**0.10** (0.14)	**−0.42** (0.18)	−0.08 (0.10)
R^2	0.00	0.03	0.01	0.05
Rho	0.61	0.59	0.58	0.73
(N)				
(Respondents)	(4483)	(4482)	(4484)	(4483)
(Occasions)	(10,008)	(10,005)	(10,004)	(10,009)

Note: Robust standard errors (clustered within GSS sampling areas) are given in parentheses. **Bold** coefficients have associated p values of 0.05 or less

[a]Reference categories for categorical variables are: (marital status) never-married; (labor force status) other, including students, homemakers, etc.; (residence) town or rural area

successive panel interviews, so we can examine the associations between such transitions and changes in socializing that were reported. Table 5.6 presents estimates for fixed-effect models that predict socializing from life course states; these adjust for all time-constant respondent characteristics, observed or unobserved. The sample size for these analyses is much smaller than that in Table 5.4, so much less power to detect significant associations is available. Across occasions of measurement, respondents display relatively strong proclivities toward particular forms of socializing, as indicated by the rho values in Table 5.6.

In general, regression coefficients in Table 5.6 are similar in sign but smaller in magnitude than the corresponding estimates from the cross-sectional analyses (Table 5.4). Entry into marriage is associated with significant decreases in the frequency of socializing with friends and visiting bars. It is not, however, linked to increased time with relatives. While almost all estimated associations between rises in the numbers of children in a household and changes in non-familial socializing are negative, they are small and insignificant for the most part. There are indications that having very young children slightly reduces neighboring, however, and that visits to bars decline a bit among those with additional children of elementary school age.

Several other findings regarding employment and residence also align with those in the cross-sectional analyses. Full-time employment is linked with fewer visits with neighbors and with an increase in socializing at bars, but not with spending more time with friends. Additional socializing with friends does, however, accompany entry into part-time employment. Residential moves from rural places into urban or suburban ones entail a rise in socializing with friends and a decline in seeing neighbors; the estimated coefficients for seeing relatives are also negative, but not statistically significant.

Table 5.6 contains one significant finding that did not emerge in the cross-sectional analyses: entry into the labor force—on either a full- or part-time basis—is linked to spending fewer social evenings with relatives, while no such association is evident in Table 5.4. One might conjecture that this divergence in findings reflects the short-term (2-year) changes captured by the panel data, and that labor force participants might adapt and restore their familial contacts to pre-entry levels after longer durations of employment. Alternately, reduced contact with family upon employment could be a phenomenon specific to the recent period (2006–2014) covered by the panel data, rather than the four decades spanned by the cross-sectional data.

Inspection of gender-related interactions yields only a few suggestive findings bearing on the prospect that transitions affect men and women differentially. The three significant differences found, however, take a similar form, indicating that a transition reduces socializing among women while making no difference among men. Specifically, relocating from a town or rural area to a suburb is accompanied by less socializing with relatives among women, but not among men; additional pre-school children lower socializing with friends among women only; and adding teenage children is associated with fewer visits to bars for women, but not men. None of these interactions emerged in the cross-sectional analyses, however (see Table 5.5).

The longitudinal analyses of network activity in Table 5.6 lend support to the main premise on which this chapter rests, that life course transitions can prompt changes in social networks. Though the panel and cross-sectional analyses are not consistent in all respects, the fixed-effect estimates offer stronger evidence that changes involving marriage, children, employment, and residence alter the rhythms of informal social lives.

Summary and Conclusion

This chapter argues that life course events shape social networks by both creating and eliminating opportunities for contact with others. Entering different life course states makes new types of people accessible, while limiting contact with other types of potential associates. Transitions in the life course can prompt changes in the composition of social networks, as well as in the frequency of different forms of network activity.

The General Social Survey data on social networks and informal socializing activity presented here offer considerable support for the perspective set forth.

Family-related life course states, particularly marital status, shape contacts with relatives: currently married persons tend to confide in kin and spend more time socializing with them, and are correspondingly less involved with non-familial associates. Entry into the paid workforce expands the number of readily available coworkers, making it more likely that confiding networks will include workplace colleagues. Some competition across foci of activity is evident, as employed people appear somewhat less apt to draw their confidants from the family or the residential neighborhood, and likewise have fewer social contacts with neighbors.

In line with Moen's (2001) observations about the gendering of the life course, the chapter investigated the possibility that life course states and social networks covary in different ways for men and women. The findings obtained are far from conclusive, and many of the differences detected are only modest in magnitude. They do convey several hints, however, that marriage and the presence of children may indeed hold different implications for the social lives of wives/mothers and husbands/fathers.

Notwithstanding our emphasis on life course transitions as events that shape opportunities for contact and thereby serve to constrain network formation, individual preferences and the human agency stressed by Elder (1994) surely affect the social networks that actually take form. Certainly individuals are able to exercise discretion within a structure of opportunities. Indeed, some may opt to enter a context or focus of activity because of the prospects it offers for network building (Burt 1992). Settings also may be chosen for other reasons, though, and not all network consequences of contextual choices are anticipated ex ante (Small 2009). Selection into a context or focus, then, serves to narrow—sometimes dramatically—the range of alternatives within which individuals may exercise agency.

The lines of analysis pursued here could be productively extended in several ways. More extensive network data, covering forms of social contact other than confiding and socializing (e.g. instrumental and informational assistance) could be informative. Longer-term longitudinal studies could enable a better parsing-out of the degree to which networks reflect the availability of contact opportunities versus preferences for associates of particular types. More recent data on confiding too would be helpful, especially in light of ongoing changes in the positions of women and men within families and the workforce.

As well, many questions can be posed about whether particular combinations of life course states—e.g. of marital, parental, and employment statuses—give rise to unique social network configurations. One might also ask, in line with Elder's (1985) emphasis on historical time as a context in which life courses unfold, whether particular states or transitions are more strongly linked to network phenomena during different periods. Finally, pursuing the directions opened by Kalmijn's (2003) study of the shared social networks of spouses and partners could yield insights into social networks as a means via which life courses are linked, and how transitions in a subject's life course may ramify into the networks of his/her alters. The idea that life course states are associated with structured opportunities for contact, however, is likely to be one element to be taken into consideration while pursuing any of these interesting directions beyond this chapter's line of inquiry.

References

Alwin, D. F. (2012). Integrating varieties of life course concepts. *The Journals of Gerontology Series B: Psychological Sciences and Social Sciences, 67*(2), 206–220.

Antonucci, T. C., & Akiyama, H. (1987). Social networks in adult life and a preliminary examination of the convoy model. *Journal of Gerontology, 42*(5), 519–527.

Balbo, N., & Barban, N. (2014). Does fertility behavior spread among friends? *American Sociological Review, 79*(3), 412–431.

Bernardi, L., & Klärner, A. (2014). Social networks and fertility. *Demographic Research, 30*(22), 641–670.

Bidart, C., & Lavenu, D. (2005). Evolutions of personal networks and life events. *Social Networks, 27*(4), 359–376.

Blau, P. M. (1977). *Inequality and heterogeneity: A primitive theory of social structure*. New York: Free Press.

Blau, P. M., & Schwartz, J. E. (1984). *Cross-cutting social circles: Testing a macrosociological theory of intergroup relations*. New York: Academic.

Burt, R.S. (1984). Network items and the general social survey. *Social Networks 6*(4), 293–339.

Burt, R. S. (1986). A note on sociometric order in the general social survey network data. *Social Networks, 8*(2), 149–174.

Burt, R. S. (1992). *Structural holes: The social structure of competition*. Cambridge, MA: Harvard University Press.

Chua, V. (2013). Categorical sources of varieties of network inequalities. *Social Science Research, 42*(5), 1236–1253.

Chua, V., Mathews, M., & Loh, Y. (2016). Social capital in Singapore: Gender differences, ethnic hierarchies, and their intersection. *Social Networks, 47*, 138–150.

Cornwell, B., Laumann, E. O., & Schumm, L. P. (2008). The social connectedness of older adults: A national profile. *American Sociological Review, 73*(2), 185–203.

Crossley, N., Bellotti, E., Edwards, G., Everett, M. G., Koskinen, J., & Tranmer, M. (2015). *Social network analysis for ego-nets*. London: Sage.

Degenne, A., & Lebeaux, M. (2005). The dynamics of personal networks at the time of entry into adult life. *Social Networks, 27*(4), 337–358.

Elder, G. H. (1985). Perspectives on the life course. In G. H. J. Elder (Ed.), *Life course dynamics: Trajectories and transitions, 1968–1980* (pp. 23–49). Ithaca: Cornell University Press.

Elder, G. H. (1994). Time, human agency, and social change: Perspectives on the life course. *Social Psychology Quarterly, 57*(1), 4–15.

Elder, G. H. (1995). The life course paradigm: Social change and individual development. In P. Moen, G. H. Elder, & K. Lüscher (Eds.), *Examining lives in context: Perspectives on the ecology of human development* (pp. 101–139). Washington, DC: American Psychological Association.

Feld, S. L. (1981). The focused organization of social ties. *American Journal of Sociology, 86*(5), 1015–1035.

Fischer, C. S. (1977). Perspectives on community and personal relations. In C. S. Fischer, R. M. Jackson, C. A. Stueve, K. Gerson, & L. M. Jones (Eds.), *Networks and places: Social relations in the urban setting* (pp. 1–16). New York: Free Press.

Fischer, C. S. (1982). *To dwell among friends: Personal networks in town and city*. Chicago: University of Chicago Press.

Fischer, C. S. (2009). The 2004 GSS finding of shrunken social networks: An artifact? *American Sociological Review, 74*(4), 657–669.

Fischer, C. S., & Oliker, S. J. (1983). A research note on friendship, gender, and the life cycle. *Social Forces, 62*(1), 124–133.

Goffman, E. (1961). *Asylums: Essays on the social situation of mental patients and other inmates*. Garden City: Anchor Books.

Hammer, M., Gutwirth, L., & Phillips, S. L. (1982). Parenthood and social networks. *Social Science & Medicine, 16*(24), 2091–2100.
Heise, D. R. (1972). Employing nominal variables, induced variables, and block variables in path analysis. *Sociological Methods and Research, 1*(2), 147–173.
Hurlbert, J. S., & Acock, A. C. (1990). The effects of marital status on the form and composition of social networks. *Social Science Quarterly, 71*(1), 163–174.
Jonczyk, C. D., Lee, Y. G., Galunic, C. D., & Bensaou, B. M. (2016). Relational changes during role transitions: The interplay of efficiency and cohesion. *Academy of Management Journal, 59*(3), 956–982.
Kahn, R. L., & Antonucci, T. C. (1980). Convoys over the life course: Attachment, roles, and social support. In *Life-span development and behavior* (Vol. 3, pp. 253–286). New York: Academic.
Kalmijn, M. (2003). Shared friendship networks and the life course: An analysis of survey data on married and cohabiting couples. *Social Networks, 25*(3), 231–249.
Kalmijn, M. (2012). Longitudinal analyses of the effects of age, marriage, and parenthood on social contacts and support. *Advances in Life Course Research, 17*(4), 177–190.
Lois, D. (2016). Types of social networks and the transition to parenthood. *Demographic Research, 34*(23), 657–688.
Marsden, P. V. (1987). Core discussion networks of Americans. *American Sociological Review, 52*(1), 122–131.
Marsden, P. V. (1990). Network diversity, substructures, and opportunities for contact. In C. Calhoun, M. Meyer, & W. R. Scott (Eds.), *Structures of power and constraint: Papers in honor of Peter M. Blau* (pp. 397–410). New York: Cambridge University Press.
Marsden, P. V., & Smith, T. W. (2012). Appendix: The general social survey project. In P. V. Marsden (Ed.), *Social trends in American life: Findings from the general social survey since 1972* (pp. 369–378). Princeton: Princeton University Press.
Marsden, P. V., & Srivastava, S. B. (2012). Trends in informal social participation: 1974–2008. In P. V. Marsden (Ed.), *Social trends in American life: Findings from the general social survey since 1972* (pp. 240–263). Princeton: Princeton University Press.
Marshall, V. W., & Mueller, M. M. (2003). Theoretical roots of the life-course perspective. In *Social dynamics of the life course: Transitions, institutions, and interrelations* (pp. 3–32). New York: Walter de Gruyter.
McCannell, K. (1988). Social networks and the transition to motherhood. In R. M. Milardo (Ed.), *Families and social networks* (pp. 83–106). Beverly Hills: Sage.
McPherson, J. M., & Smith-Lovin, L. (1982). Women and weak ties: Differences by sex in the size of voluntary organizations. *American Journal of Sociology, 87*(4), 883–904.
Moen, P. (2001). The gendered life course. In R. H. Binstock & L. K. George (Eds.), *Handbook of aging and the social sciences* (5th ed.). New York: Academic.
Mollenhorst, G., Volker, B., & Flap, H. (2014). Changes in personal relationships: How social contexts affect the emergence and discontinuation of relationships. *Social Networks, 37*, 65–80.
Moore, G. (1990). Structural determinants of men's and women's personal networks. *American Sociological Review, 55*(5), 726–735.
Morgan, D. L., Neal, M. B., & Carder, P. (1997). The stability of core and peripheral networks over time. *Social Networks, 19*(1), 9–25.
Munch, A., McPherson, J. M., & Smith-Lovin, L. (1997). Gender, children, and social contact: The effects of childrearing for men and women. *American Sociological Review, 62*(4), 509–520.
Paik, A., & Sanchagrin, K. (2013). Social isolation in America: An artifact. *American Sociological Review, 78*(3), 339–360.
Sarkisian, N., & Gerstel, N. (2016). Does singlehood isolate or integrate? Examining the link between marital status and ties to kin, friends, and neighbors. *Journal of Social and Personal Relationships, 33*(3), 361–384.
Small, M. L. (2009). *Unanticipated gains: Origins of network inequality in everyday life*. New York: Oxford University Press.

Stueve, C. A., & Gerson, K. (1977). Personal relations across the life-cycle. In C. S. Fischer, R. M. Jackson, C. A. Stueve, K. Gerson, & L. M. Jones (Eds.), *Networks and Places: Social Relations in the Urban Setting* (pp. 79–98). New York: Free Press.
Verbrugge, L. M. (1977). The structure of adult friendship choices. *Social Forces, 56*(2), 576–597.
Wellman, B., Wong, R. Y., Tindall, D., & Nazer, N. (1997). A decade of network change: Turnover, persistence and stability in personal communities. *Social Networks, 19*(1), 27–50.
Whitt, H. P. (1986). The sheaf coefficient: A simplified and expanded approach. *Social Science Research, 15*(2), 174–189.

Peter V. Marsden is the Edith and Benjamin Geisinger Professor of Sociology at Harvard University. His areas of specialization are social organization, especially formal organizations, social networks, social science methodology and the sociology of medicine.

Part III
Marriage and Family Networks

Chapter 6
Calling on Kin: The Place of Parents and Adult Children in Egocentric Networks

Shira Offer and Claude S. Fischer

Close kin, particularly parents and adult children, have, barring any dramatic estrangement, a distinctive role in individuals' support networks by virtue of their lifelong connections and the extent to which people rely on them through time. According to a recent Pew Research Center report, 60% of Americans provided practical support, such as help with errands and housework, to their aging parents in the previous year (Pew 2015). Over half reported giving in-kind assistance and almost two-thirds financial assistance to their adult children (see also Robinson and Schoeni 2010; Schoeni and Ross 2005). Time-diary studies suggest that parents and their adult children interact even more frequently and that most of them engage in mundane yet meaningful social exchanges on a weekly, and often daily, basis (Fingerman et al. 2016). Relationships between parents and adult children are assumed to be "special" and different from other types of relations due to the high level of emotional involvement and strong feelings of commitment they entail (Finch and Mason 1993; Silverstein et al. 2006; Wellman and Wortley 1990). Yet variation exists in the functions and quality of close kinship ties. In recent decades, major demographic, economic, and normative changes have affected the availability of immediate kin and altered the dynamics of intergenerational relationships (see reviews in Bengtson 2001; Johnson 2000; Swartz 2009).

The research reported here is supported by National Institute of Aging Grant R01 AG041955-01 (Claude S. Fischer, PI). We thank the editors of this volume and other members of the UCNets Project for helpful comments.

S. Offer (✉)
Department of Sociology and Anthropology, Bar Ilan University, Ramat Gan, Israel
e-mail: Shira.Offer@biu.ac.il

C. S. Fischer
Department of Sociology, University of California, Berkeley, CA, USA
e-mail: Fischer1@berkeley.edu

D. F. Alwin et al. (eds.), *Social Networks and the Life Course*, Frontiers in Sociology and Social Research 2, https://doi.org/10.1007/978-3-319-71544-5_6

In the present study we use data from the first wave of the UCNets project, a longitudinal study of personal networks, life events, and health in the greater San Francisco Bay Area, to learn in an inductive way about the role that close kin play in people's personal networks. Specifically, we ask: (1) Who has parents or adult children available and accessible to help them? (2) Given that such immediate family are available, who reports an active connection to parents or adult children? (3) For people who have an active connection to parents or adult children, what role do these kin play in their network? And (4) to what extent is their connection related to other characteristics of their relationships? Recent sociological studies of familial exchanges have typically examined relations with kin in general without making a distinction between immediate and more distant kin. By contrast, gerontological research has mainly focused on the parent-adult child dyad and treated it somewhat in isolation from its broader social context. Our analytic approach is different. We use an egocentric network methodology, which collects data on to whom individuals are connected and the characteristics of those connected people; it does not prompt respondents to specifically consider their ties to kin. Hence, this study provides an unusually rich exploration of the role played by close kin, not presuming their importance but instead locating them within people's larger spheres of activity and personal networks.

Among the findings discussed below is evidence of the interdependence of generations and, in particular, of the interdependence both upward and downward by the "sandwich" generation; the pervasiveness of gender differences in how much and what kinds of support parents and children provide one another; differences suggestive of a gendered division of labor in generational relationships; the continuing importance of geographical proximity for many aspects of filial ties; and paradoxical class differences in ties to parents. Overall, our findings indicate that social involvement with close kin is high and that kin play an important role in support systems.

Background

Much variability exists in the extent to which people are involved with and rely on kin for support. We know, for example, that getting married often has the paradoxical consequence of creating new, formal kin ties with in-laws but also reducing interaction with other types of kin, including parents, and the amount of support received from them; widowhood and divorce often have the reverse effect (Gerstel and Sarkisian 2006; Sarkisian and Gerstel 2008; Guiaux et al. 2007; Kalmijn 2012; Morgan and March 1992). Another important determinant of involvement with kin is gender. Numerous studies show that for both cultural and structural reasons women have more frequent contact with family members and are more likely to engage in social exchanges with them than do men (e.g., Hogan et al. 1993; Fischer 1982; Roschelle 1997; Sarkisian and Gerstel 2004; Wellman and Wortley 1990). Specifically, adult daughters more often provide support to aging parents than do adult sons (Lawton et al. 1994; Rossi and Rossi 1990; Silverstein et al. 1995; Silverstein et al. 2006). Differences in involvement with kin by race and ethnicity have also been widely documented. Research portrays a rather complex picture with results varying by gender, generation, and the type of support examined. By and large they suggest that whites more frequently engage in the exchange of emotional and financial support with kin whereas blacks and Latinos are more likely to live with or in close proximity to kin. These differences, however, are mostly explained by the lower socioeconomic status of blacks and Latinos, which affects both their level of need and the amount of resources available for exchange (Hogan et al. 1993; Lee and Aytac 1998; Sarkisian and Gerstel 2004; Sarkisian et al. 2007).

We also know that education and income matter for social involvement with kin. More educated people tend to live farther from kin and are, at least proportionately, less involved with kin than are less educated people (Chan and Ermisch 2015; Compton and Pollak 2009; Fischer 1982; Kalmijn 2006). Yet, the higher-educated also tend to have kin networks with the greatest upward reach in class standing (Goldstein and Warren 2000), providing at least a latent source of greater social support. Although reliance on kin constitutes an important coping strategy in low-income people's struggle to make ends meet (e.g., Domínguez and Watkins 2003; Edin and Lein 1997; Nelson 2005), research suggests that overall they receive lower levels of support, particularly financial support, than people with higher incomes (Hogan et al. 1993; Roschelle 1997; Goldstein and Warren 2000). The greater ability of wealthier parents to help their young adult children in the transition into adulthood has important implications for the reproduction of class, as well as racial, inequalities (see review in Swartz 2009).

Despite the abundant literature on kin relations, there is still much we do not know about the contexts, modalities, and shapers of kin support. One such shaper of people's involvement with immediate family is simply their availability. Obviously, an older person with a single child who lives a thousand miles away is in a different situation than one with three children who live nearby. Important demographic shifts that have occurred in the last three to four decades have had a profound impact on the number and types of kin available for intergenerational relations. Most notably, declining mortality and fertility rates have led to longer years of shared lives between generations but with fewer adult children available to provide support to aging parents in times of need. At the same time, smaller families also means that parents have more resources to share with each of their adult children (Bengtson 2001). The higher prevalence of divorce and single-parenthood has further contributed to the diversification of family forms and intergenerational relations (see also Johnson 2000).

Another important source of variation is residential mobility. Movers are likely to move away from kin in response to better educational and occupational opportunities (Pugh 2015; Rosenfeld and Kim 2005). And while new communication technologies have made it easier for family members to stay in touch regardless of their geographical location, some forms of support, such as taking care of a sick relative or providing help with childcare, are facilitated by physical proximity. The relatively smaller role of kin among the better-educated that earlier research has found may "simply" reflect their higher tendency to move long distances (Fischer 2002), as well as their lower birth rates.

Yet availability and accessibility are not the whole story. People's lifestyles vary from less to more kin-centered. Some spend considerable time with and rely extensively on kin; others choose to rely less on relatives and more on non-kin (Agneessens et al. 2006; Giannella and Fischer 2016) and those lifestyle variations may in turn reflect differences by socioeconomic status, generation, and culture. For example, Hansen (2005) shows in her in-depth study of the networks of care of children that families who adhered to the ideology of self-sufficiency and independence of the nuclear family, typically families of middle-class background, tended to restrict their involvement with the extended family and relied on them less often for help with childcare than other families. The quality of kin relationships may be especially important in this context. Some scholars have suggested that in contemporary society, relationships with close kin have become less motivated by felt obligation and, similarly to other ties, more motivated by felt closeness and affection (Beck and Beck-Gernsheim 1995; Finch and Mason 1993; Van Gaalen and Dykstra 2006). In support of this view, research has shown that people feel more motivated to help kin with whom they get along and to whom they feel affection and love (Fingerman et al. 2016; Silverstein et al. 2006).

Overall, the extensive research on involvement with kin suggests that family networks are flexible and dynamic. The major goal of this study is to examine the scope and correlates of the availability and accessibility of parents and adult children and, given that these ties exist, to gain insights into the role they play in people's larger networks. To address these issues we draw on the first wave of the UCNets project, described below.

Data and Measures

The UCNets project has collected extensive descriptions of personal networks from two samples of respondents in the greater San Francisco Bay Area: 690 respondents aged 50 to 70 and 495 respondents aged 21 to 30 completed wave 1 of the panel survey.

Sampling We drew samples from six San Francisco Bay Area counties, using address-based methods, sending solicitation letters to households randomly selected from 30 randomly-selected census tracts. The letters invited any member of the household who was either 21 to 30 years old or 50 to 70 years old to join the panel study, a commitment entailing being interviewed three times over about a 4-year period. The study focused on these two specific age groups to maximize the number of key transitions and life events respondents would likely experience between waves of the survey. The letter offered escalating payments for each interview in order to entice staying on the panel. It directed would-be respondents to call in or to use a web site to register. The screening procedure randomly assigned qualifying respondents to either a face-to-face interview (75% of cases) or a web survey (25%).

Table 6.1 Sample characteristics by age group: Percentages (n in parentheses)

	21–30 year-olds	50–70 year-olds
Male (n = 495, 690)	32%	36%
Married (n = 495, 689)	11	46
Ethnicity/race (n = 485, 672)		
White	48	72
Latino	10	5
Asian	25	8
Black and other	17	15
BA or higher degree (n = 484, 667)	77	71
Family income $75 K or higher (n = 482, 664)	23	55
New resident in current town (n = 494, 688)	60	6
Born in California (n = 485, 669)	51	41

The in-person and online instruments were substantively identical; later reports will address mode effects. This outreach procedure sufficed for the 50–70 year-olds; to reach enough 21–30 year-olds, however, we had to resort to extra means, as described below.

The overall yield from the letters was low, we estimate at about 10%, which would be expected given (a) the narrow age criteria for qualifying; (b) the multi-year commitment; and (c) generally declining survey response rates (National Research Council 2013). Young respondents were especially difficult to recruit. We therefore supplemented the initial, address-drawn sample of 162 young adults with an additional 36 recruited through previous respondents and an additional 297 recruited through social media (Facebook solicitation allows one to target a region—the Bay Area, here—and specific ages.)[1] Our field contractor, *Nexant*, collected the data from the middle to the end of 2015. In the end, 522 older respondents were interviewed face-to-face and 168 did the survey online; 141 young respondents were interviewed face-to-face and 354 did the survey online (which includes the referred and Facebook-recruited respondents). Our final sample, described in Table 6.1, skews toward women and the better-educated. It is, however, diverse in various demographic dimensions and we use those as controls in our models.

Measures First, the UCNets survey instrument took a rough "census" on the existence and location of various types of kin. Most relevant to this paper, it asked respondents if their mothers and fathers were still alive and, if so, whether each of the parents lived within a one-hour drive.[2] It also asked respondents if they had any

[1] We wish to thank Eric Giannella for his help with recruiting respondents through social media.

[2] Because our main interest in the present study is in the relationships people have with their parents and adult children who do not live with them, we excluded cases where respondents indicated that their mother or father lived with them. In future research we plan to examine the effect of co-residence on the parent-adult child relationship.

adult children or step-children who did not live with them, how many of each, and whether any of them lived within a one-hour drive.

Second, the UCNets instrument solicited the names of the people, or alters, to whom respondents were connected by asking several "name-eliciting' questions. The protocol then applied several "name-interpreting" questions to the list of alters to obtain descriptions of the named individuals and of the ties they had with the respondents. We focus here on five types of name-eliciting connections. We asked respondents to name the people with whom they:

1. *Socialized*—the people with whom they usually got together and did social activities such as going out to restaurants, concerts, plays, clubs, sports, other events, or hanging out (up to 9 names);
2. *Confided in or sought advice*—two name-eliciting questions: those whom they confided in about relationships, important life experiences, and the like, and the people whose advice they sought or would seek to help make an important life decision, for example, about taking a job, family issues, or health problems (up to 6 names for each item here and for each of the remaining questions)[3];
3. *Practical help* – the people who had given the respondent practical help in the previous few months, such as moving furniture, doing repairs, picking up something at the store, looking after a child, and giving a ride;
4. *Emergency help* – The people whom the respondent would ask if she or he were seriously injured or sick and needed some help for a couple of weeks with things such as preparing meals and getting around; and
5. *Provides support* – the people whom the respondent helped out practically, or with advice, or in other kinds of ways at least occasionally. While topics 2–4 refer to the respondent as the actual or potential recipient of support, this one treats the respondent as a provider of support.

The instrument then asked respondents to specify how each person whom they named was related to them, choosing among a list of predetermined categories (e.g., parent, child, sibling, neighbor, friend, coworker, and so forth). We identified mothers, fathers, adult daughters, and adult sons living outside the respondents' households.[4] We were then able to calculate the percentage of kin elicited for each type of connection, such as the percentage of mothers (out of all mothers) who were named in the socializing question, or the percentage of sons (out of all sons) who provided practical help. Additionally, we created a global measure of inclusion in the network

[3] UCNets originally included two separate questions for confide and advise. Because conceptually both of these items refer to the domain of emotional support we treat them in this study as one type of connection. Preliminary analyses revealed much overlap in the names elicited by these two questions.

[4] We do not know the exact age of the person named. Respondents were only asked if the person they mentioned was of the same age or older than they were. Thus we cannot know for sure that the children mentioned here were all adults. Nevertheless, the likelihood that respondents will have children below age 18 who do *not* live with them is expected to be small and therefore not likely to introduce much bias in the results.

(referred to as "*in network*"), indicating whether the relative in question was named in at least one of the five name-eliciting questions.

Additionally, we used information about the characteristics of the relationship between the respondent ego and each named alter. These include *emotional closeness*, measured by a yes/no question asking whether the respondent feels close to the alter; and *physical proximity*, a yes/no question asking whether the alter lives within one hour drive from the respondent.[5]

Finally, we examined a series of sociodemographic characteristics of the respondent. *Gender* is coded as a dummy (0 = "female"; 1 = "male"). Recall that UCNets gathered information among two age groups: 21–30 year-olds and 50–70 year-olds. We ran some of the analyses separately for each age group and included age as a control in others. In the latter case we made a distinction within the older cohort between respondents aged 50–59 and those aged 60–70. Married is coded as a dummy (0 = "no"; 1 = "yes"). In some of the analyses, for example when we estimated the factors associated with naming adult children in the network, we also controlled for the (natural log) number of adult daughters and sons the respondent had. *Ethnicity/Race* is measured with three dummies: Latino, Asian, black and other, with white used as the reference category. Education level is coded as a dummy indicating whether the respondent had a BA or higher degree. Family income refers to either the total household income for respondents who were married or living with a partner or other relative, or the individual income for respondents who lived alone (or with roommates). Income is measured with a dummy indicating whether the income (before taxes) was $75,000 or higher (0 = "no"; 1 = "yes"). We included two additional measures to capture the respondent's residential history and potential migration: whether the respondent had been living in current town for two or fewer years, referred to as *new resident in current town*, and whether the respondent was *born in California* (0 = "no"; 1 = "yes").

Table 6.1 shows the distribution of the sociodemographic variables by age group. Overall, both samples were predominantly female. Many more of the older sample, unsurprisingly, were married. The two age groups also appeared to significantly vary by ethnicity and race. About half of the young respondents were either Asian, Latino, black, or "other," whereas the older ones were overwhelmingly white (more than 70%). Not surprisingly, older respondents had higher incomes. No meaningful difference was observed for level of education; about 70% of respondents in both age groups had a BA or higher degree (about 30% of the young respondents were still engaged in schooling of some kind.) Sixty percent of the younger respondents had lived in their current town for two or fewer years, compared to only 6% among the older age group. The younger respondents, however, were more often born in California.

[5] With these aggregated-level data it was not possible to know whether the adult children who lived close to the respondent were the ones who were actually included in the network.

Findings

Descriptive Results: The Availability, Accessibility, and Mobilization of Close Kin

Table 6.2 presents a first, descriptive look at the availability, accessibility, and mobilization of kin. Because the raw numbers are subject to methods effects and because our samples are regionally and cohort specific, we should attend to internal comparisons rather than the absolute values. The results show differences by age group and the relative's gender. Not surprisingly, almost all 21–30 year-olds reported parents who were alive, while most 50–70 year-olds had one or both parents deceased. Younger respondents were less likely to live near their parents, either mother or father, than older ones (about one fourth versus 40%). These results are somewhat unexpected. Considering their 30 or more years of opportunities for migration, older respondents might have drifted farther away from their parents. These results, however, may reflect the tendency of the young generation to move away from their family of origin in search of educational and occupational opportunities and that of the older generation to have their elderly parents live close to them so that they can more easily provide assistance to them. Given living mothers, the young were much more likely than the old to list their mothers in response to the name-eliciting questions (61% versus 36%). No such difference was found for reporting a father in the network (approximately 45%). We discuss in later analyses (see Table 6.5) the particular roles those parents played in each cohort's lives.

Table 6.2 Kin availability: Percentage of respondents reporting parents or adult children who are alive, in close geographic proximity, and in the reported network, by age group

	21–30 year-olds (n = 495)	50–70 year-olds (n = 690)
Mother: alive	98%	38%
Of those alive: within one hour drive	25	41
Of those alive: named in network	61	36
Father: alive	92	21
Of those alive: within one hour drive	24	40
Of those alive: named in network	48	42
Adult daughters: at least one	–	37
At least one within one hour drive	–	57
At least one in network	–	60
Mn number alive (*SD*)	–	1.49 (0.73)
Mn prop daughters in network (*SD*)	–	0.56 (0.48)
Adult sons: At least one	–	37
At least one within one hour drive	–	61
At least one in network	–	55
Mn number alive (*SD*)	–	1.46 (0.74)
Mn prop sons in network (*SD*)	–	0.50 (0.48)

Table 6.2 further indicates that among the 50–70 year-olds almost 40% had at least one adult daughter or adult son. Given a living child, it appears that sons were slightly more likely than daughters to live within one-hour drive from the parent, whereas daughters were slightly more likely than sons to be named in the network by the parent. Consistent with the latter trend respondents included on average slightly more adult daughters than sons in their network (means of 0.56 versus 0.50).

These numbers are consistent with the general findings in the literature that mothers play a more critical role in Americans' lives than do fathers. They also suggest that daughters are only slightly more likely than sons to be part of the network but, as we will show in Table 6.5, the role that daughters assume in the network of their aging parents is substantially different from that of sons.

The Sociodemographic Correlates of the Availability, Accessibility, and Mobilization of Close Kin

In the next stage we examined the socio-demographic factors that are independently associated with the availability, accessibility, and mobilization of close kin. Tables 6.3 and 6.4 present the results of a series of logistic regression models accounting for the roles of parents and adult children, respectively. For each type of kin, we tested three models to predict the likelihood of (1) having the relative alive; (2) given that the relative is alive, that he or she lived within one hour drive; and (3) drawing on the name-eliciting data, that he or she appears in the respondent's network in one or more of the five delineated roles. We present the effects as odds ratios. The results for parents, displayed in Table 6.3, show that having a mother or father alive was largely a matter of age, although there is a suggestion that high-income was also positively associated with the likelihood of having a living father. This result is not surprising considering the well-documented beneficial effect of socioeconomic status on health.

The next models examined the sociodemographic factors associated with living within one hour drive from the parent. Not much in the respondent's background was independently associated with the chances that a parent lived nearby, with the exception of age, marital status, and state of origin. The models predicting accessibility show that, given that the parent was alive, by and large older respondents were more likely than younger ones to have a mother or father living within one hour drive from them. Married respondents were almost two times (OR = 1.81) more likely to have a father, but not a mother, who lived nearby than their non-married counterparts, a non-obvious finding. Whether the respondent was born in California appeared as an important determinant of having either parent within a one hour drive from them. Although we do not know about the full migration history of the respondents (e.g., they could have moved out of the state at some point before the survey and then come back to California), nor do we know about the migration history of the parent, this result suggests that respondents born in California and their parents remained rooted in their state of origin.

Table 6.3 Likelihood of kin availability: Odds ratios from logistic regression models predicting respondents' reports on the availability, accessibility and network inclusion of parents

	Mother			Father		
	Alive	Within one hour drive[a]	Named in network[a]	Alive	Within one hour drive[a]	Named in network[a]
Age: 21–30 (reference)						
50–59	0.03***	2.51***	0.39***	0.05***	3.57***	0.72
60–70	0.01***	2.62**	0.27***	0.01***	1.15	0.27**
Male	0.87	0.79	0.92	1.03	0.92	1.15
Married	0.85	1.31	0.75	1.20	1.81*	0.85
Ethnicity-race: white (reference)						
Latino	1.29	0.95	1.30	1.23	0.67	1.30
Asian	1.10	0.87	0.61*	1.07	1.06	0.62*
Black and other	1.29	1.23	0.98	1.06	1.39	0.74
BA or higher degree	1.17	0.94	2.15***	1.29	0.85	2.45***
Family income $75 K or higher	1.21	0.74	1.35	1.64*	0.65	1.24
New resident in current town	0.63	0.78	1.60*	1.32	0.96	1.65*
Born in California	0.81	5.13***	0.81	1.43	7.51***	1.09
Parent lives within one hour drive	–	–	2.90***	–	–	3.08***
Constant	58.76***	0.16***	0.65	5.84***	0.10***	0.26***
−2 log likelihood	852.36	766.11	893.69	747.67	564.80	731.87
N of respondents	1140	721	721	1140	581	581

[a]Estimate refers to respondents whose parent is alive
*$p < .05$. **$p < .01$. ***$p < .001$ (two-tailed tests)

The models predicting inclusion in the network showed that older respondents were less likely than younger ones to name their parents in the network. Asians were less likely than whites to name living parents. Education level turned out to be an important determinant of network inclusion. Highly educated respondents (i.e., those with a BA or higher degree) were substantially more likely to name their mothers ($OR = 2.15$) and fathers ($OR = 2.45$) in the network than those with a lower level of education. Additionally, recently-arrived respondents more often named a parent in their networks. Finally, geographic proximity was another important factor; parents who lived nearby were likelier to appear as part of the respondent's network than those who lived farther away. Later analyses (see Table 6.5) examine which specific kinds of interactions produced these associations.

Table 6.4 repeated the analyses with the adult daughters and sons of the older cohort. Having an adult child living outside the household was largely a matter of demographics: Older and married respondents, as well as those born in California,

Table 6.4 Likelihood of kin availability: Odds ratios from logistic regression models predicting respondents' reports on the availability, accessibility, and network inclusion of adult children

	At least one adult daughter			At least one adult son		
	Alive	Within one hour drive[a]	Named in network[a]	Alive	Within one hour drive[a]	Named in network[a]
Age: 50–59 (reference)						
60–70	1.93***	1.84*	1.69	2.76***	3.08***	1.92*
Male	0.76	1.43	0.90	1.06	1.02	1.69
Married	2.06***	0.92	0.95	2.32***	1.43	1.20
Ln number of daughters	–	1.49	0.91	–	1.10	0.91
Ln number of sons	–	0.96	0.87	–	1.51	1.65
Ethnicity-race: white (reference)						
Latino	1.32	1.18	5.76*	1.79	4.62*	2.87
Asian	0.64	2.66	1.24	1.04	1.39	1.46
Black and other	0.99	1.05	1.75	1.23	0.90	1.52
BA or higher degree	0.64**	0.61	0.55	0.76	0.72	1.00
Family income $75 K or higher	0.91	1.06	1.47	0.94	0.98	1.15
New resident in current town	1.28	0.56	1.54	1.28	0.53	2.02
Born in California	1.55**	1.99**	0.93	1.39*	1.74*	0.80
Adult child lives within one hour drive	–	–	7.19***	–	–	3.61***
Constant	0.38***	0.64	0.38	0.20***	0.53	0.18***
−2 log likelihood	826.48	318.41	272.64	810.27	305.37	298.23
N of respondents	659	249	249	659	245	245

[a]Estimate refers to respondents whose adult child is alive
*$p < .05$. **$p < .01$. ***$p < .001$ (two-tailed tests)

were more likely to report having at least one adult child. Respondents with a BA or higher degree were less likely to have an adult child (significantly so in the case of daughters) than their less well educated counterparts.

Given that they had adult children and controlling for the number of adult daughters and sons, the oldest respondents (those aged 60–70) were more likely to report that at least one of their children, either a daughter or a son, vlived within one hour drive from them. These results most likely reflect the greater need for support of the oldest. Latinos were over four times ($OR = 4.62$) more likely to live near a son (but not a daughter) than whites. Respondents who were born in California were almost two times more likely to have at least one adult daughter ($OR = 1.99$) or son ($OR = 1.74$) living nearby compared to those born elsewhere.

As to respondents actually naming daughters or sons in their networks, conditional on having adult children and the number of adult children, Table 6.4 shows that 60–70 year-old parents were significantly more likely to mention at least one adult son in their network than were parents in their 50s. Latinos were substantially

Table 6.5 Types of connection to kin: Differences in mean percentage of respondents reporting a connection to kin, by gender of kin

	Parents		Adult children		Siblings		Other relatives	Non-kin
	Mothers	Fathers	Daughters	Sons	Sisters	Brothers		
21–30 year-olds								
Socialize	16%	14%	–	–	29	31	36	62
Confide/advise	76	69	–	–	64	42***	30	37
Practical help	29	33	–	–	26	30	28	20
Emergency help	55	45*	–	–	29	25	26	20
Provide support to alter	31	17***	–	–	61	55	29	37
n (of relatives by type)	317	229	–	–	171	134	299	3340
50–70 year-olds								
Socialize	37%	32%	50	46	32	32	51	58
Confide/advise	58	55	46	35*	66	50***	23	38
Practical help	19	21	24	34*	15	17	15	18
Emergency help	33	25	47	43	38	31	24	24
Provide support to alter	54	53	59	58	37	37	34	35
n (of relatives by type)	107	53	251	213	335	191	686	4411

Notes: Percentages calculated as number of specified kin named to the specific eliciting question divided by the total number of such kin named in the network
Significance tests for differences by gender of the kin among parents (i.e., mothers versus fathers), adult children (i.e., daughters versus adult sons), and siblings (i.e., sisters versus brothers)
$*p < .05$. $**p < .01$. $***p < .001$ (two-tailed tests)

more likely to include at least one adult daughter in their network as compared to whites. Geographic proximity mattered a great deal. Respondents were significantly more likely to name an adult child in their network if at least one of their children lived nearby.[6] The independent association of having a daughter nearby ($OR = 7.19$) was especially pronounced and substantially higher than that of having a son nearby

[6]We also examined whether family composition was associated with the likelihood of living near parents and adult children and with naming them in the network. One could plausibly argue, for example, that a widowed mother would be more likely than a mother whose partner is alive to live near one of her adult children, or that an aging parent would be less likely to name her adult children in the network if she has living siblings. We tested for these possibilities by including the existence of other kin (e.g., spouses and siblings) in the model. None of these associations was found significant, nor did they alter the results reported in Tables 6.3 and 6.4.

(*OR* = 3.61). Unlike previous research suggesting that relying on adult children for support varies substantially by the marital status of the parent (see reviews in Polenick et al. 2017; Swartz 2009), Table 6.4 shows no independent association. It is possible that the lack of effect resulted from our comparison of the married to the non-married, a category that included both divorced, never-married, and widowed respondents (unfortunately, due to the sample size we could not examine these groups separately).[7]

The Role of Close Kin in the Network

We now turn to examine the question of what specific role parents and adult children reportedly played in respondents' lives. For this analysis, we shifted from the respondent (i.e., ego) as the unit of analysis to the listed parents and children (i.e., alters) as the units of analysis: 424 mothers, 282 fathers, 251 daughters, and 213 sons. We focused on five kinds of connections to kin: socializing, confiding/being advised, receiving practical help, anticipating emergency help, and providing support to alter. The results displayed in Table 6.5 show systematic variations by type of connection, type of kin, the gender of the relative, and age group. For comparison purposes we also show the results for siblings (sisters and brothers), other relatives, and non-kin. These ties all play a distinct role in personal networks and their consideration is important in order to capture the broader picture of it, but this is beyond the scope of the present study. We plan to examine the meaning of different types of kin, as well as that of non-kin, for social involvement in future research. In this study we focus on intergenerational relations between parents and adult children.

Multiple comparisons are possible – by type of role, by type of relative, and by age group. We start by examining the role of parents in the networks of young respondents. Their answers suggest that they looked to their parents for emotional support and emergency help. More than two-thirds of the parents whom young respondents listed at all appeared in answer to the confide or advise questions (76% and 69% for mothers and fathers, respectively) and approximately half of them were mentioned as someone respondents would turn to in the case of an emergency. Approximately one-third of the parents were mentioned as providers of practical support. Relatively few parents of the 21–30 year-olds appeared as social companions or recipients of help. Also note that respondents were more likely to name their mothers than fathers as potential providers of emergency support (55% as compared to 45%) and more often indicated providing support to the mother than to the father (31% as compared to 17%).

Older respondents named their parents in distinctively other roles. They named their parents as confidants or advisers (although less so than younger respondents), but then most often as recipients of help and as social companions. Put simply, the

[7] There may have been, of course, other, unnamed adult children who got no support. Our network measure does not account for this possibility.

young respondents appeared to rely on their parents in times for emotional and instrumental support, but were otherwise only modestly involved with them, while older respondents reported helping their parents and spending social time with them, but not much depending upon them. These results suggest that middle-aged parents provide a safety-net for their young adult children while elderly parents play a more complex role in the lives of their middle-aged children.

Table 6.5 further looks at the various roles played by adult children in the networks of the older cohort. Overall, involvement was quite high. Almost the same proportion of 50–70 year-old respondents' grown children got help (about 60%) as did those respondents' parents (about 54%).[7] This finding provides a nice illustration of the crucial role of parents in late mid-life, "sandwiched" between two generations, in helping both the young and the elderly. It is noteworthy that respondents were as likely to help their adult daughters as sons in the network. At the same time, adult children apparently provided important support for their 50–70 year-old parents. More than 40% of both adult daughters and sons who were included in the network were named as emergency helpers and about half of them were named as social companions. Daughters, however, were more often named as confidants or advisors than were sons (46% versus 35%), while sons got called on for practical help more often than daughters (34% versus 24%), suggesting an emotional versus practical division of labor by gender of adult child.

A comparison to other kin and non-kin in the network further emphasized the distinct role played by close relatives as a major source of emotional and instrumental support in the lives of the respondents. By and large, the results of Table 6.5 show that non-kin mainly assumed the role of social companions in the network and were less often named as providing emotional support, especially among young respondents. By contrast, siblings, especially sisters, were often named as confidants or advisors and as providers of instrumental support. Their social involvement in the networks of the older respondents appeared to be as important as that of parents, but less so than that of adult children. Among the 21–30 year-olds, however, siblings assumed a less important role as potential helpers during emergencies than did parents, but they were more often mentioned as social companions.

Variation in the Role of Close Kin in the Network by Characteristics of the Relationship

Finally, in the last set of analyses (see Table 6.6), we tested the extent to which the roles assumed by parents and children in the network were associated with other characteristics of their relationships. What kinds of bonds to the kin went along with what kinds of support that they provided (or received)? Again using the named relatives as units of analysis, we focus on three major attributes of the relationship: degree of emotional closeness, geographic proximity, and frequency of contact. The

Table 6.6 Variations in connections to kin: Differences in mean percentage of respondents reporting specified connection to kin by relationship characteristics (closeness and geographic proximity)

	Closeness (feels close to)		Lives within one hour drive	
	Yes	No	Yes	No
Mothers				
Socialize	25	14**	39	11***
Confide/advise	82	51***	65	76**
Practical help	29	21	35	22**
Emergency help	54	37***	60	41***
Provide support to mother	42	25***	50	28***
N	288	136	161	263
Fathers				
Socialize	19	15	29	10***
Confide/advise	75	53***	53	74***
Practical help	30	31	38	26*
Emergency help	46	34*	50	35**
Provide support to father	24	23	37	17**
N	167	115	107	175
Daughters				
Socialize	52	43	59	33***
Confide/advise	52	29***	46	48
Practical help	28	15*	31	14**
Emergency help	49	43	57	29***
Provide support to daughter	64	43**	59	59
N	190	63	167	86
Sons				
Socialize	49	40	55	31***
Confide/advise	39	23*	33	39
Practical help	38	23*	36	31
Emergency help	44	38	49	31**
Provide support to son	58	55	57	57
N	162	53	140	75

* $p < .05$. ** $p < .01$. *** $p < .001$ (two-tailed tests)

results displayed in the first two columns of Table 6.6 show that parents, mothers and fathers, whom respondents reported as "close" tended to be the ones whom they said provided emotional support and emergency assistance. Respondents who felt close to their mothers were also more likely to socialize with her. No such effect was observed for fathers.

Similarly, adult children, both daughters and sons, were more often reported as "close" when they also played the role of confidant or advisors and also providers of practical support. By contrast, expecting emergency assistance from adult children was not related to how close the parent felt to them. This result seems to suggest that parents expect that they can turn to adult children for support when acute needs arise regardless of how close they feel, perhaps reflecting the norm of filial obligation. Interestingly, reporting that one provided help to mothers and daughters was likelier if the respondent also reported feeling closer to those mothers or daughters, but was not the case for either fathers or sons.

As expected, geographic proximity (examined in the next two columns of Table 6.6) was an important correlate of socializing with immediate kin. Mothers, fathers, daughters and sons were all more likely to be named as someone with whom the respondent socialized when they lived nearby. It makes sense to assume that geographic distance would also matter for the provision of mundane practical help, such as home repairs and childcare, but that it would be less of a factor in emergency situations. By and large, however, geographic proximity was an important correlate of both types of support. Respondents were more likely to name their mother, father, and adult daughter as the provider of both practical and emergency support when those relatives lived nearby rather than farther away. For sons, only emergency help was significantly related to geographic proximity. These findings may perhaps reflect the desire not to impose on close kin who lived far away. Geographic proximity also appeared to be an important factor when we examined the data from the opposite perspective, switching the unit of analysis from children to parents. Proximity did not matter for parents' reporting that they provided support to their adult children, but it did matter for parents' report of providing support to their own aging parents. Respondents were more likely to report helping their parents if they lived close to them than if they lived farther away.

Considering that recent technological developments have made it easier for people to communicate with members in their network regardless of their location, it is not surprising that physical distance was not associated with the likelihood of confiding or advising with adult children. This is consistent with previous research showing that emotionally supportive ties tended to be maintained over long geographic distances (Viry 2012). Interestingly, however, mothers and fathers were more likely to be named as confidents or advisors if they lived *farther* away than if they lived nearby. A possible explanation for this seemingly odd finding has to do with a selection effect by which parents get included in the network at all. In this case, it may result from having many respondents naming distant parents only in this role, as the high percentages reported in Table 6.6 (76% and 74% for mother and fathers, respectively) and the results in Table 6.5 seem to imply (cf. Fischer 1977, pp. 172–77).

Conclusion

Using the UCNets data, we have been able to place the dynamics of parent-child relations within the larger context of people's support and exchange networks. Overall, our findings highlight the high level of connections between young adult children and their aging parents and the important place each has in the others' systems of support. Yet we found substantial variation in the availability, accessibility, and mobilization of close kin.

We found that the likelihood of having adult children, as well as the likelihood of socially engaging with them, increased with age. By contrast, the likelihood of having parents and of naming them in the network declined with age. This trend may be due to the greater needs of older as compared to younger parents, which may be attended at least partially by their adult children, but it could also reflect the rise in intergenerational stake that both parents and children experience as they grow older (Giarrusso et al. 1995). Older parents reported spending time and engaging in social activities with their adult children. They also named their adult children as confidents or advisors and as an important source of support during emergency situations. These same parents, however, also reported providing much support to their adult children. In fact, and consistent with previous research showing that in most American families intergenerational support typically flows downstream from the parents' to the children's generation (Fingerman et al. 2011; Fingerman et al. 2013; Logan and Spitze 1996), it appeared that the 50–70 year-old parents in our sample played a greater role as providers of support to their young adult children than the reverse. About 60% of the parents indicated that they provided support to their adult children. This finding was echoed in the adult children's report, with a large percentage mentioning their parents as providers of emotional and instrumental support.

Interestingly, and unlike previous research (e.g., Chan and Ermisch 2015; Lawton et al. 1994), we found that geographic proximity between generations increased with age. That is, elderly parents were more likely to live near their adult children than were middle-aged parents. This finding may have important implications for intergenerational relations because geographic proximity is likely to facilitate face-to-face interactions and the exchange of support (Grundy and Shelton 2001; Lawton et al. 1994; Ward et al. 2014). Indeed, we found that geographic proximity was a major determinant of the inclusion of close kin in the network. Mothers, fathers, adult daughters, and adult sons were all more likely to be named in the network if they lived within one-hour drive to the respondent than if they lived farther away. Our results showed that geographic proximity mattered much for the chances of socializing with close kin and for receiving support from them in both mundane and emergency situations. Altogether, they suggest that, even in the internet age and with the widespread availability of digital communication technologies, geographic proximity still matters (see review in Mok et al. 2010). By facilitating shared experiences, geographic proximity may contribute to reinforcing intergenerational bonds, which in turn may encourage children's provision of support to their aging parents (Silverstein et al. 2006; Ward et al. 2014). Geographic proximity, however, did not matter for the receipt of emotional support. This finding is consistent with previous research showing the limited effect of geographic dispersion on the emotional supportiveness of personal contacts (Viry 2012).

Level of education was another important determinant of parents' inclusion in the network. However, unlike previous research (Kalmijn 2006; Lawton et al. 1994; Greenwell and Bengtson 1997; Grundy and Shelton 2001), we found a positive, not negative, association between education and social engagement with aging parents. That is, highly educated respondents were more likely to include their mother and father in the network than those with a lower level of education. This finding resonates with studies showing more frequent social exchanges among families of higher as compared to lower socioeconomic status (Hogan et al. 1993; Roschelle 1997), and may perhaps suggest a lower level of family conflict among the better educated.

Furthermore, we did not find a significant association between level of education and the likelihood of living close to the parent's home. Previous studies have indicated that the highly educated face greater labor market opportunities and are thus more inclined to migrate from their place of origin in search of jobs that would fit their education level and skills (Kalmijn 2006). Our findings, by contrast, seem to support the view that in contemporary society it has become more difficult for most people, especially in the young generation and regardless of educational status, to accumulate financial resources, develop careers, and obtain jobs that would provide stability and grant control over one's geographic location (Greenwell and Bengtson 1997; Pugh 2015).

Although we did not find any differences by the *respondent's* gender in the availability, accessibility, and general inclusion in the network of parents, we did find differences by the gender of the *named relatives*. Mothers played a very important and specific role in their adult children's lives; they were substantially more likely to be named as a source of emergency support for their children than were fathers. With respect to adult children, consistent with the abundant literature on gender and involvement with kin (Rossi and Rossi 1990; Silverstein et al. 1995; Silverstein et al. 2006), we found that overall daughters were slightly more likely than sons to be included in their parents' network. The gender gap was relatively small in size and therefore should not be overstated. More interesting, however, were the results suggesting a gendered division of labor in the caretaking of aging parents; we found that daughters were more often named as providers of emotional support than sons whereas sons, more so than daughters, tended to be called upon for practical help. Nevertheless, our results did not reveal a difference in the likelihood of mobilizing daughters versus sons during emergencies, which suggests that both daughters and sons may be motivated by a strong sense of filial obligation to provide support to aging parents when acute needs arise. Our finding that the parent's mentioning of an adult child, regardless of the child's gender, as someone to rely on in the case of an emergency was not related to how emotionally close the parent felt to that child further supports this possibility.

The quality of the relationship between parents and adult children, measured in this study with emotional closeness, was another important factor that helped explain variation in the role played by close kin in the network and the kin's gender (see also Wellman and Wortley 1990). Overall, we found that respondents tended to mention their immediate kin as confidants or advisors when they felt emotionally close to them. Emotional closeness was also related to the perception that the parent, either mother or father, would provide support in the case of an emergency. Yet our findings further revealed that respondents were substantially more likely to report that they provided support to their mothers and adult daughters if they felt emotionally close to them, but no such effect was observed for fathers and sons. Previous research has suggested that the motivation to help kin differs by gender. For example, Silverstein et al. (1995) found that while daughters tended to provide support to aging parents out of affection for them, sons mainly helped their parents out of a sense of obligation and therefore the amount of assistance they provided to them was not related to the quality of their relationship. Following this rationale, our finding may reflect the different ways by which men and women frame their involvement and willingness to socially engage with close kin.

Finally, this study allowed for an examination of familial relationships across multiple generations and it underscores the particular position of middle-aged parents as a "sandwich" generation. This concept has been originally applied when referring to parents in their 40s and 50s who simultaneously care for dependent children and frail elderly parents. Scholars, however, have noted that in light of recent demographic changes a more common situation is that of parents in late midlife (those 50–70 year-olds whom we examined in this study) who have both at least one surviving parent and one adult child who is still economically dependent on them (Grundy and Henretta 2006). These parents' "sandwich" experience is the result of both the increase in longevity of the older generation and the longer time it takes today for the younger generation to transition into adulthood and reach independence (Fingerman et al. 2011; Fuerstenberg 2010; Swartz 2009). Our findings showed that parents in late mid-life were highly and simultaneously involved in the provision of support to both their adult children and elderly parents. This finding has important implications for the well-being of the middle generation, as well as for members of the generations above and below them. In future research we plan to examine how relationships and network dynamics across multiple generations change over time in response to the occurrence of various life-events and transitions, which are likely to affect both the level of need and amount of resources at the disposal of different family members.

To conclude, the findings presented here clearly suggest that even though families have undergone significant changes over the last few decades, changes that have been extensively discussed in the sociological literature, social involvement with close kin is high. Aging parents and their adult children socially engage with each other in a variety of ways and their relationships constitute an important source of emotional and instrumental support in both routine and emergency situations.

References

Agneessens, F., Waege, H., & Lievens, J. (2006). Diversity in social support by role relations: A typology. *Social Networks, 28*, 427–441. https://doi.org/10.1016/j.socnet.2005.10.001.

Beck, U., & Beck-Gernsheim, E. (1995). *The normal chaos of love*. Polity Press.

Bengtson, V. L. (2001). Beyond the nuclear family: The increasing importance of multigenerational bonds. *Journal of Marriage and Family, 63*, 1–16. https://doi.org/10.1111/j.1741-3737.2001.00001.x.

Chan, T. W., & Ermisch, J. (2015). Proximity of couples to parents: Influences of gender, labor market, and family. *Demography, 52*, 379–399. https://doi.org/10.1007/s13524-015-0379-0.

Compton, J., & Pollak, R. A. (2009). *Proximity and coresidence of adult children and their parents: Description and correlates*. Ann Arbor: University of Michigan Retirement Center.
Domínguez, S., & Watkins, C. (2003). Creating networks for survival and mobility: Social capital among African-American and Latin-American low-income mothers. *Social Problems, 50*, 111–135. https://doi.org/10.1525/sp.2003.50.1.111.
Edin, K., & Lein, L. (1997). *Making ends meet: How single mothers survive welfare and low-wage work*. New York: Russell Sage Foundation.
Finch, J., & Mason, J. (1993). *Negotiating family responsibilities*. London: Routledge.
Fingerman, K. L., Lindsay, L., Pitzer, M., Chan, W., Birditt, K. S., Franks, M. M., & Zarit, S. (2011). Who gets what and why: Help middle-aged adults provide to parents and grown children. *Journal of Gerontology: Social Sciences, 66*, 87–98. https://doi.org/10.1093/geronb/gbq009.
Fingerman, K. L., Sechrist, J., & Birditt, K. S. (2013). Changing views on intergenerational ties. *Gerontology, 59*, 64–70. https://doi.org/10.1159/000342211.
Fingerman, K. L., Kim, K., Tennant, P. S., Birditt, K. S., & Zarit, S. H. (2016). Intergenerational support in a daily context. *The Gerontologist, 56*, 896–908. https://doi.org/10.1093/geront/gnv035.
Fischer, C. S. (1977). *Networks and places: Social relations in the urban setting*. New York: Free Press.
Fischer, C. S. (1982). *To dwell among friends*. Chicago: The University of Chicago Press.
Fischer, C. S. (2002). Ever-more rooted Americans. *City & Community, 1*, 175–194. https://doi.org/10.1111/1540-6040.00016.
Fuerstenberg, F. F., Jr. (2010). On a new schedule: Transitions to adulthood and family change. *The Future of Children, 20*, 67–87.
Gerstel, N., & Sarkisian, N. (2006). Marriage: The good, the bad, and the greedy. *Contexts, 5*, 16–21. https://doi.org/10.1525/ctx.2006.5.4.16.
Giannella, E., & Fischer, C. S. (2016). An inductive typology of egocentric networks. *Social Networks, 47*, 15–23. https://doi.org/10.1016/j.socnet.2016.02.003.
Giarrusso, R., Stallings, M., & Bengtson, V. L. (1995). The intergenerational stake hypothesis revisited: Parent-child differences in perceptions of relationships 20 years later. In V. L. Bengtson, K. W. Schaie, & L. M. Burton (Eds.), *Adult intergenerational relationships: Effects of societal change* (pp. 227–263). New York: Springer.
Goldstein, J. R., & Warren, J. R. (2000). Socioeconomic reach and heterogeneity in the extended family: Contours and consequences. *Social Science Research, 29*, 382–404. https://doi.org/10.1006/ssre.2000.0676.
Greenwell, L., & Bengtson, V. L. (1997). Geographic distance and contact between middle-aged children and their parents: The effects of social class over 20 years. *Journal of Gerontology, 52*, S13–S26.
Grundy, E., & Henretta, J. C. (2006). Between elderly parents and adult children: A new look at the intergenerational care provided by the 'sandwich generation'. *Ageing & Society, 26*, 702–722. https://doi.org/10.1017/S0144686X06004934.
Grundy, E., & Shelton, N. (2001). Contact between adult children and their parents in Great Britain 1986–99. *Environment and Planning, 33*, 685–697. https://doi.org/10.1068/a33165.
Guiaux, M., Van Tilburg, T., & Van Groenou, M. B. (2007). Changes in contact and support exchange in personal networks after widowhood. *Personal Relationships, 14*, 457–473. https://doi.org/10.1111/j.1475-6811.2007.00165.x.
Hansen, K. V. (2005). *Not-so-nuclear families: Class, gender, and networks of care*. New Brunswick: Rutgers University Press.
Hogan, D. P., Eggeben, D. J., & Clogg, C. C. (1993). The structure of intergenerational exchanges in American families. *American Journal of Sociology, 98*, 1428–1458.
Johnson, C. (2000). Perspectives on American kinship in the later 1990s. *Journal of Marriage and the Family, 62*, 623–639. https://doi.org/10.1111/j.1741-3737.2000.00623.x.
Kalmijn, M. (2006). Educational inequality and family relationships: Influences on contact and proximity. *European Sociological Review, 22*, 1–16. https://doi.org/10.1093/esr/jci036.

Kalmijn, M. (2012). Longitudinal analyses of the effects of age, marriage, and parenthood on social contacts and support. *Advances in Life Course Research, 17*, 177–190. https://doi.org/10.1016/j.alcr.2012.08.002.

Lawton, L., Silverstein, M., & Bengtson, V. L. (1994). Affection, social contact, and geographical distance between adult children and their parents. *Journal of Marriage and the Family, 56*, 57–68. https://doi.org/10.2307/352701.

Lee, Y., & Aytac, I. A. (1998). Intergenerational financial support among whites, blacks, and Latinos. *Journal of Marriage and the Family, 60*, 426–441. https://doi.org/10.2307/353859.

Logan, J., & Spitze, G. D. (1996). *Family ties: Enduring relations between parents and their grown children*. Philadelphia: Temple University Press.

Mok, D., Wellman, B., & Carrasco, J. (2010). Does distance matter in the age of the internet? *Urban Studies, 47*, 2747–2783. https://doi.org/10.1177/0042098010377363.

Morgan, D. L., & March, S. J. (1992). The impact of life events on networks of personal relationships: A comparison of widowhood and caring for a spouse with Alzheimer's disease. *Journal of Social and Personal Relationships, 9*, 563–584. https://doi.org/10.1177/0265407592094006.

National Research Council. (2013). Nonresponse in social science surveys: A research agenda. In R. Tourangeau, & T. J. Plewes (Eds.), *Panel on a research agenda for the future of social science data collection, committee on national statistics*. Division of Behavioral and Social Sciences and Education. Washington, DC: The National Academies Press.

Nelson, M. K. (2005). *The social economy of single motherhood: Raising children in rural America*. New York: Routledge.

Pew Research Center. (2015). *Family support in graying societies: How Americans, Germans and Italians are coping with an aging population*. http://www.pewsocialtrends.org/2015/05/21/family-support-in-graying-societies/. Accessed 1 Nov 2015.

Polenick, C. A., Zarit, S. H., Birditt, K. S., Bangerter, L. R., Seidel, A. J., & Fingerman, K. L. (2017). Intergenerational support and marital satisfaction: Implications of beliefs about helping aging parents. *Journal of Marriage and Family, 79*, 131–146. https://doi.org/10.1111/jomf.12334.

Pugh, A. (2015). *The tumbleweed society: Working and caring in an age of insecurity*. New York: Oxford University Press.

Robinson, K., & Schoeni, R. F. (2010). *Disparities in familial financial assistance to young adults: Initial findings*. Ann Arbor: Institute for Social Research.

Roschelle, A. R. (1997). *No more kin: Exploring race, class, and gender in family networks*. Thousand Oaks: Sage.

Rosenfeld, M., & Kim, B. (2005). The independence of young adults and the rise of interracial and same-sex unions. *American Sociological Review, 70*, 541–562. https://doi.org/10.1177/000312240507000401.

Rossi, A. S., & Rossi, P. H. (1990). *Of human bonding: Parent–child relations across the life course*. New York: Aldine de Gruyter.

Sarkisian, N., & Gerstel, N. (2004). Kin support among blacks and whites: Race and family organization. *American Sociological Review, 69*, 812–837. https://doi.org/10.1177/000312240406900604.

Sarkisian, N., & Gerstel, N. (2008). Till marriage do us part: Adult children's relationships with their parents. *Journal of Marriage and Family, 70*, 360–376. https://doi.org/10.1111/j.1741-3737.2008.00487.x.

Sarkisian, N., Mariana, G., & Gerstel, N. (2007). Extended family integration among Euro and Mexican Americans: Ethnicity, gender and class. *Journal of Marriage and Family, 69*, 40–54. https://doi.org/10.1111/j.1741-3737.2006.00342.x.

Schoeni, R., & Ross, K. (2005). Material assistance from families during the transition to adulthood. In R. A. Settersten, F. F. Furstenberg Jr., & R. G. Rumbaut (Eds.), *On the frontier of adulthood: Theory, research, and public policy* (pp. 396–416). Chicago: University of Chicago Press.

Silverstein, M., Parrott, T. M., & Bengtson, V. L. (1995). Factors that predispose middle-aged sons and daughters to provide social support to older parents. *Journal of Marriage and Family, 57*, 465–475. https://doi.org/10.2307/353699.

Silverstein, M., Gans, D., & Yang, F. (2006). Intergenerational support to aging parents: The role of norms and needs. *Journal of Family Issues, 27*, 1068–1084. https://doi.org/10.1177/0192513X06288120.

Swartz, T. T. (2009). Intergenerational family relations in adulthood: Patterns, variations, and implications in the contemporary United States. *Annual Review of Sociology, 35*, 191–212. https://doi.org/10.1146/annurev.aoc.34.040507.134615.

Van Gaalen, R. I., & Dykstra, P. A. (2006). Solidarity and conflict between adult children and parents: A latent class analysis. *Journal of Marriage and Family, 68*, 947–960. https://doi.org/10.1111/j.1741-3737.2006.00306.x.

Viry, G. (2012). Residential mobility and the spatial dispersion of personal networks: Effects on social support. *Social Networks, 34*, 59–72. https://doi.org/10.1016/j.socnet.2011.07.003.

Ward, R., Deane, G., & Spitze, G. (2014). Life-course changes and parent–adult child contact. *Research on Aging, 36*, 568–602. https://doi.org/10.1177/0164027513510325.

Wellman, B., & Wortley, S. (1990). Different strokes for different folks: Community ties and social support. *American Journal of Sociology, 96*, 558–588.

Shira Offer is an Associate Professor in the Department of Sociology and Anthropology at Bar Ilan University, in Israel, and a visiting lecturer at the University of California at Berkeley. She studies social networks, social support, gender inequality, and family relationships.

Claude S. Fischer is Professor of the Graduate School in Sociology at the University of California. His interests lie in personal networks, social history, social psychology, and technology.

Chapter 7
Changes in Spousal Relationships over the Marital Life Course

Paul R. Amato and Spencer L. James

Social scientists have learned a great deal about marriage since the first empirical studies were conducted in the 1930s (Burgess and Cottrell 1939; Terman et al. 1938). We know, for example, about the correlates of marital quality, the predictors of divorce, and the consequences of marital conflict and divorce for health and general wellbeing. Despite many decades of research, however, gaps remain in our understanding of how spousal relationships change over the marital life course. These gaps are due partly to the scarcity of long-term longitudinal studies of married people, especially studies based on nationally representative samples. Although some studies have examined long-term trends in marital happiness, few have focused on other marital dimensions, such as the frequency of shared activities or conflict. Moreover, we know little about how marital trajectories differ between spouses who divorce and those who remain continuously married.

To address these gaps in our understanding, we show how three dimensions of marital relationships—happiness, participation in shared activities, and discord—change over time in a nationally representative (U.S.) sample of married people. We focus on the relationship trajectories of two particular groups: those who remain continuously married and those who divorce. We also consider whether relationship trajectories vary by gender, marriage order, and education. We accomplish these goals using pooled time series analyses (with random and fixed effects models) and 20 years of panel data from the Marital Instability over the Life Course (MIOLC) study. These analyses cast light on several theoretical perspectives on stability and change in marriage.

P. R. Amato (✉)
Department of Sociology, Pennsylvania State University, State College, PA, USA
e-mail: pxa6@psu.edu

S. L. James
School of Family Life, Brigham Young University, Provo, UT, USA

D. F. Alwin et al. (eds.), *Social Networks and the Life Course*, Frontiers in Sociology and Social Research 2, https://doi.org/10.1007/978-3-319-71544-5_7

Theoretical Perspectives

Three general ways of thinking about changes in spousal relationships appear in the research literature. *Marital stability perspectives* stress the homeostatic nature of spousal relationships. The enduring dynamics perspective (Huston et al. 2001) assumes that spouses have stable traits, such as genetic predispositions, personalities, attachment styles, and relationship skills that affect the quality of their interaction. These factors lead to stable patterns of interaction in the early years of marriage—or even prior to marriage. Because relationship dynamics crystallize early, interpersonal problems typically emerge in the early years of marriage and endure over time. Karney and Bradbury's (1995) vulnerability-stress-adaptation model also emphasizes the stable traits that people bring to relationships, such as a tendency to experience negative affect (neuroticism) or make problematic attributions about a partner's behavior. These factors not only increase the level of discord in relationships, but also impair people's ability to cope with stressful circumstances that arise during marriage. In summary, relationship stability perspectives suggest that (a) most of the risk factors that lead to divorce are present at the start of marriages, and (b) relationship characteristics tends to be stable over many years because the individual and couple traits that shape relationships change slowly, if at all.

Huston and colleagues also outlined two *marital decline perspectives*, based on the idea that most marriages are harmonious during the newlywed stage but deteriorate over time (Huston et al. 2001). The disillusionment perspective suggests that people enter marriage with romanticized and idealized images of their spouses. After the newlywed years, however, people become disillusioned with their marriages as they move beyond romanticized fantasies and adopt more realistic views of their spouses' limitations. As disappointment sets in, feelings of satisfaction and love begin to wane, and feelings of ambivalence and doubt emerge. A related perspective based on the notion of emergent distress assumes that all married couples begin as affectionate and loving partners. During the early years they may even avoid conflict to maintain a positive emotional tone. But as time passes, an accumulation of disagreements, expressions of negative sentiment, and troubling behavior leads to relationship distress. Because conflict arises in all relationships, declines in attraction to one's spouse are normative.

Another marital decline perspective was advanced by Pineo (1961). According to this view, spouses marry at a time when they are most compatible. As the years pass, however, individuals change in random, largely unanticipated ways. These changes lead to incompatibility and a poorer relationship fit. These ideas are consistent with exchange theory (Sabatelli and Shehan 1993), which assumes that spouses "exchange" valued characteristics that each brings to the marriage. Changes in these characteristics over time tend to disrupt the equity of the exchange and lead to unhappiness.

A related decline perspective can be drawn from sociological life course theory (Elder 1998), which assumes that relationships are shaped by the timing and sequencing of events and the roles that spouses enter and leave during marriage. According to this view, the positive feelings reported by newlyweds tend to decline as couples struggle with the challenges of rearing young children, paying off mortgages, dealing with work-family conflict, caring for aging relatives, and experiencing age-related decrements in health (VanLaningham et al. 2001). In other words, the accumulation of normative but stressful events, obligations, and circumstances creates "wear and tear" on marriages and consumes much of the time that couples might otherwise devote to relationship-strengthening activities.

Although they appear frequently in the research literature, the theoretical models described thus far may be too pessimistic. It is true, as noted earlier, that some individuals possess negative traits that undermine relationships. But other individuals possess positive traits that strengthen relationships, such as honesty, generosity, trust, conscientiousness, good communication skills, the willingness to compromise, and a knack for resolving disagreements peacefully. Correspondingly, some people are able to allocate their time effectively and find a reasonable balance between life course demands and the needs of their marriages. Moreover, all individuals—even if those with difficult personalities—have the capacity to learn, adapt, and grow. These positive traits make it possible to adapt to changing circumstances and deal with the inevitable problems that arise in relationships and in life more generally (Hawkins et al. 2007). According to a *marital resilience perspective,* not all spouses are doomed to see the quality of their relationships erode over time. Although marriages headed for divorce may deteriorate, spouses with resilient relationships can maintain—or even improve on—the generally positive relationship dynamics that characterize the early years of marriage (Canary et al. 2002). From this perspective, spending many years together provides opportunities for couples to experience even deeper levels of appreciation, closeness, and contentment.

Empirical Evidence

Does previous research provide support for any of the three theoretical models—based on the notions of stability, decline, and resilience—outlined earlier? Although many longitudinal studies of marital quality can be found in the literature, few have lasted longer than 5 years. Moreover, most longitudinal studies have involved only two waves of data and, hence, are unable to detect nonlinear patterns of change. Despite these limitations, a consistent finding in this literature is that marital satisfaction declines over the first few years of marriage (e.g., Kurdek 1999; Lindahl et al. 1998). How marital quality changes after this, and whether couples that eventually divorce begin their marriages with troubled relationships, is less clear.

In an early study, Pineo (1961) reported on 400 married couples first studied in the 1930s and followed up 20 years later. Husbands as well as wives reported general declines in a variety of relationship characteristics between interviews, including satisfaction, love, intimacy, and shared activities. Vaillant and Vaillant (1993) followed 169 male college students and their wives (first studied in the 1930s and

1940s) for 40 years. Among husbands, marital adjustment declined during the first 15 years of marriage then stabilized, whereas among wives, marital adjustment declined continuously. (Wives reported especially large declines in resolving disagreements.) VanLaningham, Johnson, and Amato (2001) used 17 years of national data from the first five waves of the MIOLC study (initiated in 1980) and found that marital happiness declined continuously at all marital durations, with no upturn in the later years of marriage.

More recently, Birditt et al. (2012) followed 320 newlywed couples for 16 years and found a general (average) decline in marital happiness for wives as well as husbands. The authors also used mixture modeling to show that not all spouses followed the same trajectory, however. James (2015) used data from 2604 women in the 1979 National Longitudinal Survey of Youth who reported on their marriages between 1992 and 2010. Reports of happiness and communication declined modestly but continuously, on average, whereas reports of conflict were curvilinear (increasing and then declining after the first decade). James also used mixture modeling to demonstrate heterogeneity in these trajectories.

Taken together, the studies by Pineo (1961), Vaillant and Vaillant (1993), VanLaningham et al. (2001), Birditt et al. (2012), and James (2015) are consistent in showing that spousal relationships tend to become less positive over time. The latter two studies also show, however, that not all couples follow the same pattern of decline. Moreover, no studies have considered how the relationship trajectories of continuously married spouses differ from the relationship trajectories of spouses who end their marriages in divorce.

Contributions of the Current Investigation

To assess the three general theoretical perspectives outlined earlier, we draw on the MIOLC study. This data set has four advantages for the current inquiry: (1) it is based on a randomly selected national sample of married individuals, (2) it is relatively large with over 2000 cases, (3) it contains multiple-item measures of several relationship dimensions, and (4) it includes six waves of data collected over a 20-year period. A disadvantage is that it was initiated in 1980, which means that the results may not be generalizable to more recent marriage cohorts. Nevertheless, the MIOLC continues to be a useful data set available for understanding long-term changes in marital relationships.

The current study is similar in certain respects to VanLaningham et al. (2001), which also used the MIOLC. The two studies differ in several important respects, however. First, the VanLaningham et al. study was conducted before the final (6th) wave of data (collected in 2000) was available, whereas we use all six waves of data. The additional wave makes it possible to extend the range of marital duration estimates with greater precision. Second, VanLaningham et al. did not examine marital quality trajectories for respondents who divorced—a central focus of the current study. Third, VanLaningham et al. focused only on marital happiness, whereas the current study includes three conceptually distinct relationship dimensions. Fourth, although VanLaningham et al. provided suggestive evidence that period effects were present in their data, they did not directly test or control for them. The current study, in contrast, includes controls for period effects that can distort estimates of marital duration effects.

To summarize, the current study reveals how three spousal relationship dimensions (happiness, shared activities, and discord) change over the marital life course. A central goal is to consider how relationships change for spouses who either divorce or remain together. Can the troubled relationships of divorced spouses be observed in the initial years of marriage, as the marital stability perspective suggests? Or do these relationships begin happily and then decline abruptly, as the marital decline perspective suggests? What about spouses who remain continuously married? Do they also report declines in relationship quality, as the marital decline perspective suggests? Or do they report consistently positive relationships, or even improvement in relationship quality, as the marital resilience perspective suggests?

In addition to focusing on divorce, we consider whether relationship trajectories vary with gender (husband versus wife), marriage order (first versus higher-order marriages), and education (college versus non-college). Since Jessie Bernard's (1982) discussion of "his" and "her" marriages, gender differences in marriage have been of broad interest to family scholars (Jackson et al. 2014). Marriage order is of interest because, since the rise in divorce rates in the 1960s and 1970s, an increasing percentage of marriages have been remarriages for one or both spouses (Bramlett and Mosher 2002). With respect to education, college and non-college educated spouses differ substantially on a variety of marital behaviors, including age at marriage, having children prior to marriage, and the probability of ending a marriage in divorce (Cherlin 2014). Whether these two groups also differ with respect to relationship trajectories is not clear.

Method

Sample

Our analysis was based on the 20-year MIOLC study (Booth et al. 2000). The target population consisted of all married individuals in households in the contiguous United States with a telephone, both spouses present, and both spouses 55 years of age or less in 1980. Telephone interviewers used random digit dialing to select a sample of households and a second random procedure to select either the husband or wife for an interview. Seventeen percent of targeted individuals could not be reached after 20 calls. Of those individuals contacted, 78% gave complete interviews. The final sample consisted of 2034 married persons. When compared with U.S. Census data, the sample was representative of married individuals with respect to age, race, household size, home ownership, presence of children, and region of the country, although there was an overrepresentation of women—a common

Table 7.1 Sample descriptive statistics

	Mean	Standard deviation	Standard error
Age	35.58	9.16	0.23
Duration of marriage in 1980 (years)	12.84	9.19	0.23
Gender (1 = wife)	0.60	–	0.01
Marriage order (1 = remarried)	0.14	–	0.01
College graduate (1 = yes)	0.19	–	0.01
Divorced during study (1 = yes)	0.19	–	0.01
NonHispanic white (1 = yes)	0.88	–	0.01
Cohabitation prior to marriage (1 = yes)	0.17	–	0.01
Children during marriage (1 = yes)	0.72	–	0.01

Note: Sample statistics are based on the number of cases (N = 1617) rather than the number of observations. Standard deviations are not shown for binary variables

outcome in surveys. The sample was tracked and re-interviewed in 1983, 1988, 1992, 1997, and 2000, with re-interview rates of 78%, 84%, 89%, 88%, and 87%, respectively.

The data set for the current analysis included pooled data from all six waves. Respondents contributed records for each wave in which they were married and participating in the study. An advantage of pooled time series analysis is that it allows cases to contribute all available data, irrespective of attrition (Johnson 1995). Only respondents who participated in two or more waves of data collection were included in the analysis, however. The analytic sample involved 7076 observations (records) from 1617 individuals. Of these individuals, 790 remained married and continued through the final interview in 2000, 313 divorced, 77 experienced the death of a spouse, and the remaining 437 dropped out of the panel. Of those respondents who divorced or experienced the death of a spouse during the study, 89 remarried and reported on their new relationships in two or more waves. We included these observations in the analyses. One advantage of including these remarried cases is that it weakened the correlation between duration of marriage and year of interview.

In 1980 the mean ages of wives and husbands were 35 and 37, respectively. The majority of respondents (88%) were white, and 17% had cohabited with their spouses prior to marriage. The majority of couples (72%) were parents in 1980, although some no longer had children living at home. (See Table 7.1 for a summary of sample descriptive statistics.)

Variables

Relationship Characteristics Marital happiness was based on ten items. Sample items included, "How happy are you with the amount of understanding you receive from your spouse?...with the amount of love and affection you receive?...with your sexual relationship?...with your marriage overall?" Responses were scored in the direction of greater happiness (1 = *not too happy*, 2 = *pretty happy*, 3 = *very happy*), and the mean response served as the scale score. Alpha reliability coefficients ranged from .87 to .88 across waves.

To measure shared activities, respondents were asked how often they engaged in six activities with their spouses: eating dinner, shopping, visiting friends, working on projects around the house, and going out for recreation. Responses were scored in the direction of frequent interaction (1 = *never*, 4 = *almost always*), and the mean response served as the scale score. Alpha reliability coefficients ranged from .64 to .69 across waves.

General relationship discord was a composite based on three sub-scales. To assess marital problems, respondents were asked about the presence of 13 problems in their marriages, including whether they or their spouses get angry easily, have feelings that are easily hurt, are jealous, are critical, avoid talking, or have had extra-marital sex. The total number of reported problems served as the measure. Marital conflict was based on five items, including "In general, how often do you disagree with your spouse?" (1 = *never*, 5 = *very often*), and "How many serious quarrels have you had with your spouse in the last two months?" (0–4 or more). The mean response across the five items served as the scale score. Divorce proneness is the propensity to divorce and includes both a cognitive component (e.g., thinking that one's marriage is in trouble) and a behavioral component (e.g., talking with one's spouse about divorce). The scale included 13-items, such as "Has the thought of divorce or separation ever crossed your mind?" Because the sum of the items was positively skewed, the log (base 10) served as the scale score. The three scales (problems, conflict, and divorce proneness) were equally weighted (using Z scores) and added to produce a measure of general relationship discord. The reliability for the composite was 0.85 across all waves.

Marital Duration Marital duration was measured in years and was time-varying in the analysis. In 1980 this variable ranged from 0 to 38 with a mean of 12.8 (S = 9.2). In 2000 (the final survey year) this variable ranged from 20 to 58 with a mean of 33.1 (S = 8.9). The longitudinal data set included 242 spouses who had been married for 2 years or less at the time of the first interview, and 205 spouses who had been married for 40 years or longer at the time of the final interview. We also included a quadratic term (years married squared) to capture nonlinear trends.

Divorce As noted earlier, 313 spouses (19%) divorced during the study. Divorce was treated as a time-invariant variable in the analysis because the focus was on spouses who ever divorced, irrespective of when the event occurred.

Gender The respondent's gender was included in all analyses (0 = *husband*, 1 = *wife*). The majority of respondents (60%) were female.

Marriage Order Marriage order was coded 0 = first marriage for the respondent, 1 = second or higher order marriage for the respondent (14% of respondents were in second or higher-order marriages). In an alternative specification, we scored this variable 1 if it was a second or higher-order marriage for the respondent *and* the respondent's spouse, but the results were identical to those reported later.

College Graduate The respondent's education was coded 0 = not a college graduate, 1 = college graduate (19% of respondents were college graduates). In alternative specifications, we scored this variable 1 if the respondent *and* the respondent's spouse were college graduates, but the results were identical to those reported in the main analysis.

Periods Period effects were estimated by including dummy variables for each survey year (1983, 1988, 1992, 1997, and 2000), with 1980 serving as the omitted reference category.

Attrition Of all the respondents interviewed in 1980, 53% no longer were participating in the panel by 2000 (including respondents who died). We relied on a variation of Heckman's (1979) two-step method to correct for attrition bias. We relied on logistic regression to model the attrition of respondents from the panel and used the resulting equation to calculate the probability of dropping out of the panel for each case. Attrition was more common among African Americans, relatively young or old spouses, renters, spouses with little education, spouses married for only a few years, and spouses living in the south. This variable was included as a control variable in the random effects models.

Analysis

We estimated the statistical models with the xtreg procedure in Stata. We estimated random and fixed effects models because each has offsetting advantages and disadvantages. Random effects models allowed us to estimate regression coefficients for divorce, gender, marriage order, and college—four of the central variables in our study. Fixed effects models (unlike random effects models) allowed us to control for all unobserved time-invariant variables, including demographic characteristics and stable personality traits that may affect attrition. Fixed effects models also allowed us to control for cohort effects, given that year of birth and age at marriage are fixed. Fixed effects models do not allow for the inclusion of time-invariant variables, however, so we could not use them to estimate regression coefficients for divorce, gender, marriage order, and college. We could, however, model interaction terms between these variables and marital duration, which was sufficient for our purposes. It is common for researchers working with pooled time series data to compare the results of both types of models (e.g., Teachman 2011; Turney and Carlson 2011). To the extent that random and fixed effects models yield comparable findings, confidence in the conclusions is strengthened.

Although a good deal of attrition occurred in the panel study (as noted earlier), missing data among cases participating in each wave was modest and represented no more than 1% of observations for the variables used in the analysis. For this reason, we relied on listwise deletion to deal with within-wave missing data.

Prior to analysis, the relationship variables (happiness, shared activities, and discord) were transformed to Z scores (mean = 0, standard deviation = 1). Doing so made it easier to assess the magnitude of change over time and to make comparisons across outcomes.

Results from Random Effects Models

Overall Trends

Table 7.2 shows the equations (unstandardized coefficients) for all three spousal relationship variables. We begin by focusing on the Model 1 results without the interaction terms. For marital happiness, the negative coefficient for years married (−.015) and the positive coefficient for years married squared (.0003) indicated a curvilinear trend. Not surprisingly, spouses who eventually divorced reported lower levels of happiness (−.710 of a standard deviation) than did spouses who remained married. Consistent with many studies, wives reported less happiness than did husbands (−.187 of a standard deviation). The dummy variables for survey year reveal that marital happiness declined during the 1980s and 1990s but rebounded in 2000. Finally, the significant coefficient for attrition (−.495) indicates that spouses with a high probability of dropping out of the sample reported less happiness—a result that supports the usefulness of controlling for attrition bias.

The results for the shared activities were comparable to the results for happiness in some respects. In particular, the negative coefficient for years and the positive coefficient for years squared in Model 1 indicate a curvilinear trend. In addition, spouses who divorced reported fewer activities than did spouses who remained married, and wives reported fewer activities than did husbands. Respondents with a high probability of attrition reported fewer activities than did respondents with a low probability. Finally, the coefficients for survey years reveal that shared activities declined substantially during the years of the study, with an especially large drop in the final year of the study. With respect to discord, the Model 1 equation shows a significant decline over time, and the quadratic term was not significant. Consistent with earlier results, discord was higher among spouses headed for divorce than for spouses who remained together and higher among wives than husbands. The dummy variables for year of survey suggest that discord increased during the 1980s and 1990s.

Figure 7.1 shows the overall trajectories of marital happiness, shared activities, and discord, based on the Model 1 equations with all covariates set at their means. Note that happiness declined during the first 20 years of marriage and then stabilized. The amount of decline was modest, however, and represented only about one-fifth of a standard deviation. Shared activities also declined during the first

Table 7.2 Random effects regression of spousal relationship characteristics on marital duration

	Marital happiness		Shared activities		Marital discord	
	Model 1	Model 2	Model 1	Model 2	Model 1	Model 2
Years married	−.015***	−.006	−.027***	−.021***	−.013***	−.021***
	(.004)	(.004)	(.004)	(.004)	(.004)	(.004)
Years married^2	.0003***	.0002*	.001***	.001***	−.0001	−.0001
	(.0001)	(.0001)	(.0001)	(.0001)	(.0001)	(.0001)
Divorce	−.710***	−.116	−.539***	−.182	.740***	.194*
	(.057)	(.100)	(.054)	(.100)	(.058)	(.098)
Divorce × years	–	−.048***	–	−.035**	–	.054***
		(.012)		(.013)		(.011)
Divorce × years^2	–	−.0001	–	.0003	–	−.0004
		(.0004)		(.0004)		(.0004)
Female	−.187***	−.196***	−.129**	−.134**	.149**	.157***
	(.044)	(.044)	(.041)	(.041)	(.045)	(.045)
Remarried	−.043	−.070	−.003	−.017	.010	.034
	(.063)	(.063)	(.059)	(.059)	(.064)	(.065)
College	.044	.034	.029	−.034	−.006	.002
	(.057)	(.056)	(.052)	(.052)	(.058)	(.058)
1980	–	–	–	–	–	–
1983	−.187***	−.184***	−.166***	−.163***	.075**	.072**
	(.025)	(.024)	(.026)	(.026)	(.023)	(.023)
1988	−.253***	−.257***	−.367***	−.367***	.150***	.152***
	(.032)	(.032)	(.032)	(.032)	(.031)	(.031)
1992	−.267***	−.291***	−.384***	−.393***	.239***	.256***
	(.039)	(.039)	(.039)	(.039)	(.039)	(.039)
1997	−.244***	−.291***	−.374***	−.395***	.143**	.181***
	(.049)	(.049)	(.048)	(.048)	(.049)	(.049)
2000	.016	−.051	−1.160***	−1.190***	−.108	.033
	(.056)	(.057)	(.055)	(.055)	(.056)	(.057)
Attrition	−.495*	−.636**	−.523*	−.595**	.453	.575*
	(.233)	(.232)	(.218)	(.218)	(.238)	(.238)
Constant	.463***	.343***	.605	.539***	.083	.182**
	(.058)	(.059)	(.056)	(.057)	(.059)	(.060
R squared	.056***	.101***	.105***	.107***	.110***	.110***

Note: Table values are unstandardized regression coefficients with standard errors in parentheses. Sample sizes are 1616–1618 cases (6618–6705 observations), depending on the equation
* $p < .05$. ** $p < .01$. *** $p < .001$ (two-tailed)

20 years of marriage (about one fourth of a standard deviation). After 25 years of marriage, however, shared activities began to increase, and by year 40 this variable was about as high as it had been in the first year of marriage. Finally, discord between spouses declined continuously and represented a drop of nearly two thirds of a standard deviation over a 40-year period.

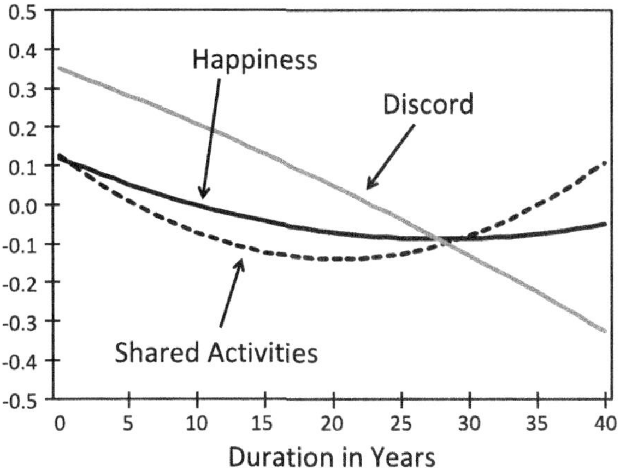

Fig. 7.1 Marital happiness, shared activities, and discord by duration of marriage in years (random effects models)

Trends for Spouses Who Divorced or Remained Married

The Model 2 equations in Table 7.2 show the results of interacting divorce and marital duration. For marital happiness, the divorce × years married coefficient was negative and statistically significant (−.048). This result indicates that marital happiness declined more steeply over time for spouses who divorced than for spouses who remained together. The coefficient for divorce in Model 2 was low and not significant (−.116). This result indicates that the gap in marital happiness between spouses who either divorced or remained together was modest in the first year of marriage (that is, at year = 0) but became larger in subsequent years.

With respect to shared activities, the divorce × years married interaction term in Model 2 was negative and significant. This result indicates that participation in shared activities declined more steeply for spouses who divorced than for spouses who remained together. Moreover, the coefficient for divorce in Model 2 was low and not significant, which indicates that the gap between spouses who either divorced or remained together was small in the first year of marriage. With respect to discord, the divorce × years married interaction term also was significant and positive. This result indicates that discord increased more steeply over time for spouses who divorced than for spouses who remained together. Contrary to the results for happiness and shared activities, however, the *b* coefficient for divorce was significant (.194), which indicates that even in the first year of marriage, spouses who later divorced reported more conflict than did spouses who remained together.

Figure 7.2 shows the estimated trajectories for spouses who divorced and remained married, based on the coefficients in Model 2 (Table 7.2) with all covariates set at their means. In the first year of marriage, spouses who later divorced reported slightly (but not significantly) less happiness than did spouses who remained together. Spouses headed for divorce revealed a sharp decline in happiness in subsequent years, however, dropping about one standard deviation within 20 years—assuming that they stayed married for that long. Spouses who did not divorce exhibited a different trajectory, with an almost imperceptible decline in happiness during the first two decades of marriage (5% of a standard deviation) followed by a small increase (10% of a standard deviation) during the next two decades.

Trajectories of shared activities for divorced and continuously married spouses also are shown in Fig. 7.2. Spouses who divorced scored slightly lower at the beginning of the marriage than did spouses who remained together. Shared activities in the divorced group declined two thirds of a standard deviation during the first two decades of marriage. The mean for the continuously married group also declined, albeit more gradually, and bottomed out after 20 years, with an overall decline of about one fifth of a standard deviation. The frequency of shared activities increased again in subsequent years and by 36 years had returned to where it started at the beginning of the marriage.

Finally, spouses who divorced reported more discord (conflict, problems, and divorce proneness) in the first year of marriage than did spouses who remained together. Moreover, discord increased over time for spouses headed for divorce, whereas it declined over time for spouses who remained together. The decline in discord for continuously married spouses represented 85% of a standard deviation over 40 years—a large change.

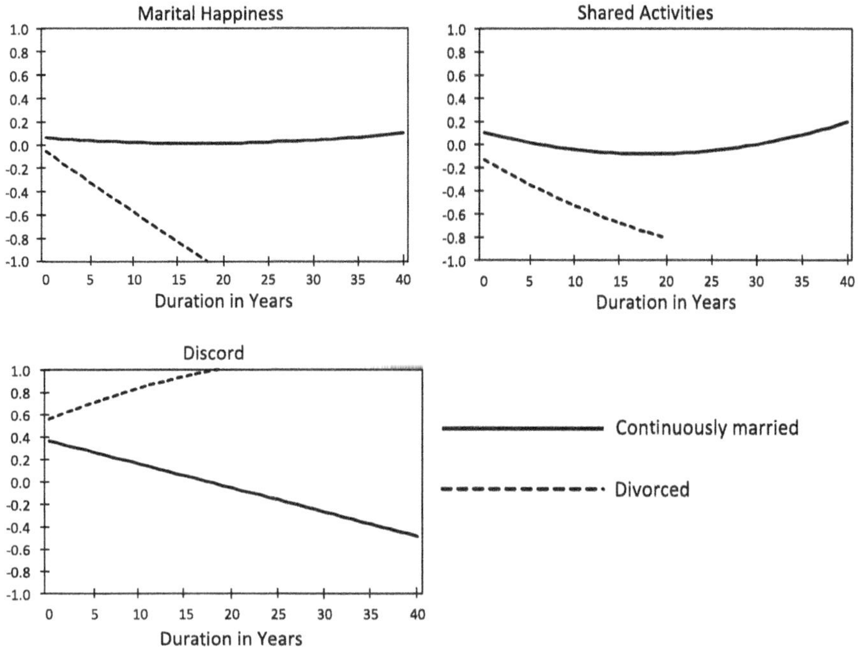

Fig. 7.2 Spousal relationships by divorce and duration of marriage in years (random effects models)

Gender Differences

In subsequent models (not shown), we examined differences between husbands and wives by including interaction terms between gender and years married, years married squared, and divorce. No two- or three-way interaction terms were significant for the frequency of shared activities. For happiness and discord, however, the three-way interaction terms (gender × years married × divorce) were statistically significant (all $p < .05$). The corresponding three-way interaction for shared activities only approached significance ($p = .09$).

Figure 7.3 shows the marital happiness trajectories separately for husbands and wives. Husbands and wives headed for divorce reported declines in marital happiness, but the decline was steeper for wives than for husbands. Among wives who remained continuously married, marital happiness changed little. Among husbands who remained continuously married, marital happiness increased modestly (about one-tenth of a standard deviation) but significantly. These results are consistent with prior research showing that wives tend to be report less marital happiness and more relationship problems than do husbands (Amato et al. 2007; Jackson et al. 2014). The current results indicate, however, that the gap between husbands and wives grew larger over time, irrespective of whether couples stayed together or divorced.

Although the three-way interaction between gender, divorce, and the number of years married was only marginally significant for shared activities ($p = .09$), we include a figure for this outcome for the sake of completeness. As was the case for marital happiness, reports of shared activities declined more steeply among wives headed for divorce than among husbands. The trends for husbands and wives who remained together were essentially identical.

Figure 7.3 also illustrates gender differences in the trajectories of discord. Among wives in marriages that ended in divorce, reports of discord started at a relatively high level in the first year of marriage and increased substantially over time. Among husbands in marriages that ended in divorce, in contrast, reports of discord were relatively high in the first year of marriage and changed little after that. As with marital happiness, wives headed for divorce held especially dismal views of their relationships as the years passed. Among marriages that remained intact, wives reported more discord early in the marriage than did husbands. Over time, however, both wives and husbands reported less discord, with the two trajectories converging after 30 years of marriage.

Results for Other Variables

Spouses in first marriages did not differ from spouses in second or higher-order marriages with respect to happiness, shared activities, or discord. Moreover, marriage order did not interact with divorce or gender with respect to any relationship outcomes. Although second (and higher-order marriages) are more likely than first marriages to end in divorce (Bramlett and Mosher 2002), marriage order does not

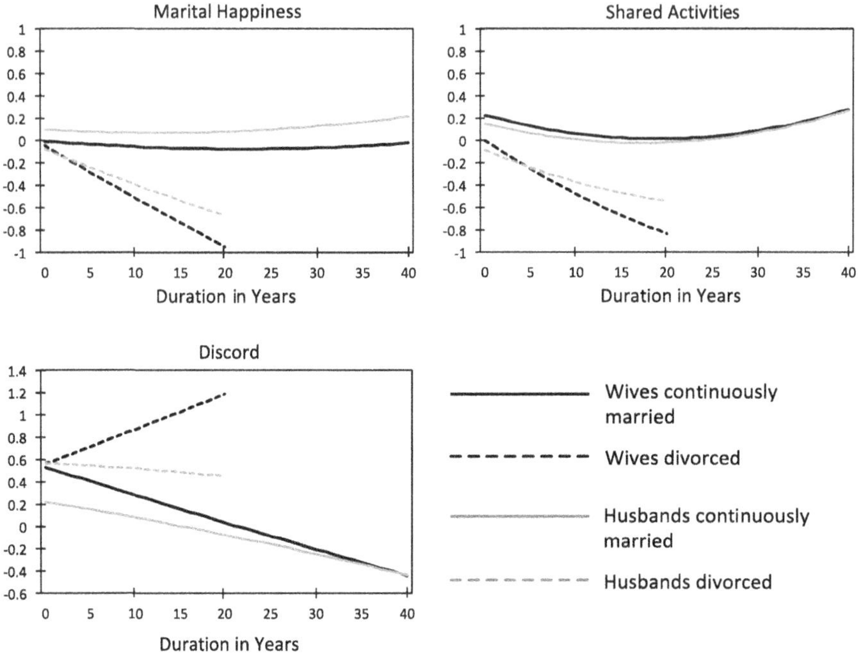

Fig. 7.3 Spousal relationships for divorced and continuously married wives and husbands (random effects models)

appear to be related to how spouses evaluate their marriages. These results are consistent with several prior studies (e.g., Amato et al. 2007; White and Booth 1985). Presumably, higher-order marriages often end for reasons other than poor relationship quality (such as holding positive attitudes toward divorce, having low commitment to the relationship, or wishing to escape from stepchildren).

Spouses with college degrees did not differ from spouses without college degrees on any relationship outcome. Moreover, education did not interact with divorce or gender in any statistical model. Although divorce rates tend to be lower for spouses with college degrees (Cherlin 2014), having a college degree does not appear to be related to reports of relationship quality—at least in the marriage cohort considered in the current study.

The dummy variables reflecting year of study consistently produced significant results. These period effects are shown in Fig. 7.4, with all other variables in the models set at their means. Happiness and discord reflected one another, with happiness showing declines followed by an increase, and discord showing increases followed by a decline. In contrast, participation in shared activities declined continuously during the years of the study and dropped especially sharply between 1997 and 2000.

It is difficult to determine the cause of period effects like these. Economic recessions in 1980–82 and 1991–91 were associated with increases in unemployment, declines in the real earnings of men, and more family poverty. Starting in the mid

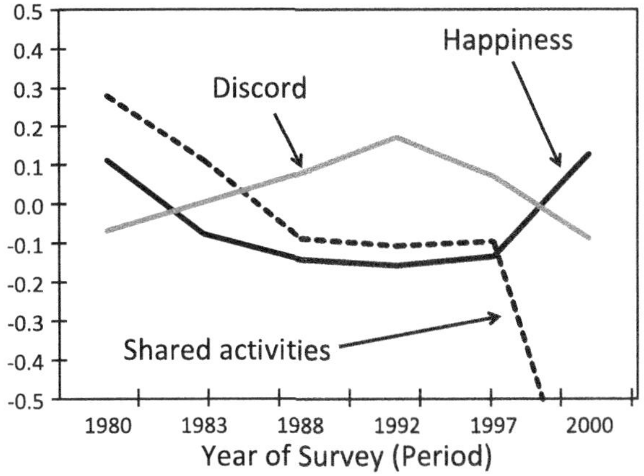

Fig. 7.4 Spousal relationship dimensions by year of survey (random effects models)

1990s and continuing through 2000, however, the U.S. economy expanded, leading to increases in employment and wages and declines in economic hardship (Gould et al. 2013). These trends may have had negative (and later, positive) effects on marital relationships. Wives' employment expanded during the 1980s and 1990s, which led to greater work-family conflict and tension over gender role (Amato et al. 2007). Moreover, the high rate of female employment in 2000 may have suppressed the frequency of shared activities in that year to an unusually low level. In addition, many observers have argued that American culture became more individualistic after the 1960s (Amato et al. 2007; Cherlin 2004)—another trend that may have decreased the frequency of interaction between spouses. Any of these factors, or a combination of them, could have been responsible for the changes shown in Fig. 7.4.

Fixed Effects Models

The results of fixed effects models are shown in Table 7.3. These equations should be compared with the Model 2 equations in Table 7.2. Divorce status, gender, marriage order, college attendance, and the attrition variable are not in the fixed effects equations because they are time invariant. Although it was not possible to include divorce, it was possible to include interaction terms for years married × divorce (and the other time invariant variables).

The equations in Table 7.3 are similar in many respects to those in Table 7.2. The interactions between divorce and years married were significant and in the expected direction for all three outcomes. A disadvantage of fixed effects models is that they cannot show difference between groups of spouses in the first year of marriage. Because no between-person variance is modeled (only within-person variance) everyone essentially starts in the "same place." Nevertheless, consistent with the results from the random effects models, the fixed effects models reveal that all aspects of relationship quality deteriorated relatively quickly among spouses headed

Table 7.3 Fixed effects regression of spousal relationship characteristics on marital duration

	Marital happiness	Shared activities	Discord
Years married	−.008	−.042***	.006
	(.006)	(.007)	(.006)
Years married²	.0002*	.0005***	−.0001
	(.0001)	(.0001)	(.0001)
Divorce years	−.072***	−.040**	.055***
	(.013)	(.014)	(.013)
Divorce × years²	.0002	.0001	−.0002
	(.0004)	(.0004)	(.0004)
1980	–	–	–
1983	−.178***	−.102***	.064
	(.027)	(.030)	(.026)
1988	−.237***	−.192***	−.046
	(.047)	(.050)	(.044)
1992	−.280***	−.138	−.032
	(.066)	(.071)	(.062)
1997	−.274**	−.046	−.224**
	(.091)	(.098)	(.088)
2000	−.048	−.689***	−.426***
	(.107)	(.115)	(.101)
Constant	.295***	.733***	−.066
	(.070)	(.076)	(.067)
R squared	.081***	.180***	.079***

Note: Table values are unstandardized regression coefficients with standard errors in parentheses. Sample sizes are 1616–1618 cases (6618–6705 observations), depending on the equation
* $p < .05$. ** $p < .01$. *** $p < .001$ (two-tailed)

for divorce. Among spouses who did not divorce, marital happiness declined slightly and then increased again after about 20 years of marriage—a result directly comparable to the random effects model. Shared activities declined by about three fourths of a standard deviation and then stabilized after 30 years of marriage among spouses in continuously intact marriages. This result differs from the random effects models, which suggested that shared activities increased again after 20 years of marriage. Finally, the level of discord among spouses who remained married increased slightly, but this trend was not statistically significant (see Table 7.3). This contrasts with the random effects result, which suggested that discord declined continuously.

General Discussion

The current investigation considered the evidence for three theoretical perspectives on spousal relationships over the life course. Most studies on this topic have been limited by relatively short time frames of 5 years or less (e.g., Huston et al. 2001;

Kurdek 1999; Lavner and Bradbury 2010). Other studies with longer time frames have involved samples of limited size and geographical range, often without the benefit of probability sampling (e.g., Birditt et al. (2012); Pineo 1961; Vaillant and Vaillant 1993). The current study, in contrast, was based on a large, randomly selected national sample with six waves of data collected over a 20-year period.

Relationship stability perspectives assume that relationship characteristics crystallize quickly and remain constant over time. This continuity reflects the role of stable personal traits such as personalities, genetic predispositions, attachment styles, and social skills, in shaping relationship outcomes (Karney and Bradbury 1995; Huston et al. 2001). If this perspective is correct, then differences between spouses who divorce or remain together should be apparent from the very beginning of the marriage. Contrary to this assumption, however, our random effects models (Table 7.2 and Fig. 7.2) indicated that the differences between spouses who either divorced or stayed married were modest in the first year of marriage. Gaps between these two groups widened considerably, however, as the first decade of marriage unfolded. Our analysis, therefore, provided limited support for the relationship stability perspective.

Relationship decline perspectives assume that marital quality gradually deteriorates for most spouses. This deterioration occurs for several reasons: Spouses become disillusioned as they learn more about one another (Huston et al. 2001), conflict inevitably emerges and takes its toll on relationships (Huston et al. 2001), spouses become increasingly different from one another over time and drift apart (Pineo 1961), and stressful events and social demands accumulate over the life course (VanLaningham et al. 2001). Our random and fixed effects results indicate that this perspective accurately describes the trajectories of spouses who end their marriages in divorce, but it does not apply to spouses who remain married. Marital happiness does not decline, on average, among spouses in stable marriages. Indeed, our results suggest that marital happiness increases slightly in the later years of marriage, especially for husbands. We also find no evidence that relationship discord increases over time for spouses who avoid divorce. Instead, discord either declines (random effects model) or remains constant (fixed effects model). It is true that the frequency of shared activities declines in long-term marriages, although interaction either stabilizes (fixed effects model) or increases again in the later years of marriage (random effects model). This decline in shared activities may occur because spouses in long-term marriages develop new interests or friendships outside of the relationship. Even if one accepts the fixed effects result, however, spouses in long-term marriages appear to be as happy as they had been in the early years of marriage and experience no more conflict.

Our results suggest that the pessimistic conclusions of previous studies may have been due to three limitations: (1) not having longitudinal data of sufficient duration to capture improvements in marital quality in the later years of marriage, (2) failing to separate couples headed for divorce from couples who remain married, thus depressing aggregate levels of relationship quality in the pooled sample, and (3) failing to control for period effects that can shift mean levels of relationship quality downward during particular historical periods. Contrary to previous work, the current study offers a more optimistic view of how marriages change, at least among spouses who avoid divorce. Our results provide the strongest support for the marital resilience model. Although many marriages end unhappily, a substantial number of spouses are able to maintain satisfying and cohesive marital bonds for many decades.

This paper is not without limitations. First, although the MIOLC is a nationally representative sample of married Americans 55 or younger, these data were originally collected in 1980, and it is possible that more recent marriage cohorts display different patterns of change over time. Second, as is typical of longitudinal studies, the data set suffered from a significant degree of attrition. Although we attempted to correct for attrition bias, this is always a source of concern in longitudinal research. Third, although our total sample included 1617 cases, our estimates of how trajectories began and concluded were based on smaller subsamples. In particular, our estimates of marital quality in the first 2 years of marriage were based on only 242 individuals and 56 divorces. Fourth, although our fixed effects analyses controlled for cohort differences in mean levels of marital quality, our analysis assumed no cohort differences in how marital quality changes over time. Cohort × duration interactions could cause some of our estimates to be misleading. Given the difficulty of disentangling marital duration, period, and cohort effects, we do not test this assumption here. Finally, we only had data from one spouse in each marriage, so we cannot see how changes in one spouse's reports are related to changes in the other spouse's reports.

In the present study, different trajectories were estimated from known groups based on divorce and gender. Mixture modeling—an increasingly common method in the social sciences—makes it possible to estimate trajectories when groups are unknown, and a few recent studies have demonstrated that this method can be applied usefully to study marital relationships (Anderson et al. 2010; Birditt et al. 2012; Kamp Dush et al. 2008; Kamp Dush and Taylor 2012; Lavner and Bradbury 2010). Although more work along these lines could be done with the MIOLC, new sources of long-term data on marriage will become available as ongoing longitudinal studies, such as the National Longitudinal Surveys of Youth (NLSY1979 and NLSY1997), continue into the future. Ultimately, however, a better understanding of how relationships change in more recent marriage cohorts will require the collection of new longitudinal data—an expensive and long-term commitment on the part of researchers, although one that seems worthwhile.

Trajectories of marital quality unfold within the context of many life course events and transitions, such as shifts into and out of employment, having children, the departure of children from the household, and obligations to aging parents. Although the current study documented how marital quality changes over time, we did not focus specifically on how trajectories of marital quality are related to other life course phenomena. Future research could make these linkages more explicit.

The current study was able to examine an unusually wide span of the marital life course. Although divorce is common these days, about half of all marriages last a lifetime, and the long-term outlook for most of these marriages is upbeat, with happiness and interaction remaining high and discord declining. This optimistic perspective is not sufficiently acknowledged or appreciated in the social science literature on marriage, which has tended to assume that relationship quality declines continuously for the majority of couples. Our theoretical understanding may have been unduly influenced by the many studies of the early years of marriage—studies that include many couples that will divorce *after* the study is completed. Incorporating insights from the study of long-term, stable marriages may be a useful corrective to this literature.

References

Amato, P. R., Booth, A., Johnson, D. R., & Rogers, S. J. (2007). *Alone together: How marriage in America is changing*. Cambridge, MA: Harvard University Press.

Anderson, J. R., Van Ryzin, M. J., & Doherty, W. J. (2010). Developmental trajectories of marital happiness in continuously married indivdiuals: A group-based modeling approach. *Journal of Family Psychology, 24*, 587–596.

Bernard, J. (1982). *The future of marriage*. New Haven: Yale University Press.

Birditt, K. S., Hope, S., Brown, E., & Orbuch, T. L. (2012). Developmental trajectories of marital happiness over 16 years. *Research in Human Development, 9*, 126–144.

Booth, A., Johnson, D. R., Amato, P. R., & Rogers, S. J. (2000). *Marital instability over the life course: A six-wave panel study*. Ann Arbor: Inter-University Consortium for Political and Social Research.

Bramlett, M. D., & Mosher, W. D. (2002). *Cohabitation, marriage, divorce, and remarriage in the United States, Series 23, Number 22*. Washington, DC: National Center for Health Statistics.

Burgess, E. W., & Cottrell, L. S. (1939). *Predicting success or failure in marriage*. New York: Prentice-Hall.

Canary, D. J., Stafford, L., & Semic, B. A. (2002). A panel study of the associations between maintenance strategies and relational characteristics. *Journal of Marriage and Family, 64*, 395–406.

Cherlin, A. J. (2014). *Labor's love lost: The rise and fall of the working-class family in America*. New York: Russell Sage Foundation.

Elder, G. H. (1998). The life course as developmental theory. *Child Development, 69*, 1–12.

Gould, E., Mishel, L., & Shierholz, H. (2013). *Already more than a lost decade: Income and poverty trends continue to paint a bleak picture*. Economic Policy Institute. http://www.epi.org/publication/lost-decade-income-poverty-trends-continue/ Accessed 18 July 2016.

Hawkins, A. J., Fowers, B. J., Carroll, J. S., & Yang, C. (2007). Conceptualizing and measuring marital virtues. In S. L. Hofferth & L. M. Casper (Eds.), *Handbook of measurement issues in family research* (pp. 67–83). Mahweh: Lawrence Erlbaum.

Heckman, J. (1979). Sample selection bias as a specification error. *Econometrica, 47*, 153–161.

Huston, T. L., Caughlin, J. P., Houts, R. M., Smith, S. E., & George, L. J. (2001). The connubial crucible: Newlywed years as predictors of marital delight, distress, and divorce. *Journal of Personality and Social Psychology, 80*, 237–252.

Jackson, J. B., Miller, R. B., Oka, M., & Henry, R. G. (2014). Gender differences in marital satisfaction: A meta-analysis. *Journal of Marriage and Family, 76*, 105–129.

Johnson, D. (1995). Alternative methods for the quantitative analysis of panel data in family research: Pooled time-series models. *Journal of Marriage and Family, 57*, 1065–1077.

Kamp Dush, C. M., & Taylor, M. G. (2012). Trajectories of marital conflict across the life course: Predictors and interactions with marital happiness trajectories. *Journal of Family Issues, 33*, 341–368.

Kamp Dush, C. M., Taylor, M. G., & Kroeger, R. A. (2008). Marital happiness and psychological well-being across the life course. *Family Relations, 57*, 211–226.

Karney, B. R., & Bradbury, T. N. (1995). The longitudinal course of marital quality and stability: A review of theory, method, and research. *Psychological Bulletin, 118*, 3–34.
Kurdek, L. (1999). The nature and predictors of the trajectory of change in marital quality for husbands and wives over the first 10 years of marriage. *Developmental Psychology, 35*, 1283–1296.
Lavner, J. A., & Bradbury, T. N. (2010). Patterns of change in marital satisfaction over the newlywed years. *Journal of Marriage and Family, 72*, 1171–1118.
Lindahl, K., Clements, M., & Markman, H. (1998). The development of marriage: A 9-year perspective. In T. N. Bradbury (Ed.), *The developmental course of marital dysfunction*. Cambridge, MA: Cambridge University Press.
Pineo, P. C. (1961). Disenchantment in the later years of marriage. *Marriage and Family Living, 23*, 3–11.
Sabatelli, R. M., & Shehan, C. L. (1993). Exchange and resource theories. In P. G. Boss, W. J. Doherty, R. LaRossa, W. R. Schumm, & S. K. Steinmetz (Eds.), *Sourcebook of family theories and methods: A contextualapproach* (pp. 385–411). New York: Plenum.
Spencer, J. L. (2015). Variation in marital quality in a national sample of divorced women. *Social Science Research, 49*, 16–30.
Teachman, J. (2011). Modeling repeateable events using discrete-time data: Predicting marital dissolution. *Journal of Marriage and Family, 73*, 525–540.
Terman, L. M., Buttenwieser, P., Ferguson, L. W., Johnson, W. B., & Wilson, D. P. (1938). *Psychological factors in marital happiness*. New York: McGraw-Hill.
Turney, K., & Carlson, M. J. (2011). Multipartnered fertility and depression among fragile families. *Journal of Marriage and Family, 73*, 570–587.
Vaillant, C. O., & Vaillant, G. E. (1993). Is the U-curve of marital satisfaction an illusion? A 40-year study of marriage. *Journal of Marriage and the Family, 55*, 230–239.
VanLaningham, J., Johnson, D. R., & Amato, P. R. (2001). Marital happiness, marital duration, and the U-shaped curve: Evidence from a five-wave panel study. *Social Forces, 78*, 1313–1341.
White, L. K., & Booth, A. (1985). The quality and stability of remarriages: The role of stepchildren. *American Sociological Review, 50*, 689–698.

Paul R. Amato is the Arnold and Bette Hoffman Emeritus Professor of Family Sociology and Demography at Pennsylvania State University. His research intrests include the causes and consequences of separation and divorce, marriage and marital quality, parent-child relationships, psychological distress and well-being over the life course.

Spencer L. James is an Assistant Professor in the School of Family Life, Brigham Young University. His research focuses on marriage and the family.

Part IV
Childhood and Adolescent Social Networks

Chapter 8
The Evolution of Youth Friendship Networks from 6th to 12th Grade: School Transitions, Popularity and Centrality

Diane H. Felmlee, Cassie McMillan, Paulina Inara Rodis, and D. Wayne Osgood

This chapter focuses on the crucial role of friendship networks in adolescent life. Previous work documents numerous benefits of strong friendship connections for young people, with improvements in health (Ueno 2005; Umberson et al. 2010), academic outcomes (Vaquera and Kao 2008), economic prospects (Shi and Moody 2017), and prosocial behavior (Rodkin and Hanish 2007). Social networks also play an important role in influencing the quality and stability of informal and intimate relationships (e.g., Felmlee 2001; Flynn et al. 2014). Yet, with few exceptions (e.g., Moody et al. 2011), we know little about the ways in which the crucial, linked bonds of youth friendships evolve and change, especially over extended intervals of time. The bulk of research on young people's friendship networks concentrates instead on cross-sectional data based on small samples or on relatively short panel studies. Literature reviews and meta-analyses call for more longitudinal studies and designs in this area (Newcomb and Bagwell 1995; Poulin and Chan 2010). One of the main purposes of this study, therefore, is to examine changes in youth friendship networks over a relatively long period of time.

The developmental processes of aging and maturation over the life course, as well as fluctuations in contextual factors, are apt to contribute to substantial alterations in adolescent friendships, creating patterns that may not be readily visible on the basis of one or two data points. In addition, almost all young people experience significant life transitions when they matriculate from elementary school to middle school and then from middle to high school. These transitions pose noteworthy challenges that are likely to influence youth friendships substantially. A better understanding of these types of changes in adolescents' social networks can provide additional information to support students as they progress through adolescence.

D. H. Felmlee (✉) · C. McMillan · P. Inara Rodis · D. W. Osgood
Department of Sociology and Criminology, Pennsylvania State University, University Park, PA, USA
e-mail: dhf12@psu.edu

D. F. Alwin et al. (eds.), *Social Networks and the Life Course*, Frontiers in Sociology and Social Research 2, https://doi.org/10.1007/978-3-319-71544-5_8

Greater knowledge of shifting relationship patterns also can help to inform developmental life course theories.

The first purpose of this study is to document changes in youth friendship networks over six years, beginning in 6th grade and ending in 12th. Second, building on a life course perspective, we examine the degree to which two life transitions for young people influence their friendship networks, those of departing elementary school to attend middle school and leaving middle school to attend high school. Our primary focus will be on changes in two central social network dimensions, those of indegree, or popularity, and network centrality. We use data from the Promoting School-Community Partnerships to Enhance Resilience (PROSPER) study, which provides us with a uniquely large sample of over 50 adolescent friendship networks. We begin with an overview of relevant literature.

Adolescent Friendship Networks

Friendships prove to be valuable for youth in a number of ways. For instance, these intimate relationships help adolescents manage the pressures of growing up, as well as provide them with opportunities to develop independence outside of their families and imitate routines they learn from observing adults (Bagwell and Schmidt 2011; Giordano 2003). Additionally, adolescents' social networks influence the socialization of several developmental trajectories, including those associated with education (Vaquera and Kao 2008), health (Umberson et al. 2010), and supportive and problematic behavior (Rodkin and Hanish 2007).

Considerable research contributes to an understanding of the social network properties that shape youth friendships and their behavior (Felmlee and Faris 2013). For example, centrality in adolescent friendship networks influences academic outcomes (Calvó-Armengol et al. 2009), school aggression and victimization (Faris and Felmlee 2014), and prosocial and antisocial behavior styles (Gest et al. 2001). The multiple network connections of parents, romantic partners, and peers also contribute to shape the stability and quality of adolescent friendships (Flynn et al. 2014). In addition, social ties in adolescence have consequences for health outcomes (Umberson et al. 2010), and likewise, health affects adolescents' friendship ties. Youth who are in good, as compared to poor, health, for example, tend to be located in relatively central, network positions (Haas et al. 2010). Furthermore, the school and classroom ecology and structure in which many close relationships form affect youth friendship network patterns (McFarland et al. 2014).

It is important to note, too, that the effects of peer relations do not necessarily end in adolescence, and can last well into adulthood. Characteristics of early friendships, such as their quality and an individual's degree of isolation, for instance, significantly and robustly predict health quality in adulthood. Youth friendships are associated with the risk of cardiovascular disease 20 years later (Caspi et al. 2006), the prevalence of metabolic syndrome (Gustafsson et al. 2012), and various other physical health outcomes for adults (Allen et al. 2015). Early friendships also are linked to higher levels of self-worth in adulthood (Bagwell et al. 1998) and to young adults' patterns of interaction on social networking websites (Mikami et al. 2010). Furthermore, the number of friendships that an individual receives in adolescence is an indicator of future economic success; a one standard deviation increase in popularity increases earnings by 5.3% 15 years later (Shi and Moody 2017).

One characteristic of social networks on which we focus here is popularity. There are two broad ways of conceptualizing and measuring popularity in network research: perceived popularity and sociometric popularity (e.g., McElhaney et al. 2008). Perceived popularity measures how individual students see their own position within the school setting. Sociometric popularity measures how well-liked an adolescent is by his or her peers by counting the number of friendship nominations received from other students (network indegree). Perceived popularity remains useful when discussing the ways in which students' own perceptions of social acceptance may emanate from sources other than school peers, such as friends outside the school (McElhaney et al. 2008). Sociometric popularity, on the other hand, aids in placing an adolescent within the social context of his or her school setting. Moreover, high sociometric popularity is associated generally with several outcomes, such as prosocial behaviors (Allen et al. 2005; McElhaney et al. 2008; Moody et al. 2011), low levels of aggression (e.g., Faris and Felmlee 2014), and friendship stability (Bowker 2004; McElhaney et al. 2008; Moody et al. 2011). In this study, we examine measures of individual sociometric popularity, or social network indegree, which is also used as a measure of social network centrality. In addition, we examine two other measures of network centrality, betweenness and Bonacich, which will be discussed in more detail later.

Life Course Perspective

According to Benner (2011), a life course paradigm is particularly useful in furthering our knowledge of transitions in the American educational system, helping to place micro-level processes in their broader social context (see also Langenkamp 2011). Thus, we extend our social network approach to incorporate a life course perspective to better understand the ways in which young people's relationships evolve over a sequence of several school years. Multiple concepts characterize the life course framework (Alwin 2012), and in this chapter we focus on two that are of particular relevance to our topic, those of "linked lives" and "life transitions." The life course principle of "linked lives" (Elder 1994) posits that we must understand the lived experiences of individuals as occurring interdependently within a network of social relationships. One of the main goals during the life stage of adolescence is to establish and maintain friendships, that is, social connections that move beyond the family of origin (Wrzus et al. 2013). The friendship ties of youth formed within their school systems represent notable examples of linked lives worthy of investigation.

Kahn and Antonucci (1980) refer to the concept of "linked lives" as a convoy that consists of essential resources for behavior and well-being that follows people throughout the life course, and yet evolves over time. Relationships within the inner core of the convoy, such as those with close family members, tend to remain highly stable, whereas the distal connections of acquaintances and neighbors are more likely to fade away over progressive life stages (Wrzus et al. 2013).

The concept of "life transitions" represents a second elemental component of the life course paradigm that is pertinent to our project. Transitions refer to life altering events that are positioned within overall life course trajectories and encompass events that can change abruptly, such as shifts in labor force entry and exit, marriage and divorce, and entry into new levels of education (Elder 1985). Life course transitions represent turning points that are embedded in people's trajectories, and ones that often dramatically alter peoples' experiences and subsequent life paths. Educational shifts made from attendance at one level of schooling to another represent life transitions that are normative, that is, they are routine changes undertaken by many children and youth throughout our society. According to Kohli (2007), established programs in our society regulate sequential progressions through life, and these sequences produce the "institutionalized life course." Normative school transitions can be thought of as one such institutionalized, or standardized, life course progression.

The Evolution of Youth Friendships

There are a number of reasons to expect that the friendships of young people will vary considerably over the life stages of childhood and adolescence. To begin with, the formative biological, cognitive, and emotional developmental changes during these stages likely prompt multiple fluctuations in informal ties. The size of the social network expands from early childhood into the onset of adolescence and puberty, for example, increasing in numbers of both same and cross gender friendships (Feiring and Lewis 1991). Moreover, a number of children and adolescents undergo a major readjustment and paring down of their social networks due to relatively common, geographic moves undertaken by families in the U.S. (South and Haynie 2004). As youth enter their teenage years they also face repeated alterations in the ecological contexts of their social interactions, and these can either shrink or expand occasions for peer interaction. Typical growth in school and classroom size as young people progress through the educational system, for instance, is apt to inhibit the development of close relationships. Novel opportunities to engage in sports and clubs could enhance the chances of establishing a new friend (Schaefer et al. 2011), but also contribute to the loss of former ties between adolescents who no longer share common activities.

Although the bulk of research on youth friendships tends to be cross-sectional (Newcomb and Bagwell 1995), several recent studies utilize longitudinal designs. Over-time investigations tend to uncover evidence of extensive fluctuations in youth's social ties (e.g., Berndt and Hawkins 1985; Bowker 2004; Branje et al. 2007; Chan and Poulin 2007; Hartl et al. 2015; McElhaney et al. 2008; Parker and Seal 1996; Poulin and Chan 2010; Selfhout et al. 2008). For instance, about half of friendships change over the school year (e.g., Berndt and Hoyle 1985; Bowker 2004; Değirmencioğlu et al. 1998), and the likelihood of friendship alterations increases further as the time period between points of measurement lengthens. Based on a subset of the sample of the same schools used in the current study, only one in seven (15%) of friendships that began in 6th grade persisted until the 9th grade (Moody et al. 2011). Beginning with 7th grade and ending in the senior year of high school, Hartl et al. (2015) followed youth for an even longer period and revealed that only a tiny fraction of friendships (1%) remained stable over this more extensive period of time (see also Chap. 9, in this volume); almost all friendship network ties changed completely.

Given the elevated levels of friendship instability during the school years, it may not be surprising that research tends to find that youth report fewer friendships over time (e.g., Berndt et al. 1999; Hardy et al. 2002; Kingery et al. 2011; Temkin et al. 2015). Moreover, older youth lose more friendships than those who are younger. Berndt and Hoyle (1985), for example, find that unlike elementary students, 8th graders lost more friends than they gained over the course of the school year. Friendships that are not reciprocal, that is, those not reported by both members, tend to be particularly unstable (Berndt and Keefe 1995; Değirmencioğlu et al. 1998; Hardy et al. 2002; Moody et al. 2011; Sentse et al. 2014), whereas friendships between those with more in common last longer (Hafen et al. 2011; Hartl et al. 2015; Selfhout et al. 2009). Finally, as students age, the quality of their friendships increases (Berndt and Hawkins 1985; Bowker 2004; Selfhout et al. 2008), which suggests that although quantity may shrink, the value of the existing friendships may improve.

Social network researchers are often interested in identifying which individuals are the most central, or the most important and prominent, in the network (Wasserman and Faust 1994). In the current study, we use three common measures of friendship network centrality: indegree, Bonacich, and betweenness. While all three measures quantify the importance of an individual's unique location in a network, each is defined and calculated differently. Indegree, which is often conceptualized as sociometric popularity, is a simple sum of the number of friendship nominations received by each individual. Bonacich centrality expands upon the concept of indegree by not only considering the number of nominations received by a student, but by weighting an individual's centrality by the popularity of each nominator. Accordingly, students with high Bonacich centrality receive many friendship nominations from other, highly popular students, whereas those low in centrality receive few (or no) nominations from popular peers. Betweenness centrality, on the other hand, is a measure of how frequently a given individual falls on the shortest path of ties that connects any two other network members. Betweenness is interpreted as the degree to which an actor connects disparate parts of the network. Those high in betweenness friendship centrality provide a link between students who otherwise would be distantly, or not at all, connected.

We use all three centrality measures to test our first hypothesis regarding changes in friendship over time. As a result of the findings in the extant literature, as well as our lengthy study, we first hypothesize that individual-level sociometric centrality will decrease over the course of the study from 6th to 12th grade. The time span under consideration is, to the best of our knowledge, one of the longest periods that has been considered in current research.

H1: Friendship network popularity and centrality will decrease over time from 6th grade until 12th grade, as measured by indegree (or sociometric popularity), Bonacich centrality, and betweenness centrality.

Normative School Transitions

Every fall, countless children and adolescents embark on a trip to a new school as they matriculate to the next level in the U.S. system of education. This change in schooling often represents a risky time for youth, both on an academic and social level (Langenkamp 2010), and one which entails a range of taxing adjustments. For example, normative transitions are often associated with more challenging academics and placements in classrooms with numerous new classmates. When young people move between schools, they also must adjust to different teachers, mentors, counselors, coaches, and support staff. In other words, school transitions are characterized by changes from routine to unfamiliar and unpredictable environments (Caspi and Moffitt 1993), which may have long-lasting implications.

Research repeatedly finds that students' grades, school engagement, and academic outcomes suffer following a change in schools (Blyth et al. 1983; Kingery et al. 2011; Roderick 2003; Seidman et al. 1994). Making a transition to a new high school, rather than staying in the same school, for example, is associated with a lower likelihood of achieving high grades throughout the high school years (Felmlee et al. 2018). In contrast, much less research examines the possible social and emotional consequences associated with matriculation to a new school. Those that do examine emotional consequences find that youth exhibit higher levels of anxiety and depression (e.g., Benner and Graham 2009; Newman et al. 2007) and lower levels of self-esteem (e.g., Barber and Olsen 2004; Blyth et al. 1983; Hirsch and Rapkin 1987; Seidman et al. 1994; Wigfield et al. 1991).

Research that examines the social ramifications of school transitions often documents negative consequences. For example, transitions to new schools are associated with fewer close friendships (Berndt and Hawkins 1985), high levels of turnover in best friends (Aikins et al. 2005), increases in loneliness (Benner and Graham 2009), and a decrease in the numbers of reciprocated friendships and old friends (Hardy et al. 2002). A few studies, on the other hand, uncover mixed results or no negative effects (e.g., Temkin et al. 2015; Wallis and Barrett 1998; Weiss and Bearman 2007). Additional research documents that the consequences of school changes also depend on the number of schools involved in the shift. When multiple feeder schools, rather than a single feeder school, matriculate into one higher level school, adolescents experience less connected friendships, higher friendship instability across the transition, and increased social distance and segregation (Temkin et al. 2015). Friendship quality matters as well. High quality friendships, or those with more intimacy, openness, and warmth, demonstrate greater stability during matriculation to a new school than do those of lower quality (Aikins et al. 2005). Finally, students who encounter several transitions during their educational career face even higher penalties associated with their compounded school changes (Blyth et al. 1983; Crockett et al. 1989; Temkin et al. 2015).

The majority of studies that follow children and adolescents during the period before and after a school transition concentrate on the shift from elementary to middle school (Benner 2011), in part, because this transition is believed to be particularly demanding for youth (Barber and Olsen 2004; Blyth et al. 1983; McDougall and Hymel 1998). Yet the shift to high school can be difficult as well, and this transition has important, long-term implications for adolescents (Benner 2011). As a result, the current study considers the effects of both types of transitions – elementary school to middle school and middle school to high school.

Much of the existing research on school transitions also focuses solely on the year prior to and the year immediately following a move to a different school (Benner 2011). While this allows scholars to examine the immediate consequences of a major life transition, studies of possible long-term consequences are not possible, given the limited time frame of most data sources. Moreover, negative costs of such an event may be limited primarily to the period directly following a transition, such that adolescents actually recover or return to their pre-transition statuses sometime after the move (Barber and Olsen 2004; Blyth et al. 1983; Wallis and Barrett 1998; Wigfield et al. 1991). Longer longitudinal study designs are needed to investigate such a possibility. Furthermore, with few exceptions (e.g., Tempkin et al. 2015; Weiss and Bearman 2007), research does not directly compare outcomes in schools that experience transitions with those in schools without such transitions (Benner 2011). These comparisons are necessary to control for universal, developmental changes that occur among youth, regardless of school changes, and also influence their friendships.

One main goal of this project, therefore, is to examine the direct effects of school transitions on friendship networks over an extended period of time from 6th grade to 12th grade. By examining networks over the latter half of adolescence, this study is able to examine whether the consequences of school transitions are long-lasting. Furthermore, we consider the timing of the transition, whether it occurs between 6th and 7th grade or 8th and 9th grade, and hypothesize that school transitions at both times will be damaging for popularity and centrality. These two transitions represent the modal times to transition in our sample, with 84.31% experiencing a school transition between 8th and 9th grade and 35.29% experiencing a transition between 6th and 7th grades. Finally, we not only follow students over a particularly lengthy period, we also directly compare outcomes for students in schools that transition with those in non-transition schools.

H2: Friendship network popularity and centrality will all decline following normative school transitions, as measured by indegree (or sociometric popularity), Bonacich centrality, and betweenness centrality.

Data and Methods

Sample

We analyze data on 14,462 students who attended middle and/or high school at one of 28 small public school districts that participated in the Promoting School-Community Partnerships to Enhance Resilience (PROSPER) study. Participating districts were required to enroll between 1300 and 5200 students, 15% of which must have been eligible for free or reduced lunch. All school districts were located in rural or semi-rural communities, half of which were located in Iowa and the other half were located in Pennsylvania. Half of the schools in the study were randomly assigned to participate in both family- and school-based substance abuse prevention programs during respondents' 6th and 7th grade years.

Two different cohorts participated in the study: the first includes students who entered 6th grade in 2002 and the second includes those who entered in 2003. Students completed self-administered surveys during the fall and spring semesters of their 6th grade year and during the spring semesters of their 7th through 12th grade years, resulting in eight waves of data that each include an average of roughly 9000 students. Response and participant retention rates were generally high, with response rates varying from 86–90% across the eight waves and students participating in an average of 4.18 waves of the study. Students who participated were asked to nominate up to seven of their closest within school and within grade friends and approximately 83.0% of these nominations were successfully tied to other students participating in the study. It was necessary to omit five friendship networks from our analysis because of irregularities (e.g. one school was affected by a fire), resulting in a final sample of 51 networks.

Definition of Variables

At each wave of the study, participants were asked, "Who are your best and closest friends in your grade?" They were able to nominate a maximum of two "best friends" and up to five "other close friends," permitting each student to nominate as many as seven peers. For the current study, we only consider nominations of within-community and within-grade friends, from which we constructed a total of 51 global friendship networks.

Normative school transitions are one of the independent variables of interest in our study. All districts in our sample transitioned students at least one time during the course of the study and six districts transitioned youth twice. However, the districts vary in the timing of their transitions: 35.3% transition students between 6th and 7th grade, 84.3% transition them between 8th and 9th grade, and 7.8% did so between 9th and 10th grade. To specifically test for the effect of school transitions, we include two binary variables in our models. One measures the effect of transitions between 6th and 7th grade and one measures the effect of transitions between 8th and 9th grade (1 = experienced transition). Due to small sample sizes, we did not include a binary variable modeling transitions experience between 9th and 10th grade. Despite exhibiting different transition patterns, the school districts are relatively alike. All districts are located in communities that have similar population sizes, median household incomes, average test scores, dropout rates, and proportions of students on free/reduced lunch.

We add several control variables that also could be associated with an individual's tendencies to both nominate friends and receive nominations from their peers. Binary indicators are included to control for the state where the school is located (0 = Pennsylvania, 1 = Iowa), cohort (1 = first cohort), gender (1 = girl), race (1 = white), free/reduced lunch status (1 = receives free/reduced lunch), and living with both biological parents (1 = lives with both). Additionally, we include measures of school adjustment and bonding (measured using 8 survey items, with a higher score indicating greater adjustment/bonding), delinquency (measured using 12 survey items, with a higher score indicating higher delinquency), and school performance (1 = mostly F's, 5 = mostly A's).

Centrality Measures and Plan of Analysis

We consider individual students' positions in their social networks by examining three measures of individual centrality: indegree, Bonacich, and betweenness centrality. We first calculated indegree, or a count of the friendship nominations that each student receives from his or her peers (Wasserman and Faust 1994). Previous research often uses indegree as a measure of individual popularity (Moody et al. 2011; Valente et al. 2005). While students could only nominate a maximum of seven friends, there was no limit to the number of nominations a student could receive. In our sample, the highest indegree student received 20 friendship nominations.

Our second network measure, Bonacich centrality, not only considers the number of nominations received by a student; it also considers how popular these students are in the overall network. A student with high Bonacich centrality would not only receive multiple friendship nominations, but these nominations would be from other, highly popular students. Finally, we consider betweenness centrality, a measure calculated by first summing the total number of geodesics (i.e. shortest paths that connect all pairs of students) in the entire network. Then, for each focal student we calculate the proportion of geodesics on which he or she is situated. Students located on many of these shortest paths are assigned high betweenness scores, indicating that they play a crucial role in connecting a friendship network.

To test our research questions regarding the relationship between school transitions and individual centrality, we apply ordinary least squares (OLS) and negative binomial regressions to our data. OLS models are used to predict the effect of transitions on our continuous measures of centrality, Bonacich and betweenness. Negative binomial regressions predict the effect of transitions on indegree, a count measure of centrality.

Results

Descriptive Statistics

There are slightly more girls in the sample than boys and 84.9% of the students are white (see Table 8.1). Over all eight waves, the average indegree, or number of friendship nominations received by each student, was 3.343, yet some students receive as many as 20 or as few as 0 nominations. Average Bonacich centrality over the eight waves was 0.763, where a measure of 1 approximately corresponds to an individual who does not have particularly high or low centrality. This indicates that, on average, Bonacich centrality tends to be relatively low. Finally, average individual betweenness centrality was 0.017, suggesting that when we consider all of the shortest paths that connect each possible pair of students, an average student would intersect 1.7% of these paths.

Table 8.1 Descriptive statistics averaged over waves 1–8

	Mean	S.D.	Max.	Min.
Indegree	3.343	2.676	0	20
Bonacich centrality[a]	0.763	0.589	0	4.555
Betweenness centrality[a]	0.017	0.028	0	0.466
Transition after 6th Grade	0.353	–	0	1
Transition after 8th Grade	0.843	–	0	1
Transition after 9th Grade	0.078	–	0	1
Cohort 1	0.491	–	0	1
Iowa	0.507	–	0	1
Female	0.515	–	0	1
White	0.849	–	0	1
Free/reduced lunch	0.268	–	0	1
School adjustment & bonding	3.723	0.751	1	5
Lives with both bio. parents	0.604	0.489	0	1
Grades	4.041	0.902	1	5
Delinquency	1.472	2.437	0	12

[a]Statistics are for the non-transformed centrality measures

Table 8.2 Average measures of individual centrality by wave

	Indegree		Bonacich[a]		Betweenness[a]	
	Mean	S.D.	Mean	S.D.	Mean	S.D.
6th (Fall)	3.355	2.635	0.785	0.574	0.023	0.035
6th (Spring)	3.824	2.842	0.805	0.563	0.022	0.032
7th	4.041	2.962	0.814	0.554	0.020	0.027
8th	3.931	2.781	0.821	0.547	0.019	0.026
9th	3.402	2.584	0.781	0.582	0.016	0.024
10th	2.934	2.392	0.733	0.613	0.015	0.026
11th	2.562	2.236	0.697	0.626	0.012	0.023
12th	2.224	2.052	0.636	0.637	0.010	0.021

[a]Statistics are for the non-transformed centrality measures

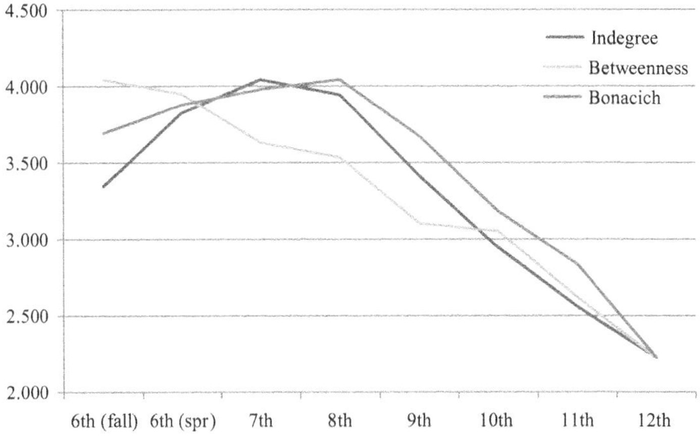

Fig. 8.1 Normalized average centrality scores by grade scaled by the minimum and maximum of indegree [2.224, 4.041]

Individual Centrality Over Time

After considering how average individual centrality varies across the eight waves of our study, it is clear that average individual centrality tends to reach its maximum in early adolescence (See Table 8.2 and Fig. 8.1).[1] Average betweenness reaches its peak during 6th grade (0.023), indegree does so in 7th (4.041), and Bonacich in 8th (0.821). After reaching this maximum, average centrality declines steadily until

[1] Due to the different ranges of each centrality measure (see Table 8.1), we normalize each measure of centrality and then scale the normalized values so that their minimum and maximum reflect those of indegree. This normalization technique is only used in Fig. 8.1 in order to better visualize how the overall trends in individual centrality relate to one another. When interpreting our findings, we will refer to the actual averages of each centrality measure which are presented in Table 8.2.

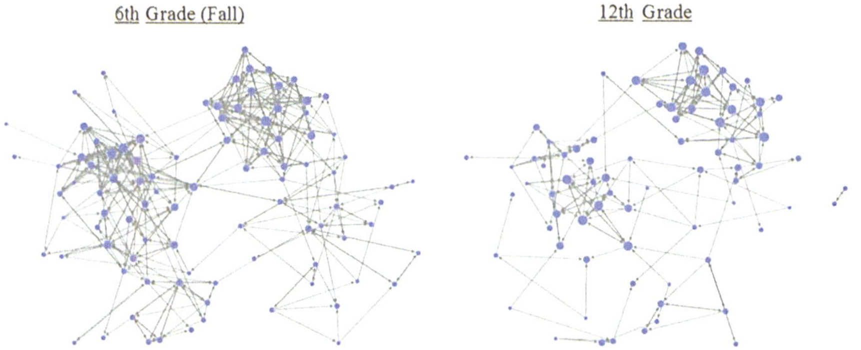

Fig. 8.2 Friendship networks in a small school district during 6th and 12th grade
Nodes are sized by indegree. 12th grade nodes have been locked in place so that each node is in the same exact location as it was in 6th grade. Isolates and missing nodes were removed from both graphs

12th grade when all three centrality measures reach their minimum value (betweenness = 0.010, indegree = 2.224, Bonacich = 0.636).

To further illustrate how individual centrality varies over time, we present illustrations of two network graphs in Fig. 8.2. Both graphs illustrate friendship networks from a small school in our sample at two different time points. In each graph, circles represent students, lines represent friendship ties, and arrows indicate the direction of each friendship nomination. Circles have been sized to reflect indegree, so that larger circles are more popular. Students' locations in the friendship network visualization have been locked in place, meaning that a student's location in the 6th grade graph is the same as his or her location in the twelfth grade graph. Over time, there are two core friendship groups that remain relatively intact: one is located on the left half of the graph and the other is located on the right. The network is heavily segregated by gender. Most girls are situated on the left side of the graph, while most boys are on the right side. In 6th grade, each group appears to be particularly well connected; students tend to be friends with many of the peers in their same group, often those of the same gender. However, in 12th grade, each group appears to be substantially less connected than they were during the first wave of the study. There are fewer friendship ties in 12th grade, less gender segregation, and the two larger groups appear to be further partitioned into sub-groups.

School Transitions and Centrality

To better understand why this decline in centrality occurs during late adolescence, we further considered the role played by school transitions. Using negative binomial regressions, we present two models where respondent indegree, or popularity, is the dependent variable. The 7th grade model only includes respondents who participated in the survey during their 7th grade year, and the 9th grade model only includes respondents who participated in their 9th grade year. Students who did not attend school during either of these years were not included in our analysis, because it was not possible to measure how this normative transition was associated with their individual centrality.

The effects for several covariates are significant and in the expected direction. In 7th and 9th grade, both girls and whites received more nominations than boys and non-whites, respectively. Those who received free or reduced lunch tended to be less popular. Living with both biological parents and earning higher grades were significantly associated with higher indegree. 7th graders with higher levels of delinquency tended to attract more friendship nominations, however this association was not significant in the 9th grade model.

As hypothesized, school transitions are negatively associated with receiving friendship nominations. Students attending schools that experience a transition between 6th and 7th grade receive fewer friendship nominations in 7th grade, the year immediately following the transition ($b = -0.069$, $p < 0.001$) (see Table 8.3). In other words, a student who changed schools received roughly 7% fewer nominations in their 7th grade year compared to those who did not transition. Similarly, students who transition between 8th and 9th grade also receive fewer friendship nominations in 9th grade than do their peers who do not transition at this time ($b = -0.078$, $p < 0.01$). These students tend to receive almost 8% fewer nominations than their peers who did not experience this school transition.

To test whether these school transitions had long-term effects on individual indegree we also ran identical models on samples of students from each grade level (analyses available on request). We find that transitions to middle school that occur between 6th and 7th grade depress popularity, as hypothesized, but this effect is significant only in the year immediately following the transition. On the other hand, transitions occurring between 8th and 9th grade appear to have long term effects on individual popularity. In both 11th and 12th grade, for example, students who transitioned to high school between 8th and 9th grade received significantly fewer friendship nominations than those who did not experience such a transition. In one exception, the 8th to 9th grade transition was not associated with significant differences in popularity for 10th graders. This exception is likely a function of additional school changes that occurred in several districts between 9th and 10th grades, a transition that also was associated with lower indegree, or popularity.

The relationship between changing schools between 8th and 9th grade and average individual indegree, or friendship popularity, throughout adolescence can be visualized in Fig. 8.3. During 6th through 8th grade, average indegree tends to be similar among all students. However, students who change schools between 8th and 9th grade have significantly lower average indegree in 9th grade, the year directly following the transition, as compared to those who remain within the same school between 8th and 9th grade. With the exception of 10th grade, this pattern continues for all later grades, suggesting that normative school transitions have long-term consequences on friendship networks and individual popularity. Changing schools

Table 8.3 Negative binomial regression on indegree for students in grades 7 and 9

	7th Grade		9th Grade	
Transition After 6th	−0.069	***		
	(0.016)			
Transition After 8th			−0.078	**
			(0.024)	
Girl	0.219	***	0.218	***
	(0.016)		(0.016)	
White	0.083	***	0.124	***
	(0.023)		(0.024)	
Free/Reduced Lunch	−0.263	***	−0.246	***
	(0.018)		(0.020)	
School Bonding	−0.012		0.017	
	(0.012)		(0.013)	
Lives with Both Bio. Parents	0.093	***	0.105	***
	(0.017)		(0.017)	
Grades	0.105	***	0.106	***
	(0.010)		(0.010)	
Delinquency	0.016	***	0.006	
	(0.004)		(0.003)	
Number of Students	0.000	***	0.000	***
	(0.000)		(0.000)	
Iowa	0.012		−0.015	
	(0.015)		(0.018)	
Cohort 1	−0.007		−0.011	
	(0.015)		(0.016)	
Constant	0.913	***	0.674	***
	(0.061)		(0.065)	
n	8893		8923	
Pseudo R^2	0.019		0.021	
ln alpha	−1.387	***	−1.384	***
	(0.032)		(0.036)	
Log likelihood	−20,880		−19,798	
Wald Chi Square (11)	825.52	***	827.80	***

Standard errors for b-coefficients are in parentheticals.
$^{**}p < 0.01$, $^{***}p < 0.001$

between 8th and 9th grade not only reduces friendship popularity in the year directly following the transition, it continues to be negatively associated with popularity throughout students' high school experiences.

Bonacich and Betweenness Centrality Next, we examine the association between school transitions in regressions in which two other measures of network centrality,

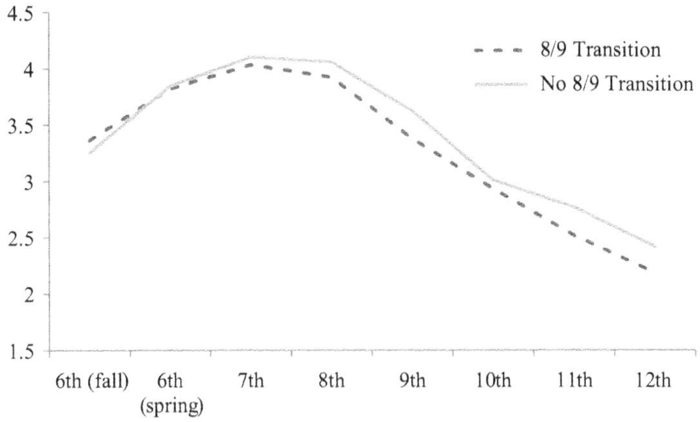

Fig. 8.3 Average indegree for students experiencing a transition to a new school from 8th grade to 9th grade compared to those who did not change schools between 8th and 9th grades
Note: Differences in average indegree were statistically significant for 9th, 11th, and 12th grade, as confirmed by a two-tailed t-test ($p < 0.05$). Differences for all other grades were not statistically significant

or importance, serve as the dependent variables, the transformed Bonacich[2] and the transformed betweenness[3] centrality measures (see Table 8.4). For both centrality variables, an OLS regression is estimated for 7th and 9th grade respondents, because those grades represent the years that follow typical school transitions in our data. Overall, control variables show similar patterns as those discussed in the indegree model. Furthermore, these results complement the previous findings regarding school transitions and popularity. In 7th grade, students that recently experienced a school transition, as compared to those who did not transition, have Bonacich centrality measures that are significantly lower ($b = -0.031$, $p < 0.001$). This trend is also observed among 9th grade students who recently transitioned; those who just started high school tend to have lower Bonacich centrality measures when compared to their non-transitioning peers ($b = -0.078$, $p < 0.01$). In the 7th grade model for betweenness, experiencing a recent transition is again associated with lower centrality ($b = -0.023$, $p < 0.001$). However, in the 9th grade model, the coefficient

[2] In friendship data, measures of Bonacich centrality tend to be heavily skewed because popularity tends to be a rare phenomenon. Because of this skew, we transform our measures on Bonacich Centrality by using the following procedure: first, extreme outliers, or those with Bonacich scores above 3.25, were recoded to equal 3.25. Less than 0.1% of all cases reported scores this high, and this score was more than four standard deviations greater than the mean. After recoding, we took the square root of the updated parameter to reduce skew.

[3] In our data, variance for individual betweenness is highly dependent on network size (Osgood et al. 2013) and, like Bonacich centrality, the distribution tends to be positively skewed. With these issues in mind, we apply the following transformation to our betweenness measures: each original score is multiplied by the ratio of the individual's network size to the mean size of the 51 total networks in our sample (mean = 214 students). Then, the cube root is taken of the result.

Table 8.4 OLS regression on Bonacich and betweenness centrality for students in post-transition grades, Grades 7 and 9

	Bonacich				Betweenness			
	7th Grade		9th Grade		7th Grade		9th Grade	
Transition Post-6th	−0.031	***			−0.023	***		
	(0.007)				(0.003)			
Transition Post-8th			−0.078	**			−0.004	
			(0.024)				(0.004)	
Student Network Size	0.000	**	0.000		0.000	***	0.000	**
	(0.000)		(0.000)		(0.000)		(0.000)	
Iowa	−0.033		−0.002		0.017	***	−0.009	**
	(0.007)		(0.008)		(0.003)		(0.003)	
Cohort 1	−0.001		−0.010		−0.002		0.000	
	(0.006)		(0.007)		(0.003)		(0.003)	
Girl	0.119	***	0.070	***	0.037	***	0.036	***
	(0.016)		(0.007)		(0.003)		(0.003)	
White	0.049	***	0.089	***	0.014	**	0.019	***
	(0.010)		(0.010)		(0.004)		(0.004)	
Free/Reduced Lunch	−0.136	***	−0.131	***	−0.025	***	−0.028	***
	(0.007)		(0.009)		(0.003)		(0.003)	
School Bonding	−0.011	*	0.035	***	−0.001		0.012	***
	(0.005)		(0.006)		(0.002)		(0.002)	
Lives with Both Parents	0.032	***	0.062	***	0.004		0.012	***
	(0.007)		(0.007)		(0.003)		(0.003)	
Grades	0.058	***	0.072	***	0.010	***	0.012	***
	(0.004)		(0.004)		(0.002)		(0.002)	
Delinquency	0.006	**	0.000		0.001		0.001	
	(0.002)		(0.001)		(0.001)		(0.001)	
Constant	0.516	***	0.324	***	0.123	***	0.049	***
	(0.026)		(0.028)		(0.011)		(0.011)	
R^2	0.137		0.157		0.051		0.069	
n	8893		8923		8893		8923	

for experiencing a transition between 8th and 9th grade is no longer significant, but is still in the expected direction ($b = -0.004$).[4] Again, transitions between 8th and 9th grade appear to be associated with long-term declines for both centrality measures, while transitions between 6th and 7th grade were only detrimental in the short term.

[4]Patterns of school transitions can be complex, and we consider only the modal prototypes for our sample (i.e., shifts from 6th to 7th and 8th to 9th grade). A larger sample of schools is needed to compare the possible influence of alternative configurations.

Supplemental Analyses

In analyses not shown here, we found no evidence that the effects of school transitions on friendship centrality differed for boys and girls by including interactions between gender and the school transition variables. Both boys and girls experience significant declines in popularity and centrality following these types of school changes.

We also explored alternative explanations that, in addition to school transitions, may help illuminate the steep decline observed in all three measures of network popularity and centrality during late adolescence. First, we considered whether the decline in popularity is associated with romantic relationships, which become increasingly common as adolescents progress through high school. As a result of a process known as dyadic withdrawal, individuals in romantic relationships tend to report smaller friendship networks than their single peers (Johnson and Leslie 1982). However, in our sample, dyadic withdrawal does not appear to explain the decline in network popularity. Even though more students report romantic relationships at the later waves of the survey, respondents who report these relationships tend to make between 21% and 42% *more* friendship nominations than their single peers. There is no evidence that adolescents are replacing their friendship ties with romantic partners, and the increase in dating relationships does not appear to explain the simultaneous decline in friendship centrality.

As noted earlier, our measures of friendship centrality only consider within-grade nominations. It is possible that the decline that is observed is the result of an increase in friendships with peers in other grades, friendships which may form more frequently as adolescents enter high school. However, our supplementary analyses suggest that this is unlikely to be the case. Students were asked to report how many out-of-grade friends they had in the last five waves of the survey. Starting in 8th grade, respondents reported an average of 5.81 out-of-grade friends. By 12th grade, this average had slightly decreased to 5.67 friends. Since the number of out-of-grade friends did not increase in late adolescence, it is unlikely that out-of-grade friends supplant in-grade friends over the secondary school years.[5]

Discussion

In sum, we document a striking pattern of change in student's social ties over a six year period, highlighting the importance of examining the friendship networks of youth over an extended period of time. Adolescents' degree of centrality, or prominence, in their friendship network diminishes substantially over time,

[5] Changes in missing data over time do not appear to account for the decline in network centrality, furthermore. The decrease in degree over time, for example, also is apparent in the number of names per respondent written down in the raw data, prior to coding of the names.

subsequent to peaks that occur during middle school, as depicted by all three of our network centrality measures. Average network popularity, or indegree, and our weighted popularity measure, Bonacich centrality, both increase until 7th or 8th grade, and then drop continuously until they reach their lowest level in 12th grade. Betweenness centrality, which reflects the tendency to act as an intermediary between disconnected sections of the network, shows steady decreases that begin in the spring of 6th grade and also continue through until the end of high school. This overall pattern of shrinking social network centrality occurs for those in all types of schools, regardless of patterns in school transitions.

There could be several explanations for the decline in measures of network popularity and centrality during secondary school. Contextual changes in education likely contribute. The relatively large size of most secondary classes, as compared to those in middle school, could make it increasingly difficult to maintain multiple friendships, for instance. Other explanations focus on the social maturation of youth as they proceed through the teen years. As youth age, their friendships become closer and more involved (e.g., Berndt and Hawkins 1985; Bowker 2004), and so older youth may focus their social energies on smaller numbers of friends, with whom they are more intimate. Furthermore, as youth enter the later teen years, develop more independence from families, and begin to drive themselves to social engagements, they gain additional control over their interactions. Such control might lead to increased time spent largely with an inner circle of friends.

We also see that normative school transitions that take place between levels of education are linked to reductions in the degree to which adolescents find themselves positioned in central and popular locations in their friendship networks. As expected, and while controlling for other factors, our measures of network centrality tend to exhibit decreases following a school transition that occurs either from elementary to middle school or from middle to high school. With one exception (betweenness centrality for the high school transition), the declines in centrality were statistically significant for the various types of centrality and for both levels of school transitions. Furthermore, this additional drop in network centrality associated with the high school transition extends over the course of high school. Those high school seniors who had changed schools between 8th and 9th grade continued to be chosen as friends by significantly fewer classmates, on average, than those who did not experience such a school transition. In other words, we see long-term detrimental, social effects of the high school transition that remain for a period of four years, lasting from 9th through 12th grade.

The detrimental effect of school transitions on social relationships likely occurs for several reasons. Adolescents often have relatively few opportunities to interact with former friends after leaving a feeder school, for instance, and instead face situations in classes, clubs, and athletic activities in which they encounter numerous new peers. The lack of mutual contact with old friends is apt to lead to the deterioration of previous friendships, while the formation of close bonds with new acquaintances likely takes time to unfold. In addition, young people shift from a situation in which they are the oldest, and most experienced, members of their schools, into an environment in which they occupy the "lowest rung of the ladder" in the school-wide, social system. This experience of reduced status makes those who completed a transition less socially prominent and increases their vulnerability to social exclusion. School mobility also severs relationships with familiar teachers, counselors, and coaches, some of whom may have eased young people's paths to social connectedness, by encouraging their involvement in school activities and providing emotional support. Moreover, the academic challenges inherent in a novel, more difficult, learning environment likely influence adolescents' social ties. A new high school, for example, may enforce unique and demanding educational expectations for achievement that make it difficult to find the time required to maintain one's informal connections.

A number of key concepts from a life course perspective help to place our findings in a broader, theoretical context. The life course concept of linked lives, for example, provides a direct connection to the social network framework employed in our study. Our findings illustrate that the social convoy of networked lives that carries youth along over the bumps and disequilibria during primary and secondary schooling undergoes a dramatic contraction into a smaller number of main friendships. Presumably many early ties, and those most peripheral, are lost, while a more durable core remains (Wrzus et al. 2013). The life course notion of transitions represents another key life course concept that gives impetus to our work. Our analyses contribute additional support for the argument that major life transitions can substantially alter an individual's life path. Here we see that the normative, life transition of matriculating to a new school decreases adolescents' likelihood of being central in their friendship networks. The importance that a life course framework places on following individuals over critical life cycle periods of growth and change also is reinforced by the intriguing long-term friendship network patterns revealed in our longitudinal study. More generally, our research demonstrates the utility of building on both the life course and social network paradigms in examining social processes.

In addition to the unique theoretical focus, the strengths of our study include the longitudinal design, the large sample of youth and networks, and our ability to directly compare students who experience school transitions with those who do not. Nevertheless, there remain certain limitations. For example, our networks do not include data regarding friendships that occur either outside of grade or outside of school, and therefore our conclusions are limited to the effects of transitions on within grade friendships. While supplementary analyses suggest that estimates of these other types of friendships do not alter our main conclusions, additional research is required to explore this issue more formally. Moreover, our sample consists largely of rural and semi-rural schools. Schools from large urban locations are underrepresented, and more research is needed in such settings.

We also do not have information regarding young people's satisfaction with their friendships. It remains possible that although friendship network popularity and centrality decline over time, the smaller numbers of friendships that remain are more rewarding to individuals than were the larger numbers of past friendships. As mentioned previously, as youth mature, they may learn to concentrate their social efforts on a particularly satisfying, select group of confidants. Some also may seize upon a shift to a more promising educational and social setting as an opportunity to reinvent themselves and then expand, rather than shrink, their social network (e.g., Weiss and Bearman 2007). Nevertheless, the modal experience of decreasing network centrality over time reported here likely leads many teenagers to feel that they are becoming peripheral to their own social group, and such feelings could be stressful and deleterious. For others the ramifications may be even more dire, leading to isolation and increased loneliness (Benner 2011), disengagement from social activities, and enhancing the likelihood of dropping out of school (Neild 2009). Additional research is needed to investigate the emotional and academic consequences for teens of the friendship trends described in this project.

In conclusion, the friendship network popularity and centrality of young people diminishes remarkably during the period between 6th and 12th grade. This decline is accelerated when youth matriculate to a new school either between 6th and 7th grade, or between 8th and 9th grade and the negative effects can persist through high school. Our study calls attention to this noteworthy phenomenon in which the linked lives of adolescents experience significant paring down during secondary school. Furthermore, the social handicaps that are accrued early in adolescence, triggered in part by a normative life transition, likely do not end in 12th grade. These disadvantages have the potential to accumulate over the life course and portend subsequent problems for adults, highlighting the need for further study.

Acknowledgments The authors thank Duane Alwin and David Johnson for helpful comments on our work. This research was supported in part by the W.T. Grant Foundation (8316) and National Institute on Drug Abuse (RO1-DA08225; T32-DA-017629; F31-DA-024497), and uses data from PROSPER, a project directed by R. L. Spoth and funded by grant RO1-DA013709 from the National Institute on Drug Abuse. Support also came from the Pennsylvania State University and the National Science Foundation under an IGERT award # DGE-1144860, Big Data Social Science.

References

Aikins, J. W., Bierman, K. L., & Parker, J. G. (2005). Navigating the transition to junior high school: The influence of pre-transition friendship and self-system characteristics. *Social Development, 14*(1), 42–60.

Allen, J. P., Porter, M. R., McFarland, F. C., Marsh, P., & McElhaney, K. B. (2005). The two faces of adolescents' success with peers: Adolescent popularity, social adaptation, and deviant behavior. *Child Development, 76*(3), 747–760.

Allen, J. P., Uchino, B. N., & Hafen, C. A. (2015). Running with the pack: Teen peer-relationship qualities as predictors of adult physical health. *Psychological Science, 26*(10), 1574–1583.

Alwin, D. F. (2012). Integrating varieties of life course concepts. *The Journals of Gerontology: Series B, 67B*(2), 206–220.

Bagwell, C., & Schmidt, M. E. (2011). *Friendships in childhood & adolescence*. New York: Guilford Press.

Bagwell, C. L., Newcomb, A. F., & Bukowski, W. M. (1998). Preadolescent friendship and peer rejection as predictors of adult adjustment. *Child Development, 69*(1), 140–153.

Barber, B., & Olsen, J. (2004). Assessing the transitions to middle and high school. *Journal of Adolescent Research, 19*(1), 3–30.
Benner, A. D. (2011). The transition to high school: Current knowledge, future directions. *Educational Psychology Review, 23*(3), 299–328.
Benner, A. D., & Graham, S. (2009). The transition to high school as a developmental process among multiethnic urban youth. *Child Development, 80*(2), 356–376.
Berndt, T. J., & Hawkins, J. A. (1985). *The effects of friendships on students' adjustment after the transition to junior high school*. Paper presented at the meeting of the American Educational Research Association, Chicago.
Berndt, T. J., & Hoyle, S. G. (1985). Stability and change in childhood and adolescent friendships. *Developmental Psychology, 21*(6), 1007.
Berndt, T. J., & Keefe, K. (1995). Friends' influence on adolescents' adjustment to school. *Child Development, 66*(5), 1312–1329.
Berndt, T. J., Hawkins, J. A., & Jiao, Z. (1999). Influences of friends and friendships on adjustment to junior high school. *Merrill-Palmer Quarterly (1982-), 45*(1), 13–41.
Blyth, D., Simmons, R., & Carlton-Ford, S. (1983). The adjustment of early adolescents to school transitions. *The Journal of Early Adolescence, 3*(1–2), 105–120. https://doi.org/10.1177/027243168331008.
Bowker, A. (2004). Predicting friendship stability during early adolescence. *The Journal of Early Adolescence, 24*(2), 85–112.
Branje, S. J. T., Frijns, T., Finkenauer, C., Engels, R., & Meeus, W. (2007). You are my best friend: Commitment and stability in adolescents' same-sex friendships. *Personal Relationships, 14*(4), 587–603.
Calvó-Armengol, A., Patacchini, E., & Zenou, Y. (2009). Peer effects and social networks in education. *The Review of Economic Studies, 76*(4), 1239–1267.
Caspi, A., & Moffitt, T. E. (1993). When do individual differences matter? A paradoxical theory of personality coherence. *Psychological Inquiry, 4*(4), 247–271.
Caspi, A., Harrington, H., Moffitt, T. E., Milne, B. J., & Poulton, R. (2006). Socially isolated children 20 years later: Risk of cardiovascular disease. *Archives of Pediatrics & Adolescent Medicine, 160*(8), 805–811.
Chan, A., & Poulin, F. (2007). Monthly changes in the composition of friendship networks in early adolescence. *Merrill-Palmer Quarterly, 53*(4), 578–602.
Crockett, L., Petersen, A., Graber, J., Schulenberg, J., & Ebata, A. (1989). School transitions and adjustment during early adolescence. *The Journal of Early Adolescence, 9*(3), 181–210.
Değirmencioğlu, S. M., Urberg, K. A., Tolson, J. M., & Richard, P. (1998). Adolescent friendship networks: Continuity and change over the school year. *Merrill-Palmer Quarterly (1982-), 44*(3), 313–337.
Elder, G. H. (1994). Time, human agency, and social change: Perspectives on the life course. *Social Psychology Quarterly, 57*(1), 4–15.
Elder, G. H., & Social Science Research Council (U.S.). (1985). *Life course dynamics: Trajectories and transitions, 1968–1980*. Ithaca: Cornell University Press.
Faris, R., & Felmlee, D. (2014). Casualties of social combat: School networks of peer victimization and their consequences. *American Sociological Review, 79*(2), 228–257.
Feiring, C., & Lewis, M. (1991). The development of social networks from early to middle childhood: Gender differences and the relation to school competence. *Sex Roles, 25*(3–4), 237–253.
Felmlee, D. H. (2001). No couple is an island: A social network perspective on dyadic stability. *Social Forces, 79*(4), 1259–1287.
Felmlee, D., & Faris, R. (2013). Interaction in social networks. In J. DeLamater & A. Ward (Eds.), *Handbook of social psychology* (pp. 439–464). Dordrecht: Springer. Retrieved May 24, 2017, http://link.springer.com/chapter/10.1007/978-94-007-6772-0_15
Felmlee, D., McMillan, C., Inara Rodis, P., & Osgood, D. W. (2018). Falling behind: Lingering costs of the high school transition for youth friendships and GPA. *Sociology of Education*, 91(2).

Flynn, H. K., Felmlee, D. H., & Conger, R. D. (2014). The social context of adolescent friendships parents, peers, and romantic partners. *Youth Society, 49*(5), 679–705.
Gest, S. D., Graham-Bermann, S. A., & Hartup, W. W. (2001). Peer experience: Common and unique features of number of friendships, social network centrality, and sociometric status. *Social Development, 10*(1), 23–40.
Giordano, P. C. (2003). Relationships in adolescence. *Annual Review of Sociology, 29*(1), 257–281.
Gustafsson, P. E., Janlert, U., Theorell, T., Westerlund, H., & Hammarström, A. (2012). Do peer relations in adolescence influence health in adulthood? Peer problems in the school setting and the metabolic syndrome in middle-age. *PLoS One, 7*(6), e39385.
Haas, S. A., Schaefer, D. R., & Kornienko, O. (2010). Health and the structure of adolescent social networks. *Journal of Health and Social Behavior, 51*(4), 424–439.
Hafen, C. A., Laursen, B., Burk, W. J., Kerr, M., & Stattin, H. (2011). Homophily in stable and unstable adolescent friendships: Similarity breeds constancy. *Personality and Individual Differences, 51*(5), 607–612.
Hardy, C. L., Bukowski, W. M., & Sippola, L. K. (2002). Stability and change in peer relationships during the transition to middle-level school. *The Journal of Early Adolescence, 22*(2), 117–142.
Hartl, A. C., Laursen, B., & Cillessen, A. H. N. (2015). A survival analysis of adolescent friendships the downside of dissimilarity. *Psychological Science, 26*(8), 1304–1315.
Hirsch, B. J., & Rapkin, B. D. (1987). The transition to junior high school: A longitudinal study of self-esteem, psychological symptomatology, school life, and social support. *Child Development, 58*(5), 1235–1243.
Johnson, M. P., & Leslie, L. (1982). Couple involvement and network structure: A test of the dyadic withdrawal hypothesis. *Social Psychology Quarterly, 45*(1), 34.
Kahn, R. L., & Antonucci, T. C. (1980). Convoys over the life course: Attachment roles and social support. *Life Span Development, 3*, 253–267.
Kingery, J. N., Erdley, C. A., & Marshall, K. C. (2011). Peer acceptance and friendship as predictors of early adolescents' adjustment across the middle school transition. *Merrill-Palmer Quarterly (1982-), 57*(3), 215–243.
Kohli, M. (2007). The institutionalization of the life course: Looking back to look ahead. *Research in Human Development, 4*(3–4), 253–271.
Langenkamp, A. G. (2010). Academic vulnerability and resilience during the transition to high school: The role of social relationships and district context. *Sociology of Education, 83*(1), 1–19.
Langenkamp, A. G. (2011). Effects of educational transitions on students' academic trajectory: A life course perspective. *Sociological Perspectives, 54*(4), 497–520.
McDougall, P., & Hymel, S. (1998). Moving into middle school: Individual differences in the transition experience. *Canadian Journal of Behavioural Science/Revue Canadienne Des Sciences Du Comportement, 30*(2), 108–120.
McElhaney, K. B., Antonishak, J., & Allen, J. P. (2008). They like me, they like me not: Popularity and adolescents perceptions of acceptance predicting social functioning over time. *Child Development, 79*(3), 720–731.
McFarland, D., Moody, J., Diehl, D., Smith, J., & Thomas, R. (2014). Network ecology and adolescent social structure. *American Sociological Review, 79*(6), 1088–1121.
Mikami, A. Y., Szwedo, D. E., Allen, J. P., Evans, M. A., & Hare, A. L. (2010). Adolescent peer relationships and behavior problems predict young adults' communication on social networking websites. *Developmental Psychology, 46*(1), 46–56.
Moody, J., Brynildsen, W. D., Osgood, D. W., Feinberg, M. E., & Gest, S. (2011). Popularity trajectories and substance use in early adolescence. *Social Networks, 33*(2), 101–112.
Neild, R. C. (2009). Falling off track during the transition to high school: What we know and what can be done. *The Future of Children, 19*(1), 53–76.
Newcomb, A. F., & Bagwell, C. L. (1995). Children's friendship relations: A meta-analytic review. *Psychological Bulletin, 117*(2), 306–347.

Newman, B. M., Newman, P. R., Griffen, S., & O'Connor, K. (2007). The relationship of social support to depressive symptoms during the transition to high school. *Adolescence, 42*(167), 441.

Osgood, D. W., Ragan, D. T., Wallace, L., Gest, S. D., Feinberg, M. E., & Moody, J. (2013). Peers and the emergence of alcohol use: Influence and selection processes in adolescent friendship networks. *Journal of Research on Adolescence: The Official Journal of the Society for Research on Adolescence, 23*(3).

Parker, J. G., & Seal, J. (1996). Forming, losing, renewing, and replacing friendships: Applying temporal parameters to the assessment of children's friendship experiences. *Child Development, 67*(5), 2248–2268.

Poulin, F., & Chan, A. (2010). Friendship stability and change in childhood and adolescence. *Developmental Review, 30*(3), 257–272.

Roderick, M. (2003). What's happening to the boys?: Early high school experiences and school outcomes among African American male adolescents in Chicago. *Urban Education, 38*(5), 538–607.

Rodkin, P. C., & Hanish, L. D. (2007). *Social network analysis and children's peer relationships* (Vol. 118). San Francisco: Jossey-Bass.

Schaefer, D. R., Simpkins, S. D., Vest, A. E., & Price, C. D. (2011). The contribution of extracurricular activities to adolescent friendships: New insights through social network analysis. *Developmental Psychology, 47*(4), 1141.

Seidman, E., Allen, L., Aber, J. L., Mitchell, C., & Feinman, J. (1994). The impact of school transitions in early adolescence on the self-system and perceived social context of poor urban youth. *Child Development, 65*(2), 507–522.

Selfhout, M., Branje, S., & Meeus, W. (2008). The development of delinquency and perceived friendship quality in adolescent best friendship dyads. *Journal of Abnormal Child Psychology, 36*(4), 471–485.

Selfhout, M. H. W., Branje, S. J. T., ter Bogt, T. F. M., & Meeus, W. H. J. (2009). The role of music preferences in early adolescents' friendship formation and stability. *Journal of Adolescence, 32*(1), 95–107.

Sentse, M., Kiuru, N., Veenstra, R., & Salmivalli, C. (2014). A social network approach to the interplay between adolescents' bullying and likeability over time. *Journal of Youth and Adolescence, 43*(9), 1409–1420. https://doi.org/http://dx.doi.org.ezaccess.libraries.psu.edu/10.1007/s10964-014-0129-4.

Shi, Y., & Moody, J. (2017). Most likely to succeed: Long-run returns to adolescent popularity. *Social Currents, 4*(1), 13–33.

South, S. J., & Haynie, D. L. (2004). Friendship networks of mobile adolescents. *Social Forces, 83*(1), 315–350.

Temkin, D. A., Gest, S. D., Osgood, D. W., Feinberg, M., & Moody, J. (2015). Social network implications of normative school transitions in non-urban school districts. *Youth & Society*, 0044118X15607164.

Ueno, K. (2005). The effects of friendship networks on adolescent depressive symptoms. *Social Science Research, 34*(3), 484–510.

Umberson, D., Crosnoe, R., & Reczek, C. (2010). Social relationships and health behavior across the life course. *Annual Review of Sociology, 36*(1), 139–157.

Valente, T. W., Unger, J. B., & Johnson, C. A. (2005). Do popular students smoke? The association between popularity and smoking among middle school students. *Journal of Adolescent Health, 37*(4), 323–329.

Vaquera, E., & Kao, G. (2008). Do you like me as much as i like you? Friendship reciprocity and its effects on school outcomes among adolescents. *Social Science Research, 37*(1), 55–72.

Wallis, J., & Barrett, P. (1998). Adolescent adjustment and the transition to high school. *Journal of Child and Family Studies, 7*(1), 43–58.

Wasserman, S., & Faust, K. (1994). *12th grade nodes have been locked in place* (Vol. 8). Cambridge: Cambridge University Press.

Weiss, C. C., & Bearman, P. S. (2007). Fresh starts: Reinvestigating the effects of the transition to high school on student outcomes. *American Journal of Education, 113*(3), 395–421.
Wigfield, A., Eccles, J. S., Mac Iver, D., Reuman, D. A., & Midgley, C. (1991). Transitions during early adolescence: Changes in children's domain-specific self-perceptions and general self-esteem across the transition to junior high school. *Developmental Psychology, 27*(4), 552–565.
Wrzus, C., Hänel, M., Wagner, J., & Neyer, F. J. (2013). Social network changes and life events across the life span: A meta-analysis. *Psychological Bulletin, 139*(1), 53–80.

Diane H. Felmlee is Professor of Sociology and Demography at Pennsylvania State University and Research Associate in the Population Research Institute. Her interests lie at the intersection of social networks and life course studies, pursuing research on aggression and friendship networks, cyberbullying, and gender inequalities.

Cassie McMillan is a graduate student in the Department of Sociology and Criminology at Pennsylvania State University.

Paulina Inara Rodis is a graduate student in the Department of Sociology and Criminology at Pennsylvania State University.

D. Wayne Osgood is Professor Emeritus of Criminology and Sociology in the Department of Sociology and Criminology at Pennsylvania State University. His research interests include the connection of adolescents' friendship networks to delinquency and other problem behaviors during adolescence and early adulthood.

Chapter 9
Best Friends for Now: Friendship Network Stability and Adolescents' Life Course Goals

Robert Faris and Diane H. Felmlee

Introduction

Of all the possible life goals for young Americans, perhaps the most common and conventional are to finish school and begin a family. These are each important in their own right. Educational aspirations inspire shorter term, specific achievement objectives, which are then associated with increased effort and subsequent degree attainment (Domina et al. 2011; Harackiewicz et al. 2002; Duncan et al. 1972). The desire for a family has long predicted ultimate fertility (Coombs 1974). These aspirations—for completing education and forming a family—are important organizers of the life course, guiding critical choices with lifelong implications.

There is no logical reason these different goals should be linked, no *a priori* reason to expect youth who want to go to college also want to start a family. Despite this, these goals are not, by and large, selected *a la carte*, and most young people seek to accomplish all of them at some point (Nurmi 1992). This is because these are more than personal goals, they are the culturally accepted hallmarks of adulthood. And while there are other routes to adulthood, few who reach these milestones would be mistaken for an adolescent. Indeed, *society as we know it* depends on the near-universal reproduction of these core life goals. They are taken for granted not only by those who hold them, but by scholars as well, who have tended to focus either on the tendency to form goals at all (regardless of content), or on one particular type of life goal, such as educational aspirations, rather than this cultural

R. Faris (✉)
Department of Sociology, University of California at Davis, Davis, CA, USA
e-mail: rwfaris@ucdavis.edu

D. H. Felmlee
Department of Sociology and Criminology, Pennsylvania State University, University Park, PA, USA
e-mail: dhf12@psu.edu

D. F. Alwin et al. (eds.), *Social Networks and the Life Course*, Frontiers in Sociology and Social Research 2, https://doi.org/10.1007/978-3-319-71544-5_9

package of goals. We are unaware of any studies examining the joint adoption of educational and familial goals.

Here, we examine the social processes by which this package of goals assumes importance for adolescents, concentrating our investigation on the dynamics of school-based friendship networks. Inspired by the life course tradition as well as by social psychological conceptions of the self, we advance an argument centered on the role of stable and enduring friendships in shaping adolescents' life goals.

We begin our analyses by developing a series of measures of tie stability and examine friendship stability for a sample of school-aged youth over a relatively extended period of time. Next, we investigate the possible consequences of friendship impermanence on outcomes for young people, by testing for the effects of stability on adolescents' future life goals. We argue that adolescents' tendency to embrace life goals regarding plans for schooling and family is influenced not only by the goals of their friends, but by how long those friendships have lasted. We examine our arguments using a panel study of over 1600 adolescents in North Carolina. The data include school social network information, derived from individual friendship nominations, from seven waves of data collection spanning 4.5 years. The three cohorts included in the study are followed from 6th, 7th, and 8th grade through 10th, 11th, and 12th grade. We close with a discussion of methodological issues and future research directions.

Theory and Literature

Life Goals

The bulk of research on life goals focuses on their consequences rather than their origins. The former are generally positive in nature. Goal-orientation is not only a temporary state, but may cumulate into a more stable personal trait, with additional positive consequences for life chances (Payne et al. 2007). But the benefits of life goal formation can be immediate: Among adolescents, for example, merely thinking and writing about life goals—whatever they may be— significantly increases subjective well-being (King et al. 2016) and reduces illness-related visits to health centers (Harrist et al. 2007). Having life goals is negatively associated with juvenile delinquency (Newberry and Duncan 2001), and youth who invest meaning in their goals are less likely to abuse alcohol or engage in other health risk behaviors (Williams et al. 2000b; Palfai and Weafer 2006). Aside from categorizing them as extrinsic or intrinsic, this body of research generally sidesteps the substantive details of the goals themselves, focusing more on the contrast between those who have them and those who do not.

Meanwhile, the literatures that explicitly consider the substance of these goals—for educational attainment and family planning—are too vast to be adequately summarized here, although we can offer a few important insights to be gleaned. First, these literatures are largely separated by substantive, theoretical, methodological, and disciplinary divisions. Second, to the extent that scholars attempt to explain the formation of these goals, as opposed to their consequences, they have largely focused on individual, structural, or familial factors (e.g., Sewell and Shah 1968). The literature on educational aspirations more thoroughly investigates peer influences, from early work on supportive peers (Duncan et al. 1968), to research on tracking (Hallinan 1982; Buchmann and Dalton 2002), to economic research on peer effects via random assignment (B. Sacerdote 2001). With respect to family planning, peer influences have generally been limited to sexual behavior (e.g., Bearman and Brukner 2015) or actual fertility itself (Brown and Theobold 1999), rather than the desire for such. Finally, in both fields, the influence of peers has been restricted to attitudinal or behavioral modeling, and research has yet to explore the effect of the structure or dynamics of peer relationships, focusing, in other words, on what one's friends think and do, rather than changes to those friendships. We hope to contribute to both literatures by addressing the joint embrace of educational and familial aspirations and by showing how they are shaped by the dynamics of peer relationships, particularly their instability.

Peer Relationships

A major task of childhood and adolescence involves the establishment of peer friendship ties (e.g., Berndt 2002). Much research has been conducted on the developmental implications of the characteristics and strength of these ties (e.g., Billy and Udry 1985; Demir and Urberg 2004; Nangle et al. 2003), invariably concluding that friendship quality is positively associated with psychosocial adjustment. Friendships between children and youth offer social support and serve as the context for social, emotional, and cognitive development (e.g. Berndt 2002; Hartup 1996). The presence of a friend also helps to buffer the effects of negative experiences on young people (Adams et al. 2011). Youth who lack friends, on the other hand, display a range of difficulties, such as loneliness, lower social competence, and less self-confidence (e.g., Hartup 1996; Newcomb and Bagwell 1995). Fortunately, relatively few adolescents are friendless. However, the state of friendlessness is not the only form of isolation, and the bonding on display in snapshots of a student body—either actual photos in a yearbook, or those depicted in social media—belies the fragile and fleeting nature of so many adolescent friendships. This, we argue, is a second and far more prevalent form of social isolation, and one that cannot be detected in such snapshots.

Much research has been conducted on the developmental implications of the characteristics and strength of friendships (e.g., Billy and Udry 1985; Demir and Urberg 2004; Nangle et al. 2003), invariably concluding that friendship quality is positively associated with psychosocial adjustment. Yet a meta-analysis of friendship research found that the majority of analyses are conducted in the cross section (Newcomb and Bagwell 1995) and thus at least until recently, the temporal dimension of friendships has been relatively neglected. Scholars repeatedly call for greater attention to this topic (e.g., Hartup 1996; Newcomb and Bagwell 1995), arguing that in order to be of substantial value to a young person, friendships must be long-lasting (Poulin and Chan 2010).

The relatively small number of studies on temporal patterns of friendships that do exist document considerable volatility in the networks of children and adolescents. Estimates of instability or stability vary, depending upon the grade level, the definition of friendship, and the study duration. Studies of instability over relatively short time periods of 1–5 months find that approximately one-third of children's friendships shift in composition (Chan and Poulin 2007; Poulin and Chan 2010). Several investigations that examine variation over a school year report a friendship stability/instability rate of approximately 50%, based on samples from 7th grade (Bowker 2004), grade school and middle school (Berndt and Hoyle 1985; Branje et al. 2007), and within middle and high school (Değirmencioğlu et al. 1998). The few studies that cover lengthier interludes document even higher levels of fluctuations in friendships. One such investigation reports that approximately only one in seven (15%) friendship nominations made by 6th–9th graders lasted for 4 years (Moody et al. 2011). Another finds that a scant 1% of 7th grade friendships survived until 12th grade; that is, 99% of friendships were unstable (Hartl et al. 2015). Thus, for the majority of youth, we expect relatively high levels of instability in friendships over time.

The Life Course Convoy of Linked Lives

Patterns of change and transition in close, social relationships remain critical to consider, according to a life course perspective (Elder 1994). Furthermore, people's relationships form a network of "linked lives" that prove key to their development (Elder 1998). For example, the social convoy model maintains that individuals form a network of relationships that accompanies them over the life course (Kahn and Antonucci 1980). The social convoy consists of the linked lives of core members, especially family, who remain consistent. Peripheral relationships are less stable and can terminate with changes in roles or locations (Antonucci and Akiyama 1987). The social convoy model primarily has been used to explain changes in older adult, life course transitions (Antonucci and Akiyama 1987; Kahn and Antonucci 1980), but the logic applies equally well to the relations of youth (Wrzus et al. 2013). The model suggests that having a stable convoy of core friendships, as well as family members, is likely to prove valuable to young people as they transition through the many adjustments associated with the life course evolution from the stage of childhood to that of early adulthood.

Temporal patterns in the friendships of children and youth tend to support the argument that friendship stability does, indeed, yield benefits, whereas instability is costly. Greater instability in popularity (e.g., network indegree) in either direction, for example, contributes to increased substance use on the part of adolescents

(Moody et al. 2011). Changes in social connections also exhibit links to bullying and aggression. Overtly aggressive kids have difficulty maintaining friendships (Ellis and Zarbatany 2007), and friendship stability is associated with low rates of aggression victimization (Poulin and Chan 2010). Moreover, mobile adolescents who relocate within or between communities, and by definition likely undergo substantial network alterations, also experience a host of negative, social outcomes (South and Haynie 2004). Damaging outcomes, which can be long-lasting, include a decrease in popularity, centrality, and prestige in friendship networks.

At the same time, there remain a few exceptions or qualifications to the typical effects of youth friendship stability and instability. The retention of an identical pattern of social ties within the school year may not be beneficial in certain situations for young people. The experience of constant, relative isolation over time can be detrimental (Witvliet et al. 2010), for example, as can the stability of problematic friendships. Behavioral problems increase on the part of students who retain 6th grade friendships with peers who already are high in behavioral problems (Berndt et al. 1999). In addition, declines in network size may not produce costly outcomes in cases in which shrinkage is associated with the ending of troublesome connections. Decreases in friendship size for kids at a summer camp were not problematic, for instance, apparently because the terminated relationships had been conflictual (Parker and Seal 1996). Furthermore, certain positive outcomes associated with stable friendships can depend on the quality of the maintained friendships. The endurance of high quality, but not low quality, friendships contributes to increases in sociability and leadership (Berndt et al. 1999) for junior high students.

Conceptualization and Consequences of Friendship Instability

Given that friendship networks can fluctuate in a multitude of ways (Parker and Seal 1996), the concept of stability represents a complex dimension of close ties. Youth can lose friendships, form new ones, renew old friendships, or replace one friend with another. Friendship networks, thus, can expand as new ties are added, shrink as ties are dissolved, or remain unchanged. Seeming steadiness in network size over time also can hide instances of variability. In cases in which the same number of new and old ties enter and exit an individual's network, size will remain constant and thus mask considerable shifts in friendships. For this reason, we focus on friendship *consistency*, specifically, the number of times the same friendship nominations were repeated over the period of observation.

Consistent, durable friendships ground adolescents, laying a foundation for a coherent sense of self upon which expectations for the future can be erected. During a formative stage of the life course, lasting friendships reinforce an adolescent's identity, while limiting the range of possibilities it can take. Unmoored from these bonds, adolescents whose friendships are fleeting are free to reinvent themselves and to drift. Experiencing such turnover in their social lives, they are also more likely to orient themselves to the present instead of planning for the future (Gould

2003). Additionally, the investment and commitment required to maintain friendships across the vagaries of middle and high school are also likely associated with goal orientation. For these reasons, we propose our primary hypothesis: *Adolescents with more consistent friendships over time will care more about finishing high school, going to college, and starting a family.*

Sources of Instability and Potential Confounders

We expect a good deal of change to occur among the friendships of youth, especially over longer periods of time. There are a great many reasons for turnover, each of which could potentially confound the relationship between friendship consistency and future life goals. Friendship changes originate in three different domains: (1) the external context, (2) individual characteristics of the youth, and (3) processes at the dyad or peer group level.

First, external events and context shape the opportunities that children and adolescents confront in forming and maintaining close ties with a peer. A number of such external influences exist. The most obvious, and potentially powerful event consists of moving between schools and/or communities. The rate at which U.S. children change schools has grown over time, due both to switches between public and private schools as well as to residential mobility (Swanson and Schneider 1999). This type of external move likely entails dramatic fluctuations in social networks, with the ending of established friendships and the initiation of new ones, as youth enter new schools and perhaps novel neighborhoods and communities, as well. Second, even for many youth who remain within the same school system, shifts in classroom composition that typically occur between grades are apt to influence their friendship networks. The size of such an effect may depend on the degree to which particular classrooms foster distinct opportunities to maintain and initiate social ties, such as interaction during class time and joint activities.

Moreover, the large majority of U.S. children experience at least two major school transitions, beginning with the shift from primary to middle school, and later, the transition from middle to high school. Both of these experiences typically present significant challenges for youth, and each type of transition significantly reduces friendship popularity and network centrality (see Chapter in this volume). In addition, other noteworthy, contextual factors affect the social networks of students as they progress through the school system, in particular, extracurricular activities. Joint participation in extracurricular activities, such as sports, music, art, and school clubs, is associated with current friendships among youth and the development of new friendships, even over a period of 8 months (Schaefer et al. 2011). School clubs and activities facilitate friendships by providing opportunities for interaction with peers and a chance to engage with others in common interests.

Characteristics of children and youth themselves also can affect patterns of developing, maintaining, and ending social ties. Children suffering from depression, for example, are more apt than their non-depressed peers to experience friendship instability between months (Chan and Poulin 2007). Externalizing behavior and lower levels of prosocial behavior on the part of a youth relate to friendship instability in clique membership (Witvliet et al. 2010). Age of the individual, on the other hand, has a positive association with stability (Değirmencioğlu et al. 1998).

Finally, interaction processes at the level of the dyad or peer group also contribute to the solidity of social connections. Involvement in aggression, either as perpetrator or victim, for instance, is not uncommon in schools and can embroil friends (Faris and Felmlee 2014; Felmlee and Faris 2016), yet it also increases the likelihood of terminating friendships (Ellis and Zarbatany 2007). In addition, strategies for the resolution of conflict used by friends predict 7th grade friendship stability, with boys' friendship endurance enhanced by minimization strategies, and that of girls improved instead by confrontation (Bowker 2016). Demographic or other differences between friends also can reduce the duration of the relationship; interracial friendships, for example, are less stable than those within the same racial group (Hallinan and Williams 1987). Finally, network size also represents one component that relates negatively to friendship permanence, with large networks demonstrating particularly high levels of alterations in ties over time (Chan and Poulin 2007). This may be due to the greater availability of alternative friendships, which also predicts network change (Branje et al. 2007).

Accordingly, we examine sources of peer influence on the life goals of youth by investigating the effect of fleeting, versus enduring, peer friendships on these goals. Based on previous findings in the literature reviewed above, we control for a range of factors that may be associated with friendship stability in our multivariate analyses. For example, empirically we account for residential moves, school transitions, and participation in extracurricular activities. In addition, we include measures for internalizing and externalizing symptoms as well as age. We also control for involvement in bullying and aggression, either as victim or perpetrator, as well as social network centrality and social isolation. Furthermore, because friendship duration is linked to various indicators of friendship quality, we include measures for reciprocity and average emotional closeness felt for friends. Finally, we also control for the prior importance of life goals (averaged across all prior waves of data) as well as friends' life goals, to capture peer influence processes.

Data and Methods

Data for this analysis come from the *Contexts of Adolescent Substance Use* (hereafter, *Contexts*), a large, longitudinal social network panel survey of adolescents in three counties in North Carolina. At the outset, all students in grades 6th, 7th, and 8th (cohort 1, 2, and 3, respectively) who were attending one of the 19 public schools in the three counties were eligible to participate, and eligibility was extended to any student who joined those grades in the study schools. Paper surveys were administered in schools by trained data collectors every 6 months, starting with wave 1 in the spring of 2001, until wave 6, in the fall of 2004. The 7th and final wave of data was collected 1 year after wave 6, in the fall of 2005. Both students and parents were given the opportunity to refuse to participate in the study which was funded by the NIH and the CDC and approved by the Institutional Review Board of the University of North Carolina at Chapel Hill. Response rates were high, ranging from 89% (wave 1) to 73% (wave 7), and 7174 students participated in at least one wave of data collection.

Analytic Sample

After wave 5, however, the largest county dropped out of the study (for reasons unrelated to the project), cutting the sample by more than half, to 3379 eligible students. Because we are interested here in longer term outcomes, we focus on future life goals as observed in wave 7, the last moment of observation before the oldest cohort graduated from high school. While 2406 students participated in wave 7, 793 of them were excluded because they did not participate in any prior wave of data. Our analytic sample thus includes the 1613 students who participated in wave 7 and at least one other wave, and who had valid responses on the life goals scale. We used multiple imputation with ten imputations to address missing data on independent variables. We also identified and removed four influential outliers (with extremely low values on goals and extremely high values on other measures), resulting in a final sample of 1609.

Measures

The dependent variable, ***future life goals***, is observed at wave 7 and is a scale comprised of three items measuring the importance (in four levels, from "not at all important" to "very important") of: "finishing high school," "going to college," and "having a happy family life" (alpha = 0.71 at wave 7, and averaged 0.75 in prior waves). The key independent variable, ***friendship consistency***, was derived from the friendship network questions asking students to name up to five of their best friends (out of school nominations were allowed, but are treated as missing). It is defined as the average number of times each friendship nomination was made across all waves of participation, divided by the number of waves in which the student participated. Take, for example, a student, *A*, who participated in five waves of data collection. If *A* nominated *B* in all five waves, and nominated *C* in one wave, *A*'s average number of nominations would be 3 (the average of 5 and 1), and her friendship consistency would be 3/5 = 0.6. If *A* had nominated all new friends at each wave, her friendship consistency would be 1/5 = .2. The measure ranges from 0.14, which indicates that a student participated in all seven waves and never repeated a friendship nomination, to 1, which indicates that the student had no changes in her friendship nominations across all waves of participation. We also test a variety of other approaches to measuring this concept, discussed in detail in the robustness section below.

At the individual level, we control for participation in extracurricular activities, specifically, ***academic honors clubs, sports, service clubs, yearbook,*** and ***performing arts***, each of which is a binary indicator that is averaged across all waves of participation (so 1 indicates that the student was in honors at every wave of participation, and so on). We control for two symptoms of internalizing symptoms: ***anxiety*** (average alpha = 0.88) is measured by a scale of the following items: "I felt sick in my stomach," "I got mad easily," "I had trouble getting my breath [don't count asthma or exercise]," "I was tired a lot," "I worried about what was going to happen," "I worried when I went to bed at night," "I often worried about bad things happening to me" (Reynolds and Richmond 1979). ***Depression*** (average alpha = 0.90) is a scale of the following items: "I hated myself," "I was a bad person," and "I did everything wrong" (Angold et al. 1995). ***Delinquency*** (average alpha = 0.75) was measured by the frequency the student "skipped school," "damaged school or other property that did not belong to you," "cheated on a test," and "gone to school but skipped class" (Farrell et al. 2000).

At the family level, we control for a ***single parent home*** and ***no parent attended college*** using binary indicators. ***Parental attachment*** (alpha average = 0.80) is measured by the following (asked about each parent): "how often does he/she hug or kiss you?", "how close do you feel toward him/her?", and "how close do you think she feels toward you?" We control for ***residential move*** with a binary indicator of whether the student's family residence changed at all during the study period. Finally, in the peer context, we controlled for social status using Bonacich social network centrality.

We initially anticipated that life goals might be influenced not only by the overall average level of social network centrality, but by the *trajectory* of centrality. Accordingly, we estimated within-individual OLS regressions of centrality with time (in years) and time squared (to capture nonlinearity) as the independent variables. This produces estimates of ***initial centrality, centrality slope, and centrality quadratic.*** Aggression and victimization were measured as the number of schoolmates the student "picked on or was mean to," and the number who "picked on or were mean to you." We also estimated within-individual regressions for these variables (although without a quadratic term because these questions were only introduced at wave 4), yielding ***initial aggression, aggression slope, initial victimization,*** and ***victimization slope.*** We control for ***social isolation*** using a binary indicator of lacking friends (e.g., degree = 0), averaged across prior waves. ***Friends' goals*** is the average life goal score of the friends nominated by the respondent at wave 6. ***Reciprocity*** represents the percent of friendship nominations that were reciprocated, averaged across prior waves. Finally, ***closeness to friends*** was an average of how close (on a four point scale, from "very close" to "not close at all") the respondent felt toward her friends, averaged across prior waves. We also control for gender, race and ethnicity, and grade in school. We estimate our models using OLS regressions including school fixed effects to adjust for unobserved heterogeneity across schools.

Results

Descriptive

The sample consists of 57% females and 43% males, with approximately half white (49%), 42% African-American, 3% Latino/a, and 5% other race/ethnicities. Students participated in honors clubs and performing arts about a quarter of the time, service clubs about a third of the time, and sports over half. They felt anxious more often than they felt depressed. Family conflict was relatively uncommon, and most students felt close to their parents. Both aggression and victimization tended to decline over time, on average.

Perhaps not surprisingly, we find that most students are invested in their future: The scale average for future goals was 2.83 out of a maximum of 3 (Table 9.1), meaning that most adolescents view graduating from high school (97%), going to college (80%), and having a happy family life (89%) are "very important." This figure is nearly identical to the average of the prior waves, implying substantial stability in goal orientation.

Friendship Stability

We find evidence of a high degree of turnover in friendship nominations: The average friendship consistency score was 0.35 (Table 9.1), which is equivalent to a student participating in six waves of data collection and replacing all her friends after every two waves (or every school year). Indeed, the average number of times a given friendship nomination was made is 2.1, and 49% of all adolescents had an average score of 2 or less—meaning that friends were nominated no more than two times, on average, over the course of the study. As can be seen in Fig. 9.1, the distribution of the average number of times a friend was nominated is skewed, ranging from a low of 1 to a high of close to 5, with a mode of 2, and a mean of 2.1. Nearly one-third (31%) of students in the sample replaced friends at every wave of participation. Meanwhile, only 10% had completely stable friendship networks.

The instability of adolescent friendships can be visualized more clearly in Fig. 9.2, which shows the friendship network of the largest school in the study. The leftmost panel shows the full network, and the next panel removes friendships that only existed in one wave, the next panel removes those only in two waves, and so on, until there are only a very few left. In addition to their transitory nature, most friendships were not reciprocated, and entailed only moderate levels of emotional closeness (Table 9.1).

Table 9.1 Descriptive statistics with missing data imputed

Variable	Mean	SD	Min.	Max.
Future goals[a]	2.83	0.41	0.00	3.00
Friendship consistency	0.35	0.16	0.14	1.00
Academic honors clubs	0.27	0.32	0.00	1.00
Sports	0.56	0.39	0.00	1.00
Service clubs	0.32	0.33	0.00	1.00
Yearbook	0.14	0.22	0.00	1.00
Performing arts	0.26	0.34	0.00	1.00
Anxiety	1.75	0.86	0.00	4.00
Depression	0.99	0.92	0.00	4.00
Delinquency	0.35	0.42	0.00	3.50
Cumulative GPA	2.84	0.65	1.00	4.00
Single parent home	0.34	0.47	0.00	1.00
No parent attended college	0.36	0.48	0.00	1.00
Family conflict	1.04	0.89	0.00	4.00
Attachment to parents	2.22	0.54	0.00	3.00
Any residential move	0.12	0.32	0.00	1.00
Friends' life goals	2.83	0.32	0.00	3.00
Initial network centrality	53.78	56.27	−899.22	511.37
Network centrality slope	2.65	53.09	−373.78	706.53
Network centrality quadratic	−1.67	15.84	−128.46	150.38
Initial victimization	0.80	1.42	−1.20	14.40
Victimization slope	−0.37	1.18	−11.20	3.60
Initial aggression	0.74	1.18	−1.00	7.20
Aggression slope	−0.33	1.00	−5.60	3.20
Social isolation	0.02	0.13	0.00	1.00
Average friendship reciprocity	0.33	0.21	0.00	1.00
Average closeness to friends	1.95	1.02	0.00	3.00
Prior life goals	2.86	0.29	0.00	3.00
Female	0.57	0.50	0.00	1.00
Male	0.43	0.50	0.00	1.00
White	0.49	0.50	0.00	1.00
African-American	0.42	0.49	0.00	1.00
Latino/a	0.03	0.16	0.00	1.00
Other minority	0.05	0.22	0.00	1.00
10th grade	0.36	0.48	0.00	1.00
11th grade	0.36	0.48	0.00	1.00
12th grade	0.28	0.45	0.00	1.00
School 1	0.02	0.13	0.00	1.00
School 2	0.50	0.50	0.00	1.00
School 3	0.22	0.41	0.00	1.00
School 4	0.27	0.44	0.00	1.00

N = 1609

[a]Life goals: graduating from high school, going to college, and having a happy family life

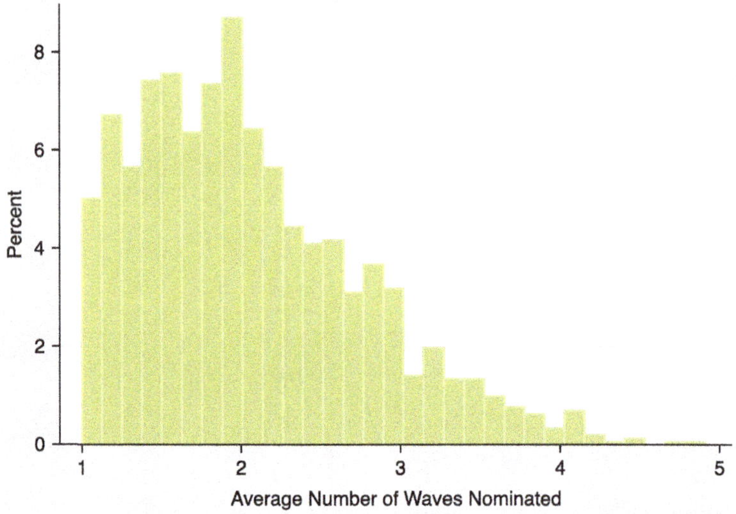

Fig. 9.1 Distribution of friendship duration

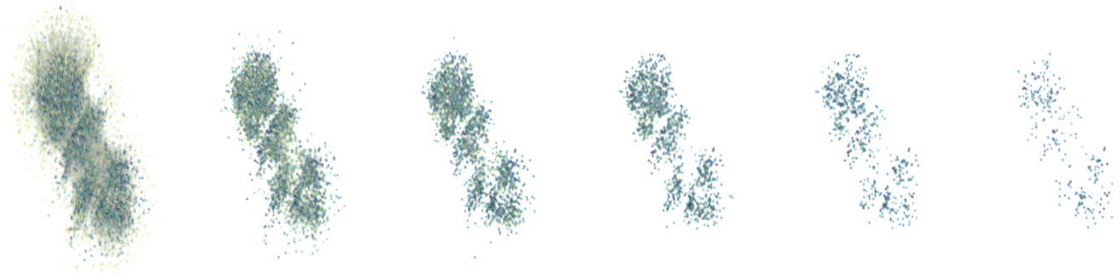

Fig. 9.2 Fleeting and enduring friendships

Life-Course Goals

Turning to the multivariate results (Table 9.2), we find that friendship consistency is significantly associated with strongly held future goals, as expected. The modal or average youth in our sample, that is, one who changed friends at every wave, had a below average predicted life goals score of 2.788, compared to 2.995 for those who maintained consistent friendships (Model 1). This is a relatively large effect size (coefficient = 0.23), considering that we control for the prior average level of life goals and how stable these goals are: 75% of students' life goals at wave 7 were within 0.23 of their prior average. Adding individual factors to the model reduces the size of the friendship consistency coefficient, but it remains a significant effect (Model 2).[1]

[1] In subsequent models we detected four influential outliers, all of which had above average levels of friendship consistency (average = 0.45), but extremely low investment in future goals (average = 0.25). In models 2–4, friendship consistency was not statistically significant when these cases were included, but had a significant positive effect in model 1 regardless of their inclusion.

Table 9.2 OLS regression of life goals[a] on individual, family, and peer factors

	Model 1		Model 2		Model 3		Model 4	
	β	S.E.	β	S.E.	β	S.E.	β	S.E.
Friendship consistency	0.237**	(0.083)	0.186*	(0.085)	0.180*	(0.085)	0.177*	(0.089)
Individual								
Academic honors clubs			−0.024	(0.041)	−0.030	(0.041)	−0.024	(0.041)
Sports			−0.014	(0.027)	−0.020	(0.027)	−0.024	(0.027)
Service clubs			0.009	(0.037)	0.006	(0.037)	0.004	(0.037)
Yearbook			−0.004	(0.049)	0.006	(0.049)	0.003	(0.049)
Performing arts			0.046	(0.032)	0.041	(0.032)	0.036	(0.033)
Anxiety			−0,009	(0.016)	−0.003	(0.016)	−0.004	(0.016)
Depression			−0.010	(0.015)	0.000	(0.015)	−0.002	(0.016)
Delinquency			0.047	(0.025)	0.057*	(0.025)	0.052*	(0.025)
Cumulative GPA			0.051**	(0.019)	0.046*	(0.019)	0.044*	(0.020)
Family								
Single parent home					0.013	(0.021)	0.012	(0.021)
No parent attended college					−0.033	(0.022)	−0.031	(0.022)
Family conflict					−0.036**	(0.014)	−0.036**	(0.014)
Attachment to parents					−0.005	(0.021)	−0.003	(0.021)
Any residential move					0.023	(0.032)	0.025	(0.033)
Peers								
Friends' life goals							0.038	(0.040)
Initial network centrality							0.000	(0.001)
Network centrality slope							0.001	(0.001)
Network centrality quadratic							0.003	(0.004)
Initial victimization							0.011	(0.020)
Victimization slope							0.002	(0.023)
Initial aggression							0.015	(0.022)
Aggression slope							0.009	(0.026)
Social isolation							−0.050	(0.096)

(continued)

Table 9.2 (continued)

	Model 1		Model 2		Model 3		Model 4	
	β	S.E.	β	S.E.	β	S.E.	β	S.E.
Average friendship reciprocity							−0.002	(0.052)
Average closeness to friends							0.007	(0.010)
F (df)	30.97***	(11)	17.98***	(20)	14.82***	(25)	10.28***	(36)

N = 1609

*p < 0.05; **p < 0.01; ***p < 0.001

[a]Life goals: graduating from high school, going to college, and having a happy family life. All models control for prior life goals, gender, race/ethnicity, grade in school, and school fixed effects (not shown)

The only individual-level factor significantly associated with life goals is GPA: Compared to a C-student, a straight-A student has a 0.10 higher predicted life goal value. Somewhat surprisingly, family factors seem to have little influence on the importance of these life goals (model 3). Only family conflict has a negative effect, albeit a small one: The difference in predicted life goals between youth from the most peaceful household and the most conflictive is 0.144. Surprisingly, delinquency also emerges as a significant, but *positive*, predictor of life goals, such that youth who skip class and cheat on tests the most often are likely to care more about their future life goals. This effect only becomes significant once family-level factors are controlled, suggesting a suppressed effect (the correlation between goals and delinquency is −0.13). Finally, adding in peer factors—including friends' life goals, adolescent network centrality, and several measures of friendship quality—has no effect on future life goals (model 4). In addition to prior life goals, all models control for gender, race/ethnicity, grade in school, and school fixed effects, but the only significant demographic factor is gender, with boys holding weaker future goals than girls (not shown).

Robustness Checks

In order to increase confidence that these results are not highly dependent on mondel specification, we engaged in a number of robustness checks. First, because our dependent variable is not normally distributed, we also estimated ordered logit models with a dependent variable that took on three levels (a value of 1 when future goals was less than 2 [3% of the sample], a value of 2 when future goals fell between 2 and 3 [21% of the sample], and a value of 3 when future goals was also 3 [76% of the sample]). Results were not substantively different. Second, we include a far greater number of controls in our models than is customary, and thus run the risk of overcontrolling. However, removing any of our controls either has no substantive effect on our results, or strengthens the effect of friendship consistency. Third, because of the complexity of measuring friendship consistency over a seven-wave panel study, we tested a series of alternative measures, including: the average number of times friends were nominated, the average number of times friends were nominated and also reciprocated (also as a percent of the number of waves of participation), as well as the *maximum* number of times a friend was nominated (and again, as a percent of waves of participation), which captured the idea that an adolescent may experience significant benefits so long as they had one enduring friendship. We found substantively similar results in all cases.

Fourth, because our dependent variable is somewhat novel, we also estimated models of each specific goal separately, finding that friendship consistency had a positive association with the importance of going to college and having a happy family life, but did not significantly affect the importance of graduating from high school—most likely because there was so little variation on this item (97% of students said this was very important). Fifth, our data asked students to name their five best friends using school rosters, and out-of-school friends were excluded from network measures. While we know nothing about the stability of these friendships, we were able to control for the average number of out-of-school friends. This had no substantive effect on the key independent variables and was not statistically significant. Finally, we tested for nonlinearity in the effect of friendship consistency, anticipating that unchanging, "frozen" friendship networks might not have the same effects. The quadratic term, however, was not significant.

Discussion and Conclusion

Most adolescents in our study experienced high rates of turnover in their friendships, with nearly one-third of them replacing all of their friends with new ones every 6 months. On average, friends were nominated no more than two times over the four and one-half years of the study. Only one in ten maintained stable friendships at every wave of observation. Our findings of high turnover resonate with those of the few extended, longitudinal studies on this topic, which found that between 1% (Hartl et al. 2015) to 15% (Moody et al. 2011) of friendships remained stable over a period of multiple years.

We expected students who lacked long-lasting friendships to find it more difficult to develop a grounded sense of who they are and where they want to go, as compared to those with more enduring friendships and deeper social roots. This appears to be the case: Friendship consistency was significantly associated with greater investment in future life goals. Furthermore, our supplementary analyses suggested that having at least one, stable friendship is of particular importance. These patterns were true even after controlling for an extraordinary range of individual, family, and peer factors, and also under a variety of model specifications.

Our findings reinforce key concepts and tenets of a life course perspective regarding youth development. Here we see that having a stable, "social convoy" of friendships aids young people as they navigate the bumps and turns in the process of progressing through middle and high school. Our results highlight the argument that social processes operate via a network of linked lives (Elder 1998), which in this case consists of a set of interconnected friendships that prove beneficial during adolescence.

Although we constructed numerous alternative measures of friendship stability, and obtained similar findings with those measures, we acknowledge the complexity of longitudinal change in friendship composition and the inherent difficulty in adequately capturing the concept in a simple measure. In addition, the association between friendship consistency and investment in future life goals is robust, but also highly endogenous. This makes it difficult to discern causal relationships, because the unobserved personal characteristics that help maintain committed friendships through the vagaries of middle and high school are also likely to be associated with goal orientation. We attempted to mitigate concerns about causal relationships by using a longitudinal design, lagging our dependent variable, and controlling for many potential confounders. Nonetheless, this issue of causal effects deserves further inquiry, and we hope future researchers exploit exogenous sources of friendship instability—changes in school feeder patterns, for example—to address this matter.

We note, too, that we lack information on the quality of friendships. Maintaining high quality friendship ties and letting go of problematic ones can have particular benefits for adolescents (Berndt et al. 1999); presumably our findings would be even stronger if we examined the stability of high quality friendships. A final puzzle in our study concerns the extremely, and perhaps alarming, high level of instability experienced by the modal student in our sample. If friendship change is so common, and endurance so rare, then what does this mean for adolescents' social lives and life outcomes? Our robustness checks indicate that, although there appear to be few downsides to completely stable friendship networks, much of the benefit of stability can be obtained by having at least one unwavering friendship. An unanswered question worthy of further consideration, therefore, concerns how much turnover is tolerable before adverse outcomes occur. Finally, we hope that future research explores a wide range of outcomes associated with friendship instability, and whether youths with stable personal relationships are more likely to achieve, and not just set, future goals.

References

Adams, R. E., Santo, J. B., & Bukowski, W. M. (2011). The presence of a best friend buffers the effects of negative experiences. *Developmental Psychology, 47*(6), 1786–1791.

Angold, A., Costello, E. J., Messer, S. C., Pickles, A., Winder, F., & Silver, D. (1995). Development of a short questionnaire for use in epidemiological studies of depression in children and adolescents: Factor composition and structure across development. *International Journal of Methods in Psychiatric Research, 5*(4), 237–249.

Antonucci, T. C., & Akiyama, H. (1987). Social networks in adult life and a preliminary examination of the convoy model. *Journal of Gerontology, 42*(5), 519–527.

Bearman, P. S., & Brückner, H. (2015). Promising the future: Virginity pledges and first intercourse1. *American Journal of Sociology*, 106(4), 859–912.
Berndt, T. J. (2002). Friendship quality and social development. *Current Directions in Psychological Science, 11*(1), 7–10.
Berndt, T. J., & Hoyle, S. G. (1985). Stability and change in childhood and adolescent friendships. *Developmental Psychology, 21*(6), 1007–1015.
Berndt, T. J., Hawkins, J. A., & Jiao, Z. (1999). Influences of friends and friendships on adjustment to junior high school. *Merrill-Palmer Quarterly, 45*(1), 13–41.
Billy, J. O. G., & Udry, J. R. (1985). Patterns of adolescent friendship and effects on sexual behavior. *Social Psychology Quarterly, 48*(1), 27–41.
Bowker, A. (2004). Predicting friendship stability during early adolescence. *The Journal of Early Adolescence, 24*(2), 85–112.
Bowker, A. (2016). Predicting friendship stability during early adolescence. *The Journal of Early Adolescence, 24*(2), 85–112.
Branje, S. J. T., Frijns, T., Finkenauer, C., Engels, R., & Meeus, W. (2007). You are my best friend: Commitment and stability in adolescents' same-sex friendships. *Personal Relationships, 14*(4), 587–603.
Brown, B. B., & Theobald, W. (1999). How peers matter: A research synthesis of peer influences on adolescent pregnancy. In *Peer potential: Making the most of how teens influence each other*. National Campaign to Prevent Teen Pregnancy.
Buchmann, C., & Dalton, B. (2002). Interpersonal influences and educational aspirations in 12 countries: The importance of institutional context. *Sociology of Education, 75*(2), 99–122.
Chan, A., & Poulin, F. (2007). Monthly changes in the composition of friendship networks in early adolescence. *Merrill-Palmer Quarterly, 53*(4), 578–602.
Coombs, L. C. (1974). The measurement of family size preferences and subsequent fertility. *Demography, 11*(4), 587.
Değirmencioğlu, S. M., Urberg, K. A., Tolson, J. M., & Richard, P. (1998). Adolescent friendship networks: Continuity and change over the school year. *Merrill-Palmer Quarterly, 44*(3), 313–337.
Demir, M., & Urberg, K. A. (2004). Friendship and adjustment among adolescents. *Journal of Experimental Child Psychology, 88*(1), 68–82.
Domina, T., Conley, A. M., & Farkas, G. (2011). The link between educational expectations and effort in the college-for-all era. *Sociology of Education, 84*(2), 93–112.
Duncan, O. D., Featherman, D. L., & Duncan, B. (1972). *Socioeconomic background and achievement*. New York: Seminar Press.
Duncan, O. D., Haller, A. O., & Portes, A. (1968). Peer influences on aspirations: A reinterpretation. *American Journal of Sociology, 74*(2), 119–137.
Elder, G. H., Jr. (1994). Time, human agency, and social change: Perspectives on the life course. *Social Psychology Quarterly, 57*(1), 4–15.
Elder, G. H., Jr. (1998). The life course as developmental theory. *Child Development, 69*(1), 1–12.
Ellis, W. E., & Zarbatany, L. (2007). Explaining friendship formation and friendship stability: The role of children's and friends' aggression and victimization. *Merrill-Palmer Quarterly, 53*(1), 79–104.
Faris, R., & Felmlee, D. (2014). Casualties of social combat: School networks of peer victimization and their consequences. *American Sociological Review, 79*(2), 228–257.
Farrell, A. D., Kung, E. M., White, K. S., & Valois, R. F. (2000). The structure of self-reported aggression, drug use, and delinquent behaviors during early adolescence. *Journal of Clinical Child Psychology, 29*(2), 282–292.
Felmlee, D., & Faris, R. (2016). Toxic ties: Networks of friendship, dating, and cyber victimization. *Social Psychology Quarterly, 79*(3), 243–262.
Gould, R. V. (2003). Collision of wills: How ambiguity about social rank breeds conflict. Chicago: University of Chicago Press.

Hallinan, M. T., & Williams, R. A. (1987). The stability of students' interracial friendships. *American Sociological Review, 52*(5), 653–664.
Harackiewicz, J. M., Barron, K. E., Tauer, J. M., & Elliot, A. J. (2002). Predicting success in college: A longitudinal study of achievement goals and ability measures as predictors of interest and performance from freshman year through graduation. *Journal of Educational Psychology, 94*(3), 562–575.
Harrist, S., Carlozzi, B. L., McGovern, A. R., & Harrist, A. W. (2007). Benefits of expressive writing and expressive talking about life goals. *Journal of Research in Personality, 41*(4), 923–930.
Hartl, A. C., Laursen, B., & Cillessen, A. H. N. (2015). A survival analysis of adolescent friendships the downside of dissimilarity. *Psychological Science, 26*(8), 1304–1315.
Hartup, W. W. (1996). The company they keep: Friendships and their developmental significance. *Child Development, 67*(1), 1–13.
Hallinan, M. T. (1982). Classroom racial composition and children's friendships. *Social Forces, 61*(1), 56.
Kahn, R. L., & Antonucci, T. C. (1980). Convoys over the life course: Attachment, roles, and social support. In P. B. Baltes & O. Brim (Eds.), *Life-span development and behavior* (Vol. 3, pp. 253–267). New York: Academic.
King, L. A. (2016). The health benefits of writing about life goals. *Personality and Social Psychology Bulletin, 27*(7), 798–807.
Moody, J., Brynildsen, W. D., Osgood, D. W., Feinberg, M. E., & Gest, S. (2011). Popularity trajectories and substance use in early adolescence. *Social Networks, 33*(2), 101–112.
Nangle, D. W., Erdley, C. A., Newman, J. E., Mason, C. A., & Carpenter, E. M. (2003). Popularity, friendship quantity, and friendship quality: Interactive influences on children's loneliness and depression. *Journal of Clinical Child & Adolescent Psychology, 32*(4), 546–555.
Newberry, A. L., & Duncan, R. D. (2001). Roles of boredom and life goals in juvenile delinquency. *Journal of Applied Social Psychology, 31*(3), 527–541.
Newcomb, A. F., & Bagwell, C. L. (1995). Children's friendship relations: A meta-analytic review. *Psychological Bulletin, 117*(2), 306–347.
Nurmi, J.-E. (1992). Age differences in adult life goals, concerns, and their temporal extension: A life course approach to future-oriented motivation. *International Journal of Behavioral Development, 15*(4), 487–508.
Palfai, T. P., & Weafer, J. (2006). College student drinking and meaning in the pursuit of life goals. *Psychology of Addictive Behaviors, 20*(2), 131–134.
Parker, J. G., & Seal, J. (1996). Forming, losing, renewing, and replacing friendships: Applying temporal parameters to the assessment of children's friendship experiences. *Child Development, 67*(5), 2248–2268.
Payne, S. C., Youngcourt, S. S., & Beaubien, J. M. (2007). A meta-analytic examination of the goal orientation nomological net. *Journal of Applied Psychology, 92*(1), 128–150.
Poulin, F., & Chan, A. (2010). Friendship stability and change in childhood and adolescence. *Developmental Review, 30*(3), 257–272.
Reynolds, C. R., & Richmond, B. O. (1979). Factor structure and construct validity of 'What I think and feel': The revised children's manifest anxiety scale. *Journal of Personality Assessment, 43*(3), 281–283.
Sacerdote, B. (2001). Peer effects with random assignment: Results for Dartmouth roommates. *The Quarterly Journal of Economics, 116*(2), 681–704.
Schaefer, D. R., Simpkins, S. D., Vest, A. E., & Price, C. D. (2011). The contribution of extracurricular activities to adolescent friendships: New insights through social network analysis. *Developmental Psychology, 47*(4), 1141–1152.
Sewell, W. H., & Shah, V. P. (1968). Social class, parental encouragement, and educational aspirations. *American Journal of Sociology, 73*(5), 559–572.
South, S. J., & Haynie, D. L. (2004). Friendship networks of mobile adolescents. *Social Forces, 83*(1), 315–350.

Swanson, C. B., & Schneider, B. (1999). Students on the move: Residential and educational mobility in America's schools. *Sociology of Education, 72*(1), 54–67.
Williams, G. C., Hedberg, V. A., Cox, E. M., & Deci, E. L. (2000b). Extrinsic life goals and health-risk behaviors in adolescents. *Journal of Applied Social Psychology, 30*(8), 1756–1771.
Witvliet, M., Brendgen, M., Lier, v., Pol, A. C., Koot, H. M., & Vitaro, F. (2010). Early adolescent depressive symptoms: Prediction from clique isolation, loneliness, and perceived social acceptance. *Journal of Abnormal Child Psychology, 38*(8), 1045–1056.
Wrzus, C., Hanel, M., Wagner, J., & Neyer, F. J. (2013). Social network changes and life events across the life span: A meta-analysis. *Psychological Bulletin, 139*(1), 53–80.

Robert Faris is an Associate Professor in the Sociology Department at the University of California at Davis. His research investigate the dynamics of social networks through time and their implications for the life course.

Diane H. Felmlee is Professor of Sociology and Demography at Pennsylvania State University and Research Associate in the Population Research Institute. Her interests lie at the intersection of social networks and life course studies, pursuing research on aggression and friendship networks, cyberbullying, and gender inequalities.

Chapter 10
Problems at Home, Peer Networks at School, and the Social Integration of Adolescents

Robert Crosnoe, Julie Skalamera Olson, and Jacob E. Cheadle

Families and schools represent two of the major settings of adolescent life. They often seem like distinct settings—physically separate, of course, but also psychologically separate, as young people exit home and then spend the day separate from parents at school before leaving school behind to return to their families (Parcel et al. 2010; Schneider and Coleman 1993). Social and behavioral scientists often magnify this perceived distinctness by conceptualizing these two settings in different ways and studying them separately from each other. The family is typically viewed as an intimate context of interpersonal processes (e.g., communication, interaction) that are difficult or inappropriate to manipulate from the outside, and it is usually evaluated in terms of social psychological qualities. The school is typically viewed as an institutional context of organizational processes (e.g., pedagogy, curriculum) that are subject to external manipulation through policy, and it is usually evaluated in terms of more concrete markers of performance. This distinctness

This research used data from Add Health, a program project designed by J. Richard Udry, Peter S. Bearman, and Kathleen Mullan Harris and funded by a grant P01-HD31921 from the National Institute of Child Health and Human Development, with cooperative funding from 17 other agencies. Special acknowledgment is due Ronald R. Rindfuss and Barbara Entwisle for assistance in the original design of Add Health. Persons interested in obtaining data files from Add Health should contact Add Health, Carolina Population Center, 123 W. Franklin Street, Chapel Hill, NC 27516 (www.cpc.unc.edu/addhealth/contract.html). The authors acknowledge the support of grants from the National Institute of Alcohol Abuse and Alcoholism (R21AA020045-01, PI: Robert Crosnoe; R03AA019479, PI: Jacob Cheadle) and from the National Institute of Child Health and Human Development (R24 HD42849, PI: Mark Hayward; T32 HD007081-35, PI: R. Kelly Raley). Opinions reflect those of the authors and not necessarily those of the granting agencies.

R. Crosnoe (✉) · J. S. Olson
Department of Sociology, University of Texas, Austin, TX, USA
e-mail: crosnoe@austin.utexas.edu

J. E. Cheadle
Department of Sociology, University of Nebraska, Lincoln, NE, USA

D. F. Alwin et al. (eds.), *Social Networks and the Life Course*, Frontiers in Sociology and Social Research 2, https://doi.org/10.1007/978-3-319-71544-5_10

in public and scholarly discourse belies the interconnected nature of families and schools. Not only do the same interpersonal dynamics that make families what they are also characterize the developmental contexts found in schools, families and schools influence each other in complex ways that need to be better understood (Crosnoe 2004).

The purpose of this study is to explore this interconnectedness between the interpersonal processes of families and schools by examining the degree to which parent-adolescent relations at home have implications for adolescent-peer relations at school. Integrating insights from psychology, sociology, and neuroscience, it asks: Are adolescents who are alienated from parents at risk of feeling socially marginalized at school, and what is the nature of their social relationships that would make them feel that way? To answer these questions, we apply a range of analytical techniques (including stochastic actor based longitudinal social network modeling) to network data in the large sample of U.S. high schools in the National Longitudinal Study of Adolescent to Adult Health (Add Health). Beyond answering these specific developmental questions, this research bridges several disciplinary lines, illustrates core theoretical concepts (e.g., ecological mesosystems), and shows how to capture the nesting of social relations within settings while improving causal inference.

Schools as Educational Institutions and Social Contexts

Educational experiences affect the life course in fundamental ways. These effects go beyond the role of academic credentials and skill development in long-term socioeconomic attainment. Where young people go to school and what happens in those schools shapes their social psychological development, which then affects how they transition into and though adulthood (Alexander et al. 2014; Wells 2010; Barber et al. 2001; Eccles and Barber 1999).

In the particular case of high schools, these developmental effects are rooted in the peer environment organized by high schools when they bring together many young people for long periods of time in an academically (and often racially and socioeconomically) stratified space. The peers that adolescents are exposed to and they interactions they have with these peers in and around the school over time structure identity development and sense of self, provide resources for coping, present challenges to overcome, socialize into world view, set the opportunity structure for behavioral experimentation, and facilitate individuation from parents (Crosnoe 2011). Thus, how high school shapes the future is not just about classes and test scores but also about the climate of the peer culture and how adolescents are integrated into it.

Connecting Schools to Families

High schools do not operate in vacuum. They are part of a developmental ecological consisting of many other contexts in which young people live their lives. In many ways, the school and the family are the most critical of these contexts during the early life course, as they are the settings in which young people spend the most time and that so powerfully shape their current experiences and future prospects (Parcel et al. 2010; Crosnoe 2004). In ecological terms (see Bronfenbrenner and Morris 2006), the family may operate alongside the school with parallel but largely independent influences on the adolescent (the microsystem), or the family's influences on adolescents may be intricately tangled up with the influences of the high school (the mesosystem).

In one example of such mesosystem influences, what is happening in one of these contexts shapes what is happening in the other, which then influences the adolescents living their lives in both. Traditionally, the most common way that scholars have viewed such a connection between families and schools was as a direct path through parents' active or passive choice of where their adolescents attend school. Parents actively select a high school for adolescents, or adolescents are passively selected into a high school through such parental factors as socioeconomic status. In both ways, the parent affects the peer environment to which the adolescent will be exposed, given that the high school is the primary setting of peer life (McFarland and Pals 2005; Milner 2004; Moody and White 2003; Coleman 1961). This direct path is in line with Harris' controversial argument (1998) that the only lasting non-genetic effects parents have on the kinds of adults their children will turn out to be is through their power to influence peer exposure, primarily through school selection.

Another way to consider this mesosystem connection between families and schools is to go deeper into parent-adolescent relationship. Parenting processes shape who adolescents are and the competencies and capacities that they take into the peer world that make them accepted or rejected, sociable or withdrawn, leaders or followers. Thus, how parents parent has implications for how adolescents interact with, engage in, and perceive the peer contexts that they encounter at the schools into which their parents have selected them (Giordano 2003; Bronfenbrenner 1986).

A Focus on Problems in Both Contexts

Take, for example, the potential implications for positive peer relations at school of experiencing negative relations with parents, such as when adolescents are disconnected from their parents through conflict or alienation. What will their social lives at school be like? Theory and research from multiple disciplines suggest that, rather than looking for or finding social support at school that they lack at home, such adolescents may struggle socially at school. Theoretical perspectives, like human ecology, emphasize the overlap in social and psychological experiences at home and school and how experiences in one set the stage for experiences in the other. The general argument is that problems at home will interfere with development of the social competencies and capacities that are necessary to navigating the peer world successfully, such as confidence, agreeableness, and perspective-taking (Crosnoe 2011; Giordano 2003; Collins et al. 2009).

Developmental research suggests a socioemotional pathway connecting relationships with parents at home to relationships with peers at school. In short, secure attachments with parents facilitate the social and emotional skills that allow adolescents to form close relationships with peers. Disruptions to that attachment with parents, therefore, may mean that adolescents do not have the personal resources (or even motivation) to bond with the peers that they encounter at school (Schneider et al. 2001). If young people feel alienated from parents, who are supposed to love them more than anyone, what are their chances of successfully finding their place in the more complex and shifting social currents of the high school peer context? In support of this socioemotional mechanism is ample evidence that attachment with parents and attachment with peers are correlated. Indeed, a meta-analysis of 43 studies reported that the correlation between the two was .27 (.31 for attachment with mothers, .22 for attachment with fathers) (Gorrese and Ruggieri 2012).

Neuroscience research suggests a different pathway connecting relationships with parents at home to relationships with peers at school, one that also concerns socioemotional skills but is more directly tied to brain development. In short, negative relationships with parents can shape brain development in critical ways that blunt the sensitivity of adolescents to their peer relations. For example, a series of studies by Dahl and colleagues linked parent-adolescent discussion tasks to virtual peer interaction games while scanning adolescents' brains with fMRI (functional magnetic resonance imaging). The affective networks of adolescents' brains, such as the lentiform nucleus, were more active than their cognitive control networks, such as the dorsolateral prefrontal cortex, when adolescents experienced negativity from mothers. When interacting with peers in more positive ways, these same adolescents demonstrated reduced activity in the parts of their brains that organize emotional responses to social stimuli, such as the bilateral amygdala. These findings suggest that the brain rewires in response to family negativity to protect adolescents from that emotional and psychological threat, but this protective response desensitizes them too broadly, so that they are less reactive to even the positive aspects of their peer relations (Lee et al. 2015; Tan et al. 2014). As a result, adolescents with problems at home may derive less benefit from peer relations even though they need these social and emotional benefits the most.

Connecting these different disciplinary insights and the mechanisms that they suggest, adolescents who have problematic relationships with parents at home may be less embedded in and sensitive to peer relations at school, so that they are less motivated to engage with peers, less connected to peers, and less reactive to peers and peer relations in positive and negative ways. A consequence of home life, therefore, would by marginalization at school.

Study Hypotheses

Based on this integration of diverse perspectives on connections between adolescents' home and school lives, we pose two sets of hypotheses. The first hypothesis is that adolescents with problems at home will be less likely to feel socially integrated at school, both when they are isolated and when they objectively seem to be connected to others. The idea here is that their feelings of integration will be less reactive to their social resources at school. The second hypothesis is that adolescents with problems at home will cluster together—through homophily or from lack of other alternatives—in at school. If so, the expected weaker link between having friends at school and feeling socially integrated at school among adolescents with problems at home may be due to the fact that their friends come into these relationships with similar interpersonal disadvantages.

Methods

Data and Sample

Add Health is a nationally representative survey that launched in 1994 and has followed adolescents into adulthood over the next two decades (Harris et al. 2009). The schools included in the study were randomly selected through a sampling frame stratified by region, urbanicity, school size, school type, and racial composition based. Data collection began with an In-School Survey in 1994 with all 90,118 7-12th graders in the 132 middle and high schools selected for the sample. This census-like survey was then used to generate a nationally representative subsample of 20,745 students selected across schools by gender and grade. This sample group then completed an In-Home Interview in 1995 (Wave I), 1996 (Wave II), 2001–2002 (Wave III), and 2007–2008 (Wave IV). Add Health designated 16 schools as *saturated*, meaning that all students, rather than a random sample, participated in the In-Home Interviews.

Given our interest in adolescence and high school, the analytical sample for this study included adolescents who participated in the In-School Survey and the Waves I–II In-Home Interviews during high school. Restricting the analytical sample to adolescents who participated in these three data collections necessarily excluded the Wave I high school seniors, who were purposely dropped from the core sampling frame in Wave II by Add Health investigators before being added back in later waves. Furthermore, some of our analytical techniques (e.g., Simulation Investigation for Empirical Network Analysis, SIENA; see below) required near-complete network data. To maintain a comparable sample across all analyses, therefore, we focused on adolescents in the two high schools with the most complete network data: Sunshine, a large and predominantly White high school, and Jefferson, a moderately sized and predominantly minority high school. Thus, the final analytical sample included 2699 adolescents attending Sunshine or Jefferson.

Missing data within this sample were estimated through special techniques, as described below, and we employed longitudinal sampling weights to account for study design effects and to address differential attrition from the core sample across waves. Of note is that we also compared the results of non-SIENA models (which did not require a focus on the two high schools in question) to equivalent models estimated with the full In-School Survey through Wave I-II longitudinal sample (n = 13,568). This comparison revealed virtually no difference in the focal coefficients between these unrestricted and restricted samples.

Measures

Table 10.1 presents the univariate descriptive statistics for all variables included in analyses.

Feelings of Fitting in at School Drawing on earlier work with Add Health (Crosnoe 2011), we created a scale with five variables from the Waves I–II In-Home Interviews. Adolescents reported how much they got along with other students, felt close to people at their school, and felt like they were part of their school, felt socially accepted, and felt loved and wanted. Their responses were dichotomized to indicate that the adolescent felt accepted, felt wanted, had no trouble with other students, felt close to other students, and/or felt part of the school. These binary variables were summed to create a scale ranging from 0–5, where higher values represent more perceived integration.

Friendship Network During the In-School Survey, adolescents nominated up to five female and five male friends. These nominations can be used to create multiple individual-level and school-level measures that capture the friendship network and the standing of the adolescent within it. In some models, the presence of a friendship tie (and its continuation over time) served as the outcome of interest. In other models, adolescents' in-degree nominations (number of friends nominated by them, gauging sociability) and their out-degree nominations (number of friends who nominate them, gauging popularity) were used as key independent variables.

Negative Relationships with Parents In Wave I, respondents were asked to agree or disagree with the statement that, "most of the time your mother [and father] is warm and loving toward you." Responses were coded such that higher values represented stronger agreement with the statement (1 = strongly agree; 2 = agree; 3 = neither agree nor disagree; 4 = disagree; 5 = strongly disagree) for both parents, separately. Comparison of models with a similar scale of adolescents' perceptions that their mothers and fathers cared about them yielded similar results.

Sociodemographic Covariates A set of characteristics was measured to account for sociodemographic variability and important spurious factors: gender (1 = female),

Table 10.1 Univariate descriptive statistics ($n = 2699$)

	Mean (SE)/%	
Feelings of fitting in at school		
Wave I	3.91	(1.239)
Wave II	3.98	(1.194)
Friendship network		
In-degree nominations	4.243	(3.499)
Out-degree nominations	4.267	(2.979)
Negative relationships with parents	4.322	(0.827)
Mother		
Strongly agree	48.76%	
Agree	40.12%	
Neither agree/disagree	6.99%	
Disagree	2.83%	
Strongly disagree	1.30%	
Father		
Strongly agree	37.66%	
Agree	42.56%	
Neither agree/disagree	12.63%	
Disagree	4.85%	
Strongly disagree	2.31%	
Covariates		
Gender (female)	49.94%	
Age	16.258	(1.471)
Parent education		
Less than high school	12.54%	
High school	31.63%	
Some post-secondary	22.16%	
College graduate	23.43%	
Post-graduate degree	10.23%	
Two biological parent household	27.83%	
Race/ethnicity		
Non-Hispanic white	49.57%	
Non-Hispanic black	14.66%	
Hispanic	19.51%	
Non-Hispanic Asian	13.81%	
Other/multi-racial	2.33%	

age at Wave I, parent education (highest level among any residential parents; 1 = less than high school, 2 = high school graduate, 3 = some post-secondary education, 4 = college graduate, 5 = post-graduate degree), family structure at Wave I (1 = lives with both biological parents, 0 = other family form), and race/ethnicity (dummy variables for non-Hispanic White, non-Hispanic Black, Hispanic, non-Hispanic Asian, and other/multi-racial).

Analytical Strategy

The first hypothesis considered the links among adolescents' relationships with parents, their sociometric positions in their peer networks, and their perceived social integration. This hypothesis called for individual-level analyses. We estimated a series of models regressing the feelings of fitting in scale on the focal parenting factors (negative relationships with mothers and fathers) and the covariates, and then added interactions between the parenting and network variables. Because the fitting in scale was measured at both Waves I and II, we employed a lagged modeling structure in which the Wave II scale was the dependent variable and the Wave I scale was a covariate, effectively modeling changes in fitting in over time. These individual-level analyses were performed in Mplus, which estimated all missing data with full information maximum likelihood (FIML) based on available data.

The second hypothesis concerned homophily between adolescents based on their relationships with parents, which drew on data from the two saturated schools of interest. This aim called for a dyadic-level analysis within the context of the full network in each school. The SIENA model estimates changes in the friendship network over time and how such changes are predicted by focal factors (Snijders 1996). Coefficients are calculated using a method of moments estimator summarizing changes in the network statistics between observations combined with an agent-based simulation model that updates the parameters, estimates uncertainties, and provides an actor-based interpretational framework. The simulation model decomposes network changes into a series of the smallest possible transitions in one tie at a time for a randomly chosen focal adolescent. Here, we estimated changes in friendship networks with ties possible among all adolescents in a school, using the parenting of adolescents as predictors of any changes in ties. The models also took into account the reverse path in which friendship ties could theoretically predict changes in the quality of parent-adolescent relationships.

In the SIENA models, the *alter*, *ego*, and *ego-alter interaction* effects are selection mechanisms central to understanding how parent-adolescent relationships are related to popularity (alter; number of friendship nominations received), sociability (ego; number of nominations made), and homophilous selection (ego-alter). These effects can refer to a creation process, in which a friendship that does not exist at one wave forms by the next wave (as opposed to not), as well as a continuation process, in which a friendship persists across waves (as opposed to dissolving). Additional parameters include structural effects for reciprocity and transitive network closure (e.g., transitive triplets: $i \rightarrow k$ become friends when $i \rightarrow j \rightarrow k$).

Results

Only 11% of adolescents in our analytical sample of students at Sunshine and Jefferson high schools did not agree that their mothers were warm and loving, with the proportion rising to 19% for fathers. When comparing the extremes (strongly agree vs. strongly disagree), some differences in the network positions of adolescents with good and poor relationships with parents are evident, although not consistent. Comparisons of mean number of peer nominations in the network data suggest a social advantage for having bad relationships with mothers (mean number of times nominated: 4.86, mean number of nominations made: 5.00) over having good relationships with mothers (4.49, 4.69). Yet, adolescents with bad relationships with fathers were at a social disadvantage (2.72, 3.41) compared to those with good relationships with their fathers (4.40, 4.54). These patterns should be viewed with caution, however, because the overall correlation between the two parent variables (mother, father) and the two peer variables (in-degree, out-degree) were all weak, typically .10 or below (in contrast to the correlation between parent and peer attachment discussed earlier). Moreover, the parent variables were not associated with either peer variable once the covariates were taken into account.

Testing Hypothesis 1

The results for the individual-level analyses of feelings of fitting in at Sunshine and Jefferson are presented in Table 10.2. The significant coefficients for both of the parent variables suggest a tendency for adolescents with more negative relationships with parents to have fewer feelings of fitting in at school, net of Wave I feelings; in other words, more perceived social marginalization from year to year. This association was slightly stronger for negative relationships with fathers (each point increase on this variable was associated with a 11% standard deviation reduction on the feelings of fitting in at school scale) than for negative relationships with mothers (8%). The difference between having the best and worst relationship with fathers equaled about 40% of a standard deviation on the feelings of fitting in scale.

Interestingly, we found orthogonal results in side analyses that switched out the fitting in at school outcome with a measure of involvement with peers (the sum of binary items for each nominated friend about whether, in the past week/weekend, the adolescent had gone to the friend's house, hung out somewhere with the friend, talked on the telephone with the friend, and spent time with the friend averaged across all nominated friends; see Crosnoe and Elder 2004). The results of the mother and father coefficients in this model were roughly the same as in Model 1 in Table 10.2 but in the opposite direction (*b* for mother not warm and loving = .09 $p < .10$ in the two-school sample and .12 $p < .05$). Thus, adolescents with negative relationships with parents tended to spend more time with friends but feel less socially integrated at school.

Table 10.2 Results from regression models predicting feelings of fitting in at School at wave II by relationships with parents

	b Coefficient (SE)			
	Model 1		Model 2	
Mother not warm and loving	−0.109	*		
	(0.053)			
Father not warm and loving			−0.125	**
			(0.045)	
Feelings of fitting in at school (wave I)	0.394	***	0.389	***
	(0.039)		(0.039)	
Covariates				
Gender (female)	−0.056		−0.065	
	(0.067)		(0.067)	
Age	−0.017		−0.014	
	(0.020)		(0.020)	
Parent education	−0.046		−0.048	
	(0.029)		(0.030)	
Two-biological parent household	−0.018		−0.030	
	(0.069)		(0.069)	
Race/ethnicity				
Non-Hispanic black	−0.237	*	−0.239	*
	(0.117)		(0.116)	
Hispanic	−0.022		−0.009	
	(0.120)		(0.122)	
Non-Hispanic Asian	−0.217		−0.212	
	(0.153)		(0.152)	
Other/multi-racial	0.343	*	0.371	*
	(0.154)		(0.157)	
Constant	3.162	***	3.186	***
	(0.404)		(0.408)	

Note: $n = 2699$; † $p < .10$, * $p < .05$, ** $p < .01$, *** $p < .001$

Following this interesting pattern of results, we estimated a second model with the fitting in scale as the dependent variable, adding interactions between each parent variable and each peer network variable. Did the link between negative relationships with parents and feelings of fitting in differ depending on adolescents' "objective" social positions in school? The parent variables did not interact with the out-degree peer variables. In other words, the inverse association between negative relationships with mothers and feelings of fitting in at school did not vary as a function of how popular adolescents were—adolescents got no interpersonal boost from having others nominate them as friends).

Negative relationships with parents did interact with out-degree peer nominations (i.e., the number of others adolescents nominated as friends). For interpretation, we graphed the predicted score on the Wave II feelings of fitting in scale for youth with different combinations between relationships with parents (strongly

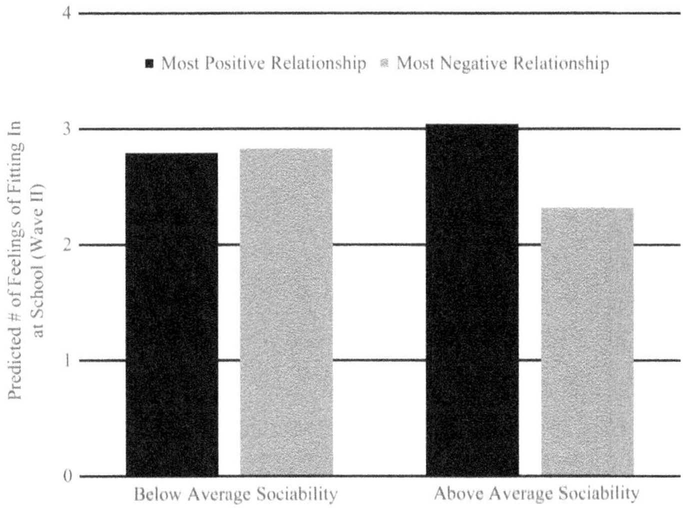

Fig. 10.1 Adolescents' feelings of fitting in at school, by relationships with mothers and number of friends nominated by adolescents

agreed and disagreed with the statement about parents being warm and loving) and out-degree peer nominations (nominated above- and below-average number of friends for the sample). Figure 10.1 graphs these predicted values for relationships with mothers.

The inverse association between negative relationships with mothers and feelings of fitting in at school did vary as a function of how sociable adolescents were, such that the gap in feelings of fitting in at school between youth with positive and negative relationships with their mothers was greater among the most sociable. Thus, if adolescents had negative relationships with mothers, they were more likely to claim lots of friends while not feeling socially integrated.

These results provide partial support for the first hypothesis. Adolescents with more negative relationships with parents tended to feel more marginalized, even when they spent a lot of time with friends, and they appeared to derive less social psychological benefit from seemingly positive network positions at school.

Testing Hypothesis 2

The second hypothesis involved dyadic-level modeling, and so we turned to SIENA. This technique captures stability/change in networks over time and has several important features, such as allowing for dynamic friendship patterns (friendship creation and/or continuation and controlling for a range of network dependencies (such as reciprocation and mutual friends, which are features of networks that can affect the likelihood of friendship ties).

Table 10.3 Partial results from SIENA models predicting changes in friendship ties between waves I and II by the relationships with parents

	Coefficient	
	Sunshine	Jefferson
Negative relationship with parent (alter effect)	.01	.00
Negative relationship with parent (ego effect)	−.03	.01
Similar relationships with parents (creation)	−.56	−.66
Similar relationships with parents (continuation)	.82***	−.77

Note: $n = 826$ (Sunshine) and 1683 (Jefferson)
*** $p < 0.001$

Table 10.3 presents the partial results of the model for featuring negative relationships with mothers as the focal factor. It revealed that adolescents who had negative relationships with their mothers were no more or less likely than other adolescents to be nominated as friends (alter) or to nominate friends (ego) in either high school. The only instance of homophily concerned continuation in Sunshine. In this high school, adolescents who had negative relationships with their mothers were no more or less likely than any two other adolescents to become friends (creation), but they were significantly more likely to maintain a friendship over time once they formed it. This significant homophily pattern, however, was reduced to non-significance by the inclusion of the network dependency variables.

The dyadic analyses, therefore, provided only limited support for the hypothesis about homophily between adolescents with negative relationships with their parents. We found only one example of such homophily, and it appeared to be more about the larger network in which the two adolescents came together.

Conclusion

Overall, we cannot say that the link between problems at home and the social outcomes of high school students was a strong one. When we did see some evidence of such a link and explored it, however, it did usually suggest some possible spillover between home and school.

If adolescents felt alienated from or rejected by parents, they were less likely to feel socially integrated at school, even when they were highly involved with friends. This spillover appeared to worsen when they thought that they had friends at school. These two patterns (where perceptions do not line up with network positions or behavior) suggest a possible "alone in the crowd" effect (see Crosnoe 2011) in which adolescents were seemingly connected to others but felt disconnected. One possible reason that they felt this way might have been that those other adolescents who appeared to be their most enduring friends also had problems at home. To the extent that adolescents with problems at home may have fewer social resources to bring into their friendships, the friendships that form between two such adolescents might not be as socially integrating. They might have less to give each other.

If the developmental and neuroscience evidence suggesting a problematic link between maternal negativity and adolescents' socioemotional skills (e.g., less ability to connect with others, blunted sensitivity to peer relations) is right, then we should expect to see less pronounced effects of problems with parents on having friends or the number of friends (a quantity metric). We would also expect to see more pronounced effects on the substance of any friendships that do form and last (a quality metric). The next step in this research, therefore, is to see how the continuation of friendships between adolescents who each have problems at home factors into perceived social integration/marginalization of both adolescents at school. Add Health allows such an examination, but the truth is that this valuable data set is getting old. The young people were in high school two decades ago. A new Add Health—with its pioneering longitudinal network design—needs to be fielded. Such a future endeavor could also correct some of the substantive limitations of Add Health, such as the fact that it is far more useful for mapping out networks of relationships than for exploring the interpersonal and affective processes going on inside these relationships.

References

Alexander, K., Entwisle, D., & Olson, L. (2014). *The long shadow: Family background, disadvantaged urban youth, and the transition to adulthood*. New York: Russell Sage Foundation.

Barber, B. L., Eccles, J. S., & Stone, M. R. (2001). Whatever happened to the jock, the brain, and the princess? Young adult pathways linked to adolescent activity involvement and social identity. *Journal of Adolescent Research, 16*, 429–455.

Bronfenbrenner, U. (1986). Ecology of the family as a context for human development: Research perspectives. *Developmental Psychology, 22*, 723–742.

Bronfenbrenner, U., & Morris, P. (2006). The bioecological model of human development. In W. Damon & R. M. Lerner (Eds.), *Handbook of child psychology, Volume 1: Theoretical models of human development* (pp. 993–1028). Hoboken: Wiley.

Coleman, J. S. (1961). *The adolescent society: The social life of teenagers and its impact on education*. New York: Free Press of Glencoe.

Collins, W. A., Welsh, D., & Furman, W. (2009). Adolescent romantic relationships. *Annual Review of Psychology, 60*, 631–652.

Crosnoe, R. (2004). Social capital and the interplay of families and schools. *Journal of Marriage and Family, 66*, 267–280.

Crosnoe, R. (2011). *Fitting in, standing out: Navigating the social challenges of high school to get an education*. New York: Cambridge University Press.

Crosnoe, R., & Elder, G. H. (2004). Family dynamics, supportive relationships, and educational resilience during adolescence. *Journal of Family Issues, 25*, 571–602.

Eccles, J. S., & Barber, B. L. (1999). Student council, volunteering, basketball, or marching band. *Journal of Adolescent Research, 14*(1), 10–43

Giordano, P. C. (2003). Relationships in adolescence. *Annual Review of Sociology, 29*, 257–281.

Gorrese, A., & Ruggieri, R. (2012). Peer attachment: A meta-analytic review of gender and age differences and associations with parent attachment. *Journal of Youth and Adolescence, 41*, 650–672.

Harris, J. R. (1998). *The nurture assumption: Why children turn out the way that they do*. New York: Free Press.

Harris, K. M., Halpern, C. T., Whitsel, E., Hussey, J., Tabor, J., Entzel, P., & Richard Udry, J. (2009). *The National longitudinal study of adolescent health: Research design*. Retrieved June 5, 2011. http://www.cpc.unc.edu/projects/addhealth/design

Lee, K. H., Siegle, G. J., Dahl, R. E., Hooley, J. M., & Silk, J. S. (2015). Neural responses to maternal criticism in healthy youth. *Social Cognitive and Affective Neuroscience, 133*.

McFarland, D. A., & Pals, H. (2005). Motives and contexts of identity change: A case for network effects. *Social Psychology Quarterly, 68*, 289–315.

Milner, M. (2004). *Freaks, geeks, and cool kids: American teenagers, schools, and the culture of consumption*. New York: Routledge.

Moody, J., & White, D. R. (2003). Social cohesion and embeddedness: A hierarchical conception of social groups. *American Sociological Review, 68*, 103–127.

Parcel, T. L., Dufur, M. J., & Zito, R. C. (2010). Capital at home and at school: A review and synthesis. *Journal of Marriage and Family, 72*, 828–846.

Schneider, B., & Coleman, J. S. (1993). *Parents, their children, and schools*. Boulder: Westview.

Schneider, B. H., Atkinson, L., & Tardif, C. (2001). Child–parent attachment and children's peer relations: A quantitative review. *Developmental Psychology, 37*, 86–100.

Snijders, T. A. B. (1996). Stochastic actor-oriented models for network change. *The Journal of Mathematical Sociology, 21*(1–2), 149–172.

Tan, P. Z., Lee, K. H., Dahl, R. E., Eric, R., Nelson, E., Stroud, L., Siegle, G. J., Morgan, J. K., & Silk, J. (2014). Associations between maternal negative affect and adolescent's neural response to peer evaluation. *Developmental Cognitive Neuroscience, 8*, 28–39.

Wells, A. S. (2010). *Both sides now: The story of school desegregation's graduates*. Berkeley: University of California Press.

Robert Crosnoe holds the Rapoport Centennial Professorship and is Chair of Sociology at the University of Texas at Austin. His interests are broadly in human development, education, family, health and immigration.

Julie Skalamera Olson is a doctoral candidate in sociology at the University of Texas at Austin, and a graduate student trainee at the Population Research Center. She is interested in the emergence of health disparities during adolescence and the transition to adulthood.

Jacob E. Cheadle is a Happold Associate Professor of Sociology at the University of Nebraska-Lincoln. His interests are in the intersection of social and biological processes in the creation of individual variation in health and social functioning.

Part V
Gender and Social Networks

Chapter 11
Who Wants the Breakup? Gender and Breakup in Heterosexual Couples

Michael J. Rosenfeld

Introduction

It is a well-established fact that most divorces in the US are wanted primarily by the wife. In Goode's (1956) sample of recently divorced women from the 1940s in Detroit, about two thirds of the recently divorced women described themselves as the initiators of their divorces.[1] More recent US data show a similar pattern, with roughly two thirds of divorces wanted by the wife (Brinig and Allen 2000; England and Kilbourne 1990; Pettit and Bloom 1984; Sayer et al. 2011; Sweeney 2002). Most divorces are wanted by the wife not only in the US, but in Europe (Charvoz et al. 2009; Kalmijn and Poortman 2006) and Australia (Hewitt 2009; Hewitt et al. 2006) as well.

The fact that wives have been more likely to want divorce implies that wives were less satisfied with their marriages than their husbands, at least among couples who divorced. Gender inequality in who wants to break up is one way to measure gender differences in satisfaction within romantic relationships. Do nonmarital relationships experience breakup in a gendered way similar to marriages? The prior

---

This project was generously supported by the National Science Foundation, grants SES-0751977 and SES-1153867, M. Rosenfeld P.I., with additional funding from Stanford's Institute for Research in the Social Sciences and Stanford's UPS endowment. Previous versions of this paper were presented at the 2015 Penn State "Together through Time" conference organized by Duane Alwin, and at the 2015 American Sociological Association meetings in Chicago. Thanks to Daniel Schneider, Amanda Mireles, Duane Alwin, Diane Felmlee, Derek Kreager, and the Stanford Graduate Family Workshop for comments.

[1] Goode (1956) reported 105 divorces initiated by the husband, 264 initiated by the wife, and 56 mutually initiated divorces. Counting the mutual divorces as 50% female initiated yields 69% female initiation (see also Table 11.1 below).

M. J. Rosenfeld (✉)
Department of Sociology, Stanford University, Stanford, CA, USA
e-mail: mrosenfe@stanford.edu

D. F. Alwin et al. (eds.), *Social Networks and the Life Course*, Frontiers in Sociology and Social Research 2, https://doi.org/10.1007/978-3-319-71544-5_11

literature on the gender of breakup has explored breakup in heterosexual marriage exclusively. In this paper, I use a new longitudinal study of relationships and breakups in the US. I compare the data on who wanted the breakup for married couples, nonmarital cohabiting couples, and couples who are not married and who have not cohabited. I examine the gender of breakup for both marital and nonmarital relationships with quantitative data for the first time.

Some of the prior explanations for women's predominance in wanting divorce (for instance, that women are more sensitive to relationship difficulties) apply equally well to marital and to nonmarital relationships. Other explanations for women's predominance in wanting divorce rely on the uniquely gendered history (and therefore uniquely gendered current reality) of heterosexual marriage. The central question addressed below is whether the gender of who wants breakups in nonmarital unions is consistent with, or inconsistent with hypotheses that have previously been offered to explain women's agency in initiating divorce.

Explanations for Why Women Are More Likely to Want Divorce

1. *Sensitivity to Relationship Issues*

One plausible explanation offered for why women are more likely to want divorce is that women are more sensitive to relationship difficulties (Heaton and Blake 1999; Sweeney 2002). If women are more attuned to a relationship difficulty, they may be more likely to see the difficulty as requiring action, and eventually make the decision to exit from the relationship. The hypothesis that women are more sensitive to relationship problems leads to a corollary that women would be more likely to want breakups than men across all types of relationships and contexts. The corollary that women would have a leading role in breakup across all relationship contexts is consistent with research on the longevity of same-sex couples, which has usually shown that lesbian couples in committed relationships have a higher breakup rate than gay male couples in committed relationships (Blumstein and Schwartz 1983; Rosenfeld 2014).

2. *Marriage as a Gendered Institution*

Heterosexual marriage is an institution built on centuries of gendered law and common law (Weitzman 1981). Despite the institution of marriage changing and adapting (Cherlin 2004) and becoming more diverse in terms of who marries whom (Rosenfeld 2007), feminist scholars view heterosexual marriage as a gendered institution (Berk 1985), which is a potential reason why wives might selectively want divorce. By gendered institution, scholars mean that heterosexual marriage reproduces and reifies traditional gender roles for men and women (Berk 1985; Shelton and John 1993). In their description of the post-1960 gender revolution as a stalled revolution, Hochschild and Machung (1989) describe how wives' careers were constrained by their husbands' expectations that the afternoon and evening shift of housework and childcare was fundamentally women's work. Even husbands and wives who thought of themselves as holding gender egalitarian ideals were found by Hochschild and Machung to be living (and justifying to themselves) traditional gender expectations of childcare and housework as women's work.

More recent research on the transition from cohabitation to marriage continues to show that traditional gender expectations are re-enforced at the threshold of marriage for heterosexual couples. Brown (2000) found that heterosexual couples were especially likely to marry if the man had high earnings. Weisshaar (2014) found that among heterosexual couples, earnings between partners became more unequal as the couples transitioned from cohabitation to marriage. Sassler and Miller (2011) found that among young heterosexual couples, men had the privilege of asking their partner to marry, meaning men controlled the marriage decision. Bass (2015) found that among young heterosexual couples planning to marry, men pressured their fiancées to adopt the man's family surname. Most women in the US continue to take their husbands' surnames when they marry (Johnson and Scheuble 1995), even though the laws that required wives to take their husband's surname were phased out in the 1970s (Scheuble and Johnson 1993). Wives' adoption of their husbands' surnames is an example of heterosexual marriage as a gendered institution with current gender practice rooted in a gender inegalitarian past.

Feminist literature on marriage argues that heterosexual marriage is not only gendered, but fundamentally asymmetric and inegalitarian as well. Jessie Bernard (1982) famously wrote: "There are two marriages, then, in every marital union, his and hers. And his... is better than hers." The feminist critique of heterosexual marriage is consistent with wives being more likely than husbands to want to divorce. The feminist critique of heterosexual marriage, however, has less direct application to nonmarital heterosexual relationships. Nonmarital heterosexual relationships generally involve lower levels of commitment, fewer children, and nonmarital unions are less influenced by the legal and cultural history of marriage as a gendered institution (Cherlin 2009; Poortman and Mills 2012; Rosenfeld 2014).

Time use studies (Bianchi et al. 2006) suggest that between 1965 and 2000, married fathers had increased their share of unpaid family caregiving, but that married mothers still did about two thirds of the housework. Frisco and Williams (2003) showed that not only were men doing less housework than their wives in the US in the 1980s, but that marriages in which the wife felt they were doing more than their share of the housework were especially likely to end in divorce. The slow pace of gender role change within heterosexual marriage is one key reason why the feminist revolution is seen as an unfinished, or stalled revolution (England 2010; Gerson 2010; Hochschild and Machung 1989; Ridgeway 2011).

Research on housework has consistently found that the gender housework gap was larger in marriage than in nonmarital cohabiting relationships (Davis et al. 2007; Gupta 1999; Shelton and John 1993; South and Spitze 1994). Married men resist housework to an extent that cannot be explained by practical considerations and constraints (such as the presence of children or men's higher earnings, see Brines 1994; Shelton and John 1993).

3. *Power Differentials within Relationships*

A third potential explanation for who wants divorce or breakup relates to the relative power of the partners or spouses within the relationship. The power differential theory of divorce assumes that the spouse with better prospects beyond the current relationship is more likely to want to break up (Sayer et al. 2011). By external measures, husbands' power has generally exceeded wives' power. Husbands tend to be older than wives (England and McClintock 2009), though the power advantage of being older might dissipate or even reverse as individuals age into their later years. Husbands have always had higher earnings on average than wives (though the gender earnings gap has narrowed over time, see Vanneman 2006). Research in online dating markets shows that single women's attractiveness to men declines more sharply over the adult life course than single men's attractiveness to women (Rudder 2014). Wallerstein and Blakeslee's (1989) reported that older women were more likely to be "losers" in divorce.

If women are most in romantic demand when they are young, and older men are more in demand as heterosexual partners as they age (Rudder 2014), the power theory of relationships implies that divorce should become more male-initiated as couples age. The realities of gendered divorce fit uneasily with power theory, however: despite men's various power advantages (being older than their wives, earning more, and ageing into greater demand as heterosexual partners), women have been the initiators of about two thirds of all divorces from the 1940s to the present. Furthermore, as I show below, female initiation of divorce does not vary significantly by age.

An alternate version of the power theory of relationships suggests that women's *lack* of power within heterosexual marriages is the reason that women choose to exit marriages (England and Kilbourne 1990). Lacking power within the relationship to give sufficient voice to their dissatisfactions, women may choose to exit (Hirschman 1970). As Sayer et al. (2011) noted, the vast literature on determinants of divorce (with some notable exceptions cited above) has usually failed to distinguish between divorces wanted by the wife versus divorces wanted by the husband.

Hypotheses

Consistent with prior literature:

Hypothesis 1 Women want the clear majority of heterosexual divorces.

Corollary 1a Women's tendency to want divorce is robust to multivariate controls from the individual or couple level.

If the reason that most divorces are wanted by the wife is that marriage is a uniquely gendered institution, then nonmarital unions should have a more egalitarian breakup pattern.

Hypothesis 2 In nonmarital heterosexual couples, neither gender dominates in who wants breakups.

If women are more sensitive to relationship shortcomings, then:

Hypothesis 3 Self-reported relationship quality has a stronger effect on women wanting to break up than on men wanting to break up.

If Hypothesis 3 is supported by the data, we also expect that the divergent gender sensitivity to relationship quality would mediate the association between gender and who wants to break up.

Corollary 3a Different gender responses to relationship quality explain (at least partly) the prevalence of women wanting breakups.

The simplest version of the power theory of relationships gives the initiative to the partner with more power or status. Therefore:

Hypothesis 4 Individuals with more power, more status, or more income are more likely to want to break up.

Data and Methods

The How Couples Meet and Stay Together surveys (HCMST; Rosenfeld et al. 2015) started with a nationally representative survey of 2538 adults who had partners of a different gender in 2009, and included follow-up with the same individuals covering wave 2 in 2010, wave 3 in 2011, wave 4 in 2013, and wave 5 which ended in early 2015. I supplement the individual-level and couple-level analysis of HCMST data with data on marital satisfaction from the General Social Survey (GSS; Smith et al. 2013), and data on the prevalence of marriage from the US Census and American Community Surveys (Ruggles et al. 2015).

The HCMST subjects were initially recruited into the study through a nationally representative random digit dialing (RDD) telephone survey, so the HCMST sample is nationally representative (Chang and Krosnick 2009; Rosenfeld and Thomas 2012). Subjects who did not have Internet access at home were given Internet access by survey firm Knowledge Networks/GfK (hereafter KN/GfK).[2]

[2]The response rate to HCMST wave 1 was 71%. Including the initial RDD phone contact and agreement to join the KN/GfK panel (recruitment rate 32.6%) which took place months or years before HCMST wave 1, and the respondents' completion of the initial KN/GfK demographic survey (profile rate 56.8%) which also predated HCMST wave 1 by months or years, the composite overall response rate for the wave 1 HCMST survey is .71*.326*.568 = 13% (Callegaro and DiSogra 2008). Despite the low overall response rate of multistage KN/GfK surveys compared to single stage RDD surveys, the quality of data derived from the KN/GfK panel has been shown to equal or exceed the quality of data derived from industry standard RDD surveys (Chang and Krosnick 2009; Fricker et al. 2005), in part because KN/GfK gathers information from subjects at each survey stage. Among subjects eligible for follow-up, the response rate was 85% at wave 2, 73% at wave 3, 60% at wave 4, and 46% at wave 5. The key determinant of response to the HCMST follow-up surveys was not any factor that predicts couple longevity (such as relationship

In the 6 years of exposure to the risk of breakup from early 2009 to early 2015, HCMST recorded 385 breakups of heterosexual couples. Of the 385 subjects who reported breakup of a heterosexual union, all but 12 answered the question about which partner had wanted the breakup more.[3] The number of subjects in heterosexual unions that broke up between waves 1 and 5 of HCMST was reduced by 2 when subjects were removed from analysis for inconsistent report of own gender, yielding the final count of 371 breakups reported in Table 11.1, below.

Table 11.1 Women's role in the breakup of married and nonmarital heterosexual relationships

	Number of breakups	Pct reporting that both partners equally wanted to break up	Weighted mean of women wanting the breakup, pct	SE of mean	95% confidence interval
Married	92	19	69	4.3	(61, 78)
Reported by women	43		78	5.8	(66, 89)
Reported by men	49		63	6.4	(50, 75)
Nonmarital, have cohabited as a couple	76	32	56	5.3	(47, 65)
Reported by women	40		59	6.6	(46, 72)
Reported by men	36		52	6.8	(39, 66)
Nonmarital, never cohabited	203	35	53.4	2.8	(47.9, 58.9)
Reported by women	104		60	4.1	(52, 68)
Reported by men	99		47	3.9	(39, 55)

Source: How Couples Meet and Stay Together, breakups from waves 2–5, covering 2009–2015. Data weighted by weight variable "weight2." Women's role is scored as follows: 0 if the male partner wanted the breakup more, 0.5 if both partners equally wanted the breakup, and 1 if the female partner wanted the breakup more. Unweighted breakup outcomes are as follows: for married couples, 92 breakups: 18 wanted by the husband, 18 mutual breakups, 56 wanted by the wife. For 76 nonmarital cohabiter breakups: 24 wanted by the man, 24 mutual breakups, 28 wanted by the woman. For 203 breakups of non-cohabiting never married couples: 58 wanted by the man, 61 mutual breakups, 84 wanted by the woman

duration or marriage), but whether the respondent was still in the KN/GfK panel at the time of the follow-up survey, which is why loss-to-follow-up does not bias estimates of breakup in HCMST. In separate analyses (available from the author) I replicate a key model from Table 11.2 with weights that are adjusted for attrition (McGuigan et al. 1997), and I show that the attrition-adjusted weights and the standard weights yield the same results.

[3]Among the 12 subjects for whom the gender of who wanted the breakup was not reported, 6 subjects had their breakup status identified post-hoc from text answers in wave 5, so they did not see the 'who wanted the breakup' question.

In waves 2–5 of HCMST, respondents who reported that their relationship with their spouse or partner from wave 1 was no longer intact were asked: "Between you and (partner name), who wanted the (divorce/separation/breakup) more?" Respondents were offered 3 alternatives: "I wanted the (divorce/separation/breakup) more;"(Partner name) wanted the (divorce/separation/breakup) more;" and "We both equally wanted the (divorce/separation/breakup)." Literature on women's initiation of divorce shows that the average of female predominance in divorce initiation is similar whether one examines the records of who files for divorce, or who wanted the divorce more, or who initiated the divorce (Brinig and Allen 2000; Pettit and Bloom 1984; Sayer et al. 2011; Sweeney 2002), though in individual couples the person who initiates the breakup need not be the same person as the person who most wanted the breakup.[4]

The measure of relationship quality in HCMST is a 1–5 scale, treated as a continuous variable, measured at wave 1, with higher values meaning higher relationship quality (5 is "excellent," 4 is "good", 3 is "fair, 2 is "poor", and 1 is "very poor"). Relationship duration is the time varying duration, in years, since the couple first became romantically involved. Control of relationship duration is necessary to preclude the potential bias of left censored observations (Yamaguchi 1991). The income difference between partners was determined at wave 1 by the question "Between you and (partner name), who earned more income in 2008?" with the options "I earned more," "we earned about the same amount," and "(partner name) earned more." Both female partner's college degree status and the educational gap between female and male partners are based on educational attainment at wave 1. The number of minor children in respondent's household and household income for the prior 12 months are both time varying variables drawn from the 5 KN/GfK background surveys. I deflated household income to 2009 dollars by the Consumer Price Index, and then took its natural logarithm.

Methodologically, I rely on discrete time multinomial logistic regression to distinguish between competing gendered breakup outcomes (Box-Steffensmeier and Jones 2004; Kalmijn and Poortman 2006). My multinomial logistic regressions are weighted using the weight variable "weight2." An alternate set (available from the author) of event history multinomial logistic models which uses robust standard errors and clustering to account for the non-independence of repeated observations of the same couple yields the same substantive conclusions. I present the unclustered event history analysis in Table 11.2 below to preserve model fitting by likelihood maximization, and to preserve BIC goodness of fit tests based on likelihood maximization.

The univariate analysis in Table 11.1 compares three couple types: married couples, non-marital couples who have cohabited, and nonmarital couples who have never cohabited. For Table 11.2, the multinomial logistic regressions, I compare

[4] HCMST data include only one subject from each couple. Sayer et al. (2011) used data from the National Survey of Families and Households, which included both spouses' report on who wanted the divorce. Sayer et al. found consistency between husbands' and wives' reports (about who wanted the divorce more), net of the ego bias effect I discuss below.

Table 11.2 Coefficients (and standard errors) from competing risks discrete time weighted multinomial logistic models for break-up (compared to non-breakups) for heterosexual couples who were married or who have coresided

	Model 1				Model 2				Model 3			
Predictors:	(1a) Male wanted breakup	(1b) Both wanted breakup	(1c) Female wanted breakup	(1d) Female-other difference	(2a) Male breakup	(2b) both wanted break up	(2c) Female breakup	(2d) Female-other difference	(3a) Male Breakup	(3b) both wanted break up	(3c) Female wanted breakup	(3d) Female-other difference
Married	−2.56***	−2.88***	−1.79***	0.92**	−2.40***	−2.71***	−1.66***	0.89**	−2.06***	−2.43***	−1.21***	1.04**
	(0.32)	(0.34)	(0.23)	(0.33)	(0.32)	(0.33)	(0.23)	(0.33)	(0.39)	(0.40)	(0.28)	(0.39)
Subject female	−0.32	−0.43	0.25	0.62+	0.38	−0.19	0.19	0.09	0.48	−0.27	0.19	0.09
	(0.32)	(0.32)	(0.23)	(0.32)	(0.48)	(0.48)	(0.34)	(0.48)	(0.49)	(0.49)	(0.35)	(0.50)
Her relationship quality					−0.46+	−0.68**	−0.89***	−0.33	−0.35	−0.90***	−0.88***	−0.24
					(0.27)	(0.25)	(0.13)	(0.23)	(0.27)	(0.26)	(0.14)	(0.24)
His relationship quality					−1.16***	−0.94***	−0.94***	0.12	−1.22***	−1.00***	−0.94***	0.16
					(0.21)	(0.22)	(0.17)	(0.23)	(0.23)	(0.24)	(0.18)	(0.25)
Female's age									−0.0043	−0.056***	−0.027**	0.003
Female has BA									−0.15	−0.26	−0.34	−0.13
Female more ed									0.46	−0.23	0.35	0.23
1/(Rel Duration)									0.11	−1.23	0.04	0.60
Same income (ref his more)									0.27	1.70***	0.79*	−0.20

Female more income									−0.29	−0.65	−0.003	0.47
ln of HH income (2009 $)									−0.40*	−0.07	−0.18	0.05
Num of minor children in HH									−0.007	−0.006	0.10	0.11
Subject is black									−0.28	1.32**	−0.17	−0.70
df	6				12				57			
LRT	186.3				291.99				375.4			
BIC	−141.0				−201.4				55.1			

Source: HCMST, waves 1–5, for years 2009_2015. For each model, N of couples = 1904 (used as the basis for BIC), and N of couple-months = 95,006. Regressions analytically weighted by weight variable "weight2,". Models exclude 9 subjects whose self-reported gender changed across survey waves. Relationship quality (5 point scale, rescaled so that 0 is best and −5 is worst), female partner's educational attainment, race, evangelical Christianity (3 terms, all insignificant, included in Model 3 but not shown), and relative income of partners both measured at wave 1. Time varying variables are marital status, living with children, age, relationship duration, and household income (in 2009 dollars). Coefficients for four ethnic/racial groups other than black not shown above. The direct effect of gender (for women with relationship quality of zero, model 2 and 3), is not reported in the table. Female-Other Difference is (with letters indicating columns in the table above): $D = C-((B + A)/2)$. $^{*}P < 0.05$; $^{**}P < 0.01$; $^{***}P < 0.001$, two tailed tests

married couples to nonmarital cohabiting couples, and exclude the couples who have never cohabited because some aspects of the power dynamics of couples apply less well to couples who have not cohabited.

The couple-month dataset used for the event history models in Table 11.2 begins with the month of wave 1 of HCMST, and ends with the month of breakup or the month of last contact. I randomly allocated the month of breakup for couples who broke up in the approximately 12 months between wave 1 and wave 2, as month of breakup was not asked in wave 2.[5] The 3 models in Table 11.2 each include 1904 heterosexual couples (reduced via listwise deletion from a maximum of 2262 couples) and 95,006 couple-months of exposure to the risk of breakup.

Results

Table 11.1 and Fig. 11.1 show the percentage of heterosexual couple breakups in HCMST waves 2–5 whose breakup was wanted more by the woman. If the woman wanted the breakup more, that is scored as "1"; if the man wanted the breakup more, that is scored as "0"; and if both partners wanted the breakup equally, that is scored as "0.5." Table 11.1 shows that women accounted for 69% of the breakups of heterosexual marriages, consistent with the approximately two thirds of divorces wanted by wives reported in other studies (England and Kilbourne 1990; Heaton and Blake 1999; Sayer et al. 2011; Sweeney 2002). Even though only 92 breakups of heterosexual marriages were recorded in the data, the 69% of marital breakups wanted by women is significantly different from 50%, with a 95% confidence interval ranging from 61% to 78%.[6]

For heterosexual cohabiters, Table 11.1 shows 76 breakups were recorded, and of these breakups 56% were wanted by the woman. The 95% confidence interval for the gender of who wanted breakup among nonmarital heterosexual unions was 47–65%, which includes 50%, meaning that the gender of breakup for nonmarital heterosexual couples was not significantly different from 50%. Cohabitation proved

[5] For married couples who broke up between wave 1 and wave 2, whose annual rate of breakup was less than 2%, breakups were randomly distributed to months between wave 1 and wave 2. For unmarried couples, breakup rate was much higher in the early stages of the relationship; the breakup rate was more than 60% per year for unmarried couples who had been together for less than a year (Rosenfeld 2014), meaning the breakups would have been distributed more in the beginning of the year than in the end of the year between wave 1 and wave 2. To accommodate the front-loading of breakups of nonmarital unions in the period between wave 1 and wave 2, I used the following function: $M_b = (M_e) r^{\left(\frac{2+rd}{1+rd}\right)}$ Where M_b is the allocated month of breakup after wave 1, M_e is the number of months elapsed between wave 1 and wave 2, r is a random uniform number between zero and 1, and rd is relationship duration in years. For short relationship duration, the random factor is nearly squared, reducing the allocated months before breakup.

[6] Standard errors are defined by $SE = {sd}/{\sqrt{n}}$, where sd is the standard deviation, and n is the sample size in each category.

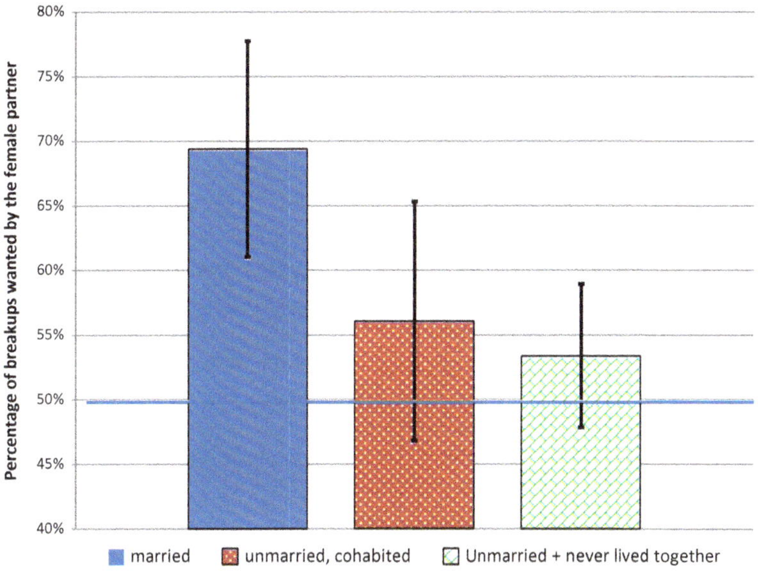

Fig. 11.1 Percentage of breakups of heterosexual couples wanted by the female partner
Source: How Couples Meet and Stay Together, breakups from waves 2–5, covering 2009–2015. Data weighted by weight variable "weight2." See Table 11.1 for more details. Bars represent the average, with 95% confidence intervals. For married, n = 92, for unmarried cohabiters, n = 76, for unmarried and never lived together, n = 203

to have no effect on the gender of breakup for nonmarital couples. Among the non-cohabiting nonmarital unions, 53.4% of the breakups were wanted by the woman, which was not significantly different from the 50% gender parity level and also not significantly different from the 56% rate of female wanted breakups recorded among the cohabiting couples.

Table 11.1 and Fig. 11.1 support Hypothesis 1 (that most divorces would be wanted by the wife) and Hypothesis 2 (that breakup among nonmarital heterosexual couples would be gender neutral). Table 11.1 and Fig. 11.1's support for Hypotheses 1 and 2 is strengthened by the observation that coresidence (and the relationship commitment that coresidence implies) appears to have had no effect on the gender of relationship breakup, whereas heterosexual marriage was firmly associated with women wanting to break up. Table 11.1 shows that mutual breakup was substantially more common in nonmarital breakups (32% for cohabiters and 35% for non-cohabiters) than in marital breakups (19%).

For the gender of nonmarital breakup, there are no published results to compare HCMST to. Is it possible that the person who wanted the breakup is recalled less accurately in nonmarital relationships? One reason that it might be easier to recall who wanted a marital breakup is that divorces require a court petition (which one spouse alone can file), while nonmarital breakups are generally accomplished without paperwork or formalities.

Despite the informality of nonmarital breakups, the nonmarital breakups in HCMST do not show signs of being subject to greater recall bias than the marital breakups. Most breakups in HCMST were reported within a year of occurrence. If the true recollection of who wanted the nonmarital breakup was subject to more recall bias, we would expect to see more ego bias (i.e. the subject, in their recollection of the breakup, giving themselves more agency over the breakup) in the nonmarital breakups.[7] Yet, as Table 11.1 shows, the ego bias appears to be strongest for the married couples, at 78−63 = 15%. Second, subjects' open-ended reports of why they broke up suggest clarity on the respondents' parts about who wanted the breakup. Explanations for breakup include: "I wasn't in love with him anymore, he was selfish, immature. I was ready to move on and find better love;" or "I'm not really sure. She just wanted it to end;" or: "We had a mutual break up ..., we knew that we would never end up getting married as we belong to different religion. However, we had a nice relationship till the time we were together and she is still my very good friend."

Multivariable Tests

Table 11.2 shows coefficients from a series of three competing risk discrete time event history models, for couples who were married or who cohabited. Each model compares competing risk outcomes: male partner wanted the breakup, mutual breakup, or female partner wanted the breakup (compared to non-breakups). Model 1, the simplest model, includes only marriage and subject gender as predictors. Column D of each model tests the difference between predictors of breakups that women wanted compared to the breakups that were wanted either by men or by both partners.[8] The gender difference coefficients (column D of each model) identify which factors explain gendered differences in who wanted to break up. I compare the women-wanted breakups to all other breakups because it is women's unique role in wanting breakups that is of particular interest here. When a coefficient in column

[7] Table 11.1 demonstrates a pattern of ego bias in the reporting of who wanted the breakup, a bias which is evident in similar fashion in every prior study that has surveyed divorced individuals and asked them (after the divorce) who wanted or who initiated the divorce (Charvoz et al. 2009; Hewitt et al. 2006; Kalmijn and Poortman 2006; Sayer et al. 2011). By ego bias, I mean that individuals magnify (after the fact) their own agency in the breakup, so that the rate at which women are reported to want the breakup is lower for male survey respondents compared to female survey respondents. Table 11.1 understates the difference in the percentage of breakups wanted by the woman between married couples (69%) and nonmarital cohabiting couples (56%) because of ego bias. The marital breakups in Table 11.1 were reported by a sample that was majority male, while the nonmarital breakups were reported by a sample that had a slight majority of female respondents. In model 1 of Table 11.2 below, controlling for only marital status and the gender of the subject, the marital gender gap in who wanted the breakup was highly significant.

[8] The coefficient for the gender contrast is $D = C-((A + B)/2)$, where A is the coefficient for men wanting breakup, B, is the coefficient for both wanting breakup, and C is the coefficient for women wanting the breakup.

D of Table 11.2 is positive and significant, that indicates that the attribute in that row is associated with women especially wanting the breakup (net of other predictors of breakup).

Model 1 shows that marriage was negatively associated with breakup, regardless of who wanted the breakup. Being married reducing the log odds of breakups that men wanted by 2.56, and reduced the log odds of mutual breakups by 2.88. Being married also reduced the log odds of women wanting to breakup, but by a smaller amount, by 1.79. In Model 1, women had a higher log odds of wanting marital breakups by 0.92 (column D of Model 1) so the odds of women wanting breakup were $e^{0.92} = 2.51$ times higher than other kinds of breakups for married couples, and the gender gap in wanting marital breakups was significant at the 0.01 level, supporting Hypothesis 1.

Model 2 adds a control for relationship quality (at wave 1) interacted with respondent gender. Note that control for relationship quality does not substantially diminish the gender difference coefficient for marriage (0.89 in Model 2, column D compared to 0.92 in Model 1, column D). In Model 2, being married increased the odds ratio that women wanted the breakup by $e^{0.89} = 2.44$ compared to male initiated and mutual breakups. Relationship quality coefficients that are more negative indicate that better relationship quality (at wave 1) depressed the log odds of breakup. The more negative the relationship quality coefficient, the more sensitive respondents were to relationship quality (in terms of better relationship quality protecting couples more against breaking up). Models 2 and 3 show no significant gendered effects of perceived relationship quality on which partner wanted to break up, because the coefficients in column D of Models 2 and 3 show no significant gender differences in the effect of his or her relationship quality. Table 11.2 provides no support for Hypothesis 3 (that relationship quality has a stronger effect on women wanting to break up) and no evidence for Corollary 3a (that different gender responses to relationship quality would explain women's role in wanting divorce).

Model 3 adds controls for female partner's age, income gap, female partner's education, education gap, household income, number of minor children, subject's race, evangelical Christian identity for both partners (the Christian identity controls were all non-significant, and are not shown), and relationship duration, operationalized as $\frac{1}{\text{r.d.}}$ where r.d. is relationship duration (in years). The $\frac{1}{\text{r.d.}}$ term fit the data better than the untransformed r.d. term because of the sharp decline in breakup rate during the first two years of relationships (Rosenfeld 2014). A positive significant coefficient for $\frac{1}{\text{r.d.}}$ would indicate that longer relationship duration was associated with lower log odds of breakup. Model 3 includes several potential predictors of breakup that allow for tests of Hypothesis 4, specifically whether individuals with more power or more status within the relationship were more likely to want to break up. None of the power differential hypotheses are supported by Model 3. Model 3 shows that females having higher income had no significant effect on which gender partner wanted to break up. Model 3 shows that female partner's age did not have a

Table 11.3 Relationship quality at wave 1 for married and nonmarital respondents in heterosexual unions, by gender

	All wave 1 subjects			Excluding subjects who later broke up		
	Married	Nonmarital, cohabiting	Nonmarital, non cohabiters	Married	Nonmarital, cohabiters	Nonmarital, non cohabiters
Men	4.61	4.22	4.25	4.65	4.35	4.42
Women	4.46	4.29	4.34	4.50	4.37	4.49
N	1826	251	446	1733	189	219
Male-female difference	0.15***	−0.07	−0.09	0.15***	−0.02	−0.07

Source: HCMST wave 1 data, relationship quality scores weighted by variable "weight2." Relationship quality was scored on a 1–5 scale, 5 being the best relationship quality. Relationship quality, Marriage and Coresidence were measured at wave 1, excluding individuals with inconsistent gender reports in later waves of the background survey

* $P<0.05$; ** $P<0.01$; *** $P<0.001$, two tailed tests

gendered effect on who wanted to break up. The lack of significance of all of the power differential coefficients in column 3d, and the similarity of the key gender difference coefficient for marriage across models (0.92 in Model 1 column D, 0.89 in Model 2 column D, 1.04 in Model 3 column D) means that power differentials in education, or income between partners do not appear to explain the women's role in wanting divorce. Model 3 with its several additional terms to test power differential hypothesis fits the data dramatically worse by the BIC standard compared to Model 2.[9]

Relationship Quality

Table 11.3 summarizes relationship quality in heterosexual couples in HCMST. The data on relationship quality show that in nonmarital cohabiting heterosexual couples, men reported relationship quality of 4.22 (with 5 meaning best, or "excellent" relationship quality) and women reported relationship quality of 4.29, not statistically different from the men. In married heterosexual relationships, the men reported relationship quality of 4.61, significantly more than the female reported relationship quality of 4.46. Even excluding all respondents who later broke up from their spouse or partner, the results remain the same: married men in HCMST reported higher

[9]Lower BIC scores correspond to better fit. The BIC for Table 11.2 Model 2 is −201.4, 256.4 points lower than the BIC for Model 3. A difference of 256.4 favoring Model 2 in the BIC is a substantial difference by the standards of the parsimony-favoring BIC, it corresponds to a probability of less than 10^{-54} that Model 3 is the better fitting model (Raftery 1995). The N of couples, 1904, was used as the relevant sample size in calculating BIC. Model 3 fits somewhat better than Model 2 by the Likelihood Ratio Test standard: the chisquare difference of 375.4−291.99 = 83.4 on 57−12 = 45 degrees of freedom yields an upper tail P value of 0.0004.

relationship quality than married women (Corra et al. 2009), whereas men and women in nonmarital unions report more similar levels of relationship quality.

For respondents in heterosexual marriages at wave 1, 69.2% of the husbands and 60.1% of the wives reported that relationship quality was "excellent," or 5 points out of 5 on the relationship quality scale, while 6.0% of husbands and 11.1% of wives reported that their relationship quality was "fair," "poor," or "very poor." Note also that Table 11.2 above showed that neither differences in relationship quality between husbands and wives nor gender differences in the association between relationship quality and breakup explain why women seek most divorces. Table 11.3 provides an explanation: women's relationship quality is slightly lower than men's relationship quality in marriage regardless of whether the marriage later broke up.[10]

Table 11.4 reports a series of OLS regressions predicting relationship quality for men and women in heterosexual marriages at HCMST wave 1, to determine if there were any relational or sociodemographic factors that might explain why married women report lower relationship quality than married men. Table 11.4 shows that while age had a U-shaped association with marital quality, and wives' high earnings were negatively associated with marital quality, and evangelical respondents married to evangelicals had higher marital quality than non-evangelicals, none of these factors moderated or interacted with women's report of lower marital quality (compared to men; note the consistency of the female coefficient across models 1–3). There are demographic and life course predictors of marital happiness, but the marital happiness gap between husbands and wives does not appear to be a function of age, life course, individual socioeconomic status, or demography. Table 11.4 therefore provides no evidence to support Hypothesis 4 (that power inequalities, some of which are age related, might explain women's lower marital satisfaction).

Figure 11.2 shows a smoothed graph of husbands' and wives' marital quality by age, smoothed by lowess regressions (Cleveland 1979). The gender marital satisfaction gap is constant in Fig. 11.2 across the adult age distribution; both husbands and wives in their early 40s report substantially lower marital satisfaction than their younger and their older peers. The lack of an age interaction with the gender marital satisfaction gap is further evidence against Hypothesis 4.

Figure 11.3 shows a smoothed time trend of marital satisfaction for men and for women from the GSS, 1973–2014. In Fig. 11.3, marital satisfaction in the US declined in the 1970s and 1980s, a period when the divorce rate was rising. Despite changes in average marital satisfaction over time, the gender marital satisfaction gap in the GSS has remained fairly stable over historical time. Although the gender marital satisfaction gap in the GSS data amounts to only a difference of 3.6% across all years (with 65.2% of husbands and 61.6% of wives saying their marriage is "very happy"), and Fig. 11.3 reflects a good deal of noise in the measured gender gap within years (where the sample size is much smaller) the gender gap in marital

[10]The relationship quality question in HCMST was re-asked in wave 4. Relationship quality did not change significantly between wave 1 and wave 4 for male respondents or female respondents who married their different gender partner between wave 1 and wave 4.

Table 11.4 Predicting relationship quality for individuals in heterosexual marriages from HCMST Wave 1, OLS regression coefficients and robust standard errors

	Model 1	Model 2	Model 3
Female	−0.16***	−0.16***	−0.13**
	(0.042)	(0.042)	(0.042)
Wife's age		−0.22**	−0.027***
		(0.0071)	(0.0077)
Wife's age squared		0.00026***	0.00030***
		(0.000067)	0.000069
Relationship duration (years)		−0.0032	−0.00096
		(0.0020)	(0.0024)
Earnings gap (ref: husband earned more)			
Equal earnings		−0.019	−0.017
		(0.066)	(0.064)
Wife earned more		−0.16**	−0.15**
		(0.058)	(0.057)
Evangelicals (ref: both Evangelical)			
Wife evangelical		−0.28**	−0.28**
		(0.10)	(0.097)
Husband evangelical		−0.17	−0.16
		(0.11)	(0.11)
Neither evangelical		−0.093*	−0.13**
		(0.045)	(0.044)
Wife has BA			0.098*
			(0.048)
Ln household income			0.073
			(0.038)
Respondent black			−0.24*
			(0.10)
Times married			0.074
			(0.039)
Num children <2 years old			−0.10
			(0.077)
df	1	9	17
N	1752	1752	1752
R-square	0.011	0.0415	0.0612
BIC	−11.9	−7.0	16.3

Source: HCMST wave 1 data, relationship quality scores weighted by variable "weight2." Relationship quality was scored on a 1–5 scale, 5 being the best relationship quality. Interactions between gender of respondent and who earned more, wife's age, and evangelical Christianity were all not significant, so not included above. Four additional race/ethnicity categories not shown
* *P*<0.05; ** *P*<0.01; *** *P*<0.001, two tailed tests

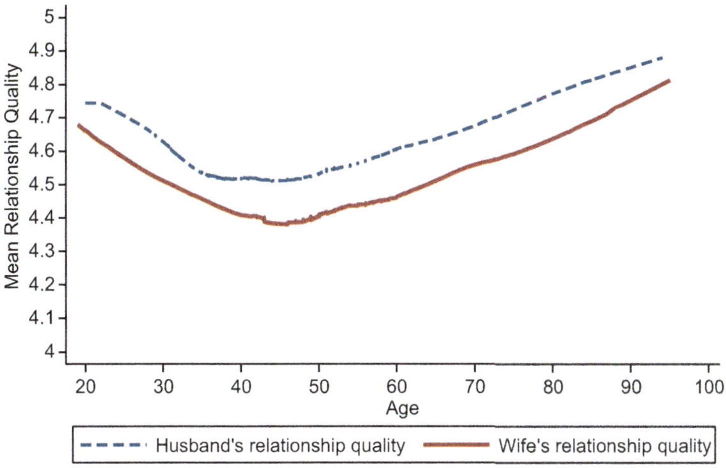

Fig. 11.2 Relationship quality (5 is best) for husband and wives by age smoothed data from HCMST wave 1
Source: HCMST, wave 1 (2009), heterosexual married couples only. Relationship quality is a 5 point scale with 5 being excellent, 4 being good. Unweighted data smoothed by lowess local regressions with bandwidth = 0.8

satisfaction is highly significant, with no significant change in the marital satisfaction gender gap over historical time (significance determined by logistic regressions not shown).

Conclusion

Most divorces in the US are wanted by the wife. In this paper I suggest (for the first time) that the gender gap in relationship satisfaction and the gender gap in who wants the breakup are unique to heterosexual marriage. Nonmarital heterosexual unions have a gender neutral breakup pattern and a gender neutral pattern of relationship satisfaction. Neither women's supposedly greater sensitivity to relationship problems, nor income gaps, nor education gaps, nor conservative religious identity, nor woman's age, nor the presence of children explain why women are so much more likely than men to desire exit from heterosexual marriage, but no more likely than men to desire exit from nonmarital heterosexual unions. The uniquely gendered character of the heterosexual marriage tie is consistent with the view that heterosexual marriage is a gendered institution (Berk 1985; Shelton and John 1993).

The HCMST, GSS, and US Census data I use in this paper do not allow for in-depth insight into marriages that would be required to shed light on how gender is

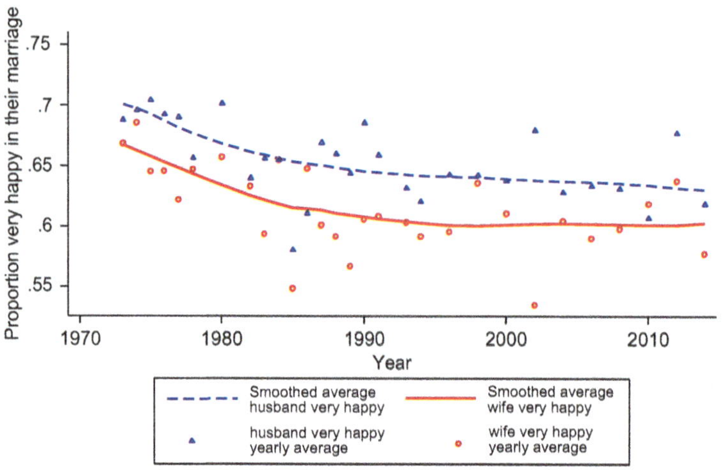

Fig. 11.3 Marital happiness for husbands and wives in the GSS, 1973–2014 smoothed by lowess regressions
Source: unweighted data from GSS, variable HAPMAR, n = 28,362. Question text: "Taking all things together, how would you describe your marriage?", with answers 1 "Very Happy," 2 "Pretty Happy," and 3 "Not Too Happy." In this figure, marital happiness equals answer 1, "Very Happy." Lowess regressions used bandwidth 0.8

enacted within marriages, and to explain what precisely leads to women's lower average rate of marital satisfaction. The specific reasons for women's greater agency in divorce remain opaque. It is also true that selection into marriage is an agentic and nonrandom activity, with the male partner usually having more agency (Sassler and Miller 2011) as marriage ties are formed. Given that men are more agentic in the formation of marital ties, relationships that reflect men's preferences about relationship gender roles may be more likely to transition to marriage. Thus, the gendered nature of marriage might reflect (men's) selection bias rather than transformation of couples' experiences after getting married.

Could women's primary role in wanting divorce be instrumental? Court-ordered spousal support and child support which follow divorce mainly benefit women. There were only 14 marriages in HCMST that ended in separation but not divorce, an insufficient number to judge whether the instrumental aspects of divorce were responsible for some of the gendering of marital breakups. The gender gap in marital satisfaction which is consistent across the life course and across historical time suggests that women's role in marital breakup is not simply introduced at the end of relationships for instrumental reasons; rather, the gender of breakup appears to be rooted in marriage itself.

While the analyses above show that women's predominant role in wanting divorce seems to be robust to power differentials between spouses and robust to perceived relationship quality, sample size limitations of HCMST should be kept in mind. Only 92 breakups of heterosexual marriages were recorded in

HCMST. Furthermore, my analyses here do not provide a model for predicting which subset of women will be particularly likely to want divorce. A substantial proportion of married people who later divorced reported at wave 1 that their relationship quality was excellent, and described the relationship as idyllic or nearly perfect, which is consistent with Vaughan's (1990) description of divorce as often taking one spouse by surprise.

Most married women are happily married, and the marital network tie remains the most stable (and some scholars would argue, the most important) network tie in the modern social world. Across 6 years of HCMST data, the weighted marital breakup rate was 1.2% per year for heterosexual married couples,[11] compared to 9.4% per year breakup rate for unmarried heterosexual couples who ever cohabited, and a 30.3% per year breakup rate for unmarried heterosexual couples who never lived together. Even though most married women are happily married, a modest difference in husbands' and wives' marital satisfaction can result in most divorces being wanted by the wife.

Wives have predominated in wanting divorce since the earliest available data on who wanted divorce from the 1940s. Wives have consistently reported lower marital satisfaction than husbands since the earliest available data from the 1970s. The lack of apparent progress over time in two key marital gender gaps (breakup and satisfaction) is consistent with the stalled gender revolution theory (Hochschild and Machung 1989).

Discussion

Because the marital union is the most stable primary network tie in American social life, the society-wide retreat from marriage has broad implications. Nonmarital unions of men and women are a nontraditional family form that is increasing over time (Rosenfeld 2007; Smock 2000) as marriage prevalence declines among adults, see Fig. 11.4.[12] Age at first marriage has grown more for women than for men in the past few decades (Rosenfeld 2007).

One paradox of gender, marriage, and the life course, is that young single women appear to desire marriage and commitment more than men do, yet married women appear to be less satisfied by their marital experiences than married men are. Figure 11.5 shows smoothed data from the 1996 and 1998 GSS. Consistent with the

[11] The unweighted annual breakup rate of heterosexual married couples through wave 5 of HCMST was 1.44%, compare to the 1.5% reported unweighted annual breakup rate of heterosexual married couples reported in Rosenfeld (2014) using the first 4 waves of HCMST.

[12] The gender gap in Figure 11.4 is driven by the sex ratio of older adults: because women live longer, women outnumber men among adults. Because the US Census Bureau has previously only counted heterosexual marriages as marriages, the count of married couples had to include a nearly equal number of men and women (excluding the small number of minors married to adults and US persons married to persons living outside the US), so the number of unmarried women had to be higher than the number of unmarried men as a function of the adult sex ratio.

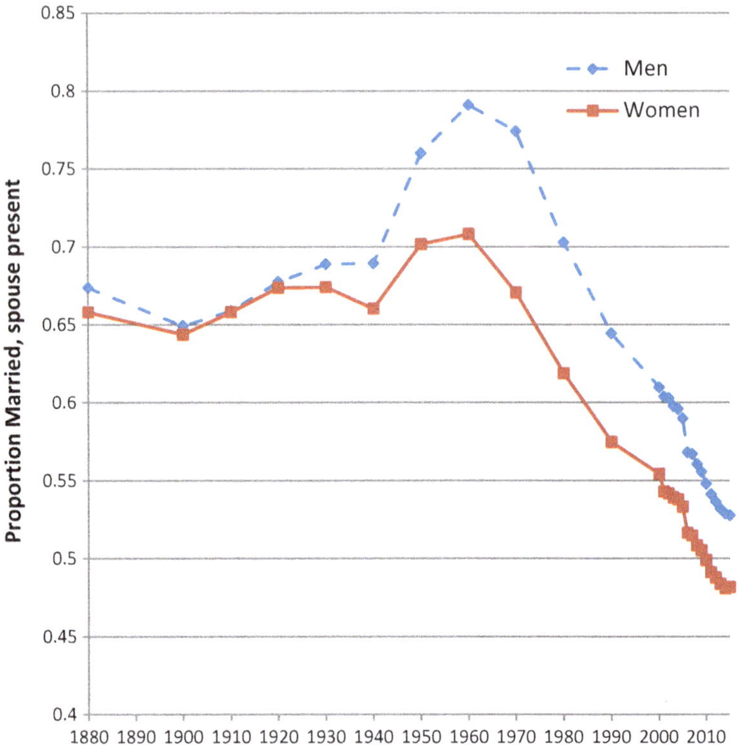

Fig. 11.4 The post-1960 decline of marriage prevalence for adults 20 years old or older in the US Source: Weighted US census microdata from ipums, 1880–2015, persons not living in group quarters

Ad Health results reported by Falcon (2014), the GSS data show that single women were more likely than single men to say they wanted to marry between age 20 and age 35, when most first marriages take place. After age 50, however, Fig. 11.5 shows that single women were substantially less likely than single men to say they wanted to marry "if the right person came along."[13] Women's lower marital satisfaction might explain part of single women's especially steep life course decline in wanting to marry.

[13] The GSS question for the variable willwed2 was fielded only in 1996 and 1998, and only to GSS respondents who were not married. The sample size of 773 respondents to willwed2 yields tests of insufficient power to show conclusively whether women's experience of prior marriage significantly discourages them from wanting to marry again (supplementary analyses available from the author). The remarriage rate for men has long been higher than the remarriage rate for women, yet this difference in remarriage rates could be explained by the surplus of unmarried women in adulthood, see Fig. 11.4.

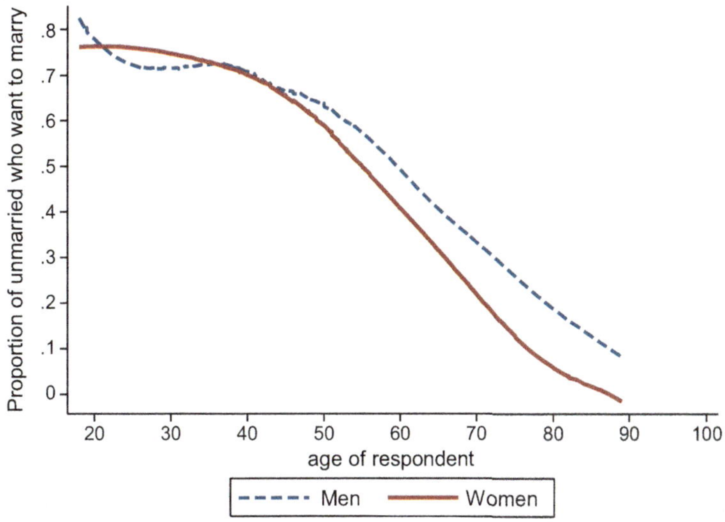

Fig. 11.5 The proportion of unmarried people who want to marry, by age and gender, from GSS 1996 and 1998
Source: General Social Survey, Willwed2 Question text: "If the right person came along, would you like to be married?" Smoothed via Lowess

References

Bass, B. C. (2015). *How couples negotiate marital surname choice*. Unpublished manuscript. Retrieved from https://sociology.stanford.edu/publications/how-couples-negotiate-marital-surname-choice

Berk, S. F. (1985). *The gender factory: The apportionment of work in american households*. New York: Plenum Press.

Bernard, J. (1982). *The future of marriage*. New Haven: Yale University Press.

Bianchi, S., Robinson, J. P., & Milkie, M. A. (2006). *The changing rhythms of American family life*. New York: Russell Sage Foundation.

Blumstein, P., & Schwartz, P. (1983). *American couples: Money, work, sex*. New York: William Morrow.

Box-Steffensmeier, J. M., & Jones, B. S. (2004). *Event history modeling: A guide for social scientists*. Cambridge: Cambridge University Press.

Brines, J. (1994). Economic dependency, gender, and the division of labor at home. *American Journal of Sociology, 100*(3), 652–688.

Brinig, M. F., & Allen, D. W. (2000). 'These boots are made for walking:' Why most divorce filers are women. *American Law and Economics Review, 2*(1), 126–169.

Brown, S. L. (2000). Union transitions among cohabitors: The significance of relationship assessments and expectations. *Journal of Marriage and the Family, 62*, 833–846.

Callegaro, M., & DiSogra, C. (2008). Computing response metrics for online panels. *Public Opinion Quarterly, 72*(5), 1008–1032.

Chang, L., & Krosnick, J. A. (2009). National surveys via RDD telephone interviewing versus the internet: Comparing sample representativeness and response quality. *Public Opinion Quarterly, 73*(4), 661–674.

Charvoz, L., Bodenmann, G., Bertoni, A., Iafrate, R., & Giuliana, C. (2009). Is the partner who decides to divorce more attractive? A comparison between initiators and noninitiators. *Journal of Divorce & Remarriage, 50*, 22–37.

Cherlin, A. J. (2004). The deinstitutionalization of American marriage. *Journal of Marriage and Family, 66*, 848–861.

Cherlin, A. J. (2009). *The marriage-go-round: The state of marriage and the family in America today*. New York: Knopf.

Cleveland, W. S. (1979). Robust locally weighted regression and smoothing scatterplots. *Journal of the American Statistical Association, 74*, 829–836.

Corra, M., Carter, S. K., Carter, J. S., & Knox, D. (2009). Trends in marital happiness by gender and race, 1973 to 2006. *Journal of Family Issues, 30*(10), 1379–1404.

Davis, S. N., Greenstein, T. N., & Marks, J. P. G. (2007). Effects of union type on division of household labor: Do cohabiting men really perform more housework? *Journal of Family Issues, 28*, 1246–1272.

England, P. (2010). The gender revolution: Uneven and stalled. *Gender and Society, 24*(2), 149–166.

England, P., & Kilbourne, B. S. (1990). Markets, marriages, and other mates: The problem of power. In R. Friedland & A. F. Robertson (Eds.), *Beyond the marketplace: Rethinking economy and society* (pp. 163–188). New York: Aldine de Gruyter.

England, P., & McClintock, E. A. (2009). The gendered double standard of aging in US marriage markets. *Population and Development Review, 35*(4), 797–816.

Falcon, M. (2014). *Racial inequalities in marriage outcomes*. (Unpublished manuscript).

Fricker, S., Galesic, M., Tourangeau, R., & Yan, T. (2005). An experimental comparison of web and telephone surveys. *Public Opinion Quarterly, 69*(3), 370–392.

Frisco, M. L., & Williams, K. (2003). Perceived housework equity, marital happiness, and divorce in dual-earner households. *Journal of Family Issues, 24*(1), 51–73.

Gerson, K. (2010). *The unfinished revolution: Coming of age in a new era of gender, work, and family*. Oxford: Oxford University Press.

Goode, W. J. (1956). *After divorce*. Glencoe: The Free Press.

Gupta, S. (1999). The effects of transitions in marital status on men's performance of housework. *Journal of Marriage and Family, 61*(3), 700–711.

Heaton, T. B., & Blake, A. M. (1999). Gender differences in determinants of marital disruption. *Journal of Family Issues, 20*(1), 25–45.

Hewitt, B. (2009). Which spouse initiates marital separation when there are children involved? *Journal of Marriage and Family, 71*, 362–372.

Hewitt, B., Western, M., & Baxter, J. (2006). Who decides? The social characteristics of who initiates marital separation. *Journal of Marriage and Family, 68*, 1165–1177.

Hirschman, A. O. (1970). *Exit, voice and loyalty: responses to decline in firms, organizatins, and states*. Cambridge, MA: Harvard University Press.

Hochschild, A., & Machung, A. (1989). *The second shift: Working parents and the revolution at home*. New York: Viking.

Johnson, D. R., & Scheuble, L. K. (1995). Women's marital naming in two generations: A national study. *Journal of Marriage and Family, 57*(3), 724–732.

Kalmijn, M., & Poortman, A.-R. (2006). His or her divorce? The gendered nature of divorce and its determinants. *European Sociological Review, 22*(2), 201–214.

McGuigan, K. A., Ellickson, P. L., Hays, R. D., & Bell, R. M. (1997). Adjusting for attrition in school-based samples: Bias, precision, and cost trade-offs of three methods. *Evaluation Review, 21*(5), 554–567.

Pettit, E. J., & Bloom, B. L. (1984). Whose decision was it? The effects of initiator status on adjustment to marital disruption. *Journal of Marriage and Family, 46*(3), 587–595.

Poortman, A.-R., & Mills, M. (2012). Investments in marriage and cohabitation: The role of legal and interpersonal commitment. *Journal of Marriage and Family, 74*(2), 357–376.

Raftery, A. E. (1995). Bayesian model selection in social research. *Sociological Methodology, 25*, 111–163.
Ridgeway, C. (2011). *Framed by gender: How gender inequality persists in the modern world.* Oxford: Oxford University Press.
Rosenfeld, M. J. (2007). *The age of independence: Interracial unions, same-sex unions, and the changing American family.* Cambridge, MA: Harvard University Press.
Rosenfeld, M. J. (2014). Couple longevity in the Era of same-sex marriage in the US. *Journal of Marriage and Family, 76*, 905–918.
Rosenfeld, M. J., & Thomas, R. J. (2012). Searching for a mate: The rise of the internet as a social intermediary. *American Sociological Review, 77*(4), 523–547.
Rosenfeld, M. J., Thomas, R. J., & Falcon, M. (2015). *How couples meet and stay together (waves 1, 2, and 3 version 3.04; wave 4 supplement version 1.02; wave 5 supplement version 1.0 ed.).* Stanford: Stanford University Libraries.
Rudder, C. (2014). *Dataclysm: Who we are when we think no one is looking.* New York: Crown Publishers.
Ruggles, S., Genadek, K., Goeken, R., Grover, J., & Sobek, M. (2015). *Integrated public use microdata series: Version 6.0.* Minneapolis: University of Minnesota.
Sassler, S., & Miller, A. J. (2011). Waiting to be asked: gender, power, and relationship progression among cohabiting couples. *Journal of Family Issues, 32*(4), 482–506.
Sayer, L. C., England, P., Allison, P. D., & Kangas, N. (2011). She left, he left: How employment and satisfaction affect women's and men's decisions to leave marriages. *American Journal of Sociology, 116*(6), 1982–2018.
Scheuble, L. K., & Johnson, D. R. (1993). Marital name change: Plans and attitudes of college students. *Journal of Marriage and Family, 55*(3), 747–754.
Shelton, B. A., & John, D. (1993). Does marital status make a difference? Housework among married and cohabiting men and women. *Journal of Family Issues, 14*(3), 401–420.
Smith, T. W., Hout, M., & Marsden, P. V. (2013). *General social survey, cumulative file 1972–2012.* Ann Arbor: Inter University Consortium for Political and Social Research.
Smock, P. J. (2000). Cohabitation in the United States: An appraisal of research themes, findings, and implications. *Annual Review of Sociology, 26*, 1–20.
South, S. J., & Spitze, G. (1994). Housework in marital and nonmarital households. *American Sociological Review, 59*(3), 327–347.
Sweeney, M. M. (2002). Remarriage and the nature of divorce: Does it matter which spouse chose to leave? *Journal of Family Issues, 23*(3), 410–440.
Vanneman, R. (2006). *Gender earnings gap.* Retrieved January 5, 2015, from http://www.vanneman.umd.edu/endofgr/cpsearn.html
Vaughan, D. (1990). *Uncoupling: Turning points in intimate relationships.* New York: Vintage Books.
Wallerstein, J. S., & Blakeslee, S. (1989). *Second chances: Men women, and children a decade after divorce.* New York: Ticknor and Fields.
Weisshaar, K. (2014). Earnings equality and relationship stability for same-sex and heterosexual couples. *Social Forces, 93*(1), 93–123.
Weitzman, L. (1981). *The marriage contract: spouses, lovers and the law.* New York: The Free Press.
Yamaguchi, K. (1991). *Event history analysis.* Newbury Park: Sage.

Michael J. Rosenfeld is Professor of Sociology at Stanford University. He is a social demographer who studies race, ethnicity, family structure, family effects and the history of the family.

Chapter 12
Gendered Life Course Transitions: The Case of Driving Cessation and Social Networks

Markus H. Schafer

Introduction

In the life course paradigm, transitions are the set of events that redirect a life trajectory—the "sequences of roles and experiences" that people experience in a given life domain (Elder et al. 2003:8). Life course transitions, of course, occur in a gendered context. As Moen (2001) maintains, men and women experience distinct life trajectories; key transitions often unfold at different points in the life course, have different implications for daily routines, and take on different meanings for personal identity. The gendered life course perspective originated through careful consideration of how institutional arrangements and labor market policies reinforce a male breadwinner/female homemaker ideal and shape the social organization of work (Moen 2011). A range of studies supports the gendered life course model, especially with respect to differences in family role transitions. Widowhood experiences, for instance, occur more frequently and at earlier average ages for women than for men (Elliot and Simmons 2011), yet take a greater toll on men's well-being (Williams and Umberson 2004). When it comes to role entries, the transition to parenthood entails a disproportionate increase in domestic responsibilities among women (Baxter et al. 2008; Sanchez and Thomson 1997), and tends to accentuate traditional male and female identities (Burke and Cast 1997).

Assertions of the gendered life course approach are also applicable to *driving cessation transitions*, a consequential turning point for many people in later life

I thank Laura Upenieks for her feedback on an earlier version of this manuscript. NSHAP data were made available by the Inter-university Consortium for Political and Social Research, Ann Arbor, MI. Neither the collector of the original data nor the Consortium bears any responsibility for the analyses or interpretations presented here.

M. H. Schafer (✉)
Department of Sociology, University of Toronto, Toronto, ON, Canada
e-mail: markus.schafer@utoronto.ca

D. F. Alwin et al. (eds.), *Social Networks and the Life Course*, Frontiers in Sociology and Social Research 2, https://doi.org/10.1007/978-3-319-71544-5_12

(Adler 2010), yet one that has not been frequently studied in the context of gender. The automobile is a ubiquitous piece of machinery whose use is commonly expected to expire at some point during a person's life. Yet observers have long noted that men and women experience this technological artifact on quite different terms (see, e.g., B.J. Bolin's [1958] amusing commentary 'Men, Women, and Cars'). Given its connection to independence and freedom—and the lack of desired transportation alternatives for many older Americans (Dickerson et al. 2007)—it is not surprising that, in general, people seek to remain a driver for as long as possible (Bryanton et al. 2010; Carp 1971; Siren and Hakamies-Blomqvist 2005). Qualitative studies indicate driving cessation limits the discretionary trips that people enjoy and use to maintain assorted social contacts (Davey 2007; Ziegler and Schwanen 2011), puts older adults in the uncomfortable and often stressful position of requesting rides from busy friends and family members (Braynton et al. 2010), and represents a powerful symbol that irreversible health decline is underway (Ziegler and Schwanen 2011). Yet little research has systematically documented how close social networks change in the aftermath of driving cessation or how such transitions may differ by gender. The purpose of this article is to extend the gendered life course perspective to the case of driving and networks in later life.

Driving Cessation as a Gendered Late-Life Course Transition

By most comparative standards, the United States is an unusually car-dependent society (Buehler 2011; Kenworthy and Laube 1996). Americans, for instance, drive in almost 85% of their daily trips and nearly 70% of U.S. adults opt for their cars when traveling a mile or less. It is clear, moreover, that driving represents a means for older adults to stay socially engaged, exercise freedom of choice, and age autonomously in the community. Yet each year hundreds of thousands of older drivers lay down their keys, making a driving cessation a common life transition as the lifespans of men and women increase (Foley et al. 2002).

For many adults, driving is a social role facilitator and multiplier; it broadens the horizons of people's social possibilities and enables them to perform role activity. Becoming unable to drive, then, represents a transition that could alter experiences such as paid employment, civic engagement, volunteering, informal friendships, or grand-parenting. Absent easy availability of public transportation, it also puts people in the position of soliciting rides from others. This changes the nature of role relationships with friends and family members and likewise alters life trajectories. Consistent with the claim that transitions often elicit "changes in status or identity" (Elder et al. 2003: 8), one of the major fears of those turning in their keys is that they will lose precious independence and be consigned to the status of a "dependent" or a "nuisance" (Bryanton et al. 2010).

There are at least three reasons why the gendered life course perspective, in particular, is relevant for considering driving cessation in later life. First, as noted by many cultural observers, there is a longstanding connection between driving and masculinity in advertising, film, and other aspects of popular culture (Conley and McLaren 2009; Redshaw 2012; Schroeder and Zwick 2004; Shackleford 1999). Such messages have deep roots and wide reach, as research from around the world suggests that driving is a more salient aspect of identity for men than for women (Ozkan and Lajunen 2005, 2006; Polk 2004), that women are disproportionately stereotyped as "poor drivers" (Berger 1986; Ekehammar et al. 2000), and that driving is a more stressful experience for women than for men (Taubman-Ben-Ari et al. 2004). The salience of driving for masculine identity may be especially prominent for current cohorts of older adults who came of age during the ascendency of the automobile (Eisenhandler 1990). These considerations in view, ceding the ability to operate a car may pose a more pronounced change in identity for older men compared to older women. Second, gender norms strongly govern the driver/passenger configuration when people ride in cars. Data from the National Household Travel Survey corroborates that when men and women are in a car, it is the man who most often drives (Santos et al. 2011). These gendered automobile norms ensure that once men can no longer drive, they are in the unfamiliar position of depending on others for rides. Many older women, on the other hand, are typically far more accustomed to the passenger seat. While relying on friends or family for a ride can be an undesirable prospect for people of either gender, the transition from able driver to dependent passenger may be more acute for men than for women. Third, though there is little research documenting gender differences in willingness to solicit rides, some studies indicate that women are more likely to seek help during times of limitation (Barbee et al. 1993). This pattern—reflecting the cultural schema that people adopt when "doing" gender (Moen 2011)—likely extends to the case of asking for rides in the aftermath of driving cessation.

Previous research reports that, regardless of age, women are disproportionately likely to stop driving, and that health status is a more important factor for determining female driving cessation than that of males (Choi et al. 2012). Nevertheless, existing research has given surprisingly little attention to gender differences in the social implications of driving cessation. The gendered life course perspective implies that men and women may experience driving cessation differently and may see different consequences in their social networks. Specifically, women may be less dependent on their own driving abilities to sustain their social networks and their sense of efficacy. It is worth noting, however, that older women are more likely than men to be unmarried and to live alone (Vespa et al. 2013), meaning that men in declining health may have more ready access to a drive-able partner than would a woman in comparable health. Accordingly, it is important to account for partnership status and transitions when assessing the impact of driving transitions (see Curl et al. 2015).

Driving Cessation and Social Connectedness: Prior Evidence and the Current Study

A growing body of literature suggests that driving cessation has negative consequences for older adults, raising the risk of health decline (Edwards et al. 2009a), depression (Fonda et al. 2001) institutionalization (Freeman et al. 2006), and death (Edwards et al. 2009b). Engagement in and through social networks is a key pathway between driving and these important health outcomes (see Berkman et al. 2000), yet few population-based studies have documented how driving cessation affects social connectedness in later life. Evidence from the Health and Retirement Survey indicates that becoming unable to drive limits formal volunteering and informal social support provision to neighbors, friends, and family, though it seems to have less impact on frequency of neighborly socializing (Curl et al. 2014). Data from an urban sample of older Baltimore residents suggest that driving cessation reduces number of friends (e.g., reporting 2–5 rather than 6+), though there was no evidence that people who stopped driving over the course of a decade spoke with their friends or family any less frequently than those who kept driving (Mezuk and Rebok 2008). These projects aside, it is notable that few studies use nationally-representative data to connect driving cessation to the themes of network contraction and decreased social autonomy—ideas central and poignant in much qualitative research (e.g., Davey 2007; Ziegler and Schwanen 2011).

To extend the existing literature, the current article will focus on social networks of older men and women—in particular, network constructs that align most closely with the themes of autonomy and empowerment in later life. First, network growth and the addition of new network members represent an expression of autonomy because they demonstrate the ability to actively replace ties lost in old age, as well as the proactive procurement of needed network resources (Cornwell and Laumann 2015). Older adults who cultivate new ties and/or see a net gain in network size are able to widen their social circle rather than resign to social isolation and network constriction in the face of late-life challenges (see Abramson 2015; Adams 1987). In this way, expanding networks also signify opportunities for active engagement and continued autonomy on into the future. An influx of new ties can present its own challenges, including the potential for disrupted routines and the possible introduction of new norms and influences within the network (Cornwell and Laumann 2015). Yet, older adults emphasize that cultivating new relationships can be mentally and physically stimulating and that is enhances their sense of autonomy and empowerment (Gabriel and Bowling 2004; McMellon and Schiffman 2002; Stevens 2001).

Network bridging potential is a second relevant construct for this study. Bridging potential refers to the maintenance of network ties with people who are themselves not directly connected (Cornwell 2011). Being a bridge between disparate social parties gives older adults alternative exchange partners and makes them less dependent on any specific network member. Therefore, older adults with relatively high (and/or increasing) bridging potential can be considered those with the greatest opportunity to demonstrate independence and autonomy. At the same time, network structures with many structural holes—i.e., unconnected members bridged by the focal individual—are the forms that place the greatest demand on an older adult (Cornwell 2009). Juggling non-overlapping relationships undoubtedly becomes an increasing challenge once someone has relinquished their car keys.

Older adults depend on their cars to accomplish a diverse set of daily tasks, and the maintenance of social networks should be no exception. I therefore hypothesize that driving cessation will shrink people's networks, make more difficult the addition of new ties, and reduce bridging opportunities. These patterns, however, may be less pronounced among women than among men, as women are most likely to actively solicit assistance from friends and family during times of hardship (Barbee et al. 1993). Such inclinations could be helpful in sustaining network connections and offset the consequences of driving cessation. And of course, the initial nature of people's networks—how close they are to their ties, whether ties are predominantly kin or non-kin—will likely influence the extent to which they go on to change after a driving transition. It is therefore important to account for existing network conditions that precede driving cessation.

Methods

Sample

Analyses use panel data from the National Social Life Health and Aging Project (NSHAP). The NSHAP is a nationally-representative sample of 3005 U.S. adults age 57-85 recruited through a multistage area probability design. NSHAP participants were first surveyed in 2005 and 2006 (hereafter, W1) and living participants were re-contacted in 2010/2011 for follow-up interviews (W2). The initial response rate was 75.5%, and 75.2% of the participants who completed W1 interviews participated again at W2. Surveys consisted of in-home interviews and leave-behind questionnaires. About 84% and 87% of respondents returned the questionnaires via mail at W1 and W2, respectively. Factoring in missing dependent variables, the final analytic sample comes to between 1173 women and 1077 men.

Measures

To measure social networks, the NSHAP team asked participants to list the people (alters) with whom they discussed important matters. In addition, participants were asked if there was "anyone (else) who is very important to you", and individuals identified were then added to the roster. *Network size* is the number of alters the respondent named during this procedure. Upon completing the network roster, respondents were asked a series of follow-up questions, including whether and how often each network alter talked to each other alter. *Bridging potential* is the number of times that the respondent connects a pair of network alters who are reported to not know one another or who speak only less than once a year. With network rosters of up to size 6, the highest possible value is 21 ((6*(6−1)/2) = 15), but the variable was top-coded at 7 because few cases had values of 8 or higher (<4% in each wave). Other follow-up information gleaned about each network tie included kin status (used to calculate proportion kin in network) and closeness to network alter (ranging from 1 "not very close" to 4 "extremely close"; used to calculate average closeness across ties).

The network protocol was repeated at W2, but with a valuable wrinkle. After establishing the network roster, NSHAP staff showed respondents a saved version of their W1 roster and ascertained whether current network alters were identical to W1 alters or whether they were new members. From this information, I create a count of *ties added*, ranging from 0 to 6 new alters. W2 information is also used to create change scores for each of the primary network variables (i.e., change in overall network size, change in bridging potential).

Consistent with earlier research (Curl et al. 2014, 2015), I operationalize *driving cessation* with a respondent reporting that he or she was "unable to drive" by W2 if no such report of driving inability was given at W1. The NSHAP survey included separate questions about daytime and nighttime driving at both waves. Participants who indicated that they could drive neither by day nor at night at W2 were coded "1", while those who denoted some ability to drive at either time were coded "0."

Covariates used in the regression analysis were selected on the basis of past research on driving cessation. For demographic traits, I include age, race/ethnicity (non-white = 1; white = 0), a series of dummy variables for partnership status (partnered both waves, partnered neither wave, became partnered, or became un-partnered), education (B.A. or higher = 1; < B.A. = 0), and logged household income (to reduce skew). Health conditions may precipitate driving cessation and declining health often co-occurs with such later-life transitions (Edwards et al. 2009a). Therefore, I adjust regression models for baseline and change score measures of the following health-related variables: *functional limitations* (average difficulty with seven activities of daily living, e.g., eating, dressing, from 0 "no difficulty" to 3 "unable to do"), count of 7 possible *chronic health problems* (e.g., cancer, diabetes), and *eyesight* (from 1 "poor" to 5 "excellent"). The Chicago Cognitive Functional Measure for assessing cognitive health was introduced at W2, so scores from this multi-dimensional measure were also incorporated as a covariate (see Shega et al. 2014 for scoring details). Finally, regression estimates were adjusted for *neighborhood density* to account for differential levels of walkability and driving dependency as well as variable likelihood of accessing public transportation. This variable was derived from NSHAP interviewer reports which scored respondents' block from 1 (buildings/houses close together) to 5 (buildings/houses far apart).

Analysis

I use Poisson and negative binomial regression to assess how driving cessation shapes networks, as all three dependent variables are counts. Models for overall network size and ties added had difficulty converging with the negative binomial estimator, so Poisson was used for those outcome variables (both variables' standard deviations were less than their mean, indicating that overdispersion is not a serious problem). In models for overall network size and for bridging potential, corresponding W1 (lagged) measures are included in order to assess change over time. Coefficients are presented as incident rate ratios (IRRs) to document the percentage change in the expected count of the dependent variable associated with driving cessation, or with a 1-unit change in other variables.

Regression models were estimated separately for men and women. Preliminary analyses examined interactions with neighborhood density to consider whether driving cessation's impact on networks was contingent upon living in more urban contexts. None of these interactions were statistically significant and are not included in the final analyses. Regression estimates employ robust standard errors to correct for the NSHAP's complex survey design and use weights to generalize findings to the relevant American population. Missing data was handled with multiple imputation using an iterated chained equations approach (Royston 2005). Regression estimates were averaged over five imputation data sets in which all study variables predicted missing values; outcome variables were used in imputation equations and cases with missing *Y*'s were removed prior to final analysis (von Hippel 2007).

Results

Unweighted descriptive statistics are shown in Table 12.1. About 21% of the 1001 women who initially indicated that they could drive reported being unable to do so by W2 ($n = 206$). Consistent with prior research, driving cessation was less common for men, as only about 7% of eligible respondents reported the transition between W1 and W2 (68 out of 1025 who initially reported being able to drive). Among men and women, adults who ceased driving tended to be older, in worse health, and with poorer eyesight than those who continued to drive. They were also less likely to have a college degree, more likely to be non-white, and more likely to live in a densely populated area. The descriptive statistics give some indication that for many of those who stopped driving between waves, health limitations were already well underway at baseline (see the worse W1 health scores across multiple dimensions among those in the driving cessation category). Estimates of how networks change from W1 to W2 will therefore be fairly conservative, as network adaptations are already likely in motion among the soon-to-be non-drivers who anticipate this transition. Respondents who already reported the inability to drive at study baseline

Table 12.1 Unweighted descriptive statistics, National Social Life Health and Aging Project (NSHAP)

Variable	Range	Women: Can still drive (n = 795)	Women: Could not drive at W1 (n = 165)	Women: Never drove (n = 7)	Women: Ceased driving by W2 (n = 206)	Men: Can still drive (n = 957)	Men: Could not drive at W1 (n = 52)	Men: Ceased driving by W2 (n = 68)
Main network factors								
Network size, W1	0–6	4.53 (1.37)	4.02 (1.57)	2.57 (1.27)	3.72 (1.57)	3.87 (1.61)	3.35 (1.55)	3.69 (1.76)
Network size, W2	0–6	4.65 (1.34)	4.27 (1.39)	3.71 (1.25)	4.02 (1.54)	4.13 (1.54)	3.17 (1.57)	3.57 (1.55)
New ties added	0–6	1.94 (1.41)	1.98 (1.55)	2.00 (1.73)	1.80 (1.54)	1.79 (1.57)	1.42 (1.55)	1.56 (1.41)
Bridging potential, W1	0–7	1.21 (2.18)	1.06 (2.16)	1.43 (2.23)	0.60 (1.57)	0.61 (1.60)	0.43 (1.35)	0.87 (1.98)
Bridging potential, W2	0–7	1.50 (2.46)	0.99 (2.01)	0.72 (1.50)	0.93 (1.93)	0.72 (1.80)	0.62 (1.61)	0.37 (1.36)
Demographics								
Age	57–85	67.03 (6.71)	72.19 (7.84)	69.86 (7.97)	72.14 (8.05)	67.18 (7.10)	70.96 (8.58)	74.46 (7.56)
Nonwhite	0–1	0.23	0.42	0.71	0.49	0.25	0.69	0.44
College	0–1	0.57	0.29	0.14	0.21	0.58	0.19	0.27
Income (logged)	4.61–14.40	10.51 (0.87)	9.64 (0.87)	9.79 (0.50)	9.63 (0.75)	10.74 (0.96)	9.57 (0.81)	10.00 (0.79)
Not partnered, both waves	0–1	0.40	0.59	0.71	0.57	0.15	0.37	0.39
Became partnered, W1 to W2	0–1	0.01	0.01	0.00	0.01	0.03	0.04	0.00
Became un-partnered, W1 to W2	0–1	0.10	0.10	0.14	0.11	0.06	0.10	0.16
Neighborhood density	1–5	3.23 (1.20)	3.40 (1.18)	3.86 (1.07)	3.49 (1.05)	3.14 (1.18)	3.43 (1.29)	3.67 (0.97)
Health								
Functional impairment, W1	0–3	0.09 (0.20)	0.45 (0.51)	0.31 (0.35)	0.23 (0.40)	0.07 (0.19)	0.49 (0.66)	0.17 (0.28)
Functional impairment Δ	−1.57–2	0.02 (0.22)	0.07 (0.48)	0.00 (0.41)	0.13 (0.38)	0.03 (0.21)	0.10 (0.60)	0.23 (0.46)
Chronic health problems, W1	0–6	1.64 (1.16)	2.34 (1.20)	2.43 (0.98)	2.07 (1.23)	1.58 (1.21)	2.06 (1.26)	2.21 (1.47)
Chronic health problems Δ	0–4	0.39 (0.59)	0.48 (0.66)	0.00 (0.00)	0.44 (0.67)	0.49 (0.70)	0.60 (0.89)	0.60 (0.79)
Eyesight, W1	1–5	3.72 (0.96)	2.90 (1.06)	3.29 (1.38)	3.05 (1.06)	3.63 (0.96)	2.35 (1.19)	3.06 (1.06)

(continued)

Table 12.1 (continued)

		Women				Men		
		Can still drive	Could not drive at W1	Never drove	Ceased driving by W2	Can still drive	Could not drive at W1	Ceased driving by W2
Variable	Range	(n = 795)	(n = 165)	(n = 7)	(n = 206)	(n = 957)	(n = 52)	(n = 68)
Eyesight Δ	−3–4	−0.08 (1.05)	−0.12 (1.14)	0.57 (1.62)	−0.09 (1.30)	−0.07 (1.08)	0.27 (1.25)	−0.16 (1.40)
Depressive symptoms, W1	1–4	1.45 (0.43)	1.73 (0.54)	1.70 (0.49)	1.65 (0.54)	1.39 (0.40)	1.71 (0.51)	1.57 (0.40)
Depressive symptoms Δ	−2.36–1.73	0.01 (0.41)	−0.11 (0.54)	−0.10 (0.50)	0.03 (0.50)	0.01 (0.39)	−0.12 (0.56)	0.04 (0.46)
Cognitive health	0–20	14.93 (3.31)	11.08 (4.19)	10.29 (3.25)	10.50 (4.44)	14.22 (3.47)	8.96 (4.68)	10.56 (4.50)
Network controls								
Closeness to network members, W1	1–4	3.19 (0.46)	3.17 (0.51)	3.35 (0.60)	3.20 (0.47)	3.09 (0.50)	3.11 (0.62)	3.09 (0.48)
Proportion kin, W1	0–1	0.64 (0.29)	0.69 (0.32)	0.87 (0.17)	0.74 (0.29)	0.70 (0.31)	0.69 (0.36)	0.70 (0.32)

were older, in worse health, poorer, less-educated, and more likely to be non-white relative to those who were able to drive at W1. This pattern held among both men and women. Only a handful of women—and no men—reported never having driven.

Tables 12.2 and 12.3 present findings on network change in the aftermath of driving cessation. One of the main highlights from these two tables is the difference between women (Table 12.2) and men (Table 12.3). There is no evidence that driving cessation produces change in women's overall network size, their likelihood of adding new network ties, or their bridging potential in close networks. For women, the incident rate ratio for each model is close to unity and each 95% confidence interval crosses that point. Men's networks, on the other hand, appear responsive to driving cessation transitions. This pattern plays out despite there being only about a third as many men who ceased driving relative to women, indicating that low statistical power should make it more difficult to detect significant differences in the former group. Net of declining physical, mental, and cognitive capacities—which often co-occur with driving cessation and which could also affect networks—men who stopped driving had networks that decreased in size by 12%. This corresponds, on average, to 0.48 fewer predicted network ties at W2 than their still-driving counterparts. Those who stopped driving added new ties at a rate 20% lower than those who kept driving, leading to a predicted value of 1.45 vs. 1.81 network additions, respectively, for those who stopped driving relative to those who continued driving. Finally, men who stopped driving were predicted to demonstrate fewer bridging opportunities than men who remained as drivers. Each of these predicted values is illustrated in Fig. 12.1.

Bridging potential is, in part, a function of network size—bigger networks provide more pairs of ties that could possibly be bridged. Supplementary results

Table 12.2 Incident rate ratios, network changes between W1 and W2, NSHAP women

	Total network size	New ties added	Bridging potential
Already ceased driving, W1[a]	1.03	1.07	0.68
	(0.97–1.08)	(0.93–1.23)	(0.44–1.05)
Never drove [a]	0.99	1.15	0.39
	(0.61–1.59)	(0.67–1.95)	(0.11–1.38)
Driving cessation [a]	0.98	0.99	0.94
	(0.92–1.05)	(0.86–1.15)	(0.62–1.44)
Demographic controls			
Age	1.00	1.00	1.02*
	(1.00–1.00)	(0.99–1.00)	(1.00–1.04)
Nonwhite	1.01	1.06	0.97
	(0.95–1.06)	(0.96–1.18)	(0.65–1.45)
College	1.05*	1.12*	1.31
	(1.01–1.09)	(1.00–1.25)	(0.97–1.76)
Income (logged)	1.01	0.94	1.00
	(0.98–1.04)	(0.88–1.01)	(0.85–1.18)
Not partnered, both waves	1.01	1.09	1.91***
	(0.97–1.05)	(0.97–1.22)	(1.45–2.53)
Became partnered, W1 to W2	1.16***	1.75***	2.71*
	(1.08–1.24)	(1.30–2.35)	(1.07–6.88)
Became un-partnered, W1 to W2	0.97	1.41***	2.00***
	(0.90–1.03)	(1.23–1.62)	(1.32–3.03)
Neighborhood density	1.01	1.00	0.99
	(0.99–1.02)	(0.96–1.04)	(0.89–1.11)
Health			
Functional impairment, W1	0.98	0.89	0.93
	(0.91–1.06)	(0.73–1.10)	(0.52–1.66)
Functional impairment Δ	0.95	0.91	0.52*
	(0.88–1.03)	(0.77–1.08)	(0.28–0.94)
Chronic health problems, W1	1.00	1.02	0.91
	(0.99–1.02)	(0.98–1.07)	(0.81–1.04)
Chronic health problems Δ	1.00	1.01	1.19
	(0.96–1.04)	(0.93–1.11)	(0.98–1.45)
Eyesight, W1	0.99	1.00	1.03
	(0.97–1.01)	(0.93–1.06)	(0.87–1.22)
Eyesight Δ	1.00	1.01	0.98
	(0.98–1.02)	(0.96–1.07)	(0.86–1.12)
Depressive symptoms, W1	0.98	0.99	1.19
	(0.92–1.04)	(0.86–1.14)	(0.81–1.73)
Depressive symptoms Δ	0.98	0.95	1.44
	(0.93–1.03)	(0.85–1.07)	(1.00–2.07)
Cognitive health	1.01***	1.00	1.05*
	(1.01–1.02)	(0.99–1.02)	(1.01–1.09)

(continued)

Table 12.2 (continued)

	Total network size	New ties added	Bridging potential
Network controls			
Network size, W1	1.08***	1.00	1.01
	(1.06–1.09)	(0.97–1.03)	(0.92–1.11)
Closeness to network members, W1	1.02	0.90	0.84
	(0.97–1.07)	(0.80–1.02)	(0.62–1.13)
Proportion kin, W1	0.97	0.53***	0.45***
	(0.89–1.05)	(0.45–0.62)	(0.29–0.71)
Bridging potential, W1			1.17***
			(1.10–1.23)
Observations	1173	1173	1173

Notes: Regression estimates are weighted and standard errors are adjusted for the complex survey design

*** $p < .001$; * $p < .05$; 95% confidence intervals shown in parentheses

[a]Reference group is those who remain driving at W2

Table 12.3 Incident rate ratios, network changes between W1 and W2, NSHAP men

	Total network size	New ties added	Bridging potential
Already ceased driving, W1 [a]	0.82*	0.78	1.51
	(0.68–0.99)	(0.52–1.18)	(0.53–4.27)
Driving cessation [a]	0.88*	0.80*	0.14**
	(0.80–0.98)	(0.64–1.00)	(0.06–0.34)
Demographic controls			
Age	1.00	1.00	1.08**
	(1.00–1.01)	(0.99–1.01)	(1.05–1.11)
Nonwhite	1.00	1.05	0.77
	(0.94–1.06)	(0.90–1.21)	(0.41–1.44)
College	0.97	0.96	1.31
	(0.91–1.02)	(0.82–1.13)	(0.78–2.21)
Income (logged)	1.02	0.96	1.15
	(0.98–1.05)	(0.90–1.04)	(0.93–1.42)
Not partnered, both waves	1.02	1.00	1.20
	(0.95–1.08)	(0.86–1.16)	(0.82–1.78)
Became partnered, W1 to W2	0.97	1.01	1.36
	(0.80–1.18)	(0.68–1.51)	(0.53–3.54)
Became un-partnered, W1 to W2	0.95	1.24	1.39
	(0.86–1.04)	(0.99–1.56)	(0.73–2.65)
Neighborhood density	1.00	1.04	1.19*
	(0.98–1.02)	(0.98–1.11)	(1.01–1.40)
Health			
Functional impairment, W1	1.11	1.09	0.78
	(0.97–1.27)	(0.80–1.48)	(0.32–1.91)

(continued)

Table 12.3 (continued)

	Total network size	New ties added	Bridging potential
Functional impairment Δ	0.97	0.92	0.76
	(0.83–1.13)	(0.73–1.16)	(0.25–2.27)
Chronic health problems, W1	0.99	1.01	0.98
	(0.97–1.02)	(0.97–1.06)	(0.82–1.16)
Chronic health problems Δ	1.00	0.99	0.89
	(0.97–1.03)	(0.90–1.08)	(0.67–1.18)
Eyesight, W1	0.98	0.98	0.84
	(0.95–1.02)	(0.91–1.05)	(0.63–1.13)
Eyesight Δ	1.01	0.99	0.81*
	(0.98–1.04)	(0.93–1.05)	(0.66–0.99)
Depressive symptoms, W1	1.00	0.95	1.25
	(0.92–1.07)	(0.80–1.14)	(0.69–2.27)
Depressive symptoms Δ	1.01	1.06	1.39
	(0.94–1.09)	(0.90–1.25)	(0.90–2.13)
Cognitive health	1.01**	1.00	1.06
	(1.00–1.02)	(0.98–1.02)	(0.99–1.14)
Network controls			
Network size, W1	1.09**	1.03	1.02
	(1.07–1.10)	(0.99–1.08)	(0.88–1.18)
Closeness to network members, W1	1.06*	0.86**	0.79
	(1.00–1.12)	(0.77–0.96)	(0.48–1.31)
Proportion kin, W1	0.94	0.53**	0.52
	(0.84–1.06)	(0.44–0.65)	(0.24–1.09)
Bridging potential, W1			1.17**
			(1.06–1.29)
Observations	1077	1077	1077

Notes: Regression estimates are weighted and standard errors are adjusted for the complex survey design

** $p < 0.01$; * $p < 0.05$; 95% confidence intervals shown in parentheses

[a]Reference group is those who remain driving at W2

reveal that about half of the association between driving and cessation and bridging potential change is explained by changing network size. That is, men who stop driving are in fewer positions of linking otherwise disconnected alters largely because they have fewer structural opportunities to serve as bridges.

Men who had already ceased driving at the baseline also had decreasing network size by W2. This may reflect ongoing consequences of driving cessation experienced just before the study's observation window (men already unable to drive by W1 were, on average, about 3.5 years older than still-driving men). Models predicting new ties and bridging potential were unable to discern differences between men who remained drivers and those who had already stopped driving by survey baseline. For the models predicting the addition of new network members, incident rate ratios associated with driving cessation and with existing driving difficulty are similar in

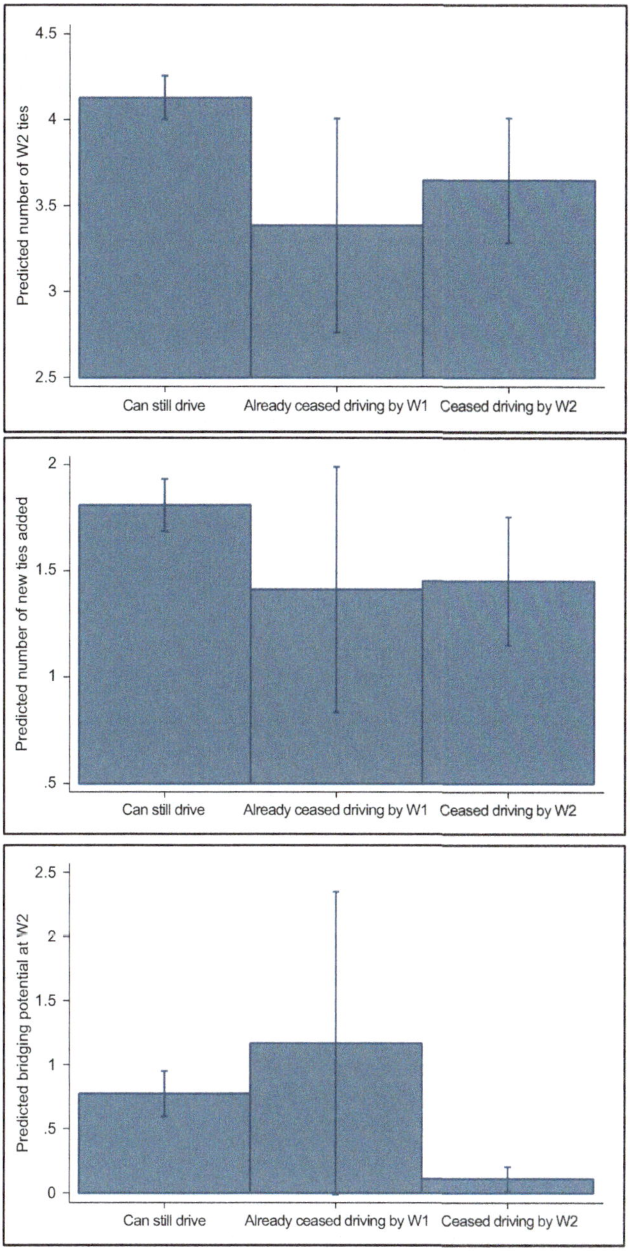

Fig. 12.1 Network changes for men
Note: Figures are calculated from Table 12.3, all other variables held at their mean

size. Confidence intervals, however, are much wider for the latter, reflecting relatively low statistical power.

Though the other covariates are not the focus of this study, it is noteworthy that partnership transitions have strong implications for women's network change. Tie replacement and more bridging opportunities arise for women in the aftermath of un-partnership (widowhood, mostly). Likewise, becoming partnered leads to a surge of new ties, heightens bridging potential, and is associated with a net increase in network size, while consistently non-partnered women have more bridging potential than their partnered counterparts. Few of the other demographic factors or health-related conditions were consistently related to network change for men and women.

Discussion

Driving is a lifeline to the social world. Becoming unable to drive can have important implications for sustaining social engagement in later life and may contribute to a downward cycle of social isolation and health decline (Edwards et al. 2009a; Fonda et al. 2001; Mezuk and Rebok 2008). The current study sought to expand existing literature by considering basic structural features of people's close networks, including size and bridging potential. Networks that expand, get regenerated with new members, and facilitate new brokerage opportunities can yield many benefits, but these structural arrangements may become challenged when older adults give up their keys. Findings from the current study reveal that driving cessation has implications for people's networks, though primarily among men.

Consistent with expectations from the gendered life course perspective, men who stopped driving saw a decline in overall network size, added fewer new network ties, and dropped in bridging potential relative to their still-driving male counterparts. Findings were unable to show that women experienced similar network changes if they stopped driving. The data do not provide a clear explanation for these gender distinctions, but the differences likely reflect a series of normative expectations and relational patterns that have accumulated over individuals' lifetimes and that permeate this cohort's lived experience (e.g., women more likely to assume the passenger role). Taken together, such factors imply that driving cessation is not experienced the same way for men and women, thereby representing the very essence of the gendered life course model (Moen 2001). What may mark a mere life transition for women may represent a trajectory-redirecting "turning point" for men.

Another noteworthy set of findings—not directly related to driving cessation but interesting nonetheless—pertain to network dynamics amidst partnership change. While prior research has reported that partnership change leads to network turnover in the form of loss and gain in network members (Cornwell 2015; Terhell et al. 2004), I am not aware of any studies which examine changes in bridging potential following partnership transitions. Moreover, relatively few studies on network change in later life have considered gender differences, though some studies have shown that widowhood erodes men's social contact more than women's (e.g., Hatch and Bulcroft 1992), while others show no gender differences on the effects of widowhood for social contact and support (e.g., Guiaux et al. 2007). Current findings reveal much network turnover amid partnership change for women, suggesting that both losing and gaining a partner in later life leads to an influx of new core ties and an expansion of bridging potential.

The current study has several key limitations. First, driving cessation is a process that typically occurs over time, yet it is treated in this article as a one-time, discrete event. More waves of data would enable a more nuanced analysis of the incremental process of driving cessation. Second, the ability-based indicator of driving cessation does not provide any information about whether the inability to drive was voluntary or coerced. There may be some cases where respondents reported they were "able" to drive, yet had actually ceased driving due to the request of a spouse or adult child. Finally, it would have been informative to have data on local public transportation and the walkability of respondents' communities. It is likely that these factors moderate the consequences of driving cessation.

Despite these limitations, the current study generates several new insights about an important, yet relatively understudied late-life transition. Driving cessation is considered an undesirable and disempowering life course event (Adler 2010; Bryanton et al. 2010; Carp 1971; Siren and Hakamies-Blomqvist 2005), yet few existing studies have considered how it shapes people's close social networks. Future research can build on these findings to trace how initial and changing network resources moderate other consequences of driving cessation, such as mental health or the sense of mastery. The gendered life course perspective would imply that men and women would respond in different ways to this transition, but personal network context could also play a gender-specific role in buffering the impact of driving cessation on well-being.

In conclusion, the current results suggest that senior services which provide transportation could consider how to facilitate social connectedness among their ridership and provide opportunities for clients to form new ties. Likewise, physicians or adult children who encourage or insist that older adults stop driving should be mindful of the senior's social network context. And, especially when it comes to older men, such advisors should consider how driving cessation may affect their pool of social resources.

References

Abramson, C. M. (2015). *The end game: How inequality shapes our final years*. Cambridge, MA: Harvard University Press.

Adams, R. G. (1987). Patterns of network change: A longitudinal study of friendships of elderly women. *The Gerontologist, 27*, 222–227.

Adler, G. (2010). Driving decision-making in older adults with dementia. *Dementia, 9*, 45–60.

Barbee, A. P., Cunningham, M. R., Winstead, B. A., Derlega, V. J., Gulley, M. R., Yankeelov, P. A., & Druen, P. B. (1993). Effects of gender role expectations on the social support process. *Journal of Social Issues, 49*, 175–190.

Baxter, J., Hewitt, B., & Haynes, M. (2008). Life course transitions and housework: Marriage, parenthood, and time on housework. *Journal of Marriage and Family, 70*(2), 259–272.

Berger, M. L. (1986, January). Women drivers!: The emergence of folklore and stereotypic opinions concerning feminine automotive behavior. *Women's Studies International Forum, 9*(3), 257–263. Pergamon.
Berkman, L. F., Glass, T., Brissette, I., & Seeman, T. E. (2000). From social integration to health: Durkheim in the New Millennium. *Social Science & Medicine, 51*, 843–857.
Bolin, B. J. (1958). Men, women, and cars. *Psychoanalysis and the Psychoanalytic Review, 45*, 113–116.
Bryanton, O., Weeks, L. E., & Lees, J. M. (2010). Supporting older women in the transition to driving cessation. *Activities, Adaptation & Aging, 34*, 181–195.
Buehler, R. (2011). Determinants of transport mode choice: A comparison of germany and the USA. *Journal of Transport Geography, 19*, 644–657.
Burke, P. J., & Cast, A. D. (1997). Stability and change in the gender identities of newly married couples. *Social Psychology Quarterly, 60*, 277–290.
Carp, F. M. (1971). On becoming an exdriver: Prospect and retrospect. *The Gerontologist, 11*, 101–103.
Choi, M., Mezuk, B., Lohman, M. C., Edwards, J. D., & Rebok, G. W. (2012). Gender and racial disparities in driving cessation among older adults. *Journal of Aging and Health, 24*, 1364–1379.
Conley, J., & McLaren, A. T. (2009). *Car troubles: Critical studies of automobility and automobility*. Burlington: Ashgate Publishing Company.
Cornwell, B. (2009). Good health and the bridging of structural holes. *Social Networks, 31*, 92–103.
Cornwell, B. (2011). Independence through social networks: Bridging potential among older women and men. *Journal of Gerontology: Social Sciences, 66B*, 782–794.
Cornwell, B. (2015). Social disadvantage and network turnover. *Journal of Gerontology: Social Sciences, 70B*, 132–142.
Cornwell, B., & Laumann, E. O. (2015). The health benefits of network growth: New evidence from a national survey of older adults. *Social Science & Medicine, 125*, 94–106.
Curl, A. L., Stowe, J. D., Cooney, T. M., & Proulx, C. M. (2014). Giving up the keys: How driving cessation affects engagement in later life. *The Gerontologist, 54*, 423–433.
Curl, A. L., Proulx, C. M., Stowe, J. D., & Cooney, T. M. (2015). Productive and social engagement following driving cessation. *Research on Aging, 37*, 171–199.
Davey, J. A. (2007). Older people and transport: Coping without a car. *Ageing & Society, 27*, 49–65.
Dickerson, A. E., Molnar, L. J., Eby, D. W., Adler, G., Bedard, M., Berg-Weger, M., Classen, S., Foley, D., Horowitz, A., Kerschner, H., Page, O., Silverstein, N. M., Staplin, L., & Trujilo, L. (2007). Transportation and aging: A research agenda for advancing safe mobility. *The Gerontologist, 47*, 578–590.
Edwards, J. D., Lunsman, M., Perkins, M., Rebok, G. W., & Roth, D. L. (2009a). Driving cessation and health trajectories in older adults. *Journal of Gerontology: Medical Sciences, 64A*, 1290–1295.
Edwards, J. D., Perkins, M., Ross, L. A., & Reynolds, S. L. (2009b). Driving status and three-year mortality among community-dwelling older adults. *Journal of Gerontology: Medical Sciences, 64A*, 300–305.
Eisenhandler, S. A. (1990). The asphalt identikit: Old age and the driver's license. *International Journal of Aging and Human Development, 30*, 1–14.
Ekehammar, B., Akrami, N., & Araya, T. (2000). Development and validation of Swedish classical and modern sexism scales. *Scandinavian Journal of Psychology, 41*, 307–314.
Elder, G. H., Jr., Johnson, M. K., & Crosnoe, R. (2003). The emergence and development of life course theory. In J. T. Mortimer & M. Shanahan (Eds.), *Handbook of the life course* (pp. 3–19). New York: Kluwer Academic.
Elliott, D. B., & Simmons, T. (2011). *Marital events of Americans: 2009*. American Community Survey Reports. Retrieved from http:// www.census.gov/prod/2011pubs/acs-13.pdf

Foley, D. F., Heimovitz, H. K., Guralnik, J. M., & Brock, D. B. (2002). Driving life expectancy of persons aged 70 years and older in the United States. *American Journal of Public Health, 92*, 1284–1289.
Fonda, S. J., Wallace, R. B., & Herzog, R. (2001). Changes in driving patterns and worsening depressive symptoms among older adults. *Journal of Gerontology: Social Sciences, 56*, S343–S351.
Freeman, E. E., Gange, S. J., Munoz, B., & West, S. K. (2006). Driving status and risk of entry into long-term care in older adults. *American Journal of Public Health, 96*, 1254–1259.
Gabriel, Z., & Bowling, A. (2004). Quality of life from the perspectives of older people. *Ageing & Society, 24*, 675–691.
Guiaux, M., van Tilburg, T., & van Groenou, M. B. (2007). Changes in contact and support exchanges in personal networks after widowhood. *Personal Relationships, 14*, 457–473.
Hatch, L. R., & Bulcroft, K. (1992). Contact with friends in later life: Disentangling the effects of gender and marital status. *Journal of Marriage and the Family, 54*, 222–232.
Kenworthy, J. R., & Laube, F. B. (1996). Automobile dependence in cities: An international comparison of urban transport and land use patterns with implications for sustainability. *Environmental Impact Assessment Review, 16*, 279–308.
McMellon, C. A., & Schiffman, L. G. (2002). Cybersenior empowerment: How some older individuals are taking control of their lives. *Journal of Applied Gerontology, 21*, 157–175.
Mezuk, B., & Rebok, G. W. (2008). Social integration and social support among older adults following driving cessation. *Journal of Gerontology: Social Sciences, 63*, S298–S303.
Moen, P. (2001). The gendered life course. In R. H. Binstock & L. K. George (Eds.), *Handbook of aging and the social sciences* (5th ed., pp. 179–196). San Diego: Academic.
Moen, P. (2011). From 'work-family' to the 'gendered life course' and 'fit': Five challenges to the field. *Community, Work, & Family, 14*, 81–96.
Ozkan, T., & Lajunen, T. (2005). Why are there sex differences in risky driving? The relationship between sex and gender-role on aggressive driving, traffic offences, and accident involvement among young Turkish drivers. *Aggressive Behavior, 31*, 547–558.
Ozkan, T., & Lajunen, T. (2006). What causes the differences in driving between young men and women? The effects of gender roles and sex on young drivers' driving behaviour and self-assessment of skills. *Transportation Research Part F: Traffic Psychology and Behaviour, 9*, 269–277.
Polk, M. (2004). The influence of gender on daily car use and on willingness to reduce car use in Sweden. *Journal of Transport Geography, 12*, 185–195.
Redshaw, S. (2012). *In the company of cars: Driving as a social and cultural practice*. Burlington: Ashgate Publishing Company.
Royston, P. (2005). Multiple imputation of missing values: Update of ice. *The Stata Journal, 4*, 527–536.
Sanchez, L., & Thomson, E. (1997). Becoming mothers and fathers: Parenthood, gender, and the division of labor. *Gender and Society, 11*(6), 747–772.
Santos, A., McGuckin, N., Nakamoto, H. Y., Gray, D., & Liss, S. (2011). *Summary of travel trends: 2009 national household travel survey*. Washington, DC: U.S. Department of Transportation.
Schroeder, J. E., & Zwick, D. (2004). Mirrors of masculinity: Representation and identity in advertising images. *Consumption Markets & Culture, 7*, 21–52.
Shackleford, B. A. (1999). Masculinity, the auto-racing fraternity, and the technological sublime: The pit stop as a celebration of social roles. *Men and Masculinities, 2*, 180–196.
Shega, J. W., Sunkara, P. D., Kotwal, A., Kern, D. W., Henning, S. L., McClintock, M. K., Schumm, P., Waite, L. J., & Dale, W. (2014). Measuring cognition: The chicago cognitive function measure in the national social life, health and aging project, wave 2. *Journal of Gerontology: Social Sciences, 69*(Supplement), S166–S176.
Siren, A., & Hakamies-Blomqvist, L. (2005). Sense and sensibility. A narrative study of older women's car driving. *Transportation Research Part F: Traffic Psychology and Behaviour, 8*, 213–228.

Stevens, N. (2001). Combating loneliness: A friendship enrichment programme for older women. *Ageing & Society, 21*, 183–202.
Taubman-Ben-Ari, O., Mikulincer, M., & Gillath, O. (2004). The multidimensional driving style inventory—Scale construct and validation. *Accident Analysis & Prevention, 36*, 323–332.
Terhell, E. L., van Groenou, M. I. B., & van Tilburg, T. (2004). Network dynamics in the long-term period after divorce. *Journal of Personal Relationships, 21*, 719–738.
Vespa, J., Lewis, J. M., & Kreider, R. M. (2013). *America's families and living arrangements: 2012*. Washington, DC: U.S. Census Bureau.
von Hippel, P. T. (2007). Regression with missing Ys: An improved strategy for analyzing multiply imputed data. *Sociological Methodology, 37*, 83–117.
Williams, K., & Umberson, D. (2004). Marital status, marital transitions, and health: A gendered life course perspective. *Journal of Health and Social Behavior, 45*(1), 81–98.
Ziegler, F., & Schwanen, T. (2011). 'I like to go out to be energised by different people': An exploratory analysis of mobility and wellbeing in later life. *Ageing & Society, 31*, 758–791.

Markus H. Schafer is an Associate Professor of Sociology and a Faculty Associate of the Institute of Life Course at the University of Toronto. His work has focused on the impact of childhood adversity on later life health, and on the role of social networks on health.

Chapter 13
How Much Can Be Expected of One Child? Consequences of Multiplexity of Mothers' Support Preferences on Adult Children's Psychological Well-Being

J. Jill Suitor, Megan Gilligan, Siyun Peng, and Marissa Rurka

The role of social support in psychological well-being has been a major area of study for social scientists for more than four decades (Carr and Umberson 2013; Umberson et al. 2010; Antonucci et al. 2014). Although much of the broader literature has focused on the benefits of support on recipients' well-being, family scholars and gerontologists have raised concerns about the detrimental consequences of these processes for individuals who *provide* support. In the present paper, we look at the consequences of support processes from the perspective of the provider, bringing together perspectives from family gerontology and social networks. Specifically, we explore whether multiplexity in older mothers' differential preferences for support from their offspring predict adult children's depressive symptoms. By multiplexity, we mean the overlap of multiple activities or exchanges within the same relationship as it is used in the broader literature on ego-centric networks (Kapferer 1969; Verbrugge 1979). By "differential preferences," we are referring to mothers' preferences for some offspring as sources of support over other children, a concept also known as mothers' differential treatment (MDT) or maternal favoritism.

Since the 1980s, both developmental psychologists and sociologists have documented that mothers' differential treatment (MDT) has detrimental consequences for their offspring in both childhood and adulthood (Feinberg and Mavis Hetherington 2001; Jensen et al. 2013; McHale et al. 2000; Peng et al. 2016; Richmond et al. 2005; Shanahan et al. 2008; Suitor et al. 2008, 2015; Young and Ehrenberg 2007). It is not surprising that being the unfavored or disfavored child is

J. J. Suitor (✉) • S. Peng • M. Rurka
Department of Sociology, Purdue University, West Lafayette, IN, USA
e-mail: jsuitor@purdue.edu; peng60@purdue.edu; mrurka@purdue.edu

M. Gilligan
Department of Human Development and Family Studies, Iowa State University, Ames, IA, USA
e-mail: mgilliga@iastate.edu

D. F. Alwin et al. (eds.), *Social Networks and the Life Course*, Frontiers in Sociology and Social Research 2, https://doi.org/10.1007/978-3-319-71544-5_13

associated with lower psychological well-being; however, studies have shown that being the favored offspring, in either childhood or adulthood, can also have detrimental consequences. In fact, the evidence in both early adulthood and midlife suggests that the presence of MDT, regardless of which child is favored, is associated with greater psychological distress, a pattern consistent with theories of both equity and social comparison. Young adults have been found to have poorer adjustment when they perceived mothers' differential treatment (Young and Ehrenberg 2007), particularly in the presence of high levels of perceptions of favoritism (Jensen et al. 2013). Similarly, perceptions of favoritism in midlife have been found to be associated with higher depressive symptoms (Pillemer et al. 2010; Suitor et al. 2015).

However, an issue that has not been investigated in this line of research is whether being favored across multiple dimensions of MDT has a greater impact on well-being than does being favored for a single dimension. In the present paper, we address this question, focusing on dimensions of MDT that, implicitly or explicitly, call for adult children to provide support to their mothers—emotional closeness, preferences for confiding, and preferences for caregiving. Specifically, we investigate whether the consequences of perceptions of mothers' differential preferences for support on children's depressive symptoms vary depending on whether offspring perceive that they are preferred for multiple dimensions of support, compared to a single dimension or no dimensions. Further, we explore whether the associations between depressive symptoms and perceptions of mothers' multiplexity differ by children's gender. To address these questions, we use data collected from 719 adult children nested within 309 later-life families as part of the Within-Family Differences Study-II.

Perceptions of Maternal Preferences for Support and Psychological Well-Being

The question we are raising—how does multiplexity within the mother-adult child tie affect children's psychological well-being—is rooted in theoretical arguments developed by Rose Coser (1991) and Stephen Marks (1977) nearly 40 years ago. This debate focused on the negative consequences of multiple roles as sources of role overload and role conflict, versus the positive consequences of multiple roles as buffers against the demands of each individual role, often referred to as "role enhancement." The hundreds of studies that have addressed the question of which argument is best supported by empirical evidence have resoundingly indicated, "It all depends on context." Context in this case refers to a combination of conditional factors, including which roles, occupied by which people, and at what point in the life course. In the case of mothers' support preferences, we propose that multiplexity is far more likely to have detrimental than positive consequences on adult children's psychological well-being, given the consistent findings regarding the association between favoritism and well-being (Jensen et al. 2013; Pillemer et al. 2010; Suitor et al. 2015; Young and Ehrenberg 2007). Thus, rather than proposing alternative arguments regarding role overload versus role enhancement, we will focus on the possible problematic consequences of multiplexity for adult children who perceive that they are their mothers' preferred sources of support in the later years.

The literature on intergenerational support can be used to suggest that multiplexity in mothers' preferences for support from their adult children has the potential to be more consequential for the well-being of offspring than do mothers' preferences for single dimensions of support. A large body of research has shown that providing support to parents can be especially "costly" in terms of time, energy, and psychological well-being when adult children simultaneously hold multiple demanding roles (Barnett 2015; Lyons et al. 2015). Although these studies consider the consequences of multiple roles associated with combining caregiving and *different* social statuses (e.g., caregiver plus spouse or worker), we propose that the same argument can be made regarding the potential consequences of enacting multiple roles *within* the same social status—in fact, with the same role partner. For example, in the role of confidant, children may be expected to be primarily nonjudgmental listeners when mothers are facing crises; however, those crises may lead children to make decisions that are at odds with the mothers' wishes, as part of the caregiver role.

Taken together, we propose that mothers' multiplex support preferences may create strain due to either time constraints or incompatible expectations between the multiple roles that comprise the multiplex relationship. As a result, depressive symptoms could be expected to be higher among adult children who perceive that they are preferred by their mothers across multiple dimensions of support. Thus, we hypothesize that there will be an association between perceived mothers' multiplex support preferences and adult children's depressive symptoms.

Gender, Perceived Preferences, and Multiplexity

Up to this point, we have discussed the association between mothers' multiplex support preferences and adult children's psychological well-being without taking gender of the adult child into consideration. However, the literature on support to parents and well-being suggests that the experiences of adult sons and daughters as sources of support differ; this is greatly due to gendered variations in the strength of ties (Putney and Bengtson 2001; Rossi and Rossi 1990; Suitor and Pillemer 2006; Suitor et al. 2016), the expectations for support (Suitor et al. 2015), and the actual history of support exchanges between mothers and their offspring (Leopold et al. 2014; Pavalko 2011; Suitor et al. 2006, 2015). These patterns lead us to propose two alternative hypotheses rather than a single hypothesis.

On one hand, there is compelling evidence that the consequences of providing support to older mothers, particularly when occupying other demanding roles, takes a greater toll on daughters' than sons' psychological well-being (Barnett 2015; Bookwala 2009). Such a pattern is not surprising, considering that the standards for daughters regarding providing support to their parents, particularly their mothers, is much higher than those for sons (Suitor et al. 2015). From childhood, daughters are socialized to emphasize their interpersonal relationships, particularly within the family, and to develop their skills as sources of support (Chodorow 1978; Gilligan 1982); in contrast, sons are encouraged to emphasize independence from family and develop instrumental skills (Chodorow 1978; Gilligan 1982). These gendered socialization patterns are particularly evident regarding care to family members across the life cycle (Bianchi et al. 2006, 2012; Sayer et al. 2004). Beginning in childhood, mothers are expected to play a greater role in care to children than are fathers (Bernard 1975; Bianchi et al. 2006; Sayer et al. 2004; Noddings 1984); these gendered expectations remain strong in later-life families when older parents are in need of care from adult children (Glenn 2010; Pavalko 2011).

Further, ties between mothers and daughters are typically substantially closer and more intense than are any other gender combinations, particularly in adulthood (Putney and Bengtson 2001; Rossi and Rossi 1990; Suitor and Pillemer 2006; Suitor et al. 2015). Thus, it is not surprising that daughters are substantially more likely to become caregivers, particularly primary caregivers, to their mothers (Leopold et al. 2014; Pillemer and Suitor 2006, 2014). Not only are daughters substantially more likely than sons to become their mothers' caregivers, but mothers overwhelming prefer daughters over sons to fill this role (Suitor et al. 2013).

Based on this pattern of greater investment in maternal ties by daughters than sons, we propose multiplex support preferences will be associated with higher depressive symptoms for daughters. However, we propose an alternative argument, based on the same literature. Because daughters are socialized across the life course to invest more in their ties with their mothers, increased pressure from multiplex support ties is somewhat normalized; however, when sons are faced with the belief that their mothers prefer high levels of support from them, this deviates from societal expectations and from their own experiences, and therefore they may experience greater distress than daughters. We will explore both of these hypotheses.

Additional Factors That May Predict Adult Children's Depressive Symptoms

It is important to control for several characteristics of adult children that have been found to predict depressive symptoms and within-family differences in mothers' favoritism and disfavoritism. These include child's age, educational attainment, marital status, employment, and self-rated health. In some cases, the controls we have included have not been found to predict patterns of favoritism or disfavoritism; however, we have included them due to their strong role in psychological well-being. This is the case for age, physical health, and employment status (Suitor and Pillemer 2007; Suitor et al. 2013). Specifically, physical health and employment predict lower depressive symptoms (Clarke et al. 2011; Schieman and Glavin 2011), whereas age has been found to have a curvilinear relationship to depressive symptoms (Clarke et al. 2011). Educational attainment and marital status have each been found to predict both maternal differentiation and depressive symptoms; mothers are more likely to favor offspring who have completed more education and have stable marriages (Suitor and Pillemer 2007; Suitor et al. 2013, 2016). Educational attainment and marital status also predict depressive symptoms, with those who are better educated and married reporting lower symptoms than those less educated and unmarried (Clarke et al. 2011). Finally, one family-level characteristic—race—has been found to predict both mothers' likelihood of differentiating and adult children's perceptions of differentiation for some dimensions of maternal favoritism and disfavoritism (Peng et al. 2016; Suitor et al. 2016). We included all of these variables as controls throughout the analyses.

In summary, we hypothesize that adult children's perceptions of multiplexity regarding their mothers' preferences for support will be associated with higher depressive symptoms. Further, we propose alternative hypothesizes regarding the differential consequences of multiplexity on the depressive symptoms of sons and daughters. On one hand, socialization and the history of the relationship may lead daughters to experience higher depressive symptoms when they perceive multiplex support preferences from their mothers; on the other hand, the counter-normative nature of mothers' multiplex support preferences may lead to higher depressive symptoms among sons than daughters.

Methods

The data used in the present analyses were collected as part of the Within-Family Differences Study (WFDS). The design of the WFDS-I involved selecting a sample of mothers 65–75 years of age with at least two living adult children and collecting data from mothers regarding each of their children. The first wave of interviews was conducted between 2001 and 2003; the original study was expanded to include a second wave of data collection from 2008–2011 (WFDS-II). With the exception of race and educational attainment, all of the data for the present analyses were collected at T2.

Procedures

Massachusetts city and town lists were used as the source of the WFDS-I sample. With the assistance of the Center for Survey Research (CSR) at the University of Massachusetts, Boston, the researchers drew a probability sample of women ages 65–75 with two or more children from the greater Boston area. The T1 sample consisted of 566 mothers, which represented 61% of those who were eligible for participation, a rate comparable to that of similar surveys in the 2000s (Wright and Marsden 2010). (For a more detailed description of the WFDS-I and II designs, see

Suitor and Pillemer 2006 and Suitor et al. 2013, where portions of this section have been published previously.)

For the follow-up study (WFDS-II), the survey team attempted to contact each mother who had participated in the original study. At T2, 420 mothers were interviewed. Of the 146 mothers who participated at only T1, 78 had died between waves, 19 were too ill to be interviewed, 33 refused, and 16 could not be reached. Thus, the 420 represent 86% of mothers who were alive at T2. Comparisons between the mothers alive at T2 who did and did not participate revealed that they differed on only education and subjective health; those who participated were better educated and in better health. Comparison of the T1 and T2 samples revealed that the respondents differed on subjective health, educational attainment, marital status, and race. Mothers who were not interviewed at T2 were less healthy, less educated, and less likely to have been married at T1; they were also more likely to be Black.

Following the interviews, mothers were asked for contact information for their adult children; at T2, 81% of the mothers provided contact information – a rate higher than typically found in studies of multiple generations (Rossi and Rossi 1990; Kalmijn and Liefbroer 2011). In cases in which the mother was not interviewed at T2, information from T1 was used to contact adult children at T2. Seventy-five percent of the adult children for whom contact information was available agreed to participate, resulting in a final sample of 826 children nested within 360 families. Analyses comparing mothers with no participating children and mothers who had at least one participating child revealed no differences between these two groups in terms of race, marital status, education, age or number of children, but that daughters, marrieds, and those with higher education were slightly more likely to participate, consistent with other studies with multiple generations (Kalmijn and Liefbroer 2011; Rossi and Rossi 1990).

The analytic sample for this paper includes 719 adult children nested within 309 families. The sample was restricted to adult children: (a) whose mothers were alive at the time of the child's T2 interview; (b) who had at least one living sibling at T2; and (c) whose families had been identified as Black or non-Hispanic white. Using these criteria, 64 children whose mothers had died between T1 and T2 were omitted, as were nine children who had no living siblings at T2, and 18 children who were Asian or Hispanic. Further, 16 children were omitted because they were missing data on variables of central interest. In 13 of the 309 families, the mother died during the period of data collection, such that some offspring were interviewed before and some after her death; only data from the children interviewed prior to her death were included in the analytic sample for this paper.

Table 13.1 presents demographic information for the adult children and their mothers in this subsample

Table 13.1 Demographics of adult children and mothers in analytic sample

	Means, SD, %	
	Mothers (n = 309)	Adult children (n = 725)
Age in years (s.d.)	77.9 (3.1)	49.4 (5.7)
Race (in %)		
White	77.0	79.8
Black	23.0	20.2
Sex (female)	100.0	57.8
Marital status (in %)		
Married	40.8	64.4
Cohabiting	1.0	5.6
Divorced/separated	12.3	13.7
Widowed	46.0	2.4
Never married	0.0	14.0
Education (in %)		
Less than high school	17.5	5.1
High school graduate	43.3	24.6
Some college	13.6	13.1
College graduate	12.6	34.6
Graduate school	12.6	22.5
Number of children (s.d.)	3.7 (1.6)	1.9 (1.5)

Measures

Depressive Symptoms

To measure depressive symptoms we employed the 7-item version of the Center for Epidemiological Studies Depression (CES-D) Scale (Ross and Mirowsky 1988). The CES-D asks respondents how often in the past week they have felt a certain way. It should be noted that the CES-D was not intended for use as a diagnostic tool; rather, it provides a valid and reliable means for ordering individuals on the basis of the frequency and severity of their symptoms. The CES-D's reliability and validity for use in community surveys has been clearly established (Radloff 1977). The items composing the scale are: (a) Everything I did was an effort; (b) I had trouble getting to sleep or staying asleep; (c) I felt lonely; (d) I felt sad; (e) I could not get going; (f) I felt I could not shake off the blues; and (g) I had trouble keeping my mind on what I was doing. In this sample, the scale ranged from 7–28, with a mean of 11.6 (SD = 4.6) and an Alpha coefficient of .84.

Independent Variables

The variables regarding children's perceptions of mothers' support preferences used in the present analyses were collected at T2. To create the perceived maternal support preferences measures, each offspring was asked: (a) To which child in your family is your mother the most emotionally close? (b) Which child in the family would your mother be most likely to talk to about a personal problem? (c) If your mother became ill or disabled and needed help on a day-to-day basis, which of your siblings would your mother prefer help her? Children's responses to each question were coded: 1 = child perceives that mother prefers him or herself; and 0 = child does not perceive mother as preferring any particular offspring or child perceives that mother prefers another child in the family. We chose this coding because adult children's perceptions that they are favored or disfavored by their mothers have been found to predict depressive symptoms in adulthood, whereas perceptions that mothers favored or disfavored their siblings have not (Suitor et al. 2015).

Control Variables

Family Level Characteristics Race was measured by asking the mothers to select from a card listing several races and ethnicities (e.g., White, Black or African-American, Hispanic or Latina, Native American, Asian). They were instructed that they could choose more than one race or ethnicity. The analytic sample for this paper included 574 adult children in families in which the mothers identified themselves as White and 145 in families in which the mothers identified themselves as Black. We coded race as White = 0 and Black = 1.

Adult Child Characteristics Gender was coded 0 = son; 1 = daughter. Marital status was coded as 0 = not married; 1 = married. Age at T2 was calculated as age at T1 plus 7 (the number of years between interviews). Employment was measured by asking each respondent whether he or she was currently working for a job with pay (0 = no; 1 = yes). Respondents' educational attainment was reported by their mothers at T1; categories were 1 = eighth grade or less; 2 = 1–3 years of high school; 3 = high school graduate, 4 = vocational/non-college, post high school; 5 = 1–3 years of college; 6 = college graduate; and 7 = graduate work.

Subjective health was measured by asking respondents whether their physical health was excellent (5), very good (4), good (3), fair (2), or poor (1).

Plan of Analysis

Because the 719 adult children were nested within 309 families, we used multilevel modeling, which accounts for nonindependence and allows for correlated error structure. To determine whether to use random-effects or fixed-effects models, we ran an intercept-only model, which provided the variance components to calculate the intraclass correlation coefficients (Heck et al. 2013). The intraclass correlation coefficient was .025, indicating that the family-level factors accounted for only 2.5% of the variance in adult children's depressive symptoms. Although the amount of family-level variance was small, we also conducted a Hausman test to assess the difference between within-family effects and between-family effects. The results of this test indicated that the differences were insignificant, in which case a random-effects model is generally preferred. We conducted subsequent analyses to determine whether we could identify any particular family-level characteristics that accounted for this explained variance. This set of analyses revealed that race was the only family-level characteristic to predict children's depressive symptoms; thus, we have included this variable in the MLM analyses.

To examine gender differences in the relationship between multiplexity and depressive symptoms, we conducted separate MLM analyses for sons and daughters and compared the coefficients across models (Paternoster et al. 1998):

$$t = \frac{b_1 - b_2}{\sqrt{\left(SEb_1^{\,2} + SEb_2^{\,2}\right)}}$$

Listwise deletion was used to handle missing data on the independent variables because there were fewer than 2% missing on any variable in the analyses (cf. Allison 2010). The analyses were conducted using SPSS23.

Results

Multi-level Modeling

Main Effects Models Table 13.2 displays the associations between adult children's depressive symptoms and perceived maternal preferences for support, beginning with models exploring each dimension separately and controlling for relevant family and child-level characteristics. Models 1 and 2, shown in the left columns, reveal that both perceived maternal preferences for support regarding confiding and emotional closeness predicted children's depressive symptoms. However, as shown in Model 3, mothers' preferences regarding future caregiving did not predict depressive symptoms.

Next, we tested whether perceived multiplexity of mothers' preferences for support by adult children predicted depressive symptoms. As shown in Model 4, the 3-item measure of multiplexity did not predict higher depressive symptoms compared to the individual dimensions of mothers' preferences.

Finally, we conducted the analysis using a two-item measure of multiplexity, including only preferences regarding emotional closeness and confiding. In this case, multiplexity predicted higher depressive symptoms than did either closeness or confiding alone, a difference that was statistically significant ($b = .95$; $p < .05$).

Table 13.2 Mixed model results predicting adult children's depressive symptoms (N = 719)

	Model 1		Model 2		Model 3		Model 4		Model 5	
Predictors	B	SE	B	SE	B	SE	B	SE	B	SE
Family level characteristics										
Race (1 = non-white)	−.83	.44	−.75	.44	−.75	.44	−.86*	.44	−.79	.44
Family size	−.16	.09	−.16	.09	−.21*	.09	−.14	.09	−.13	.09
Child level characteristics										
Daughter	−.04	.32	.07	.31	.16	.32	−.07	.32	−.05	.32
Age	−.04	.03	−.03	.03	−.03	.03	−.03	.03	−.03	.03
Education	−.01	.11	.00	.11	−.01	.11	−.00	.11	−.01	.11
Married	−1.98**	.35	−2.03**	.35	−2.02**	.35	−1.99**	.35	−2.01**	.35
Employed	−1.84**	.42	−1.76**	.42	−1.81**	.42	−1.78**	.42	−1.77**	.42
Health	−1.47**	.16	−1.47**	.16	−1.43**	.16	−1.47**	.16	−1.48**	.16
Perceived maternal favoritism (chose Self = 1)										
Confiding	.88**	.33								
Emotional closeness			.99**	.34						
Preferred for care					.17	.40				
3 dimension Multiplexity (confiding, closeness, care; Reference = 1)										
Chose self for none of favoritism							−.73*	.38		
Chose self for 2 dimensions of favoritism							.09	.43		
Chose self for 3 dimensions of favoritism							1.14	.62		
2 dimension Multiplexity (confiding & closeness; Reference = 1)										
Chose self for none of favoritism									−.49	.37
Chose self for 2 dimensions of favoritism									.95*	.42
Model statistics										
BIC	4091.678		4099.338		4119.794		4081.796		4081.063	
AIC	4082.547		4090.202		4110.652		4072.674		4071.938	

$^{*}p < .05$; $^{**}p < .01$

Thus, the findings reveal that this measure of multiplexity of mothers' support preferences was a stronger predictor of well-being than was either emotional closeness or confiding individually.

Gender as a Moderator

As shown in Table 13.3, we conducted separate analyses to compare the association between perceptions of mothers' support preferences and depressive symptoms for sons and daughters. We have controlled on the same set of variables as in the models shown in Table 13.2, but we present only the coefficients regarding mothers' preferences in Table 13.3. As shown in the top three rows of coefficients, preferences regarding confiding and emotional closeness predicted depressive symptoms for daughters, but not sons. Perceived mothers' preferences regarding future care did not predict depressive symptoms for either daughters or sons.

Comparing the multiplexity measures by gender indicated that the 3-item multiplexity measure (emotional closeness/confiding/future caregiving) did not predict depressive symptoms for either sons or daughters. However, the 2-item multiplexity measure (emotional closeness and confiding) predicted depressive symptoms for daughters but not sons.

We then tested for differences in the magnitude of the associations. Tests between coefficients across models by gender revealed notable and significant differences between sons and daughters regarding perceptions of mothers' preferences for emotional closeness and confiding individually ($p < .05$ for confiding; $p < .10$ for emotional closeness). Although the coefficient for the 2-item multiplexity measure predicted depressive symptoms for daughters, but not sons, the difference between the coefficients between models was not significant.

Discussion

This paper brings together perspectives from social networks and family gerontology, asking whether multiplexity plays a role in the impact of mothers' differential preferences on adult children's psychological well-being. This question is rooted in theoretical arguments developed by Rose Coser (1991) and Stephen Marks (1977) regarding the negative consequences of multiple roles as sources of role strain and role conflict (Goode 1960), versus the positive consequences of multiple roles as buffers against the demands of each individual role, often referred to as "role enhancement."

These theoretical perspectives suggest that mothers' multiplex preferences for support could have beneficial or detrimental effects on adult children's psychological well-being; however, the empirical literature on intergenerational support indicates that multiplexity in mothers' preferences for support from their adult children

Table 13.3 Mixed model results predicting adult children's depressive symptoms by gender

	Model 1				Model 2				Model 3				Model 4				Model 5			
	Sons N = 304		Daughters N = 415		Sons N = 304		Daughters N = 415		Sons N = 304		Daughters N = 415		Sons N = 304		Daughters N = 415		Sons N = 304		Daughters N = 415	
Predictors	B	SE	B	SE	B	SE	B	SE	B	SE	B	SE	B	SE	B	SE	B	SE	B	SE
Perceived maternal favoritism (chose Self = 1)																				
Confiding	-.03[a]	.53	1.47**	.41																
Emotional closeness					.39[b]	.54	1.36**	.42												
Preferred for care									.26	.80	−.03	.46								
3 dimension Multiplexity (confiding, closeness, care; Reference = 1)																				
Chose self for none of favoritism													−.16	.59	−1.29**	.51				
Chose self for 2 dimensions of favoritism													.31	.76	−.19	.52				
Chose self for 3 dimensions of favoritism													−.28	1.31	1.22	.69				

2 dimension Multiplexity (confiding, closeness; Reference = 1)																				
Chose self for none of favoritism																	−.11	.58	−.91*	.47
Chose self for 2 dimensions of favoritism																	.16	.75	1.22**	.50
Model statistics																				
BIC	1733.294		2344.720		1737.437		235.852		1737.060		2373.628		1729.279		2335.976		1731.954		2333.875	
AIC	1725.920		2336.702		173.056		2342.830		1729.679		2365.595		1721.919		2327.973		1724.587		2325.867	

$^*p < .05$; $^{**}p < .01$

$^{a}p < .05$ for the difference between coefficients across models

$^{b}p < .10$ for the difference between coefficients across models

is far more likely to be detrimental. In particular, providing support to parents has been found to take a heavy toll on offspring in terms of time, energy, and psychological well-being, especially when adult children simultaneously hold multiple demanding roles (Barnett 2015; Lyons et al. 2015). We argued that the same proposal could be made regarding the potential consequences of enacting multiple roles *within* the same social status—in fact, with the same role partner. Thus, we hypothesized that adult children who perceived that their mothers held such multiplex support preferences for them would report higher depressive symptoms.

Consistent with our expectations, multiplexity of mothers' support preferences was a stronger predictor than was any individual dimension of mothers' preferences. However, only the two-item measure including mothers' support preferences for emotional closeness and confiding predicted depressive symptoms, whereas the measure including all three dimensions did not. This finding mirrored those for each dimension separately in that both perceptions that the child was most emotionally close to the mother and that he or she was preferred as a confidant predicted depressive symptoms, whereas, perceptions that one was preferred as the mother's future caregiver did not. However, the findings went beyond this to show that the combination of perceiving that one was his or her mother's preferred child for both closeness and confiding carried a heavier toll than did perceiving that one was preferred for either dimension alone.

The relative effects of mothers' preferences regarding emotional closeness/confiding and caregiving might seem counterintuitive, particularly given that caregiving is often portrayed as primarily overwhelming and demanding (Glenn 2010). There may be several processes underlying this difference. First, although caregiving is often found to be stressful (Lin et al. 2012; Marks et al. 2008), recent findings suggest that many caregivers also experience positive dimensions of this role (Lin et al. 2012; Cheng et al. 2016). Further, the caregiving measure asked about mothers' preferences for future support, unlike the measures for emotional closeness and confiding, both of which called for the provision of support at the present time.

Another difference between emotional closeness and confiding versus future caregiving highlights why these expressive dimensions of support may be so costly in terms of psychological well-being. Being a source of emotional support and confiding is a somewhat ambiguous role, compared to caregiving, in which the expected behaviors are more clearly defined. Further, when adult children are especially close to their mothers and serve as their confidants, it may be painful as the mothers age because offspring cannot always "make things better" despite their high levels of investment in these relationships.

Finally, the gender difference in the association between depressive symptoms and mothers' preferences was quite striking in some regards, but did not meet our expectations in others. We had proposed alternative hypotheses regarding differences between sons and daughters. On one hand, we argued that the association between perceptions of mothers' multiplex support preferences and depressive symptoms would be stronger for daughters than sons, given daughters' greater investment in their relationships with their mothers (Putney and Bengtson 2001; Rossi and Rossi 1990; Suitor and Pillemer 2006; Suitor et al. 2015). On the other hand, because daughters are expected to invest more in their relationships with their mothers, we argued that sons might experience more distress than daughters if they found themselves in the counter-normative position of perceiving high support requests from their mothers.

The findings showed that the consequences of perceptions of mothers' support preferences were greater for daughters than sons. This was clearly the case for emotional closeness and confiding, and trended in that direction for the 2-item measure of multiplexity, although the difference did not reach statistical significance. The stronger effects of mothers' preferences on daughters' psychological well-being is not surprising, given the higher investment that daughters have in their relationships with their mothers than sons, and greater expectations that daughters will respond to mothers' requests for support. This pattern reveals that despite some changes in gender norms in recent decades (Bianchi et al. 2006; 2012), differences in adult daughters' and sons' relationships with their mothers continue to reflect the gendered focus on interpersonal relations in the family, as argued by classic theories of gender role development (Chodorow 1978; Gilligan 1982). Further, our findings suggest that these gendered expectations may be particularly strong in later-life families when older parents are in need of support from adult children (Glenn 2010; Noddings 1984), creating the potential for greater role confict or ambivalence for daughters than sons (Connidis and McMullin 2002).

The finding that perceiving oneself as most emotionally close and the primary confidant to one's mother predicted depressive symptoms might be interpreted as suggesting that mothers are most close to offspring whom they feel are most psychologically vulnerable. Although this argument cannot be completely ruled out using cross-sectional data, based on mothers' reports, psychological problems experienced by the adult children in the present study did not predict to which of their offspring mothers were most emotionally close or whom they preferred as confidants (Suitor and Pillemer 2007; Suitor et al. 2013). Further, longitudinal studies in childhood have shown that although children's behaviors and temperaments affect MDT, there are also clear effects of MDT on children's outcomes (Richmond et al. 2005). We suggest that a more likely interpretation of the finding of our study regarding emotional closeness and confiding is that a "cost" of perceiving oneself as most close to one's mother may be greater feelings of responsibility for the mothers' "emotional care," which increases stress. Such an argument is consistent with classic arguments regarding ambivalence and role conflict in intergenerational relations (Coser 1966; Luescher and Pillemer 1998; Merton and Barber 1963).

One additional potential limitation to the present paper is that we are concerned with individuals' perceptions of their mothers' multiplex preferences and expectations, rather than the mothers' actual preferences and expectations. However, we suggest that one's own perceptions are, in fact, more likely to be salient than are others' preferences and expectations in predicting well-being. Our perspective is consistent with empirical literature showing, for example, that perceptions of equity regarding the division of household labor play a greater role in both marital quality (cf. Frisco and Williams 2003; Grote et al. 2004; Kamo 2000; Lavee and Katz 2002; Suitor 1991; Wilcox and Nock 2006) and, for women, psychological well-being

(Robinson and Spitze 1992), than does the actual division of labor. Further, research has shown that perceptions of equity of support are stronger predictors of relationship quality than are actual exchanges of support (Sechrist et al. 2014) and that perceived social support is a stronger predictor of well-being than the actual social support received (Haber et al. 2007; McDowell and Serovich 2007; Wethington and Kessler 1986). Thus, we argue that it is not surprising that one's own perceptions of mothers' multiplex support preferences and expectations are strong predictors of adult children's psychological well-being.

In summary, the findings we have presented are consistent with classic theories of role strain and role articulation (Coser 1991; Goode 1960; Marks 1977) in that strain is especially likely to occur under circumstances in which the individual roles are highly demanding. In this case, we found that adult children reported higher levels of depressive symptoms when they perceived that their mothers preferred them over other offspring in the family for both emotional closeness and confiding—two support roles that are each demanding, ambiguous, and often place their occupants in positions in which the ability to adequately perform the roles is out of their reach. This particularly appears to be the case for daughters, who, due to the gendered nature of these support roles, are especially sensitive to the normative expectations that they both respond to their mothers' needs and successfully ameliorate their mothers' concerns. Under these circumstances, it is not surprising that multiplexity exacerbates the detrimental consequences of roles that are, individually, also taxing for individuals' well-being.

Analyses were conducted controlling on race, family size, child's age, gender, education, employment, marital status, & subjective health.

References

Allison, P. D. (2010). Missing data. In J. Wright & P. Marsden (Eds.), *Handbook of survey research* (pp. 631–658). Bingley: Emerald Group Limited.

Antonucci, T. C., Ajrouch, K. J., & Birditt, K. S. (2014). The convoy model: Explaining social relations from a multidisciplinary perspective. *Gerontologist, 54*(1), 82–92.

Barnett, A. E. (2015). Adult child caregiver health trajectories and the impact of multiple roles over time. *Research on Aging, 37*, 227–252.

Bernard, J. (1975). Adolescence and socialization for motherhood. In S. E. Dragastin & G. H. Elder Jr. (Eds.), *Adolescence in the life cycle, psychological change and social context* (pp. 227–252). Washington: Hemisphere Publishing Co.

Bianchi, S. M., Robinson, J. P., & Milkie, M. A. (2006). *Changing rhythms in American family life*. New York: Russell Sage.

Bianchi, S. M., Sayer, L. C., Milkie, M. A., & Robinson, J. P. (2012). Housework: Who did, does or will do it, and how much does it matter? *Social Forces, 91*(1), 55–63.

Bookwala, J. (2009). The impact of parent care on marital quality and well-being in adult daughters and sons. *The Journals of Gerontology Series B: Psychological Sciences and Social Sciences, 64B*(3), 339–347.

Carr, D., & Umberson, D. (2013). The social psychology of stress, health, and coping. In J. Delamater & A. Ward (Eds.), *Handbook of social psychology* (2nd ed., pp. 465–487). Dordrecht: Springer.

Cheng, S.-T., Mak, E. P. M., Lau, R. W. L., Ng, N. S. S., & Lam, L. C. W. (2016). Voices of Alzheimer caregivers of positive aspects of caregiving. *Gerontologist, 56*, 451–460.

Chodorow, N. (1978). *The reproduction of mothering*. Berkeley/Los Angeles: University of California Press.

Clarke, P. J., Marshall, V. W., House, J. S., & Lantz, P. M. (2011). The social structuring of mental health over the adult life course: Advancing theory in the sociology of aging. *Social Forces, 89*(4), 1287–1313.

Connidis, I. A., & McMullin, J. A. (2002). Ambivalence, family ties, and doing sociology. *Journal of Marriage and Family, 64*(3), 594–601.

Coser, R. L. (1966). Role distance, sociological ambivalence, and transitional status systems. *American Journal of Sociology, 72*(2), 173–187.

Coser, R. L. (1991). *In defense of modernity: Role complexity and individual autonomy*. Stanford: Stanford University Press.

Feinberg, M., & Mavis Hetherington, E. (2001). Differential parenting as a within-family variable. *Journal of Family Psychology, 15*(1), 22–37.

Frisco, M. L., & Williams, K. (2003). Perceived housework equity, marital happiness, and divorce in dual-earner households. *Journal of Family Issues, 24*(1), 51–73.

Gilligan, C. (1982). *In a different voice: Psychological theory and women's development*. Cambridge, MA: Harvard University Press.

Glenn, E. N. (2010). *Forced to care: Coercion and caregiving in America*. Boston: Harvard Press.

Goode, W. J. (1960). A theory of role strain. *American Sociological Review, 25*, 483–496.

Grote, N. K., Clark, M. S., & Moore, A. (2004). Perceptions of injustice in family work: The role of psychological distress. *Journal of Family Psychology, 18*(3), 480–492.

Haber, M. G., Cohen, J. L., Lucas, T., & Baltes, B. B. (2007). The relationship between self-reported received and perceived social support: A meta-analytic review. *American Journal of Psychology, 39*, 133–144.

Heck, R. H., Thomas, S., & Tabata, L. (2013). *Multilevel modeling of categorical outcomes using IBM SPSS*. New York: Routledge Academic.

Jensen, A. C., Whiteman, S. D., Fingerman, K. L., & Birditt, K. S. (2013). "Life still isn't fair": Parental differential treatment of young adult siblings. *Journal of Marriage and Family, 75*(2), 438–452.

Kalmijn, M., & Liefbroer, A. C. (2011). Nonresponse of secondary respondents in multi-actor surveys: Determinants, consequences, and possible remedies. *Journal of Family Issues, 32*(6), 735–766.

Kamo, Y. (2000). 'He said, she said': Assessing discrepancies in husbands' and wives' reports on the division of household labor. *Social Science Research, 29*(4), 459–476.

Kapferer, B. (1969). Norms and the manipulation of relationships in a work context. In J. C. Mitchell (Ed.), *Social networks in urban situations*. Manchester: Manchester University Press.

Lavee, Y., & Katz, R. (2002). Divison of labor, perceived fairness, and marital quality: The effect of gender ideology. *Journal of Marriage and Family, 64*(1), 27–39.

Leopold, T., Raab, M., & Engelhardt, H. (2014). The transition to parent care: Costs, commitments, and caregiver selection among children. *Journal of Marriage and Family, 76*(2), 300–318.

Lin, I.-f., Fee, H. R., & Hsueh-Sheng, W. (2012). Negative and positive caregiving experiences: A closer look at the intersection of gender and relationship quality. *Family Relations, 61*, 343–358.

Luescher, K., & Pillemer, K. (1998). Intergenerational ambivalence: A new approach to the study of parent-child relations in later life. *Journal of Marriage and Family, 60*(2), 413–425.

Lyons, J. G., Cauley, J. A., & Fredman, L. (2015). The effect of transitions in caregiving states and intensity on perceived stress among 992 female caregivers and noncaregivers. *The Journals of Gerontology Series A: Biological Sciences and Medical Sciences, 70*(8), 1018–1023.

Marks, S. R. (1977). Multiple roles and role strain: Some notes on human energy, time and commitment. *American Sociological Review, 42*(6), 921–936.

Marks, N. F., Lambert, J. D., Jun, H., & Song, J. (2008). Psychosocial moderators of the effects of transitioning into filial caregiving on mental and physical health. *Research on Aging, 30*(3), 358–389.

McDowell, T. L., & Serovich, J. M. (2007). The effect of perceived and actual social support on the mental health of HIV-positive persons. *AIDS Care, 19*(10), 1223–1229.

McHale, S. M., Updegraff, K. A., Tucker, C. J., & Crouter, A. C. (2000). Step in or stay out? Parents' roles in adolescent siblings' relationships. *Journal of Marriage and Family, 62*(3), 746–760.

Merton, R. K., & Barber, E. (1963). Sociological ambivalence. In E. Tiryakian (Ed.), *Sociological theory: Values and sociocultural change* (pp. 91–120). New York: Free Press.

Noddings, N. (1984). *Caring: A feminine approach to ethics and moral education*. Berkeley: University of California Press.

Paternoster, R., Brame, R., Mazerolle, P., & Piquero, A. (1998). Using the correct statistical test for the equality of regression coefficients. *Criminology, 36*(4), 859–866.

Pavalko, E. K. (2011). Caregiving and the life course: Connecting the personal and the public. In R. A. Settersten & J. L. Angel (Eds.), *Handbook of sociology of aging* (pp. 603–618). New York: Springer.

Peng, S., Suitor, J. J., & Gilligan, M. (2016). The long arm of maternal differential treatment: Effects of recalled and current favoritism on adult children's psychological well-being. *Journal of Gerontology: Social Sciences*. Advance Online Publication.

Pillemer, K., & Suitor, J. J. (2006). Making Choices: A within-family study of caregiver selection. *The Gerontologist, 46*(4), 439–448.

Pillemer, K., & Suitor, J. J. (2014). Who provides care? A prospective study of caregiving among adult siblings. *The Gerontologist, 54*, 589–598.

Pillemer, K., Jill Suitor, J., Pardo, S., & Henderson, C., Jr. (2010). Mothers' differentiation and depressive symptoms among adult children. *Journal of Marriage and Family, 72*, 333–345.

Putney, N. M., & Bengtson, V. L. (2001). Families, interational relationships, and kinkeeping in midlife. In M. E. Lachman (Ed.), *Handbook of midlife development* (pp. 528–570). New York: Wiley.

Radloff, L. S. (1977). The CES-D scale: A self-report depression scale for research in the general population. *Applied Psychological Measurement, 1*(3), 385–401.

Richmond, M. K., Stocker, C. M., & Rienks, S. L. (2005). Longitudinal associations between sibling relationship quality, parental differential treatment, and children's adjustment. *Journal of Family Psychology, 19*(4), 550–559.

Robinson, J., & Spitze, G. D. (1992). Whistle while you work? The effect of household task performance on women's and men's well-being. *Social Science Quarterly, 73*, 844–861.

Ross, C. E., & Mirowsky, J. (1988). Child care and emotional adjustment to wives' employment. *Journal of Health and Social Behavior, 29*(2), 127–138.

Rossi, A. S., & Rossi, P. H. (1990). *Of human bonding: Parent-child relations across the life course*. Piscataway: Transaction Publishers.

Sayer, L. C., Bianchi, S. M., & Robinson, J. P. (2004). Are parents investing less in children? Trends in mothers' and fathers' time with children1. *American Journal of Sociology, 110*, 1–43.

Schieman, S., & Glavin, P. (2011). Education and work-family conflict: Explanations, contingencies and mental health consequences. *Social Forces, 89*(4), 1341–1362.

Sechrist, J., Jill Suitor, J., Howard, A., & Pillemer, K. (2014). Perceptions of equity, balance of support exchange, and mother-adult child relations. *Journal of Marriage and Family, 76*, 285–299.

Shanahan, L., McHale, S. M., Crouter, A. C., & Wayne Osgood, D. (2008). Linkages between parents' differential treatment, youth depressive symptoms, and sibling relationships. *Journal of Marriage and Family, 70*(2), 480–494.

Suitor, J. J. (1991). Marital quality and satisfaction with the division of household labor across the family life cycle. *Journal of Marriage and Family, 53*(1), 221–230.

Suitor, J. J., & Pillemer, K. (2006). Choosing daughters: Exploring why mothers favor adult daughters over sons. *Sociological Perspectives, 49*, 139–160.

Suitor, J. J., & Pillemer, K. (2007). Mothers' favoritism in later life: The role of children's birth order. *Research on Aging, 29*, 32–55.
Suitor, J. J., Pillemer, K., & Sechrist, J. (2006). Within-family differences in mothers' support to adult children. *The Journals of Gerontology Series B: Psychological Sciences and Social Sciences, 61B*, S10–S17.
Suitor, J. J., Sechrist, J., Plikuhn, M., Pardo, S., & Pillemer, K. (2008). Within-family differences in parent–child relations across the life course. *Current Directions in Psychological Science, 17*(5), 334–338.
Suitor, J. J., Gilligan, M., & Pillemer, K. (2013). Continuity and change in mothers' favoritism toward offspring in adulthood. *Journal of Marriage and Family, 75*, 1229–1247.
Suitor, J. J., Gilligan, M., Peng, S., Jung, J. H., & Pillemer, K. (2015). Role of perceived maternal favoritism and disfavoritism in adult children's psychological well-being. *The Journals of Gerontology Series B: Psychological Sciences and Social Sciences*. Advance online publication.
Suitor, J. J., Gilligan, M., Peng, S., Con, G., Rurka, M., & Pillemer, K. (2016). My pride and joy? Predicting favoritism and disfavoritism in mother-adult child relations. *Journal of Marriage and Family, 78*(4), 908–925. Advanced online publication.
Umberson, D., Crosnoe, R., & Reczek, C. (2010). Social relationships and health behavior across the life course. *Annual Review of Sociology, 36*, 139–157.
Verbrugge, L. M. (1979). Marital status and health. *Journal of Marriage and the Family, 41*(2), 267–285.
Wethington, E., & Kessler, R. C. (1986). Perceived support, received support, and adjustment to stressful life events. *Journal of Health and Social Behavior, 27*(1), 78–89.
Wilcox, W. B., & Nock, S. L. (2006). What's love got to do with it? Equality, equity, commitment and women's marital quality. *Social Forces, 84*(3), 1321–1345.
Wright, J. D., & Marsden, P. V. (2010). Survey research and social science: History, current practice, and future prospects. In J. Wright & P. Marsden (Eds.), *Handbook of survey research* (pp. 3–26). Bingley: Emerald Group.
Young, L., & Ehrenberg, M. F. (2007). Siblings, parenting, conflict, and divorce. *Journal of Divorce & Remarriage, 47*(3–4), 67–85.

J. Jill Suitor is a Professor of Sociology at Purdue University. Her research has focused on parent-adult child relations, family caregiving, interpersonal relations and well-being.

Megan Gilligan is an Assistant Professor of Human Development and Family Studies at Iowa State University. She is interested in parent-adult child relations, adult sibling relations, and their implications for well-being.

Siyun Peng is a doctoral student in sociology at Purdue University. His research interests focus on marriage and family, health, aging and the life course.

Marissa Rurka is a doctoral student in sociology at Purdue University. Her interests are in family and gender, healthy aging, and the life course.

Part VI
Race and Social Networks

Chapter 14
Race, Social Relations and the Life Course

Duane F. Alwin, Jason R. Thomas, and Kyler J. Sherman-Wilkins

Introduction

In this chapter we investigate the potential linkage between race/ethnicity and social relationships. We discuss this topic within the framework of the "racialized life course," which argues that lives and the pathways persons follow are ordered much differently across different racial and ethnic groups. One of the key differences involves the nature of social relationships, particularly the nature of social network ties and social participation. This is an important issue because recent theorizing about present-day racial inequalities emphasize the interlocking nature of several aspects of the *racial paradigm*, including racial ideology, segregation practices, and the role of discrimination (Higginbotham 2013). Historically, of course, the most salient explanation given in the social sciences is that modern-day prejudice and racial discrimination are the key factors in creating racial inequalities (e.g., Bobo 1999; Bobo et al. 1997; Bonilla-Silva 2014; Sears and Henry 2005). Further, audit studies of discriminatory behavior have shown systematic biases against younger members of minority groups, and are clear in their implications with respect to the reflection of racial animus in hiring decisions (e.g., see Pager and Sheppard 2008; Pager et al. 2009; Quillian 2006).

Recently, social science theorizing has proposed that present-day racial inequalities are driven by a suggested "race neutral" process that does not depend upon contemporary racial prejudice and intentional discrimination, but rather focuses on the explanatory mechanisms that emphasize the self-reinforcing nature of

The authors wish to acknowledge the assistance of Judy Bowes and Kerri Weitzel in the preparation of the tables and figures for this paper

D. F. Alwin (✉) · J. R. Thomas · K. J. Sherman-Wilkins
Department of Sociology and Criminology, Pennsylvania State University, University Park, PA, USA
e-mail: dfa2@psu.edu

D. F. Alwin et al. (eds.), *Social Networks and the Life Course*, Frontiers in Sociology and Social Research 2, https://doi.org/10.1007/978-3-319-71544-5_14

institutionalized structural processes rooted in history and culture (e.g., Roithmayr 2014). These accounts emphasize family and neighborhood social networks—processes that are historically tied to slavery and the subsequent *de-jure* period of Jim Crow segregation. Present day inequalities, according to this argument, reflect in part the "locked in" nature of historically-based institutional racism, not necessarily the racist attitudes of protagonists in the contemporary social system. These views are compatible with other theorizing in the social science of race, wherein it is argued that associational ties of African-Americans, especially marital relationships, in the post-slavery era, even after centuries of change, are in many ways reproductive of the social connections of institutionalized structures that impoverished Blacks, especially African-American men, in former times (e.g., Higginbotham 2013; Patterson 1998).

In light of these arguments, this chapter takes as problematic differences among racial- ethnic groups in their social networks and associational ties. We examine black-white differences in social network ties, in addition to aspects of social participation: organizational memberships and estimates of social contact with family, friends and neighbors. Although we conceive of the problem in terms of racial and ethnic differences, we here focus primarily on black-white differences due to the small sample sizes of other ethnic groups in available data. By addressing the question of racial differences in these domains, our research is relevant to the understanding of the importance of social networks and social capital to institutional racism and its persistence. We frame these issues both in terms of the sociology of social networks and the sociology of the life course. We rely on a number of different sources of data in our investigation of these issues, but especially data on social attachments, social networks and social participation from the General Social Surveys (GSS).

To summarize the objectives of this chapter, we (1) begin with a theoretical discussion of how social networks are important in the study of the life course; (2) provide a brief overview of the link between race and the life course, from conception to death, with a focus on race and social networks; (3) review the existing literature on the relationship between race and social networks and how these relationships may potentially change over the life course; (4) present available evidence from large-scale social surveys, specifically survey data from three GSS surveys, obtained in 1985, 1987 and 2004, which used ego-centric network name generators and follow up questions regarding the composition of the network; and (5) we extend the analysis of the GSS to include two additional domains relevant to racial differences in social relationships, associational memberships and social participation.

Theoretical Background

Historically, perhaps the most salient explanation given in social psychology, and social science generally, is that modern-day prejudice and racial discrimination are the key factors in creating contemporary racial inequalities. Going beyond the psychological theories of prejudice (e.g., Allport 1954), Herbert Blumer (1958) argued that societies are stratified in "color hierarchies" and that belief systems arise from these hierarchies that justify and maintain their existence. Members of society develop schemas regarding the relative "sense of group position" allocated to different groups. These schemas are part of the culture and learned during early periods of socialization. It has been argued that the remnants of slavery were preserved in racialist thinking, reflected in attitudes and beliefs of white citizens, especially during the Jim Crow era. The general view is that "old fashioned" or Jim Crow racism has declined over the past 50–60 years in America (see Schuman et al. 1997; Bobo et al. 2012), but several scholars have argued that there remains a persistent form of "modern day racism." The latter is a contemporary racial ideology that contains just as much racial animosity tied to the sense of group position as did Jim Crow racism, and these modern-day forms of racial animosity continue to promote prejudice and discrimination. There have been several ways of articulating these modern forms of racism (e.g., Bobo 1999; Bobo et al. 1997; Bonilla-Silva 2014; Sears and Henry 2005), and these modern forms of racism continue to serve as important explanations of continuing racial inequalities (see review by Quillian 2006).

In an important contrast to this way of thinking—namely that persistent racial inequalities exist in American society results from racialized thinking on the part of the dominant white population as noted above—a new perspective has recently come on to the scene. In her book, *Reproducing Racism*, (2014), Daria Roithmayr has staked out the argument that, consistent with the "locked-in model," in other spheres (e.g. in judicial precedents, in software development, in real estate transactions, etc.), our models of racial inequality need to reframe our contemporary understanding of persistent racial gaps in American society. Roithmayr indicates that her explanation is "race neutral" with respect to contemporary racial ideologies—it is the past that has created the present-day inequalities, not present-day racism. In other words, she discounts the basic elements of contemporary theories of "modern-day racism" discussed above. To be sure, Roithmayr (2014) does not deny the existence of racial animus, and her larger claim is plausible, given the extensive empirical literature connecting social network characteristics to resource flows like social support and social capital (House et al. 1988; Lin 2001; Lin et al. 1979; Wellman 1983; Smith and Christakis 2008), employment and occupational attainment (Granovetter 1995; Lin et al. 1981), and physical and mental health (Berkman and Syme 1979; Lin et al. 2014; Litwin and Stoeckel 2013; Thoits 2011; Uchino et al. 2012; York et al. 2009). As noted earlier, consistent with Roithmayr's (2014) argument, Orlando Patterson (1998 has put forth the argument that blacks are the most isolated social group in America in the aftermath of slavery and the Jim Crow era (see also Higginbotham 2013). He argues that the roots in the institution of slavery are responsible for diminished social networks of African-Americans, especially of men. Using data from the 1985 GSS networks module, he found considerable support for smaller and more dense social networks among African-Americans. In this paper we replicate some of Patterson's (1998) findings and provide a more exhaustive empirical assessment of the relationships of race to social relationships and social participation more generally. We find there is support for Patterson's claims using the GSS network module data from 1985, 1987 and 2004, but using standard social participation measures from the GSS, we find that blacks "activate" their social networks to a greater extent than do whites.

Race and the Life Course

Many arguments have been set forth for why social networks matter, and how they may operate differently for different racial-ethnic (hereafter we simply use the term "race" but we include racial and ethnic groups in our interpretation of this term). Research indicates that race-ethnicity is intimately tied to the life course, and we argue that the linkage between race and the life course fundamentally involves the connections between social networks, race and the life course. We argue that it is important to consider a model that simultaneously integrates race, social networks, and the life course. In this chapter we investigate the potential support for this point of view, exploring the linkage between race/ethnicity and social networks within this multidimensional framework.

Racial disparities occur throughout the life span, and some of these disparities result in differences in the social worlds of racial groups. A key element in connecting these conceptual domains is the realization that *life course transitions*, such as progressing through the educational system, entering the labor force, and forming families (through marriage, divorce and parenthood), bring individuals into contact with existing social networks and social relationships. At the same time, social networks also influence life course transitions, which in turn, bring individuals into new social spaces and opportunities for developing new social ties. We argue that this process begins very early in life (see, e.g., Kuh and Ben-Shlomo 2004), as the child's social environment largely structures the potential pool of available network ties, and that the nature of these network ties differs among racial and ethnic group members over the entire life span.

One of the key elements of the differences in social worlds of race-ethnic groups are the social networks, or level of social participation of minority groups. We conceive of a "racialized life course," which results in important differences in the nature of one's social networks at important life course transitions. The idea of a "racialized life course" is conceptualized in much the same way that Phyllis Moen and her colleagues have conceptualized the "gendered life course" (Moen 2001), namely that gender (in our case, race-ethnicity) defines the nature of life and life courses. In this regard, the nature of the life course lends itself to understanding the fact that there are differences in institutionalized events, transitions and trajectories for different subgroups of society, and therefore lives are "racialized," due to those differences. There is much to cover in this topic, given that the focus begins at conception and ends at death. At the same time, there is much that we know, which we can only briefly summarize here. Our assumption is that the differences in the life courses of racial/ethnic groups result in differences in the nature of social networks, although we cannot link these directly in our empirical analysis presented here. We assume the nature of the life course lends itself to understanding the fact that there are differences in events, transitions and trajectories for different subgroups of society (in this case racial subgroups), and therefore lives are "racialized" in nature (Alwin 2012). Recent theorizing in the social sciences by African-American feminist scholars has pointed to the "intersectionality" of various ascriptive statuses, particularly race, gender, and sexuality (see Crenshaw 1991; McCall 2005; Thornton-Dill and Zambrana 2009). Intersectionality theory has a great deal to say about race differences in social networks and vice versa, the study of social networks and social relationships can help inform a variety of theoretical perspectives. Again, although our main focus here is in black-white differences, we are aware there are other ethnic experiences, and in the analysis of data presented here, in a limited number of cases (the 2004 GSS survey) we have information on Hispanics.

Race and Social Relations

The life courses of different racial and ethnic groups result in differences in the nature of their social relationships. In this section we briefly review areas of research that have suggested there are racial differences in social networks and social participation, which are developed over the racialized life course. We begin this discussion of empirical results from the General Social Survey (GSS) on race and social networks described by Orlando Patterson (1998), and then we briefly consider each of these aspects of social participation prior to investigating some of these ideas using empirical data. Specifically, we cover: (1) the growing literature on race and social networks; (2) research on associational memberships; (3) literature on race and social participation and (4) findings of race differences in the study of social support.

Social Networks

Patterson (1998) develops an historical interpretation that links the present day experiences of African-Americans to behavioral patterns connected to slavery. Among other things, he draws upon 1985 General Social Survey (GSS) network data to show that, relative to other races, blacks have networks that are smaller, denser, and consist of fewer kin. It is important to note that the GSS network measures focus attention on "core discussion networks," i.e. persons with whom they have discussed "important matters" (e.g., Fischer 1982; McAllister and Fischer 1978). He argues that not only are African Americans even more isolated from other ethnic groups than they are from each other. He suggests that low rates of marriage are "the root of the problem" (p. 155). We return to the issue of racial differences in marriage later on. The following were his key findings (Patterson 1998, pp. 152–154) with respect to racial differences in social networks using the 1985 GSS network data: (1) African-Americans have smaller numbers of persons in their core discussion networks; (2) African-American networks are highly dense, being substantially more dense than are other ethnicities; (3) Despite being more dense, the networks of African-Americans are "striking for the low proportion of ties that were kin--nearly half of African-Americans had no kin in their networks, whereas this was true of only one-quarter of European- Americans; (4) Among European-Americans, those with higher levels of schooling had less dense social networks, suggesting that higher levels of education give people access to a wider range of social contacts; the finding did not hold for African-Americans; (5) Marriage had a strong relationship to the number of kin in one's network for European- Americans, whereas there was no such relationship among African-Americans.

From these findings, Patterson concluded that African-Americans "are in the worst possible situation in regard to the composition of their social ties" (Patterson 1998, p. 154). Their networks are smaller, denser, and their range of contacts "narrower than those of other Americans" (Patterson 1998, p. 154). Further, not only do they experience impoverished social ties, African-Americans rely on ties that have the smallest proportions of kinsmen relative to all other ethnic groups, and therefore, contrary to ethnographic mythology (e.g., see Stack 1974), Patterson argues that they do not derive the benefits of family support and solidarity that is true for whites. With respect to education, African-Americans are "gaining little in terms of enlarged range of ties from their educational experiences." Similar findings held with regard to employment and social class. Employed and higher status European-Americans had less dense networks, whereas among African-Americans, there was no such relationship. We return to Patterson's results in our empirical investigation of differences in social networks with respect to race/ethnicity below, where these results are replication and extended.

In the analysis presented below, we extend Patterson's work to two additional GSS network modules, carried out in 1987 and 2004. We are in a position therefore of examining the generality of the findings from the 1985 study, using relatively consistent measures. In addition, we combine this re-analysis and replication of Patterson's analysis by turning to a number of additional measures of social network ties, not specifically driven by network methodology, but nonetheless standard concepts in the social integration literature. We look at two major constructs, the first of which is suggested by the social capital literature, namely the extent of racial differences in associational memberships (see Putnam 2000). Second, we examine racial differences in social contact with network ties, which links ultimately to the construct of social support (Kahn and Antonucci 1980).

Associational Memberships

The social capital literature has debated the appropriate role of social networks in the definition of social capital (see Sabatini 2009). In his classic treatment of social participation, the massive book *Bowling Alone* (2000, p. 280), Robert Putnam suggested that African-Americans may be distinctive in their associational memberships. Although racial differences in associational memberships were not large, his findings suggested that African-Americans belonged to more associations on average than European-Americans. The finding was substantially reduced when the data were subjected to statistical controls for educational and income differences among groups, but there was a net effect of race/ethnicity in a direction favoring African-Americans. One of the reasons for these differences had to do with the preponderance of ties to religious and ethnic organizations among African-Americans as compared to others. These findings appear to go against the information from "core discussion" network studies, suggesting that Blacks may have more associational ties than whites (Patterson 1998). However, one must bear in mind that the network data were focused, not on social participation, but on "core discussion groups." In the research we report below, we not only examine the question of the nature of race differences in network ties, but also the extent of differences in associations with religious organizations more closely, using a variety of different measures. Specifically, not only do we employ data on associational memberships, we obtain independent reports on religious group participation and attendance at religious services.

Although Patterson focused on data from the GSS, race differences in social networks, specifically among older adults, have been shown using other datasets other as well. Drawing on data from the Chicago Health and Aging Project, Barnes and colleagues (2004) found that blacks had smaller social networks than their white counterparts. Results from the National Social Life, Health, and Aging Project (NSHAP) echoes the white-black social network differential (Cornwell et al. 2008). Given our focus on the life course perspective, it is also important to note that the rate of loss in close social ties seems to be greater for blacks than for whites suggesting that the resources and social support from which older black men and women can draw is less than that of their white peers (Cornwell 2015).

Composition of Social Networks

One of the most important concepts for understanding the composition and structure of social networks is network homophily. Homophily refers to the pattern that "likes attract likes," that is people tend to connect with other who are similar to themselves in various attributes. In the present context racial homophily refers to the extent to which one's social networks tend to be racially homogenous. The literature on survey-based measures of social network ties shows that homophily in race and ethnicity represents one of the most important structuring principles with regard to social networks (McPherson et al. 2001). According to McPherseon et al. (2001, p. 420), race and ethnicity "are clearly the biggest divide in social networks today in the United States, and they play a major part in structuring the networks in other ethnically diverse societies as well." It is estimated that less than one tenth of adults with "core discussion groups" of size two or greater mention having a person of another race in their social network (Marsden 1987). With respect to baseline homophily, European Americans tend to have the most racially homogenous networks relative to other groups, African-Americans and Hispanics have moderate levels, and smaller racial and ethnic groups have the least, with their networks dominated by the majority group (Marsden 1987). The high levels of racial/ethnic homophily is not just due to baseline phenomena, racial inbreeding in social networks begins at very young ages, with African-Americans showing greater levels (McPherson et al. 2001, p. 421). The consequences resulting from these processes are that blacks are less likely to have access to "white" networks (Patterson 1998; Ibarra 1995).

Social Support

Virtually everyone agrees that one of the most important functions of social networks is the social support they provide (e.g., Wrzus et al. 2013). In the present paper we examine the extent to which social support networks operate differently for race/ethnic groups. In their attempt to address the challenges with understanding social relationships across the life span, Kahn and Antonucci (1980) introduce the "convoy model," which argues that individuals are surrounded by a personal network of close friends and family throughout the life span. In this paper, we focus on the extent of racial differences in these network ties. Kahn and Antonucci (1980) argue that this personal network is where social support is both given and received. Another important feature of the convoy is that, though it has the potential to change, there is also inherent stability (Antonucci 1985; Antonucci and Akiyama 1987; Kahn and Antonucci 1980). As individuals construct their lives, they continuously draw on their convoy for social support.

Alhough the set of network ties on which individuals draw their social suport is mainly described as close friends and family, the framework also allows for other network ties (including coworkers, neighbors, and supervisors). Indeed, Kahn and Antonucci (1980) articulated the convoy model as a series of concentric circles that surround the individual. The further away the circle is from the individual the less close the social tie, and consequently, the less amount of social support is provided. In the first empirical investigation of the convoy model, Antonucci and Akiyama (1987) describe both the structural and functional characteristics of social support convoy for a national sample of 718 adults aged 50 and older. Structurally, individuals reported a greater number of alters in their inner circle, consistent with the idea that individuals draw on social support from close and friends at older ages. There were no differences in network size, however. Moreover, the average age of alters was younger for the inner circle compared to outer circle members. It was also found that older members tend to have older network members on average. However, for the oldest old, there was also evidence for an uptick in grandchildren joining the convoy. Across all ages, there were more women in the convoy than men, and predictably, the older respondents reported knowing the convoy members for a longer period of time. Additionally, 67% of network members live within a 1 h drive and 82% were kin (including spouses). As theorized by the convoy model of social support, respondents reported giving and receiving more social support from inner circle members than their outer circles. Interestingly, there were no age differences in the number of types of support received. This runs counter to the premise that older adults receive more support as they age.

In a more recent analysis of social networks in Detroit, Michigan, Ajrouch, et al. (2001) found that older age predicted a smaller, less frequently contacted, and more geographically dispersed convoy. Additionally, important race difference were found as well. Specifically, whereas blacks reported a smaller number of alters in their convoy, they also reported more frequent contact with members as well as a greater proportion of kin in their convoy. The researchers also found an interaction effect between race and age, such that the race differences in frequency of contact and family members in the convoy decreased at advancing ages. In the following analysis, we approach the question of access to "convoy" members by several different indicators, assessing social participation.

The Present Study

Research on social networks consists not only of investigations of network characteristics and how they differ across sub-groups, but also how networks change over time (see Cornwell and Silverstein 2015; Cornwell and Schafer 2016). However, there is a general absence of research that considers the link between the life course and race. Although previous research has examined racial differences in network characteristics as well as how networks change over the life span, there is little research combining these two issues, examining the extent to which the nature of changing networks is different for whites and blacks as they age. Here we focus on network characteristics (network size, density, network composition, contact with network members), associational memberships and social participation.

Methods and Measures

The data employed in this section come from the General Social Survey (GSS), a biennial survey representative of the non-institutionalized U.S. population aged 18 and over. Specifically, we draw on the Social Networks topical modules administered in 1985, 1987 and 2004 (see Burt 1985; Marsden 1987, 1990; Marsden and Campbell 1984), as well as additional measures in the GSS involving associational memberships and social participation. In the GSS network modules, people were asked a series of questions that assess various network characteristics including size, density, strength, and composition. The questions in the topical module vary to some extent across the 3 years, but there are enough commonalities, allowing for valid comparisons at three points in time for several of our network measures, specifically network size, the kinship composition of the network, and the proportion of married individuals whose "core discussion" networks contain their spouse. As already noted, Patterson (1998) examined these relationships using the 1985 GSS network data, and in this paper we focus on replicating his findings in the additional surveys.[1]

Network Characteristics

We relied on the coding schemes used by previous researchers who used the GSS data (e.g. Marsden 1987; McPherson et al. 2006; Patterson 1998) for our operationalization of network characteristics. *Network size* indicates the number of people an individual reports as having had shared "important matters" with in the past 6 months. Responses range from zero people to six or more, which we recoded as 0–6.5. *Network density* is a measure of the mean strength of ties between various alters in the respondents' network (see Marsden 1987; McPherson et al. 2006). Obviously, density is only meaningful for respondents who mentioned more than one alter. In the following analysis, "density is coded as 0 if the respondent reports that two of their alters are total strangers, 0.5 if they are acquaintances, and 1.0 if they are especially close" (see Marsden 1987: 124; McPherson et al. 2006:357).[2] *Average frequency of contact* is a measure of the strength of the ties between the respondent and (averaged over) each of his alters. Following the lead of McPherson et al. (2006), we recode the original scale of this variable to indicate the average number of days per year the ego has contact with network members.[3] Finally, with regard to *network composition*, we employ three indicators here: number of kin in the network, whether (if married) their spouse is included in their network, and the number of black network members. The *number of kin in the network* is indicated by the number of family members (e.g., spouse, parent, child, sibling) that a respondent lists as an alter. The other composition measures are straightforward.

[1] Our analyses using the pooled GSS social networks modules control for year of survey due to potential differences in levels of network properties and/or the nature of the data in the various GSS surveys (see McPherson et al. 2006, 2009; Fischer 2009; Paik and Sanchagrin 2013). We thank Diane Felmlee for drawing this literature to our attention.

[2] We experimented with other measures of density, but none produced better results than those based on the Marsden measure. We also employed a measure of density defined as the number of ties divided by the total number of possible ties. In the present case the distribution of this variable is highly skewed, with roughly 50% of the observations having a value of 1 (100%). We thank Derek Kreager for pointing out the potential usefulness of this measure.

[3] The specific codes are as follows: "almost daily" = 365 days per year (dpy); "once a week" = 52 dpy; "once a month" = 12 dpy; and "less than once a month" = 6 dpy.

Social Participation

The GSS has for several years asked a series of questions dealing with social contact with relatives and friends. These questions are phrased as follows:

> Would you use this card and tell me which answer comes closest to how often do the following things (almost every day, once or twice a week, several times a month, about once a month, several times a year, never) … (a) spend a social evening with relatives? (SOCREL), (b) spend a social evening with someone who lives in your neighborhood? (SOCOMMUN), (c) spend a social evening with friends who lives outside the neighborhood? (SOCFREND), (d) go to a bar or tavern? (SOCBAR), (e) spend a social evening with your parents? (SOCPARS), (f) spend a social evening with a brother or sister? (SOCSIBS)

Responses to these questions were coded in 7 categories in the GSS data, ranging from 0 = never and 6 = almost every day, but given. Given the lumping of values at 0, we decided to collapse categories to create a series of binary variables expressing whether the respondent engaged in a particular type of social contact or not. In attempt to establish a more intuitive metric, we again recode the original scales to indicate the average number of days per year (dpy) the respondent has contact with relative and friends.[4]

Associational Memberships

In line with discussions of social capital, the GSS has included for several years a series of questions on memberships in social groups. The questions were as follows:

> Now we would like to know something about the groups or organizations to which individuals belong. Here is a list of various organizations. Could you tell me whether or not you are a member of each type? (a) fraternal groups, (b) service clubs, (c) veteran's groups, (d) political clubs, (e) labor unions, (f) sports groups, (g) youth groups, (h) school service groups, (i) hobby or garden clubs, (j) school fraternities or sororities, (k) nationality groups, (l) farm organizations, (m) literary, art, discussion or study groups, (n) professional or academic societies, (o) church-affiliated groups, and (p) any other groups? This sentence does not belong here. It goes with the next paragraph.

GSS constructed an index of the total number of "yeses" to these inquiries (MEMNUM), which ranges from "0" (the modal category) to "16". We collapse the high end of this code to "10 or more". We also analyze separately, the variable "church affiliated groups" (MEMCHURH).

[4]The specific codes are as follows: "almost daily" = 365 dpy; "several times a week" = 182 dpy; "several times a month" = 52 dpy; "once a month" = 12 dpy; "several times a year" = 6 dpy; "once a year" = 1 dpy; and "never" = 0 dpy.

Other Social Activities

In order to complement the above measures, we also assess the respondent's report of their church attendance and involvement in other church activities. *Church attendance* is measured as follows:

> "How often do you attend religious services?" (never, less than once a year, about once or twice a year, several times a year, about once a month, 2–3 times a month, nearly every week, every week, several times a week).

This variable is recoded in the metric of days per year (dpy) with values: "never" and "less than once per year" = 0dpy; "once a year" = 1dpy; "several times a year" = 6dpy; "once a month" = 12dpy; "2–3 times per month" = 30dpy; "nearly every week" 39dpy (assuming 75% of the weeks); "every week" = 52 dpy; and "more than once a week" = 130dpy (assuming 2.5 times per week).

Other religious participation is measured as follows:

> "How often do you take part in the activities and organizations of a church or place of worship?" (never, less than once a year, about once or twice a year, several times a year, about once a month, 2–3 times a month, nearly every week, every week, several times a week, once a day, several times a day.

This variable is also rescaled to days per year in order to provide a more meaningful interpretation of the results.[5]

Major Independent Variables

Our major independent variables in this analysis are race and sex. Race is measured in the GSS as self-identified race, using the following question: "What race do you consider yourself?" For purposes of this analysis we include only those cases that self-identified as "white" and "black." All others are excluded for analyses presented in this chapter. Sex is measured as "male" or "female," based on interviewer observations. In the present analysis we assess this variable using female = 1, male = 0. In addition, we include a variable (an interaction term) that assesses any differences in sex and race effects by categories of the other.

[5]The specific codes are as follows: The specific as follows: "never" and "less than once a year" = 0 dpy; "about once or twice a year" = 1.5 dpy; "several times a year" = 6 dyp; "about once a month" = 12 dpy; "two to three times a month" = 30 dpy (assuming 2.5 times a month); "nearly every week" = 39 dpy (assuming 75% of the weeks); "every week" = 52 dpy; "several times a week" = 182 dpy (assuming 3.5 times per week); "once a day" = 365 dpy; and "several times a day" = 1095 dpy (assuming 4 times a day).

Covariates

Our baseline models include (model 1a) race and sex, and (model 1b) race, sex and their interaction. Our subsequent models include several covariates, including marital status, age, years of schooling, and family (of origin) size, as assessed by sibship size. Marriage was based on the following GSS question: "Are you currently—married, widowed, divorced, separated, or have you never been married." For our purposes we collapse all non-married categories into one, so the variable is coded "1" for married, "0" for not married. Age is measured as chronological age, recoded from year and month of birth. Years of schooling completed is based on a series of questions, ending up with a code that reflects years of schooling from 0 to 20. Number of siblings is based on the GSS question asking about siblings. All continuous covariates are centered about the sample mean.

Analytic Strategy

Our analysis is composed of several parts. We begin by looking at the zero-order relationship between categories of race in network characteristics across the GSS survey years (1985, 1987 and 2004) (Tables 14.1, 14.2, 14.3, 14.4, 14.5 and 14.6). After establishing the basic patterns in the network characteristics, we then examine the robustness of the findings by implementing statistical controls for covariates (Table 14.7). We then examine the zero-order relationships and net effects of race on several social participation indicators and associational ties. Finally, we focus on several interaction effects of network characteristics with age and education. All analyses are weighted to make the results representative of the national population. Between survey years 1972 and 2002, sample weights are adjusted by the number of adults in the household, and the 1982 and 1987 data are adjusted for the oversample of African-Americans (using the GSS variable "OVERSAMP"). Sample weights for 2004 and later are adjusted for sub-sampling of non-respondents, the number of adults in the household, and differential non-response across areas (using the GSS variable "WTSSNR").[6]

Race and Social Relations – Empirical Results

In the following discussion we present baseline information from the GSS network modules, obtained in 1985, 1987 and 2004 concerning the relationship between race and social networks. We first attempt to replicate Patterson's (1998) results from the

[6]We followed the guidance of McPherson et al. (2006: 357) on the appropriate weights for this analysis and made every effort to reproduce their findings with respect to obtaining results that are representative of the household population of the United States.

1985 survey and test their generality in the network modules included in 1987 and 2004. In addition to the network data, we supplement these analyses by also examining several additional areas using data from the GSS, specifically self-reports of organizational/associational ties and social participation.

Network Size and Density

As noted earlier, Patterson (1998) draws on 1985 General Social Survey data to show that, relative to other races, blacks have networks that are smaller, denser, and consist of fewer kin. His findings were summarized above, and we here reproduce his basic findings (see Tables 14.1, 14.2 and 14.3) and replicate his results in the two additional surveys—1987 and 2004. In Table 14.1 we present the differences in network size by race/ethnicity from the GSS core discussion network assessments in 1985, 1987 and 2004. Note that in the 1985 and 1987 surveys it is not possible to distinguish Hispanic respondents, but we do have data on Hispanics in the 2004 survey. In the 2004 survey, it appears that Hispanic respondents fall midway between whites and blacks. Regardless of these different subsamples, in Table 14.1 we show that in all three GSS surveys there are significant differences by race/ethnicity, with African-Americans registering significantly smaller numbers of persons in their core discussion networks. Our analysis focuses primarily on relationships within

Table 14.1 Differences in network size by race/ethnicity: General Social Survey Core Discussion Network Assessments in 1985, 1987 and 2004

Panel A: Average network size							
	White	Black	Other	Hispanic	Total	F-ratio	p-value
1985	3.03	2.25	2.60	---	2.94	10.62	0.000
	(0.052)	(0.168)	(0.291)				
1987	2.70	2.18	2.62	---	2.63	32.12	0.000
	(0.037)	(0.054)	(0.102)				
	NH-white	NH-black	NH-other				
2004	2.29	1.65	1.64	1.84	2.14	7.82	0.000
	(0.063)	(0.164)	(0.225)	(0.153)			
Panel B: Sample sizes							
	White	Black	Other	Hispanic	Total		
1985	1336	151	44	---	1531		
1987	1213	537	50	---	1800		
2004	1048	203	54	117	1422		

Note: In the 1985 and 1987 surveys, it is not possible to distinguish Hispanic respondents. In the 2004 survey, whites refers to "non-Hispanic" whites, and blacks refers to "non-Hispanic" blacks

years of the GSS surveys. We do not address the relative patterns over time here, as this issue has been discussed in the literature (see McPherson et al. 2006, 2009; Fischer 2009; Paik and Sanchagrin 2013). Our later analysis uses the pooled GSS social networks modules, wherein we control for year of survey due to potential differences in levels of network properties and/or the nature of the data in the various GSS surveys.

In order to examine the robustness of these patterns, we have introduced statistical controls for marital status, age, and education, and the patterns and significance levels do not change. As a measure of the strength of within-network ties, we calculated a measure of network density in order to replicate Patterson's (1998) results. As we noted earlier, this measure assesses the extent to which members of one's network have ties with each other. If most of one's network members know each other, their network is considered relatively more dense, and "inbred" in a sense. It is considered advantageous to have a less dense network, so that one's network ties are considered to more broadly tap into the society. Recall that Patterson (1998) argued that the social networks of blacks were more dense, and that this represented a barrier to full social participation. In contrast to the findings regarding size, we were unable to reproduce Patterson's (1998) conclusions regarding network density. In Table 14.2 we present differences in network density by race/ethnicity for 1985 and 2004. Our results indicate that African-American networks are not any more dense than those of European-Americans in both years. Statistical controls for covariates did not alter these results.

Table 14.2 Differences in network density by race/ethnicity: General Social Survey Core Discussion Network Assessments in 1985 and 2004

Panel A: Average network density							
	White	Black	Other	Hispanic	Total	F-ratio	p-value
1985	0.60	0.62	0.67	---	0.60	1.13	0.3239
	(0.010)	(0.038)	(0.050)				
	NH-white	NH-black	NH-other				
2004	0.66	0.66	0.68	0.65	0.66	0.06	0.9828
	(0.013)	(0.036)	(0.082)	(0.045)			
Panel B: Sample sizes							
	White	Black	Other	Hispanic	Total		
1985	1041	89	31	---	1161		
2004	633	76	22	55	786		

Note: In the 1985 survey, it is not possible to distinguish Hispanic respondents. The 1987 survey did not include the requisite questions to calculate a density measure. In the 2004 survey, whites refers to "non-Hispanic" whites, and blacks refers to "non-Hispanic" blacks

Table 14.3 Differences in the number of network members who are kin by race/ethnicity: General Social Survey Core Discussion Network Assessments in 1985, 1987 and 2004

Panel A: Average number of network members who are kin							
	White	Black	Other	Hispanic	Total	F-ratio	p-value
1985	1.51	0.93	1.06	---	1.44	15.66	0.0000
	(0.039)	(0.102)	(0.199)				
1987	1.41	1.07	1.38	---	1.36	23.06	0.0000
	(0.029)	(0.042)	(0.138)				
	NH-white	NH-black	NH-other				
2004	1.30	0.75	0.67	0.91	1.17	16.06	0.0000
	(0.044)	(0.092)	(0.133)	(0.110)			
Panel B: Sample sizes							
	White	Black	Other	Hispanic	Total		
1985	1336	151	44	---	1531		
1987	1213	537	50	---	1800		
2004	1048	203	54	117	1422		

Note: In the 1985 and 1987 surveys, it is not possible to distinguish Hispanic respondents. In the 2004 survey, whites refers to "non-Hispanic" whites, and blacks refers to "non-Hispanic" blacks

Network Composition

In Table 14.3 we present differences in the number of network members who are kin in order to examine Patterson's (1998) finding that African Americans' networks contain a lower proportion of kinship ties. These data are available in all 3 years, 1985, 1987 and 2004. In our analyses, Patterson's conclusion with regard to the presence of kin in core discussion networks is supported without question. The results for all three surveys replicate these results—that African-Americans had significantly fewer kin in their networks compared to European-Americans. As above, in these results the estimates for Hispanics fall midway between blacks and whites. The effects of race on the number of kin in one's network is not diminished when we control for covariates.

Social Participation

There appear to be few differences in social participation by race in the GSS data for 1985 and 2004, as measured by the average frequency of contact with network members in the GSS network modules (see Table 14.4). We return to the topic of race differences in social participation below when we consider the GSS social participation measures.

Table 14.4 Differences in the mean frequency of contact with network members by race/ethnicity: General Social Survey Core Discussion Network Assessments in 1985 and 2004

Panel A: Average frequency of contact with network members (days per year)							
	White	Black	Other	Hispanic	Total	F-ratio	p-value
1985	207.82	216.53	221.53	---	208.92	0.33	0.7186
	(3.732)	(14.083)	(23.555)				
	NH-white	NH-black	NH-other				
2004	240.99	239.88	265.97	261.55	243.81	1.03	0.3772
	(4.578)	(13.541)	(22.157)	(13.863)			
Panel B: Sample sizes							
	White	Black	Other	Hispanic	Total		
1985	1234	117	40	---	1391		
2004	821	117	37	87	1062		

Note: In the 1985 survey, it is not possible to distinguish Hispanic respondents. The 1987 survey did not include the requisite questions to calculate a density measure. In the 2004 survey, whites refers to "non-Hispanic" whites, and blacks refers to "non-Hispanic" blacks

Table 14.5 Differences in the number of network members who are black by race/ethnicity: General Social Survey Core Discussion Network Assessments in 1985 and 2004

Panel A: Average number of black network members							
	White	Black	Other	Hispanic	Total	F-ratio	p-value
1985	0.02	1.85	0.20	---	0.22	77.86	0.0000
	(0.004)	(0.148)	(0.084)				
	NH-white	NH-black	NH-other				
2004	0.03	1.32	0.052	0.083	0.20	43.43	0.0000
	(0.008)	(0.114)	(0.032)	(0.035)			
Panel B: Sample sizes							
	White	Black	Other	Hispanic	Total		
1985	1336	151	44	---	1531		
2004	1048	203	54	117	1422		

Note: In the 1985 survey, it is not possible to distinguish Hispanic respondents. The 1987 survey did not include the requisite questions to calculate a density measure. In the 2004 survey, whites refers to "non-Hispanic" whites, and blacks refers to "non-Hispanic" blacks

Network Composition

Due to homophily, one of the characteristic features of social networks is that people rarely affiliate with others across racial lines. In Table 14.5 we present the average number of black network members by racial group. Blacks have vastly more black members of their networks than whites, a result that is highly statistically significant.

Race and Marriage

It has been argued that marriage is one of the most influential connections for generating the social, psychological, and economic benefits derived from social networks. Patterson (1998, p. 150) builds on this perspective to argue further that marriage, or the lack thereof, contributes importantly to the internal and external isolation of Afro-Americans. African-Americans are less likely to be married than other racial groups and, among those who are married, they are less likely to be in marriages compared to other groups (see Fig. 14.1). Census data on interracial marriage suggests that exogamy among Afro-Americans has been increasing over time, but involves less than 6% and 3% of marriages among men and women, respectively (U.S. Bureau of the Census 2015). To the extent that a social tie through marriage (and the concomitant social connections to extended family and the spouse's network) contributes to success in life, racial differences in marriage rates may be an important source of inequality (although there may be some selection operating here as well). Furthermore, relatively high rates of endogamy, particularly among

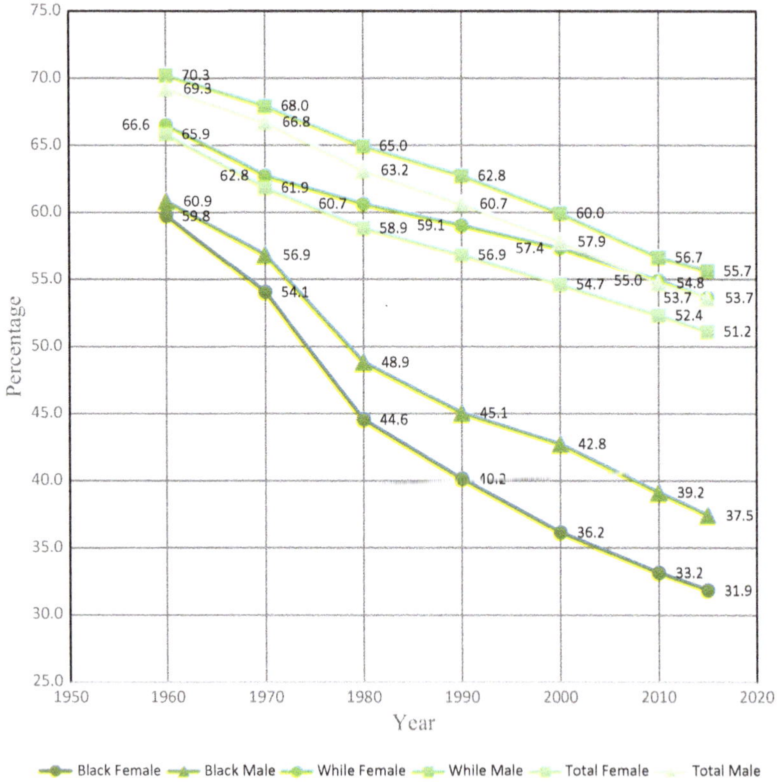

Fig. 14.1 Percentage of all persons age 15 and older in the United States who were married, by sex and race, 1960–2015

Afro-Americans, can limit social integration, cultural exchanges, and the acquisition of social capital.

U.S. Current Population Survey data on marital status help illustrate the extent of racial differences in social isolation over time. In Fig. 14.1, we present trends in the percentage of all persons age 15 and older who are married by race/ethnicity and gender. With the exception of Asians (data not shown), the percent of each demographic group that is married generally declines over time. Within this pattern, however, there are obvious racial disparities, such that Hispanics and particularly African-Americans are less likely than Asians and whites to be married. Finally, the fairly stable trend in marriage among Asians (data not shown) over the past few decades makes this the most likely group to be married in recent years.

In Patterson's analysis, marriage had a strong relationship to the number of kin in one's network for European-Americans, whereas there was no such relationship among African-Americans. We extend the analysis of this question by considering the number of network members mentioned in the GSS protocol who were spouses of the respondent. In Table 14.6 we present the differences in the proportion of married persons who include their spouse in their "core discussion" social networks by race/ethnicity from the General Social Survey Core Discussion Network Assessments in 1985, 1987 and 2004. In these analyses, as above, it is not possible to distinguish Hispanic respondents in the 1985 and 1987 surveys (in the 2004 survey, whites refers to "non-Hispanic" whites, and blacks refers to "non-Hispanic" blacks).

These results indicate that among married individuals, whites are far more likely than blacks to include their spouse in their core discussion networks. These results are highly significant, and suggest that there is something different about the nature of marital relations between race-ethnic groups. The 2004 GSS survey is the only

Table 14.6 Differences in the proportion of married individuals with their spouse in their social networks by race/ethnicity: General Social Survey Core Discussion Network Assessments in 1985, 1987 and 2004

Panel A: Proportion of married with spouse in network							
	White	Black	Other	Hispanic	Total	F-ratio	p-value
1985	0.70	0.45	0.52	---	0.68	7.81	0.0004
	(0.017)	(0.068)	(0.099)				
1987	0.78	0.57	0.82	---	0.77	13.54	0.0000
	(0.015)	(0.038)	(0.072)				
	NH-white	NH-black	NH-other				
2004	0.65	0.40	0.37	0.46	0.60	8.84	0.0000
	(0.020)	(0.064)	(0.089)	(0.074)			
Panel B: Sample sizes							
	White	Black	Other	Hispanic	Total		
1985	784	59	27	---	870		
1987	709	168	28	---	905		
2004	606	71	37	54	768		

Note: In the 1985 and 1987 surveys, it is not possible to distinguish Hispanic respondents. In the 2004 survey, whites refers to "non-Hispanic" whites, and blacks refers to "non-Hispanic" blacks

one that gives us any insight into differences among other ethnic groups, which suggests that Hispanic and African-American respondents have the lowest levels of the participation of spouses in individuals's social networks. This suggests a difference in the nature of marriage across racial-ethnic groups.

In Table 14.7 we present the net racial/ethnic differences in our network charateristics, controlling for a number of additional covariates, namely race, sex, age, schooling, number of siblings, and marital status. The results presented in this table indicate that our earlier conclusions about racial differences in the above discussion hold, after controlling for relevant covariates. Among the covariates, the principal variables that affect network characteristics are sex, schooling, marital status and to some extent age. In general, females have larger social networks, which include a greater number of kin, and are more likely to include their spouse. Married people

Table 14.7 Net effects of race, sex and covariates and interactions of race and key predictors

	Network characteristics					
Panel A: Main effects						
	Network size	Network density	Kin in network	Blacks in network	Spouse in network	Contact w/ network
Predictor variables						
Constant	2.846***	0.642***	−0.023	−0.080**	0.709*	264.061***
Network size	---	−0.017**	0.382***	0.071***	1.521***	−23.760***
Race (black = 1)	−0.501***	−0.009	−0.205***	0.857***	0.375***	−13.210
Sex (female = 1)	0.189***	0.004	0.206***	−0.012	1.026	18.478***
Age (centered)	−0.005**	0.001**	−0.001	0.000	0.979***	−1.367***
Schooling (centered)	0.140***	−0.015***	−0.035***	−0.008***	1.085***	−4.540***
Number of sibs	0.000	0.000	0.014*	0.000	0.996	−0.070
Marital status (married = 1)	0.139**	0.055***	0.438***	0.016	---	30.581***
Survey year = 1987	−0.363***	---	0.003	−0.219***	1.855***	---
Survey year = 2004	−0.800***	0.047**	−0.008	0.012	1.084	16.003**
R^2 [see note]	0.124	0.061	0.328	0.298	0.130	0.182
Panel B: Interaction effects						
	Network size	Network density	Kin in network	Blacks in network	Spouse in network	Contact w/ network
Race x age	−0.003	−0.002	−0.007*	−0.001	1.003	−0.429
Race x schooling	−0.072**	0.006	0.008	0.010	0.853**	−4.051
Sample sizes	4534	1875	4534	4534	2420	2341

Note: The R^2 for "spouse in network" is a "pseudo R^2" based on the log-likelihood statistics taken from the unweighted estimates; in all other cases, it is an R^2 adjusted for degrees of freedom. *** $p < 0.001$ ** $p < 0.01$ *$p < 0.05$

also have larger and more dense networks, including greater numbers of kin. Greater amounts of schooling similarly increase the number of network members, and with more education, the less dense are one's social network contacts. More schooling also diminishes the number of kin in one's networks. Finally, with age, ones' networks shrink (Morgan 1988; Cornwell et al. 2008), and become slightly more dense with slightly fewer kin. Despite these additional influences, our findings with respect to racial differences are robust with respect to these statistical controls.

In addition, in Table 14.7 we present the results of our tests for interaction effects of race with age and education in affecting the network characteristics. Several significant interactions are reported in these results. We find that there is an interaction of race with education in affecting network size. As reported above, network size increase with greater amounts of schooling—this is true for both groups (see Fig. 14.2), but the relationship is much weaker for blacks compared to whites. In addition, we find there is a race by education interaction effect on the probability that ego's spouse is in his/her network. For whites, with increases in education there is an increase the likelihood of having a spouse in one's network, whereas for blacks, the probability of having a spouse in one's network declines with increasing education (see Fig. 14.3).

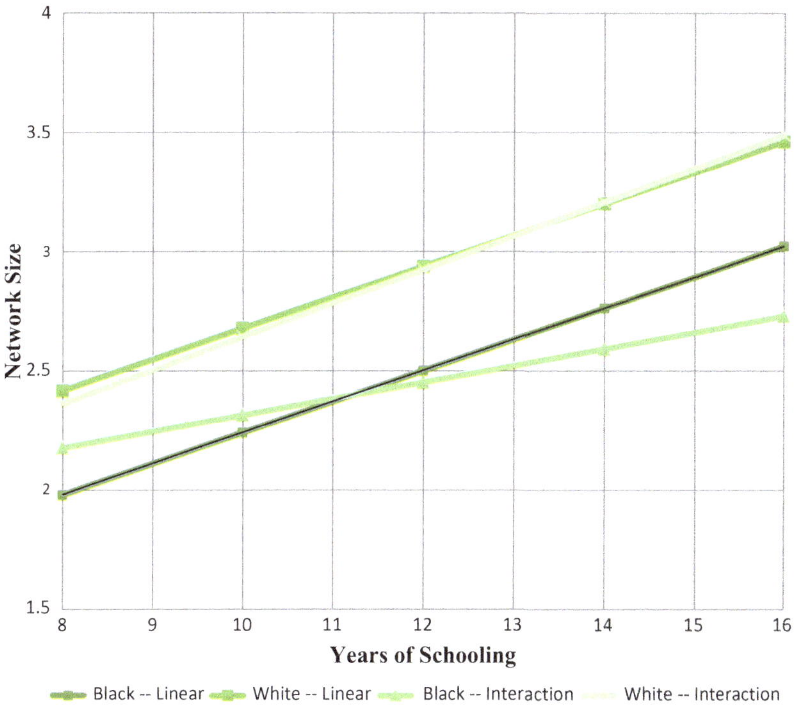

Fig. 14.2 Race by education interaction effect for network size

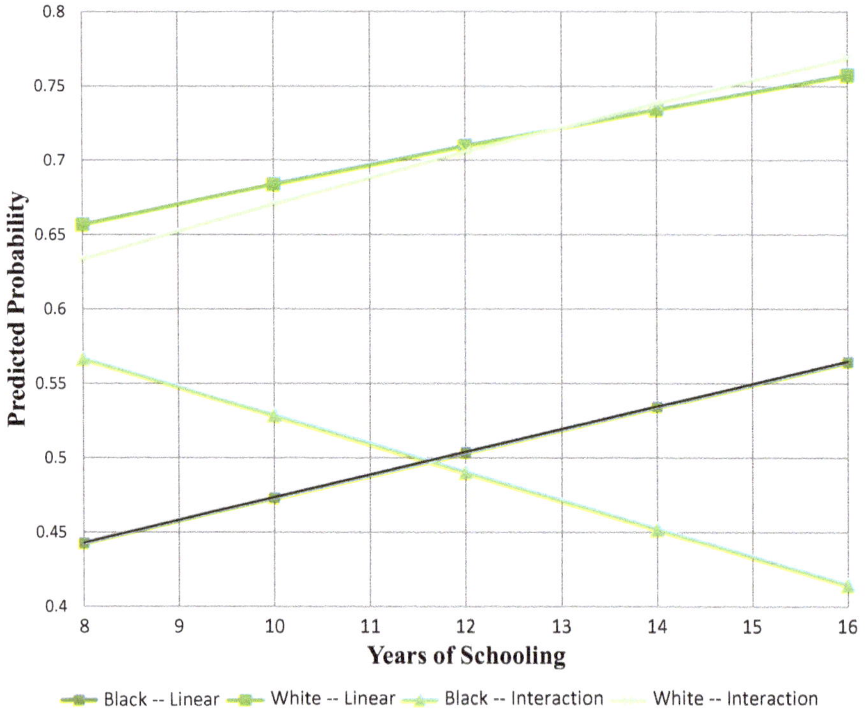

Fig. 14.3 Race by education interaction effect for probability of spouse in network

Finally, we note that age (as a proxy for life course) is linked differently to some network characteristics for blacks compared to whites. For example, the loss of kin in one's network that happens with increasing age is even more dramatic for blacks than for whites (see Fig. 14.4). This is an area that requires further study.

GSS Social Participation Measures

In Table 14.8 we summarize an analysis of differences by race/ethnicity in the GSS social participation measures. These measures, described above, assess the extent to which the respondent spends time with relatives, friends and neighbors. As shown in Table 14.8, African Americans have higher levels of social participation relative to whites. We estimated a series of regressions with each of our measure of social participation or associational membership was on a set of predictors that included race (black vs. white), sex, age (centered at the mean), marital status (married vs. unmarried), education (centered at the mean), and number of siblings. In the case of the social participation measures we also employed a social participation summary score based on a composite of the separate measures. In Table 14.8 we present the raw race differences, accompanied by the coefficient for race in these regressions, and its level of significance net of these other factors.

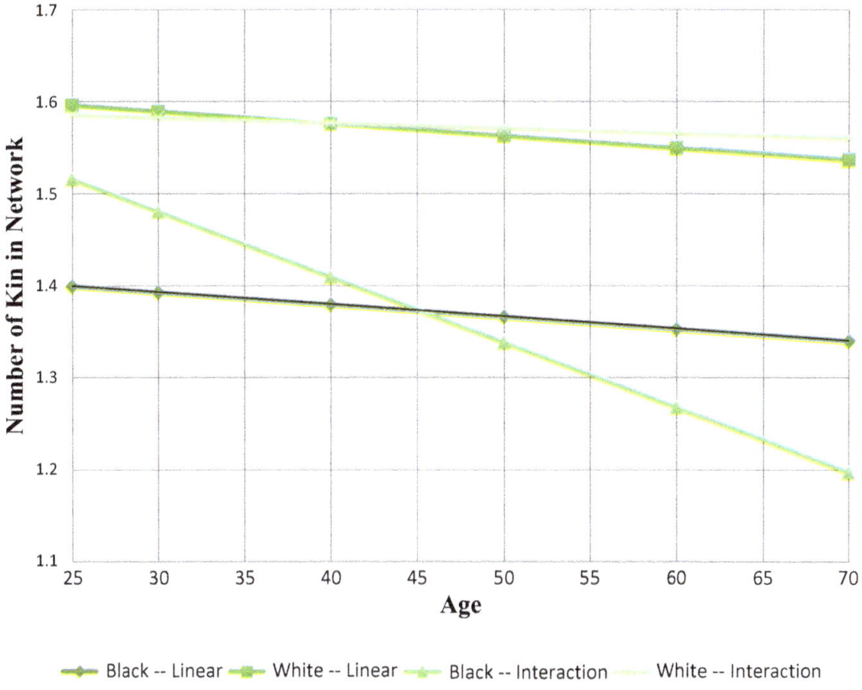

Fig. 14.4 Race by age interaction effect for number of kin in network

Table 14.8 Differences in social participation and associational connections by race/ethnicity: General Social Survey Measures

Panel A: Social participation measure						
	White sample size	White days per year	Black sample size	Black days per year	Regression coefficient	Log-odds coefficient (ordered logit)
SOCREL	29,552	92.4	5082	124.1	21.51***	0.2219***
SOCOMMUN	29,529	61.0	5072	78.7	12.44***	0.0482
SOCFREND	29,542	60.3	5073	67.6	3.75*	0.0142
SOCBAR	29,517	25.5	5065	21.1	−4.45***	−0.2777***
SOCPARS	11,281	48.9	1799	75.3	17.39***	0.1087*
SOCSIBS	11,272	44.2	1795	85.9	28.40***	0.1491*
Summary	11,167	333.0	1777	450.5	78.34***	---
Panel B: Measures of associational ties						
	White sample size	White mean	Black sample size	Black mean	Regression coefficient	Log-odds coefficient (ordered logit)
NUMMEMS	17,510	1.8076	2736	1.4851	0.0103	−0.0226
MEMCHURCH[a]	17,392	0.3439	2722	0.4342	---	0.5432***
ATTEND	49,894	25.4	8699	34.0	8.20***	0.5072***
RELACTIV	12,815	11.2	2484	20.1	9.17***	0.6805***

Note: [a]MEMCHURCH is a binary indicator with the mean indicating the proportion responding "yes" and the log-odds coefficent corresponding to a logistic regression model (as opposed to an ordered logit)

*** $p < 0.001$ ** $p < 0.01$ *$p < 0.05$

Of some interest here is the fact that across most of the social participation variables blacks have greater logged-odds of ever socializing with others. Blacks spend more time with their relatives, including parents and siblings, and members of the community. They also spend more time with friends than whites, although this difference is only marginally significant. What is also of interest is Blacks are less likely to meet with friends at a bar, the only negative effect on participation in the table. All of these patterns are robust with respect to statistical controls for sociodemographic characteristics. The highly significant differences shown in this table for socializing with familial others (relatives, parents and siblings), as well as the results for members of the community, challenges some of the ideas advanced about the impoverishment of blacks' social networks in the above discussion.

In addition to these findings, there were statistically significant race by sex interactions for socializing with a neighbor and socializing with parents and siblings (results not presented here). However, the interaction term became insignificant for socializing with parents and siblings when age and other sociodemographic characteristics were added as statistical controls.

Associational Connections

One of the measures indicated by the literature on social capital involves the level of involvement in associational memberships. This was the basic idea of Putnam, namely that organizational ties are decreasing across generations (Putnam 2000). It turns out that blacks report fewer organizational memberships than whites, as shown in panel B of Table 14.8. However, this is explained away by sociodemographic characteristics. In the GSS samples, blacks are more likely to be members of a church, to engage in religious activities, and to attend religious services. There is also a significant race by sex interaction for church attendance (results not shown here), which suggest that black women are the most likely to attend church services.

Discussion and Conclusion

In this chapter we have argued that one of the key differences in the social worlds of different racial and ethnic groups is the nature of their social networks, and more broadly, the nature of their social participation. We have developed the idea of a "racialized life course," in which the nature of the life course depends intimately on racial and ethnic experiences. In this regard, the nature of the life course lends itself to understanding the fact that there are differences in institutionalized events, transitions and trajectories for different subgroups of society, and therefore lives are "racialized," due to those differences.

At the beginning of this chapter, we drew attention to one of the contemporary institutionalist arguments regarding racial inequalities in modern society, which made a case for the impoverished nature of blacks' social networks, differences that lock in black disadvantage across a wide variety of outcomes, and which as a consequence serve to reproduce racism over time (Roithmayr 2014). We coupled this type of reasoning with F. Michael Higginbotham's concept of the *racial paradigm* and with Orlando Patterson's analysis of the history of the African-American family in the context of its roots in the institution of slavery. According to Patterson (1998), based on an extensive analysis of the 1985 GSS social network module data, the associational ties of African-Americans, including marital relationships, in the post- slavery era, even after centuries of change, are in many ways reproductive of the social connections of institutionalized structures that impoverish Blacks, especially African-American men (e.g., Patterson 1998). Patterson (1998 has argued that blacks are the most isolated social group in America in the aftermath of slavery and the Jim Crow era. He argued that the roots in the institution of slavery are responsible for diminished social networks of African-Americans, especially of men. He found considerable support for smaller and more dense social networks among African-Americans. In this paper we replicate some of Patterson's (1998) findings and provide a more exhaustive empirical assessment of the relationships of race to social relationships and social participation more generally. We find there is support for some of Patterson's claims using the GSS network module data from 1985, 1987 and 2004, but using standard social participation measures from the GSS, we find that blacks "activate" their social networks to a greater extent than do whites.

Our own analyses of the GSS network data provide strong evidence for black-white differences in social network characteristics. For five out of the six network characteristics analyzed, we found statistically significant differences, with blacks being disadvantaged with regards to network size, number of kin in network, frequency of contact with network members, and the likelihood of having a spouse in their network, net of gender. Blacks were also found to have a higher number of blacks in their network. The only exception to these patterns, was our analysis of network density, but these projections were challenged by the limited number of cases upon which to base an analysis of network density. More importantly, however, the race differences remained after adjusting for network size, age, education, number of siblings, and current marital status (though the magnitude of the race coefficient was reduced, and in the case of the number of blacks in one's network, slightly increased).

In contrast to these results, our analysis of the GSS associational memberships and levels of social participation reveal a different story. There are racial differences in these outcomes, but the differences largely favor blacks. Whites exceed blacks in the number of organizational memberships, but the difference is not statistically significant. There are some areas where blacks appear to be much more involved with their social networks. Blacks are much more likely to be a member of a church, to attend regularly, and to involve themselves in other (non-worship) church activities. These findings provide an interesting avenue for future research, namely to examine the idea that these alternative social network choices might compensate in some way for patterns observed with respect to racial differences in social network ties.

With the exceptions noted, our results provide strong support for the theoretical arguments of Orlando Patterson (1998) and others regarding the importance of racial differences in social networks when examining patterns of racial inequalities. The results of the above analysis go further in suggesting some of the key black-white differences, not only in the extent of network contacts, but with respect to social participation more generally. While blacks may not have large social networks, they are more likely to activate those they have, resulting in higher social participation levels than whites. Patterson's (1998) work also suggested that race interacts in important ways with other factors. In a number of cases we found statistically significant interactions, indicating that the benefits of the educational system for increasing network size and reducing network density did not accrue to blacks as compared to whites. Also, we found that the negative effects of increasing age were even more deleterious for blacks compared to whites. Simply put, black and white social lives involve social networks in different ways.

Although we believe the GSS data provide important information about racial-ethnic differences in social relationships, the findings raise a number of questions. Given the patterns observed in the GSS core discussion network assessments, one of the most fundamental of these involves the validity of the measurement of social ties. The idea of discussing "important issues" with others may have vastly different meanings across individuals, and some of this heterogeneity may reside in racial-ethnic group differences. While homophily may exist with respect to the racial composition of social networks, suggesting blacks are more isolated, our results using the GSS data on measures of social participation (i.e., contact with relatives and members of the neighborhood) and associational ties (e.g., church membership and attendance) further indicate that blacks are more likely to activate their social networks. In conclusion, although there are some apparent social network differences, but it is important to consider the possibility that the network measures assess a relatively narrow range of social relationships and do not gauge broader concepts of social participation and social capital. In fact, the social participation measures may come closer to theoretical concepts of interest.

Finally, taking the GSS network data at face value, we conclude that there is some support in these analyses for Roithmayr's (2014) "locked in" model of racial inequality. The apparent differences among racial-ethnic groups in the nature of their social relationships can clearly lead to access to fewer resources and limited social networks. There is little question that the pervasiveness of racial segregation, and the range of factors set in place by such historically-linked residential patterns, limits equal access to the resources and social networks that matter for achievement and economic well-being. Our results reinforce the conclusion that there are racial-ethnic differences in the nature of social relations. However, the case for diminishing the important role of prejudice and discrimination is incomplete, and it is too early to dismiss the significance of racial animus and discrimination in understanding racial inequalities in contemporary society.

References

Ajrouch, K. J., Antonucci, T. C., & Janevic, M. R. (2001). Social networks among blacks and whites: The interaction between race and age. *Journal of Gerontology: Social Sciences, 56B*, S112–S118.

Allport, G. W. (1954). *The nature of prejudice* (25th anniversary ed., 1979). New York: Basic Books.

Alwin, D. F. (2012). Integrating varieties of life course concepts. *Journals of Gerontology Series B: Psychological Sciences and Social Sciences, 60*(Special Issue II), 7–14.

Antonucci, T. C. (1985). Personal characteristics, social support, and social behavior. In R. H. Binstock & E. Shanas (Eds.), *Handbook of aging and the social sciences* (pp. 94–128). New York: Van Nostrand Reinhold.

Antonucci, T. C., & Akiyama, H. (1987). Social networks in adult life and a preliminary examination of the convoy model. *Journal of Gerontology, 42*, 519–527.

Barnes, L. L., Mendes de Leon, C. F., Wilson, R. S., Bienias, J. L., & Evans, D. A. (2004). A longitudinal study of black-white differences in social resources. *Journal of Gerontology: Psychological Sciences and Social Sciences, 59*, 146–153.

Berkman, L. F., & Leonard Syme, S. (1979). Social networks, host resistance, and mortality: A nine-year follow-up study of Alameda County residents. *American Journal of Epidemiology, 109*(2), 186–204.

Blumer, H. (1958). Race prejudice as a sense of group position. *Pacific Sociological Review, 1*, 3–7.

Bobo, L. (1999). Prejudice as group position: Micro-foundations of a sociological approach to racism and race relations. *Journal of Social Issues, 55*(3), 445–472.

Bobo, L., Kluegel, J., & Smith, R. A. (1997). Laissez faire racism: The crystallization of a kinder, gentler, antiblack ideology. In S. A. Tuch & J. Martin (Eds.), *Racial attitudes in the 1990s: Continuity and change* (pp. 15–42). Westport: Praeger.

Bobo, L. D., Charles, C. Z., Krysan, M., & Simmons, A. D. (2012). The real record on racial attitudes. In P. V. Marsden (Ed.), *Social trends in American life: Findings from the general social survey since 1972* (pp. 38–83). Princeton: Princeton University Press.

Bonilla-Silva, E. (2014). *Racism without racists—Color-blind racism and the persistence of racial inequality in America* (4th ed.). Lanham: Rowman & Littlefield Publishing. (Earlier editions published in 2003, 2006 and 2010).

Burt, R. S. (1985). Network items in the general social survey. *Social Networks, 6*, 293–339.

Cornwell, B. (2015). Social disadvantage and network turnover. *Journal of Gerontology Series B: Psychological and Social Sciences, 70*(1), 132–142.

Cornwell, B., & Schafer, M. (2016). Social networks in later life. In L. K. George & K. F. Ferraro (Eds.), *Handbook of aging and the social sciences* (8th ed., pp. 181–201). Waltham: Academic.

Cornwell, B., & Silverstein, M. (2015). The social network approach in gerontological research. *Journal of Gerontology Series B: Psychological and Social Sciences, 70*, 87–90.

Cornwell, B., Laumann, E. O., & Philip Schumm, L. (2008). The social connectedness of older adults: A national profile. *American Sociological Review, 73*, 185–203.

Crenshaw, K. (1991). Mapping the margins: Intersectionality, identity politics, and violence against women of color. *Stanford Law Review, 43*(6), 1241–1299.

Fischer, C. S. (1982). *To dwell among friends: Personal networks in town and city*. Chicago: University of Chicago Press.

Fischer, C. S. (2009). The 2004 GSS finding of shrunken social networks: An artifact? *American Sociological Review, 74*, 657–669.

Granovetter, M. S. (1995). *Getting a job: A study of contacts and careers*. Chicago: University of Chicago Press.

Higginbotham, F. M. (2013). *Ghosts of Jim Crow: Ending racism in post-racial America*. New York: New York University Press.

House, J. S., Umberson, D., & Landis, K. R. (1988). Structures and processes of social support. *Annual Review of Sociology, 14*, 293–318.
Ibarra, H. (1995). Race, opportunity, and diversity of social circles in managerial networks. *Academy of Management, 38*, 673–703.
Kahn, R., & Antonucci, T. C. (1980). Convoys over the life course: Attachment, roles, and social support. In P. B. Baltes & O. Brim (Eds.), *Life-span development and behavior* (Vol. 3, pp. 253–286). New York: Academic.
Kuh, D., & Ben-Shlomo, Y. (Eds.). (2004). *A life course approach to chronic disease epidemiology*. Oxford: Oxford University Press.
Lin, N. (2001). *Social capital: A theory of social structure and action*. Cambridge: Cambridge University Press.
Lin, N., Ensel, W. M., Simeone, R. S., & Kuo, W. (1979). Social support, stressful life events, and illness: A model and an empirical test. *Journal of Health and Social Behavior, 20*(2), 108–119.
Lin, N., Ensel, W. M., & Vaugh, J. C. (1981). Social resources and strength of ties: Structural factors in occupational status attainment. *American Sociological Review, 46*(4), 393–405.
Lin, S.-F., Beck, A. N., & Finch, B. K. (2014). Black-white disparity in disability among U.S. older adults: Age, period, and cohort trends. *The Journals of Gerontology. Series B, Psychological Sciences and Social Sciences, 69*(5), 784–797.
Litwin, H., & Stoeckel, K. J. (2013). Social network and mobility improvement among older Europeans: The ambiguous role of family ties. *European Journal of Ageing, 10*, 159–169.
Marsden, P. V. (1987). Core discussion networks of Americans. *American Sociological Review, 52*, 122–131.
Marsden, P. V. (1990). Network data and measurement. *Annual Review of Sociology, 16*, 435–463.
Marsden, P. V., & Campbell, K. E. (1984). Measuring tie strength. *Social Forces, 63*, 482–501.
McAllister, L., & Fischer, C. S. (1978). A procedure for surveying personal networks. *Sociological Methods and Research, 7*, 131–148.
McCall, L. (2005). The complexity of intersectionality. *Signs, 30*(3), 1771–1800.
McPherson, M., Smith-Lovin, L., & Cook, J. M. (2001). Birds of a feather: Homophily in social networks. *Annual Review of Sociology, 27*, 415–444.
McPherson, M., Smith-Lovin, L., & Brashears, M. E. (2006). Social isolation in America: Changes in core discussion networks over two decades. *American Sociological Review, 71*, 353–375.
McPherson, M., Smith-Lovin, L., & Brashears, M. E. (2009). Reply to Fischer: Models and marginals: Using survey evidence to study social networks. *American Sociological Review, 74*(4), 670–681.
Moen, P. (2001). The gendered life course. In L. George & R. H. Binstock (Eds.), *Handbook of aging and the social sciences* (pp. 179–196). San Diego: Academic.
Morgan, D. L. (1988). Age differences in social network participation. *Journal of Gerontology: Social Sciences, 43*, S129–S137.
Pager, D., & Sheppard, H. (2008). The sociology of discrimination: Racial discrimination in employment, housing, credit, and consumer markets. *Annual Review of Sociology, 34*, 181–209.
Pager, D., Western, B., & Bonikowski, B. (2009). Discrimination in a low-wage labor market: A field experiment. *American Sociological Review, 74*(5), 777–799.
Paik, A., & Sanchagrin, K. (2013). Social isolation in America: An artifact. *American Sociological Review, 78*(3), 339–360.
Patterson, O. (1998). *Rituals of blood: Consequences of slavery in two American centuries*. New York: Basic Civitas.
Putnam, R. D. (2000). *Bowling alone: The collapse and revival of American community*. New York: Simon & Schuester.
Quillian, L. (2006). New approaches to understanding racial prejudice and discrimination. *Annual Review of Sociology, 32*, 299–328.
Roithmayr, D. (2014). *Reproducing racism: How everyday choices lock in white advantage*. New York: New York University Press.

Sabatini, F. (2009). Social capital as social networks: A new framework for measurement and an empirical analysis of its determinants and consequences. *The Journal of Socio- Economics, 38*, 429–442.
Schuman, H., Steeh, C., Bobo, L., & Krysan, M. (1997). *Racial attitudes in America: Trends and interpretations* (2nd ed.). Cambridge, MA: Harvard University Press.
Sears, D. O., & Henry, P. J. (2005). Over thirty years later: A contemporary look at symbolic racism. *Advances in Experimental Social Psychology, 37*, 95–150.
Smith, K. P., & Christakis, N. A. (2008). Social networks and health. *Annual Review of Sociology, 34*, 419–429.
Stack, C. (1974). *All our kin: Strategies for survival in a Black community*. New York: Basic Books.
Thoits, P. A. (2011). Mechanisms linking social ties and support to physical and mental health. *Journal of Health and Social Behavior, 52*(2), 145–161.
Thornton-Dill, B., & Zambrana, R. E. (Eds.). (2009). *Emerging intersections of sexuality, gender and race in theory, policy and practice*. New Brunswick: Rutgers University Press.
Uchino, B. N., Bowen, K., Carlisle, M. K., & Birmingham, W. (2012). Psycholgocial pathways linking social support to health outcomes: A visit with the "ghosts" of research past, present, and future. *Social Science & Medicine, 74*, 949–957.
U.S. Census Bureau. (2015). *America's families and living arrangements*. Current Population Survey, Annual Social and Economic Supplement.
Wellman, B. (1983). Network analysis: Some basic principles. *Sociological Theory, 1*, 155–200.
Wrzus, C., Hänel, M., Wagner, J., & Neyer, F. J. (2013). Social network changes and life events across the life span: A meta-analysis. *Psychological Bulletin, 139*, 53–80.
York, E., Cornwell, B., & Waite, L. J. (2009). Social disconnectedness, perceived isolation, and health among older adults. *Journal of Health and Social Behavior, 50*(1), 31–48.

Duane F. Alwin is the inaugural holder of the Tracy Winfree and Ted H. McCourtney Professorship in Sociology and Demography at Pennsylvania State University, where he directs the Center for Life Course and Longitudinal Studies. He is also Emeritus Research Professor at the Survey Research Center, Institute for Social Research and Emeritus Professor of Sociology, University of Michigan, Ann Arbor, where he was affiliated for 23 years. His main areas of specialization include research methods, social stratification, social psychology, family and the life course.

Jason R. Thomas is a mathematical demographer who studies inequalities in health outcomes over the life course. He operates a consulting service focusing on data collection and analysis in cross-national research located in State College, Pennsylvania.

Kyler J. Sherman-Wilkins was a doctoral candidate in Sociology and Criminology at Pennsylvania State University when this paper was written. He is presently an Assistant Professor of Sociology and Anthropology at Missouri State University. His research interests focus on racial differences in health and cognitive decline in older age.

Chapter 15
Can Extracurricular Activities Reduce Adolescent Race/Ethnic Friendship Segregation?

David R. Schaefer, Sandra D. Simpkins, and Andrea Vest Ettekal

Introduction

Friendship segregation based on race and ethnicity—also referred to as racial/ethnic homophily—is one of the strongest, most obstinate characteristics of friendship networks in the U.S. (McPherson et al. 2001). Friendship segregation appears early in life and persists throughout the life course (Graham et al. 2009). In 1985, 91% of U.S. adults had no racial diversity in their close personal networks, dropping only slightly to 85% in 2004 (McPherson et al. 2006). Such extreme segregation has several consequences, oftentimes negative. At the societal level, segregated networks increase inequality, polarize beliefs and attitudes, and perpetuate disparities in health, academic achievement and other important outcomes (McPherson et al. 2001).

Adolescence may be a sensitive period in the life course for considering race/ethnicity in regard to beliefs and friendships. To begin, race and ethnicity are core components of identity (Umaña-Taylor et al. 2014); and, the development of identity during adolescence serves as the foundation of beliefs youth carry into adulthood. Because understanding who they are and how they fit within society are central

Support provided by NICHD R21-HD071885.
We are grateful for the thoughtful feedback provided by Michal Bojanowski, Ron Burt, Claude Fischer, Scott Feld, and Steven Haas.

D. R. Schaefer (✉)
Department of Sociology, University of California, Irvine, CA, USA
e-mail: drschaef@uci.edu

S. D. Simpkins
School of Education, University of California, Irvine, CA, USA

A. V. Ettekal
Department of Recreation, Park and Tourism Sciences, Texas A&M University, College Station, TX, USA

D. F. Alwin et al. (eds.), *Social Networks and the Life Course*, Frontiers in Sociology and Social Research 2, https://doi.org/10.1007/978-3-319-71544-5_15

developmental tasks of adolescence, youth may be more susceptible to influence during this period compared to other developmental periods. Indeed, adolescents' identity exploration is informed by the racial/ethnic composition of their friendship networks where these processes play out (Kornienko et al. 2015; Rivas-Drake et al. 2016). Friendships not only shape adolescents' racial/ethnic identity, but how adolescents see themselves more broadly and how they view others, including their beliefs about other groups (Hartup and Stevens 1997). Moreover, adolescents increasingly turn to their peers for guidance in a variety of decisions (Berndt 1992; Rubin et al. 2006), meaning that friend selection becomes important for structuring one's social environments concurrently and into adulthood.

According to a life course perspective, friendships during adolescence not only have implications for youth outcomes during the adolescent period, but shape youth's future life course pathways (Johnson et al. 2011; Roeser and Peck 2003). The peers youth befriend during adolescence affect adulthood through processes associated with consistency in friendship characteristics over time and friend influence on one's behaviors and attitudes (Hartup and Stevens 1997). Drawing on perpetuation theory, Wells and Crain (1994) argue that interracial contact during childhood and adolescence has a broad array of benefits for disadvantaged minorities to help them counteract forces of segregation that hinder educational attainment and occupational success. For instance, individuals with ethnically and racially diverse friendships in high school have more diverse friendships in college (Stearns et al. 2009) and the workplace (Stearns 2010). Intergroup friendships also help children develop social skills (Lease and Blake 2005), reduce prejudice and bias toward other ethnic groups (Aboud et al. 2003; Davies et al. 2011), and provide the cultural tools needed to interact in diverse settings later in life (e.g. knowledge of a wide range of music or sports; Benediktsson 2012). Given these implications, it is important to both understand the mechanisms that promote and inhibit friendship segregation and devise strategies to overcome segregation.

Historically, policies and interventions have been devised to decrease inequality and improve race/ethnic relations among youth. For instance, following *Brown v. Board of Education*, school districts across the U.S. implemented strategies (such as forced busing) in an effort to desegregate schools. Though such efforts afforded the proximity necessary for cross-race relations to develop, proximity is not a sufficient condition for the emergence of cross-race friendships – additional steps are needed. We argue that school-based extracurricular activities are a context with the potential to influence adolescent friendship segregation.

We argue that among the numerous benefits afforded by extracurricular activities (labeled ECAs), they are a setting that can create positive turning points in individuals' life course pathways. ECAs provide access to and strengthen youth's human, cultural, and social capital, including leadership development, fostering adult-youth supportive relationships, and improving youth's cognitive, behavioral, and emotional skills, even after accounting for selection factors (Mahoney et al. 2009; Vandell et al. 2015). For instance, students who participate in ECAs during adolescence are more likely to gain admission to college, earn a bachelor's degree, and have higher earnings after college – all of which have profound impacts on adult well-being (Vandell et al. 2015). Roeser and Peck (2003) found that participation in ECAs in high school provided a positive turning point for youth who had "everything going wrong in their lives during eighth grade" (p. 56) and made them twice as likely to enroll in college.

Of particular interest for the current research question is the capacity for social capital that ECAs foster by connecting youth participants to teachers, mentors, or other adult leaders, as well as peers with whom they may not otherwise associate. Regardless of the ECA focus (e.g. sports or arts), a common goal among all ECA types is to promote positive interpersonal skills and harmonious relationships among youth participants. ECAs afford opportunities for youth to develop interpersonal communication skills, improve attitudes toward others who are different than themselves, and develop friendships (Schaefer et al. 2011; Watkins et al. 2007). These social skills are key to achieving the potential decreases in racial/ethnic friendship segregation that contact through ECAs can bring. Although most ECAs are designed to promote positive interactions among youth, we argue that ECA leaders could capitalize on ECAs' established social benefits and broaden their aims to explicitly promote positive intergroup relations. ECA leaders often have more flexibility to address intergroup relations and friendships than teachers in classrooms. And, ECA involvement is more amenable to intervention and manipulation than other settings that filter friendship opportunities, such as academic tracks (Moody 2001) or neighborhoods (Mouw and Entwisle 2006). Given their pervasiveness in U.S. high schools, ECAs may be a cost-effective, ecologically valid avenue for efforts to support adolescent friendship diversity.

Empirical studies concerning the effects of ECAs on adolescent racial/ethnic friendship segregation are rare (Clotfelter 2002). However, qualitative evidence suggests that ECAs can promote intergroup friendships through shared interests and working together toward a common goal (Ettekal et al. 2015; Watkins et al. 2007). For instance, in interviewing students at a school desegregated in the 1970s, Ferrell (2008) observed that all six students interviewed commented on the power of ECAs to reduce racial tension. One former student reported "Athletics…transcends color. Kids don't see color, they play" (p. 93). Another former student reported, "a lot of the extra-curricular activities – sports, dance, theater, music – it's a whole lot different than just education. From there you learn great social skills: how to mingle and how to understand other social aspects of other races we didn't have before integration" (pp. 94–95). Findings such as these hint at the potential for ECAs to promote positive intergroup relations—whether these processes are typical in all ECAs or only under specific conditions remains to be determined.

If ECAs can successfully promote intergroup relations, they may serve as a positive turning point in adolescents' life course and lead to lasting changes because they represent a "change in the environment" or change participants' "views and expectations of other people" (Rutter 1996: p. 614). Qualitative data suggest that both mechanisms occurred in high quality organized after-school community-based programs (Watkins et al. 2007). In one example, an after-school program not only shifted adolescents' social environments by promoting positive intergroup relations, but working with cross racial/ethnic peers helped youth reconsider stereotypes, learn about people who were different than themselves and the injustices they experience, and change how they interacted with diverse peers outside of the activity (Watkins et al. 2007). As one adolescent reported, "Since there are a lot of Palestinian people or people of Palestinian descent here, I got a chance to talk to them and find out how they feel about things and how it affected their lives personally. So it's not just an issue on ABC news or something anymore. It's like, 'Well, I'm friends with this person, and you know they experienced it'" (Watkins et al. 2007: p. 391). Or as another adolescent expressed, "Like here, I chill with more people that listen to hip-hop and are more like urban, and when you really get down to it, they're not that different. It's only like the exterior stuff, but on the inside it's really all the same people" (Watkins et al. 2007: p. 392). Such experiences reflect changes among adolescents to be more sensitive to issues around diversity and social justice in their lives more broadly.

We draw upon two theories to investigate the association between ECA participation and friendship segregation. On the one hand, focus theory (Feld 1982) suggests that friendships within ECAs should be more homogeneous than in the broader school population. On the other hand, intergroup contact theory (Allport 1954; Pettigrew 1998) contends that ECAs should promote more diverse friendships than the school as a whole. This chapter unpacks these two theoretical accounts in order to provide a more comprehensive view of the contextual processes driving friend selection. Empirically, we partial out the net effects of each of these processes and evaluate the total effect of ECAs on friendship segregation.

Theories of Contextual Effects on Intergroup Relations

Focus theory and intergroup contact theory help to explain how ECAs could affect racial/ethnic friendship segregation. We propose that the seemingly contradictory implications of these theories actually operate in tandem because they focus on different aspects of the friend selection process: the pool of potential friends versus who from that pool is selected as a friend. To be clear, by racial/ethnic friendship segregation or *homophily*, we are referring to a network pattern whereby people of the same racial/ethnic group are more likely to share a tie (in this case a friendship tie) than people from different racial/ethnic groups (i.e., the proportion of same group vs. intergroup ties exceeds 0.5). Our use of the term racial/ethnic homophily itself does not imply any particular cause or reason for this pattern as multiple processes can produce racial/ethnic homophily (Wimmer and Lewis 2010).

Focus Theory

Feld observed that relationships are often centered around foci, which he described as contexts or activities that "actively bring people together or passively constrain them to interact" (1981: p. 1018). For adolescents, salient foci include families, neighborhoods, ECAs, schools, workplaces, and churches. Of interest here is the fact that foci tend to attract relatively homogenous subsets of the population (Feld 1982; Fischer et al. 1977). Foci are expected to be homogeneous on attributes related to the foci's purpose (Feld and Grofman 2009). In the case of ECAs, adolescents often participate in a particular ECA because they find it interesting, important, and something they are good at (Wigfield et al. 2015). Similarities among ECA participants in terms of how much they value the activity and their proficiency are likely to be strong during adolescence when competition for ECA slots is heightened and only those who are highly motivated are likely to persist.

Activities may also be relatively homogenous on attributes that are not directly related to the activity's purpose, yet are still related to participation. ECA participation varies systematically by youth gender, race, and SES (i.e., socioeconomic status) due to societal norms and family resources (Wigfield et al. 2015). For example, ECAs that require substantial financial investments in equipment or travel, such as sports and music, attract socioeconomically advantaged participants (Mahoney et al. 2009). When SES and race/ethnicity are correlated, certain ECAs will disproportionately draw youth from socioeconomically advantaged racial/ethnic group(s).

These initial segregation tendencies can intensify due to the way individuals hear about and join voluntary organizations like ECAs. According to McPherson (2004), organizations such as ECAs (and cultural phenomenon more generally) require "attention" from individuals in order to survive. For ECAs, attention takes the form of memberships. Membership spreads or diffuses through social networks as existing members convey information about the activity, practical details on how to participate, and legitimize it as an action. Because social networks tend toward homophily, membership diffuses across relatively homogenous sets of individuals. Consequently, members typically share similarities on many attributes, such as age, SES, and gender (McPherson 1983; McPherson and Smith-Lovin 1986).

Focus theory's contention that ECA participants are likely to be relatively homogenous in terms of race/ethnicity is consistent with prior research finding that individual activities offer less racial diversity than the school as a whole (Clotfelter 2002) and tend to draw participants from predominantly one racial/ethnic group (Schofield 1995). These conditions lead to racial/ethnic homophily because friends are disproportionately drawn from among one's ECA co-participants (Schaefer et al. 2011). The relatively homogenous nature of ECAs restricts opportunities for intergroup friendships, hence friendships among ECA co-participants should be more homophilous than the broader population. Of course, the amount of racial/ethnic homogeneity within an ECA determines the amount of friendship homophily expected by chance. If participation in an ECA is disproportionately concentrated by race/ethnicity, then homophily on race/ethnicity should be strong, whereas a more racially/ethnically diverse ECA should produce relatively weaker homophily among co-participants.

Research at different points in the life course has supported this hypothesis. For instance, adolescents participating in more heterogeneous activities have a greater proportion of friends from a different race/ethnicity (Jones et al. 2016). Among adult co-workers, Feld (1982) found that the distribution of age within departments was strongly related to age similarity among friends. Employees with a high proportion of same-age co-workers in their department reported a high percentage of same-age friends within the department. And, in considering more intimate relations, Kalmijn and Flap (2001) found that spouses who met in certain foci (e.g. schools, workplaces, voluntary associations, neighborhoods and families) exhibited more sociodemographic homophily than spouses who met outside of these foci. In sum, the expectation based on focus theory is that ECAs will demonstrate higher levels of homophily than the surrounding school context.

Intergroup Contact Theory

An alternative hypothesis is derived from intergroup contact theory (Allport 1954; Pettigrew 1998). Intergroup contact theory was originally developed by Allport in the 1950s to explain the contradictory findings on whether intergroup contact alleviated or exacerbated prejudice and negative outgroup attitudes. Allport proposed that intergroup contact would reduce prejudice and stereotypes at the root of segregation *if* the right conditions were met. Requisite conditions include (1) equal status between groups, (2) a common goal for the groups to meet, (3) interdependence in meeting their goal, and (4) support by authorities. Recent meta-analyses suggest that these conditions are not necessary as originally theorized, but rather facilitate and promote positive intergroup relations, with repeated contact and contact through a formal program having stronger effects (Pettigrew and Tropp 2006).

Pettigrew (1998) reformulated Allport's original hypothesis into a formalized theory. In so doing, he recognized the importance of friendships for overcoming prejudice, though friendships have been incorporated in variant ways over the years. Initially, Pettigrew characterized intergroup friendships as a fifth condition reasoning that contexts enabling friendships met Allport's four original conditions, in addition to affording other mechanisms, such as repeated contact and self-disclosure, that further reduce prejudice. More recently, Pettigrew and colleagues characterized friendships as a specific type of contact, rather than a condition, that is particularly effective at lowering prejudice (Davies et al. 2011). Drawing from this reformulated theoretical role of friendships, scholars have focused on *how* intergroup friendships reduce prejudice. Although important, the critical question is how intergroup friendships develop in the first place, given individual's overwhelming tendency to befriend same-race/ethnic peers throughout the life course (Graham et al. 2009). As part of that endeavor, we need to examine what opportunities support intergroup friendships.

High quality ECAs meet many of Allport's four facilitative conditions (1954) as well as those associated with strong effects in recent meta-analyses (e.g. Pettigrew and Tropp 2006). School-based ECAs are formal groups supported by school authorities that bring together youth who share similar interests and offer consistent contact over the school year. ECAs often have a common goal that requires cooperation to achieve. School sport teams, which is Pettigrew's (1998) exemplar, have an explicit common goal by competing against other schools. Other common goals include a student council fundraiser or producing a monthly newspaper. Though the four conditions of intergroup contact theory form the backbone of many ECAs, ECA contexts and leaders vary in their ability to achieve these facilitative conditions. There are times when programming of the most well-intentioned leader can go awry (Ettekal et al. 2015). To the extent ECAs exemplify these facilitative conditions, they should promote positive intergroup contact and decrease segregation (Watkins et al. 2007).

ECA research has mostly focused on friendships in general and not intergroup friendships, though a handful of exceptions exist. Adolescents have noted in qualitative studies that community-based organized activities helped them become friends with peers of different demographic groups (e.g. Watkins et al. 2007). Moody's (2001) classic study focused at the school level and suggested that the more students were exposed to outgroup members through ECAs, the lower the level of friendship segregation in the school, offering indirect evidence that ECAs can promote intergroup relations. More closely aligned with the research questions at hand, Knifsend and Juvonen (2015) found that more interethnic contact within ECAs led to a greater proportion of interethnic friendships. Though all of these studies provide evidence consistent with intergroup contact theory, none were designed to test the hypothesized effects derived from focus theory. As a result, many statistical effects that are of primary interest were simply controlled for, and the level of specificity in homophily necessary to tease apart the nuanced differences between these two theories was not addressed.

Based on intergroup contact theory, we expect that ECAs will exhibit weaker homophily than non-ECA contexts, such as the broader school. The extent to which ECAs promote intergroup friendships, however, likely depends upon how well they meet the conditions specified by intergroup contact theory.

Reconciling the Theories

Focus and intergroup contact theories make seemingly contradictory predictions regarding whether ECAs increase or decrease racial/ethnic friendship homophily. However, a closer examination reveals they are not actually in conflict. To inform this exposition, we draw upon the conceptual framework developed by McPherson et al. (2001), who attributed homophily to two general sources: baseline and inbreeding.

Although adolescents exercise agency in their choice of friends, those friendships are drawn from a set of potential ties dictated by the environment, referred to as the "opportunity structure" (Blau 1977). The capacity to form homophilous ties is contingent upon the composition of the broader population from which they are drawn. *Baseline homophily* is defined as the level of friendship similarity that would be expected by chance given the composition of the population on an attribute. For example, consider a population with two equally represented groups—perhaps half Black and half White. Assuming group members have an equal number of ties on average, then the random assignment of ties to dyads would result in a roughly equal proportion of ingroup and outgroup ties.

Baseline homophily is the target of focus theory. Focus theory makes a macro-level argument about how much homophily to expect by chance within the opportunity structure provided by ECAs. Because ECAs are expected to be more homogenous than the broader population, the baseline level of homophily within ECAs should be greater. Consequently, activity participants face restricted options when choosing co-participants as friends. Key to reconciling focus theory with intergroup contact theory is recognizing that the emphasis of focus theory is ECA composition, which should be more homogenous than the broader school population. Focus theory does not address individual level processes, such as preferences, that may also factor into friend selection. Rather, the argument relies on a comparison of chance expectations, or what would occur if friend selection processes were uncorrelated with race/ethnicity.

The second source of homophily is *inbreeding*, which refers to the amount of similarity that exists in excess of the baseline level. The most common form of inbreeding homophily is individual preferences for similar friends. People oftentimes prefer associating with similar others because such relations ease communication, reduce uncertainty, and reinforce one's identity. Additional sources of inbreeding homophily include network processes such as triad closure that *amplify* small initial tendencies toward homophily, essentially serving as a network feedback mechanism (Wimmer and Lewis 2010). Network processes in the form of social withdrawal or sociality can also create homophily if being socially active is associated with the attribute in question (Schaefer et al. 2011). For example, among two equally-sized groups, if one is more social, then that group will have more ties, which are primarily ingroup, and skew the distribution of ties toward homophily. Thus, homophily can emerge even without homophily preferences.

Inbreeding homophily is the target of intergroup contact theory. ECAs give students the chance to become acquainted, work together, and learn to rely upon one another. Interest-based groups also provide a common ground to members that neutralizes the threat of differences on other attributes (Wojcieszak and Mutz 2009). These direct experiences are argued to make pre-existing characteristics like race and ethnicity less salient. Thus, at the micro-level, ECA co-participants should have a weaker relative preference for homophily on dimensions unrelated to the activity compared to peers who are not ECA participants.

Based on this discussion, it is clear that focus theory and intergroup contact theory target different aspects of the friend selection process. Focus theory emphasizes the opportunity structure, which dictates the set of possible friendships, whereas, intergroup contact theory emphasizes the processes that operate once adolescents become involved in an ECA. In addition, these theories target different levels of analysis. At the macro level, ECAs can promote homophily by homogenizing the pool of available friends (focus theory), whereas at the micro level, ECAs can decrease the relative salience of attributes not directly related to the ECA's goals (intergroup contact theory).

The net effect of these processes within ECAs is unknown. In studying adult voluntary associations, McPherson and Smith-Lovin (1987) found evidence for homophily due to both baseline and inbreeding sources on gender, age, education, and occupation (they did not examine race/ethnicity). However, they only measured friendship pairs within voluntary associations. They did not consider friendships among non-participants and thus could not determine whether the inbreeding homophily they observed was stronger or weaker than outside of voluntary associations. Jones et al. (2016) focused on adolescent ECAs and found that the opportunity structure, as represented by ECA homogeneity, had the expected effect on total homophily. Like most studies, however, they did not differentiate between baseline and inbreeding sources of homophily. Within ECAs, we expect processes related to focus theory and intergroup contract theory to have opposing effects on friendship homophily: ECAs will exhibit more baseline homophily but weaker preferences for homophily compared to the broader population. In other words, friends in ECAs may be more similar, but have a weaker preference for similarity.

Methods

We used data from the National Longitudinal Study of Adolescent Health (Add Health), which is a nationally representative study of 7th–12th graders in the U.S. (Udry 2003). Add Health targeted more than 90,000 students in 132 schools for an in-school survey that included questions on race/ethnicity, friendships, and ECAs. This study offers unprecedented data on friendships and ECAs across a wide range of school contexts. Given its unprecedented scope, this dataset is well-suited to study questions of racial/ethnic friend segregation (Currarini et al. 2010; Goodreau et al. 2009; Moody 2001; Mouw and Entwisle 2006).

Our primary analysis draws from this sample by selecting schools with sufficient variation in race/ethnicity and ECA participation and at least a 75% response rate (to ensure the network is well-represented). These constraints resulted in a sample of 60,903 students in 108 middle and high schools.

Friendships were measured by asking students to list their 5 closest male and 5 closest female friends within the school. Race and ethnicity were based on separate questions and coded into the 4 most prevalent categories: White, Black/African American, Hispanic/Spanish, and Asian/Pacific Islander. ECA participation was determined by asking students to indicate which of 31 activities they participated in or planned to participate in during the school year. Eleven of these were sports, which we separated into male and female, giving a total of 42 distinct activities. Although Add Health sampled individuals, our unit of analysis is the ECAs to which individuals belonged. For each activity in each school, we determined which students belonged to the activity and whether those students' friends were also in the activity. We retained only those activities with at least 10 members and 10 friendships, leaving a sample of 1707 activities representing 40 of the 42 distinct types (female wrestling and male field hockey did not meet our threshold).

Measuring Homophily

The basis of homophily can be explained using three levels of ingroup vs. outgroup ties: equal, random, and observed (see Fig. 15.1). First, equal tie probability is when the proportions of ingroup and outgroup ties are equal, both at 0.5, in which case the network is neither homophilous nor heterophilous. This is a theoretical value and may not even be possible in some network contexts with highly skewed distributions. Second, random tie probability is the level of homophily that would occur by chance if ties were formed completely at random (though other operationalizations of chance are possible; see Bojanowski and Corten 2014). Depending upon the population composition, this level may be greater or less than 0.5. Third, observed tie probability is the level of homophily actually observed in a network. This level may be greater or less than either the 0.5 level and/or the random level.

We use these three levels to offer a conceptual means to partition total homophily into baseline and inbreeding sources. Total homophily is defined as the difference between equal tie probability and the observed proportion of ingroup ties. Total homophily (H_T) can be partitioned into baseline and inbreeding. Baseline homophily

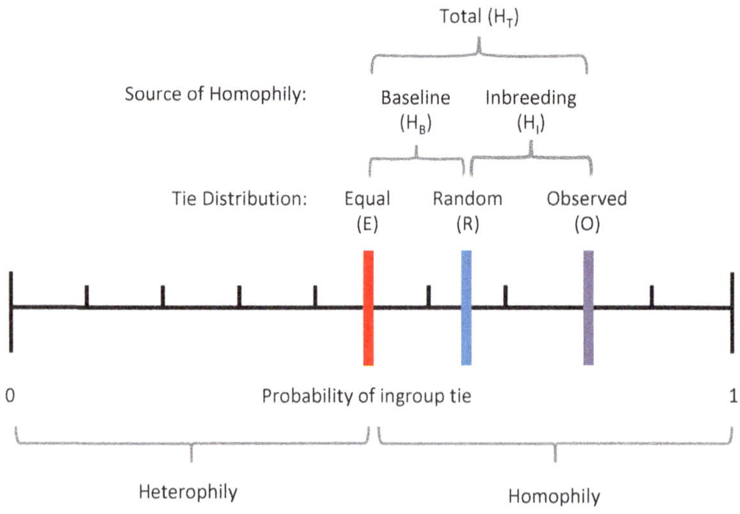

Fig. 15.1 Sources of homophily for two equally represented groups

(H_B) is represented by the difference between equal tie probability and random tie probability. As seen in Fig. 15.1, baseline homophily may reflect a positive or negative departure from equal tie probability depending upon the composition of the population. Inbreeding homophily (H_I) is represented by the departure of the observed tie probability from random tie probability. This departure may also be positive or negative; however, friendship networks are nearly universally characterized by observed homophily that exceeds random levels (McPherson et al. 2001; for an exception see Lewis et al. 2011).

We measured all three forms of homophily within each ECA and within each school as a whole. To measure homophily, we used variations of Coleman's segregation index (1958). We generalized Coleman's measure to the network level (equation 4.39 in Bojanowski and Corten 2014) and assumed friendship rates were constant across racial/ethnic groups (Goodreau et al. 2009). Coleman's original formulation compared observed homophily to what would occur if ties were formed randomly (i.e., expected). We used this original formulation as our measure of inbreeding homophily (H_I). To measure total homophily (H_T), our formula replaced the expected counts representing random tie distribution, with counts representing equal tie distribution within and between groups. For baseline homophily (H_B), the expected counts are also based on equal tie distribution, while the "observed" counts represent what would occur based on chance (i.e., the expected counts used to measure inbreeding homophily). Referring to Fig. 15.1, total homophily compares O (observed tie distribution) to E (equal tie distribution), baseline homophily compares R to E, while inbreeding homophily compares O to R (random tie distribution). Coleman's measure ranges from −1 to 1, with 1 representing the highest level of homophily.[1]

Results

We begin our investigation by examining differences between friendships for ECA participants relative to the broader school. Focus theory contends that baseline homophily (H_B) should be greater within ECAs than in the broader school. As expected, we found that the *mean* H_B across all ECAs was .36 compared to .31 for all schools. This is in the hypothesized direction of more homogeneity within ECAs than the school and was statistically significant ($t = 3.80$, $p < .001$).

A better test is to compare H_B for *each* ECA to H_B measured for the entire school in which it is situated. If ECA participation were random then we would expect H_B within ECAs to center around school level H_B. However, if ECAs serve as foci that bring similar adolescents together, then H_B should be greater within ECAs than the school in more than half the cases. This comparison revealed that 60% of ECAs were more homogenous on race/ethnicity than the school, which was statistically

[1]All else being equal, smaller groups will have a higher Coleman value. Thus, the test is biased toward greater homophily within ECAs. This bias is negligible as group size increases.

significant ($z = 8.42$, $p < .001$). Table 15.1 presents this comparison, as well as the comparison for each specific activity type. In combination, these results are consistent with focus theory's assertion that ECAs bring together relatively homogenous subsets of the broader school population.

Intergroup contact theory led to the hypothesis that ECA co-participation would weaken preferences for similar friends, resulting in lower inbreeding homophily (H_I) among ECA co-participants. Making a similar comparison as above, we found that the *mean* H_I across all ECAs was .38, compared to .38 for the broader school mean ($t = .03$, $p = .97$). This nonsignificant difference also emerged when we compared *each* ECA to the broader school context. Specifically, we found that 49% of ECAs displayed greater inbreeding homophily than the school ($z = .91$, $p = .36$). The results of H_I for both the mean comparison and for each activity contradict the expectations derived from intergroup contact theory. Thus, we have no evidence that ECAs reduced preferences for racial/ethnic inbreeding homophily.

Lastly, we calculated total homophily (H_T) for friendships within ECAs and for the broader school contexts. The objective of this analysis was to determine the net effect of baseline and inbreeding sources of homophily on friendship segregation. We found the *mean* H_T was .59 across all ECAs and .62 across all schools, a statistically significant difference ($t = 3.88$, $p < .001$). That is, we found less total homophily for ECAs than for schools overall. However, when we compared H_T for *each* activity to the broader school, we found that only 51% of the ECAs had greater total homophily than the broader school, which was equivalent to chance ($z = .91$, $p = .36$). These results suggest that some ECAs can reduce total homophily, but overall the combination of baseline and inbreeding homophily had no effect on friendship racial/ethnic segregation.

Heterogeneity Within ECAs

Thus far, we have found greater support for the predictions of focus theory than for intergroup contact theory. However, our analysis has treated all activities equally, ignoring whether or not they meet the facilitating conditions described in intergroup contact theory. ECAs vary in whether participants share a common goal; for instance, sports teams are more likely to involve participants coming together to meet a common challenge than academic clubs (Larson et al. 2006). Although we do not have detailed data on each specific activity, we categorized each activity based on their general characteristics and developmental experiences they typically afford (e.g. Larson et al. 2006). In this manner, we evaluated the effects of the following four ECA attributes: interdependence, team sport, number of friendships in the ECA, and contact sport (see Table 15.1 for coding). Interdependence (i.e., whether participants were required to work together to succeed in the activity, such as winning a game or putting on a performance), team sport (i.e., sports where adolescents play as a team, such as volleyball and field hockey, in contrast to individual sports, such as swimming), and friendship opportunities (i.e., the number of

Table 15.1 Extracurricular activity coding and homophily rates relative to school

				Activity coding			% ECA H ≥ School H		
ECA	Mean size	# of schools	Friendship #	Interdependence	Team sport	Contact sport	Baseline	Inbreeding	Total
Band	84.4	92	168.8	1	0	0	69.6	39.3	64.3
Softball (girls)	47.2	73	45.7	1	1	0	76.7	50.8	65.6
Baseball (boys)	62.1	87	62.2	1	1	0	70.1	43.8	45.0
Basketball (girls)	45.2	88	54.0	1	1	1	54.5	42.1	46.1
Basketball (boys)	65.4	101	76.7	1	1	1	36.6	54.1	38.8
Book Club	35.0	1	64.0	0	0	0	100.0	100.0	100.0
Cheerleading	50.2	91	57.2	1	0	0	61.5	59.5	59.5
Choir	70.0	80	101.9	1	0	0	56.3	54.3	51.4
Computer Club	38.8	12	24.0	0	0	0	50.0	50.0	50.0
Debate	33.7	19	26.7	0	0	0	57.9	50.0	43.8
Drama	61.2	56	81.2	1	0	0	73.2	53.8	53.8
Field Hockey (girls)	48.3	4	58.8	1	1	1	50.0	0.0	25.0
FFA	47.5	15	51.5	0	0	0	86.7	50.0	60.0
Football (girls)	12.0	1	11.0	1	1	1	99.0	99.0	99.0
Football (boys)	79.9	89	99.7	1	1	1	40.4	36.4	27.3
French Club	45.1	36	42.1	0	0	0	66.7	51.9	55.6
German Club	33.8	8	22.6	0	0	0	100.0	20.0	40.0
History Club	32.5	6	27.8	0	0	0	66.7	75.0	75.0
Honor Society	68.7	73	109.4	0	0	0	75.3	47.6	65.1
Ice Hockey (girls)	65.0	1	45.0	1	1	1	100.0	100.0	100.0
Ice Hockey (boys)	32.5	8	24.0	1	1	1	100.0	0.0	50.0
Latin Club	62.2	9	63.0	0	0	0	77.8	42.9	85.7
Math Club	41.1	33	44.6	0	0	0	60.6	51.7	44.8
Newspaper	38.1	50	31.6	1	0	0	72.0	42.1	52.6
Orchestra	58.4	14	58.3	1	0	0	57.1	46.2	53.8
Science Club	48.2	29	66.5	0	0	0	55.2	46.2	53.8
Soccer (girls)	44.1	39	43.7	1	1	1	66.7	53.1	59.4
Soccer (boys)	46.6	51	42.6	1	1	1	72.5	44.2	48.8
Spanish Club	68.1	56	80.4	0	0	0	41.1	58.0	46.0
Student Council	52.0	79	68.1	1	0	0	58.2	38.5	50.8

(continued)

Table 15.1 (continued)

ECA	Mean size	# of schools	Friendship #	Activity coding: Interdependence	Activity coding: Team sport	Activity coding: Contact sport	% ECA H ≥ School H: Baseline	% ECA H ≥ School H: Inbreeding	% ECA H ≥ School H: Total
Swimming (girls)	35.2	27	20.6	0	0	0	66.7	40.9	63.6
Swimming (boys)	32.3	6	17.5	0	0	0	66.7	60.0	40.0
Tennis (girls)	32.7	31	25.5	0	0	0	83.9	52.4	71.4
Tennis (boys)	30.9	25	23.2	0	0	0	72.0	70.6	64.7
Track (girls)	46.6	69	44.1	0	0	0	52.2	58.3	46.7
Track (boys)	46.4	65	38.9	0	0	0	40.0	50.0	43.5
Volleyball (girls)	50.2	60	63.5	1	1	0	58.3	58.5	58.5
Volleyball (boys)	31.8	8	22.0	1	1	0	75.0	66.7	100.0
Wrestling (boys)	41.9	29	28.2	0	0	1	51.7	30.4	34.8
Yearbook	48.2	86	40.3	1	0	0	55.8	58.2	49.3
Total[a]	54.6	1707	63.3	0.67	0.36	0.24	60.2	48.9	51.1

[a]Totals for activity codes represent the proportion of activities in the sample of each type

friendship ties among co-participants) are derived directly from intergroup contact theory (Allport 1954; Pettigrew 1998). Contact sport, which includes sports characterized by physical contact among players (e.g. football, soccer), was derived from literature suggesting that physical contact provides a more intimate level of familiarity that can help overcome outgroup prejudices (Chappell 2002). Although we only expected these factors to affect inbreeding homophily, we evaluated their effects on baseline and total homophily as an exploratory step.

In the following analyses, the outcome of interest was the difference between school and ECA measures of homophily. For each analysis, we estimated a model using each activity measure to predict the school-ECA homophily differential. We used a multilevel model, to account for the nesting of activities within schools, and included effects to control for activity size, school type (i.e., middle school, high school or combination), school size, school diversity, region of country, and community type (i.e., urban, suburban, rural).

Our analysis of interdependence and friendship opportunities focused on all ECAs. We expected that interdependence would reduce inbreeding homophily. However, the models revealed no differences in any source of homophily based upon the interdependence of participants in the activity (H_B: $b = -.01, p = .32$; H_I: $b = -.02, p = .10$; H_T: $b = -.01, p = .26$). Turning to Pettigrew's notion of friendship opportunities, we expected a negative association between number of friendships in the activity and inbreeding homophily. By contrast, the models indicated that number of friendships in an ECA were positively related to all three forms of homophily

(H_B: $b = .06$, $p < .001$; H_I: $b = .03$, $p = .02$; H_T: $b = .05$, $p < .001$). Activities with more friendships were more likely to have each form of homophily than the school at large.

The remaining two comparisons were specific to the subset of sport ECAs. In comparing team (vs. individual) and contact (vs. non-contact) sports, we found no differences in any form of homophily between team and individual sports (H_B: $b = .01$, $p = .31$; H_I: $b = -.03$, $p = .15$; H_T: $b = -.01$, $p = .77$). However, we found that contact sports had lower levels of each source of homophily than the overall school (H_B: $b = -.03$, $p = .02$; H_I: $b = -.04$, $p = .01$; H_T: $b = -.05$, $p = .003$). That is, contact sports drew a more diverse set of participants, exhibited weaker preferences for homophily, and had less friendship segregation overall than non-contact sports.

These analyses attempted to discern whether activities that conformed to intergroup contact theory reduced friendship segregation. There is a sizeable amount of measurement error as we were only able to roughly estimate the correspondence between ECAs and the theory's facilitating conditions. Although limited, this offers some evidence that when ECAs meet certain conditions, such as the case with contact sports, they can reduce racial/ethnic homophily.

Reflecting on Moody's Findings

It is informative to contrast our findings with Moody (2001), who was interested in how school desegregation following *Brown v. Board of Education* impacted friendship segregation—in essence, whether more integrated schools actually created more integrated friendship networks. At the school level, he found a curvilinear effect of school integration on friendship segregation whereby greater diversity was associated with increasing segregation, with this trend reversing at the very highest levels of diversity (Fig. 15.2). Another of Moody's key findings—and pertinent to our question—was that ECA diversity offset friendship segregation. Schools with more racially/ethnically integrated ECAs displayed lower rates of inbreeding homophily.

His results for ECAs stand in contrast to our mostly null results regarding the effect of ECAs on inbreeding homophily. To shed more light on the subject, we replicated Moody's main analysis, but with activities (not schools) as the unit of analysis. Although Moody framed the question in terms of the effect of school composition on preference for homophily, it is analogous to our conceptualizations of baseline and inbreeding homophily. To facilitate this comparison, we adopted his measures: an odds ratio to measure inbreeding homophily and the index of qualitative variation (IQV) to measure baseline homophily. Note, IQV is a measure of *diversity* and has the opposite valence as our measure of baseline homophily. Using our measures produced equivalent findings.[2]

[2]The correlation between baseline homophily measures is −.995; measures of inbreeding are correlated at .65.

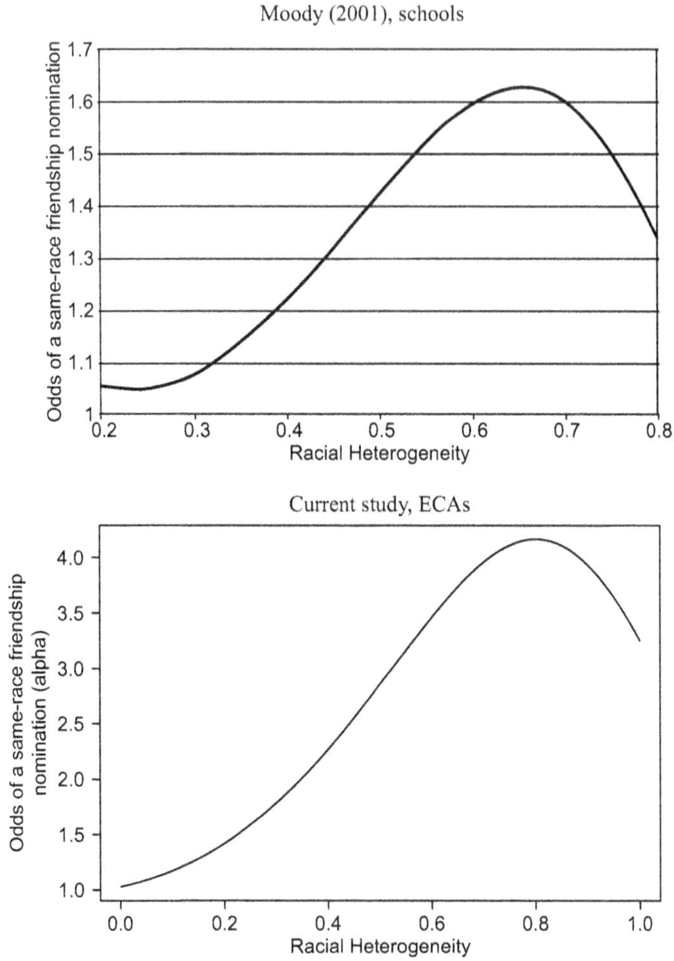

Fig. 15.2 Associations between school and ECA race/ethnic composition and race/ethnic inbreeding homophily

Note: We used a multilevel model, to account for the nesting of activities within schools, and included effects to control for activity type (academic, art, leadership, sport), activity size, school type (middle, high or combination), school size, school diversity, region of country, and community type (urban, suburban, rural). Odds of same race friendship is an indicator of inbreeding homophily.

To test for the curvilinear effect Moody found, we regressed inbreeding homophily on IQV as well as squared and cubed transformations of IQV. Results indicated that the effect of IQV (compositional diversity) was nonlinear as indicated by significant squared and cubed terms. As the predicted values in Fig. 15.2 show, these results are strikingly similar to Moody's. At both the ECA and school levels, more diversity was associated with a stronger preference for same-race/ethnic friends. However, this pattern tapered off at the highest levels of diversity. The only seeming differences between our results and Moody's are in (1) effect magnitude (y-axis), which is attributable to remaining differences between measures,[3] and (2) the x-axis displayed a greater range of diversity for ECAs than for schools.

These results suggest that the processes Moody documented at the school level also play out at the ECA level. If this is the case, then why do we reach a different conclusion from Moody as to whether ECAs decrease inbreeding preferences? Although our main analysis paralleled Moody's test quite closely, several differences remain that could account for this discrepancy. A key difference is that Moody considered all friendships within a school whereas we only considered friendships occurring among activity co-participants. It is possible that ECA diversity has effects on friendship that extend beyond the particular activity.[4] For instance, by offering the chance to learn about members of other groups, diverse ECAs may promote intergroup friendships between participants in the particular activity and non-participants. Such a process would be captured in Moody's analysis, but actually obscure the difference between ECAs and the broader school in our analysis. In addition, from a methodological perspective, our focus on ECAs resulted in more observations (compared to schools), but also more noise given the smaller size of ECAs and imprecision in measuring co-participation (i.e., the presence of varsity and junior varsity teams would affect calculations at the ECA level more than at the school level). Thus, our results may be overly conservative.

Additional Analyses

The results thus far paint a rather pessimistic view of how ECAs affect friendship segregation, especially in considering the policy prospects of manipulating ECA composition as a means to reduce friendship segregation. It is important to consider, however, that inbreeding homophily is an indicator of only one aspect of segregation—namely network level segregation that departs from chance expectation given the ECA's composition. It is informative to also consider how ECA composition affects overall racial/ethnic segregation (i.e., total homophily), which is closer to what is experienced at the individual level. Thus, as a final step we tested how ECA composition affects total homophily. This model replicated the one in the previous section, though with the dependent variable specified as total homophily. To be consistent with the previous models, we retained IQV as the measure of ECA composition.

[3] The odds ratio we use is equivalent to Moody's α as a measure of *gross segregation*. Moody's figure is based on *net segregation* (β), which was calculated using a statistical model (e.g. ERGM) to control for other friend selection factors. The smaller size of ECAs, relative to schools, precludes us from taking this approach. Moody found that the two measures exhibited similar patterns with β smaller on average than α.

[4] Feld (1982) observed such a pattern: the proportion of friends outside one's department who were similar to oneself was greater for workers in less diverse departments.

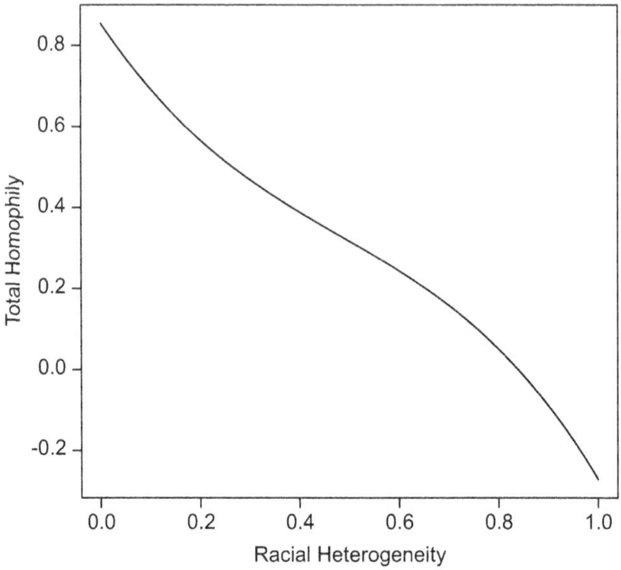

Fig. 15.3 Total homophily based on ECA racial heterogeneity (IQV)

Results indicated that total homophily was weaker in more diverse ECAs. As shown in Fig. 15.3, this effect was non-linear, however its trend was downward throughout the complete range of ECA composition. Thus, at all levels, increasing activity diversity led to a greater proportion of intergroup friendships within ECAs. As previous models showed, this was not enough to reduce inbreeding homophily (e.g. preferences). However, it may provide exposure to and experience with out-group members that help promote and strengthen intergroup relations later in the life course.

Discussion

Middle and high schools are influential times and places in the life course for adolescents' intergroup relations. Developmental changes place an increasing emphasis on friendship networks, at the same time that ethnic/racial identity issues become more salient (Umaña-Taylor et al. 2014). Cross ethnic/racial interactions and friendships during this time may have implications for individual's beliefs and ability to develop intergroup friendships in other settings in the later phases of life (Hartup and Stevens 1997; Johnson et al. 2011; Stearns et al. 2009). Moreover, for disadvantaged minorities, intergroup friendships provide access to important resources and capital that can enhance educational, occupational, and health outcomes.

Given these outcomes, persisting racial/ethnic friendship segregation during adolescence sets a disturbing precedent. From a policy standpoint, the high school context may be the last chance to reach the majority of the youth population in order to promote friendships among peers from different racial/ethnic groups. Following high school, students move to a range of contexts; many enter the workforce, while others attend college, where they have much more autonomy in selecting their courses, activities, and relationships. Given that previous work suggested that extracurricular activities have the potential to alter individuals' life course trajectories in terms of educational attainment (Roeser and Peck 2003), part of our goal was to test their potential in terms of cross-ethnic/racial friendships.

Our approach was informed by two theories—focus theory and intergroup contact theory—that offer seemingly contradictory hypotheses. To reconcile these theories, we distinguished between total homophily and its constituents: (1) baseline homophily, based on the composition of the opportunity structure, and (2) inbreeding homophily that arises due to non-random selection forces (McPherson et al. 2001). Baseline homophily reflects the structure that provides opportunities as well as constraints on friendships (which are the aim of focus theory). Within this structure, individuals make decisions regarding their friendships (which intergroup contact theory emphasizes). Distinguishing between these two levels offers a more complete understanding of how ECAs shape friendship segregation.

Our main finding was that ECAs were associated with lower friendship segregation on race/ethnicity, with the effect primarily operating through baseline homophily. The more opportunities students had to befriend members of a different race/ethnicity, the more such friendships developed. We did not see clear-cut or strong effects of ECAs on inbreeding homophily, such as would be expected if ECAs affected adolescents' preferences for ingroup friends. Under the right circumstances, ECAs help bridge group differences and promote positive intergroup relationships (Watkins et al. 2007); however, this did not seem to characterize ECAs as a whole in the Add Health data.

Although ECAs on average did not reduce adolescents' preferences for same-race/ethnic friends, there was one type of ECA that promoted cross-racial/ethnic friendships. Participants of contact sports consistently exhibited lower preferences for same-ethnic/racial friends than the school at large. Contact sports are most likely to meet the facilitative conditions articulated by Allport; thus, this finding provides some support for intergroup contact theory. Though it is curious that team sports did not produce the same decreases in preferences (i.e., inbreeding homophily), one possible reason we did not see stronger more consistent effects is that ECAs vary dramatically in quality (Mahoney et al. 2009; Vandell et al. 2015). ECA quality is a key ingredient to having a positive impact on youth development. The extent to which ECAs conform to the four facilitative conditions of intergroup contact theory and the extent to which leaders promote positive intergroup contact and how they handle intergroup conflict are aspects of quality that are likely integral to influence positive intergroup relationships (Watkins et al. 2007). Great strides have been made over the last few decades in defining program quality and ensuring that ECAs meet quality standards. It is possible that such improvements since the collection of Add Health data could translate into larger impacts on inbreeding homophily within today's ECAs.

Even when ECA diversity does not reduce inbreeding preferences concurrently, there may be other positive effects given that ECA diversity reduced baseline homophily. Following Davies et al. (2011), if ECAs can increase the number of intergroup friendships then intergroup attitudes should improve. In addition, there are likely longstanding effects of exposure to diverse peers during adolescence as outlined by perpetuation theory. Namely, intergroup friendships in high school can (1) increase the likelihood of choosing integrated social settings (e.g. more diverse workplaces), (2) help develop the skills to interact in diverse settings, (3) offer access to valuable opportunities (i.e., social capital), and (4) provide motivation for greater academic and occupational achievement (Stearns 2010). ECAs may have such positive long-term effects on intergroup relations even when they do not conform to the requirements of intergroup contact theory and weaken preferences for homophily. That is, increasing the frequency of friendships between members of different racial/ethnic groups may still provide many of the desired benefits of integration, include more equal access to education and labor market outcomes, even if they do not produce short-term changes in friendship preferences.

Implications

Theoretical Our integration of focus theory with intergroup contact theory led us to conceptualize friendships within ECAs as a two-level process involving who selects into the ECA and, within ECAs, who selects whom as a friend. Although both levels are important for understanding the source of intergroup friendship, a disproportionate amount of research has focused on the second level—what occurs once individuals are in a setting. However, there is likely an endogenous element to this process—individuals have agency in choosing the contexts and networks that provide their friendship opportunities (Kossinets and Watts 2009). For instance, adolescents may select into ECAs because their friends are involved, or in order to become friends with certain peers. Moreover, intergroup attitudes and diverse friendships—factors often treated as outcomes—likely play a role in determining who selects into a particular ECA setting. Selecting into a racially or ethnically diverse setting is only likely to occur once an individual's prejudice has fallen below some threshold (Binder et al. 2009). The endogenous nature of ECA participation allows for feedback effects on friendship that are worth considering. Kossinets and Watts (2009) speculated that endogenous selection of friends and activities can cumulate over time, magnifying even small tendencies toward homophily and leading toward racially/ethnically segregated groups. Thus, we call for future theoretical models that more fully articulate the complex associations between ECA participation, friendship, and the attitudes and beliefs at the heart of prejudice. Such efforts would benefit from the call by Johnson et al. (2011) to consider processes at work earlier in the life course that lead some adolescents to select into more diverse settings and/or be more susceptible to the positive effects of outgroup contact during adolescence.

Methodological Our findings have broader implications for the study of friendship segregation. All too often, studies of friendship segregation and its effects on development only consider a single source of homophily. Studies focused on total homophily have found that the diversity of ECAs promoted friendship diversity (Jones et al. 2016; Knifsend and Juvonen 2015). However, because they used a measure of *total* homophily, they were unable to distinguish whether the reductions in friendship segregation they observed were due to changes in preferences, or simply the greater availability of more diverse peers, a distinction with important theoretical and policy implications. By contrast, Moody (2001) utilized several measures of *inbreeding* homophily to reach his conclusion that schools with more integrated ECAs exhibited weaker preferences for homophily. This is a better measure when the research question is related to intergroup preferences as an outcome, as is often the case when evaluating intergroup contact theory, but does not give an indication of changes in the raw number of intergroup friendships. When researchers evaluate only one type of homophily, their results are not so much inaccurate as they are incomplete.

Policy and Practice Given evidence that ECAs can facilitate positive intergroup relationships (Watkins et al. 2007), is it possible to design ECAs to enhance this outcome? Focus theory and intergroup contact theory point to different intervention levers. First, focus theory points to manipulating the composition of ECAs to make them more heterogeneous, which should naturally lead to more intergroup friendships (given support we found for its effects on baseline homophily). A first step is to identify why certain racial/ethnic groups are under-represented within particular activities and devise strategies to overcome those barriers. Very different strategies will be required if the obstacles are cultural, socioeconomic (e.g. financial, transportation), or interest- or skill-based (e.g. because the activity requires cumulative skills, whose prior acquisition is correlated with race/ethnicity).

Second, what can be done to promote intergroup friendships within racially/ethnically diverse ECAs? Support for intergroup contact theory was weak at best given the modest reductions we saw in inbreeding homophily (e.g. preferences). However, this finding is likely because ECAs on average did not meet Allport's facilitative conditions. ECAs can alter preferences, as we found for contact sports and which is consistent with prior findings (Chappell 2002), but likely require more concerted effort focused specifically on promoting intergroup friendships than is typically the case. For this step, adult leaders are critical given their role in structuring the activity. Leaders often receive limited training and feel unprepared to effectively handle issues related to race/ethnicity that can be emotionally charged and surrounded by hesitation and trepidation. In addition, such efforts would require contending with the fact that activities vary greatly in their objectives (e.g. sports vs. academic clubs) and structure.

An open question is why ECAs were more homogenous than the school population only 60% of the time. In other words, 40% of ECAs were more diverse than the student body from which they were drawn. Though we have few empirical referents (see Clotfelter (2002) for an exception), this low level is surprising given the expectations from focus theory and ecological theory. It suggests that the processes that drive membership extend beyond the network effects emphasized by ecological theory. It may be that some ECAs are readily accessible to students regardless of race/ethnic background. For instance, we would expect more diverse ECA membership if information about the activity were widespread, the activity was normatively legitimate, and membership requirements were low. For diversity to be relatively greater within ECAs than the school as we observed 40% of the time, there must be forces at work that push some numerical minority groups toward participation, or restrict a numerical majority groups' participation rates. One possibility is that participation in ECAs is a way for minorities to gain status (Chappell 2002).

Conclusion

ECAs offer a promising route to reduce friendship segregation during adolescence and into adulthood, though one that is underutilized and all too often bereft of conscientious and purposeful planning. Our results suggest that although gathering diverse youth within an ECA can lessen individuals' typical tendencies toward homophily, additional support and concerted effort by leaders may be needed to bridge differences and promote adolescents' preferences for diverse friendships. This focus on adolescence is key as adolescents are developing the cognitive capacities to understand intergroup relations at the same time they gain the autonomy to begin building their own social ecologies. Though our focus was on racial/ethnic segregation, ECAs effects could extend to members of stigmatized groups, such as overweight, immigrant, or LBGTQ youth. Common efforts grounded in extracurricular activities can help to reduce friendship segregation on such attributes, improving life outcomes and promoting societal level integration.

References

Aboud, F. E., Mendelson, M. J., & Purdy, K. T. (2003). Cross-race peer relations and friendship quality. *International Journal of Behavioral Development, 27*, 165–173.

Allport, G. (1954). *The nature of prejudice*. New Jersey: Doubleday Anchor Books.

Benediktsson, M. O. (2012). Bridging and bonding in the academic melting pot: Cultural resources and network diversity. *Sociological Forum, 27*, 46–69.

Berndt, T. J. (1992). Friendship and friends' influence in adolescence. *Current Directions in Psychological Science, 1*, 156–159.

Binder, J., Zagefka, H., Brown, R., Funke, F., Kessler, T., Mummendey, A., Maquil, A., Demoulin, S., & Leyens, J.-P. (2009). Does contact reduce prejudice or does prejudice reduce contact? A longitudinal test of the contact hypothesis among majority and minority groups in three European countries. *Journal of Personality and Social Psychology, 96*, 843–856.

Blau, P. M. (1977). *Inequality and heterogeneity*. New York: Free Press.

Bojanowski, M., & Corten, R. (2014). Measuring segregation in social networks. *Social Networks, 39*, 14–32.

Chappell, B. (2002). Race ethnicity and sport. In A. Laker (Ed.), *The sociology of sport and physical education* (pp. 92–109). London: Routledge.
Clotfelter, C. T. (2002). Interracial contact in high school extracurricular activities. *The Urban Review, 34*, 25–46.
Currarini, S., Jackson, M. O., & Pin, P. (2010). Identifying the roles of race-based choice and chance in high school friendship network formation. *Proceedings of the National Academy of Sciences, 107*, 4857–4861.
Davies, K., Tropp, L. R., Aron, A., Pettigrew, T. F., & Wright, S. C. (2011). Cross-group friendships and intergroup attitudes: A meta-analytic review. *Personality and Social Psychology Review, 15*, 332–351.
Ettekal, A. V., Simpkins, S. D., Menjivar, C., & Delgado, M. Y. (2015). "No, that's not me!" ... "Just teach me with respect": A mixed method study of culturally responsive organized activities. (Manuscript in preparation).
Feld, S. L. (1981). The focused organization of social ties. *American Journal of Sociology, 86*, 1015–1035.
Feld, S. L. (1982). Social structural determinants of similarity among associates. *American Sociological Review, 47*, 797–801.
Feld, S. L., & Grofman, B. (2009). Homophily and the focused organization of ties. In P. Bearman & P. Hedström (Eds.), *Oxford handbook of analytical sociology* (pp. 521–543). Oxford: Oxford University Press.
Ferrell, J. A. (2008). *A magnet school and desegregation: A case study of Booker T. Washington high school, 1975–1980*. Dissertation, Oklahoma State University.
Fischer, C. S., Jackson, R. M., Ann Stueve, C., Gerson, K., Jones, L. M., & Baldassare, M. (1977). *Networks and places: Social relations in the urban setting*. New York: Free Press.
Goodreau, S. M., Kitts, J. A., & Morris, M. (2009). Birds of a feather, or friend of a friend?: Using exponential random graph models to investigate adolescent social networks. *Demography, 46*, 103–125.
Graham, S., Taylor, A. Z., & Ho, A. Y. (2009). Race and ethnicity in peer relations research. In K. H. Rubin, W. M. Bukowski, & B. Laursen (Eds.), *Handbook of peer interactions, relationships, and groups* (pp. 394–413). Guilford Press.
Hartup, W. W., & Stevens, N. (1997). Friendships and adaptation in the life course. *Psychological Bulletin, 121*, 355–370.
Johnson, M. K., Crosnoe, R., & Elder, G. H. (2011). Insights on adolescence from a life course perspective. *Journal of Research on Adolescence, 21*, 273–280.
Jones, G. J., Carlton, T. A., Bocarro, J. N., Bunds, K. S., & Edwards, M. B. (2016). The salience of sport in cross-race friendship selection. *Journal of Amateur Sports, 2*, 73–98.
Kalmijn, M., & Flap, H. (2001). Assortative meeting and mating: Unintended consequences of organized settings for partner choices. *Social Forces, 79*, 1289–1312.
Knifsend, C. A., & Juvonen, J. H. (2015). *Extracurricular activities in multiethnic middle schools: Ideal context for positive intergroup attitudes?* (Unpublished manuscript).
Kornienko, O., Santos, C. E., & Updegraff, K. E. (2015). *Friendship networks and ethnic-racial identity development: Contributions of social network analysis*. (Forthcoming chapter).
Kossinets, G., & Watts, D. J. (2009). Origins of Homophily in an evolving social network. *American Journal of Sociology, 115*, 405–450.
Larson, R. W., Hansen, D. M., & Moneta, G. (2006). Differing profiles of developmental experiences across types of organized youth activities. *Developmental Psychology, 42*, 849–863.
Lease, A. M., & Blake, J. J. (2005). A comparison of majority-race children with and without a minority-race friend. *Social Development, 14*, 20–41.
Lewis, K., Gonzalez, M., & Kaufman, J. (2011). Social selection and peer influence in an online social network. *Proceedings of the National Academy of Sciences, 109*, 68–72.
Mahoney, J., Vandell, D., Simpkins, S., & Zarrett, N. (2009). Adolescent out-of-school activities. In R. M. Lerner & L. Steinberg (Eds.), *The handbook of adolescent psychology: Vol. 2. Contextual influences on adolescent development* (3rd ed., pp. 228–269). Hoboken: Wiley.

McPherson, M. (1983). An ecology of affiliation. *American Sociological Review, 48*, 519–532.
McPherson, M. (2004). A Blau space primer: Prolegomenon to an ecology of affiliation. *Industrial and Corporate Change, 13*, 263–280.
McPherson, J. M., & Smith-Lovin, L. (1986). Sex segregation in voluntary associations. *American Sociological Review, 51*, 61–79.
McPherson, M., & Smith-Lovin, L. (1987). Homophily in voluntary organizations: Status distance and the composition of face-to-face groups. *American Sociological Review, 52*, 370–379.
McPherson, J. M., Lynn, S.-L., & Cook James, M. (2001). Birds of a feather: Homophily in social networks. *Annual Review of Sociology, 27*, 415–444.
McPherson, M., Smith-Lovin, L., & Brashears, M. E. (2006). Social isolation in America: Changes in core discussion networks over two decades. *American Sociological Review, 71*, 353–375.
Moody, J. (2001). Race, school integration, and friendship segregation in America. *American Journal of Sociology, 107*, 679–716.
Mouw, T., & Entwisle, B. (2006). Residential segregation and interracial friendship in schools. *American Journal of Sociology, 112*, 394–441.
Pettigrew, T. F. (1998). Intergroup contact theory. *Annual Review of Psychology, 49*, 65–85.
Pettigrew, T. F., & Tropp, L. R. (2006). A meta-analytic test of intergroup contact theory. *Journal of Personality and Social Psychology, 90*, 751–783.
Rivas-Drake, D., Umaña-Taylor, A., Schaefer, D. R., & Medina, M. (2017). Ethnic-racial identity and friendships in early adolescence. *Child Development, 88*, 710–724.
Roeser, R. W., & Peck, S. C. (2003). Patterns and pathways of educational achievement across adolescence: A holistic-developmental perspective. *New Directions for Child and Adolescent Development, 101*, 39–62.
Rubin, K., Bukowski, W., & Parker, J. (2006). Peer interactions, relationships, and groups. In W. Damon, R. M. Lerner, & N. Eisenberg (Eds.), *Handbook of child psychology: Volume 3. Social, emotional, and personality development* (6th ed., pp. 571–645). New York: Wiley.
Rutter, M. (1996). Transitions and turning points in developmental psychopathology: As applied to the age span between childhood and mid-adulthood. *International Journal of Behavioral Development, 19*, 603–626.
Schaefer, D. R., Kornienko, O., & Fox, A. M. (2011a). Misery does not love company: Network selection mechanisms and depression homophily. *American Sociological Review, 76*, 764–785.
Schaefer, D. R., Simpkins, S. D., Vest, A. E., & Price, C. (2011b). The contribution of extra-curricular activities to adolescent friendships: New insights through social network analysis. *Developmental Psychology, 47*, 1141–1152.
Schofield, J. W. (1995). Promoting positive intergroup relations in school settings. In W. D. Hawley & A. W. Jackson (Eds.), *Toward a common destiny: Improving race and ethnic relations in America* (pp. 257–289). San Francisco: Jossey-Bass.
Stearns, E. (2010). Long-term correlates of high school racial composition: Perpetuation theory reexamined. *Teachers College Record, 112*, 1654–1678.
Stearns, E., Buchmann, C., & Bonneau, K. (2009). Interracial friendships in the transition to college: "Do birds of a feather flock together once they leave the Nest?". *Sociology of Education, 82*, 173–195.
Udry, J. R. (2003). *The national longitudinal study of adolescent health (add health)*, waves I & II, 1994–1996; wave III, 2001–2002 [machine-readable data file and documentation]. Chapel Hill: Carolina Population Center, University of North Carolina at Chapel Hill.
Umaña-Taylor, A. J., Quintana, S. M., Lee, R. M., Cross, W. E., Rivas-Drake, D., Schwartz, S. J., Syed, M., Yip, T., Seaton, E., & Ethnic and Racial Identity in the 21st century Study Group. (2014). Ethnic and racial identity during adolescence and into young adulthood: An integrated conceptualization. *Child Development, 85*, 21–39.
Vandell, D. L., Larson, R. W., Mahoney, J. L., & Watts, T. W. (2015). Children's organized activities. In R. M. Lerner (Series Ed.), & M. H. Bornstein, & T. Leventhal (Volume Eds.), *Handbook of child psychology and developmental science; Vol. 4. Ecological settings and processes* (7th ed., pp. 305–344). Hoboken: Wiley.

Watkins, N. D., Larson, R. W., & Sullivan, P. (2007). Bridging intergroup difference in a community youth program. *American Behavioral Scientist, 51*, 380–402.

Wells, A. S., & Crain, R. L. (1994). Perpetuation theory and the long-term effects of school desegregation. *Review of Educational Research, 64*, 531–555.

Wigfield, A., Eccles, J., Fredricks, J., Simpkins, S., Roeser, R., & Schiefele, U. (2015). Development of achievement motivation and engagement. In R. M. Lerner (Series Ed.), & C. Garcia Coll, & M. Lamb (Volume Eds.), *Handbook of child psychology and developmental science: Vol. 3. Social and emotional development* (7th ed., pp. 657–700). Hoboken: Wiley.

Wimmer, A., & Lewis, K. (2010). Beyond and below racial homophily: ERG models of a friendship network documented on Facebook. *American Journal of Sociology, 116*, 583–642.

Wojcieszak, M. E., & Mutz, D. C. (2009). Online groups and political discourse: Do online discussion spaces facilitate exposure to political disagreement? *Journal of Communication, 59*, 40–56.

David R. Schaefer is an Associate Professor in the Department of Sociology, University of California at Irvine. His research is centered on social networks, with emphases on health, adolescence, and delinquent populations. He investigates how social networks impact critical developmental and health-related outcomes, as well as how people acquire their respective network positions.

Sandra D. Simpkins is Professor in the School of Education, University of California at Irvine. Her work is aimed at the understanding how families, friendships, and social position factors (such as ethnicity and culture) shape adolescents' organized after-school activities and motivation.

Andrea Vest Ettekal is an Assistant Professor in Youth Development in the Department of Recreation, Park and Tourism Sciences at Texas A&M University. Her research investigates the antecedents, experiences, and outcomes of youth development program participation, as well as program design, implementation, and evaluation. Within the field of youth development programs, she has a special interest in peer relationships, sports, and character development.

Part VII
Tracking Social Networks Through Time

Chapter 16
Structure by Death: Social Network Replenishment in the Wake of Confidant Loss

Benjamin Cornwell and Edward O. Laumann

There have been enormous advances over the past few years in our understanding of the nature and consequences of *change* within individuals' social networks – especially for older adults (Cornwell et al. 2015). Contrary to the stereotype of later life as a period of idleness and isolation, research shows that older adults maintain a very dynamic social existence by remaining active in networks composed of people and various local institutions (e.g., Cornwell et al. 2008; Kohli et al. 2009; c.f., Cumming and Henry 1961). In fact, older adults may be even more socially connected than younger and middle-aged adults in some respects, especially in terms of their involvement in local community institutions (e.g., Chatters et al. 1999; Einolf 2009; Rotolo and Wilson 2004; c.f., Komp et al. 2012).

It is not just that older adults remain well connected – it is that they tend to do so despite experiencing massive changes in their social environments. Later life is full of major life-course transitions (Elder 1985; George 1993; Heinz and Marshall 2003; Settersten and Mayer 1997) – including retirement, bereavement, health decline, and the emptying of the familial nest – which often drastically alter the composition and structure of one's social network (e.g., Crisp et al. 2015; Kahn and Antonucci 1980; Crosnoe and Elder 2002; Moen et al. 1992; Perry and Pescosolido

The National Social Life, Health, and Aging Project is supported by the National Institutes of Health (R01AG021487, R37AG030481, R01AG033903), which also provided partial funding for this research. We wish to thank Duane Alwin, Diane Felmlee, Derek Kreager, Mario Luis Small, Erin York Cornwell, and participants at the "Together through Time: Social Networks and the Life Course" conference at The Pennsylvania State University in May 2015 for providing useful suggestions.

B. Cornwell (✉)
Department of Sociology, Cornell University, Ithaca, NY, USA
e-mail: btc49@cornell.edu

E. O. Laumann
Department of Sociology, University of Chicago, Chicago, IL, USA
e-mail: e-laumann@uchicago.edu

D. F. Alwin et al. (eds.), *Social Networks and the Life Course*, Frontiers in Sociology and Social Research 2, https://doi.org/10.1007/978-3-319-71544-5_16

2012; Pillemer et al. 2000; Schafer 2013; Shaw et al. 2007; van Tilburg 1998; Wrzus et al. 2013). A key insight from the social-gerontological literature is that older adults tend to respond and adapt well to any social network losses or increased isolation that accompany such changes. In fact, these changes are usually closely preceded, accompanied, or followed by the addition of new network members (Cornwell et al. 2014).[1]

Nonetheless, considerable debate remains in the literature with respect to whether older adults: (1) see network loss as an opportunity to shrink their social networks; or (2) actively attempt to adapt to and compensate for losses in an effort to remain as socially connected as possible (see Atchley 1989; Bloem et al. 2008; Charles and Carstensen 2010; Cornwell and Laumann 2015; Donnelly and Hinterlong 2010; Lamme et al. 1996; Zettel and Rook 2004).[2]

These are important questions for several reasons. For one, we know that social network changes can have major consequences for individuals. In extreme cases, the undesired loss of a close network member results in bereavement, grief, and depression (Galatzer-Levy and Bonanno 2012; Gerstorf et al. 2010; Ghesquiere et al. 2013; Vable et al. 2015). The *death* of a network member in particular is an irreparable, and often exogenous, shock over which the individual has little or no control. Regardless of their cause, network losses have long-term, downstream implications, especially if one depended on the lost network member for companionship, support, or other resources. Research shows that network losses can have negative health implications, especially if those lost contacts are not somehow replaced (e.g., see Cornwell and Laumann 2015; Eng et al. 2002; Giordano and Lindstrom 2010; Holtzman et al. 2004; Kroenke et al. 2008; Seeman et al. 2011; Thomas 2012). In other cases, network losses may be experienced as minor disturbances, if they are noticed at all, as secondary consequences of broader life-course transitions (e.g., moving from one neighborhood to another), as normal network churn, or as intentional network replacement. Unfortunately, how network change manifests in later life – and how that shapes individuals' networks – is unclear.

Our overarching goal in this paper is to examine a particularly consequential aspect of change in older adults' social networks – namely, the loss of a network member due to death or some other cause, such as severe health problems. We are particularly interested in the extent to which older adults add new confidants to their networks during a period of network loss, which could be a sign of successful adaptation. We want to understand not only the likelihood of network replenishment, but also what factors predict whether older adults report any new network additions. We are particularly interested in what role age plays in this process. In light of conflicting theories and findings about how aging relates to network tie loss, cultivation,

[1] It is important to note, however, that adaptation can be hampered by social and material disadvantage (see Cornwell 2015; Fischer and Beresford 2015; Schafer and Vargas 2016).

[2] Older adults are often active in cultivating new social relationships (e.g., by meeting new neighbors, volunteering), irrespective of whether they have experienced losses or difficult life-course transitions. As a result, many older adults' networks grow instead of decline in size (Cornwell and Laumann 2015; Cornwell et al. 2014).

and turnover (Atchley 1989; Charles and Carstensen 2010; Cornwell et al. 2014; Cumming and Henry 1961; Lamme et al. 1996), is it unclear how older adults will respond to the loss of a close network member. While some argue that network loss will lead to network shrinkage, others argue that older adults respond and adapt to these changes by recruiting new people into their closest social networks.

The Later Life-Course Dynamics of Network Change

We begin by briefly reviewing research that highlights why it is important to understand network change in later life. We then discuss some of the mechanisms through which social networks change during this period. Finally, we discuss the relationship between different types of network change in later life, including network loss, growth, and turnover.

Why This Matters

Later life is a time of several major life-course transitions – retirement, widowhood, the emptying of the familial nest, and health decline – that can have a major effect on social connectedness (e.g., see Choi and Ha 2011; Cornwell 2011). Thus, many researchers are interested in how older adults engineer or otherwise respond to the loss of important network members (McLaughlin et al. 2011). The loss of weak ties to neighbors, acquaintances, and fellow voluntary association members can have important implications or older adults' abilities to maintain their independence and access to resources outside of the family (Cornwell 2011; Cornwell and Laumann 2011; Martire et al. 2002; Silverstein et al. 1996; Warner et al. 2011). And the loss of especially close network members – such as one's spouse – can be utterly devastating.

Much research has considered the *social-psychological* implications of the loss of network members, usually with a focus on the death of a close friend or family member. This form of loss often precipitates an immediate psychological bereavement process, sometimes involving depression and loneliness (see Galatzer-Levy and Bonanno 2012; Ghesquiere et al. 2013; Vable et al. 2015). Losses of this sort are seen as highly psychologically destabilizing experiences (Gerstorf et al. 2010). This destabilizing quality of social network change also involves some subtle structural aspects. Network losses can result in a reshuffling of social influences and norms (see Deflem 1989). Furthermore, social network members develop routine patterns of interaction and exchange that are central to the coordination of social support and informal social control. Changes in one's social network may impair the internal support functions of one's network through the disruption of established routines of contact and communication among one's contacts. The loss of a particularly central network member, such as one's spouse, for example, can severely handicap a network's capacity to coordinate on one's behalf because it removes the most deeply embedded member of one's network (see Cornwell 2012; Kalmijn 2003).

But it is important to bear in mind that network loss is not inherently detrimental, and may be healthy in some cases. Some social relationships are stressful or even dangerous, such as contentious and abusive relationships (e.g., Kouvonen et al. 2011; Umberson et al. 2010). Being connected to individuals who are unhealthy or who encourage and/or engage in unhealthy behavior can, on balance, be detrimental to one's health (e.g., Barrington et al. 2009; Christakis and Fowler 2008; Eisenberg et al. 2005). In some such cases, network change (whether it is desired or not) may yield a more beneficial and enjoyable array of social contacts. This relates to the focus of this paper, which deals with the possibility that older adults replenish their networks by cultivating new contacts in the wake of network loss.

It has been shown that the process of cultivating new social ties, which can happen in several ways, can be beneficial (see Bidart and Lavenu 2005; Cornwell and Laumann 2015; Degenne and Lebeaux 2005; Sasovova et al. 2010). By resuscitating dormant ties, for example, people can recover lost social capital (Levin et al. 2011). The cultivation of new social relationships from scratch can be beneficial as well. The process of cultivating new (or dormant) social relationships may involve experimenting with new social contexts or venues, deviating from pre-established routines, trying new activities, and paying greater attention to self-presentation (see Sasovova et al. 2010). Breaking out of old routines involves more physical and cognitive effort, which may have a variety of health benefits (see Cornwell and Laumann 2015).

Given these observations, we do not assume that the loss of network members is inherently detrimental. Rather, we believe that, in most cases, network loss is inextricably linked to concurrent or sequential processes of tie cultivation (which may or may not involve tie replacement, per se). For the remainder of this paper, therefore, we consider not just tie loss, or the addition of new ties, but rather *the relationship between* the loss and addition of social network members.

Dynamics of Tie Loss and Replacement

Later life is a time of major life-course transitions. The life-course perspective (Elder 1985; George 1993) underscores the implications of various later-life challenges for older adults' social integration (e.g., see Crosnoe and Elder 2002; Kahn and Antonucci 1980; Pillemer et al. 2000). For older adults, the most important transitions include the emptying of the familial nest, retirement, health decline, and bereavement. The main thrust of much of the early, foundational research on social network change was that this period of upheaval and isolation inevitably leads to the diminution of one's social roles and positions (e.g., due to retirement), deep personal loss (e.g., widowhood), and the voluntary surrendering of large reserves of network ties and resources (Cumming and Henry 1961). The focus in more recent years has turned toward the issue of the circumstances under which older adults' social networks change, including the possibility that older adults' networks grow as well as shrink in the wake of life-course changes.

This newer perspective culminates from work that shows that many older adults turn role transitions from one social domain (e.g., retirement from paid work) into opportunities to become more socially active in other domains (e.g., volunteering, leisure activities). Thus, more recent accounts emphasize older adults' engagement in social and community activities and efforts to compensate for the loss of social ties through the cultivation of new ones (Cornwell et al. 2014; Donnelly and Hinterlong 2010; Johnson and Mutchler 2014; Lamme et al. 1996).

Consistent with both the contrasting perspectives that emphasize (1) the voluntary shedding of social ties (e.g., Cumming and Henry 1961) and those that emphasize (2) active efforts at compensation, adaptation, and network growth (e.g., Atchley 1989; Lamme et al. 1996) in the wake of life-course transitions, research shows that later life is a period of considerable network change. Recent work shows that very few older adults experience complete stability, even within the closest, most stable regions of their personal social networks. For example, Cornwell et al. (2014) report that 93.1% of non-institutionalized older Americans reported that at least one confidant was lost or added during the five-year study period. The majority of respondents reported that they both lost and added at least one confidant between waves. In this sense, later life is typically characterized by *both network decline and network growth* – in short, dynamics. This study focused on some of the strongest, most stable types of ties in older adults' social networks, so it likely understates the amount of change that older adults typically face within their everyday social environments.

What is less well understood is how the losses from and additions to older adults' social networks that emerge during such life-course transitions are related to each other. Losses and gains may be concurrent, sequential, or orthogonal processes. Our goal in this paper is to better understand the typical nature of this relationship. Fortunately, previous social-gerontological research has addressed this issue, and provides some guidance. It is this work that suggests that in order to understand how network losses are related to network additions, one has to scrutinize *the reasons behind* network change.

Specific Life-Course Transitions and Network Change For a wide variety of reasons, the process of aging has complex and sometime contradictory relationships with social network size and structure. First, it is worth noting that social gerontologists distinguish between changes in older adults' networks that are voluntary or planned and changes that are not voluntary. Most research highlights the role of life-course transitions that are generally unavoidable. Much work suggests that these transitions play a major role in shaping older adults' networks, both in terms of overall social integration and in terms of structural features of networks such as composition and density. While retirement can increase connectedness to kin and the community (e.g., through volunteering), it often results in a loss of weak ties and more restricted network range – especially for men (e.g., see Cornwell et al. 2008; Hatch and Bulcroft 1992). Likewise, health decline reduces individuals' abilities to maintain relationships, particularly weak ties or peripheral contacts (Cornwell 2009; Haas et al. 2010; Schafer 2011, 2013; Schaefer et al. 2011; Thomas 2011).

The literature conveys mixed messages regarding the consequences for social network structure of one of the most jarring types of changes that typify the experiences of later life – network member *death*. Some scholars point to the surge of support that often follows the loss of a close tie, other work documents increases in social activity following widowhood, while others focus on the likelihood of greater social isolation and loneliness (e.g., Ferraro 1984; Donnelly and Hinterlong 2010; Ha and Ingersoll-Dayton 2011; Li 2007; Utz et al. 2002; Wrzus et al. 2013). Unfortunately, few scholars have scrutinized the issue of the death of close contacts from a social networks perspective, so little known about its implications for network dynamics. Furthermore, most social-gerontological research on bereavement focuses on widowhood, and less attention has been given to loss as a factor within the larger boundaries of one's personal social circles. Because of its weight, we will come back to the issue of network member death throughout this paper.

Some research juxtaposes the kinds of life-course developments just discussed against social network changes that are purposefully and sometimes proactively engineered by older adults. The argument there is that dwindling life spans lead older adults to carefully tailor their networks – particularly by forsaking weak ties and casual acquaintances in favor of spending their remaining time enjoying stronger, more emotionally rewarding relationships (Charles and Carstensen 2010).

Network Additions from Network Losses Also relevant to this study is research which suggests that *network changes are related to each other.* Paramount here is the assumption that network losses often motivate subsequent tie cultivation (i.e., as a form of replacement).[3] From this perspective, the challenges of later life – such as the death of a close friend or family member – are are inevitable. What matters most is how older adults respond to these events. Several studies show that older adults exhibit positive, adaptive responses to later-life transitions that may otherwise threaten their social connectedness. Continuity and activity theories in particular hold that people grow accustomed to certain social roles and activities during their lives and attempt to maintain them in the midst of later-life transitions (Atchley 1989; Donnelly and Hinterlong 2010; Moen et al. 1992; Thoits 1992; Utz et al. 2002). Because of this, the loss of social ties sparks efforts by individuals to adapt – which they do by cultivating new social relationships and by becoming more involved in community activities (Donnelly and Hinterlong 2010; Lamme et al. 1996; Li 2007; Mutchler et al. 2003).

Indeed, research shows that people who adjust to challenging later-life transitions by remaining socially active tend to be happier and healthier, both because they maintain their prior access to social resources and because of the physical activity and mental stimulation that is inherent in the adaptation process itself (Depp and Jeste 2006; Hao 2008; Jang and Chiriboga 2011; Kahana et al. 2012; Mitchell and Kemp 2000; Park 2009; Schwingel et al. 2009). Therefore, it is important to

[3] For now, we set aside the question of how accurate this assumption is. It is beyond the scope of this paper, and the available data, to discern whether network losses precede network additions. It is likely that in some cases people begin to develop new ties before shedding old ones. Indeed, the addition of new friends may lead to the loss of old ones.

consider the possibility that rather than providing older adults with a desirable opportunity to pare down their networks, network loss actually spurs network replenishment efforts among older adults, either to replace lost ties or in a proactive effort to shore up one's social network in anticipation of loss.

Despite the wealth of theoretical resources for motivating this analysis, little is known about how older adults' networks change in the wake of the loss of close network members. Here we examine how network tie additions relate to the loss of preexisting network ties. We are also mindful of how these additions relate to specific sources of network loss. We pay particular attention to network loss due to the *death* of a network member – in part because of its finality, because of its potential consequences for older adults, and also because it is a source of loss that is largely exogenous. Studying this form of network loss provides unique insight into how older adults cope with losses that are largely beyond their control. We carry out this analysis using the first nationally representative data on egocentric social network change in later life, which we will now describe.

Data and Analysis

We use data from two waves of the National Social Life, Health, and Aging Project (NSHAP), a nationally representative, population-based panel study funded by the National Institutes on Health. The NSHAP focuses on understanding connections between older adults' social lives and well-being. Wave 1 was conducted in 2005–6 and consisted of in-home interviews with 3005 community-dwelling older adults between the ages of 57 and 85 (see Smith et al. 2009). The sample was selected using a multi-stage area probability design that oversampled by race/ethnicity, age, and gender. The final response rate for Wave 1 was 75.5%. In 2010–11, NSHAP conducted a second wave of interviews (Wave 2). Of the 3005 baseline respondents, 744 (24.8%) were lost to some form of attrition, primarily mortality. NSHAP's Wave 2 response rate from among eligible surviving baseline respondents (N = 2548) is 88.7%. All things considered, NSHAP re-interviewed 75.2% of baseline respondents, yielding a panel of 2261 older adults.

Network Connectedness and Network Change

Network data were collected at both waves. At Wave 1, all respondents were asked to list up to five people with whom they discuss "things that were important to you" during the past year (Cornwell et al. 2009). This procedure generally elicits strong social network ties – ties through which social influence and resources (like social support) are most likely to flow (see Bailey and Marsden 1999; Perry and Pescosolido 2010; Ruan 1998; Straits 2000). However, there is some recent work that suggests that the important matters name generator allows for the addition of ties that are weak or trivial as far as core discussion networks go (see Bearman and Parigi 2004; Small 2013). To assess the importance, intensity, and functions of these network ties, the NSHAP also asked respondents to provide information about the their relationship with each confidant, including the type of the relationship (e.g., friend, child), frequency of contact, and emotional closeness. The NSHAP also gauged the functional specificity of respondents' network ties (Perry and Pescosolido 2015) by asking them how likely they were to talk to each of their named confidants about medical matters or health issues. Another important feature of social networks for health is network density (Ashida and Heaney 2008; Haines et al. 1996), which reflects the extent to which network members are connected to each other. Therefore, the NSHAP also asked respondents to specify how frequently each of their network members interacts with each of their other network members.

Assessment of Network Change Our primary interest is in the possibility that additions to older adults' personal social networks over time are associated with losses in their social networks. Not only were the same network data collected at Wave 2, but the NSHAP also employed a computer-based technique to record specific changes that occurred within older adults' social networks between Wave 1 and Wave 2. At Wave 2, interviewers first collected each respondent's confidant roster and preliminary information about respondents' relationships with confidants, as was done at Wave 1. The respondent's Wave 1 roster was preloaded into the CAPI instrument and was not visible to the respondent while completing this step. After the respondent completed the Wave 2 roster, the CAPI displayed a visual representation that linked matches between the Wave 1 and Wave 2 rosters (see Fig. 16.1).

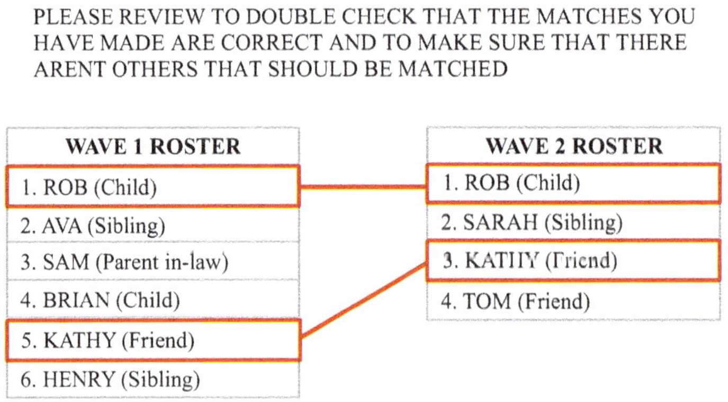

Fig. 16.1 Sample screenshot of the CAPI interface used by a hypothetical NSHAP respondent to match her Wave 1 network members to her Wave 2 network members
Note: The names that appeared in the original screenshot of the rosters above have been replaced with pseudonyms. The names of and other information concerning respondents' network members at Wave 1 were preloaded from their original Wave 1 surveys in the CATI system, which was programmed to display a visual representation linking matches between the respondent's Wave 1 and Wave 2 rosters. Respondents were asked to confirm that any changes in network personnel were depicted correctly

The respondent was asked to verify if these computer-programmed matches were correct, and was given the opportunity to correct any mismatches. The Wave 1 roster line corresponding to a given Wave 2 alter was then recorded.

This approach makes it possible to see specific changes in network membership between waves and thus to infer which confidants were lost, added, and retained over the five-year period. This is an improvement over previous approaches to network change, which would merely judge differences in overall network size between waves, and thus could not distinguish between turnover and stability (see Cornwell et al. 2014; Feld et al. 2007; Small et al. 2015). We count as "lost" any alter who was named as a confidant at Wave 1 who is not named in any of R's Wave 2 network rosters (A, B, or C). We count as "new" any alter who was not named in any of the network rosters at Wave 1 (A, B, or C) but who appears as a confidant at Wave 2. Following the roster matching exercise, respondents were asked to provide additional information about any Wave 1 alters who were not named at Wave 2. In these cases, interviewers inquired: "I noticed that in our last interview in (YEAR), you also listed (NAME) as someone with whom you discuss important matters, but you did not list (NAME) this time. Is (NAME) still living?" If the respondent responded "Yes," the interviewer asked: "What is the main reason you are no longer in touch with (NAME)?" Respondents were provided with a small preset list of reasons from which to choose (e.g., R's or alter's health problems, change in residence). If none of these were chose, a brief open-ended explanation was recorded. For the purposes of this paper, we focus mainly on the issue of whether a Wave 1 confidant died or was lost for any other reason.

Predictors

We are interested in the extent to which older adults add new network members to their confidant rosters between waves. We control for a number of relevant network, socio-demographic, life-course, and other social factors.

Network Member Loss and Death Our main independent variables concern whether respondents lost people from their Wave 1 confidant network. We expect that whether new confidants are added to a network in the wake of confidant loss depends on how Wave 1 network members were lost in the first place. Therefore we include separate controls for whether: (1) any Wave 1 confidant died between waves; and (2) whether any Wave 1 confidant was removed by the respondent from the network roster for some other reason.

Life-Course Factors and Transitions Several life-course factors likely co-vary with age and network structure, including marital status at baseline (currently married/partnered, widowed, separated/divorced, never married) and employment status (currently working, retired, or out of the work force). Older adults' networks are also shaped by their health and well being, so we include three measures to capture this. For one, we construct an index comprised of 9 items ($\alpha = 0.87$) that assess how much difficulty respondents have with these kinds of tasks ("functional impairment"). We also include a control for depressive symptoms. For this, we use a modified CES-D scale ($\alpha = 0.78$), which is based on responses to ten ordinal questions that assess things like how often respondents felt sad during the past week. Our measure leaves out respondents' answers to an item that is frequently included in the CES-D scale which asks about their experiences with loneliness, as including this measure increases endogeneity in analyses that consider the association between social connectedness and mental health (York Cornwell and Waite 2009). We also include a general five-level ordinal measure of self-rated health (1 = "poor", 5 = "excellent").

Sociodemographic and Network-Structural Controls Because network structure is highly gendered, we include a control for R's gender (male/female). Social disadvantage is also an important predictor of network structure in later life. To account for this, we control for ethnicity (white, African-America, Latino, or other) and education ($\leq$ high school, some college, or college/professional degree).

How a network changes will also likely depend on the nature of the network at baseline. For example, networks that are composed of more confidants and primarily strong ties will have less room for growth. Therefore we include a number of network-structural controls, including: (1) A set of indicators of the size of the confidant network (Roster A) at baseline; (2), the proportion of those confidants who are kin; (3) the average extent of emotional closeness R feels to his/her confidants; and (4) R's average frequency of interaction with his/her confidants.[4] Note that the inclusion of the last three measures means that the analysis is only relevant to respondents who listed at least one confidant at Wave 1 (which excludes 2.3% of the Wave 1 sample). Finally, to capture exposure to the broader community, we control for the respondent's frequency of religious services attendance.[5] Descriptive statistics of key variables are presented in Table 16.1.

[4] One of our criteria for counting a Wave 1 confidant as "lost" is that the confidant does not appear in any of the network rosters (A, B, or C) at Wave 2. The likelihood of moving to a different roster (but not truly being dropped from the network) thus depends on whether respondents listed anyone in Rosters B or C at Wave 1. We therefore include two controls for whether respondents listed anyone in Roster B or Roster C at Wave 1. In addition, we include a measure of the number of non-network members whom the respondent listed in his/her household roster (Roster D). Co-residents represent potential close network members in many cases.

[5] The NSHAP also collected information about the frequency with which respondents did the following within the past year: (1) socialize with friends or relatives; (2) do volunteer work; and (3) attend meetings of organized groups. This information was collected via a leave-behind questionnaire (LBQ), resulting in the loss of 481 cases from the baseline sample. We use the religious attendance measure, therefore, as a proxy measure, to attenuate selection bias caused by nonresponse on the LBQ. However, supplemental analysis that use these other measures suggest that the main findings regarding the association between forms of network loss and network recruitment do not differ when these alternative measures are used. These supplemental analyses are available upon request.

Table 16.1 Descriptions and weighted means and standard deviations of key variables (N = 2119)[a]

Variable		Mean	s.d.
Any new confidants	Indicator of whether R reported a confidant (Roster A) at W2 who was not named in Rosters A, B, or C at W1	.765	.424
Any confidants died	Indicator of whether R reported a confidant (Roster A) at W1 who died at some point between W1 and W2	.213	.409
Any other losses	Indicator of whether R reported a confidant (Roster A) at W1 who was not named in Rosters A, B, or C at W2 for some reason other than death	.651	.477
Female	Indicator of whether R is female	.514	.500
African-American	Indicator of whether R is non-Hispanic African-American	.099	.297
Latino	Indicator of whether R is Latino	.071	.257
Other ethnicity	Indicator of whether R is some other race/ethnicity	.025	.156
≤High school	Indicator of whether R had only high school education or less	.452	.498
Some college	Indicator of whether R had only some college education	.299	.458
Widowed	Indicator of whether R was a widow at W1	.170	.376
Sep/div	Indicator of whether R was separated or divorced at W1	.113	.317
Never married	Indicator of whether R had never been married at W1	.165	.371
Retired	Indicator of whether R was retired at W1	.522	.500
Out of work force	Indicator of whether R was out of work force at W1 for other reason	.128	.334
Functional health	R's self-rated ability to complete each of 7 activities of daily living on their own at W1. Responses range from "unable to do" (=1) to "no difficulty" (=4) (α = .841). Items are averaged together. Range: −4.790–.390.	.057	.657
Depressive symptoms	Average of R's standardized responses to 10 ordinal items from the CES-D scale assessing depressive symptoms. Responses range from "rarely or none of the time" (=0) to "most of the time" (3). Items are averaged together. Range: −.602–2.832.	−.019	.563
	R listed one confidant at W1	.115	.319
	R listed two confidants at W1	.158	.365
W1 network size	R listed three confidants at W1	.191	.393
	R listed four confidants at W1	.165	.371
	R listed five or more confidants at W1 (*ref. category*)	.371	.483
Kin composition	Proportion of W1 confidants who were kin	.678	.330
Emotional closeness	Average ordinal rating (1 = "not very close", 4 = "extremely close") of how close R is to each confidant at W1. Range: 1–4.	.824	.253
Frequency of contact	Average ordinal rating (1 = < once per year, 8 = every day) of how often R interacts with each confidant at W1. Range: 2.8–8.	6.880	.856

[a]Estimates are weighted using NSHAP W1 person-weights (adjusted for attrition and selection at W2). Estimates are calculated for all respondents who are in the final models predicting functional impairment

Modeling Strategy

Our goal is to understand how the above factors relate to older adults' addition of new confidants between waves. Because confidant networks tend to be small, and are capped at five, we attenuate floor and ceiling effects in the count of confidants added by predicting simply whether (yes/no) respondents named any new confidants at Wave 2 who were not named in any of the rosters at Wave 1. This is a dichotomous indicator of network additions, so logistic regression is appropriate in this case (Cox and Snell 1989). Because we are interested in how age shapes the association between confidant death, loss, and network additions, we stratify the analysis by age. Consistent with previous work that uses the NSHAP data, we divide age into three groups: 57–64, 65–74, and 75–85. The same predictors are used in all three models. We then use post-estimation Wald tests to assess any differences between groups in terms of the coefficients of specific predictors. The final sample includes 2119 respondents.

Attrition and Selection Adjustment All of our models take into account the clustering and stratification of NSHAP's sample design, and include NSHAP-supplied weights to account for respondents' differential probabilities of selection (with post-stratification adjustments for non-response) at Wave 1. It is also important to take into account the non-random loss of respondents due to attrition, which introduces selection bias. We use a complete-case form of missing data adjustment. We begin by creating a variable for each of the 3005 Wave 1 respondents that indicates whether they were part of the final Wave 2 sample. We predict this using a logit model, with socio-demographic variables, health, and other factors entered as predictors of attrition. From this, we derive a predicted probability that each Wave 1 respondent appears in the analysis. We take the inverse of this probability and multiply it by the NSHAP-supplied weight for that person at Wave 1. Using these adjusted weights in the models give more weight to individuals who were less likely to be in the Wave 2 sample, effectively moving estimates closer to where they would have been had all baseline respondents made it into the Wave 2 sample (Morgan and Todd 2008).

Findings

We begin by providing a general sense of the extent and nature of network change among the NSHAP respondents during the five-year study period. First, a total of 73.3% of respondents in the final sample reported that they lost at least one of their confidants between waves. Altogether, 21.3% of respondents in the final sample reported that at least one of their Wave 1 confidants died between waves, and over three times as many (65.1%) reported that they lost at least one confidant for some other reason (e.g., retirement). A larger proportion of the sample (76.5%) reported that they added at least one new confidant between waves. Initial examination

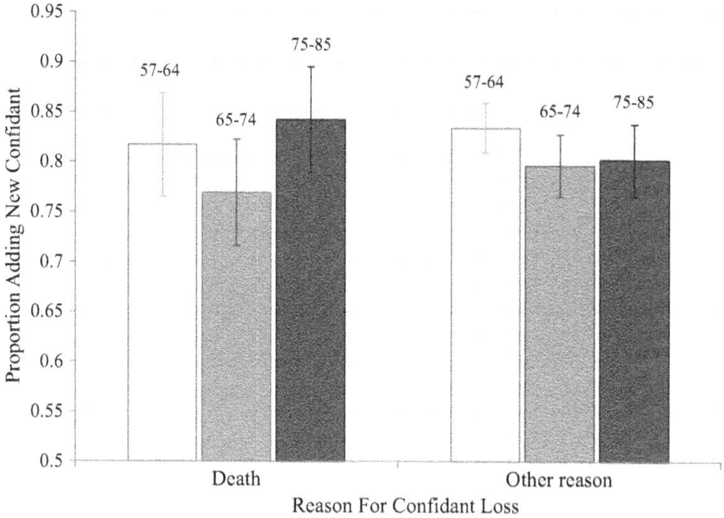

Fig. 16.2 Observed proportion of respondents in different age groups who added new confidants at Wave 2 after experiencing different forms of Wave 1 network loss
Note: 95% confidence intervals are shown at the tops of the bars. All estimates are weighted

suggests that these changes are related to each other. Fully 80.4% of those respondents who lost a Wave 1 confidant for any reason added at least one new confidant, compared to 65.6% of those who did not lose any Wave 1 confidants.

We are interested in how the tendency to add new network members relates to age. Figure 16.2 shows the proportions of people in different age groups who added at least one new confidant at Wave 2 in the wake of a network loss. In general, these numbers are high. For example, 83.4% of those who were between 57 and 64 at baseline added a new network member when they lost a confidant for some reason other than death, compared to 80.2% among those between the ages of 75 and 85. Note that these estimates are not significantly different from each other. When considering those who had experienced at least one confidant death, we see similar estimates. Of those respondents in the younger age group who experienced the loss of at least one confidant, 81.7% added at least one confidant at Wave 2, compared to 84.2% among the oldest age group (differences are not significant).

We now turn to the multivariate analysis predicting whether respondents added any confidants. Results of the logistic regression analysis, disaggregated by age group, are presented in Table 16.2. First, we note how socio-demographic and life-course measures relate to the odds of adding a new confidant. Neither race/ethnicity nor employment status is significantly associated with network additions. Several other life-course measures are significant in these models. In general, women are more likely than men to report adding new confidants to their networks, both in the youngest (OR = 1.581, $p < .05$) and the oldest (OR = 1.746, $p < .05$) age groups. Second, having less education is generally associated with greater likelihood of

Table 16.2 Odds ratios from logistic regresson models predicting whether respondents named any new network members at Wave 2 (N = 2119)[a]

	Age group		
Predictor	57–64 (N = 810)	65–74 (N = 794)	75–85 (N = 515)
Any confidants died	1.188 (.403)	1.517 (.483)	2.430** (.772)
Any other losses	2.027* (.596)	3.149*** (.696)	2.886*** (.789)
Female	1.581* (.336)	.989 (.205)	1.746* (.466)
African-American	1.203 (.415)	.853 (.288)	.801 (.361)
Latino	.767 (.232)	1.502 (.606)	.666 (.193)
Other ethnicity	3.489 (3.214)	2.031 (1.310)	1.027 (.833)
≤High school	1.116 (.292)	.793 (.260)	2.348* (.744)
Some college	1.201 (.314)	1.130 (.289)	1.856 (.769)
Widowed	1.721 (.871)	1.435 (.340)	.778 (.266)
Separated/divorced	2.679† (1.390)	1.315 (1.019)	.562 (.492)
Never married	.556 (.226)	1.613 (.919)	2.149 (1.440)
Retired	1.169 (.285)	.829 (.200)	.805 (.351)
Out of work force	.572† (.168)	.808 (.302)	.521 (.258)
Functional health	.612* (.137)	2.719*** (.724)	1.089 (.226)
Depressive symptoms	1.253 (.252)	1.075 (.274)	.760 (.228)
W1 network size (reference = five)			
One confidant	2.056 (1.006)	2.899** (1.021)	9.388*** (4.807)
Two confidants	2.077† (.805)	3.672*** (1.191)	5.452*** (2.190)
Three confidants	1.718 (.610)	3.015** (.970)	1.531 (.529)
Four confidants	1.613 (.557)	1.076 (.304)	1.611 (.566)
Kin composition	.309** (.117)	.344** (.104)	.412 (.227)
Emotional closeness	.339† (.196)	2.065 (1.109)	.651 (.422)
Frequency of contact	1.068 (.169)	1.009 (.099)	.766 (.172)
F statistic (df = 27, 24)	3.10**	2.49*	4.67***
FWD R^2	.046	.054	.052

†p < .10, *p < .05, **p < .01, ***p < .001 (two-sided tests)
[a]Estimates are weighted using NSHAP W1 person-weights (adjusted for attrition and selection at W2). All models are survey-adjusted and include additional controls for baseline measures of the respondent's self-rated overall health, frequency of attendance at religious services, indicators of whethe the respondent listed anyone in Rosters B or C at Wave 1, number listed in Roster D (the household roster), and the intercept

adding new confidants, significantly so in the oldest category with respect to having nothing more than a high school diploma (OR = 2.348, $p < .05$). Marital status is only marginally related to network additions. In the youngest age group, being separated or divorced is linked to network additions (OR = 2.679, $p < .07$). Health also matters, though not in a consistent manner. In the youngest age group, functional health is negatively associated with the addition of new confidants (OR = .612, $p < .05$), whereas in the middle age group functional impairment is positively associated with the odds of adding a new confidant (OR = 2.719, $p < .001$).

Confidant Losses, Deaths, and Additions

We are particularly interested in how the loss of confidants, due to death or other causes, relate to subsequent network additions in different age groups. Our main finding in this respect is that both forms of network loss are generally positively, rather than negatively, associated with the likelihood of adding new confidants at Wave 2. In the youngest age group, those who lost network members for any reason other than death were about twice as likely as those who did not experience any confidant losses to add a new network member (OR = 2.03, $p < .05$). A similar trend is seen among those in the middle age group, where those who experienced any non-death loss were over three times as likely to report a new confidant addition at Wave 2 (OR = 3.15, $p < .001$). In the oldest age group, both forms of network loss are independently associated with subsequent confidant additions. Those who experienced the death of a network member were almost two and a half times as likely to report a new confidant addition (OR = 2.43, $p < .05$), and those who lost network member for other reasons were 2.9 times as likely to report such an addition (OR = 2.87, $p < .001$), as those who did not experience such losses.

The trend across age groups is an important takeaway. In general, network losses are more likely to lead to new additions as age increases. This is especially true with respect to the coefficient representing confidant mortality. In the youngest age group, the coefficient does not approach significance (OR = 1.19, $p = .61$), but it is significant in the oldest age group. In addition, the coefficient for confidant death in the oldest age group is (marginally) significantly greater in magnitude than the corresponding coefficient in the youngest age group (Adjusted Wald $F = 2.95$, $p = .09$).

We see a similar pattern with respect to network-structural controls. In general having a larger network at baseline (and more kin in one's network) is negatively associated with the odds of subsequent network growth. The finding regarding network size is more highly significant and greater and magnitude for those who had very few confidants at Wave 1. Those who had only one or two confidants at Wave 1 were much more likely than those who had the largest networks to name new confidants at Wave 2. Notice that this is especially true among the oldest age group. The coefficients indicating having only one or two confidants at Wave 1 for the oldest age group are more (marginally) highly significant than the corresponding coefficients for the of the youngest age group (Adjusted Wald tests: $F = 4.56$, $p < .05$; $F = 3.18$, $p = .08$, respectively).

New Confidants and Replenished Networks

We are also interested in whether and how aging relates to the types of network ties older adults cultivate when they experience loss, and the implications of those replenishment patterns for the structure of older adults' social networks. Table 16.3 shows the characteristics of the people who were added as confidants between

Table 16.3 Characteristics of the relationships between NSHAP respondents and new confidants who were added at Wave 2[a]

Characteristics of new confidant ties	Age group 57–64	65–74	75–85	N[b]
Confidant type				
Spouse/partner	.055	.028	.036	1246
Other kin	.596	.606	.587	1246
Friend	.576	.544	.536	1246
Other non-kin	.161	.227*	.234[†]	1246
R has ≥ weekly contact with confidant	.696	.751[†]	.770[†]	1245
R is ≥ "very close" to confidant	.659	.651	.624	1246
R has known confidant ≥6 years	.799	.760	.800	1246
Confidant knows any of R's other confidants	.690	.673	.671	1225

[†]p < .10, *p < .05, **p < .01, ***p < .001 (Survey-adjusted Wald tests of mean differences from 57–64 age group)
[a]Estimates apply only to respondents who lost at least one wave 1 confidant and aded at least oe new wave 2 confidant. Estimates are weighted using NSHAP wave 1 person-level weights (adjusted for attrition and selection at wave 2)
[b]Estimates are provides for all cases that have non-missing data for the measure in question

waves from among those who lost someone. The top row shows the proportion of people in each age group who reported a new spouse or partner in their Wave 2 confidant roster. This number is low for each group. It is 5.5%, for example, for respondents between the ages of 57 and 64 who lost a confidant, and slightly more than half that for the older age groups. Cultivation of other types of ties – especially other types of kin, and new friends – is far more typical in all age groups. For example, between 58.7% and 60.6%% of people in each age group reported that they added some other type of kin contact as a confidant. In general, the differences between age groups with respect to the composition of newly developed ties are relatively small. But it is important to note that members of the youngest age group are less likely than the middle age group (Adjusted Wald $F = 5.75$, $p > .05$) and marginally less likely than the oldest age group ($F = 3.66$, $p = .06$) to name other non-kin (non-friend) contacts (e.g., neighbors) as confidants at Wave 2.

Finally, is the cultivation of confidants that have certain structural properties (e.g., tie strength) related to age? Table 16.3 shows that members of the youngest age group report marginally less frequent interaction with their new confidants than do members of the older age groups. But the main takeaway from the estimates that are presented in this table is the overall similarity across age groups with respect to the compositional profile of the new confidants that were added between waves. Even the differences between the youngest and the oldest age groups with respect to the composition of new confidants is slight. In fact, nowhere do we see statistical significance at the .05 level with respect to differences in tie strength or network-structural features (frequency of interaction, closeness, duration of relationship, or network density) of new confidant ties across the three age groups.

Conclusion and Discussion

How older adults adapt to changes within their social environments – particularly with respect to the loss of network members – is drawing increasing attention within the social-gerontological literature due to its wide-ranging potential implications for individuals (Cornwell and Laumann 2015; Eng et al. 2002; Giordano and Lindstrom 2010; Holtzman et al. 2004; Seeman et al. 2011; Thomas 2012). Following life-course approaches to the issue of social integration (e.g., Crosnoe and Elder 2002; Elder 1985; George 1993; Kahn and Antonucci 1980; Heinz and Marshall 2003; Moen et al. 1992; Pillemer et al. 2000; Settersten and Mayer 1997), we have focused in this paper on how older adults' networks change in response to the loss of confidants amidst various life-course transitions such as retirement, widowhood, and health decline. We found no significant differences between the youngest and oldest age groups with respect to their overall tendency to add new confidants to their networks. Age is related, however, to how these individuals responded to the loss of a network member. The loss of network members in general was associated with an increased likelihood of cultivating new network members. This tendency toward replenishment holds when network members were lost due to death as well – and particularly so among the oldest adults in the sample (those who are in their late 70s and 80s).

These findings highlight several issues that warrant further attention in social-gerontological research. The first issue has been a point of contention in social gerontology for half a century. Our findings challenge the popular image of older adults as: (1) passive victims of network loss; or (2) people who desire to shrink their social networks as they age. On the contrary, our data suggest that older adults respond to the loss of network members more as an opportunity to cultivate new (or to turn to alternative) relationships than as an opportunity to pare down one's social network. Several findings suggest this. First, later life is characterized more by net growth than by decline in these network ties. Second, the oldest adults in this sample were significantly more likely to add discussion partners when their baseline networks are small. Third, new additions to social networks were much more likely to be non-kin than kin. Fourth, the oldest adults were the most likely to follow the death of a confidant with the addition of a new one. A key question is how the oldest adults in the sample accomplish these things. We do not know to what extent older adults replenish their confidant networks: (1) by rekindling dormant ties from the past; (2) by merely shifting attention to others in the nearby environment who were already available; or (3) by making proactive efforts to cultivate completely new ties in the community. These are crucial questions for future work in network-gerontology.

Our analysis of the new ties that older adults cultivate suggests that it is unlikely that tie replenishment in later life (at least within the context of confidant networks) is driven primarily by an interest in creating the closest, most intimate social networks possible. The oldest adults in our sample exhibit a slight tendency to turn to non-kin (especially friends) as opposed to starting new partnerships or turning to siblings or other family members. Apart from this, according to virtually every indication, the oldest adults' (who are in their 80s) new confidants are no more close, their ties are no more strong, and their reconstituted networks are no more dense than the new relations that are developed by younger-old adults who are in their 60s. These findings pose a challenge to scholarly perspectives that suggest that older adults either gradually disengage from social circles or consciously pare down their networks to an ever-shrinking core of contacts.

The second issue concerns why the oldest adults in the sample were the most likely to add new network members in the wake of confidant mortality. There are several potential explanations. This finding is consistent with the idea that older adults get better at adapting to loss or death in their personal networks as they get older and experience it more often. They have better-developed scripts for coping with loss. Second, there may be a selection process at play here, in that those who survive the longest (the oldest adults) are better at replacing ties because they were healthier to begin with (thus contributing to their longevity). Similarly, those in the oldest age group may have survived so long in part because they have always been better at adapting to changes in their social networks, replacing lost ties, and cultivating new confidants. Third, these findings are consistent with continuity and compensation theories (Donnelly and Hinterlong 2010; Lamme et al. 1996; Li 2007; Mutchler et al. 2003; Utz et al. 2002), which suggest that older adults are more committed to preserving the level of network resources to which they are accustomed. These findings may reflect the fact that younger-old adults have less stable environments because they are still in the midst of retirement, residential mobility, and the emptying of the familial nest. This would be consistent with research on network change in younger age groups as well, which shows that changes in one's social circumstances often lead to considerable replacement within the discussion network (e.g., Small et al. 2015). In this sense, the findings reported here reflect a pattern of network change that is event in the more general population. Another explanation is that the oldest adults in the sample may have reached a more stable everyday routine, which could make it easier to achieve homeostasis in the face of network shocks. Finally, it is conceivable that, with age, people become more proactive in their efforts to cultivate new social resources when they perceive or anticipate a lack of social ties. This possibility is supported by the finding that among the oldest adults in the sample, those whose baseline networks were small were the most likely to add new confidants. Unfortunately, we do not have the data necessary to determine the relative significance of these different perspectives.

This analysis has several limitations that are important to bear in mind. For one, due to the NSHAP's focus on close, personal social networks, we are limited in what we can say about social network change or how it relates to age. This is partly intentional, as we are interested in what happens to only the most consequential ties in older adults' social networks. We are unable to shed light on changes in other aspects of older adults' networks, including rates of turnover with respect to their weaker ties and peripheral contacts. Several theories suggest that older adults shed weaker ties at greater rates than other types of ties (e.g., Cumming and Henry 1961; Charles and Carstensen 2010), so such losses may or may not results in the type of tie replacement that we cover here. An additional limitation is that we cannot establish the sequential order of network losses and replacements. It may be that the cultivation of new ties precedes the loss of older ones in some cases. This may even take place in the case of confidant mortality. For example, it is possible that the prospect of a confidant's death, if it is imminent, prompts people to proactively seek out new contacts as sources of support and companionship. For this and other reasons, our models are likely plagued by endogeneity. Data on the timing of and reasons behind older adults' network losses and additions would provide crucial context for understanding when and why certain kinds of network changes occur. Regardless, our findings provide evidence of a heretofore-underexplored process of network replacement in particular, which will hopefully provide new avenues for future research on the dynamics of networks later in the life course.

References

Ashida, S., & Heaney, C. (2008). Differential associations of social support and social connectedness with structural features of social networks and the health status of older adults. *Journal of Aging and Health, 20*, 872–893.

Atchley, R. C. (1989). The continuity theory of normal aging. *The Gerontologist, 29*, 183–190.

Bailey, S., & Marsden, P. V. (1999). Interpretation and interview context: Examining the general social survey name generator using cognitive methods. *Social Networks, 21*, 287–309.

Barrington, C., Latkin, C., Sweat, M. D., Moreno, L., Ellen, J., & Kerrigan, D. (2009). Talking the talk, walking the walk: Social network norms, communication patterns, and condom use among the male partners of female sex workers in La Romana, Dominican Republic. *Social Science & Medicine, 68*, 2037–2044.

Bearman, P., & Parigi, P. (2004). Cloning headless frogs and other important matters: Conversation topics and network structure. *Social Forces, 83*, 535–557.

Bidart, C., & Lavenu, D. (2005). Evolutions of personal networks and life events. *Social Networks, 27*, 359–376.

Bloem, B. A., van Tilburg, T. G., & Thomése, F. (2008). Changes in older Dutch adults' role networks after moving. *Personal Relationships, 15*, 465–478.

Charles, S. T., & Carstensen, L. L. (2010). Social and emotional aging. *Annual Review of Psychology, 61*, 383–409.

Chatters, L. M., Taylor, R. J., & Lincoln, K. D. (1999). African American religious participation: A multi-sample comparison. *Journal for the Scientific Study of Religion, 38*, 132–145.

Choi, N. G., & Ha, J.-H. (2011). Relationship between spouse/partner support and depressive symptoms in older adults: Gender difference. *Aging & Mental Health, 15*, 307–317.

Christakis, N. A., & Fowler, J. H. (2008). The collective dynamics of smoking in a large social network. *New England Journal of Medicine, 358*, 2249–2258.

Cornwell, B. (2009). Good health and the bridging of structural holes. *Social Networks, 31*, 92–103.

Cornwell, B. (2011). Independence through social networks: A comparison of older men's and women's bridging potential. *Journals of Gerontology B: Psychological and Social Sciences, 66B*, 782–794.

Cornwell, B. (2012). Spousal network overlap as a basis for spousal support. *Journal of Marriage and Family, 74*, 229–238.

Cornwell, B. (2015). Social disadvantage and network turnover. *Journals of Gerontology: Social Sciences, 70*, 132–142.

Cornwell, B., & Laumann, E. O. (2011). Network position and sexual dysfunction: Implications of partner betweenness for men. *American Journal of Sociology, 117*, 172–208.

Cornwell, B., & Laumann, E. O. (2015). The health benefits of network growth: New evidence from a national survey of older adults. *Social Science & Medicine, 125*, 94–106.

Cornwell, B., Laumann, E. O., & Schumm, L. P. (2008). The social connectedness of older adults: A national profile. *American Sociological Review, 73*, 185–203.

Cornwell, B., Schumm, L. P., Laumann, E. O., & Graber, J. (2009). Social networks in the nshap study: Rationale, measurement, and preliminary findings. *The Journals of Gerontology Series B: Psychological Sciences and Social Sciences, 64*(suppl 1), i47–i55.

Cornwell, B., Schumm, L. P., Laumann, E. O., Kim, J., & Kim, Y.-J. (2014). Assessment of social network change in a national longitudinal survey. *Journals of Gerontology Series B: Psychological Sciences and Social Sciences, 69*, S75–S82.

Cornwell, B., Marcum, C., & Silverstein, M. (2015). The social network approach in gerontological research. *Journals of Gerontology: Social Sciences, 70*, 87–90.

Cox, D. R., & Snell, E. J. (1989). *Analysis of binary data* (2nd ed.). New York: Chapman & Hall.

Crisp, D. A., Windsor, T. D., Butterworth, P., & Anstey, K. J. (2015). Adapting to retirement community life: Changes in social networks and perceived loneliness. *Journal of Relationships Research, 6*, e9.

Crosnoe, R., & Elder, G. H., Jr. (2002). Successful adaptation in the later years: A life course approach to aging. *Social Psychology Quarterly, 65*, 309–328.

Cumming, E., & Henry, W. E. (1961). *Growing old: The process of disengagement*. New York: Basic Books.

Deflem, M. (1989). From anomie to anomia and anomic depression: A sociological critique on the use of anomie in psychiatric research. *Social Science & Medicine, 29*, 627–634.

Degenne, A., & Lebeaux, M.-O. (2005). The dynamics of personal networks at the time of entry into adult life. *Social Networks, 27*, 337–358.

Depp, C., & Jeste, D. V. (2006). Definitions and predictors of successful aging: A comprehensive review of larger quantitative studies. *American Journal of Geriatric Psychiatry, 14*, 6–20.

Donnelly, E. A., & Hinterlong, J. E. (2010). Changes in volunteer activity among recently widowed older adults. *The Gerontologist, 50*, 158–169.

Einolf, C. J. (2009). Will the boomers volunteer during retirement? Comparing the baby boom, silent, and long civic cohorts. *Nonprofit and Voluntary Sector Quarterly, 38*, 181–199.

Eisenberg, M. E., Neumark-Sztainer, D., Story, M., & Perry, C. L. (2005). The role of social norms and friends' influences on unhealthy weight-control behaviors among adolescent girls. *Social Science & Medicine, 60*, 1165–1173.

Elder, G. H., Jr. (Ed.). (1985). *Life course dynamics*. Ithaca: Cornell University Press.

Eng, P. M., Rimm, E. B., Fitzmaurice, G., & Kawachi, I. (2002). Social ties and change in social ties in relation to subsequent total and cause-specific mortality and coronary heart disease incidence in men. *American Journal of Epidemiology, 155*, 700–709.

Feld, S. L., Suitor, J. J., & Hoegh, J. G. (2007). Describing changes in personal networks over time. *Field Methods, 19*, 218–236.

Ferraro, K. F. (1984). Widowhood and social participation in later life isolation or compensation? *Research on Aging, 6*, 451–468.

Fischer, C. S., & Beresford, L. (2015). Changes in support networks in late middle age: The extension of gender and educational differences. *The Journals of Gerontology Series B: Psychological Sciences and Social Sciences, 70*, 123–141.

Galatzer-Levy, I. R., & Bonanno, G. A. (2012). Beyond normality in the study of bereavement: Heterogeneity in depression outcomes following loss in older adults. *Social Science & Medicine, 74*, 1987–1994.

George, L. K. (1993). Sociological perspectives on life transitions. *Annual Review of Sociology, 19*, 353–373.

Gerstorf, D., Röcke, C., & Lachman, M. E. (2010). Antecedent-consequent relations of perceived control to health and social support: Longitudinal evidence for between-domain associations across adulthood. *Journal of Gerontology: Psychological Sciences, 66B*, 61–71.

Ghesquiere, A. M., Shear, K., & Duan, N. (2013). Outcomes of bereavement care among widowed older adults with complicated grief and depression. *Journal of Primary Care & Community Health, 4*, 256–264.
Giordano, G. N., & Lindstrom, M. (2010). The impact of changes in different aspects of social capital and material conditions on self-rated health over time: A longitudinal cohort study. *Social Science & Medicine, 70*, 700–710.
Ha, J.-H., & Ingersoll-Dayton, B. (2011). Moderators in the relationship between social contact and psychological distress among widowed adults. *Aging & Mental Health, 15*, 354–363.
Haas, S. A., Schaefer, D. R., & Kornienko, O. (2010). Health and the structure of adolescent social networks. *Journal of Health and Social Behavior, 51*, 424–439.
Haines, V. A., Hurlbert, J., & Beggs, J. J. (1996). Exploring the determinants of support provision: Provider characteristics, personal networks, community contexts, and support following life events. *Journal of Health and Social Behavior, 37*, 252–264.
Hao, Y. (2008). Productive activities and psychological well-being among older adults. *Journals of Gerontology Series B: Psychological Sciences and Social Sciences, 63*, S64–S72.
Hatch, L. R., & Bulcroft, K. (1992). Contact with friends in later life: Disentangling the effects of gender and marital status. *Journal of Marriage and the Family, 54*, 222–232.
Heinz, W. R., & Marshall, V. W. (Eds.). (2003). *Social dynamics of the life course: Transitions, institutions, and interrelations*. New York: Aldine de Gruyter.
Holtzman, R. E., Rebok, G. W., Saczynski, J. S., Kouzis, A. C., Doyle, K. W., & Eaton, W. W. (2004). Social network characteristics and cognition in middle-aged and older adults. *Journal of Gerontology Series B: Psychological Sciences, 59*, P278–P284.
Jang, Y., & Chiriboga, D. A. (2011). Social activity and depressive symptoms in Korean American older adults: The conditioning role of acculturation. *Journal of Aging and Health, 23*, 767–781.
Johnson, K. J., & Mutchler, J. E. (2014). The emergence of a positive gerontology: From disengagement to social involvement. *The Gerontologist, 54*, 93–100.
Kahana, E., Kelley-Moore, J., & Kahana, B. (2012). Proactive aging: A longitudinal study of stress, resources, agency, and well-being in late life. *Aging & Mental Health, 16*, 438–451.
Kahn, R. L., & Antonucci, T. C. (1980). Convoys over the life course: Attachment, roles, and social support. *Life-Span Development and Behavior, 3*, 253–286.
Kalmijn, M. (2003). Shared friendship networks and the life course: An analysis of survey data on married and cohabiting couples. *Social Networks, 25*, 231–249.
Kohli, M., Hank, K., & Künemund, H. (2009). The social connectedness of older Europeans: Patterns, dynamics and contexts. *Journal of European Social Policy, 19*, 327–340.
Komp, K., van Tilburg, T., & van Groenou, M. B. (2012). Age, retirement, and health as factors in volunteering in later life. *Nonprofit and Voluntary Sector Quarterly, 41*, 280–299.
Kouvonen, A., Stafford, M., De Vogli, R., Shipley, M. J., Marmot, M. G., Cox, T., Vahtera, J., Väänänen, A., Heponiemi, T., Singh-Manoux, A., & Kivimäki, M. (2011). Negative aspects of close relationships as a predictor of increased body mass index and waist circumference: The Whitehall II study. *American Journal of Public Health, 101*, 1474–1480.
Kroenke, C. H., Kubzansky, L. D., Adler, N., & Kawachi, I. (2008). Prospective change in health-related quality of life and subsequent mortality among middle-aged and older women. *American Journal of Public Health, 98*, 2085–2091.
Lamme, S., Dykstra, P. A., & van Groenou, M. I. B. (1996). Rebuilding the network: New relationships in widowhood. *Personal Relationships, 3*, 337–349.
Levin, D. Z., Walter, J., & Murnighan, J. K. (2011). Dormant ties: The value of reconnecting. *Organization Science, 22*, 923–939.
Li, Y. (2007). Recovering from spousal bereavement in later life: Does volunteer participation play a role? *Journals of Gerontology Series B: Psychological Sciences and Social Sciences, 62*, S257–S266.
Martire, L. M., Stephens, M. A. P., Druley, J. A., & Wojno, W. C. (2002). Negative reactions to received spousal care: Predictors and consequences of miscarried support. *Health Psychology, 21*, 167–176.

McLaughlin, D., Adams, J., Vagenas, D., & Dobson, A. (2011). Factors which enhance or inhibit social support: A mixed-methods analysis of social networks in older women. *Ageing and Society, 31*, 18–33.

Mitchell, J. M., & Kemp, B. J. (2000). Quality of life in assisted living homes: A multidimensional analysis. *Journals of Gerontology Series B: Psychological Sciences, 55B*, P117–P127.

Moen, P., Dempster-McClain, D., & Williams, R. M., Jr. (1992). Successful aging: A life-course perspective on women's multiple roles and health. *American Journal of Sociology, 97*, 1612–1638.

Morgan, S. L., & Todd, J. J. (2008). A diagnostic routine for the detection of consequential heterogeneity of causal effects. *Sociological Methodology, 38*, 231–281.

Mutchler, J. E., Burr, J. A., & Caro, F. G. (2003). From paid worker to volunteer: Leaving the paid workforce and volunteering in later life. *Social Forces, 81*, 1267–1293.

Park, N. S. (2009). The relationship of social engagement to psychological well-being of older adults in assisted living facilities. *Journal of Applied Gerontology, 28*, 461–481.

Perry, B. L., & Pescosolido, B. A. (2010). Functional specificity in discussion networks: The influence of general and problem-specific networks on health outcomes. *Social Networks, 32*, 345–357.

Perry, B. L., & Pescosolido, B. A. (2012). Social network dynamics and biographical disruption: The case of "first-timers" with mental illness. *American Journal of Sociology, 118*, 134–175.

Perry, B. L., & Pescosolido, B. A. (2015). Social network activation: The role of health discussion partners in recovery from mental illness. *Social Science & Medicine, 125*, 116–128.

Pillemer, K., Moen, P., Wethington, E., & Glasgow, N. (Eds.). (2000). *Social integration in the second half of life*. Baltimore: Johns Hopkins Press.

Rotolo, T., & Wilson, J. (2004). What happened to the "long civic generation"? Explaining cohort differences in volunteerism. *Social Forces, 82*, 1091–1121.

Ruan, D. (1998). The content of the general social survey discussion networks: An exploration of the general social survey discussion name generator in a Chinese context. *Social Networks, 20*, 247–264.

Sasovova, Z., Mehra, A., Borgatti, S. P., & Schippers, M. C. (2010). Network churn: The effects of self-monitoring personality on brokerage dynamics. *Administrative Science Quarterly, 55*, 639–670.

Schaefer, D. R., Kornienko, O., & Fox, A. M. (2011). Misery does not love company: Network selection mechanisms and depression homophily. *American Sociological Review, 76*, 764–785.

Schafer, M. H. (2011). Health and network centrality in a continuing care retirement community. *Journals of Gerontology B: Psychological and Social Sciences, 66B*, 795–803.

Schafer, M. H. (2013). Structural advantages of good health in old age: Investigating the health-begets-position hypothesis with a full social network. *Research on Aging, 35*, 348–370.

Schafer, M. H., & Vargas, N. (2016). The dynamics of social support inequality: Maintenance gaps by socioeconomic status and race? *Social Forces, 94*, 1795–1822.

Schwingel, A., Niti, M. M., Tang, C., & Ng, T. P. (2009). Continued work employment and volunteerism and mental well-being of older adults: Singapore longitudinal ageing studies. *Age and Ageing, 38*, 531–537.

Seeman, T. E., Miller-Martinez, D. M., Merkin, S. S., Lachman, M. E., Tun, P. A., & Karlamangla, A. S. (2011). Histories of social engagement and adult cognition: Midlife in the U.S. study. *The Journals of Gerontology Series B: Psychological Sciences and Social Sciences, 66B*, i141–i152.

Settersten, R. A., Jr., & Mayer, K. U. (1997). The measurement of age, age structuring, and the life course. *Annual Review of Sociology, 23*, 233–261.

Shaw, B. A., Krause, N., Liang, J., & Bennett, J. (2007). Tracking changes in social relations throughout late life. *The Journals of Gerontology Series B: Psychological Sciences and Social Sciences, 62*, S90–S99.

Silverstein, M., Chen, X., & Heller, K. (1996). Too much of a good thing? Intergenerational social support and the psychological well-being of older parents. *Journal of Marriage and the Family, 58*, 970–982.

Small, M. L. (2013). Weak ties and the core discussion network: Why people regularly discuss important matters with unimportant alters. *Social Networks, 35*, 470–483.
Small, M. L., Pamphile, V. D., & McMahan, P. (2015). How stable is the core discussion network? *Social Networks, 40*, 90–102.
Smith, S., Jaszczak, A., Graber, J., Lundeen, K., Leitsch, S., Wargo, E., & O'Muircheartaigh, C. (2009). Instrument development, study design implementation, and survey conduct for the national social life, health, and aging project. *Journals of Gerontology Series B: Psychological Sciences and Social Sciences, 64B*, i20–129.
Straits, B. C. (2000). Ego's important discussants or significant people: An experiment in varying the wording of personal network name generators. *Social Networks, 22*, 123–140.
Thoits, P. A. (1992). Identity structures and psychological well-being: Gender and marital status comparisons. *Social Psychology Quarterly, 55*, 236–256.
Thomas, P. A. (2011). Gender, social engagement, and limitations in late life. *Social Science & Medicine, 73*, 1428–1435.
Thomas, P. A. (2012). Trajectories of social engagement and mortality in late life. *Journal of Aging and Health, 24*, 547–568.
Umberson, D., Crosnoe, R., & Reczek, C. (2010). Social relationships and health behavior across life course. *Annual Review of Sociology, 36*, 139–157.
Utz, R. L., Carr, D., Nesse, R., & Wortman, C. B. (2002). The effect of widowhood on older adults' social participation: An evaluation of activity, disengagement, and continuity theories. *The Gerontologist, 42*, 522–533.
Vable, A. M., Subramanian, S. V., Rist, P. M., & Glymour, M. M. (2015). Does the "widowhood effect" precede spousal bereavement? Results from a nationally representative sample of older adults. *The American Journal of Geriatric Psychiatry, 23*, 283–292.
van Tilburg, T. (1998). Losing and gaining in old age: Changes in personal network size and social support in a four-year longitudinal study. *Journals of Gerontology Series B-Psychological Sciences & Social Sciences, 53B*, S313–S323.
Warner, L., Ziegelmann, J., Schüz, B., Wurm, S., Tesch-Römer, C., & Schwarzer, R. (2011). Maintaining autonomy despite multimorbidity: Self-efficacy and the two faces of social support. *European Journal of Ageing, 8*, 3–12.
Wrzus, C., Hänel, M., Wagner, J., & Neyer, F. J. (2013). Social network changes and life events across the life span: A meta-analysis. *Psychological Bulletin, 139*, 53–80.
York Cornwell, E., & Waite, L. J. (2009). Social disconnectedness, perceived isolation, and health among older adults. *Journal of Health and Social Behavior, 50*, 31–48.
Zettel, L. A., & Rook, K. S. (2004). Substitution and compensation in the social networks of older widowed women. *Psychology & Aging, 19*, 433–443.

Benjamin Cornwell is a Professor in the Department of Sociology, Cornell University. His research interests center on the implications of socially networked and sequenced social processes for individuals and organizations.

Edward O. Laumann is the George Herbert Mead Distinguished Service Professor in the Department of Sociology at the University of Chicago and is affiliated with several research centers there. He has pioneered in the study of social networks. Among his many studies of social networks includes their role in promoting sexually transmitted infections.

Chapter 17
Changes of Personal Network Configuration Over the Life Course in the USA: A Latent Class Approach

Yoosik Youm, Edward O. Laumann, and Keunbok Lee

Introduction

One of less studied issues in social network research is change in social network composition over the life course. While many studies examine the association between personal relationships and the aging process, most of these focus on a single average trajectory of personal network change rather than on personal networks or the proportion of relationship types. To understand changes in social relationships over a lifetime, it may more informative to describe and compare types of network composition across age groups. Instead of selecting particular age groups and describing social relationships using a single linear measurement, this study attempts to figure out types of configuration in terms of social relationships, and then test changes in the distribution of each network type over the course of a life.

The composition of social network members is closely linked with different life stages. In the normal course of life, people mainly interact with family members at the early stages and then expand their social radius to include friends. After joining the labor market, people enter into a social cycle with their groups of coworkers. Marriage typically means that a person has a primary interaction partner. In addition, childbirth and the rearing of children also bring about prominent changes in social relationships. During late middle age, adult children may depart from their social cycles, while coworkers and friends become their main partners

Y. Youm (✉)
Department of Sociology, Yonsei University, Seoul, South Korea
e-mail: yoosik@gmail.com

E. O. Laumann
Department of Sociology, University of Chicago, Chicago, IL, USA

K. Lee
Department of Sociology, University of California, Berkeley, CA, USA

D. F. Alwin et al. (eds.), *Social Networks and the Life Course*, Frontiers in Sociology and Social Research 2, https://doi.org/10.1007/978-3-319-71544-5_17

in terms of social interaction. At the end of the life course, it is expected that coworkers will gradually fade out from social relationships due to retirement, and that adult children will re-enter into social interaction. While this hypothetical story of changing social relationships over the life course does not imply the existence of normative or stereotypical types of social network composition at each life stage, it is worth testing a set of unexamined questions based on this perspective. Particularly, we examine four questions in this chapter. First, how many different network compositions are there? Second, are the different types of network composition variously distributed across age groups? Third, does general happiness vary across different types of network composition? Fourth, do the effects of network composition on happiness vary over the life course?

Theory

Social Network Changes Over the Life Course: Changes in the Size and Proportion of Relationship Types

Personal relationships vary over the life course and are affected by normative life events as well as unexpected or non-normative events. While it is still unclear how social relationships are configured across each life stage and how they differ in composition over the life process, prior studies concur in their finding that personal networks usually expand from the adolescent period to early adulthood (Feiring and Lewis 1991), and gradually shrink with the onset of age (Marsden 1987; Schnittker 2007; Cornwell et al. 2008; Wrzus et al. 2013). In their meta-analysis of 277 social network studies on adolescent and elderly respondents, Wrzus et al. established that the size of personal networks increases significantly in the adolescent and young adult population, and shows little change until the early 30s. Personal network size then gradually shrinks, and people aged over 65 tend to have a significantly smaller personal network size compared with the young population (Wrzus et al. 2013).

This decrease in personal network size that elderly people experience is mainly caused by attrition of peripheral social relationships. Kahn and Antonuncci conceptualized the social support network model, also called the "convoy model," which describes the core members of a social support network as a convoy group who have close relationship with each other and provide each other with support (Kahn and Antonucci 1980). Convoy network members such as close family and spouses are assumed to maintain stable relationship with individuals, whereas peripheral network member relationships, for example, those with coworkers, neighbors, or acquaintances, tend to be relatively unstable over the life course (Kahn and Antonucci 1980; Antonucci and Akiyama 1987).

The distinction between core and peripheral social relationships is also evident in the socio-emotional selectivity model theory, which explains the changes in personal networks over the life course based on a shift in the psychological motivation for social interaction. Carstensen argues that the psychological motivation to interact experienced by people in the adolescent and early adulthood periods is mainly derived from their inclination to acquire information, whereas people in the later stages of life are motivated by the goal of emotional regulation (Carstensen 1991, 1992). During the early stages of life, knowledge and information from interaction with diverse acquaintances is sufficiently valuable that the negative consequences on self-identity and emotional status caused by interaction with non-close partners can be ignored. However, social interaction for the sake of emotional regulation becomes more salient with aging, and older people are therefore likely to spend more time and energy on interaction with close groups of people rather than acquaintances (Carstensen 1991). Empirical research conducted on this theory has shown that in the period of old age, reduction in contact frequency mainly occurs in relationships with acquaintances whose function is to provide information and knowledge, whereas interaction with close people such as spouses and children remains relatively stable over the life course (Carstensen 1995). In another study on a case in Germany, Lang and Carstensen found that the oldest respondents, who were aged over 90, had significantly fewer acquaintances in their personal network than those in their 80s, but the number of close relationships did not differ between the two groups (Lang and Carstensen 1994).

Although all provide different explanations, both the theories and the empirical studies on this subject concur on the finding that personal network size gradually shrinks throughout adulthood, mainly due to the attrition of non-close relationships.

Normative Life Events and Social Relationships: Necessity for the Composition Approach

The life events that most people experience at certain age stages also affect changes in personal networks with regard to their compositional aspects. Normative life events such as entering school or the labor market, marriage, childbirth, and retirement provide or constrain opportunities to meet and develop social relationships. When entering school or the labor market during early adulthood, people tend to interact with many others through their school or work place. Thus, the proportion of non-family relationships, for example, with friends, coworkers, or acquaintances, increases in personal networks (Feiring and Lewis 1991; Morrison 2002). Meanwhile, the family members involved in personal networks may not change, and young adults are likely to maintain frequent interaction with their parents and any siblings they may have.

Marriage is another crucial life event that can alter personal relationships and usually occurs during the early to middle period of adulthood. Typically, marriage offers an opportunity to introduce the spouses' family members and friends into each other's personal networks. Marriage or cohabitation increases the proportion of mutual friends between partners in their individual personal relationships (Milardo 1982; Johnson and Leslie 1982) However, the chance to interact with new people introduced through a spouse's network does not necessarily imply an expansion of social relationships, because people's selection of preferable interaction partners is usually based on similarity, attraction, or homophily tendency (Byrne 1971; Sprecher and Felmlee 2000; McPherson et al. 2001). Other studies on the association between marriage and social relationships point to the dyadic withdrawal hypothesis, which argues that friendship networks tend to become smaller as individuals become involved in romantic relationships and marriage (Johnson and Leslie 1982; Milardo 1982; Surra 1985; Stein et al. 2016; Kalmijn 2003). Through marriage, therefore, individuals' personal networks tend to change as new people are added from their spouse's social relationships. However, this is subject to the constraints of the selection process and may also weaken relationships with other non-overlapping friendships.

Childbirth and the nurturing of children are examples of further events that lead to changes in social network membership. The transition to parenthood not only shifts the relationship within a family from a dyad between spouses to a three-person system, it also impacts on an individual's personal network composition (Belsky and Rovine 1984; Bost et al. 2002). From pregnancy to shortly after the postpartum period, a mother's and father's personal network size tend to shrink due to lessening contact with peripheral relationships, which is mainly down to time constraints. Meanwhile, parents with a newborn baby are likely to maintain and concentrate on relationships with family members, other parents with a similar-aged child, or neighbors (Belsky and Rovine 1984; Wellman et al. 1997).

A change in the personal network is also expected during retirement. Certain types of social relationship, particularly coworker networks, are inevitably reduced or terminated in a retiree's personal network. In his 1992 study, Tilburg found that relationships with colleagues waned after retirement, while the size of a retiree's personal network and the level of reciprocity in terms of social support exchange remained consistent (van Tilburg 1992, 2003). Thus, with respect to the convoy model, while personal network configurations may change in retirement and subsequently due to a decrease in peripheral relationships such as with colleagues, there is usually a continuation or increase in the proportion of core network members in a retired individual's personal network (Kahn and Antonucci 1980; Antonucci and Akiyama 1987).

In sum, changes in personal networks with regard to size and composition over the life course are significantly linked with normative life events. The association between life events and personal networks causes an individual's network composition to differ between various age stages over the course of a life.

Life Course Path and Heterogeneity of Personal Network Configurations Within an Age Group

Since timing and life events vary between people, life events are associated not just with changes in the size and composition of personal networks throughout the life course, but also with the heterogeneity of personal network composition within certain age groups. For example, married people's personal networks may differ from those of unmarried people, even when these two groups are of the same age. The timing of entry into the labor market, child rearing, or retirement also varies across individuals. Thus, the composition of personal networks affected by life events inevitably differs across groups of peoples of a similar age.

While few studies test the heterogeneity of network composition within particular age groups, empirical studies employing typology methods reveal the different combinations of social relationships within an age group, particularly in the older population. Litwin, for example, identified five different types of social network composition in an elderly Israeli population (Litwin 2001). In his study, 30% of the respondents were assigned to a "diverse" network type in which members enjoyed frequent interaction with family members, friends, and neighbors. In contrast, some of the other respondents' social interactions tended to be concentrated on either family, neighbors, or friends. Furthermore, about a fifth of his sample seemed to be almost isolated in terms of social interaction. Elders in this type of network are less likely to interact with adult children, friends, and neighbors. Different types of personal network in the old age population are also reported in various regions such as Europe, the United States, and Japan (Wenger 1997; Takahashi et al. 1997; Fiori et al. 2006).

Although a significant amount of research has proven the heterogeneity of social network composition within similar age groups according to the timing and occurrence of life events, there are, to our knowledge, no empirical studies that attempt to depict the distribution of different types of network composition within certain age groups and trace the changes in distribution of these network types across different age groups.

Social Network Types and General Happiness

Many empirical studies and theories concur on the significant association between social relationships and well-being. Obviously, isolation from social relationships negatively impacts psychological well-being and causes issues such as depression, unhappiness, and anxiety as well as physical health problems (Cohen and Wills 1985; Thoits 1985, 1995; Bosworth and Warner Schaie 1997; Chu et al. 2010). People with little or no social interaction may suffer from lack of the necessary social resources that would typically result from interaction. Or lack of social interaction implies insecurity in terms of social identity, which has emerged and been approved, altered, and reproduced by social relationships (Thoits 1983). Thus, social isolation results in lower levels of happiness and opens the door to a risk of psychological distress and anxiety.

Variations of the effect of social relationships on well-being have also been observed in non-isolated populations. In effect, the quality and supportiveness of social interaction mediate the effect of social relationships on well-being. For example, in older age groups particularly, friendship ties are more supportive and crucial for maintaining an individual's wellness than obligatory relationships such as those with family members (Antonucci 2001; Litwin and Landau 2000; Fiori et al. 2006). However, support from family members in people's transition to parenthood functions in a positive way to buffer individuals' psychological distress (Bost et al. 2002).

The different effects of social relationships according to types of relationship role and supportiveness of individuals' well-being imply that the configuration of an individual's personal network has different impacts over the life course. Active interaction with friends may offer a more positive influence on maintaining individual wellness, since it is based on the provision and acquisition of new knowledge and information during adolescence and early adulthood (Carstensen 1991). Such interaction may also help the elderly to feel loved and supported during the late stages of life (Fiori et al. 2006). Parents may function as primary support givers during the early life stages, but the effectiveness of their support may gradually decrease and, at the elderly stage, parents will typically become support receivers. Thus, in terms of the life course, the configuration of social networks and their effects on well-being should be examined according to life stages.

In sum, this study aimed to describe the changing of personal networks in their compositional aspects and to test the effects of network composition on well-being, especially happiness and its variations across the life course. We expect the findings to indicate that personal network composition will differ according to the age groups during which certain normative life events are assumed to occur. However, this does not mean that personal network composition is expected to be homogenous within an age group. Rather, we expect that different types of social network will coexist in each age period. While people who are isolated from social interactions may constantly show lower levels of well-being over their life course, the effects of personal network compositions on happiness among non-isolated people may vary over their life course.

Data and Method

Data for present chapter are drawn from the social network module in 2002 General Social Survey which collected a general social network information of respondents aged over 18 year old. We only analyzed sample who completed the social network questionnaires (N = 975).

We used seven social network variables; how frequently respondents visit their parents, siblings, adult children, how many they have close friends in a neighbor, work place or other social domains, and whether they had a marital partners or not. The GSS survey used four categories of kin ties in a set of social network questions; father, mother, sibling (brother and sister), and children. We merged father and mother into one, 'parents'. In addition to the four kin categories, we established variable labeled 'spouse' drawn from marital status information, in which we assumed that spouse tie should be included in network composition for married respondents. The degree of visiting kin was measured on seven categories from 'Lives in a same household (1) to 'Less often' (7) in original survey. We dichotomized these variables using 'visiting at least one month' as the cut-off point. As for the non-kin ties, we used variables which measured a number of friends. The data divides the term 'Friends' into 'close friend living near respondent', 'close friend at a work place' and 'other friend'. Respondents provided a number of each category of friends as marking from 'none (0)' to 'more than 10 friends'(10). We dichotomized the number of three types of friends into 'no friend (0)', and 'more than one friend (1)'.

Table 17.1 shows the basic statistics of social network variables. 45.13% of study sample reported that they had a spouse (e.g., married). 36.41% of respondents lived with or visited their brothers or sisters at least once a month. 25.44% lived with their children or visited once a month. 39.59% answered that they lived with or visited their parents at least once a month. As for the non-kin ties, more than two-thirds respondents has more than one close friend in neighbors (69.03%) and other close friends (84.82%), while less than half of respondent (49.74%) reported more than one close friends at their work place.

Happiness is measured from the question 'Taken all together, how would you say things are these days… would you say that you are very happy, pretty happy, or not too happy?". Respondents' general happiness are coded as 'very happy (1)', 'pretty happy(2)', and 'not too happy(3)'. In our analysis, happiness variable was dichotomized into 'very happy' and 'less than very happy'. 31.08% reported that they were in general 'very happy', and rest of sample said that they are 'less than very happy'.

We categorized respondent' age into six categories from '18–29 year old (1)' to 'over 70 years old(6)'. Distributions of respondents in each age group are around about 20% for the 20s to the 40s (19.69% for 20s, 22.36% for 30s, 21.44% for 40s), and 15.18% of respondents are in the 50s, 9.95% in the 60s, and 11.38% of respondents are older than 70 year old. Race, gender and education level also were used in our analysis. 81.13% respondents are White, 13.33% are African American and 5.54% identified themselves as Asian and other race. 47.79% are male, and others are female. As for the education level, 55.28% have high school diploma, 6.97% has junior college degree, 15.90% finished bachelor level education, and 9.74% has more than master degree. Proportion of respondents who were educated less than high school level is 12.10% among our study sample.

Our analysis has three steps; first, grouping personal networks, second, estimating the distribution of network composition types in each age group, and third, examining varying effect of network composition types on the level of general happiness. In a first step, we conduct an explanatory latent class analysis which aims to figure out distinctive sub-clusters which differ in the composition of alters

Table 17.1 Descriptive statistics for using variables

Variables	Value	N	%
Spouse (married)	Not have	535	54.87
	Have	440	45.13
Siblings	Visit less than one per month or not have	620	63.59
	Live with or visit more than once a month	355	36.41
Children	Visit less than one per month or not have	727	74.56
	Live with or visit more than once a month	248	25.44
Parent	Visit less than one per month or not have	589	60.41
	Live with or visit more than once a month	386	39.59
Close friends at work place	Not have	490	50.26
	More than one	485	49.74
Close friends at nieghborhood	Not have	302	30.97
	More than one	673	69.03
Other close Friends	Not have	148	15.18
	More than one	827	84.82
Age Group	18–29 years old	192	19.69
	30–39 years old	218	22.36
	40–49 years old	209	21.44
	50–59 years old	148	15.18
	60–69 years old	97	9.95
	More than 70 years old	111	11.38
Gender	Male	466	47.79
	Female	509	52.21
Race	White	791	81.13
	Black	130	13.33
	Other	54	5.54
Education level	Less than high school	118	12.10
	High school	539	55.28
	Junior college	68	6.97
	Bachelor	155	15.90
	Graduate	95	9.74
Happiness	Very happy	303	31.08
	Less than very happy	672	68.92

from each other. Then, the second step model test the different distribution of each sub-cluster across the six age groups. Based on the result from former steps, we conducted a set of logistic regressions which tests the impact of network composition types on happiness. There are two sets of logistic regression. In the first regression model, we test the effect of network composition types as including age as controlling variable. And we separately run the logistic regressions model by the age group. The final latent class models in the first and second step analysis was evaluated their goodness of fit with x2, and L2 statistics. The logistic regression runs with the three-step method, which estimates the effect of latent variable on the external variable as reducing the bias in parameter estimate due to the classification error in latent class model (Vermunt 2010).

Result

Typology of Personal Network Configuration

Through the explanatory latent class analysis, we found six mutually distinctive types of network composition and their distribution varied across the age-group. The number of sub-types of social network compositions was confirmed with the goodness of fit statistics. Table 17.2 shows the statistics for explanatory latent class models which are conducted based upon different number of latent sub-clusters from one to seven. With chi-square criteria, model 3 and following models shows well fit on observed data ($p > 0.1$). In selecting the best model, we compared log-likelihood statistics between models which tests whether newly added parameters significantly improve model fitness or not. A result presented in last two columns in Table 17.2 indicates Model 6 is better than Model five ($p < 0.01$), while Model 7 did not significantly improve the fitness compared with Model 6 ($p > 0.1$). Thus we choose the Model 6 as our final model which means that observed patterns of social interaction with seven different types of alters can be summarized with six latent subgroups.

Age-group variable as a covariate were added into the six-latent class model (Model 6) which tested whether the distribution of six latent sub-clusters varies across the age group. Model 8 assumes that the distribution is not differed among age-groups, while model 9 allowed the variance of proportion of six-latent sub-clusters across the age-groups. BIC, L2 and X2 statistics were dramatically reduced in Model 9 compared with Model 8, which confirms that the distribution of six-latent classes were differ across the six age-groups.

The six types of network composition can be described with conditional probabilities which indicate the possibility to frequenlty contact with kin members and have more then one non-kins given the probability of belonging in each latent sub-clusters. Table 17.3 presents a set of conditional probabilities estimated from Model 9 in Table 17.2. For example, respondents who belong to the first cluster are 74% likely to report that they lived with or visited their siblings at least more than once, and only 21.2% likely to be married. Figure 17.1 plots the conditional probabilities of interaction with seven network members for six latent sub-clusters. Based upon the distribution of conditional probabilities in each latent sub-clusters, we labeled each group; the first cluster is the ‘Single, with family and friend’ group. People assigned in the first cluster are mostly unmarried and frequently interact with their kin (i.e., parents, and siblings) and their friends at neighborhood and other friends. The second cluster, labeled as the ‘Married, with Coworker, Friends, and Neighbors’ group, seems to have more interact with non-kin relations than kin ties. They have friends at their neighborhood, work place, and have more than one other close friend with high probability, while the probability of contact with parents and siblings is obviously low. The third group, labeled as the ‘Single, with Friends and Neighbors’, seems to be highly likely to interact with their close friends and neighbors, but the probabilities of interacting with parents, and siblings are very low. They are most likely to be unmarried and not have children. Compared with former three clusters,

Table 17.2 Goodness of fit statistics for atent class models

		BIC(LL)	L^2	X2	df	p-value	ΔL^2	p-value
Model1	1-Cluster	8068.246	330.82	372.94	120	0.00	.	.
Model2	2-Cluster	7938.339	146.26	152.66	112	0.01	184.56	0.00
Model3	3-Cluster	7965.968	119.23	117.33	104	0.18	27.03	0.00
Model4	4-Cluster	8005.347	103.96	96.21	96	0.47	15.28	0.05
Model5	5-Cluster	8043.685	87.64	82.84	88	0.64	16.32	0.04
Model6	***6-Cluster***	***8078.24***	***67.54***	***63.54***	***80***	***0.91***	20.10	0.01
Model7	7-Cluster	8126.019	60.66	54.51	72	0.94	6.88	0.55
Model 8	6-cluster+agegroup null	8040.499	1095.62	1234.80	715	0.00	.	.
Model 9	6-Cluster+agegroup	7645.704	530.16	616.63	690	0.98	565.46	0.00

Table 17.3 Conditional probability of interacting with network members

	Single, with family and friends	Married, with friends, coworkers and neighbors	Single, with friend and neighbors	Married, with children, friends, and neighbors	Children, friends, and neighbors	Poor ties:
	24.85%	21.38%	18.78%	15.93%	14.09%	4.98%
Married	0.2118	0.9577	0.0448	0.6336	0.5048	0.2598
Contact siblings	0.7413	0.202	0.2244	0.3051	0.2336	0.276
Contact children	0.0431	0.0248	0.0007	0.9792	0.5188	0.1769
Contact parents	0.9801	0.2445	0.182	0.3637	0.0215	0.1132
Has coworkers	0.5821	0.6866	0.5276	0.5644	0.0579	0.169
Has neighbors	0.6673	0.7072	0.7302	0.6745	0.8269	0.2304
Has friends	0.8107	0.9118	0.9194	0.8622	0.8975	0.3121

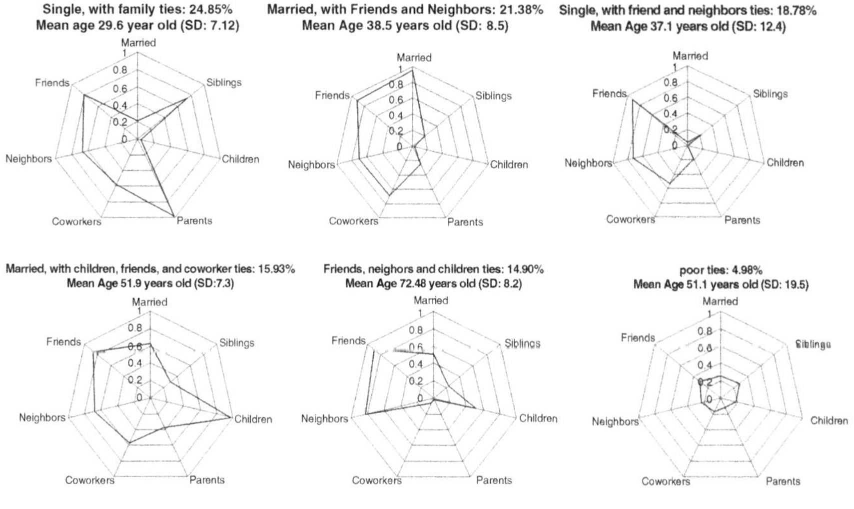

Fig. 17.1 Six types of network composition

respondents belonged to the fourth cluster show highest conditional probability of interaction with their children. They also seem to keep interaction with friends, and neighbors, whereas parents and siblings have lower conditional probabilities. The members of this cluster are 63.4% likely to be married. This group is labeled as the 'Married with Children, Friends and Neighbors'. In the fifth group, we named 'Friends and Neighbor with Children', respondents mainly interact with friends and neighbors. The probabilities of interacting with children and being married are

Table 17.4 Distribution of six-network composition types across the six age groups

Age	Single, with family ties (%)	Married, with friends and neighbors (%)	Single, with friend and neighbors ties (%)	Married, with children, friends, and coworker ties (%)	Friends, neighbors and children ties (%)	Poor ties (%)
20s	59.11	8.57	26.47	0.02	0.01	5.82
30s	41.64	33.56	23.90	0.04	0.69	0.17
40s	17.03	39.44	13.94	21.78	0.78	7.04
50s	1.33	22.69	21.71	49.30	0.51	4.46
60s	0.02	3.04	19.11	37.83	36.02	3.98
70s	0.06	0.02	0.23	0.16	88.90	10.63

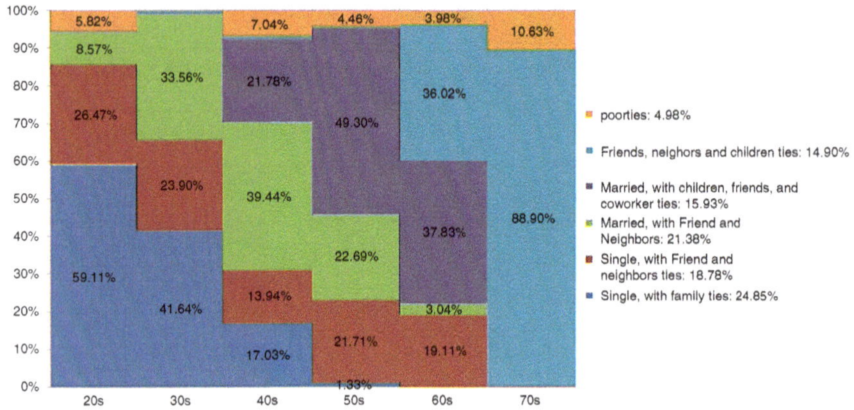

Fig. 17.2 Distribution of types of network composition in each age group

moderate (50.5 for being married and 51.9 for interacting with children). The last class interestingly has very lower probabilities of interaction with all types of social ties. We called this group as the 'Poor tie' group.

Personal Network Composition and Life-Course

Distribution of each of six network composition types varies through the life course. Table 17.4 and Fig. 17.2 show the distribution of network composition types in each age group. Across the age group, some types of network composition fades out, and other types of networks composition became a dominant network composition. The 'Single with Family and Friends' groups are concentrated on 20s and 30s, whereas its proportion dramatically decreases after 40s. More than 85% of 20s are likely to belong in either of the 'Single with Family and Friends' or 'Single with Friends and Neighbor' group (59.1% for 'the single with family and friends', and 26.5% for the single with Friends and Neighbors'). In 40s, proportion of the 'Married with friends and coworkers' raises up to 33.6%, meanwhile the two single classes still remains with substantial size of proportions. More than half of population aged in 40s (about 62%) belonged to either of 'Married, with Friends, Coworkers, and Neighbor' group or 'Married, with Children, Friends, and Neighbors' group. It implies that many of people in early middle age accomplished to build an independent family through the marriage and child birth. However, Fig. 17.1 also shows that about 30% of the 40s still remain in single status with mainly interact with their kin ties (17.3% for the 'Single, with Parents and Siblings' and 13.94% for the 'Single, with Friends and Neighbors'). In the 50s, the 'Married, with Children, Friends, and Neighbor' group became a dominate type of social network composition (49.3%). And 22.6% of the 50s were assigned in the 'Married with Friends, Neighbors and Coworker' group. It may be a reasonable guess that member of this group did not have a child yet or their child is under 18 years-old. Among people in the 60s, 37% belongs to the 'Married with Children, Friends, and Neighbors' group, and the proportion of 'Friend and Neighbors, with Children' group upsurges up to 36% from 0.5% in the 50s. During the latest life stage after 70 years old, most people's social network seems to be composed with their children, friends and neighbors. 88.9% of the 70s were assigned to the 'Friend and Neighbors and Children' group. Member of this groups have a spouse tie with moderate level. As regarding their age, the dominance of children and, friends, and nieghbors may be, at least partially, due to the widowhood. After losing loved one, old peoples are likely to contact more frequntly with other social network members, particulary with thier children and sibligns (Guiaux et al. 2007).

In addition to the changing of network composition through the life course, there are two notable points. First, the poor tie group distributed relatively evenly through the age groups, except in the 30s. Second, the proportion of 'Single, with Friends, and Neighbor' group in each age group is relatively constant around 20%, except in 40s, and 70s. The 'Poor tie' group distributed in each age group ranged from 4.5% to 10.6%, while the proportion of this group in the 30s is less than 1%. Among the 20s, 5.25% were assigned into this group, and it is little bit larger in the 40s with 7%. While its size seems to be reduced through 50s and 60s (4.5% for the 50s and 4% for the 60s), it surged up to 10.6% among the oldest old people (older than 70 years old). It apparently shows that the isolated population in terms of social interaction concentrated on the latest life stage, but it also seems to be true that the non-negligible amount of population in each age group also may be socially isolated.

As for the 'Single, with Friends and Neighbors' group, the distinctive characteristics of this group compared with other groups is that they are much less likely to contact with their parents and siblings, and their marital status kept remaining as single through the life course. Another interesting aspect of this group is that their distribution in each age group is relatively constant. Although the proportion of this group peaked up in the 20s with 26.5%, this group keeps its proportion around 20% from the 30s to the 60s. The absence of spouse and kinship ties in personal network may imply different meaning according to the life stage. During the 20s and 30s, the majority of this age groups still remaining as single. Thus, the absence of spouse in the 'Single, with Friends and Neighbors' may be treated as normal, whereas the absence of interaction with parents and siblings of this group may associated with a certain abnormal status compared with others who contact with their family ties. From the middle-age stage, majority of social network composition is two married group which compose social network with married partner, and non-kin ties, or children. The 'Single, with Friends and Neighbors' may have a distinctive characteristic from other two married groups in terms of the absence of spouse and children in their social networks.

In sum, first, we found that there are six distinctive types of social network compositions, and the distribution of those network composition types varies across the age group. The changing of distribution of each type of social networks across the life stage, in general, implies that a certain network members gradually wane out from the social interaction, while others have been got into social cycle. For example, spouse and children seems to enter into social networks from the early middle age, and the proportion of parents and siblings in social interaction gradually faded out by aging. The interaction with friends and neighbors, in contrast, seems to be relatively constant in all age groups. Second, while each type of social networks peaked up in its percentage in a certain age group, it does not necessarily means that a certain type of network emerged as the dominant and standard network composition in a particular age group. Rather it is more reasonable understanding that different types of network composition are layered with varying degree in each age-group. Third, among those layered types of network composition, we found two interesting groups (or deviant groups) which seem to be either isolated from all kinds of social interaction or constantly missing a kinship ties (i.e., parent, siblings and spouse). The isolated population (e.g., the 'poor tie' group) was detected in each age group with ranged from 4% to 10%. And the network composition without spouse, parents, and children was relatively constantly distributed from 20s to 60s with about 20%.

In next section, we examined the effects of social network composition on the level of general happiness, particularly focusing on two deviant groups.

Happiness

Studies tested the effects of social relationship on psychological status have been reported that negative outcome for population with isolated social relationship (Cohen and Wills 1985; Thoits 1985, 1995; Chu et al. 2010). The previous studies lead the hypothesis that the 'Poor ties' group would show the lower level of happiness. In addition, we expected that the 'Single with friend and neighbor' group would show low level of happiness in some life stages due the constant missing of family and spouse ties in their social relationship.

Table 17.5 shows the result from the set of logistic regressions in which the general happiness level was regressed on the six-types of network composition as controlling age, gender, race, and education level. As we expected, coefficients in the first column in Table 17.5 indicate that person belonged to the 'Poor tie' group are more likely to report poor happiness than the' Single with family and friend ties'

Table 17.5 Ordinal logistic regression for the general happiness

		All	20s	30s	40s	50s	60s	70s
General happiness		Coef.	Coef.	Coef.	Coef.	Coef.	Coef.	Coef.
Cluster	Single, with family ties	(ref)	(ref)	(ref)	0.460	1.093	0.3303	0.311
	Married, with friends and Neighbors	−0.250	−0.833	−0.485	(ref)	0.269	0.5206	0.255
	Single, with friend and neighbors ties	1.120***	0.898*	1.806**	2.894**	0.615	0.9332	0.273
	Married, with children, friends, and coworker ties	0.174	0.238	0.191	0.933**	(ref)	(ref)	0.259
	Friends, neighbors and children ties	−0.376	0.234	1.317	0.976	0.450	0.5601	(ref)
	Poor ties	3.063**	1.489	0.279	2.629**	2.602	0.3265	3.241**
	Age	−0.006	0.033	0.113**	0.026	−0.051	0.045	−0.031
Gender	Male(ref)							
	Female	0.122	0.328	0.122	0.351	−0.151	0.561	−0.624
Race	White(ref)							
	Black	0.193	0.294	0.132	0.129	−0.026	1.170	−0.126
	Other	0.525	0.348	0.136	1.337	−0.019	3.572**	.
Education	LT high school (Ref)							
	High school	−0.010	0.115	0.192	0.379	0.254	−0.941	−0.403
	Junior college	−0.607	1.517	−0.179	−1.905	−0.800	−0.026	−0.049
	Bachelor	−0.404*	−0.706	−0.121	−0.255	0.188	−1.644	−1.509
	Graduate	0.031	−1.423	0.916	0.414	0.191	−0.267**	−0.845
Constant		0.395	−0.7498	−3.776*	−1.858	2.856	−2.737	2.581
N		975	192	218	209	148	97	111

* p<0.1, **p<0.05, ***p<0.01.

group. Also, the 'Single, with Friend and neighbors' group shows significantly lower level of general happiness compared with the 'Single, with Family and Friends ties'.

While we estimated the effects of the type of network composition as controlling age, it may provide more detail information of the association between network composition types and general happiness to separately examine the association by age groups. For example, it may be possible that the 'Single, with Friends and Neighbors' group was not less happy compared with the 'Single, with Family and Friend' group in the 20s, whereas they may show significantly lower happiness level than the 'Married, with Friends and Neighbors' in the 40s. To examine varying effects of network types across the age group on the happiness, we conducted a set of logistic models for each age group.

The result from logistic model for each age group is presented in from second to seventh column in Table 17.5. Coefficients from seven logistic regressions indicate that members in the 'Single, with friends and neighbors' group constantly shows the lower level of happiness from 20s to 40s, while there is no statistically significant difference in level of happiness across network compositions in 50s and 60s group. Regarding with that the 'Single with friends and neighbors' group constantly distributed from 20s to 60s with range from14% to 26%, this result implies that the absence of family ties and spouse may salient in happiness particularly during 20s to 40s.

Conclusion

The goal of this chapter is to figure out a set of typologies of personal network compositions and to describe the distribution of these networks over the life course. In addition, we aim to test the effect of personal network typologies on general happiness. The results of our analysis demonstrate that six different types of personal network composition are distributed to varying degrees over the life course. In addition, each type of personal network has different implications for an individual's happiness according to age group.

Our first step was to identify six different types of personal network composition based on the combination of marital status and the presence of kin and non-kin relationships. The most distinctive network type among the six network compositions is the "poor tie" type, in which members have few or no interaction partners in their personal networks. The other five types of personal network can be summarized based on the proportion of spouse, kin, and non-kin relationships that feature in them. Two of the groups do not have a spouse, while the others are likely to include their marital partners in their personal networks. The difference between the two single groups (i.e., single with family and single with friends and neighbors) lies in contact with parents and siblings. The "single with family ties" group shows a high likelihood of interacting with parents and siblings, as well as other non-kin ties. Meanwhile, social interactions of people in the "single with friends and neighbors" group is concentrated on non-kin relationships. Of the married groups, the "married with friends and neighbors" group also shows a non-kin-dominant personal network composition, except that most members in this group have a spouse. The "married with friends, neighbors, coworkers, and children" group shows a high likelihood of interaction with their children as well as with other non-kin ties. Lastly, members in the "friends, neighbors, and children" group are also likely to report their children as interaction partners but have few work-related contacts in their personal networks.

Since previous network typology studies have focused on the elderly population and used different network questions, it is not possible to make a direct comparison between our findings and the results of other typology studies. However, Fiori et al. 2006 study and Litwin and Shiovitz-Ezra's 2011 research may be worth mentioning in terms of understanding the non-kin-dominant social network types in our results (i.e., single with friends and neighbors, and married with friends and neighbors). Unlike other network typology studies conducted in Israel and Europe (e.g., Litwin 2001; Wenger 1997), the above researchers found that there is a group of elderly Americans who have little interaction with spouses and children, but show an average level of contact with friends or through attendance at religious services (i.e., the "non-family restricted" group in Fiori et al. and the "congregant" group in Litwin and Shiovitz-Ezra). Fiori her colleagues suggest that the personal network comprising few family members but a moderate level of contact with friends may be one of the unique aspect of American culture in social interactions. Thus, the absence of interaction with family members does not necessarily increase overall isolation (Fiori et al. 2006). In our findings, the two network types showing no frequent contact with parents, siblings, and children (i.e., the "single with friends and neighbors" and the "married with friends, neighbors, and coworkers" groups) may also reflect this tendency in American society.

Second, the six types of personal network composition are differently distributed across age groups. The "single with family ties" group who show frequent contact with parents and siblings, as well as with other non-kin ties, shows the highest proportion during the 20s and is gradually reduced until the 50s. The groups who reported active interactions with children (i.e., the "married with children, friends, coworkers, and neighbors" and "friends, neighbors, and children" groups) show become dominant types in the 40s and most prevalent in the later life stage. The varying proportions of the six network composition types across the age groups is obviously related to normative life events. Over 60% of the two single groups (i.e., the "single with family ties" and the "single with friends and neighbors" groups) are composed of people in their 20s and 30s, whereas the proportion of the two married groups (i.e., the "married with friends, neighbors, and coworkers" and the "married with friends, neighbors, and children" groups) increases during the middle-age periods. This distributional difference between single and married groups across age groups is coupled with the timing of marriage in the population. According to the 2002 US census, 70% of people in their 20s reported that they did not have a spouse, while less than 32% of people aged from 30 years old to 64 years old reported the absence of a spouse due to divorce, being widowed, being separated, or never having married. In the elderly population over 65 years old, 54.4% of the population stated that they had a spouse (United States Census Bureau 2002).

Emerging social network types involving contact with children from the 40s can be understood with the timing of childbirth. In America, the average age at which women gave birth to their first child in the year 2000 was 24.9 years (National Center for Health and Statistics). Since our data focuses on interaction with children aged over 18, it is evident that adult children begin to enter into personal networks from the 40s. The disappearance of coworkers from personal networks in the elderly population is also a finding of previous studies in which the proportion of work-related relationships was found to reduce significantly after retirement (van Tilburg 1992, 2003).

In addition to the changing proportion in each network type over various age groups, our findings also indicate that different types of network composition coexist within the same age group. Particularly, the "poor tie" group was found in most age groups. While its proportion peaked in the elderly population with 10%, more than 4% of people in their 20s, 30s, 40s, and 50s showed a low likelihood of interaction with any relationships. This result shows that a socially isolated population exists at most of life stages. Another interesting group is the "single with friends and neighbors" group, which is characterized by the absence of a marital spouse and low contact frequency with family members. This group was constantly detected from the 20s to the 60s in proportions ranging from 14% to 27%. The lack of contact with parents and siblings in young (ages 20 to 39 years) may be attributed to several reasons, such as coming from a single-child family, early separation from parents due to attending school or getting a job in a different region from where they grew up, or the postponement of marriage. Meanwhile, members of this group who are aged between 30 and 60 years may have different reasons for the absence of a marital partner and little contact with adult children; for example, they might have experienced the divorce or death of a spouse and remained unmarried during the middle-aged period. In terms of children, they may simply not have had children or their children may have been born to them at a later age, precluding them from forming mature social relationships with their children. It is also possible that members of this group merely have a tendency to build their social relationships outside of family. While profiling and testing the detailed characteristics of isolated and non-family network composition across the age groups is beyond the scope of this study, the existence of these two groups in each age group implies the heterogeneity of personal networks in a given life stage, and it may also be associated with different trajectories of life events.

Last, we examined the effect of network composition types on general happiness. As expected from the findings of previous studies, the absence of social relationships reduces the level of general happiness. These results confirm that socially isolated people tend to suffer from lack of social resources that can help them to maintain their wellness, or from insecure social identities gathered from social interaction (Thoits 1983). One notable finding is that members of the "single with friends and neighbors" group also showed significantly lower happiness levels than others. And this significant difference is mostly observed in 20s, 30s, and 40s. This result may imply that not only the lack of overall social contacts, but also the absence of family members and spouse from the early adulthoods to middle aged negatively impact on an individual's well-being.

Regarding the association between personal network composition and life events and trajectory of life-course, several important quetsions remain for furture research. For example, it would be interesting to trace the individual trajectory in terms of changing network compositions at various age stages, and to examine what social and psychological factors underlie the different paths of individuals' lives. At the same time, the cross-sectional nature of our data prevents us from testing the reverse causality between general happiness and network composition. While it is possible, for example, that little contact with family members causes lower levels of happiness at certain life stages, the unhappiness of individuals may lead their family members to avoid interaction with them. Other factors such as a negative personal history with family members involving, for example, serious disagreements or ecumenical conflict, may cause separation from family and general unhappiness. In order to explore these issues, future studies should conduct research using longitudinal data.

In conclusion, this chapter suggests that personal network composition varies across the life course and different types of personal network may coexist within the same age periods. Changes and heterogeneity of personal network configuration may be associated with timing, paths, and the occurrence of life events. Furthermore, an individual's well-being may vary according to types of network composition across the life course.

References

Antonucci, T. C., & Akiyama, H. (1987, September 1). Social networks in adult life and a preliminary examination of the convoy model. *Journal of Gerontology, 42*(5), 519–527.

Antonucci, T. C. (2001). Social relations: An examination of social networks, social support, and sense of control. In J. E. Birren & K. W. Schaie (Eds.), *Handbook of the psychology of aging* (pp. 427–453). San Diego: Academic Press.

Belsky, J., & Rovine, M. (1984). Social-network contact, family support, and the transition to parenthood. *Journal of Marriage and Family, 46*(2), 455–462.

Bost, K. K., Cox, M. J., Burchinal, M. R., & Payne, C. (2002). Structural and supportive changes in couples' family and friendship networks across the transition to parenthood. *Journal of Marriage and Family, 64*(2), 517–531.

Bosworth, H. B., & Warner Schaie, K. (1997, September 1). The relationship of social environment, social networks, and health outcomes in the seattle longitudinal study: Two analytical approaches. *The Journals of Gerontology Series B: Psychological Sciences and Social Sciences, 52B*(5), P197–P205.

Byrne, D. E. (1971). *The attraction paradigm*. New York: Academic.

Carstensen, L. (1991). Selectivity theory: Social activity in life-span context. *Annual Review of Gerontology and Geriatrics, 11*, 195–217.

Carstensen, L. L. (1992). Social and emotional patterns in adulthood: Support for socioemotional selectivity theory. *Psychology and Aging, 7*(3), 331–338.

Carstensen, L. L. (1995). Evidence for a life-span theory of socioemotional selectivity. *Current Directions in Psychological Science, 4*(5), 151–156.

Surra, C. A. (1985). Courtship types: Variations in interdependence between partners and social networks. *Journal of Personality and Social Psychology, 49*(2), 357–375.

Stein, C. H., Bush, E. G., Ross, R. R., & Ward, M. (2016). Mine, yours and ours: A configural analysis of the networks of married couples in relation to marital satisfaction and individual well-being. *Journal of Social and Personal Relationships, 9*(3), 365–383.

Cohen, S., & Wills, T. A. (1985). Stress, social support, and the buffering hypothesis. *Psychological Bulletin, 98*(2), 310–357.

Cornwell, B., Laumann, E. O., & Philip Schumm, L. (2008, April 1). The social connectedness of older adults: A national profile. *American Sociological Review, 73*(2), 185–203.

Feiring, C., & Lewis, M. (1991, April). The transition from middle childhood to early adolescence: Sex differences in the social network and perceived self-competence. *Sex Roles, 24*(7–8), 489–509.

Fiori, K. L., Antonucci, T. C., & Cortina, K. S. (2006, January 1). Social network typologies and mental health among older adults. *The Journals of Gerontology Series B: Psychological Sciences and Social Sciences, 61*(1), P25–P32.

Guiaux, M., Van Tilburg, T., & Broese Van Groenou, M. (2007, September 1). Changes in contact and support exchange in personal networks after widowhood. *Personal Relationships, 14*(3), 457–473.

Johnson, M. P., & Leslie, L. (1982). Couple involvement and network structure: A test of the dyadic withdrawal hypothesis. *Social Psychology Quarterly, 45*(1), 34–43.

Kahn, R. L., & Antonucci, T. C. (1980). Convoys over the life course: Attachment, roles, and social support. In P. B. Baltes & O. G. Grim (Eds.), *Life-span development and behavior* (Vol. 3, pp. 253–286). New York: Academic.

Kalmijn, M. (2003, July). Shared friendship networks and the life course: An analysis of survey data on married and cohabiting couples. *Social Networks, 25*(3), 231–249.

Lang, F. R., & Carstensen, L. L. (1994). Close emotional relationships in late life: Further support for proactive aging in the social domain. *Psychology and Aging, 9*(2), 315–324. https://doi.org/10.1037/0882-7974.9.2.315.

Litwin, H. (2001, August 1). Social network type and morale in old age. *The Gerontologist, 41*(4), 516–524.

Litwin, H., & Landau, R. (2000, June). Social network type and social support among the old-old. *Journal of Aging Studies, 14*(2), 213–228.

Litwin, H., & Shiovitz-Ezra, S. (2011, June 1). Social network type and subjective well-being in a national sample of older americans. *The Gerontologist, 51*(3), 379–388.

Marsden, P. V. (1987). Core discussion networks of Americans. *American Sociological Review, 52*(1), 122–131.

McPherson, M., Smith-Lovin, L., & Cook, J. M. (2001). Birds of a feather: Homophily in social networks. *Annual Review of Sociology, 27*, 415–444.

Milardo, R. M. (1982). Friendship networks in developing relationships: Converging and diverging social environments. *Social Psychology Quarterly, 45*(3), 162–172.

Morrison, E. W. (2002, December 1). Newcomers' relationships: The role of social network ties during socialization. *Academy of Management Journal, 45*(6), 1149–1160.

Thoits, P. A. (1995). Stress, coping, and social support processes: Where are we? What next? *Journal of Health and Social Behavior, 35*, 53.

Chu, P. S., Saucier, D. A., & Hafner, E. (2010). Meta-analysis of the relationships between social support and well-being in children and adolescents. *Journal of Social and Clinical Psychology, 29*(6), 624–645.

Schnittker, J. (2007, August 1). Look (Closely) at all the lonely people age and the social psychology of social support. *Journal of Aging and Health, 19*(4), 659–682.

Sprecher, S., & Felmlee, D. (2000, December 1). Romantic partners'perceptions of social network attributes with the passage of time and relationship transitions. *Personal Relationships, 7*(4), 325–340.
Takahashi, K., Tamura, J., & Tokoro, M. (1997, October 1). Patterns of social relationships and psychological well-being among the elderly. *International Journal of Behavioral Development, 21*(3), 417–430.
Thoits, P. A. (1983). multiple identities and psychological well-being: A reformulation and test of the social isolation hypothesis. *American Sociological Review, 48*(2), 174–187. https://doi.org/10.2307/2095103.
Thoits, P. A. (1985). Social support and psychological well-being: Theoretical possibilities. In I. G. Sarason & B. R. Sarason (Eds.), *Social support: Theory, research and applications* (NATO ASI Series 24, pp. 51–72). Dordrecht: Springer.
United States Census Bureau. (2002). *America's families and living arrangements*. Retrieved from https://www.census.gov/data/tables/2002/demo/families/families-living-arrangements.html
van Tilburg, T. (1992, August 1). Support networks before and after retirement. *Journal of Social and Personal Relationships, 9*(3), 433–445.
Van Tilburg, T. (2003, December). Consequences of men's retirement for the continuation of work-related personal relationships. *Ageing International, 28*(4), 345–358.
Vermunt, J. K. (2010). Latent class modeling with covariates: Two improved three-step approaches. *Political Analysis, 18*(04), 450–469.
Wellman, B., Wong, R. Y.-l., Tindall, D., & Nazer, N. (1997, January). A decade of network change: Turnover, persistence and stability in personal communities. *Social Networks, 19*(1), 27–50.
Wenger, G. C. (1997, November 1). Social networks and the prediction of elderly people at risk. *Aging & Mental Health, 1*(4), 311–320.
Wrzus, C., Hänel, M., Wagner, J., & Neyer, F. J. (2013). Social network changes and life events across the life span: A meta-analysis. *Psychological Bulletin, 139*(1), 53–80.

Yoosik Youm is Professor in the Department of Sociology at Yonsei University, South Korea. His interests include medical sociology, organizations, and social networks.

Edward O. Laumann is the George Herbert Mead Distinguished Service Professor in the Department of Sociology at the University of Chicago and is affiliated with several research centers there. He has pioneered in the study of social networks. Among his many studies of social networks includes their role in promoting sexually transmitted infections.

Keunbok Lee is a Ph.D. candidate in Department of Sociology at the University of California, Berkeley. His research interests include social networks, life course, social stratification, and inequality.

Part VIII
Inter-generational Social Networks

Chapter 18
Trajectories of Mother-Child Relationships Across the Life Course: Links with Adult Well-Being

Jennifer L. Doty and Jeylan T. Mortimer

The life course perspective highlights the importance of linked lives, recognizing that social influence is transmitted through "a network of shared relationships" (Elder 1998, p. 4). Families and parents, in particular, occupy a key location in social networks, and in the context of youth development may play a more salient role than neighborhood and school (Furstenberg 1999; Parcel et al. 2010). Parent-child relationships predict close relationships with peers (Sroufe 2005), grandparents (Attar-Schwartz et al. 2009; Swartz et al. 2014), and romantic partners (Jager 2011; Seiffge-Krenke et al. 2010). Furstenberg and Hughes (1995) distinguished between close ties within families (i.e., those with greater depth or intensity) and ties outside of families (i.e., those with greater breadth); here we focus on the depth, or closeness, of the mother-child relationships. Some identify the mother-child bond as the strongest family tie throughout the life course (Gilligan et al. 2015), and supportive mother-child relationships early in life are associated with child well-being into adulthood (e.g., Englund et al. 2011).

The life course approach draws attention to the continuity of network ties over time. A prospective, longitudinal view of mother-child relationships across time is important to understand child development and adult outcomes. Parent-child relationships can range from being a source of continuing support to a source of long-term discord (e.g., vanGaalen and Dykstra 2006). Across time, patterns of closeness with parents extending across adolescence, young adulthood, and adulthood may differ among subgroups of the population. Although some have found stability in

J. L. Doty (✉)
Division of General Pediatrics and Adolescent Health, Department of Pediatrics, University of Minnesota, Minneapolis, MN, USA
e-mail: dotyx093@umn.edu

J. T. Mortimer
Department of Sociology, University of Minnesota, Minneapolis, MN, USA
e-mail: morti002@umn.edu

D. F. Alwin et al. (eds.), *Social Networks and the Life Course*, Frontiers in Sociology and Social Research 2, https://doi.org/10.1007/978-3-319-71544-5_18

parent-child relationships across time (e.g., Schenk and Dykstra 2012; Tsai et al. 2013), a variety of parent-child relationship patterns are evident (McGue et al. 2005; Seiffge-Krenke et al. 2010; vanGaalen and Dykstra 2006). The assumption that average parent-child relationship measures, either within or across time, best represent the experience of all people, or even most people, can be misleading and obscure the experiences of individuals who differ substantially (George 2009; Jung and Wickrama 2008). In the current study, we seek to understand how adult well-being differs depending on patterns of mother-child relationships over time.

An abundant literature focuses on mother-child relationships in adolescence, but less research has examined the mother-child relationship from adolescence to young adulthood or continuing further into adulthood. Below, we review longitudinal studies on parent-child closeness from adolescence to young adulthood, focusing on trajectories of relationship experience across time. Next, we consider continuity and change in parent-child relationships later in the life course, from young adulthood to adulthood. Though much of the research assesses parents in general, we focus on mothers where possible. We then review research that connects relationships with parents, particularly mothers, with the adjustment and health of adult children. Finally, we describe the data and present findings based on our present study.

Parent-Child Closeness from Adolescence to Young Adulthood

On average, children report high levels of closeness with their parents before adolescence, but closeness tends to diminish in early adolescence, and then increases or stabilizes in late adolescence (Shanahan et al. 2007; Tsai et al. 2013). Adolescents generally report that they feel closer to mothers than fathers (Tsai et al. 2013; Williams and Kelly 2005), and this may be in part because mothers spend more time with their children than fathers during adolescence (Laursen and Collins 2009; Williams and Kelly 2005). However, girls report less closeness with mothers than boys in early adolescence (Laursen and Collins 2009; Tsai et al. 2013). In another study, mothers' and fathers' levels of warmth were higher with their same sex children than with the opposite sex child (Shanahan et al. 2007).

Rather than examining average closeness, a German study found that unique latent trajectories of mother-child relationships in adolescence were related to romantic relationships in young adulthood (Seiffge-Krenke et al. 2010). Growth mixture models revealed three patterns of mother-child relationships with different patterns of closeness and negativity. The three pathways of mother-child relationships predicted connectedness, sexual attraction, and anxiety in romantic relationships at two time points in young adulthood. This study underscores the merit of examining various patterns of mother-child relationships over time rather than an aggregate mean score that hides variability. However, few studies have examined mother-child relationships over the transition to adulthood (Bucx and van Wel 2008; Tsai et al. 2013).

The nature of parent-child relationships changes as children enter young adulthood. Moving out of the parental home is associated with a weakening of the parent-child bond; with increased independence and autonomy of young adult children, there is less emotional reliance on parents (Aquilino 1997; Bucx and van Wel 2008). Young adults from diverse ethnic backgrounds spend more time engaged with other people and activities and less of their leisure time with parents and siblings (Fuligni and Masten 2010). An analysis of college students' answers to open ended questions found that most reported an improvement in their relationships with parents after transitioning into a university setting (Lefkowitz 2005). In contrast, another qualitative study of parents revealed that as young adults develop autonomy, some parents (primarily mothers) have a hard time letting go, which may create tension in the relationship (Kloep and Hendry 2010).

In an 8-year longitudinal study, Tsai et al. (2013) found that although the quality of relationships with mothers declined in adolescence, they stabilized in young adulthood. Throughout both developmental time periods, young people reported closer relationships with mothers than with fathers. Little variation in parent-child relationships by gender or ethnicity was found. However, these analyses were based on aggregate data, and the mean trends may obscure the experiences of subgroups (George 2009; Jung and Wickrama 2008).

Some studies have linked parents' emotional and instrumental support for young adults with the quality of earlier parent-child relationships. Levitt et al. (2007) examined parent-child relationships at two time points across the transition out of high school. They found stability in father-child relationships but improvement in mother-child relationships. Parents' support in young adulthood was positively associated with young adults' satisfaction with father and mother relationships. In another study, young people who were close to mothers in adolescence tended to receive more instrumental support later, in young adulthood, than those who were less close, but closeness to fathers was associated with less support (Swartz et al. 2011). These studies indicate the importance of examining relationships with mothers and fathers separately.

Parent-Child Relationships from Young Adulthood into Adulthood

Evidence suggests that life course transitions impact parent-child relationships in young adulthood. Young adults whose parents divorce report high relationship quality with mothers and emotional support from mothers but emotional distance from fathers (Riggio 2004). Life course transitions in adult children's lives, such as marriage, parenthood, or divorce, are also associated with change in the relationships adults have with their parents (Aquilino 1997; Sarkisian and Gerstel 2008). A national study of adult children found that those who were married were less likely than their non-married counterparts to live nearby their parents or to give and receive financial or practical support (Sarkisian and Gerstel 2008). Additionally, mothers are generally more involved with adult children than fathers (McHale et al. 2003). Having children at a young age predicted a weaker parent-child bond, but having children at an older age strengthened this bond (Bucx and van Wel 2008). Another study found that marriage, cohabitation, and employment were associated with a closer relationship with parents in young adulthood, but becoming a parent was not (Aquilino 1997). Timing, of central importance in life course analysis, may be a relevant consideration (Elder and Giele 2009). Parent-child relationships in adulthood may be negatively affected by transitions that are perceived as occurring "off-time," or early in relation to cultural norms, but they may be positively affected by "normatively" timed transitions.

Using the first wave of data from a panel in the Netherlands, Van Gaalen and Dykstra (2006) identified five latent classes of parent-child relationships in adulthood:

1. "harmonious" relationships similar to friendships,
2. "ambivalent" relationships with mutual support given but with some tension,
3. "obligatory" relationships focused on care-taking,
4. "affective" relationships with mainly emotional support given and received, often over a distance, and
5. "discordant" relationships with low likelihood of contact or support.

Mothers were more likely than fathers to be in the group with harmonious relationships, perhaps filling a role as kinkeepers. Although this study found variation between groups of participants, in a three-year follow-up study, Schenk and Dykstra (2012) found very little change across time within these classes. The authors suggest that only a substantial change in circumstances, such as a parental divorce or moving apart, influences parent-child relationship patterns. They conclude that parent-child relationships need to be followed for longer periods of time to detect change. What is lacking in this literature is a prospective view of parent-child relationships that bridges the span between childhood and adulthood.

Parent-Child Relationships and Well-Being over the Transition to Adulthood

A wealth of evidence demonstrates that the quality of parent-adolescent relationships is positively associated with adolescent physical health and mental health (Amato 1994; Andersson 2014; Lippold et al. 2014; Merten and Henry 2011; Videon 2005). However, less is known about whether the benefits of close parent-child relationships in adolescence extend into adulthood. Retrospectively, adults who report earlier warmth with parents have better physical health (e.g., Andersson 2014). One study documented a cascading positive effect of attachment to parents in childhood on peer relationships and romantic relationships, which in turn, were related to adult functioning (Englund et al. 2011). The parent-child bond in adolescence and young adulthood was found to be associated with general well-being at three time points over 6 years during the transition to adulthood (Bucx and Van Weil 2008). In a

German study (Buhl 2007), young adults transitioning from college into the workplace were clustered in two groups: those with increased well-being and those with decreased well-being. Reports of low conflict with mothers during college were associated with increased well-being a few years later during the transition to work. These studies imply that parent-child relationships have an influence on well-being across the transition to adulthood.

Prior studies have also examined parent-child relationship quality and well-being in the adult years, particularly depressive symptoms and self-esteem. In a cross-sectional study, a close relationship with mother in young adulthood was negatively associated with depressive symptoms, but no relationship was found between a close relationship with fathers or peers and depression symptoms (Norwood et al. 2013). Another study found young adult women who reported feeling rejected by mothers in the last month were more likely to report depression (Thompson et al. 2009). A longitudinal study of young adults from age 18 to 25 found conflict with mothers at age 18 was positively associated with depression at 18 and a decline in depression over time (Galambos and Kotylak 2011), perhaps because mother-child relationships improved or because mother-child relationships lost salience over time.

One criticism of this literature is that self-reported parent-child relationship quality and depression may be confounded. Concerned parents may spend more time with, and give more attention to, a depressed child. Reverse causality would be indicated if parents become more supportive when children are struggling with depression (Restifo and Bögels 2009). Moreover, depressed children may tend to see their parents in a less than positive light. However, when researchers observed parent-child interactions (rather than collecting self-report data), clinically depressed and subclinically depressed adolescents were found to have more conflict with, and less support from, parents than those without depression symptoms (Sheeber et al. 2007). Furthermore, a prospective Dutch study found a negative bidirectional relationship between adolescents' depressive symptoms and relationship quality with both mothers and fathers for two cohorts of early and middle adolescents over 4 years as they approached adulthood (Branje et al. 2010).

Self-esteem not only buffers against depression (Sowislo and Orth 2013), but is considered a marker of well-being in its own right (Du-Bois and Flay 2004). In a cross-sectional study, self-worth was found to mediate the relationship between perceived attachment with mothers and depression among young adults (Kenny and Sirin 2006). Although differences between mothers' and fathers' influence have been found in some studies, together these studies suggest that high quality, close parent-adolescent relationships are crucial for mental health and well-being, particularly with regards to depression and self-esteem.

Some evidence suggests that parents may act as buffers against negative health outcomes when young adults face life stress. Young adults' report of warm relationships with mothers is associated with lower cortisol levels, suggesting that support from mothers helps young adults cope with stress and ultimately reduces health risks (Lucas-Thompson 2014). In another study of college students, communication with parents on weekend days was associated with less risky drinking during the first year of college, which is often a stressful transition for young adults (Small et al. 2011). Negative life events, such as bereavement, parents' divorce, or an adult child's relationship problems, may affect both adult well-being (Luhmann et al. 2012) and relationships with parents (Kaufman and Ulenberg 1998). However, few studies have prospectively examined both life events and parent-child relationships in relation to well-being beyond young adulthood. This study fills this gap and applies a life course approach to the understanding of adult well-being by considering trajectories of mother-child relationships.

The Current Study

Although the association between mother-child relationship quality and adolescent well-being is established, little is known about the association of long-term mother-child relationship trajectories and adult well-being. Parent-child relationships are unique in social networks because they are not chosen. Because there is no selection into or out of the mother-child relationships, a focus on the trajectory of relationship strength is appropriate. Research indicates that close relationships with parents in childhood have a distal effect on well-being in adulthood (Englund et al. 2011; Fluori and Buchanan 2003). However, scant research has followed the trajectory of parent-child relationships from adolescence, through young adulthood, and into adulthood. Most research has assessed average effects at single points in time rather than taking a person-centered approach to examine multiple trajectories of relationship quality over time. In the current study, we focus on perceived relationships with mothers, as research has demonstrated the importance of examining relationships with fathers and mothers separately rather than combining them (e.g., Seiffge-Krenke et al. 2010). Additionally, since mother-child relationships are a key source of support within families across the life-span (Gilligan et al. 2015), understanding different trajectories of closeness with mothers may shed light on protective and risk factors for adult mental health.

This research advances the field in two ways. First, unlike most prior studies, this study considers perceived closeness with mothers across the life course through three developmental periods (adolescence, young adulthood, and adulthood). In doing so, we sought to answer the following research questions: Are there subpopulations of individuals who experience different patterns of relationships with mothers over this span of the life course? If so, how many trajectories of mother-child closeness from adolescence to adulthood best fit the data? Using growth mixture models, we empirically identify distinct trajectories; variation in the sample is characterized by patterns over time that may represent subgroups in the larger population (Jung and Wickrama 2008). Second, we examine the relationships between closeness trajectories, revealed by growth mixture models, and adult mental health, taking into account background variables, mental health in adolescence, and negative life events. We hypothesized that adult self-esteem will be higher and depressed mood lower when there are high levels of perceived closeness with mothers from adolescence to adulthood.

Methods

Participants

The Youth Development Study is a longitudinal study of youth in the Midwest of the U.S. as they transition into adulthood. This study collected data from two generations: G1, the natural parents or stepparents/guardians of the participants and G2, the adolescents who were followed over time. The present study uses background data from G1 and relational and mental health outcome data from G2. In 1987, YDS participants ($N = 1139$) were recruited as ninth graders from the St. Paul, Minnesota public school district via random sampling. A probit analysis comparing the consenting sample (64%) to those who did not consent using 1980 census data showed no significant differences in socioeconomic contextual variables (Finch et al. 1991).

The first four waves of data were collected while the participants were in high school (1988–1991); parents of the students were also mailed surveys in 1988 and 1991. After high school, participants completed surveys for waves 5–19 via mail every one or two years. The current study uses data from wave 1 (1988), wave 4 (1991), wave 8 (1995), wave 12 (2000), wave 16 (2005), wave 18 (2009), and wave 19 (2011). The sample included individuals who answered questions about closeness with the same person they considered as their mother in both adolescence and adulthood ($n = 966$). Those retained in recent waves were more likely to be female, White, and to have an employed parent than the baseline sample, reflecting patterns of attrition (Staff and Mortimer 2007; Swartz et al. 2011). For demographics, see Table 18.1.

Measures

Quality of Relationships with Primary Mother Figure We operationalized quality of mother-child relationships through child reports of closeness with mother from adolescence to adulthood at 6 time-points: wave 1 (age 15), wave 4 (age 18), wave 8 (age 22), wave 12 (age 27), wave 16 (age 32), and the most recent information from either wave 18 (age 36) or 19 (age 38). For waves 1 and 4, respondents had the opportunity to answer questions regarding the mother they lived with (natural parent, step-parent, or guardian) and a parent they did not live with (natural parent or step-parent).

In waves beyond high school (waves 8–19), respondents were asked to report closeness with their primary female parent. The primary mother designated in these waves was matched to responses in waves 1 and 4. Categorical variables were created indicating which parent the G2 respondent chose as the primary mother figure most often over time, including at least one time point in adolescence (waves 1 and 4) and one time point in adulthood (waves 8 to 19). Categories included the following: natural mother (biological or adopted parent), stepmother, and guardian (rela-

Table 18.1 Demographic characteristics of full and analytic sample

	Initial sample ($N = 1139$)	G2 individuals who reported mother closeness ($n = 966$)[a]
G1		
Household income (1988)	60.5%	59.1%
35 K or less		
Household education (1988)	41.1%	40.3%
High school or less		
G2		
Female gender	52.0%	55.6%
White	65.1%	70.3%
Primary parent over time		
Natural father	–	83.7%
Step father or guardian	–	16.3%
Natural mother	–	96.5%
Step mother or guardian	–	3.5%
Lived with natural father (1988)	75.6%	75.4%
Lived with natural mother (1988)	86.4%	94.5%

Note: [a]Analytic sample for closeness with mother

tive, foster parent, or other). Some respondents answered about different mother figures at different time points; when this occurred, responses that did not refer to the primary mother (the female parent respondents chose to answer about most often over time) were dropped from the analysis. Although 23.9% of respondents had missing data at waves 18/19 because of attrition or answering about a different mother figure, these respondents were retained using full information maximum likelihood but contributed fewer data points to the analysis.

At wave 1, 92.7% (1056/1139) of respondents answered questions about a natural mother, and 8.0% (91/1139) of respondents answered closeness questions about a step-mother or female guardian (at wave 1, responses about more than one mother figure were possible). Over time, 96.5% (932/966) consistently answered questions about a primary mother they identified as a natural mother in waves 1 and 4, and 3.5% (34/966) consistently answered questions about a primary mother they identified as a step-parent or guardian in waves 1 and 4.[1]

Perceived closeness to mother at each time point was measured by a 4-item scale: "How close do you feel to her?", "When you are faced with personal concerns and decisions, do you talk them over with her?", "How often does she talk over important decisions that she has to make with you?", and "How often does she listen

[1] Using a question about whether a G1 parent had recently remarried at each time point, descriptive analyses were conducted to assess stability of stepparent relationships (e.g., to ensure that answers about stepmothers did not refer to different stepmothers at different time points). Only one out of those who identified stepmothers as a primary parent indicated that one of their parents remarried. Thus, 97% of respondents with stepmothers indicated no ambiguity about their primary mother figure, suggesting that relationships with stepmothers had a highly stable referent.

Table 18.2 Mean and standard deviation of perceived closeness scales

	Perceived closeness with mother (*n* = 966)
	M (*SD*)
Wave 1 (1988)	2.93 (0.74)
Wave 4	2.90 (0.76)
Wave 8	3.18 (0.74)
Wave 12	3.12 (0.77)
Wave 16	3.12 (0.73)
Wave 18/19	2.81 (0.54)

to your side of an argument?" At each time point, a scale was computed by averaging the responses (1 = *not close/often*; 4 = *close/often*). Reliability for the perceived closeness with mother scales ranged from $\alpha = .78$ to $\alpha = .91$ (for means, see Table 18.2).

Self-Esteem At both wave 1 (when respondents were freshmen in high school) and wave 18/19 (when respondents were in their 30's), self-esteem was measured by the 7-item Rosenberg Self-Esteem scale ($\alpha = .72$; Rosenberg 1965); for example, "I feel I have a number of good qualities", "I certainly feel useless at times" (reversed), and "On the whole, I am satisfied with myself."

Depressed Mood At both wave 1 (when respondents were freshman in high school) and wave 18/19 (when respondents were in their 30s), depressed mood was measured by a 4-item scale from the Mental Health Inventory ($\alpha = .91$; Veit and Ware 1983), for example, "How much in the past month have you felt downhearted and blue?" and "Have you been moody or brooded about things?"

Negative Life Events At wave 8 and subsequently, respondents were provided a check list of life events and asked to "indicate which events have happened to you recently (last year, two years ago, 3 years ago, or 4 years ago)." Life events included 15 possible events, for example: serious personal injury, break-up of a romantic relationship, or death of a close friend. Events from young adulthood (wave 8) to adulthood (wave 18/19) were cumulated across waves.

Demographic Variables Gender of G2 respondents at wave 1 was provided in response to the question "What is your sex?" (1 = *male*; 2 = *female*) and from school reports. At wave 1, G1 respondents answered the following question regarding income: "What was your total household income in 1987 before taxes?" and a variable with income in thousands of dollars was calculated from fathers' report, or mothers if fathers' data were unavailable. Parental education, the highest reported educational attainment reported by G1 father or mother at wave 1 (1991), ranged from 1 = *elementary or junior high school* to 7 = *Ph.D. or professional degree.* Race of G2 respondents was coded as a dichotomous variable (0 = *non-White*; 1 = *White*).

Analysis

The analysis proceeded in two stages: the first identified trajectories of closeness with mother, and the second examined differences in adult well-being by trajectories of closeness with mothers. To determine the number of trajectories of mother-child closeness that best fit the data, growth mixture models (GMM) were first conducted using MPlus, version 7.2. GMM allows an examination of trajectories using a person-centered approach rather than a variable-centered approach (Jung and Wickrama 2008). This method identifies unobserved subgroups within a population, accounting for variation within subgroups, and has been recommended as appropriate for the analysis of trajectories over time guided by life course theory (George 2009).

Observed data, statistical criteria, and theoretical considerations guided the selection of the optimal number of classes. The model with the lowest Akaike information criterion (AIC) and Bayesian information criterion (BIC), a significant Lo-Mendell-Rubin adjusted likelihood ratio test (LMR-LRT), and a significant bootstrapped likelihood ratio test (BLRT) were considered the best fit statistically (Nylund et al. 2007). The BIC and the BLRT, however, have been shown to be the best indicators of model fit (Nylund et al. 2007) and were deferred to in this study in case of inconsistent evidence. An average entropy of .80 has been considered high entropy (Clark and Muthén 2009) and indicates adequate classification of individuals (i.e., low entropy would suggest that individuals are not clearly fitting into one class or another). Classes were also examined to ensure that they were conceptually distinct, or in other words, to ensure they described distinct pathways of closeness over time.

In the second stage of analysis, to address the hypothesis that trajectories of perceived mother-child closeness relate to adult self-esteem and depressed mood, we used posterior probabilities to define "membership in" the three trajectories. Using Stata, version 14.0, adult depressed mood and self-esteem were regressed on these categorical variables; background variables (gender, race, G1 income, and G1 education), depressed mood and self-esteem in adolescence, and negative life events were included in the models.[2]

Results

Sample means and standard deviations of closeness with mothers across time are presented in Table 18.2. Latent growth classes were then estimated for perceived closeness with mothers (see Fig. 18.1).

[2]Missing data was addressed using full information maximum likelihood or multiple imputation depending on the capacity of the statistical software (Johnson and Young 2011).

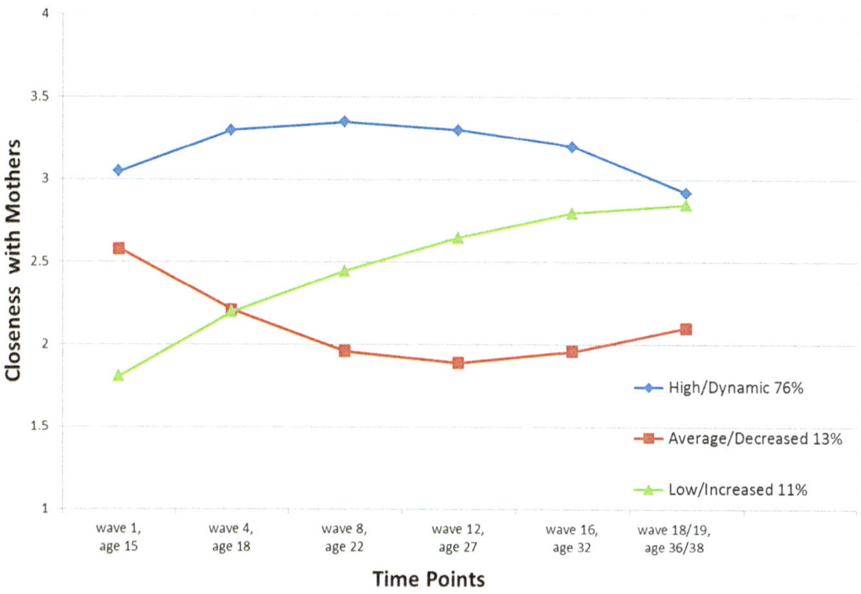

Fig. 18.1 Three trajectories of perceived closeness with mothers ($n = 966$) from wave 1 (1988) to wave 18/19 (2009/2011)

Latent Classes

To address the research question of the best way to measure perceived closeness with mothers over time and to identify the number of trajectory classes that best fit the data, we tested latent growth one-, two-, three-, and four-class solutions.[3] A three-class solution with quadratic slopes proved the best fit to the data (see Table 18.3). Both the AIC and BIC for the three-class solution were lower than the two-class and the four-class solutions. Although the LMR-LRT was not significant, the BLRT indicated that the three-class solution was a significantly better fit than the two-class solution ($p < 0.00$). In addition, the entropy was .76. Further, observational evidence suggested that a three-class solution was best: random selection of observed data (n = 300) demonstrated three patterns that mirrored the estimated curve of the classes.

The first class, labeled *High/Dynamic* was the largest (n = 737; 79.4%). On average, this class had high levels of closeness with mother at wave 1, as indicated by the intercept ($\beta = 3.05$, $SE = 0.19$, $p < .000$). The slope of closeness with mothers from adolescence through young adulthood increased significantly over time

[3]Growth mixture models were also conducted for perceived closeness with fathers from adolescence to adulthood. However, the resulting entropy (separation between classes) was low, suggesting that treating perceived closeness with fathers as a continuous variable was preferable (results available upon request).

Table 18.3 Fit statistics for growth mixture models identifying trajectories of perceived closeness with mother ($n = 966$)

Number of classes	Log likelihood	Free parameters	AIC	BIC	LMR-LRT	BLRT	Entropy
Closeness with mother							
1 linear	−4726.80	11	9475.59	9529.59	–	–	–
2 linear	−4667.42	14	9431.07	9431.07	$p < .000$	$p < .000$	.76
3 linear	−4651.97	17	9337.95	9429.79	$p = .029$	$p < .000$	.79
1 quadratic	−4532.90	15	9095.81	9168.90	–	–	–
2 quadratic	−4464.61	19	8967.21	9059.80	$p < .000$	$p < .000$	.79
3 quadratic	−4449.35	23	8944.70	9056.78	$p = .89$	$p < .000$	.76

($\beta = 0.30$, $SE = 0.14$, $p < .026$). However, the quadratic term indicated that the rate of increase significantly slowed over time ($\beta = -0.07$, $SE = 0.02$, $p < .000$), signifying dynamic, but relatively high closeness over time.

The second class, labeled *Average/Decreased* was relatively small compared to the first class ($n = 125$, 12.9%). On average, this class had fairly high levels of initial closeness at wave 1 ($\beta = 2.58$, $SE = 0.84$, $p = .002$). The direction of the slope was negative but not significant ($\beta = -0.44$, $SE = 0.35$, $p = .205$), and the positive quadratic term was marginally significant ($\beta = 0.07$, $SE = 0.040$, $p = .075$). Although the slope did not indicate a significant change in closeness with mother per unit increase of time, a post hoc paired sample t-test revealed a significant, negative difference in mean closeness with mother at wave 1 and at wave 18/19 (M difference = −0.26, $SD = 0.81$, $p < .000$).

The third class, labeled *Low/Increased* was the smallest ($n = 104$, 10.8%). On average, this class had low levels of estimated closeness with mother at wave 1, indicated by the intercept ($\beta = 1.81$, $SE = 0.17$, $p < .000$). The direction of the slope was positive but not significant ($\beta = 0.45$, $SE = 0.94$, $p = .634$), and the quadratic term was negative but not significant ($\beta = -0.05$, $SE = 0.17$, $p = .784$). Although the slope did not indicate a significant change in closeness with mother per unit increase of time, a post hoc paired sample t-test revealed a significant, positive difference in mean closeness with mother at wave 1 and at wave 18/19 (M difference = 1.11, $SD = 0.62$, $p < .000$). No significant correlation between intercept and slope emerged in any of the closeness to mother classes, indicating a lack of relationship between the baseline closeness and change in closeness over time.

Multinomial Logistic Regression

Next, we used posterior probabilities to define "membership in" the three trajectories; the entropy indicated adequate separation between classes. A multinomial logistic regression was conducted to determine which background variables predicted class membership (see Table 18.4). Highly-educated parents invest in

Table 18.4 Multivariate multinomial logistic regression of variables associated with trajectories of perceived closeness with mother ($n = 966$)

	Low/Increasing			Average/Decreasing		
	RRR	*SE*	*p*	*RRR*	*SE*	*p*
Male	0.52	0.14	.012	0.96	0.19	.836
White	1.84	0.56	.045	0.88	0.19	.549
G1 income	0.99	0.01	.046	0.99	0.06	.014
G1 education	0.14	0.06	.000	0.96	0.10	.680

Note: Reference pathway = High/dynamic closeness; *RRR* = relative risk ratio

developmentally targeted parenting and spend time managing experiences and activities as their children approach adolescence; these activities may be interpreted by adolescents as supportive (Kalil et al. 2012). In contrast, parents in low socioeconomic status (SES) households tend to allow children to participate in more informal activities, which often do not afford the same opportunities for building human capital (Lareau 2011). Compared to the *High/Dynamic* class, parental educational attainment at wave 1 was a significant, negative predictor of the *Low/Increased* class, and those in the *Average/Decreased* and *Low/Increased* classes were likely to have lower household income at wave 1. Also, compared to the *High/Dynamic* class, those in the *Low/Increased* class were significantly more likely to be female and White.

Regression Model

Depressed Mood In Model 1, we considered the *Low/Increased* trajectory and the *Average/Decreased* trajectory in relation to depressed mood in adulthood, with High/Dynamic as the reference group (see Table 18.5). In the first model, both the *Low/Increased* trajectory and the *Average/Decreased* trajectory were positively related to depressed mood compared to the *High/Dynamic* trajectory. In model 2, we added background variables (gender, race, G1 income, and G1 education), which may be related to mental health and render the association between relationship trajectories and mental health spurious. We found that both the *Low/Increased* trajectory and the *Average/Decreased* trajectory associations with depressed mood remained significant. In model 3, we added depressed mood at wave 1 to determine whether the trajectories were associated with change in depressed mood over time. Although depressed mood at wave 1 was a significant predictor, the relationship between the *Low/Increased* trajectory and depressed mood remained marginally significant, and the relationship between the *Average/Decreased* trajectory and depressed mood remained statistically significant. Finally, in model 4, we included negative life events to determine whether they may mediate the effects of the trajectories on depressed mood. That is, at-risk trajectories may be associated with more negative life events, which then lead to greater depressed mood.

Table 18.5 Adult depressed mood modeled on trajectories of perceived closeness with mothers from adolescence to adulthood ($n = 966$)

	Model 1		Model 2		Model 3		Model 4[b]	
	B	*SE*	*B*	*SE*	*B*	*SE*	*B*	*SE*
Low/increased[a]	0.25*	0.10	0.23*	0.10	0.18+	0.10	0.16+	0.10
Average/decreased[a]	0.23**	0.08	0.22**	0.08	0.20*	0.08	0.20*	0.08
Male			−0.08	0.06	−0.04	0.06	−0.03	0.06
White			−0.04	0.06	−0.05	0.06	−0.07	0.06
G1 income			0.00	0.00	0.00	0.00	0.00	0.00
G1 education			−0.07+	0.04	−0.07	0.04	−0.07+	0.04
Depression W1					0.15***	0.03	0.14***	0.03
Negative life events							0.01*	0.00

Note: [a]Reference group is the High/Dynamic trajectory of perceived closeness with mothers over time; [b]$R^2 = .06$
+<.10; *p < .05; **p < .01; ***p < .001

In the final model, the *Average/Decreased* trajectory of closeness with mother remained associated with higher adult depressed mood compared to the *High/Dynamic* trajectory, after controlling for demographic variables, depressed mood in adolescence, and negative life events ($B = 0.20$, $SE = 0.08$, $p = .014$). This indicates that negative life events did not mediate the relationship between an initially low and increasing trajectory of mother-child relationship quality and depressed mood. The *Low/Increased* trajectory of closeness with mother was also associated with greater depressed mood in adulthood compared to the high closeness trajectory, albeit marginally after controlling background variables, depressed mood in adolescence, and negative life events ($B = 0.16$, $SE = 0.10$, $p = .097$). In the final model, a marginally significant, negative association was found between education and depressed mood in adulthood ($B = -0.07$, $SE = 0.04$, $p = .057$); a significant, positive association between depressed mood at wave 1 and in adulthood ($B = 0.14$, $SE = 0.03$, $p < 0.00$); and a significant, positive association was found between negative life events and depressed mood in adulthood ($B = 0.01$, $SE = 0.00$, $p = .010$). As a robustness check, we substituted closeness with mother at wave 1 for the trajectories in the model. Wave 1 closeness was not a significant predictor of depressed mood in adulthood ($B = -0.01$, $SE - 0.01$, $p = .171$).

Self Esteem In model 1, we considered the *Low/Increased* trajectory and the *Average/Decreased* trajectory in relation to self-esteem in adulthood (see Table 18.6). In the first model, both the *Low/Increased* trajectory and the *Average/Decreased* trajectory were negatively related to self-esteem compared to the *High/Dynamic* trajectory. In model 2, we added background variables (gender, race, income, and education) and found that the *Low/Increased* trajectory and the *Average/Decreased* trajectory negative associations with self-esteem remained significant. In model 3, we added self-esteem at wave 1, which was significantly related to self-esteem in adulthood. The negative relationship between the *Low/Increased* trajectory and self-esteem was dampened but remained marginally significant, and the negative rela-

Table 18.6 Adult self-esteem modeled on trajectories of perceived closeness with mothers from adolescence to adulthood (*n* = 966)

	Model 1		Model 2		Model 3		Model 4[b]	
	B	*SE*	*B*	*SE*	*B*	*SE*	*B*	*SE*
Low/increased[a]	−0.22**	0.07	−0.20**	0.07	−0.12⁺	0.07	−0.11	0.07
Average/decreased[a]	−0.20***	0.05	−0.19***	0.05	−0.17**	0.05	−0.18***	0.05
Male			0.05	0.04	0.00	0.04	−0.01	0.04
White			−0.01	0.04	0.02	0.04	0.04	0.04
G1 income			0.00	0.00	0.00	0.00	0.00	0.00
G1 education			0.05⁺	0.02	0.05*	0.02	0.05*	0.02
Self-esteem W1					0.28***	0.04	0.28***	0.04
Negative life events							*−0.01***	*0.00*

Note: [a] Reference group is the high/dynamic trajectory of perceived closeness with mothers over time; [b]$R^2 = .11$
⁺<.10; *p < .05; **p < .01; ***p < .001

tionship between and the *Average/Decreased* trajectory and depressed mood remained significant.

In the final model, we included negative life events to determine whether they may mediate the effects of the trajectories on depressed mood. The *Average/Decreased* trajectory of closeness with mother remained negatively associated with lower self-esteem in adulthood compared to the *High/Dynamic* trajectory of closeness with mother trajectory, after controlling for demographic variables, self-esteem in adolescence, and negative life events ($B = -0.18$, $SE = 0.05$, $p < 0.00$). Negative life events did not mediate the relationship. A significant, positive association was found between education and self-esteem in adulthood ($B = 0.05$, $SE = 0.02$, $p = .030$); a significant, positive association was found between self-esteem in adolescence and self-esteem in adulthood ($B = 0.28$, $SE = 0.04$, $p < 0.00$); and a significant, negative association was found between negative life-events and self-esteem in adulthood ($B = -0.01$, $SE = 0.00$, $p = 0.01$). Again, as a robustness check, we substituted closeness with mother at wave 1 for the trajectories in the model, and wave 1 closeness was not a significant predictor of self-esteem in adulthood ($B = 0.01$, $SE = 0.01$, $p = .277$), suggesting the importance of examining trajectories of relationship quality rather than initial starting points.

Discussion

Guided by the life course perspective, this study used growth mixture modeling to identify unique trajectories of mother-child relationships from adolescence, through young adulthood, to adulthood and examined the relationship of these trajectories with well-being in adulthood. One of the goals of growth mixture modeling is to determine whether a continuous or a categorical approach to the data is most appropriate. In this study, three patterns of perceived closeness with mothers from adolescence to adulthood emerged. The majority of participants were likely to be in a class with a high, dynamic closeness with their primary mother figure over time. A second group of participants tended to report average closeness with their mother in adolescence and slightly lower closeness on average in adulthood. In adulthood, these individuals experienced greater depressed mood and lower self-esteem compared to those with relatively high but dynamic closeness. A third group of participants tended to report low closeness with their mother in adolescence and higher closeness in adulthood. These individuals also experienced greater depressed mood in adulthood compared to those with relatively high but dynamic closeness. These findings were not attributable to background variables, selection to the trajectories on the basis of prior mental health, or the frequency of negative life events after adolescence, suggesting that different social processes with regards to mother-child relationships across the life course are associated with well-being in adulthood.

The majority of respondents were in the *High/Dynamic* class of perceived closeness with their mothers, which was associated with greater psychological well-being than the two other classes. These respondents had relatively high closeness with mothers over time compared to the other two classes, which increased slightly on average during young adulthood. Based on past research, which has characterized mother-child relationships as the strongest family relationship (Gilligan et al. 2015), the finding that most children reported a close relationship across the life course was expected. Although past research found stability in mother-child relationships from adolescence to young adulthood (Tsai et al. 2013), others have found that closeness with mothers increased during the transition to adulthood (Levitt et al. 2007). Our research confirms the latter pattern, as the majority of young adults in our sample followed a trajectory of relatively high and increasing closeness with mothers.

The finding that relatively close relationships with mothers over time were related to low depressed mood and high self-esteem implies that emotionally supportive relationships with mothers may help adult children cope not only with everyday life stress, but also in the face of cumulative negative life events. Consistent with this interpretation, Lucas-Thompson (2014) found that young adults who reported having a warm relationship with their mothers tended to have low levels of cortisol, a sign of effective coping. Past research has also shown that instrumental support from parents to adult children, such as financial support or living in the parents' home, was less abundant when children reported poor relationships with mothers as adolescents (Swartz et al. 2011). The current study extends past research, which has also shown health benefits for young adults with close ties to mothers (Buhl 2007; Norwood et al. 2013), by demonstrating an association between mother-child relationship trajectories and well-being later in adulthood. This is congruent with life course theory, which contends that linked lives have a long reaching effect across time.

The demonstrated effect of maternal relationships on well-being across phases of development also underscores the idea that key social relationships, or proximal relationships within social networks, may have a strong influence over the life course. Often analyses from the social network perspective examine the breadth of social networks (i.e., the number of friends a child has or the number of people an individual can rely on for support). Evidence suggests that weak ties may be enable an individual to "get ahead" by providing connections to influential people or resources (Lin 2001; Putnam 2000). However, emotionally close ties, or proximal ties, enable an individual to "get by" in difficult times (Putnam 2000), and the current study suggests that close ties with mothers have a long-term impact on well-being. In some ways, proximal ties may be more durable than that of shorter-term relationships. This study indicates that it is important, for those working from both the life course and social network perspectives, to include measures of relationship depth (e.g., emotional closeness) across time.

Life course theory also suggests that patterns of closeness with mothers may be influenced by historical contexts. Social construction of motherhood has emphasized mothers as primary caregivers (Gilligan et al. 2015; Palkovitz et al. 2014). Children in this cohort, born in the early 1970s, experienced a time of great social change as many mothers were entering or re-entering the world of work, and families were becoming more prone to instability and dissolution (Furstenberg 2010).

For these children, instability in the mother-child relationship may have been especially stressful. Gilligan et al. (2015) found that estrangement from mothers in adulthood only occurred in 11% of families, making poor relationships with mothers a relatively unique phenomenon that may have ripple effects on other family relationships and well-being. Evidence from the current study suggests that those who experienced instability in their relationship with their mother over the transition to adulthood reported lower well-being later in adulthood.

Both at-risk trajectories, in which participants had experienced poor relationships with mothers in the past (*Low/Increased*) or concurrently (*Average/Decreased*), were related to higher depressed mood even after accounting for background variables, depressed mood in adolescence, and negative life events. These findings underscore the importance of mother-child relationships both in adolescence and later in adulthood with respect to adult children's mental health and well-being. Similarly, research has found that poor relationships with mothers in the past (Galambos and Kotylak 2011) or more recently (Thompson et al. 2009) were related to depressive symptoms in young adulthood. Additionally, we found that those whose closeness decreased in adulthood tended to have low self-esteem. This suggests that mother-child relationships continues to exert influence on adult children's self-image as predicted by life course theory. An alternative explanation is that those with low self-esteem (or more depressive symptoms) in adulthood negatively influenced their concurrent relationship with their mother or had negatively colored perceptions of the relationship. The concept of linked lives suggests mutual influence throughout the life course.

Strengths, Limitations, and Future Directions

The strengths of this research include the use of prospective data to examine perceived parent-child closeness, the use of GMM to examine differential patterns of closeness with mothers over time, and the use of the life course perspective to inform associations between these patterns and adults' well-being. While much of the past work linking parent-child closeness through adolescence, young adulthood, and adulthood has been retrospective, this work adds to the literature by using 23 years of prospective data. We did not find that baseline mother-adolescent relationships predicted well-being in adulthood, which underscores the importance of examining patterns across time. Additionally, life course scholars have recently called for analyses that identify heterogeneous populations rather than relying heavily on mean scores (e.g., George 2009). This study takes an innovative approach by using GMM to examine patterns of trajectories in longitudinal data. Finally, this research is grounded in the life course principle that linked lives have a long-term impact across the life course and provides further evidence for this principle.

Notwithstanding the strengths of this study, limitations must be acknowledged. First, this sample cannot be generalized to the population at large. At the beginning of the study in 1988, the YDS panel was representative of public school students in a large Midwestern city. However, attrition has resulted in a sample with more women and fewer minorities than those who began the study, and the findings cannot be generalized to the original sample. Second, this study follows one cohort across time and may not be generalizable to parent-child dyads in other historical periods. The population of this city has become much more ethnically diverse since then. Third, in the current study, because the outcomes of adult well-being were self-reported, an individuals' depressed mood or self-esteem in adulthood could have influenced their contemporaneous report of their relationship with their parents (though adult mental health would not have influenced prior reports). However, in the current study, we reported higher depressed mood for both those who experienced relatively low closeness with mother in adolescence and those who exhibited low closeness with mother in adulthood.

While this study has taken the first steps toward understanding differences in patterns of perceived parent-child closeness over time, future studies should examine social support, both emotional and instrumental, in parent-child relationships across the life course using large, nationally representative samples. This approach may further illuminate processes that contribute to variation in parent-child relationships over time. Cross-lagged analyses may also illuminate how the personality characteristics of both parents and children may influence the parent-child relationship across the life course. Long-term follow up to randomized controlled parenting interventions could help determine how changes in parenting can affect parent-child relationships later in life. These methods have the potential to explain causal mechanisms.

In addition, growth mixture modeling could be expanded to identify subgroups in the population, studied longitudinally, who feel close to a large number of individuals in their social networks over time, including parents, siblings, spouses and cohabiting partners, co-workers, friends, and mentors; subgroups who feel close to very few people in their networks; and those who manifest close ties to different clusters of people in their networks. The investigator could then examine the extent to which particular configurations of network ties at different points in the life course are associated with mental health.

In sum, the current study took an initial step in identifying trajectories of closeness with mother across adolescence, young adulthood, and adulthood. These trajectories were found to be linked to adult well-being. Perceived closeness with highly salient individuals may matter more than the breadth of contacts throughout a social network for well-being at key points in the life course. Further research integrating social network and life course concepts and methods is needed to substantiate this hypothesis.

Acknowledgements This work was supported by Grant R01HD044138 from the Eunice Kennedy Shriver National Institute of Child Health & Human Development. The Youth Development Study was supported by grants, "Work Experience and Mental Health: A Panel Study of Youth," from the National Institute of Child Health and Human Development (HD44138) and the National Institute of Mental Health (MH42843). The findings and conclusions in this report are those of the authors and do not represent the views of the sponsors.

References

Amato, P. R. (1994). Father-child relations, mother-child relations, and offspring psychological well-being in early adulthood. *Journal of Marriage and the Family, 56*(4), 1031–1042.

Andersson, M. A. (2014). The long arm of warm parenting: A sex-matching perspective on adult children's physical health. *Journal of Family Issues, 37*(7), 879–901. http://doi.org/10.1177/0192513X14532256.

Aquilino, W. S. (1997). From adolescent to young adult: A prospective study of parent-child relations during the transition to adulthood. *Journal of Marriage and Family, 59*(3), 670–686. https://doi.org/10.2307/353953.

Attar-Schwartz, S., Tan, J., & Buchanan, A. (2009). Adolescents' perspectives on relationships with grandparents: The contribution of adolescent, grandparent, and parent–grandparent relationship variables. *Children and Youth Services Review, 31*(9), 1057–1066. https://doi.org/10.1016/j.childyouth.2009.05.007.

Branje, S. J., Hale, W. W., III, Frijns, T., & Meeus, W. H. (2010). Longitudinal associations between perceived parent-child relationship quality and depressive symptoms in adolescence. *Journal of Abnormal Child Psychology, 38*(6), 751–763. https://doi.org/10.1007/s10802-010-9401-6.

Bucx, F., & van Wel, F. (2008). Parental bond and life course transitions from adolescence to young adulthood. *Adolescence, 43*(169), 1–88.

Buhl, H. M. (2007). Well-being and the child–parent relationship at the transition from university to work life. *Journal of Adolescent Research, 22*(5), 550–571. https://doi.org/10.1177/0743558407305415.

Clark, S., & Muthén, B. (2009). *Relating latent class analysis results to variables not included in the analysis*. Retrieved from https://www.statmodel.com/download/relatinglca.pdf

DuBois, D. L., & Flay, B. R. (2004). The healthy pursuit of self-esteem: Comment on and alternative to the Crocker and Park (2004) formulation. *Psychological Bulletin, 130*(3), 415–420. https://doi.org/10.1037/0033-2909.130.3.415415.

Elder, G. H. (1998). The life course as developmental theory. *Child Development, 69*(1), 1–12. https://doi.org/10.1111/j.1467-8624.1998.tb06128.x.

Elder, G. H., & Giele, J. Z. (2009). *The craft of life course research*. New York: Guilford Press.

Englund, M. M., Sally, I., Kuo, C., Puig, J., & Collins, W. A. (2011). Early roots of adult competence. *International Journal of Behavioral Development, 35*(6), 490–496. https://doi.org/10.1177/0165025411422994.

Finch, M. D., Shanahan, M. J., Mortimer, J. T., & Ryu, S. (1991). Work experience and control orientation in adolescence. *American Sociological Review, 56*(5), 597–611.

Flouri, E., & Buchanan, A. (2003). The role of father involvement in children's later mental health. *Journal of Adolescence, 26*(1), 63–78. https://doi.org/10.1016/S0140-1971(02)00116-1.

Fuligni, A. J., & Masten, C. L. (2010). Daily family interactions among young adults in the United States from Latin American, Filipino, East Asian, and European backgrounds. *International Journal of Behavioral Development, 34*(6), 491–499. https://doi.org/10.1177/0165025409360303.

Frank, F. F., & Hughes, M. E. (1995). Social capital and successful development among at-risk youth. *Journal of Marriage and the Family, 57*(3), 580–592.

Furstenberg, F. F. (1999). *Managing to make it: Urban families and adolescent success*. Chicago: University of Chicago Press.

Furstenberg, F. F. (2010). On a new schedule: Transitions to adulthood and family change. *The Future of Children, 20*(1), 67–87. https://doi.org/10.1353/foc.0.0038.

Galambos, N. L., & Kotylak, L. A. (2011). Transformations in parent-child relationships from adolescence to adulthood. In B. Laursen & W. A. Collins (Eds.), *Relationship pathways: From adolescence to young adulthood* (pp. 23–42). Los Angeles: Sage.

George, L. K. (2009). Conceptualizing and measuring trajectories. In G. H. Elder & J. Z. Giele (Eds.), *The craft of life course research* (pp. 163–186). New York: Guilford Press.

Gilligan, M., Suitor, J. J., & Pillemer, K. (2015). Estrangement between mothers and adult children: The role of norms and values. *Journal of Marriage and Family, 77*(4), 889–908. https://doi.org/10.1111/jomf.12207.

Jager, J. (2011). Convergence and nonconvergence in the quality of adolescent relationships and its association with adolescent adjustment and young-adult relationship quality. *International Journal of Behavioral Development, 35*(6), 497–506. https://doi.org/10.1177/0165025411422992.

Johnson, D. R., & Young, R. (2011). Toward best practices in analyzing datasets with missing data: Comparisons and recommendations. *Journal of Marriage and Family, 73*(5), 926–945. https://doi.org/10.1111/j.1741-3737.2011.00861.x.

Jung, T., & Wickrama, K. A. S. (2008). An introduction to latent class growth analysis and growth mixture modeling. *Social and Personality Psychology Compass, 2*(1), 302–317. https://doi.org/10.1111/j.1751-9004.2007.00054.x.

Kalil, A., Ryan, R., & Corey, M. (2012). Diverging destinies: Maternal education and the developmental gradient in time with children. *Demography, 49*(4), 1361–1383. https://doi.org/10.1007/s13524-012-0129-5.

Kaufman, G., & Uhlenberg, P. (1998). Effects of life course transitions on the quality of relationships between adult children and their parents. *Journal of Marriage and the Family, 60*(4), 924–938. Retrieved from http://www.jstor.org/stable/353635.

Kenny, M. E., & Sirin, S. R. (2006). Parental attachment, self-worth, and depressive symptoms among emerging adults. *Journal of Counseling & Development, 84*(1), 61–71.

Kloep, M., & Hendry, L. (2010). Letting go or holding on? Parents' perceptions of their relationships with their children during emerging adulthood. *The British Journal of Developmental Psychology, 28*(4), 817–834. https://doi.org/10.1348/026151009X480581.

Lareau, A. (2011). *Unequal childhoods: Class, race, and family life* (2nd ed.). Berkeley: University of California Press.

Laursen, B., & Collins, W. (2009). Parent-child relationships during adolescence: Contextual influences on adolescent development. In B. Laursen & W. Collins (Eds.), *Handbook of adolescent psychology: Vol. 2. Contextual influences on adolescent development* (3rd ed., pp. 3–42). Hoboken: Wiley.

Lefkowitz, E. S. (2005). "Things have gotten better": Developmental changes among emerging adults after the transition to university. *Journal of Adolescent Research, 20*(1), 40–63. https://doi.org/10.1177/0743558404271236.

Levitt, M. J., Silver, M. E., & Santos, J. D. (2007). Adolescents in transition to adulthood: Parental support, relationship satisfaction, and post-transition adjustment. *Journal of Adult Development, 14*(1–2), 53–63. https://doi.org/10.1007/s10804-007-9032-5.

Lin, N. (2001). *Social capital: A theory of social structure and action*. New York: Cambridge University Press.

Lippold, M. A., McHale, S. M., Davis, K. D., Almeida, D. M., & King, R. B. (2014). Experiences with parents and youth physical health symptoms and cortisol: A daily diary investigation. *Journal of Research on Adolescence, 26*(2), 226–240. https://doi.org/10.1111/jora.12186.

Lucas-Thompson, R. G. (2014). Relationship quality with parents, stressful life events, and cortisol production in emerging adulthood. *Emerging Adulthood, 2*(2), 92–104. https://doi.org/10.1177/2167696813503313.

Luhmann, M., Hofmann, W., Eid, M., & Lucas, R. E. (2012). Subjective well-being and adaptation to life events: A meta-analysis. *Journal of Personality and Social Psychology, 102*(3), 592. https://doi.org/10.1037/a0025948.

McGue, M., Elkins, I., Walden, B., & Iacono, W. G. (2005). Perceptions of the parent-adolescent relationship: A longitudinal investigation. *Developmental Psychology, 41*(6), 971–984. https://doi.org/10.1037/0012-1649.41.6.971.

McHale, S. H., Crouter, A. C., & Whiteman, S. D. (2003). The family contexts of gender development in childhood and adolescence. *Social Development, 12*(1), 125–148. https://doi.org/10.1111/1467-9507.00225.

Merten, M. J., & Henry, C. S. (2011). Family structure, mother–daughter relationship quality, race and ethnicity, and adolescent girls' health risks. *Journal of Divorce & Remarriage, 52*(3), 164–186. https://doi.org/10.1080/10502556.2011.556966.
Norwood, S. J., Rawana, J. S., & Brown, A. (2013). Eating disturbances, interpersonal relationships, and depressive symptoms among emerging adults. *The New School Psychology Bulletin, 10*(1), 44–53. Retrieved from http://nspb.net/index.php/nspb/article/view/217.
Nylund, K. L., Asparouhov, T., & Muthén, B. O. (2007). Deciding on the number of classes in latent class analysis and growth mixture modeling: A monte carlo simulation study. *Structural Equation Modeling, 14*(4), 535–569. https://doi.org/10.1080/10705510701575396.
Palkovitz, R., Trask, B. S., & Adamsons, K. (2014). Essential differences in the meaning and processes of mothering and fathering: Family systems, feminist and qualitative perspectives. *Journal of Family Theory & Review, 6*(4), 406–420. https://doi.org/10.1111/jftr.12048.
Parcel, T. L., Dufur, M. J., & Zito, R. C. (2010). Capital at home and at school: A review and synthesis. *Journal of Marriage and Family, 72*(4), 828–846. https://doi.org/10.1111/j.1741-3737.2010.00733.x.
Putnam, R. D. (2000). *Bowling alone: The collapse and revival of American community*. New York: Simon & Schuster.
Restifo, K., & Bögels, S. (2009). Family processes in the development of youth depression: Translating the evidence to treatment. *Clinical Psychology Review, 29*(4), 294–316. https://doi.org/10.1016/j.cpr.2009.02.005.
Riggio, H. (2004). Parental marital conflict and divorce, parent-child relationships, social support, and relationship anxiety in young adulthood. *Personal Relationships, 11*(1), 99–114. https://doi.org/10.1111/j.1475-6811.2004.00073.x.
Rosenberg, M. (1965). *Society and the adolescent self-image*. Princeton: Princeton University Press.
Sarkisian, N., & Gerstel, N. (2008). Till marriage do us part: Adult children's relationships with their parents. *Journal of Marriage and Family, 70*(2), 360–376. https://doi.org/10.1111/j.1741-3737.2008.00487.x.
Schenk, N., & Dykstra, P. A. (2012). Continuity and change in intergenerational family relationships: An examination of shifts in relationship type over a three-year period. *Current Perspectives on Aging and the Life Cycle, 17*(3), 121–132. https://doi.org/10.1016/j.alcr.2012.01.004.
Seiffge-Krenke, I., Overbeek, G., & Vermulst, A. (2010). Parent–child relationship trajectories during adolescence: Longitudinal associations with romantic outcomes in emerging adulthood. *Journal of Adolescence, 33*(1), 159–171. https://doi.org/10.1016/j.adolescence.2009.04.001.
Shanahan, L., McHale, S. M., Crouter, A. C., & Osgood, D. W. (2007). Warmth with mothers and fathers from middle childhood to late adolescence: Within- and between-families comparisons. *Developmental Psychology, 43*(3), 551–563. https://doi.org/10.1037/0012-1649.43.3.551.
Sheeber, L. B., Davis, B., Leve, C., Hops, H., & Tildesley, E. (2007). Adolescents' relationships with their mothers and fathers: Associations with depressive disorder and subdiagnostic symptomatology. *Journal of Abnormal Psychology, 116*(1), 144. https://doi.org/10.1037/0021-843X.116.1.144.
Small, M. L., Morgan, N., Abar, C., & Maggs, J. L. (2011). Protective effects of parent–college student communication during the first semester of college. *Journal of American College Health, 59*(6), 547–554. https://doi.org/10.1080/07448481.2010.528099.
Sowislo, J. F., & Orth, U. (2013). Does low self-esteem predict depression and anxiety? A meta-analysis of longitudinal studies. *Psychological Bulletin, 139*(1), 213. https://doi.org/10.1037/a0028931.
Sroufe, L. A. (2005). Attachment and development: A prospective, longitudinal study from birth to adulthood. *Attachment & Human Development, 7*(4), 349–367.
Staff, J., & Mortimer, J. T. (2007). Educational and work strategies from adolescence to early adulthood: Consequences for educational attainment. *Social Forces, 85*(3), 1169–1194. https://doi.org/10.1353/sof.2007.0057.

Swartz, T. T., Kim, M., Uno, M., Mortimer, J., & O'Brien, K. B. (2011). Safety nets and scaffolds: Parental support in the transition to adulthood. *Journal of Marriage and Family, 73*(2), 414–429. https://doi.org/10.1111/j.1741-3737.2010.00815.x.

Swartz, T. T., Mortimer, J. T., & McLaughlin, H. (2014, October 9–11). *Family ties across three generations*. Society for longitudinal and life course studies, Lausanne, Switzerland.

Thompson, R. J., Dizén, M., & Berenbaum, H. (2009). The unique relations between emotional awareness and facets of affective instability. *Journal of Research in Personality, 43*(5), 875–879. https://doi.org/10.1177/0265407509106721.

Tsai, K. M., Telzer, E. H., & Fuligni, A. J. (2013). Continuity and discontinuity in perceptions of family relationships from adolescence to young adulthood. *Child Development, 84*(2), 471–484. https://doi.org/10.1111/j.1467-8624.2012.01858.x.

van Gaalen, R. I., & Dykstra, P. A. (2006). Solidarity and conflict between adult children and parents: A latent class analysis. *Journal of Marriage and Family, 68*(4), 947–960. https://doi.org/10.1111/j.1741-3737.2006.00306.x.

Veit, C. T., & Ware, J. E. (1983). The structure of psychological distress and well-being in general populations. *Journal of Consulting and Clinical Psychology, 51*(5), 730–742.

Videon, T. M. (2005). Parent-child relations and children's psychological well-being do dads matter? *Journal of Family Issues, 26*(1), 55–78. https://doi.org/10.1177/0192513X04270262.

Williams, S. K., & Kelly, D. F. (2005). Relationships among involvement, attachment, and behavioral problems in adolescence: Examining father's influence. *The Journal of Early Adolescence, 25*(2), 168–196. https://doi.org/10.1177/0272431604274178.

Jennifer L. Doty is a postdoctoral fellow in the Department of Pediatrics at the University of Minnesota. Her interests focus on leveraging parent-child relationships to promote health and well-being.

Jeylan T. Mortimer is a Professor in the Department of Sociology and director of the Life Course Center at the University of Minnesota. Her areas of specialization are the life course, youth development, social psychology, and work.

Chapter 19
Linked Religious Lives Across Generational Time in Family Lineages: Grandparents as Agents of Transmission

Merril Silverstein and Vern L. Bengtson

Introduction

Cultural scholars have noted that over the last half century several core social institutions have weakened in American society, among them organized religion and the family (Putnam 2000). At the same time, intergenerational family life has received increased attention, particularly the role played by grandparents as inculcators of social values (Goyer 2012; King and Elder 1999) and material advantages in their grandchildren (Chan and Boliver 2013; Mare 2011). In this analysis we take advantage of a three-generation study to examine whether grandparents convey their religious beliefs, attitudes, and practices to their grandchildren, taking into account the religious contributions of parents and martial disruption in the parental generation.

Religious Change and Continuity in Families

Religious orientations have changed remarkably in recent decades in response to social trends toward greater individualism and weakening voluntary associations (Putnam 2000). After hitting a peak in the mid-1950s, formal religious involvement declined in an American society that became increasingly secularized (Bellah et al. 1985; Hout and Fischer 2002; Wuthnow 1988). Most recently there has been a substantial increase in the representation of "nones"—those who say they have no religious affiliation—in the young adult population (Hout and Fischer 2002;

M. Silverstein (✉)
Department of Sociology, Syracuse University, Syracuse, NY, USA
e-mail: merrils@syr.edu

V. L. Bengtson
School of Social Work, University of Southern California, Los Angeles, CA, USA

D. F. Alwin et al. (eds.), *Social Networks and the Life Course*, Frontiers in Sociology and Social Research 2, https://doi.org/10.1007/978-3-319-71544-5_19

Pew Forum 2015). In 2014 the unaffiliated represented more than one-third of Millennials in the U.S. adult population (Pew Forum 2015). Much of the historical change in religiosity is attributed to Baby Boomers who broadened what it means to lead a religious life as a private spiritual matter (Roof 1999), and recent cohorts of young adults who have rejected religion outright (Chaves 2011).

On the basis of the evidence cited above, it might be expected that religious continuity between generations has declined over recent decades and that the influence of grandparents, in particular would be marginal at best. However, there is strong evidence that religion is reproduced within lineages across generations (Min et al. 2012). Religiosity may be stabilized within families through informal socialization, formal religious training, and behavioral modeling (Sherkat 2003).

Religious transmission across generations has analogs in other forms of intergenerational cultural transmission. There is a large literature showing how cultural information in the form of beliefs, values, and attitudes is transmitted from one generation to another (see Schönpflug 2008). For instance, research shows strong parental effects on the socio-political orientations of young adults (Alwin et al. 1991). We maintain that the influence of parents and grandparents on the religiosity of descending generations will be stronger than their influence on secular values, such as political views, which continue to be shaped by peers and the wider social environment into young adulthood (Alwin 2013). By contrast, religious training is primarily a domestic concern and religious identity is largely forged in the childhood home. For this reason, intergenerational transmission of religion is expected to be stronger and less resistant to change than it would be for other comparable forms of transmission. Indeed, Schönpflug (2008) suggests that, religion, as a form of cultural knowledge, may have a "transmission advantage" by virtue of its emotional salience and ability to address existential questions about the meaning of life and death. This proposed hyper-transmissibility is consistent with findings showing stronger parent-child associations in religiosity compared to other transmissible attributes such as gender role ideology (Min et al. 2012) and formal education (Kalmijn 2015). Whether or not grandparents exert an independent influence on the religiosity of their adult grandchildren has rarely been studied, and is the focus of this study.

Evidence suggests that grandparents have maintained their importance in families by providing childcare to working parents (Hank and Buber 2009), serving as sources of emotional support (Silverstein and Marenco 2001) and conveying religious values to their grandchildren (Copen and Silverstein 2007). Studies demonstrate that grandparents are commonly in frequent contact with their grandchildren and find deep meaning in the grandparent role. Over 50% of grandparents reported seeing a grandchild at least once a week, with another 25% report seeing a grandchild every few weeks; 68% talk with a grandchild by telephone at least once a week and 26% say they communicate weekly by email, text, or Skype (Goyer 2012). Indeed, nearly 60% of grandparents feel they play a "very important role" in the lives of grandchildren (Lampkin 2012).

Contributions made by grandparents to the social, emotional, and moral development of their grandchildren are well documented in the literature (Mueller and Elder 2003; Silverstein and Ruiz 2006; Kemp 2005). This influence extends to the transmission of religious beliefs, behaviors, and traditions to grandchildren. In one national study, three out of five grandparents reported having participated in religious activities with grandchildren in the past year (Silverstein and Marenco 2001). Findings that religious grandparents are more involved with their grandchildren (King and Elder 1999) implies that more religious grandparents are well positioned to pass down their religious orientations to their grandchildren.

Greater longevity and healthy aging imply that contemporary older adults are better able to engage and interact with their grandchildren than ever before (Bengtson 2001; Swartz 2009). Indeed, frequent contact between grandparents and young grandchildren is likely to build strong relationships that extend the influence of grandparents (AARP 2012; Geurts et al. 2009).

Family Change and Intergenerational Transmission

The historic rise in divorce over the past half-century might have led to a decline in the religious influence of older generations. Divorces rates surged in the 1970s, and by 1990 one out two marriages ended in divorce, with remarriage and complex step-families becoming increasingly common (Casper and Bianchi 2001; Cherlin 2009). Family strains produced by divorce have been implicated in substantially reducing contact and emotional closeness between grandparents and grandchildren (Drew and Smith 1999). Adult children in step-families are, on average, less emotionally close to their parents—both their step-parents *and* biological parents—compared to adult children in intact families (Steinbach 2013). Relationships between grandparents and grandchildren may be indirectly affected by step-family formation due to the intermediary or linking position of parents in three-generation families. In addition, children of divorce often experience the entry of step-grandparents into their lives which may further weaken intergenerational cohesion and reduce intergenerational influence (Lussier et al. 2002).

In terms of the transmission of religion from parents to adult children, evidence suggests weaker transmission to children raised in step-families compared to those raised an intact families (Myers 1996). Similarly, Kalmijn (2015) found in the Netherlands that step-fathers, divorced fathers, and divorced mothers more weakly reproduced church attendance in their offspring than parents who never divorced. Thus, it would seem likely that grandparents' religious influence would be similarly weakened by marital disruption of their adult children. On the other hand, grandparents serve as important psycho-social resources for grandchildren who experience a parental divorce, emerging as important providers of emotional support to these vulnerable grandchildren (Cooney and Smith 1996; Gladstone 1988). This function of grandparents may mitigate against the disruptive potential of divorce for grandparent-grandchild relationships.

By extending our consideration of transmission to three-generations, we demonstrate the *linked lives* principle of the life course perspective which states that developmental pathways of family members are interdependent with each other

(Hagestad 2003). Access of grandparents to their grandchildren, which provides the opportunity to exert influence, is sensitive to the social conditions of parents who effectively serve as gatekeepers to grandchildren (Michaleski and Shackleford 2005; Mueller and Elder 2003; Geurts et al. 2009). At the extreme, an estranged parent-grandparent relationship reduces the exposure of grandparents to their grandchildren and suppresses the amount of contact between them (Drew and Silverstein 2007). Because parents serve as mediators between older and younger generations, it is plausible that marital disruption in the middle generation disrupts the strength with which they influence their grandchildren, particularly on the traditionally weaker paternal side of the family (Chan and Elder 2000).

In this chapter, we ask three basic questions: Do grandparents religiously influence their grandchildren independent of the parental generation? To what degree do grandparents indirectly influence their grandchildren through the parent generation? How does marital history of the parents' generation modify the strength of religious transmission between grandparents and grandchildren? This research, extends earlier work demonstrating religious continuity between grandparents and grandchildren (Bengtson 2013) by examining the religious influence of grandparents *net* of the influence of parents within the same multigenerational lineages.

Method

Sample Data for this analysis derive from the Longitudinal Study of Generations (LSOG), a study of 3681 respondents from 418 three- and four-generation families. Begun in 1971, the LSOG has collected eight waves of survey data through 2005 (for details see Silverstein and Giarrusso 2013). Three-generation families, consisting of grandparents (G1), parents (G2), and grandchildren (G3) were recruited through identification of potential grandfather participants randomly selected via a stratified random sampling procedure from 840,000 members of a health maintenance organization in Southern California. The intent of the study was to examine the relationship between intergenerational family relationships and mental health, with a focus on continuities and discontinuities across generations in beliefs, social attitudes, and family behaviors. Beginning in 1991, great-grandchildren (G4) began participating in the survey as they reached age 16.

The baseline LSOG sample was generally representative of the region's adult population at the time and was comprised mostly of working and middle class families. Subsequent surveys took place in 1985, 1988, 1991, 1994, 1997, 2000, and 2005. The LSOG has had high longitudinal participation rates considering the age of the original respondents, the duration of the study, the use of self-administered surveys, and the 14-year gap between the first two waves of measurement. The longitudinal response rate between 1971 and 1985 was 73%, and has averaged 80% between waves since 1985.

The multi-generation, multi-actor, and multi-panel design of the LSOG provides analytic leverage for examining change and continuity across generations within family lineages, and provides first-person assessments of subjective orientations about which proxy reports would be considered unreliable.

We used the three youngest generations from the LSOG to construct a sample of multigenerational triads consisting of G2 grandparents in 1971 (N = 257; M_{age} = 43 years), G3 parents in 1988 (N = 341; M_{age} = 37 years), and G4 grandchildren in 2000 (N = 554; M_{age} = 23). The staggered generational design maximizes standardization on age across generations and avoids the exclusion of grandparents who died over the course of the study.

It bears mentioning that for each grandchild, only one parent and one set of grandparents were represented in the data utilized. Consequently, our assessment is limited to a single lineage for each grandchild, providing a conservative estimate of grandparent and parent influence.

Measures Religiosity in each generation was assessed with survey questions that measured religious beliefs, attitudes, behavior, intensity, and values, corresponding to the. following five domains:

1. *Literalist religious beliefs* were measured by two questions assessing the strength of agreement with the following two statements: *God exists in the form as described in the Bible; All people today are descendants of Adam and Eve*). Responses for each item were coded on a four point scale ranging from "strongly disagree" to "strongly agree" and added together.
2. *Civic value of religion* was measured as the strength of agreement with the following two statements: *All children should receive religious training; Religion should play an important role in daily life*. Responses for each item were coded on a four point scale ranging from "strongly disagree" to "strongly agree" and added together.
3. *Religious participation* was measured as frequency of attendance at religious services: *How often do you attend religious services these days?* Responses are coded on a six point scale ranging from "never" to "everyday"
4. *Religious intensity* was measured by the question: *How religious are you?* Responses are coded on a six point scale ranging from "not at all religious" to "strongly religious".
5. *Religion as valued goal* was measured with an item from the Rokeach Values Inventory (Rokeach 1968) assessing the ranked importance of "religious participation, working with others in your own church or organization" in relation to eight other social values and is coded 1–9 with higher values indicating greater importance.

In 59% of families, both grandmothers and grandfathers responded to the survey. In such families, we used the higher raw score for each measure to represent the grandparent generation as a single entity. Alternative specifications, such as using the average score, produced similar results.

Using exploratory and confirmatory factor analysis (not shown) we found little evidence of a multidimensional structure for the five items and concluded that a single dimension provided the best fit to the observed data. Factor loadings were equivalent across generations, indicating a consistent measurement model. Based on the five sub-dimensions, we computed standardized factor scores within each generation. Because factor scores have a mean of zero, they provided a metric for religiosity that was relative to the central tendency in each generation. As such, factor scores offered a convenient way to control for cohort and period effects and better insured that the transmission of religiosity was assessed as an intra-familial process. Further, associations between factor scores are interpreted as correlations, which are advantageous for assessing the strength of intergenerational transmission within a fixed range of 0–1 and allowing comparisons between coefficients indicating the strength of transmission.

Control variables included the following characteristics of grandchildren: age, marital status (0 = not married; 1 = married), parental status (0 = no children; 1 = has at least one child). About one-quarter of grandchildren were married (26%) and had children (23%).

Education of grandchildren was also controlled (0 = less than college graduate; 1 = college graduate or greater). For the 15% of grandchildren who were 16–24 years of age and who did not graduate from college, education was imputed using earlier waves of data to predict the probability of college graduation from stated educational aspirations, age, and gender. With this imputation, almost half the grandchildren (49%) were considered college graduates.

Gender of grandchildren and parents were also controlled (0 = male; 1 = female). About half of grandchildren were female (52%) and somewhat more than half of parents were mothers (58%).

Marital history of parents was assessed based on whether a divorce was ever experienced (0 = intact; 1 = divorced). By casting a wide net, this liberal definition captured both the experience and sequelae of marital disruption and the presence of a step-parent (who may or may not be the parent represented in the analysis). Almost half of parents (49%) experienced a divorce.

Analytic Approach The sample for this analysis consisted of grandchildren nested within parents who are nested within grandparents. Consequently, we used hierarchical linear modeling (HLM) to properly account for this data structure and the lack of independence of family members within and across generations (Bryck and Raudenbush 1992).

Our application of HLM required specifications at three-levels. In this approach, random effects are generated for grandchildren's religiosity which are predicted by variables at parent and grandparent levels, along with cross-level interactions. At level-1, grandchild-specific variables predict grandchildren's religiosity within parent and grandparent units:

$$y_{ijk} = b_{0jk} + b_{1jk}\left(x_{ijk}\right) + e_{ijk},$$

where, y_{ijk} is grandchildren's religiosity and x_{ijk} is a characteristic of the ith grandchild within the jth parent and kth grandparent. The estimate b_{1jk} is a fixed effect slope and b_{0jk} is the random intercept evaluated as the adjusted mean value of religiosity for grandchildren of the *jth parent and the kth grandparent*, and e_{ijk} is the error term.

At level-2, or the parent-level of analysis, the random intercept from above is predicted as follows:

$$b_{0jk} = p_{00k} + p_{01k}\left(z_{0jk}\right) + r_{0jk},$$

where z_{0jk} the religiosity the *jth* parent within the *kth* grandparent and p_{01k} is the parents' religiosity transmission effect within the *kth* grandparent, p_{00k} represents the adjusted mean value of grandchildren's religiosity for the *kth* grandparent, and r_{0jk} is the error term.

Finally, at the third or grandparent level, the following equation predicts the random intercept above from grandparents' religiosity:

$$p_{00k} = g_{000} + g_{001}\left(w_{00k}\right)_{+} u_{00k}$$

where w_{00k} is religiosity of the kth grandparent and g_{001} is the effect of grandparents' religiosity on grandchildren's religiosity controlling for parents' religiosity.

To test the moderating role of divorce on the strength of grandparents' transmission, we estimated a random effect for parental divorce (z) at level-2 and estimated the following level-3 equation:

$$p_{01k} = g_{010} + g_{011}\left(w_{00k}\right) + u_{01k}$$

where g_{011} represents the effect of grandparents' religiosity on the effect of parents' divorce—the joint or interactive influence of both factors on grandchildren's religiosity.

Results

In Table 19.1, we present mean values for the five dimensions of religiosity by generation. ANOVA tests reveal that group differences were statistically significant on all dimensions. Further, post-hoc tests reveal that that the strength of religiosity generally followed a predictable generational pattern, with grandchildren expressing weaker religiosity than parents and/or grandparents. Attitudes toward the civic value of religiosity and religious intensity follow a steady decline from grandparents to parents to grandchildren. The other dimensions demonstrated discontinuity, with grandchildren and parents differing from grandparents on literalist beliefs and valuation of religion but not differing from each other. Grandchildren were significantly lower in religious attendance than their parents and grandparents. Generally, these reported generational differences indicate strong cohort effects that parallel the precipitous decline of religion in the United States over the period studied.

Table 19.1 Cross-generational comparison of religion variables

Religion Measures	Range	Grandchildren M (SD)	Parents M (SD)	Grandparents M (SD)	ANOVA F-statistic*
Literalist religious beliefs	1–4	2.60[b] (1.07)	2.70[c] (1.13)	3.10 (1.02)	15.32
Civic value of religion	1–4	2.59[ab] (0.96)	3.01[c] (0.92)	3.56 (0.59)	83.92
Religious attendance	1–6	2.77[a] (1.74)	3.22 (1.65)	3.03 (1.89)	5.34
Religious intensity	1–4	2.33[ab] (1.04)	2.69[c] (0.93)	3.10 (0.77)	46.25
Valuation of religion	1–9	3.39[b] (2.87)	3.23[c] (2.58)	4.52 (2.37)	15.03

*All F-statistics are significant at $p < .05$
Bonferonni post hoc multiple comparisons test ($p. < .05$)
[a]Grandchildren < Parents
[b]Grandchildren < Grandparents
[c]Parents < Grandparents

The results of the HLM analysis are shown in Table 19.2.. It is important to reiterate that our use of generation-specific factor scores to represent religiosity rendered cohort effects inconsequential in these analyses because religiosity in each generation is considered relative to its internal average. The first equation shows the main effects and the second equation adds an interaction term between parental divorce and grandparents' religiosity.

In the main effects model, both parents' religiosity and grandparents' religiosity predicted grandchildren's religiosity, with the effect for parents more than three times that of grandparents (.375 vs. .103, respectively). We also anticipated that grandparents would indirectly influence their grandchildren through their influence on parents. To calculate this indirect effect, we estimated the effect of grandparents on parents (.32) and multiplied this term by the direct effect of parents on grandchildren (.38) to produce indirect effect of .12. Adding this indirect effect to the direct effect of grandparents, the total effect of grandparents is .22, a moderately sized standardized coefficient which suggests a substantively meaningful religious influence of grandparents.

Other significant variables revealed that grandchildren who were married and had children tended to be more religious than their counterparts. These results suggest that religious grandchildren adopt more traditional family roles, or alternatively that these roles create the conditions for religiosity to emerge.

In order to gain a fuller understanding of the magnitude of familial similarity in religiosity, we make use of the variance components of the first equation (bottom of Table 19.2.) to calculate intra-class correlations (ICC) of grandchild religiosity for nuclear family and grandfamily clusters. The ICC expresses the strength of within cluster similarity ranging from 0 (no similarity) to 100 (perfect similarity) and is calculated as: between-cluster variance /between-cluster + within-cluster variance.

Table 19.2. Three-level hierarchical linear model predicting grandchildren's religiosity ($N_{Grandchildren} = 565$; $N_{Parents} = 341$; $N_{Grandparents} = 257$)

	Main effects model			Interaction model		
	Coefficient	*SE*	*t*-ratio	Coefficient	*SE*	*t*-ratio
Grandchild level-1						
Female	.100	.071	1.40	.098	.071	1.38
Age	.005	.012	.39	.005	.011	0.43
College graduate	−.027	.031	−0.87	−.032	.030	−1.04
Married	.328	.104	3.15**	.344	.102	3.37**
Has child	.174	.105	1.66⁺	.176	.102	1.72⁺
Parent level-2						
Female	−.059	.089	−0.67	−.064	.088	−0.73
Divorce	−.073	.092	−0.80	−.095	.093	−1.03
Religiosity	.375	.052	7.21***	.356	.053	6.66***
Grandparent level-3						
Religiosity	.103	.046	2.21*	.076	.044	1.71⁺
Intercept	−.048	.042	−1.15	−.077	.042	−1.83⁺
Cross-level interaction						
Grandparent Religiosity* Parent divorce	–	–	–	−.205	.097	−2.11*
Random effect	Variance component	Chi-Square	df	Variance component	Chi-Square	df
Error	.477	–	–	.473	–	–
$Intercept_{Parents}$	.190	514.6***	81	.140	–	–
$Intercept_{Grandparents}$	.070	297.6*	255	.021	47.1	127
$Intercept_{ParentDivorce}$				.427	60.0	127
Deviance	1395.1			1387.8		

⁺*p* < .10; **p* < .05; ***p* <. 01; ****p* < .001

The ICC for total familial resemblance (nuclear family + grandfamily) exceeded 35% and broke down to 25.8% within nuclear families and 9.5% within grandfamilies. As expected, siblings were more alike than cousins. Although grandfamily consistency was modest, the ratio between the two sources of similarity is in-line with expectations—particularly given that only one set of grandparents was observed for each grandchild.

The interaction model added a cross-level interaction between parental divorce and grandparents' religiosity. The coefficient for this interaction term was significant, implying that the direct influence of grandparents was different for grandchildren from divorced families than for grandchildren from intact families. Although the negative interaction coefficient implies weaker transmission in divorced families, its interpretation is aided by plotting predicted values based on

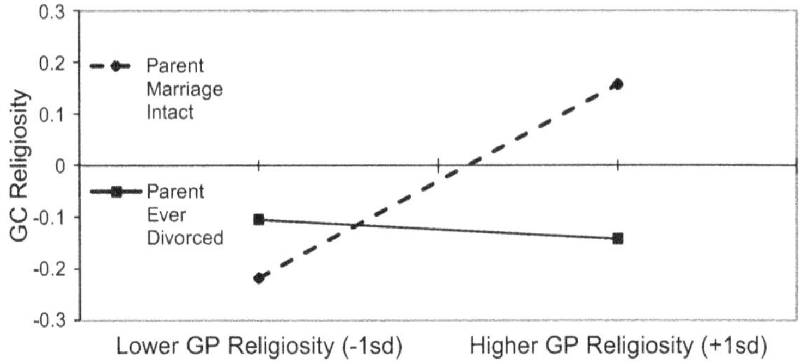

Fig. 19.1 Grandchildren's religiosity by grantparents' religiosity and parent's marital history

model coefficients. We show predictions based on −1 and +1 standard deviation units in the distribution of grandparents' religiosity, with other variables held constant at their means. Figure 19.1 demonstrates a positive association between grandparents' religiosity and grandchildren's religiosity among grandchildren in intact families. However, no such association was observed among grandchildren in divorced families; in these families, the religiosity of grandchildren was consistently low across all levels of grandparents' religiosity.

Discussion

The purpose of this investigation was to identify unique and conditional contributions of grandparents to the religiosity of their grandchildren. Analyzing data within three generation lineages spanning several decades of time, we found that grandparents influence their grandchildren independently of parents, and their influence is stronger when parents' marriages are intact than when they have experienced a divorce. This evidence supports the proposition that the multigenerational family remains a source of relative stability in core religious beliefs and attitudes, albeit with divorce as an important mitigating factor.

In addition to finding great religious change at the generation-cohort level, we also detected intergenerational religious continuity between generations within family lineages. Grandparents influenced their grandchildren directly and indirectly through socialization of their grandchildren's parents, illustrating the long reach of grandparents beyond what young adults may be fully aware. In our analysis we standardized the religiosity scores of each generation through factor analysis. Advantages to using standardized scores included the ability to "control" for cohort effects related to each generation having unique historical exposure to religious culture, and compare the strength of transmission between parents and grandparents. The total transmission effect for grandparents was somewhat more than half that for parents (.22 vs. .38), demonstrating the utility of taking a systemic view of family influence when studying the transmission of values, beliefs, and attitudes within an intergenerational context.

Our results reveal the family to be an anchoring institution within society that provides cross-generational continuity as a conservative counter-weight to social change that moves impressionable young adults to adopt novel ideologies of the immediate Zeitgeist (Alwin et al. 1991). Religion represent a prime candidate for studying this family-society tension because few aspects of life have changed so radically at the societal level while remaining so relevant at the family level.

Since we represented religiosity using factor scores, the transmission effects observed imply that families reproduce a similar rank-order of individuals in descending generations. Although the generations are, *on average*, not equivalent in their religious orientations, our results nevertheless suggest that families are stabilizing institutions—and grandparents and parents stabilizing agents—in terms of their ability to maintain the relative standing of their descendants in the shifting terrain of religious life.

Divorce in the middle generations served to inhibit religious transmission, and appeared to suppress religiosity in grandchildren regardless of the religiosity of grandparents. This effect is likely to have emerged from custody arrangements that split the influence of any one parent—and corresponding grandparents as well. In the case of remarriages, the influence of step-grandparents may be muted compared to biological grandparents, particularly when a step-parent enters the family when the grandchild is already an adolescent.

In light of custody arrangements that favor mothers and remarriage rates that favor fathers (Cherlin 2009), we also tested whether parents' gender modified the interaction between parents' divorce and grandparents' influence (not shown). However, we found that this three-way interaction was not statistically significant and, thus, cannot conclude that the lower rate of grandparents' religious transmission due to parental divorce is different in maternal vs. paternal lineages. We also did not find that grandparents' gender altered the strength of religious transmission. This is somewhat surprising given that most research on grandparenting in Western countries finds both a maternal and matrilineal advantage in grandparent-grandchild relationships (Chan and Elder 2000; Michaleski and Shackleford 2005; Uhlenberg and Hammill 1998). It may be that overall matrilineal strength is offset by patrilineal dominance in the process by which religion achieves a legacy status and is reproduced across generations. Future research with a larger sample, and one measuring both maternal and paternal grandparents in the same families, may grant the statistical power to detect lineage and gender effects. It would also be fruitful to compare gender differences between transmission of religion and transmission of other cultural content in the context of multigenerational families.

Because socialization to values invariably takes place through meaningful interaction between family members, we postulated that early exposure of grandchildren to their grandparents would enhance communication and later adoption of grandparents' religious orientations. Since religiosity of grandchildren in our study was primarily assessed in adulthood, when many grandparents were deceased, it was necessary to rely on parents' reports of contact with grandparents 20 years earlier as a proxy for early childhood contact by grandchildren. We estimated this effect as an interaction between early contact with grandparents and religiosity of grandparents. Our working hypothesis was that this interaction might explain why divorce inhibited transmission from grandparents. Although we found suggestive evidence that the amount of exposure to grandparents positively predicted the rate of transmission (not reported), the contact interaction could not be simultaneously included with the divorce interaction in the multilevel model due to sample size limitations.

We note several limitations of our research. First, the sample of families studied is less than representative of the nation as well as the region from which it derived. Extrapolation to the broader population should be done with caution. Second, our measure of religiosity was broad (though empirically verified), and may mask compositional differences in generational continuity if sub-dimensions of religiosity are differentially stable across generations. Third, the possibility that grandchildren influence the religiosity of their parents and grandparents requires consideration of a two-way flow of transmission; however, the lagged nature of the empirical design mitigates against this possibility. Finally, we did not consider religious denomination in this analysis due to the complexities of examining transitions in nominal affiliations. However, we note that previous research using this sample has found greater religious stability among grandparents who self-identified as Evangelical Protestant and Mormon (Bengtson and Silverstein in press).

In conclusion, religiosity remains a thread of influence linking both adjacent and non-adjacent generations in the family through time. We suggest that future research on this topic account for new technologies, such as social media and Skype, which will allow more frequent and low cost exchanges between grandparents and grandchildren. If these technologies increase exposure of grandchildren to grandparents, then grandparent influence may grow commensurately. In addition, owing to increases in healthy life expectancy, grandchildren will likely spend more time with grandparents, increasing opportunities for shared activities and mutual influence (Uhlenberg 2005).

Grandparents have been little considered in social science research on intergenerational transmission of beliefs and attitudes. Our results suggest that grandparents directly and indirectly influence the religiosity of their grandchildren, providing a "window" into family traditions and cultural scripts. Extending the study of intergenerational transmission to include grandparents as influential actors takes into account the wider family system of "linked lives" that shape the values and belief systems of young adults. By considering members of three-generations as embedded within micro-social networks of influence, we hope to have contributed to the mission of this volume of bridging life course and network perspectives on family life.

References

AARP. (2012). Insights and spending habits of modern grandparents. Washington, DC: AARP Research and Strategic Analysis. Retrieved from http://www.aarp.org/grandparentresearch/fullreport

Alwin, D. F. (2013). Who's talking about my generation? In M. Silversteen & R. Giarrusso (Eds.), *Kinship and cohort in an aging society* (pp. 133–158). Baltimore: Johns Hopkins University Press.

Alwin, D. F., Cohen, R. L., & Newcomb, T. M. (1991). *Political attitudes over the life span: The Bennington women after fifty years*. Madison: University of Wisconsin Press.

Bellah, R. N., Madsen, R., Sullivan, W. M., Swidler, A., & Tipton, S. M. (1985). *Habits of the heart: Individualism and commitment in American life*. New York: Harper and Row.

Bengtson, V. L. (2001). Beyond the nuclear family: The increasing importance of multigenerational relationships in American society. *Journal of Marriage and Family, 63*(1), 1–16.

Bengtson, V. L. (2013). *Families and faith: How religion is passed down across generations*. New York: Oxford University Press.

Bryck, A. S., & Raudenbush, S. W. (1992). *Hierarchical linear models: Applications and data analysis methods*. Newbury: Sage.

Casper, L. M., & Bianchi, S. M. (2001). *Continuity and change in the American family*. Thousand Oaks: Sage Publications.

Chan, T. W., & Boliver, V. (2013). The grandparents effect in social mobility: Evidence from British birth cohort studies. *American Sociological Review*, 0003122413489130.

Chan, C. G., & Elder, G. H. (2000). Matrilineal advantage in grandchild–grandparent relations. *The Gerontologist, 40*(2), 179–190.

Chaves, M. (2011). *American religion: Contemporary trends*. Princeton: Princeton University Press.

Cherlin, A. J. (2009). *The marriage-go-round: The state of marriage and the family in America today*. New York: Alfred A. Knopf.

Cooney, T. M., & Smith, L. A. (1996). Young adults' relations with grandparents following recent parental divorce. *The Journals of Gerontology Series B: Psychological Sciences and Social Sciences, 51*(2), S91–S95.

Copen, C., & Silverstein, M. (2007). Transmission of religious beliefs across generations: Do grandparents matter? *Journal of Comparative Family Studies, 38*, 497–510.

Drew, L., & Silverstein, M. (2007). Grandparents' psychological well-being after loss of contact with their grandchildren. *Journal of Family Psychology, 21*, 372–379.

Drew, L. A., & Smith, P. K. (1999). The impact of parental separation/divorce on grandparent-grandchild relationships. *The International Journal of Aging and Human Development, 48*(3), 191–216.

Geurts, T., Poortman, A. R., van Tilburg, T., & Dykstra, P. A. (2009). Contact between grandchildren and their grandparents in early adulthood. *Journal of Family Issues, 30*(12), 1698–1713.

Gladstone, J. W. (1988). Perceived changes in grandmother-grandchild relations following a child's separation or divorce. *The Gerontologist, 28*(1), 66–72.

Goyer, A. (2012). Grandparents give 'til it hurts. *Generations United: Grandparents investing in grandchildren: The MetLife Study on how grandparents share their time, values, and money.* Retrieved from http://blog.aarp.org/2012/09/08/amy-goyer-grandparents-financial-gifts

Hagestad, G. O. (2003). Interdependent lives and relationships in changing times: A life-course view of families and aging. In R. Setterston (Ed.), *Invitation to the life course: Toward new understandings of later life* (pp. 135–159). Amityville: Baywood.

Hagestad, G. O. (2006). Transfers between grandparents and grandchildren: The importance of taking a three-generation perspective. *Zeitschrift für Familienforschung, 18*, 315–332.

Hank, K., & Buber, I. (2009). Grandparents caring for their grandchildren findings from the 2004 survey of health, ageing, and retirement in Europe. *Journal of Family Issues, 30*(1), 53–73.

Hout, M., & Fischer, C. S. (2002). Why more Americans have no religious preference: Politics and generations. *American Sociological Review, 65*, 165–190.
Kalmijn, M. (2015). Family disruption and intergenerational reproduction: Comparing the influences of married parents, divorced parents, and stepparents. *Demography, 52*(3), 811–833.
Kemp, C. L. (2005). Dimensions of grandparent-adult grandchild relationships: From family ties to intergenerational friendships. *Canadian Journal on Aging/La Revue canadienne du vieillissement, 24*(02), 161–177.
King, V., & Elder, G. H., Jr. (1999). Are religious grandparents more involved grandparents? *Journal of Gerontology: Social Sciences, 54*, S317–S328.
Lampkin, C. L. (2012). *Insights and spending habits of modern grandparents*. Washington, DC: AARP: Research and Strategic Analysis. Retrieved from http://www.aarp.org/research
Lussier, G., Deater-Deckard, K., Dunn, J., & Davies, L. (2002). Support across two generations: children's closeness to grandparents following parental divorce and remarriage. *Journal of Family Psychology, 16*(3), 363.
Mare, R. D. (2011). A multigenerational view of inequality. *Demography, 48*(1), 1–23.
Michaleski, R. L., & Shackleford, T. K. (2005). Grandparental investment as a function of relational uncertainty and emotional closeness with parents. *Human Nature, 16*, 293–305.
Min, J., Silverstein, M., & Lendon, J. P. (2012). Intergenerational transmission of values over the family life course. *Advances in Life Course Research, 17*(3), 112–120.
Monserud, M. (2008). Intergenerational relationships and affectual solidarity between grandparents and young adults. *Journal of Marriage and Family, 70*, 182–195.
Mueller, M. M., & Elder, G. H. (2003). Family contingencies across the generations: Grandparent-grandchild relationships in holistic perspective. *Journal of Marriage and Family, 65*(2), 404–417.
Myers, S. M. (1996). An interactive model of religiosity inheritance: The importance of family context. *American Sociological Review, 61*, 858–866.
Pew Forum on Religion and Public Life. (2015). *US public becoming less religious*. Washington DC: Pew Research Center. Retrieved from http://pewforum.org/reports.
Putnam, R. D. (2000). *Bowling alone: The collapse and revival of American community*. New York: Simon and Schuster.
Rokeach, M. (1968). *Beliefs, attitudes and values: A theory of organization and change*. San Francisco: Jossey-Bass.
Roof, W. C. (1999). *Spiritual marketplace: Baby boomers and the remaking of American religion*. Princeton: Princeton University Press.
Rosenfeld, M. J. (2007). *The age of independence: Interracial unions, same-sex unions, and the changing American family*. Cambridge, MA: Harvard University Press.
Ruiz, S., & Silverstein, M. (2007). Relationships with grandparents and the emotional well-being of late adolescent and young adult grandchildren. *Journal of Social Issues, 6*, 793–808.
Schönpflug, U. (Ed.). (2008). *Cultural transmission: Psychological, developmental, social, and methodological aspects*. New York: Cambridge University Press.
Sherkat, D. E. (2003). Religious socialization: Sources of influence, influences of agency. In M. Dillon (Ed.), *Handbook of the sociology of religion* (pp. 151–163). Cambridge, MA: Cambridge University Press.
Silverstein, M., & Bengtson, V. L. (Forthcoming). How grandparents influence the religiosity of their grandchildren: A mixed methods study of three-generation American families. In V. Timonen (Ed.), *Grandparenting practices around the world*. Bristol: Policy Press.
Silverstein, M., & Giarrusso, R. (Eds.). (2013). *Kinship and cohort in an aging society: From generation to generation*. Baltimore: Johns Hopkins University Press.
Silverstein, M., & Marenco, A. (2001). How Americans enact the grandparent role. *Journal of Family Issues, 22*, 493–522.
Silverstein, M., & Ruiz, S. (2006). Breaking the chain: How grandparents moderate the transmission of maternal depression to their grandchildren. *Family Relations, 55*, 601–612.

Steinbach, A. (2013). Family structure and parent–child contact: A comparison of native and migrant families. *Journal of Marriage and Family, 75*(5), 1114–1129.
Swartz, T. T. (2009). Intergenerational family relations in adulthood: Patterns, variations, and implications in the contemporary United States. *Annual Review of Sociology, 35*, 191–212.
Uhlenberg, P. R. (2005). Historical forces shaping grandparent-grandchild relationships: Demography and beyond. In M. Silverstein (Ed.), *Intergenerational relations across time and place* (pp. 77–97). New York: Springer.
Uhlenberg, P., & Hammill, B. G. (1998). Frequency of grandparent contact with grandchild sets: Six factors that make a difference. *The Gerontologist, 38*(3), 276–285.
Wuthnow, R. (1988). *The restructuring of American religion: Society and faith since world war II.* Princeton: Princeton University Press.

Merril Silverstein is the Marjorie Cantor Endowed Professor in Aging, Maxwell School of Citizenship and Public Affairs and Falk College of Sport and Human Dynamics at Syracuse University. His areas of specialization include population aging, health and functioning, intergenerational family dynamics and relationships, and longitudinal methods.

Vern L. Bengtson is an emeritus member of the faculty at the Leonard Davis School of Gerontology at the University of Southern California and an adjunct professor at the USC School of Social Work. He is known for his pathbreaking studies of intergenerational relationships over time in the context of aging individuals and a changing society.

Part IX
Exploring the Potential of Social Networks as Mechanisms for Prevention

Chapter 20
A Life Course and Networks Approach to Prison Therapeutic Communities

Derek A. Kreager, Martin Bouchard, George De Leon, David R. Schaefer, Michaela Soyer, Jacob T. N. Young, and Gary Zajac

Life course criminology, the branch of the discipline aimed at understanding within-individual offending across time, has gained considerable traction over the past two decades (Blokland and Nieuwbeerta 2010; Osgood 2012; Wakefield and Apel 2016). Central interests for life course criminologists have been explaining if, why, and how offenders desist from crime as they age (Bushway and Paternoster 2013). Consistent with the broader life course perspective (Elder 1994, 1998), desistance researchers have focused much of their efforts on understanding how social role transitions (e.g., marriage, parenthood, and employment) coincide with crime deceleration or cessation (Sampson and Laub 2003). Implied in this literature is the

---

Authors following the first author contributed equally and are listed in alphabetical order. This research is supported by grants from the National Science Foundation (1457193) and National Institutes of Health (NIAAA 1R211AA023210-01A1). The content is solely the responsibility of the authors and does not necessarily represent the official views of the respective agencies. We thank Bret Bucklen and the Pennsylvania Department of Corrections administrative staff for their valuable support of this project.

D. A. Kreager (✉) · G. Zajac
Department of Sociology and Criminology, Pennsylvania State University, University Park, PA, USA
e-mail: dkreager@psu.edu

M. Bouchard
School of Criminology, Simon Fraser University, Burnaby, Canada

G. De Leon
Department of Psychiatry, New York University, New York, NY, USA

D. R. Schaefer
Department of Sociology, University of California, Irvine, CA, USA

M. Soyer
Department of Sociology, Hunter College, New York, NY, USA

J. T. N. Young
School of Criminology and Criminal Justice, Arizona State University, Tempe, AZ, USA

D. F. Alwin et al. (eds.), *Social Networks and the Life Course*, Frontiers in Sociology and Social Research 2, https://doi.org/10.1007/978-3-319-71544-5_20

life course tenet of linked lives, such that role transitions are accompanied by increased social embeddedness, which in turn has consequences for individual behavioral trajectories over time. More recent desistance theorists have expanded the area to emphasize another life course theme, human agency, arguing that offenders actively select themselves into social roles that create opportunities for identity transformation and criminal desistance (Maruna 2001; Giordano et al. 2002, 2007). Together, desistance theory and research have moved life course principles into mainstream criminology and motivated a spate of empirical research aimed at testing theory-driven hypotheses.

Although clearly contributing to criminological theory and research, it is less apparent how findings from desistance studies directly translate into effective social policy and crime intervention strategies. Desistance research commonly finds that serious offenders are unlikely to successfully transition to the roles most associated with desistance (King et al. 2007). Moreover, even when such offenders do manage to take on positive roles, the proposed mechanisms propelling the transitions (i.e., marriage, chance, "bottoming out", or personal revelation) appear outside of direct policy manipulation (Sampson and Laub 2003; Maruna 2001; Paternoster and Bushway 2009). The result is that most crime interventions associated with life course research, such as ex-inmate employment services and family counseling, have disappointing success rates and inevitably miss the population most at risk of recidivating (Bushway and Apel 2012; Visher et al. 2005).

An interesting exception to this pattern is the prison-based therapeutic community (TC), a substance abuse treatment modality aimed at identity transformation and reduced relapse risk through inclusive positive peer settings within controlled carceral settings (De Leon 2000; Stevens 2013). Prison TCs are able to enroll high-risk inmates into treatment because (1) TC completion can be a compulsory step toward parole (i.e., coercive control) and (2) the TC offers many inmates an attractive alternative to the general inmate population. Inmates unlikely to select themselves into positive social relationships outside of prison can nevertheless become embedded in such a community while confined. This exposure may then provide a "hook for change" (Giordano et al. 2002) and help explain why prison TCs, compared with other treatment modalities, demonstrate the most consistent reductions in post-release recidivism and drug relapse rates (Mitchell et al. 2012a, b).

In this paper, we connect TC philosophy and practice in prison settings with social network and life course principles. Specifically, we draw on the concept of linked lives and social network analysis to understand the mechanisms underlying prison TC effectiveness. In so doing, we build a research agenda for investigating and evaluating prison TCs that may also inform other network interventions. Finally, we demonstrate the feasibility and promise of such an approach with a pilot study conducted in a single TC housed in a men's maximum-security Pennsylvania prison.

Background

Mass imprisonment, the longstanding "War on Drugs," and the strong correlation between substance use and crime have created a drug crisis in American prisons. In the 2012 Arrestee Drug Abuse Monitoring Program (ONDCP 2013), over 60% of adult male arrestees tested positive for at least one drug. Rates of substance abuse in prison are similarly high, with over 50% of inmates in the 2004 Survey of Inmates in State and Federal Correctional Facilities meeting the DSM-IV criteria for drug dependence or abuse (Mumola and Karberg 2006). This survey also showed that one-third of state inmates were under the influence of drugs at the time of their most recent offense, and fully two-thirds were regular drug users. Moreover, prison-based efforts to treat drug-addiction remain incommensurate with inmate needs. It is estimated that only one in five inmates needing substance abuse treatment receive *any* form of treatment while imprisoned (Belenko and Peugh 2005). Mumola and Karberg (2006) found that while 39% of state and federal inmates who reported drug use in the month before their arrest participated in some sort of drug treatment while incarcerated, only 14% were treated in any sort of structured program facilitated by a trained professional, such as a therapeutic community. A large number of the over 600,000 inmates released from prison per year will therefore continue to struggle with substance dependency, resulting in increased recidivism, negative drug-related health consequences (e.g., overdose, infectious disease, malnutrition, etc.), and poor social integration. It is not surprising that the provision of evidence-based prison drug rehabilitation programming is a high priority for correctional policymakers and government health agencies alike (Steyee 2013; NIDA 2002).

The therapeutic community (TC) is a promising addiction treatment modality in prison contexts. Prison TCs are direct descendants of self-help organizations that emphasize drug abstinence through individual responsibility and group interaction (De Leon 2000; Perfas 2004). The axioms of TC theory, such as "community as method" and "you alone can do it, but you cannot do it alone," highlight the mutual self-aid and social learning principles at the heart of the TC approach (NIDA 2002). These principles are what distinguish TCs from more individualistic rehabilitation strategies, such as drug replacement or cognitive behavioral therapy (De Leon 2000). Prison TCs typically segregate drug-addicted inmates into adjoined living and working areas outside the general inmate population for periods of 3–12 months. Although there is some variation in the actual structure of prison TCs, they all share the philosophy that mutual aid between residents is the basis for successful treatment. Residents therefore share responsibility for monitoring and providing feedback for one another's behavior (De Leon 2000). Feedback from residents (directed at one another) typically consists of positive affirmations (termed "push-ups") for actions that are in accord with TC norms and corrections (termed "pull-ups") for behaviors inconsistent with TC norms (Warren et al. 2013a, b). In prison settings, "push-ups" and "pull-ups" are commonly recorded by peers, reviewed by staff, and discussed in group settings. Consistent with operant conditioning principles, "push-ups" and "pull-ups" should increase treatment engagement by extinguishing previously learned maladaptive behaviors and promoting behaviors consistent with a drug-free lifestyle (Akers 2009).

Changes in the number and content peer relations should also accompany the TC treatment process. TC theory views addicted persons as self-reliant, untrusting, and affiliated with criminal peers (De Leon 2000). These interrelated personal characteristics are modified in the TC through positive peer interactions, role-modeling, and group activities (Wexler and Prendergast 2010). Through TC participation, isolated individuals are expected to progress over time into trusting and respected community members willing to assist new TC residents. By recognizing the interdependence of their behavior and the duty to their peers, TC residents are expected to open themselves to meaningful social relationships and embed themselves into community norms and responsibilities.

The use of TCs in prisons is becoming widespread, with a 2007 nationwide prison survey finding that approximately 30% of state prisons provided some form of TC programming (Taxman et al. 2007). Moreover, experimental evaluations of TC effectiveness at reducing recidivism and drug relapse are encouraging, particularly when compared with alternative modalities. In the most comprehensive systematic review of incarceration-based drug treatment to date, Mitchell et al. (2012a, b) compared program effects (i.e., post-release recidivism and relapse) from 74 experimental and quasi-experimental evaluations conducted between 1980 and 2011. They concluded that, compared to counseling, narcotic replacement, and boot camp programs, "The most consistent evidence of treatment effectiveness came from evaluations of TC programs," and "Policymakers seeking effective interventions for incarcerated substance abusers are most likely to find success with programs that intensively focus on the multiple problems of substance abusers, such as TC programs" (Mitchell et al. 2012a, b: 30). These observed positive TC effects are consistent with TC-specific evaluations before and since (Bahr et al. 2012; Jensen and Kane 2012; Sacks et al. 2012; Welsh and Zajac 2013).

Incentivizing Prosocial Peer Integration

One reason why TCs may be effective in reducing recidivism is that they explicitly address a main challenge facing incarceration-based treatment programs – prison itself. Although incarcerated inmates commonly report that their confinement experience will place them on a positive behavioral trajectory, the structure and environment of prison are not conducive for lasting change (Soyer 2014). The coerciveness endemic to American prisons prevents inmates from acting creatively and autonomously, thereby reducing opportunities for substantive change. It is very difficult for offenders to experience a desired non-deviant identity through interactions with supportive pro-social others who can solidify this identity shift (Giordano et al. 2002). Unsurprisingly, ex-prisoners are often ill-equipped to maintain their desistance once they are confronted with inevitable disappointments and temptations post-release.

In contrast to the de-humanization and bureaucratization common to prison life, TCs are structured to enable identity shifts congruent with redemption and desistance. TCs operate as a network of peers, a community that reinforces positive behavioral patterns. What makes TC communities different from the prisons in which they are embedded is that their primary function is to help individuals with severe cognitive and behavioral disorders to *change themselves* (De Leon 2000). While prisons offer little opportunity for inmates to have a non-deviant identity verified by supportive others, TCs are explicitly designed to do so. The TC emphases on residential trust, community accountability, and shared experiences elevate peers as primary change agents.

TCs' reliance on trust and prosocial interactions may be risky propositions. Their effectiveness rests on active involvement in a positive peer community, but the inmates most in need of this treatment are, by definition, likely to be mistrustful of others and resist prosocial peers. As De Leon (2000: 60) states, "A lack, loss, or violation of trust is a distinctive marker of the substance abuser's personality and lifestyle." Most addicts' lives are littered with eroded or destroyed personal relationships, and coping strategies characterized by lying, exploitation, and denial further diminish the likelihood of establishing meaningful future relationships. Given conditions of past and present mistrust, how do prison TCs gain community members and subsequently foster positive peer engagement among those who agree to participate?

The answer to this question is that decisions to enter prison TCs do not necessitate or indicate inmates' desires for drug abstinence or community membership. Rather, inmates are likely to enter a TC as a condition for parole or to avoid chaotic, monotonous, or unsafe conditions in the general prison population (Maruna 2001; Stevens 2013). Recognizing that TC membership primarily stems from such "push" factors is important because these simultaneously explain how high-risk offenders enter a positive peer community and why they may not fully engage with treatment or community activities once they arrive. For example, an inmate who enters a TC only to meet parole board expectations may have little incentive to invest in his treatment and, if he graduates, have a relapse risk as high as when he entered. Alternatively, exposure to a positive community may alter the same inmate's outlook and identity in ways unimaginable if he had stayed in general population, making the TC experience a true life course turning point. For the typical resident, the TC experience may thus represent a "hook" for behavioral change, but grabbing this opportunity remains a highly uncertain affair. It is exactly this uncertainty that makes understanding the mechanisms at the core of TC effectiveness so important.

The above discussion parallels research on alternatives to incarceration for drug offenders, best exemplified by adult drug courts. Drug courts divert addicted offenders into alternative criminal justice programming that emphasizes extensive drug treatment, monitoring, and judicial discretion (Gonzales et al. 2006). Like prison TCs, offenders must agree to participate in drug court and the threat of sanctions (i.e., incarceration) is maintained throughout program completion. We argue that the coercive capacity of both programs increase the likelihood that high risk individuals take up the delivered treatment. As with TC research, large scale randomized trials have demonstrated strong effects of drug courts in reducing long term drug use and crime (Mitchell et al. 2012a, b; Rempel et al. 2012).

The above discussion is consistent with several life-course perspectives of criminal desistance, including Giordano et al.'s (2002) theory of cognitive transformation and Paternoster and Bushway's (2009) identity theory of desistance. For Giordano et al. (2002), prosocial relationships serve as "hooks for change" that offenders latch onto as they actively attempt to rewrite their personal narratives, transform their identities, and direct themselves on a path to desistance. Paternoster and Bushway's (2009) argument similarly relies on identity change to explain desistance, but emphasizes the subjective realization of the costs of offending as the mechanism for this transformation. Individuals must deliberately identify the "feared self" (what one does not want to be) and attempt to transition to a "possible self" (what one wants to and can become). For both theories, prosocial relationships between and among staff and residents in TCs provide daily verification and support of identify transformations. In particular, interactions among residents and staff provide a language and supportive framework for offenders to create their own redemption scripts. In these redemption scripts, residents' criminal pasts are not viewed as shameful or to be knifed off, but rather as necessary preludes to "going straight" or desisting from crime/substance abuse (Maruna 2001). Through the TC peer network, inmates are able to experience non-deviance as creative actors. Their non-deviant identities are anchored in social experiences rather than being solely cognitive or socially disconnected individual exercises. In this way, the environment of a TC is designed to empower residents to fundamentally change the ways in which they understand themselves, their offending histories, and their beliefs about life after prison (Stevens 2013). This theorized interaction between social structure and agency is highly consistent with both TC philosophy and the life course perspective.

A Network Approach

An approach explicitly focused on the structure and dynamics of relationships among prison TC residents is *necessary* for understanding the effectiveness of this treatment modality. Necessary because the treatment philosophy, goals, and their implementation are all inherently relational (i.e., focused on "linked lives") and because the peer-driven mechanisms associated with prison TC effectiveness remain untested (De Leon 2000; Mitchell et al. 2012a, b).

Approaching TC research from a network perspective acknowledges within-individual processes central to life course and desistance literatures, such as human agency and identity transformation, but gives equal emphasis to the social structure (or regular patterns of relationships) that empower and constrain individual behavior in a given context (Wellman and Berkowitz 1988). Applied to prison TCs, a network approach therefore focuses on the patterns of relationships among inmate residents themselves, and how those relationships co-evolve with treatment

Table 20.1 Network-based hypotheses derived from therapeutic community philosophy

Resident-Level
1. TC Residents should move from the periphery to the core of the unit network structure over time.
2. The number and strength of peer ties should increase as residents progress through treatment.
3. The ratio of peer affirmations to peer corrections should increase as residents progress through treatment.
4. Nominations of respect and influence should flow from residents early in the program to those later in the program.
5. Residents highly engaged in the treatment should be more influential and central in the TC network.
Unit-Level
1. TC networks should be cohesive with high friendship tie density.
2. TC networks should have high trust reciprocity.
3. TC networks should lack subgroups associated with non-TC characteristics (e.g., race, religion, hometown, etc.)
4. TC networks should be hieararchical, with senior residents shown greater respect and stronger peer influence than junior residents.
5. TC networks should have local instability, where residents change positions over time, but global stability, where community structure remains relatively stable over time.

outcomes (e.g., engagement, graduation, and desistance) over time (Kreager et al. 2016, 2017; Schaefer et al. 2017). Although residents regularly interact with staff, TCs are designed such that key mechanisms of change operate through residents' relationships with one another. Such relationships take many forms, including informal ties of friendship, trust, assistance, and respect. These kinds of ties constitute the informal "peer network" that is our primary focus. Other relational aspects of TCs include formal relationships created through pre-defined roles (e.g., peer leaders), and formalized interactions through the application of affirmations/corrections aimed at reinforcing program goals.

The network mechanisms underlying TC effectiveness are easily extracted directly from TC philosophy. We can thus generate testable hypotheses for how individual residents are expected to interact with the TC structure as they progress through treatment (i.e., inmate-level) and what the TC network should look like to facilitate resident identity transformation and long-term desistance (i.e., unit-level). Doing so helps to operationalize TC concepts using network measures and allows for analyses of the resulting data using network methods. Below, we first discuss resident-level network processes as they relate to De Leon's (2000) TC program stages (induction, primary treatment, and re-entry) and connect these with life course concepts of turning points and linked lives. We subsequently outline theoretically-driven hypotheses for unit-level network processes. We summarize these various hypotheses in Table 20.1.

Inmate-Level Network Dynamics

The TC program is implemented in phases that recognize residents' specific challenges and requirements as they progress through treatment. The overall (i.e., global) TC network structure is designed as a revolving hierarchy where junior residents replace senior residents as they move through the phases to eventual graduation. Ideally, the roles, structure, privileges, and processes of a TC remain stable over time, even though membership changes as residents transition through the system.

Induction The first stage of treatment "is to assimilate the individual into the community" as rapidly as possible (De Leon 2000: 196). This entails that peers introduce themselves to the inductee, the inductee is included in daily activities, he or she is provided a work assignment, and the community rules, structure, and norms are thoroughly explained. Connecting this process with network ideas, we would expect inmates entering a prison TC to initially be at the periphery of the unit's peer network structure, with few ties and relatively weak relationships. This marginal status should be magnified for inductees who generally mistrust others, which is often assumed to accompany addiction. They may have network ties based on preexisting relationships, for instance through serving time together before entering the TC, but fewer ties on average compared to more senior residents.

Primary Treatment As residents are gradually immersed in the unit structure and daily activities, "community expectations for the residents' full participation in all activities and roles increases, as does the intensity of group process and peer and staff counseling. Job functions become more complex, privileges grant wider latitude, and seminar content expands to address a wide variety of themes related to recovery and right living" (De Leon 2000: 199). The increased treatment engagement in this stage should be accompanied by stronger relationships with a broader set of fellow residents, resulting in movement from the periphery to the core of the TC social structure. By the completion of primary treatment, the individual should be in a position of respect among community members, which in network terms should correspond to receiving more positive tie nominations (e.g., friendship, trust, and respect) from others. In other words, residents in this stage should move from the periphery to the core of the community and interactions should shift from primarily receiving information and advice to primarily providing these resources. Relative to the induction stage, where the individual is expected to have more outgoing than incoming ties, during the primary treatment stage the ratio of incoming to outgoing ties should reach parity and, toward the end of the stage, the individual should have more incoming ties.

This shift may best be captured in changing patterns of peer affirmations ("pushups") and corrections ("pull-ups") as residents progress through treatment. Inmates entering the TC should receive peer corrections as they learn, and potentially resist, program rules. As in their entrance to the broader prison environment, incoming TC residents will tend to observe the behavior of others to get a feel for the setting

(Maruna 2001). As members familiarize themselves and begin to comply with unit rules, they should receive more affirmations and fewer corrections. As individuals identify the behavioral aspects of a "possible self" (what one wants to and can become Paternoster and Bushway 2009), residents should recognize problematic behavior and reward behavior consistent with identity transformation. Moreover, the sources of influence should change over time, such that residents will become increasingly responsible for unit administration and begin to "pay it forward" by shaping the attitudes and behaviors of new community members. By the completion of the primary treatment stage, residents should be highly influential for other residents' attitudes and behaviors and therefore the sources for the majority of sent affirmations and corrections.

Re-entry The goal of the final treatment stage is "to facilitate the individual's separation from the residential community and to complete his or her successful transition to the larger society" (De Leon 2000: 201). During this period, the resident should be increasingly exposed to his or her post-treatment context and helped to establish roles and social relationships in that future environment. Consistent with Maruna's (2001) "redemption script," the re-entry resident is expected to carry the TC philosophy outside of the unit and instruct others in need of help. Such actions keep the TC resident focused on his or her recovery and embedded in prosocial networks post-graduation. In network terms, the re-entry TC resident interacts less with other residents on a day-to-day basis and therefore is less central to the network structure, but is respected by others because he or she has completed the program and is now a role-model for right living.

Unit-Level Network Structure

The ability of individual residents to undergo the identity transformation associated with TC treatment depends on the unit fidelity to TC philosophy. A TC must exhibit several distinctive network features in order to establish and maintain the community norms essential for effective treatment. These include:

Connectedness The TC is a peer-based (vs. individualized) treatment approach. Thus, everyone in the TC should have relations with other TC residents. In network terms, this interconnectedness translates to a highly dense social structure.

Mutuality Given the explicit TC goal of helping residents to develop close, trusting peer relationships, unit networks should be characterized by a high degree of mutuality whereby both members of dyads reciprocate perceptions of trust.

Lack of Disconnected Communities Social networks often divide in subgroups or communities where ties are more concentrated within groups than between groups. Indeed, TCs explicitly foster "encounter groups" during primary treatment to provide a subgroup contexts for constructive peer influence. However, to avoid group solidification, clique formation, and the prioritization of group goals above those of the community, encounter groups should be interchangeable, ephemeral, and evolving in membership. As De Leon (2000: 173) states, "Although the TC fosters peer relating, it explicitly discourages permanent peer groupings because these potentially undermine the influence of the broader family or community." Thus, subgroups based on other shared characteristics, such as race, background, or criminal histories are assumed to be counter to effective treatment outcomes and discouraged. Instead, the TC network should form a single component in which everyone is at least indirectly connected to everyone else.

Hierarchy American prison TCs rely upon senior residents to mentor and guide newer residents. Thus, some hierarchy is inevitable and encouraged. However, all residents are allowed equal voice in contributing to how the TC is run. Accordingly, the network should be both cohesive (i.e., consist of a single network component with high tie density) and hierarchical, with respected senior residents at the center of the structure (Kreager et al. forthcoming; Moody and White 2003).

Global Stability and Local Instability Social networks are continuously in flux. This should especially be the case for TCs in their aim to discourage subgroups that detract from the TC mission. While members should be developing new, trusted ties throughout their TC tenure, ties should shift in the intensity or frequency with which they're enacted. Thus, while the overall structure and kinds of positions within the TC (e.g., inductee, primary treatment resident, and re-entry resident) should remain fairly consistent over time, the individuals occupying those positions should shift as residents progress through treatment.

Summarizing the above list, we expect the ideal prison TC to exhibit a loose core-periphery network structure. This network would consist of senior residents with social ties to both newer residents and to senior peers forming the core. The periphery would then consist of newer residents with fewer and weaker ties. The ties that newer residents do form should be with senior mentors who instruct, monitor, and sanction community norms. Late stage residents would also be loosely tied to the unit network, primarily through their relationships with the core members who they themselves mentored.

Overcoming Deleterious Network Tendencies

Several common network processes can undermine TC effectiveness and shift individual and unit-level network structure away from the theoretical ideal. Many of these can lead to subgroups or clustering within the network. First is homophily, which is the tendency to form relationships with others who are similar to oneself. This occurs because people often find it easier to get along with others when they have something in common, which promotes trust among those with limited prior interactions (McPherson et al. 2001). Homophily is one of the most common processes driving social network structure but one that is potentially problematic in the TC setting. Homophily along characteristics such as race, education, gang membership, or hometown can help to promote trust among TC residents, which is an explicit goal of treatment. However, such homophily may simultaneously undermine treatment goals because the resulting clustering on non-TC characteristics pulls the unit away from the community identity and shared norms. A well-functioning TC should thus *not* contain subgroups based on characteristics that are inconsistent with the TC. To resist the inevitable tendency toward homophily, TCs establish rules about shifting Encounter Group, bunk, and work assignments.

The second network process that may subvert TC effectiveness is transitivity, which refers to the tendency for individuals to form a relationship through a mutual friend. If A befriends B, and B befriends C, then A and C should also become friends. In the TC setting, we would expect that residents who are connected are likely to share connections to the same third parties. Like homophily, triad closure can have both positive and negative consequences for meeting TC goals. Triad closure can help overcome mistrust during early relationship stages and promote the types of close relationships at the core of the TC philosophy. Nevertheless, when only transitive ties form, then networks tend toward high levels of clustering where ties are concentrated within subgroups. In addition, transitivity can increase the prevalence of homophily (Wimmer and Lewis 2010). Thus, transitivity can also create the divided networks that TCs aim to avoid.

Third, entering a TC represents a sizeable transition in one's social and living context. People entering new, established social settings experience a lot of uncertainty and often reach out to other new entrants for social support. Two people entering a new social environment may turn to one another as they try to make sense of their new environment. The more new people enter an environment together and share the same experiences (e.g., formal orientations) we would expect them to form ties to one another. Such ties can be useful if they can develop into friendship, however they also run the risk of developing into subgroups that counter the group norms. New entrants may be skeptical of the new environment and the norms espoused therein and adopt an adverse or negative attitude. Such attitudes could be reinforced were new entrants to form their own subgroups. Thus, TCs should not have strong cohorts based upon the timing of residents' entry to the unit.

Social networks are also typically characterized by unequal distributions of ties among members. Some individuals are more "popular" as indicated by receiving more incoming ties (e.g., affirmations, friendship, or respect). To some extent this is expected as residents who have been in the TC longer have had more opportunity to develop relationships and should have more ties. Thus, popularity associated with tenure is not problematic. It is important to keep in mind that more popular individuals should theoretically wield greater influence over others. This could be beneficial for TC functioning if more popular residents buy into the program and project attitudes and principles aligned with the TC purpose. However, popularity could also have negative consequences. For instance, popular residents might resist TC values. Thus, an unequal degree distribution could be problematic if it is driven by something other than TC tenure or positive TC disposition.

The success of the TC rests on being able to overcome normative network processes, or at least keep them in check. TCs must foster relationships, but encourage residents to form relationships with different kinds of people (countering homophily). TCs must promote trust between members, yet counter the tendency toward closed networks that transitivity facilitates. TCs must also be run by residents, but avoid having power concentrated in the hands of those who deviate from TC goals. Balancing these tensions can pose several challenges and likely requires continuous monitoring.

Even if TC structure meets theoretical guidelines, individuals may not move through the program as desired. It is possible that mistrust is rooted too deep in some inmates, such that they never develop close, reciprocated relationships. Indeed, some of the primary motivations for entering the TC, such as the TC being a condition for parole or a strong desire to exit general population, do not require community investment or treatment engagement. Many residents may therefore seek to "skate" through the program. Alternatively, individuals may develop relationships, but prefer to remain in tight-knit groupings that revolve around goals unrelated to TC philosophy. Such individual and group deviations should be associated with low engagement, low likelihood of graduation, and high probability of relapse. They should also be easily discernable as outside the core structure of a TC unit.

Empirical Demonstration

The network approach to understanding prison TC effectiveness holds great promise for offender rehabilitation. To illustrate its feasibility we present preliminary findings from a cross-sectional pilot study of a TC in a maximum-security Pennsylvania men's prison. An inherent limitation of this study for understanding life course transitions is that we are unable to follow individual residents through the structural and cognitive transitions expected to accompany progress in the TC program. Analyses of TC network and peer influence dynamics is the next step in this project. Nonetheless, the current examination provides an important first step toward understanding TC network structure and allows us to evaluate if the structure conforms to theoretical expectations.

The selected TC housed 28 inmate residents and 2 peer leaders (i.e., TC graduates) in a bunkhouse setting covering a 16-week treatment period. During a single visit, project personnel outlined the study to all unit residents and explained that the survey was confidential and anonymous. Each resident was then provided an informed consent form, hardcopy survey, and unit roster. At their bunks, participating inmates filled out the informed consent form and survey and non-participating inmates sat quietly until the end of the administration period. Twenty residents (71% of the unit) handed in complete surveys.[1] Surveys took approximately 45 min to complete and all were completed within 1 h.

[1] In a parallel study of a prison work unit (n=21), a computer-assisted personal interview (CAPI) was administered with a response rate of 90% (see Kreager et al. 2016). We attribute the higher

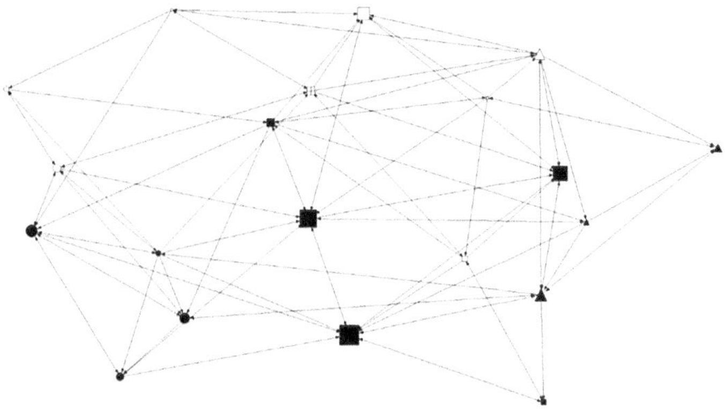

Fig. 20.1 Friendship in a prison therapeutic community (circle=new resident, square=intermediate resident, triangle=senior resident, white=white race, black=non-white race, size=number of received nominations)

To collect network information, we asked respondents to nominate unit peers that they "get along with most" (Schaefer et al. 2017). The number of nominations were restricted to 10 and, on average, inmates nominated 7 peers from the unit roster. The graph of this network is shown in Fig. 20.1. Node shapes indicate how long the residents had been in the TC (circle = 0–3 weeks, square = 4–12 weeks, and triangle = 13–16 weeks),[2] node size indicates the number of nominations each resident received from peers (larger = more nominations received), and node color indicates race (white = white, black = non-white). As can be seen, friendship ties were relatively dense (22% of possible ties were reported) and form one connected group. Of the participating residents, none was a social isolate, which is consistent with TC goals of maintaining an integrated community. Interestingly, the residents clearly cluster by their time in the program, such that new residents are more likely to get along with other new residents (left side of graph), senior residents are more likely to get along with other senior residents (right side of graph), and intermediate residents are more likely to get along with other intermediate residents (middle of graph). Due to their sandwiched status within the program, intermediate residents are also the most central to the network, receiving nominations both from new and senior-level residents, represented graphically by square nodes being larger than other nodes. The intermediate residents therefore hold strategic positions for monitoring and implementing TC activities. It is also clear from the graph that friendships cluster by race (whites are generally at the top of the graph and non-whites at the bottom), with 64% of friendship ties occurring within-race. This racial homophily is not surprising given prior network research (McPherson et al. 2001), but is incon-

response rate in that study to the one-on-one social interaction between inmate respondents and research personnel, elevating the perceived benefits of study participation from the inmates' perspectives.

[2] One respondent (shape = cross-hatch square) was missing TC duration.

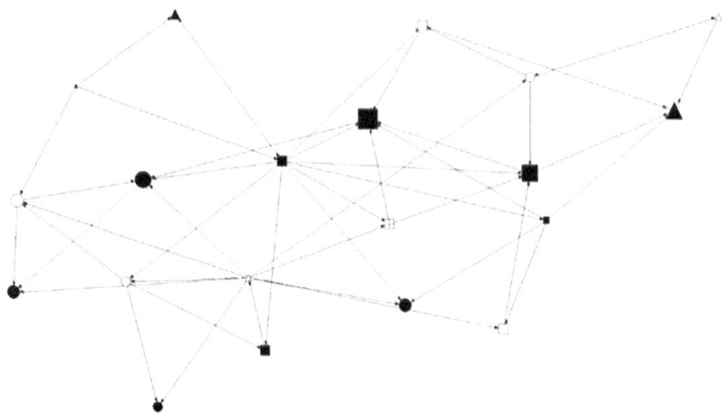

Fig. 20.2 Affirmations ("push-ups") in a prison therapeutic community (circle=new resident, square=intermediate resident, triangle=senior resident, white=white race, black=non-white race, size=number of received nominations)

sistent with TC theory as it raises concerns that racial allegiances could create obstacles to effective peer monitoring and sanctioning.

We also asked TC inmates to nominate peers to whom and from whom they sent and received affirmations (i.e., "push-ups") and corrections (i.e., "pull-ups") within 1 week of survey administration. Figure 20.2 presents the affirmation network and Fig. 20.3 presents the corrections network, with nodal attributes having the same meanings as those of Fig. 20.1. There were twice as many reported affirmations as corrections, which is similar to that found by Warren et al. (Warren et al. 2013a, b) and fits with the philosophy that social rewards are more effective than punishments for peer influence processes. Although friendship nominations generally stayed within treatment cohort, affirmations did not (Fig. 20.2). Specifically, senior inmates were more likely to send affirmations to junior residents, while the reverse was not true. The correlation between number of weeks in the program and sent affirmations was $r = .24$, whereas the correlation between number of weeks in the TC and affirmations received was $r = -.26$. In other words, those TC inmates with more experience in the program were more likely to recognize and reward behaviors consistent with TC goals exhibited by junior residents. This pattern both demonstrates the status that accompanies seniority and how TC norms are reinforced over time in the program.

The pattern of corrections (Fig. 20.3) appears quite different from affirmations. In particular, there is a clear aversion to sending corrections outside of one's program cohort. New residents (i.e., 3 weeks or less in the TC represented by circles in the graph) only sent corrections to other new residents. Intermediate residents (i.e., 4–12 weeks in TC, squares) also tended to send corrections to other intermediate residents, whereas only one of the five senior residents (13–16 weeks in TC, triangle) sent *any* corrections. Additionally, the correlation between number of weeks in the TC and sent corrections was $r = -.18$. Clearly, there is a reluctance to use corrections

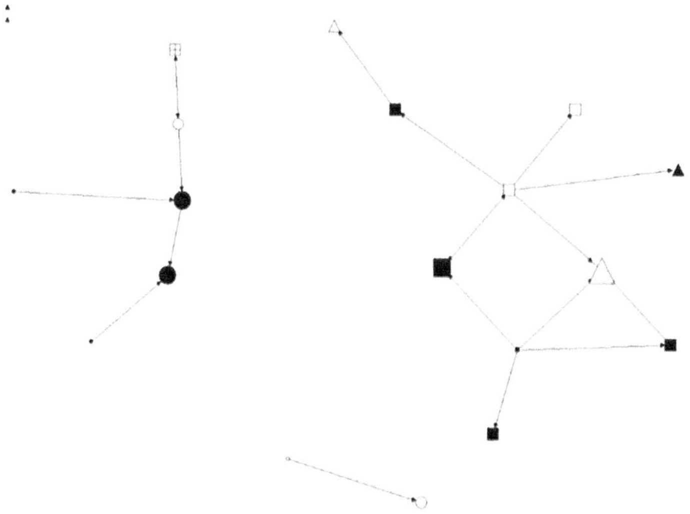

Fig. 20.3 Corrections ("pull-ups") in a prison therapeutic community (circle=new resident, square=intermediate resident, triangle=senior resident, white=white race, black=non-white race, size=number of received nominations)

as a treatment tool, particularly when these nominations span cohort boundaries or for those residents who have been in the program longer.

There is also a strong correlation between the friendship, affirmation, and correction networks. The TC residents tend to send affirmations to the same residents they get along with. The correlation between these matrices was $r = .26$. To a lesser extent, residents also sent corrections to those in their "get along with" network (matrix $r = .18$). These correlations (alongside a strong same-race preference) have implications for TC theory and practice because the clustering they represent may pose a barrier for the effective diffusion of community-wide treatment processes. If friendships, affirmations, and corrections are highly structured, then peer aid is not equally available to all TC residents.

Although clearly exploratory, our cross-sectional analyses of a single and small prison TC demonstrated the feasibility and promise of a network approach. We observed structural patterns, such as racial homophily and clustering of program corrections, that may subvert program goals. We also documented between-resident variation in structural position with the friendship, affirmation, and correction networks that may predict treatment engagement and success. Longitudinal network data collection and analyses are necessary to bear such predictions out and elucidate the social learning mechanisms at the heart of TC philosophy. We have already begun collecting such data in another prison and will estimate dynamic network models (e.g., SIENA; Snijders 1996) to uncover the peer influence and selection processes underlying TC engagement.

Discussion

Therapeutic communities receive strong support from evaluation research as effective approaches to reducing drug relapse and criminal recidivism. It would be tempting to point directly at the TC principles to explain their relative success. Yet, the truth is that therapeutic communities generate a complex set of interactions and changes among inmates that make the specification of the actual causal mechanisms underlying their success more challenging. Not all TCs are created equal, and not all of them are associated with higher than expected rates of success. As the NIDA director recently wrote, "Links between treatment elements, experiences, and outcomes need to be further studied to fully appreciate and enhance the contributions of TCs" (NIDA 2002). Delving into *why* TC treatment may or may not prove effective for drug abstinence will illuminate future avenues for measuring and improving program implementation, while also exploring which inmates benefit most from this treatment modality. From a life course perspective, we need to understand how the principles of linked lives and agency within TCs can create individual turning points in offending trajectories.

This manuscript outlines a research agenda that would provide a stronger test of the causal mechanisms responsible for lower rates of recidivism for at least some TC residents. Our interests lay both in the individual inmates and in the collective network they form within TCs. We argue that an analysis of social networks within TCs can help explain why some TCs, and some residents within a given TC, succeed where others fail. A network approach allows researchers to identity patterns in the social interactions among inmates that may both facilitate and hinder adherence to the TC principles.

Results from our pilot study suggest that some of the success of TCs may be rooted in the way in which TC inmates interact from the moment they enter the unit. Consistent with the community philosophy, we found all of the interviewed inmates were connected with at least one other resident. Additionally, we found evidence that senior residents are assuming leadership roles with regard to positive reinforcement (i.e., affirmation) of junior members. These findings support core concepts of the TC approach. However, we also found evidence that unit residents cluster by race, cohort, and peer affirmations/corrections, patterns which potentially frustrate communal goals and treatment norms. Without longitudinal data, treatment fidelity information, and observations across multiple TCs, we are reluctant to draw strong conclusions from our pilot study, but argue that this preliminary investigation demonstrates the feasibility and potential rewards of this line of inquiry. Future research in a similar vein will not only open new channels for understanding the connections between interventions and life course desistance processes, but also link these to the theory, data, and methods of the burgeoning domain of network science.

The ultimate question is how the changes individuals experience within the TC carryover outside the prison setting. In other words, does the TC intervention truly become a turning point toward desistance in the lives of ex-inmates? The peer relationships fostered within TCs will inevitably become unlinked as residents are released to the community. The TC philosophy is that residents will retain the skills and willingness to form close positive relationships, and be motivated and able to find peers who will support their continued identity transformation. Alternatively, TCs that fail to properly implement the TC philosophy, or residents who do not fully engage with the treatment, should not develop strong relationships inside or outside of prison and thus have higher rates of relapse and recidivism. The ability of a network approach to document and distinguish this variation makes it an essential tool for understanding TCs and the life course.

Finally, network processes underlying prison TCs may hold implications for understanding other behavioral interventions or socialization contexts. The idea of reference groups as influential in promoting lasting change has a long tradition within life course research. For example, Newcomb's (1952) famous Bennington Study located changes in a sample of young women's sociopolitical attitudes in the liberal contexts of a college community (see Alwin et al. 1991). Consistent with social learning expectations, significant others in the young women's college-based networks were argued to promote attitudinal change, becoming life course turning points with long-lasting effects. The current study adds to such lines of research ideas of how such communities can be deliberately established to intervene in individual trajectories and how social network theory and methods may help us to understand and evaluate peer influence processes.

References

Akers, R. L. (2009). *Social learning and social structure: A general theory of crime and deviance*. New Brunswick: Transaction Publishers.

Alwin, D. F., Cohen, R. L., & Newcomb, T. M. (1991). *Political attitudes over the life span: The Bennington women after 50 years*. Madison: University of Wisconsin Press.

Bahr, S. J., Masters, A. L., & Taylor, B. M. (2012). What works in substance abuse treatment programs for offenders? *The Prison Journal, 92*(2), 155–174.

Belenko, S., & Peugh, J. (2005). Estimating drug treatment needs among state prison inmates. *Drug and Alcohol Dependence, 77*(3), 269–281.

Blokland, A. A. J., & Nieuwbeerta, P. (2010). Considering criminal continuity: Testing for heterogeneity and state dependence in the association of past to future offending. *The Australian and New Zealand Journal of Criminology, 43*(3), 526–556.

Bushway, S. D., & Apel, R. (2012). A signaling perspective on employment-based reentry programming. *Criminology & Public Policy, 11*(1), 21–50.

Bushway, S. D., & Paternoster, R. (2013). Desistance from crime: A review and ideas for moving forward. In C. L. Gibson & M. D. Krohn (Eds.), *Handbook of life-course criminology* (pp. 213–231). New York: Springer.

De Leon, G. (2000). *The therapeutic community: Theory, model, and method*. New York: Springer Publishing.

Elder, G. H. (1994). Time, human agency, and social change: Perspectives on the life course. *Social Psychology Quarterly, 57*(1), 4–15.

Elder, G. H. (1998). The life course as developmental theory. *Child Development, 69*(1), 1–12.

Giordano, P. C., Cernkovich, S. A., & Rudolph, J. L. (2002). Gender, crime, and desistance: Toward a theory of cognitive transformation. *American Journal of Sociology, 107*(4), 990–1064.

Giordano, P. C., Schroeder, R. D., & Cernkovich, S. A. (2007). Emotions and crime over the life-course: A neo-meadian perspective on criminal continuity and change. *American Journal of Sociology, 112*(6), 1603–1661.

Gonzales, A. R., Schofield, R. B., & Schmitt, G. R. (2006). *Drug courts: The second decade*. Washington, DC: U.S. Department of Justice, Office of Justice Programs.
Jensen, E. L., & Kane, S. L. (2012). The effects of therapeutic community on recidivism up to four years after release from prison: A multisite study. *Criminal Justice and Behavior, 39*(8), 1075–1087.
King, R. D., Massoglia, M., & MacMillan, R. (2007). The context of marriage and crime: Gender, the propensity to marry, and offending in early adulthood. *Criminology, 45*(1), 33–65.
Kreager, D. A., Schaefer, D. R., Bouchard, M., Haynie, D. L., Wakefield, S., Young, J., & Zajac, G. (2016). Toward a criminology of inmate networks. *Justice Quarterly, 33*(6), 1000–1028.
Kreager, D. A., Young, J. T. N., Haynie, D. L., Bouchard, M., Schaefer, D. R., & Zajac, G. (2017). Where 'old heads' prevail: Inmate hierarchy in a men's prison unit. *American Sociological Review, 82*(4), 685–718.
Maruna, S. (2001). *Making good: How ex-convicts reform and build their lives*. Washington, DC: American Psychological Association Books.
McPherson, M., Smith-Lovin, L., & Cook, J. M. (2001). Birds of a feather: Homophily in social networks. *Annual Review of Sociology, 27*(1), 415–444.
Mitchell, O., MacKenzie, D. L., & Wilson, D. (2012a). The effectiveness of incarceration-based drug treatment on criminal behavior: A systematic review. *Campbell systematic reviews, 8*(18).
Mitchell, O., Wilson, D. B., Eggers, A., & MacKenzie, D. L. (2012b). Assessing the effectiveness of drug courts on recidivism: A meta-analytic review of traditional and non-traditional drug courts. *Journal of Criminal Justice, 40*(1), 60–71.
Moody, J., & White, D. R. (2003). Structural cohesion and embeddedness: A hierarchical concept of social groups. *American Sociological Review, 68*(1), 103–127.
Mumola, C. J., & Karberg, J. C. (2006). *Drug use and dependence, state and federal prisoners, 2004*. Washington, DC: U.S. Dept. of Justice, Office of Justice Programs, Bureau of Justice Statistics.
National Institute on Drug Abuse (NIDA). (2002). Research report series: Therapeutic community. http://archives.drugabuse.gov/researchreports/Therapeutic/. Accessed 20 Jan 2016.
Newcomb, T. M. (1952). Attitude development as a function of reference groups: The Bennington study. In G. E. Swanson, T. M. Newcomb, & E. L. Hartley (Eds.), *Readings in social psychology* (pp. 420–430). New York: Henry Holt.
Office of National Drug Control Policy (ONDC). (2013). *2012 Annual report, arrestee drug abuse monitoring program II*. Washington, DC: Executive Office of the President.
Osgood, D. W. (2012). Some future trajectories for life course criminology. In R. Loeber & B. C. Welsh (Eds.), *The future of criminology* (pp. 3–10). Oxford: Oxford University Press.
Paternoster, R., & Bushway, S. D. (2009). Desistance and the "feared self": Toward an identity theory of criminal desistance. *Journal of Criminal Law and Criminology, 99*(4), 1103–1156.
Perfas, F. B. (2004). *Therapeutic community: Social systems perspective*. Lincoln: iUniverse Inc.
Rempel, M., Zweig, J. M., Lindquist, C. H., Roman, J. K., Rossman, S. B., & Kralstein, D. (2012). Multi-site evaluation demonstrates effectiveness of adult drug courts. *Judicature, 95*(4), 154.
Sacks, J. Y., Sacks, S., Chaple, M., McKendrick, K., & Cleland, C. M. (2012). Randomized trial of a reentry modified therapeutic community for offenders with co-occurring disorders: Crime outcomes. *Journal of Substance Abuse Treatment, 42*(3), 247–259.
Sampson, R. J., & Laub, J. H. (2003). Desistance from crime over the life course. In J. T. Mortimer & M. J. Shanahan (Eds.), *Handbook of the life course* (pp. 295–309). New York: Springer.
Schaefer, D. R., Bouchard, M., Young, J. T. N., & Kreager, D. A. (2017). Friends in locked places: An investigation of prison inmate network structure. *Social Networks, 51*, 88–103.
Snijders, T. A. (1996). Stochastic actor-oriented models for network change. *Journal of mathematical sociology, 21*(1–2), 149–172.
Soyer, M. (2014). The imagination of desistance: A juxtaposition of the construction of incarceration as a turning point and the reality of recidivism. *British Journal of Criminology, 54*(1), 91.
Stevens, A. (2013). *Offender rehabilitation and therapeutic communities: Enabling change the TC way*. Abingdon: Routledge.
Steyee, J. (2013). *Program performance report: Joint/enhancement grantees of the adult drug court discretionary grant program*. Washington, DC: Bureau of Justice Assistance, U.S. Department of Justice.

Taxman, F. S., Perdoni, M. L., & Harrison, L. D. (2007). Drug treatment services for adult offenders: The state of the state. *Journal of Substance Abuse Treatment, 32*(3), 239–254.
Visher, C. A., Winterfield, L., & Coggeshall, M. B. (2005). Ex-offender employment programs and recidivism: A meta-analysis. *Journal of Experimental Criminology, 1*(3), 295–316.
Wakefield, S., & Apel, R. (2016). Criminal justice and the life course. In M. J. Shanahan, J. T. Mortimer, & M. K. Johnson (Eds.), *Handbook of the life course* (pp. 301–319). New York: Springer.
Warren, K. L., Doogan, N., De Leon, G., Phillips, G. S., Moody, J., & Hodge, A. (2013a). Short-run prosocial behavior in response to receiving corrections and affirmations in three therapeutic communities. *Journal of Offender Rehabilitation, 52*(4), 270–286.
Warren, K. L., Hiance, D., Doogan, N., De Leon, G., & Phillips, G. S. (2013b). Verbal feedback in therapeutic communities: Pull-ups and reciprocated pull-ups as predictors of graduation. *Journal of Substance Abuse Treatment, 44*(4), 361–368.
Wellman, B., & Berkowitz, S. D. (1988). *Social structures: A network approach.* Cambridge: Cambridge University Press.
Welsh, W. N., & Zajac, G. (2013). A multisite evaluation of prison-based drug treatment: Four-year follow-up results. *The Prison Journal, 93*(3), 251–271.
Wexler, H. K., & Prendergast, M. L. (2010). Therapeutic communities in United States' prisons: Effectiveness and challenges. *Therapeutic Communities, 31*(2), 157–175.
Wimmer, A., & Lewis, K. (2010). Beyond and below racial homophily: ERG models of a friendship network documented on facebook. *American Journal of Sociology, 116*(2), 583–642.

Derek A. Kreager is Professor of Sociology, Criminology, and Demography at Pennsylvania State University, Research Associate in the Population Research Institute, and Director of the Justice Center for Research. His research focuses on social networks and criminal/delinquent behavior, including the connection between the experiences of incarceration and community re-entry.

Martin Bouchard is a Professor in the School of Criminology, and the Director of the International CyberCrime Research Centre, Simon Fraser University, British Columbia. His areas of specialization include cybercrime, social networks, street gangs, organized crime, and illicit markets.

George De Leon is a Clinical Professor in the Department of Psychiatry, and Director of the Center for Therapeutic Community Research, New York University School of Medicine. He is a pioneer in the development of the therapeutic community framework and conducts research on the effectiveness of TCs.

David R. Schaefer is an Associate Professor in the Department of Sociology, University of California at Irvine. His research is centered on social networks, with emphases on health, adolescence, and delinquent populations. He investigates how social networks impact critical developmental and health-related outcomes, as well as how people acquire their respective network positions.

Michaela Soyer is an Assistant Professor in the Department of Sociology, Hunter College, and a former post-doctoral fellow at the Justice Center for Research at Pennsylvania State University. Her work focuses on delinquency, incarceration, inmate networks, re-entry and recidivism.

Jacob T. N. Young is Associate Professor in the School of Criminology and Criminal Justice at Arizona State University. He is interested in how the structure of social relations affects the diffusion of information, beliefs, norms and influence on outcomes related to delinquency and health.

Gary Zajac is a director at the Justice Center for Research at Pennsylvania State University. His main interest is in promoting research into criminal justice policy and practice.

Chapter 21
Impact of School-Based Prevention Programs on Friendship Networks and the Diffusion of Substance Use and Delinquency

Kelly L. Rulison, Scott D. Gest, Mark Feinberg, and D. Wayne Osgood

The overall aim of the present volume is to show how social network research is relevant to life course studies in terms of the theme of "linked lives," which is one of the core elements of the life course perspective articulated by Glen Elder (1998). Our chapter implements this aim by focusing on linked lives in the form of school-based friendship networks from middle school through early high school and their role in prevention programs. These programs bring an additional intersection with a life course perspective because they are designed to create a turning point at which adolescents' developmental trajectories will shift away from problem behaviors such as substance use and delinquency. The dynamic interplay between peer networks and problem behavior is a natural component of a life course perspective on the development of problem behaviors (Elder 1998; Sampson and Laub 1997), and peer networks loom large at this point of the life course for the U.S. and other western cultures. The developmental transition from classroom-based elementary school settings to larger middle school and high school settings brings substantial increases

K. L. Rulison (✉)
Department of Public Health Education, University of North Carolina at Greensboro, Greensboro, NC, USA
e-mail: klruliso@uncg.edu

S. D. Gest
Department of Human Development and Family Studies, Pennsylvania State University, State College, PA, USA

M. Feinberg
Bennett Pierce Prevention Research Center, Pennsylvania State University, State College, PA, USA

D. W. Osgood
Department of Sociology and Criminology, Pennsylvania State University, University Park, PA, USA

D. F. Alwin et al. (eds.), *Social Networks and the Life Course*, Frontiers in Sociology and Social Research 2, https://doi.org/10.1007/978-3-319-71544-5_21

in the size and complexity of peer networks (Brown and Dietz 2009) and related changes in the culture of schooling (Eccles and Roeser 2011). These increasingly complex peer networks, typically measured in terms of the friendship connections or "ties" that exist among youth, constitute a setting in which individual adolescents select particular friends who in turn expose them to potentially new attitudes and behaviors. Clarifying the interplay between these changing peer networks and problem behavior across adolescence is thus consistent with a life course emphasis on the joint influence of individual agency and social structure across major life transitions (Elder 1998).

Considerable theory and research support the assertion that adolescent substance use and delinquency are embedded within school-based friendship networks (Burgess and Akers 1966; Dishion et al. 1995; Rulison et al. 2015c). Moreover, developmental researchers have clarified the relative strength of peer selection and influence processes and have applied social network analysis to examine how problem behavior spreads, or diffuses, through peer networks (Dishion 2013; Veenstra et al. 2013), though causal inferences are constrained by reliance on non-experimental research designs. Conversely, prevention researchers have implemented experimental studies to support strong causal claims about the beneficial impact of prevention programs on individuals' behaviors (e.g., substance use initiation; Tobler et al. 2000), but insights into how peers contribute to such effects are constrained by the absence of friendship network measures in most experimental studies.

Evaluations of prevention programs implemented in the middle school years provide a unique opportunity to clarify the dynamic interplay between peer networks and problem behavior. Most prevention programs are designed to induce change at the individual level, but participants are drawn from school populations of students who have abundant opportunities for interaction. Thus, participants are embedded in peer networks that may function as a social medium through which non-participants are nonetheless exposed to its messages and effects. Documenting the spread, or diffusion, of such messages and effects and clarifying the conditions under which these diffusion processes occur in adolescence brings specificity to the linked lives and turning point themes, in the context of the general life course theory perspective that individuals both act on and are constrained by their social settings (Elder 1998; Sampson and Laub 1997).

The PROSPER Peers project was designed to leverage social network methods and measures to clarify the role of friendship networks in the impact of a community-level randomized field trial intended to reduce adolescent substance use. In an effort to begin to integrate the traditionally separate literatures of social network analysis and prevention science, we have argued that concepts and tools from social network analysis can be used to enhance our understanding of the initial impact of substance use prevention efforts (Gest et al. 2011). The goal of this chapter is to provide an overview of the PROSPER Peers project's conceptual framework regarding peers and prevention and then to summarize what we have learned about the interplay between adolescents' social networks and prevention effects on problem behavior.

Substance Use Prevention Efforts and School-Based Friendship Networks

Concepts and measures from social network analysis have great potential to contribute to the development and evaluation of school-based substance use prevention programs. Social network measures are most obviously relevant to developing and assessing intervention effects in programs that directly seek to reorganize peer interaction patterns. For example, interventions that are intended to cultivate more positive classroom peer communities through classroom meetings (Battistich et al. 2000) or cooperative learning activities (Stevens and Slavin 1995) might enhance the density and cohesion of positive sentiments among students. Network measures are also relevant to interventions that seek to promote individual-level change among all individuals within a setting. For example, by teaching all students social-emotional skills (e.g., understanding and regulating emotions, social problem-solving), some interventions seek both to reduce the behavioral risk of individual students and cultivate a more benign peer socialization environment for all students (CPPRG 1999). Such widespread individual-level changes may be associated with shifts in network processes such as the behavioral bases of friendship formation (i.e., which individuals are selected as friends), the distribution of social status, and the potential for positive and negative peer influence.

School-based substance use prevention programs typically adopt a similar strategy of promoting individual-level change among all students in a school. For example, Life Skills Training (LST; Botvin and Griffin 2004) is a school-based intervention often implemented in middle school health classes. The curriculum promotes knowledge of the consequences of drug use and builds competencies for coping with normative adolescent stressors. Multiple experimental studies demonstrate that LST is associated with slower growth in the use of substances across the secondary school years (Botvin and Griffin 2004), and our program of research seeks to go beyond previous studies by determining whether favorable changes in peer networks (i.e., fewer substance-using friends) may help sustain the positive initial individual effects.

Family-based substance use prevention programs also focus on promoting individual-level change in early adolescence. These programs are frequently offered to all parents of adolescents attending a particular school or participating in a community organization, though only a fraction of the eligible families participate (Heinrichs et al. 2005; Spoth and Redmond 2002). For example, the Strengthening Families Program: For Parents and Youth 10–14 (SFP 10–14; Molgaard et al. 1997) uses the slogan "Love and Limits" to capture its dual emphasis on promoting positive parent-adolescent relationships (e.g., compliments, communication skills) and appropriate levels of control (e.g., rules, monitoring, and consequences). Intent-to-treat analyses of experimental studies with school-level randomization demonstrated that the program dampened the growth of substance use in subsequent years, with effects maintained 10 years past baseline (Spoth et al. 1999, 2012, 2004b). From a peer network perspective, a particularly intriguing finding from this study is that students who attended schools where the program was offered, but whose families did not themselves complete the program, also showed dampened trajectories of substance use compared to similar students at schools where the program was not offered (Spoth et al. 2001). The authors suggested that the intervention effects may have diffused through contact between intervention participants and their nonintervention peers, but they did not have the data to test specific hypotheses about the extent to which social networks supported diffusion. Our program of research has addressed this possible avenue by which prevention programs my produce extended benefits.

The paper presenting out conceptual approach (Gest et al. 2011) distinguished between two different ways that substance use prevention programs may impact peer networks. First, interventions may impact the structural organization of social ties without regard to individual attributes. For example, interventions may affect the density, reciprocity, transitivity or centralization of friendship ties, or overall network cohesion (Moody and White 2003). Second, interventions may impact the behavioral dynamics linking network positions with individual behaviors through one of three different social processes. One process is peer selection based on behavioral norms. In this case, substance use prevention programs may reduce the social attractiveness of peers who use drugs by promoting anti-drug attitudes (Osgood et al. 2013). This process is depicted in Fig. 21.1. In Network A, there is strong potential for substance use to diffuse through the network because the individuals with highest influence potential (i.e., highest network centrality) are substance users. By contrast, in Network B there is weak potential for substance use to diffuse because the individuals with the highest influence potential are non-users. A second process is peer selection based on behavioral similarity, in which adolescents seek friendships with peers who are similar to themselves. In this case, there is no clear reason that prevention programs should either seek to increase or decrease the tendency for adolescents to befriend similar peers, for this process would reinforce rather than alter existing behavioral tendencies. A third process is peer influence, in which adolescents become more similar to their friends over time. The strength of this influence should determine the extent to which problem behaviors diffuse through the social network.

Notably, these same peer influence processes may shape whether intervention effects diffuse from intervention participants to non-participants. Building on diffusion of innovation theory (Rogers 2003; Valente 2010), we have identified features of adolescent friendship networks that may enhance or inhibit the diffusion of intervention effects (Rulison et al. 2015a. b). At the network level, past literature suggests that diffusion of program effects is most likely in networks that are richly interconnected, less cliquish, less hierarchical, and in which program participants are broadly distributed throughout the network (rather than all friends with each other). At the individual level, diffusion of program benefits should most affect non-participants with the most extensive connections to peers who participated in the intervention. If the intervention strongly affects participants' attitudes and behaviors, they will provide a distinctive peer context to the non-participants who choose them as friends. This distinctive peer context will in turn shape the attitudes and behaviors of the non-participants.

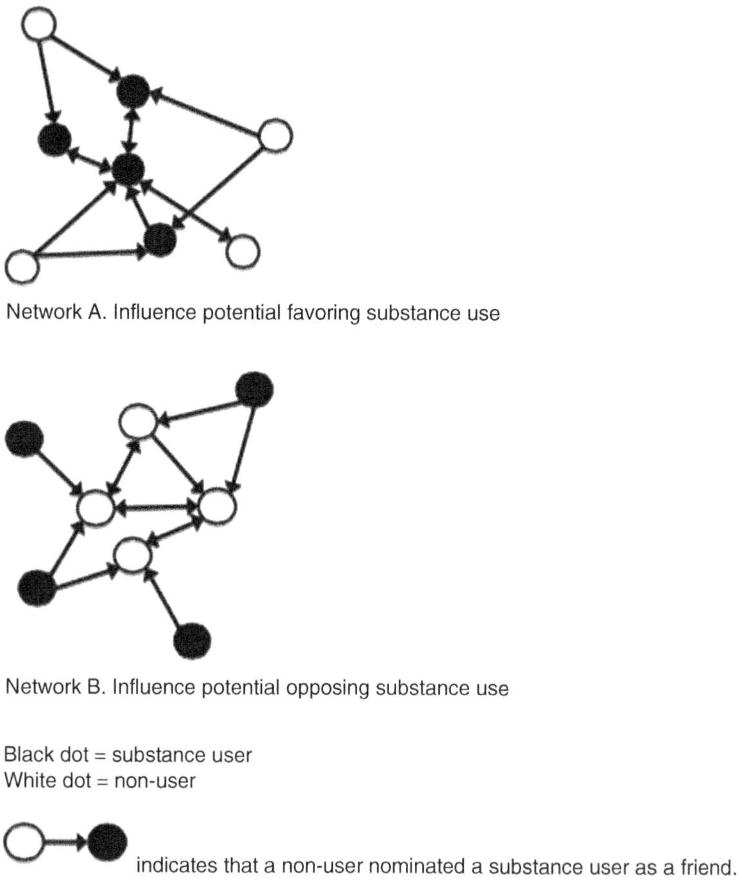

Fig. 21.1 Networks with different antisocial influence potential
Note: Reprinted with permission from Osgood et al. (2013)

By collecting social network data within the context of a larger randomized intervention trial, the PROSPER Peers project permits a strong test of hypotheses about how substance use interventions delivered during middle school can shape social networks and how these networks can in turn shape behavior. Below, we briefly describe the design of the PROSPER Peers project. We then describe some of the project's main findings concerning the role of adolescents' friendship networks in prevention programs, including how the PROSPER interventions affected friendship formation with antisocial adolescents and how network diffusion processes may contribute to program effects.

PROSPER Peers Project: Design & Measures

The PROmoting School-Community-University Partnerships to Enhance Resilience (PROSPER) Prevention Study (Spoth et al. 2004a, 2007b, 2011) is a randomized control trial conducted in 28 communities in Pennsylvania and Iowa (14 in each state). All communities were rural or semirural with at least 15% of families eligible for free or reduced-cost school lunches. After blocking districts by state, geographic area, and district size, one district of each blocked pair was randomly assigned to the intervention condition and the other to serve as a "usual practice" control. Two consecutive grade cohorts within each community participated in the study, beginning in 2001. The intervention districts implemented a universal family-focused intervention during sixth grade and a universal school-based intervention during seventh grade. As part of PROSPER, students in both cohorts were assessed in fall 6th grade (pre-intervention) and then each spring from 6th grade to 12th grade (all postbaseline). The body of work that we summarize in this chapter uses data from the first five waves (Fall 6th grade through spring 9th grade). Participation rates across these five waves ranged from 86% to 90%, with about 11,000 students completing surveys at each wave.

The PROSPER Peers Project (Osgood et al. 2013) was initiated to conduct detailed analyses of friendship network data collected as part of the PROSPER project. At each wave, students named up to two best friends and five additional close friends in their current grade and school. About 94% of survey respondents provided friendship nominations and we successfully matched 83% of the named friends to the class roster (across waves, we matched M = 4.37 to 4.92 names per respondent). At each wave, we defined separate friendship networks for each cohort at each school. A single school served each district in 9th grade, although eight of the 28 districts had multiple schools prior to 9th grade. As a result, there were 256 unique postbaseline school-, cohort-, and wave-specific networks, through 9th grade.

Interventions Each school district that was randomly assigned to the intervention condition created a community-based prevention team, led by a local university Cooperative Extension educator and based on the PROSPER Partnership Model (Spoth et al. 2004a; Spoth and Greenberg 2011). Each PROSPER team chose a family-based program (6th grade) and a school-based program (7th grade) from a menu of evidence-based options. For the family-based program, all 14 teams selected SFP10–14 (Molgaard et al. 1997). All parents of 6th grade students were invited to participate in SFP10–14; after extensive recruitment efforts 17% of families did so (Spoth et al. 2007a). During 7th grade, intervention communities chose one of three similar interventions that teachers delivered to all students in regular classes. The core logic of the three programs is more similar than different in that all address social norms, personal goal setting, decision-making, and peer group affiliation, and all share an interactive approach. Independent observations showed consistently high implementation quality.

Key Measures At each wave, students answered questions about their friendships, substance use, delinquency, attitudes, and family experiences.

PROSPER Impact on Substance Use in Adolescence

The relevance of the PROSPER Peers project for examining the role of friendship networks in prevention programming is greatly enhanced by solid evidence that PROSPER had beneficial effects on its intended outcomes. Specifically, a series of evaluations using intent-to-treat analyses (Spoth et al. 2011, 2013) demonstrated that PROSPER was associated with lower rates of substance use across adolescence, including lower past month use, frequency of use, and lifetime use across a range of substances (e.g., alcohol, tobacco, marijuana, inhalants, methamphetamines). For example, in 11th grade, students in intervention communities reported less past month use of cigarettes, marijuana, and amphetamines; and less frequent drunkenness and marijuana use. Overall, rates of growth in illicit substance use from 6th to 12th grades were significantly lower in intervention communities so that by 12th grade, lifetime use of illicit substances was 15% lower among students in the intervention communities compared to students in the control communities. These findings support the conclusion that the combination of interventions in PROSPER significantly affected substance use through the end of 12th grade (Spoth et al. 2013). Given these significant main effects of PROSPER, a detailed examination of potentially related changes in adolescent friendship networks would contribute to our understanding of intervention processes and effects.

PROSPER Impact on Prosocial Influence-Potential

The PROSPER Peer project's first empirical study of peers and prevention examined whether PROSPER altered adolescents' friendship networks toward reducing the potential for influence toward substance use (Osgood et al. 2013). We reasoned that when the social norms in a particular context support a behavior, adolescents who engage in that behavior would be more popular among their peers, and thus in a better position to influence their peers. We labeled the potential to influence others based on positional network features an actor's "influence potential." We hypothesized that PROSPER would change the behavioral dynamics of peer networks such that in intervention communities, the influence potential of prosocial students would increase relative to the influence potential of students who displayed problem behavior (see Fig. 21.1). Because students who are more centrally located in a network (e.g., receive more friendship nominations; connect pairs of other students) should have more influence potential, we examined whether the intervention networks had a relatively greater proportion of prosocial students in more central positions. To test this hypothesis, for each of the 256 school-cohort-wave networks, we determined the association of problem behavior with network centrality, which we measured as the bivariate regression coefficient, computed across the students in that network. These regression coefficients served as a network-level outcome measure.

In our analyses, we used three different measures of problem behavior: a substance use measure (based on frequency of smoking cigarettes, drinking alcohol, getting drunk and using marijuana in the past month), a substance use attitudes measure (based on 22 items) and a delinquency measure (based on 12 items). In addition, we created a single composite score of these three measures. We used six different indices of network centrality (degree, closeness, reach, betweenness, Bonacich and information), along with a composite centrality index.

We found that PROSPER significantly reduced antisocial influence potential in adolescent friendship networks, whether measured for incoming ties (i.e., being named as a friend by someone else) or undirected ties (ignoring which student did the nominating). As hypothesized, antisocial youth tended to become less central within friendship networks in intervention communities compared to the centrality of antisocial youth in control communities (see Fig. 21.2, illustrating the relationship between the composite undirected centrality and composite problem behavior measures). When we ran all 48 individual comparisons (6 centrality measures × 2 types of ties × 4 problem behavior measures), results were in the hypothesized direction in 47 cases and significant ($p < 0.05$) in 26 cases. These findings suggest an important mechanism that may account for the sustained effects of adolescent substance use prevention programs. Namely, these interventions appear to modify the behavioral dynamics of peer networks such that antisocial youth come to occupy somewhat less influential social positions, thus reducing the likelihood that antisocial behavioral will diffuse through these networks.

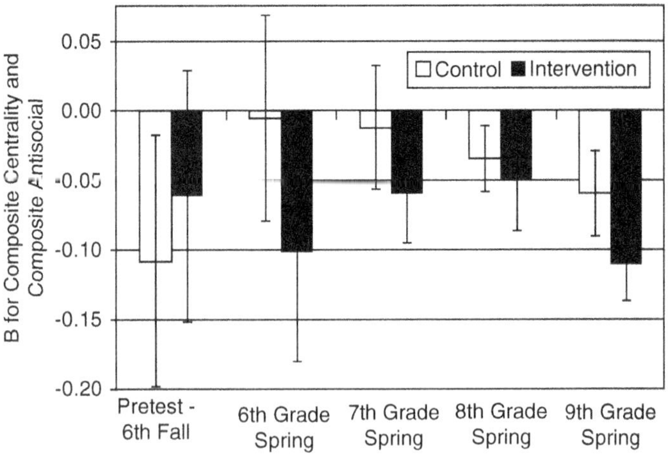

Fig. 21.2 Intervention and control means by wave for the association of composite undirected centrality with composite antisocial orientation
Note: Reprinted with permission from Osgood et al. (2013)

In sum, these analyses demonstrate that evidence-based prevention programs can alter adolescents' friendship networks in ways expected to reduce influence potential and thus reduce the diffusion of antisocial behavior. Next, we turn to our work examining the possibility that peer influence processes might create a diffusion of prevention program benefits and thereby increase program impact.

Diffusion of Intervention Impact

A pair of articles from our group has addressed the potential for program benefits to diffuse from program participants to non-participants through friendship networks (Rulison et al. 2015a, b). Typically, evaluation studies test the direct effects of an intervention on those who participated in that intervention. Yet indirect effects may also be possible because adolescents are part of larger social networks. Specifically, school-based friendship networks may be able to facilitate the diffusion of intervention effects from family-focused interventions such that non-participants benefit from the intervention even when their families do not participate. The PROSPER Peers project provides an important opportunity for testing hypotheses about whether and how diffusion occurs when an intervention is delivered to a fraction of the targeted population. First, as noted above, despite multiple efforts to recruit all families, the average participation rate in the 6th grade family program, SFP 10–14, was 17% (Spoth et al. 2007a), ranging from 5% to 46% across schools. Second, students provided friendship nominations at each wave, which allowed us to map connections between SFP10–14 participants and non-participants. Finally, our sample of 42 networks across 14 PROSPER intervention communities[1] provided a reasonable sample size of networks so that we could examine whether some networks facilitate diffusion better than others. PROSPER's corresponding large sample of students also allowed us to explore individual student-level factors that shaped diffusion.

Diffusion Processes: Network Level Influences

Our group's first article on diffusion of program effects (Rulison et al. 2015b) stemmed from our expectation that the likelihood of diffusion would be affected by features of the social network. For example, we hypothesized that diffusion would be more likely in networks with higher participation rates and in networks where participants were more representative of (i.e., similar to) non-participants. Importantly, however, other network-level features may facilitate diffusion. For

[1]There were two cohorts in each school, and some of the intervention communities had multiple middle/junior high schools; we excluded 1 network that did not to collect friendship nominations and 4 networks that had 0 or 1 SFP-participants. The final sample size was 5784 students (M = 11.8 years; 49.6% female) who were in the 42 networks.

example, it is possible for the participation rate to be the same in two networks, but in one network, almost none of the participants are named as friends whereas in the second network, the participants are named by a large number of peers. We would expect that diffusion would occur more easily in the second network, because the participants are in a position to influence more of their peers. Therefore, we also hypothesized that the network structure would affect diffusion. Specifically, we expected that diffusion would be more likely in networks that were more socially integrated (i.e., more connected, less clustered, and less hierarchal), in networks where intervention participants were widely distributed throughout the network (and thus connected to more non-participants), and in networks where participants had higher status than their non-participating peers (and thus were in a better position to influence their peers).

To illustrate how networks that are similar in terms of participation rates and representativeness can be different in terms of social network structure, we graphed the pretest social networks at two schools (Fig. 21.3). In both networks, about 22% of students participated in SFP10–14. The networks were also very similar in terms of participant representativeness for characteristics such as gender, grades, and

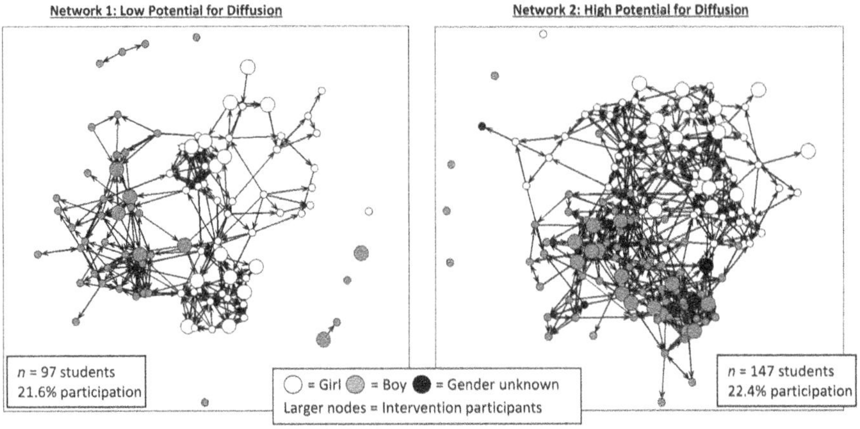

Fig. 21.3 These plots show the pretest friendship nominations (directional arrows) among 6th grade students in two networks and highlight the discriminant validity between the traditional analytic measures and SNA measures of diffusion potential. Both Network 1 (left) and Network 2 (right) had similar participation rates and were similarly representative in terms of gender (Net_1 = −0.15; Net_2 = −0.06), free lunch status (Net_1 = −0.24; Net_2 = −0.15), delinquency (Net_1 = −0.03; Net_2 = −0.06), and substance use attitudes (Net_1 = −0.08; Net_2 = −0.05), but they have very different network structure. Network 1 ranked 27th on the global network index whereas Network 2 had the highest rank. Compared to Network 2, Network 1 was less cohesive (Net_1 = 2.85 vs. Net_2 = 3.69) and more clustered (e.g., segregation index: Net_1 = 0.73 vs. Net_2 = 0.63). Several participants in Network 1 were isolated from the network, and overall the participants received fewer friendship nominations (e.g., Cohen's D for indegree: Net_1 = 0.32 vs. Net_2 = 0.09). As a result, Network 1 also had fewer non-participants within two steps of an SFP10–14 participant compared to Network 2 (58% vs. 82%)
Note: Reprinted with permission from Rulison et al. (2015b)

delinquency. Yet other network features were very different. For example, compared to Network 2 (on the right), Network 1 was less cohesive, more clustered, participants had lower status than their peers (several participants were even isolated), and fewer non-participants were connected directly (i.e., friends) or indirectly (i.e., friends of a friend) with a participant (58% vs. 82%). We expected that these features in Network 1 would inhibit diffusion by making it difficult for participants to spread attitudes and behaviors promoted by the intervention to their non-participating peers.

To test these hypotheses, we measured *network-level features* in each of the 42 intervention networks before and after the communities implemented SFP10–14 (i.e., pretest = fall 6th grade; posttest = spring 6th grade). We first tested several traditional, non-network measures of diffusion potential: participation rate and representativeness with respect to behavioral and demographic characteristics. We then tested 10 different social network analytic measures of diffusion potential.

We measured *diffusion* in each network by assessing whether the participants and non-participants became more similar to each other over time. Specifically, we created "diffusion scores" at the 1- and 2-year follow-up (i.e., spring of 7th and 8th grade) by first computing Cohen's D to compare composite substance use scores between participants and non-participants within each network; we then multiplied the absolute value of the Cohen's D value by −1, so that higher scores represented greater similarity in substance use and thus greater diffusion.

We used partial correlations to identify whether specific network-level features promote diffusion. In one set of analyses, we tested whether the *pretest* measures of each network-level feature were associated with our measure of intervention diffusion at the *1-year follow-up*. We partialled out network size and survey participation rate at the 1-year follow-up as well as the pretest diffusion score (i.e., similarity in substance use between participants and non-participants) to control for their initial similarity. The analyses also partialled out pretest SFP10–14 participation rate. We then repeated these analyses with (1) the *posttest* network measures and diffusion at the *1-year follow-up*, (2) the *pretest* network measures and diffusion at the *2-year follow-up*, and (3) the *posttest* network measures and diffusion at the *2-year follow-up*. Each analysis controlled for the corresponding measures of network size and survey participation rate (i.e., at the 1- or 2-year follow-up) and the corresponding diffusion score and SFP10–14 participation rate (i.e., at pretest or posttest).

We first explored whether *traditional non-network measures* (i.e., participation rate; behavioral and demographic representativeness) predicted network-level diffusion. We found that participation rate significantly predicted network-level diffusion scores at the 2-year follow-up (see Table 21.1). This finding is consistent with past research that demonstrated that the rate of diffusion typically accelerates once a tipping point or critical mass is reached (Rogers 2003; Valente 1995). In other words, diffusion becomes more likely when a larger proportion of the population participates, perhaps because there is a greater density of people who model and reinforce the attitudes and behaviors promoted by the intervention.

We also expected that representativeness would predict diffusion: People are more likely to adopt innovations when similar people have already adopted the

Table 21.1 Evidence of diffusion: Partial correlations between diffusion measures and substance use diffusion

Traditional measures				
	1 year follow-up		2 year follow-up	
	Pretest	Posttest	Pretest	Posttest
Participation rate represenativeness[a]	0.26	0.20	0.45**	0.43**
Demographic representativeness				
Gender	−0.30†	−0.17	0.19	0.09
Free lunch	0.19	−0.10	−0.14	−0.17
Behavioral representativeness				
Grades	−0.04	0.35*	−0.26	0.36*
Delinquency	−0.03	0.13	0.05	0.05
Substance use attitudes	0.21	−0.13	0.17	−0.37*
Average representativeness[a]	−0.02	−0.03	−0.06	0.16
SNA measures				
	1 year follow-up		2 year follow-up	
	Pretest	Posttest	Pretest	Posttest
Social integration[a,b]				
Connectivity				
Structural cohesion	−0.08	0.35*	0.30†	0.57***
Social distance	−0.20	0.34†	0.15	0.28
Clustering				
Transitivity ratio	−0.09	−0.31†	−0.22	−0.53***
Segregation index	0.16	−0.20	−0.13	−0.36*
Hierarchy (Centralization)				
Indegree	−0.31†	−0.46**	−0.25	−0.09
Betweenness	−0.26	0.05	0.20	0.04
Location of the intervention participants[a,b]				
Distribution of participants across the network				
Proportion of groups with 1+ Participant	0.01	0.13	0.19	0.25
Proportion within 2 steps of Participant	−0.03	0.13	0.36*	0.45**
Participants' relative potential for influence				
Indegree	0.09	0.09	−0.06	0.02
Betweenness	0.04	0.09	−0.44**	0.12
Global network index[a,b]	0.36*	0.49**	0.09	0.35*

Note: Reprinted with permission from Rulison et al. (2015b)

Substance use diffusion was defined as −1* (absolute difference in substance use between participants and non-participants), such that higher scores = higher diffusion. All analyses partial out network size and survey participation rate at either the 1-year or 2-year follow-up and substance use representativeness at either pretest or postest

†$p < .1$, *$p < .05$, **$p < .01$, ***$p < .001$

[a]Analyses controlled for SFP10-14 participation rate

[b]Analyses also controlled for average representativeness

innovation. The best case scenario is when potential adopters are similar to those who have adopted on all behavioral and demographic characteristics except the innovation. Thus, for intervention effects to diffuse, participants should be similar to (i.e., representative of) non-participants. For example, given the considerable gender segregation of adolescent friendship networks, it is unlikely that boys will be exposed to or adopt the attitudes and behaviors promoted by an intervention in which only girls participate. Notably, we found little evidence to support this hypothesis: There were no significant correlations between network-level diffusion scores and either demographic representativeness measure. The only behavioral representativeness measure that was positively related to the network-level diffusion score was grades at posttest. Furthermore, there were no significant correlations between the average of all of the representativeness measures and network-level diffusion scores.

We then explored whether *social network analytic measures* predicted network-level diffusion. We found that diffusion was more likely in networks that were socially integrated in terms of being richly interconnected, less cliquish, and less hierarchical. Specifically, diffusion was more likely in structurally cohesive networks (measured by mean number of "node-independent paths"; see Moody and White 2003), where students were able to interact, model, and reinforce each other's attitudes and behaviors (Valente et al. 2004). Diffusion was also more likely in less clustered networks, as measured by both Freeman's segregation index (Freeman 1978) and the transitivity ratio (Wasserman and Faust 1994). Thus, in networks that are highly clustered, with few connections between groups, diffusion may occur rapidly within groups, but it may be more difficult for intervention effects to spread to other cliques (Valente 2010). Finally, some analyses suggested that diffusion was more likely in networks that were less hierarchical. In networks that were hierarchically organized, students at the top of the hierarchy may have acted like gatekeepers to prevent intervention messages from spreading. Notably, however, we did not examine whether participant's status interacted with hierarchy. It is possible that hierarchy could facilitate diffusion when higher status students participate (and therefore overcome the tendency for hierarchy to hinder diffusion).

We found mixed support for our hypothesis that diffusion would be more likely when participants were broadly distributed across the network. We used two measures to assess the distribution of participants across the network: proportion of groups with at least one SFP10–14 participant, and the proportion of nonparticipants who were within two steps of an SFP10–14 participant (i.e., student was either friends with an SFP10–14 participant or had friends who were friends with an SFP10–14 participant). Both measures were positively related to diffusion, but only the proportion of non-participants within two steps of a participant was uniquely correlated with diffusion once we controlled for participation rate. Notably, these analyses might explain how a higher participation rate leads to more diffusion: When a greater number of students participate in the program, there are more peer groups that have at least one participant and more non-participants within two steps of a participant. Therefore, higher participation rates may facilitate diffusion by bringing non-participants into closer contact with participants.

Surprisingly, however, we found no support for our hypothesis that participants' relative status compared to their peers would be correlated with diffusion. Specifically, we used Cohen's D to quantify differences between participants' and non-participants' average indegree centrality (how often students were named as friends) as well as differences in their average betweenness centrality (the extent to which a student bridges otherwise disconnected students). Neither relative status measure had a significant positive correlation with network-level diffusion scores. These results are inconsistent with research based on opinion leaders, which shows that opinion leaders can be used to diffuse intervention messages (Campbell et al. 2008; Kelly et al. 1997; Latkin 1998; Miller-Johnson and Costanzo 2004; Valente et al. 2003; Wyman et al. 2010). Notably, we only measured exposure to the intervention (not adoption of intervention-related messages), so it is possible that higher status students were less likely to adopt intervention attitudes and behaviors: These students may not have changed their attitudes or behaviors after participating in the intervention because they might believe that doing so would cause them to lose status.

Finally, we created a global network index of diffusion potential, which was an average of the 10 social network analytic measures (standardized and scored in a consistent direction). We found that this index was positively correlated with diffusion at three of the four waves, suggesting that as a whole, social network structure facilitated diffusion.

In sum, we found that network-based measures of diffusion potential predicted diffusion benefits better than more traditional non-network measures. Participation rate predicted diffusion only at the 2-year follow-up, and average representativeness did not predict diffusion at all. By contrast, several social network features and the global network index predicted diffusion, even after controlling for participation rate and representativeness. Therefore, even though measures such as participation rate are easy to compute, they do not fully capture network-level features that facilitate diffusion.

Diffusion Processes: Individual Level Influences

After establishing that network-level features can influence diffusion of program impact, our group's next paper on diffusion sought to demonstrate the process at the individual level and explored which individual student-level features contribute to the process (Rulison et al. 2015a). We focused on two questions: (1) For a non-participant, does having more friends who participated in an intervention—i.e., the amount of *indirect exposure* to the intervention—lead to greater positive change in the non-participant's outcomes? (2) If so, what processes can explain how indirect exposure shapes non-participants' outcomes?

We examined these questions using data from the 13 intervention communities that collected friendship nominations at each wave. In these analyses, we focused primarily on data from the post-intervention waves (i.e., spring of 6th, 7th, 8th, and 9th grades). Our analytic sample included 5449 students who did not participate in SFP10–14 (i.e., nonparticipants), who completed the peer friendship nomination measure at least once, and whose nominated friends completed the survey at least once.[2] For these analyses, we focused on students' past month reports of being drunk and smoking cigarettes.

To test whether amount of indirect exposure to the intervention predicted non-participants' substance use, we first used wave-specific X^2 tests to evaluate the relationship between *total number of friends who participated in SFP (i.e., SFP-attending friends)* and each substance use outcome. Our results provide evidence of diffusion: Total number of SFP-attending friends was unrelated to substance use at baseline (before SFP10–14 was implemented) and at the immediate posttest (before intervention effects had time to diffuse). At subsequent waves, however, students with more SFP-attending friends were less likely to report past month drunkenness (Fig. 21.4a) or cigarette use (Fig. 21.4b), suggesting that intervention effects spread from participants to non-participants. Multilevel analyses (time within student within community-cohort) supported these results: Indirect exposure, measured as *cumulative proportion* of SFP-attending friends,[3] predicted past month drunkenness (adjusted Odds Ratio = 0.57) and past month cigarette use (adjusted Odds Ratio = 0.49).[4]

To identify the mediating processes that might explain how this indirect exposure to SFP reduces substance use among non-participants, we first considered the effects of SFP10–14 on program participants. Other studies have demonstrated that SFP has proximal effects on factors such as participants' parental discipline, family relationships, unstructured time use (i.e., spending time with peers without adults around), and substance use attitudes (Molgaard and Spoth 2001; Redmond et al. 1999). These proximal effects are hypothesized to then affect the more distal outcomes of the rates and frequency of participants' substance use. Both the program's effects on proximal factors and distal outcomes for intervention participants may then diffuse through peer networks and influence nonparticipants' substance use attitudes and behaviors. More specifically, we hypothesized that non-participants who have many SFP-attending friends will have more *friends* who experience less harsh and more consistent parental discipline, have better family relationships, spend less unstructured time with their peers, and have less positive attitudes toward substance use. As a result, these friends are expected to be less likely to use alcohol

[2] We did, however, use data from the 875 non-participants who were excluded because of missing friendship information and from the 889 intervention participants to calculate friends' characteristics.

[3] Measured as the average proportion of SFP-attending friends at the current wave and each previous post-intervention wave.

[4] All analyses adjusted for gender, race, network size (natural log), wave, whether the nonparticipant received free or reduced lunch, the non-participants' frequency of church attendance, family discipline, and parent-youth relationships.

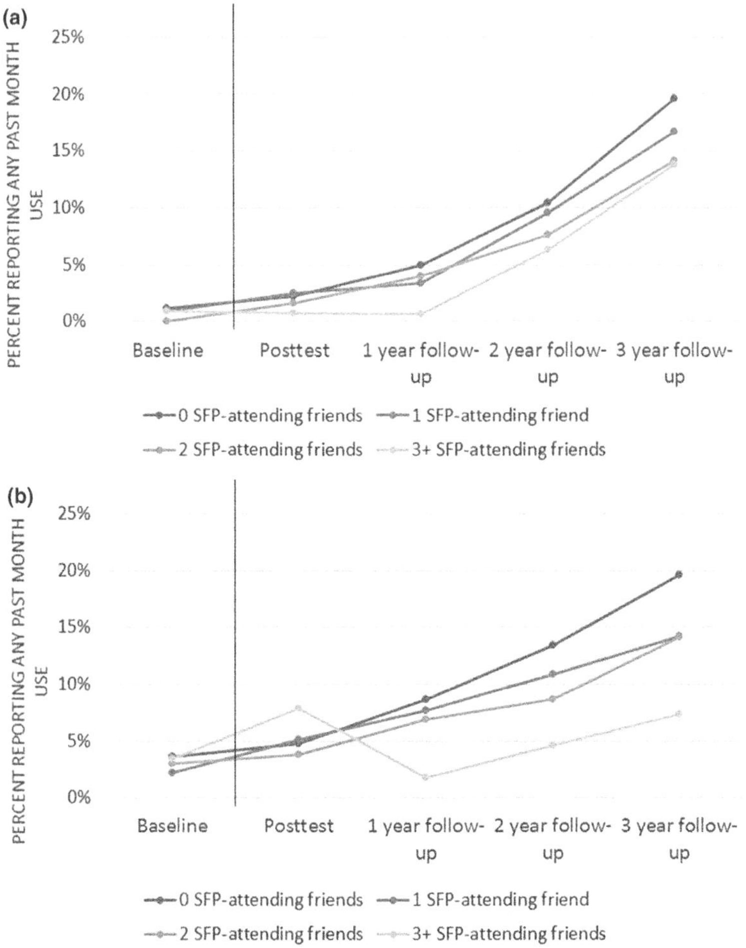

Fig. 21.4 The percent of non-participants at each wave who reported (**a**) past month drunkenness and (**b**) past month cigarette use as a function of the total number of their friends who attended SFP10–14. The vertical line indicates when SFP10–14 was implemented. Prior to (baseline) and shortly after (posttest) SFP10–14 was implemented, there were no significant differences in drunkeness or cigarette use. Significant differences emerged 1 year after SFP10–14 was implemented. At each follow-up, students with no SFP-attending friends had the highest rates of substance use whereas students with 3 or more SFP-attending friends had the lowest rates of use
Note: Reprinted with permission from Rulison et al. (2015a)

and drugs. These friends' characteristics are in turn expected to influence the distal outcome of non-participants' own substance use attitudes. Finally, these distal effects are expected to influence non-participants' own substance use behavior (See Fig. 21.5).

We tested each of the proximal mediators one at a time, and then added distal mediators (i.e., friends' substance use and non-participants' own substance use atti-

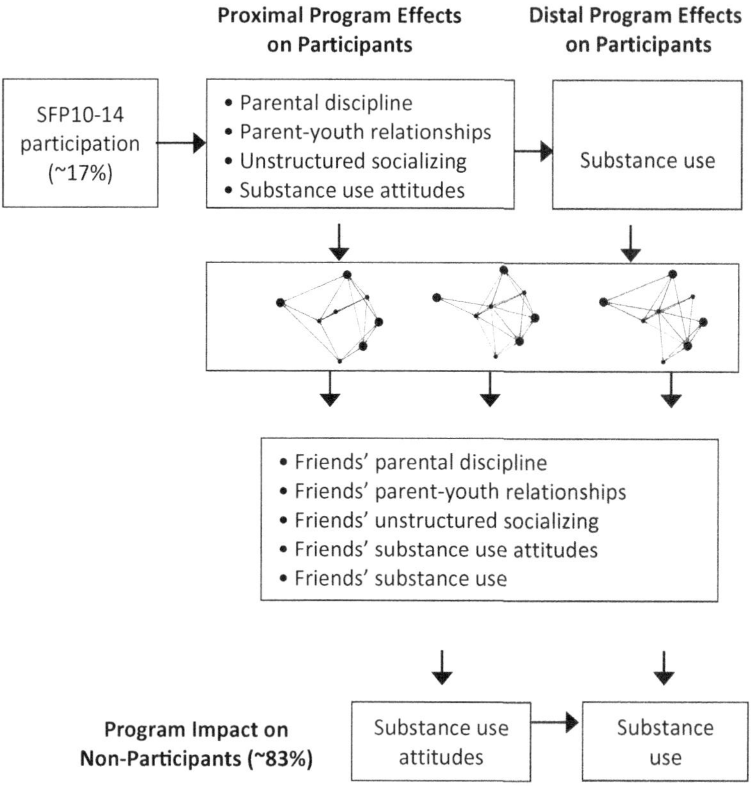

Fig. 21.5 Hypothesized process through which intervention effects diffuse from the students who participated in SFP10–14 to intervention non-participants. First, SFP10–14 has proximal and distal effects on program participants (top row). Then, non-participants are exposed to intervention participants (larger nodes) through their friendship networks (second row); some non-participants have many SFP-attending friends whereas others have few SFP-attending friends. The varying degrees of cumulative indirect exposure to SFP10–14 via friendship networks then impacts the average characteristics of non-participants' friends (third row). In turn, these friends' characteristics impact non-participants' own anti-substance use attitudes and substance use (bottom row) Note: Reprinted with permission from Rulison et al. (2015a)

tudes) one at a time (See Fig. 21.6). Overall, the mediators accounted for 63% of the total relationship between indirect exposure and drunkenness and 45% of the total relationship between indirect exposure and cigarette use. The strongest evidence of mediation was via the proximal effect on unstructured socializing, measured as the average amount of time students' spent "hanging out" with friends outside of school without adults around. This finding is consistent with past research that shows that unstructured socializing is linked with many deviant behaviors (Haynie and Osgood 2005; Light et al. 2013; Osgood and Anderson 2004; Osgood et al. 1996) and suggests that nonparticipants who have many SFP-attending friends spent less time hanging out with these friends without adults around. This result may have occurred

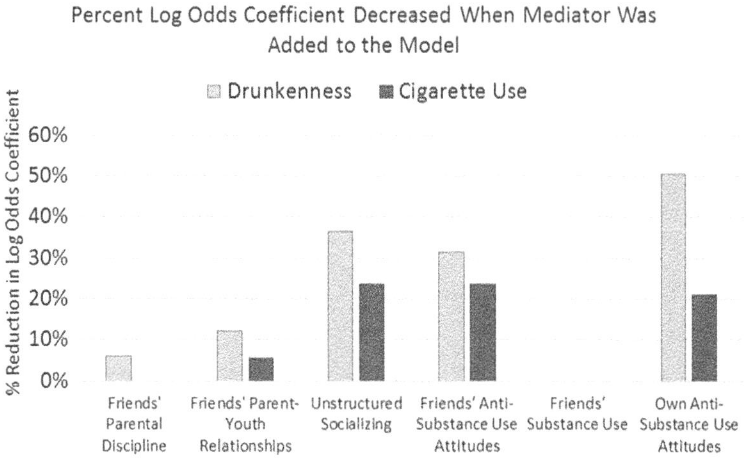

Fig. 21.6 Percent that the log odds coefficient decreased when each mediator was added to the model

because parents who participated in SFP10–14 learned the importance of parental monitoring and may have spent more time supervising their adolescents, along with their adolescents' friends.

We also found evidence of mediation via the proximal effect on participants' substance use attitudes, measured as the average of four standardized subscales related to substance use: moral attitudes, future expectations, refusal intentions, and refusal efficacy. By itself, friends' substance use attitudes mediated a higher proportion of the total relationship than the other proximal mediators; when nonparticipants' own substance use attitudes were added as predictors to the model, the proportion of indirect influence accounted for by friends' substance use attitudes dropped to almost zero. These results suggest that nonparticipants whose friends disapproved of substance use after participating in SFP10–14 were more likely themselves to develop negative attitudes toward substance use, which in turn reduced their likelihood of substance use.

By contrast, there was limited evidence of mediation via proximal program effects on friends' parenting practices, measured as friends' parent-youth relationship quality and friends' parental discipline consistency. Although both measures of parenting practices were significantly associated with nonparticipants' substance use, their influence on non-participants' substance use became non-significant after non-participants' unstructured socializing was included in the model. There was also limited evidence of mediation through friends' actual substance use. Although the proportion mediated by friends' substance use was .08–.11 when we included friends' use as the sole mediator (not shown), the influence of friends' substance use on nonparticipants' outcomes was fully accounted for when we included parenting practices, unstructured socializing, and participants' substance use attitudes in the model.

Conclusions

Life course perspectives on problem behavior (Sampson and Laub 1997) acknowledge the bidirectional influences between individuals and their social settings, and linked lives and turning points in development are central themes of the life course theory (Elder 1998). Developmental research has made clear that such bidirectional influences involving peer networks and problem behavior are evident in the processes of friendship selection and peer influence that link the lives of adolescents and their friends (Dishion 2013; Veenstra et al. 2013). Most commonly, researchers are interested in the extent to which adolescents are influenced by their peers. However, our work as part of the PROSPER project highlights two ways in which individual-level changes induced by prevention programs can produce changes in the broader peer network and potentially create developmental turning points away from problem behavior: by altering the overall influence-potential of youth who exhibit problem behavior; and by diffusing through the social medium of the network to influence youth who did not themselves participate in the prevention program. Network methods provided a critical set of tools for elucidating broad life course theory assertions about the role of active individuals in both shaping and being shaped by their social settings (Elder 1998).

Most program evaluation studies focus on the direct effects that interventions have on participants, but results from our work indicate that interventions can also have indirect effects on nonparticipants. Our first empirical study showed that an evidence-based prevention program can impact the friendship network of a student body in a way that enhances the influence of youth who do not engage in problem behavior, relative to those who do. This program effect on peer influence should help sustain the beneficial individual effects of the intervention. In addition, we found that the amount of diffusion varies across networks, with diffusion more likely to occur in networks that are more cohesive, less cliquish, and less hierarchical as well as in networks where participants are more widely distributed across the network. In addition, we found that diffusion occurs by cumulative indirect exposure through friendship networks: Those who have many SFP-attending friends were more likely to avoid substance use compared to those who had fewer SFP-attending friends. Furthermore, diffusion of SFP10–14 appears to operate by reducing opportunities for substance use (i.e., reducing unstructured, unsupervised socializing) and changing participants' substance use attitudes.

Taken together, our results to date suggest there is much to be learned from the study of how intervention effects diffuse through adolescent friendship networks, including the network conditions under which diffusion occurs and the processes that may account for the influence of participants on non-participants. Prevention researchers using randomized control trials to evaluate programs typically view such influences of participants on nonparticipants as "contamination" because they threaten the internal validity of experimental designs. Yet from a "real-world" perspective, program developers likely want to maximize such diffusion processes so that the benefits of the intervention extend beyond those who were directly targeted.

Therefore, future studies should explore strategies to actively facilitate diffusion. Such strategies could come in many forms, such as teaching students in specific network positions how to spread intervention messages (e.g., Wyman et al. 2010), trying to change features of the peer network that facilitate diffusion (e.g., try to facilitate more connected, less clustered networks), or including content that might facilitate diffusion (e.g., promoting less unstructured time with peers).

Our body of work from the PROSPER Peers project has demonstrated that integrating the study of peer selection and influence processes with the study of prevention programs has promising advantages for both developmental and prevention research traditions. Most developmental studies seeking to clarify the role of peers in the emergence of problem behavior are constrained by non-experimental designs that limit causal inferences. Conversely, prevention researchers have employed experimental designs to demonstrate the significant impact of a wide array of school- and family-based interventions on individual-level social, behavioral and academic targets; but their studies typically lack detailed measures of social network processes. Bringing a life course perspective to the study of adolescent friendship processes in the context of prevention efforts promises to strengthen our insights into how peers play a role in the development of problem behavior while offering new possibilities for enhancing the impact of prevention programs.

References

Battistich, V. A., Schaps, E., Watson, M., Solomon, D., & Lewis, C. (2000). Effects of the child development project on students' drug use and other problem behaviors. *Journal of Primary Prevention, 21*(1), 75–99.

Botvin, G. J., & Griffin, K. W. (2004). Life skills training: Empirical findings and future directions. *Journal of Primary Prevention, 25*(2), 211–232.

Brown, B. B., & Dietz, E. L. (2009). Informal peer groups in middle childhood and adolescence. In *Handbook of peer interactions, relationships, and groups* (pp. 361–376). Retrieved from https://books.google.com/books?hl=en&lr=&id=ZxqG6O28r1QC&oi=fnd&pg=PA361&dq=Informal+peer+groups+in+middle+childhood+and+adolescence&ots=3vd8HBqaus&sig=7gTHmrzJILYjm8DdX5a2Fn9pQYQ

Burgess, R. L., & Akers, R. L. (1966). A differential association-reinforcement theory of criminal behavior. *Social Problems, 14*(2), 128–147.

Campbell, R., Starkey, F., Holliday, J., Audrey, S., Bloor, M., Parry-Langdon, N., et al. (2008). An informal school-based peer-led intervention for smoking prevention in adolescence (ASSIST): A cluster randomised trial. *The Lancet, 371*, 1595–1602. https://doi.org/10.1016/s0140-6736(08)60692-3.

CPPRG. (1999). Initial impact of the fast track prevention trial for conduct problems: I. The high-risk sample. *Journal of Consulting and Clinical Psychology, 67*, 631–647.

Dishion, T. J. (2013). Stochastic agent-based modeling of influence and selection in adolescence: Current status and future directions in understanding the dynamics of peer contagion. *Journal of Research on Adolescence, 23*, 596–603. https://doi.org/10.1111/jora.12068.

Dishion, T. J., Andrews, D. W., & Crosby, L. (1995). Antisocial boys and their friends in early adolescence: Relationship characteristics, quality, and interactional process. *Child Development, 66*(1), 139–151.

Eccles, J. S., & Roeser, R. W. (2011). Schools as developmental contexts during adolescence. *Journal of Research on Adolescence, 21*, 225–241. https://doi.org/10.1111/j.1532-7795.2010.00725.x.

Elder, G. H. (1998). The life course as developmental theory. *Child Development, 69*(1), 1–12. https://doi.org/10.1111/j.1467-8624.1998.tb06128.x.

Freeman, L. C. (1978). Segregation in social networks. *Sociological Methods and Research, 6*, 411–429. https://doi.org/10.1177/004912417800600400.

Gest, S. D., Osgood, D. W., Feinberg, M. E., Bierman, K. L., & Moody, J. (2011). Strengthening prevention program theories and evaluations: Contributions from social network analysis. *Prevention Science, 12*, 349–360. https://doi.org/10.1007/s11121-011-0229-2.

Haynie, D. L., & Osgood, D. W. (2005). Reconsidering peers and delinquency: How do peers matter? *Social Forces, 84*(2), 1109–1130. https://doi.org/10.1353/sof.2006.0018.

Heinrichs, N., Bertram, H., Kuschel, A., & Hahlweg, K. (2005). Parent recruitment and retention in a universal prevention program for child behavior and emotional problems: Barriers to research and program participation. *Prevention Science, 6*, 275–286. https://doi.org/10.1007/s11121-005-0006-1.

Kelly, J. A., Murphy, D. A., Sikkema, K. J., McAuliffe, T. L., Roffman, R. A., Solomon, L. J., et al. (1997). Randomized, controlled, community-level HIV-prevention intervention for sexual-risk behaviour among homosexual men in US cities. *The Lancet, 350*, 1500–1505. https://doi.org/10.1016/s0140-6736(97)07439-4.

Latkin, C. A. (1998). Outreach in natural settings: The use of peer leaders for HIV prevention among injecting drug users' networks. *Public Health Reports, 113*, 151–159.

Light, J. M., Greenan, C. C., Rusby, J. C., Nies, K. M., & Snijders, T. A. B. (2013). Onset to first alcohol use in early adolescence: A network diffusion model. *Journal of Research on Adolescence, 23*, 487–499. https://doi.org/10.1111/jora.12064.

Miller-Johnson, S., & Costanzo, P. (2004). If you can't beat 'em...Induce them to join you: Peer-based interventions during adolescence. In J. B. Kupersmidt & K. A. Dodge (Eds.), *Children's peer relations: From development to intervention* (pp. 209–222). Washington, DC: American Psychological Association.

Molgaard, V., & Spoth, R. (2001). The strengthening families program for young adolescents: Overview and outcomes. *Residential Treatment for Children & Youth, 18*, 15–29. https://doi.org/10.1300/J007v18n03_03.

Molgaard, V. M., Kumpfer, K. L., & Fleming, E. (1997). *The strengthening families program for parents and youth 10–14: A video-based curriculum*. Ames: Institute for Social and Behavioral Research.

Moody, J., & White, D. R. (2003). Structural cohesion and embeddedness: A hierarchical concept of social groups. *American Sociological Review, 68*, 103–127.

Osgood, D. W., & Anderson, A. L. (2004). Unstructured socializing and rates of delinquency. *Criminology, 42*(3), 519–550.

Osgood, D. W., Wilson, J. K., O'Malley, P. M., Bachman, J. G., & Johnston, L. D. (1996). Routine activities and individual deviant behavior. *American Sociological Review, 61*, 635–655. https://doi.org/10.2307/2096397.

Osgood, D. W., Feinberg, M. E., Gest, S. D., Moody, J., Ragan, D. T., Spoth, R., et al. (2013). Effects of PROSPER on the influence potential of prosocial versus antisocial youth in adolescent friendship networks. *Journal of Adolescent Health, 53*, 174–179. https://doi.org/10.1016/j.jadohealth.2013.02.013.

Redmond, C., Spoth, R., Shin, C., & Lepper, H. S. (1999). Modeling long-term parent outcomes of two universal family-focused preventive interventions: One-year follow-up results. *Journal of Consulting and Clinical Psychology, 67*, 975–984. https://doi.org/10.1037/0022-006x.67.6.975.

Rogers, E. M. (2003). *Diffusion of innovations*. New York: Free Press.

Rulison, K. L., Feinberg, M., Gest, S. D., & Osgood, D. W. (2015a). Diffusion of intervention effects: The impact of a family-based substance use prevention program on friends of participants. *Journal of Adolescent Health, 57*, 433–440. https://doi.org/10.1016/j.jadohealth.2015.06.007.

Rulison, K. L., Gest, S. D., & Osgood, D. W. (2015b). Adolescent peer networks and the potential for the diffusion of intervention effects. *Prevention Science, 16*, 133–144. https://doi.org/10.1007/s11121-014-0465-3.

Rulison, K. L., Patrick, M. E., & Maggs, J. (2015c). Linking peer relationships to substance use across adolescence. In S. Brown & R. A. Zucker (Eds.), *The Oxford handbook of substance use*. New York: Oxford University Press.

Sampson, R. J., & Laub, J. H. (1997). A life-course theory of cumulative disadvantage and the stability of delinquency. *Developmental Theories of Crime and Delinquency, 7*, 133–161.

Spoth, R., & Greenberg, M. (2011). Impact challenges in community science-with-practice: Lessons from PROSPER on transformative practitioner-scientist partnerships and prevention infrastructure development. *American Journal of Community Psychology, 48*, 106–119.

Spoth, R., & Redmond, C. (2002). Project family prevention trials based in community–university partnerships: Toward scaled-up preventive interventions. *Prevention Science, 3*(3), 203–221. https://doi.org/10.1023/a:1019946617140.

Spoth, R. L., Redmond, C., & Lepper, H. (1999). Alcohol initiation outcomes of universal family-focused preventive interventions: One- and two-year follow-ups of a controlled study. *Journal of Studies on Alcohol,* (Suppl 13), 103–111.

Spoth, R. L., Redmond, C., & Shin, C. (2001). Randomized trial of brief family interventions for general populations: Adolescent substance use outcomes 4 years following baseline. *Journal of Consulting and Clinical Psychology, 69*, 627–642. https://doi.org/10.1037/0022-006x.69.4.627.

Spoth, R., Greenberg, M., Bierman, K., & Redmond, C. (2004a). PROSPER community–university partnership model for public education systems: Capacity-building for evidence-based, competence-building prevention. *Prevention Science, 5*, 31–39.

Spoth, R., Redmond, C., Shin, C., & Azevedo, K. (2004b). Brief family intervention effects on adolescent substance initiation: School-level growth curve analyses 6 years following baseline. *Journal of Consulting and Clinical Psychology, 72*(3), 535–542.

Spoth, R., Clair, S., Greenberg, M., Redmond, C., & Shin, C. (2007a). Toward dissemination of evidence-based family interventions: Maintenance of community-based partnership recruitment results. *Journal of Family Psychology, 21*, 137–146. https://doi.org/10.1037/0893-3200.21.2.137.

Spoth, R. L., Redmond, C., Shin, C., Greenberg, M., Clair, S., & Feinberg, M. (2007b). Substance-use outcomes at 18 months past baseline: The PROSPER community-university partnership trial. *American Journal of Preventive Medicine, 32*, 395–402. https://doi.org/10.1016/j.amepre.2007.01.014.

Spoth, R., Redmond, C., Clair, S., Shin, C., Greenberg, M., & Feinberg, M. (2011). Preventing substance misuse through community–university partnerships: Randomized controlled trial outcomes 4½ years past baseline. *American Journal of Preventive Medicine, 40*, 440–447. https://doi.org/10.1016/j.amepre.2010.12.012.

Spoth, R. L., Trudeau, L. S., Guyll, M., & Shin, C. (2012). Benefits of universal intervention effects on a youth protective shield 10 years after baseline. *Journal of Adolescent Health, 50*, 414–417. https://doi.org/10.1016/j.jadohealth.2011.06.010.

Spoth, R., Redmond, C., Shin, C., Greenberg, M., Feinberg, M., & Schainker, L. (2013). PROSPER community–university partnership delivery system effects on substance misuse through 6 1/2 years past baseline from a cluster randomized controlled intervention trial. *Preventive Medicine, 56*, 190–196.

Stevens, R. J., & Slavin, R. E. (1995). The cooperative elementary school: Effects on students' achievement, attitudes, and social relations. *American Educational Research Journal, 32*(2), 321.

Tobler, N. S., Roona, M. R., Ochshorn, P., Marshall, D. G., Streke, A. V., & Stackpole, K. M. (2000). School-based adolescent drug prevention programs: 1998 meta-analysis. *The Journal of Primary Prevention, 20*(4), 275–336.

Valente, T. W. (1995). *Network models of the diffusion of innovations*. Cresskill: Hampton Press.

Valente, T. W. (2010). *Social networks and health: Models, methods, and applications*. New York: Oxford University Press.
Valente, T. W., Hoffman, B. R., Ritt-Olsan, A., Lichtman, K., & Johnson, C. A. (2003). Effects of a social-network method for group assignment strategies on peer-led tobacco prevention programs in schools. *American Journal of Public Health, 93*, 1837–1843. https://doi.org/10.2105/AJPH.93.11.1837.
Valente, T. W., Gallaher, P., & Mouttapa, M. (2004). Using social networks to understand and prevent substance use: A transdisciplinary perspective. *Substance Use & Misuse, 39*, 10–12. https://doi.org/10.1081/ja-200033210.
Veenstra, R., Dijkstra, J. K., Steglich, C., & Van Zalk, M. (2013). Network-behavior dynamics. *Journal of Research on Adolescence, 23*, 399–412. https://doi.org/10.1111/jora.12070.
Wasserman, S., & Faust, K. (1994). *Social network analysis: Methods and applications*. New York: Cambridge University Press.
Wyman, P. A., Brown, C. H., LoMurray, M., Schmeelk-Cone, K., Petrova, M., Yu, Q., et al. (2010). An outcome evaluation of the sources of strength suicide prevention program delivered by adolescent peer leaders in high schools. *American Journal of Public Health, 100*, 1653–1661. https://doi.org/10.2105/AJPH.2009.190025.

Kelly L. Rulison is Associate Professor in the Department of Public Health Education at the University of North Carolina, Greensboro. Her interests include the study of the dynamic social processes and contexts that shape the development of health-risk behaviors during adolescence.

Scott D. Gest is Professor of Human Development and Family Studies at Pennsylvania State University. He uses social network methodology to study peer relationships and peer influences from childhood through adolescence.

Mark Feinberg is Research Professor of Health and Human Development in the Bennett Pierce Prevention Research Center in the College of Health and Human Development, Pennsylvania State University. His interests include family and community prevention, family relationships, and biological systems.

D. Wayne Osgood is Professor Emeritus of Criminology and Sociology in the Department of Sociology and Criminology at Pennsylvania State University. His research interests include the connection of adolescents' friendship networks to delinquency and other problem behaviors during adolescence and early adulthood.

Part X
Conclusions

Chapter 22
Strategies for Integrating Network and Life Course Perspectives

Derek A. Kreager, Diane H. Felmlee, and Duane F. Alwin

Introduction

This edited volume, and the conference that preceded it, were organized around shared topical areas (e.g., marriage, adolescence, race, etc.) largely due to pre-existing scholarly networks and research questions common to disciplinary sub-fields. However, an alternative organization that is perhaps better suited for building interdisciplinary research is to group chapters by the strategies employed to connect life course and social network concepts, data, and methods. The latter organization provides a roadmap for future research aimed at strengthening the bridge between the two perspectives and is also a useful way for us to conclude this book. In hindsight, we identified four concrete strategies utilized by authors in this volume to link perspectives: (1) social networks informing individual trajectories, (2) individual trajectories informing social networks, (3) social networks informing life transitions, and (4) life transitions informing social networks. Below we briefly discuss the theoretical foundations underlying each strategy and outline how authors in this volume used the respective strategy to link life course and network concepts.

Social Networks Informing Individual Trajectories

The idea that social relationships are influential for individual behavior is a long-standing sociological tradition. Most prominently, social psychological perspectives, such as social learning theory, assert that individuals' attitudes and behaviors are shaped by the attitudes and behaviors of significant others (Akers 2011; Bandura

D. A. Kreager (✉) · D. H. Felmlee · D. F. Alwin
Department of Sociology and Criminology, Pennsylvania State University, University Park, PA, USA
e-mail: dkreager@psu.edu

D. F. Alwin et al. (eds.), *Social Networks and the Life Course*, Frontiers in Sociology and Social Research 2, https://doi.org/10.1007/978-3-319-71544-5_22

1971; Sutherland 1947). Approached in network terms, learning theories suggest that (1) the behaviors or attitudes of an individual's social network should predict changes in his or her own behaviors or attitudes over time and (2) behaviors and attitudes are transmitted and diffuse through social network ties. Both of these network-based propositions easily connect with the life course concepts of turning points in individual trajectories, and provide a means of integrating network data and methods with a life course perspective to examine social mechanisms underlying behavioral or attitudinal change.

Within this volume, Silverstein and Bengtson provide an example of a study that examines the influence of network ties on individual trajectories. These authors draw on social learning concepts to examine the intergenerational transmission of religiosity. Using longitudinal data of grandparents, parents, and children, they apply a hierarchical linear model to demonstrate that, consistent with social learning expectations, grandparents transmit religious orientations to their grandchildren. Additionally, they found that parental divorce moderates this association, such that the association between grandparent and grandchild religiosity is weaker if the parents divorce. Approached in network terms, this mitigation results from weakening the intergenerational tie between grandparents and grandchildren because the brokers of this tie, the parents, are no longer together. In other words, religiosity is unable to fully diffuse from grandparents to grandchildren if parents divorce.

Crosnoe, Olson, and Cheadle also approach individual behavioral trajectories as influenced by network ties. In their case, ties to parents are argued to be consequential for adolescents' abilities to integrate with peers at school. They assert that experiences with parents will influence adolescents' socioemotional skills and competencies to successfully navigate school-based peer environments. Interestingly, this argument connects relational development in one domain (i.e., the family) with relational development in another domain (i.e., peer friendships). Although this link did not appear strong in their analyses, the authors did find some evidence of a spillover effect such that adolescents' negative relationships with parents carried over to weak social integration at school.

Both Suitor et al. and Doty and Mortimer explore how relationships between mothers and their adult children influence the children's psychological well-being. Suitor et al. examine whether children occupying "multiplex" social roles with their mothers, where they are called upon for multiple supportive roles, comes at psychological costs. They found that mothers who preferred a child as emotionally close and a confidant increased that child's depressive symptoms, particularly among daughters. They interpreted these findings as supportive of classic theories of role strain and role articulation. Doty and Mortimer also look at mother-child relationships and child mental health, but approach the mother-child relationship dynamically and create latent categories of these relationships over time. They find that mother-child relationships that were problematic in either adolescence or adulthood tended to be associated with greater depression and lower self-esteem for the adult children. The results of their study suggest that the influence of mother-child emotional closeness exerts lasting influences on children's self-image and mental health.

The final two chapters in the volume connect social network data and methods to individual trajectories via behavioral interventions, consistent with social learning expectations. Kreager et al. discuss how, within prison settings, group-based treatment programs rely on peer influence mechanisms to alter inmates' substance use trajectories. The authors argue that the life course transitions commonly found related to criminal desistance, including marriage, military service, parenthood, and steady employment, have proven difficult to translate into policy or miss the most at-risk population in need of change. However, the control capacity of prison provides a unique context for introducing positive peer influence for behavioral change. The therapeutic community seeks to do this for substance addicted inmates. Dynamic social network data and methods provide tools for testing the peer influence mechanisms thought to underlie the treatment program and understand how it can become a turning point in addicts' substance use trajectories.

Rulison et al. make a similar case for the potential role of social network analyses in the implementation of substance use and delinquency prevention programs in secondary schools. They argue that understanding the dynamic peer contexts of school-based friendship networks helps policy-makers understand how interventions diffuse through the social system. Approached from a life course paradigm, a network perspective prioritizes between-person interdependence and peer influence to understand how an intervention can create a turning point in adolescents' behavioral trajectories.

Individual Trajectories Informing Social Networks

Although studies of peer influence have abounded within sociology, there is also growing interest in how individuals select themselves into specific social structures, groups, and relationships, and how the creation of those relationships are structured by broader social forces (McPherson et al. 2001). Many important relationships, including marriage, friendships, and coworkers, occur after individuals are well into their lives and have accumulated experiences that shape their values, preferences, and environmental conditions. How people choose such ties then becomes important not only for statistical reasons (i.e., to remove social selection from social influence effects), but also for understanding how individuals access resources and reproduce social inequality. For example, research of assortative mating suggests that socioeconomically advantaged men and women are increasingly pairing with each other (i.e., homogamy) in heterosexual marriages that aggravate within-generation social stratification (Schwartz 2013). Approached from a life course perspective, the accumulated experiences and resources that make up individuals' lives select them into future social relationships and network structures.

In this book, several authors focus on how individuals become embedded in social relationships over time. Schaefer and Simpkins examine how experiences in extracurricular activities (ECAs) promote adolescent friendship formation, particularly between adolescents of different race/ethnic groups. Using friendship network and ECA participation data from the National Longitudinal Study of Adolescent Health, they find that, broadly, ECAs were more racially homogenous than schools as a whole and that adolescents participating in ECAs did not reduce their preferences for inbreeding homophily. Overall, the authors thus found that ECA participation did not result in adolescents selecting friends of other races or ethnicities. The exception to this pattern was contact sports, which were generally more diverse than schools and participants in these sports exhibited weaker preferences for homophily.

Youm looks at changes in individuals' networks over age. Specifically, he examines how clusters of life course transitions (e.g., marriage, parenthood) and network composition types (e.g., friends, neighbors, coworkers) vary over age. He demonstrates that change in the distribution by age of network composition relates closely to the timing of marriage and childbearing within our society. In other words, as individuals select themselves into marital and parenthood roles, their embeddedness in other social relationships also changes in predictable ways. Consistent with the social influence strategy mentioned above, Youm also finds that individuals classified as socially isolated or "single with friends and neighbors" showed lower levels of self-reported general happiness than other categories.

Burt provides an interesting examination of how business managers' network positions within their organizations vary over age. In other words, do structural advantages (i.e., access to structural holes) within an organization change with age and are there peak periods of network advantage? Additionally, at the organizational level, Burt examines if such patterns vary by organization, suggesting variations in norms related to aging and achievement. Using network data for senior managers in six organizations, Burt shows that, on average, managers tend to peak in their access to structural holes and relative achievement during middle age. However, organizations vary in these associations, with some being "old valued" where the associations have positive slopes over all age periods, and "young valued" where the associations peak early and decline with age. In sum, he shows how individual aging is linked to organizational ties and how this association varies substantially between organizational contexts.

Finally, Alwin et al. hypothesize that historical discrimination, institutional racism, and present-day inequalities result in "racialized lives" in which racial-ethnic groups experience substantially different life course trajectories, resulting in between-group differences in adult social networks and social support. With longitudinal General Social Survey data, the authors found that blacks were disadvantaged with regards to network size, number of kin in network, frequency of contact with network members, and the likelihood of having a spouse in their network, net of gender. These results remind us that individual choices and relational processes are embedded within larger historical and structural contexts that constrain opportunities and shape values in often subtle ways that result in long-term group differences and social inequality.

Social Networks Informing Life Course Transitions

A person's social networks also may affect how he or she transitions between life stages or undergoes an important and commonly occurring life event. The social capital, norms, and opportunities residing in an individual's social networks are likely to influence his or her movement into new phases of life (Portes 1998). This argument is similar to the "social networks informing life course trajectories" strategy discussed earlier, in that social relationships and peer norms are expected to influence individual behaviors. The difference, however, is that the "social networks informing life course transitions" strategy approaches social networks as informative for how individuals negotiate a shared event or experience, rather than as a turning point in individuals' behavioral trajectories.

Faris and Felmlee provide an example of this strategy when they examine the association between adolescent friendship stability and the transition to young adulthood. Specifically, they argue that adolescents with lasting friendships are better able to form strong educational and family goals as they prepare to exit adolescence. This argument moves beyond the peer influence models typical of adolescent friendship research and asserts that friendship consistency reinforces adolescents' identities and reduces uncertainty to better establish future goals. Using longitudinal social network panel data from North Carolina youth, they find that students with consistent friendships, particularly one stable friend, had greater investment in future life goals than students who lacked long-lasting friendships.

Rosenfeld also approaches a salient life course transition, divorce, from a relational perspective. He argues that the gendered context of marriage, compared to cohabitation, creates conditions less favorable for women than men, thus increasing the likelihood that women will initiate divorce. Re-stated in network terms, this argument suggests that gendered partner interdependence in marital dyads generally penalizes women and benefits men, thus increasing the odds of female-initiated divorce. Rosenfeld supports this argument using longitudinal data from the How Couples Meet and Stay Together study. His results suggest that the majority of divorces, but not cohabitation breakups, are initiated by women, and that wives report lower relationship quality than husbands. In contrast, men are just as likely as women to end non-marital relationships and report similar relationship quality in these relationships.

Finally, Amato takes a similar path as Rosenfeld when he tracks the gendered trends in happiness, discord, and shared activities that proceed divorce. Using six waves of data from the Marital Instability Over the Life Course study, Amato shows that wives, more than husbands, reported sharper declines in happiness and discord prior to divorce. And contrary to some prior research, he finds that marriages that persisted over time tended to show little deterioration in quality over the marital life course. Both Rosenfeld and Amato demonstrate that gendered interpartner dynamics within marriages are important in understanding decisions to divorce or stay together over time.

Life Course Transitions Informing Social Networks

A final strategy linking life course and network perspectives examines if significant life course transitions are mechanisms for social network change. An easily understood example of this would be leaving home at the completion of high school to pursue employment or advanced education in young adulthood. Commonly, this transition is accompanied by geographic mobility and exposure to a new set of peers potentially very different from those of the past. Navigating this transition and situating oneself within a new social structure has profound implications for identity development, behavioral change, and long-term attainment. Additionally, life course transitions may involve social relationships that alter an individual's previous social networks. For example, the interdependency and commitment of marriage may weaken ties to past friendships. Indeed, Warr (1998) asserted that marriage provides a mechanism for criminal desistance because wives pull male offenders away from criminal peers. Such explanations highlight the connections between important life events and changes in network structures and roles.

Authors in this volume commonly apply this strategy to connect social network and life course concepts. Marsden provides the most explicit example of this strategy and provides a useful literature review of the approach. Taking a "supply-side theory of structure," he focuses on how changes in social settings shift individual foci and constrain relational opportunities, resulting in changes in network structure, composition, and activities before and after life course transitions. Using longitudinal data from the General Social Survey, Marsden finds that changes in familial and employment life course states alter individuals' social relationships. Specifically, he shows that marriage shapes contacts with relatives, pulling married individuals toward familial ties and away from non-familial ties. Similarly, employment expands individuals' social networks to include coworkers, creating a relational foci that simultaneously weakens contacts with neighbors and kin.

Cornwell also connects life events with social network change, examining how the social networks of older adults are shaped by the death of a network member. Using data from the National Social Life, Health, and Aging Project (NSHAP) (see Cornwell et al. 2009), he finds that network recruitment due to the death of a network member depended on respondents' age, such that older adults were significantly more likely to replace lost confidants than were younger respondents. Consistent with a life course perspective, he argues that the experience of aging makes older adults more adept at dealing with death than their younger counterparts.

Schafer examines how a life course transition, the cessation of driving, is associated with social connectedness. Also using data from NSHAP, he finds that men, but not women, saw declines in their overall network size, fewer added network ties, and the loss of network bridging potential compared to their peers when they stopped driving. He argues that these gendered network consequences of driving cessation result from the greater normative importance of driving for men than women. As Schafer (this volume) states, "What may mark a mere life transition for women may represent a trajectory-redirecting 'turning point' for men." These findings point to intervention strategies that assist elderly men in retaining social connectedness as they stop driving.

Finally, Felmlee et al. examine how the transitions from elementary to middle school, and from middle school to high school are associated with changes in adolescents' friendship patterns. Using yearly network panel data from the PROSPER Peers study, the authors find that school transitions correlate with decreases in network centrality over time. Interestingly, the results reveal that the sociometric declines associated with the transition from middle to high school persisted into later grades, such that students who transitioned in the 9th grade received fewer friendship nominations in the 11th and 12th grades compared to students who never changed schools during this period. This pattern opens up several potential mechanisms for future investigation and highlights the importance of this particular type of life transition for social support and social capital accumulation.

Future Research

The above categories not only help authors situate their own work within prior research aimed at integrating life course and network perspectives, but also point to future directions for expanding such efforts. For example, the overwhelming majority of prior studies fall into one of the four strategies, but clearly the various strategies are not mutually exclusive and often operate in tandem. Indeed, Offer and Fischer employ multiple strategies in their chapter focused on the bidirectional associations between kin and social support. They begin their empirical analyses with a descriptive analysis of the association between age and kin relations, finding that, not surprisingly, intergenerational relationships vary significantly across age (i.e., individual trajectories inform social networks). They then shift their analyses to examine the social support roles of kin (i.e., parents and adult children) in individuals' lives (i.e., social networks inform individual trajectories), finding that the social support of close kin varies across individuals' ages and relationship characteristics. Although challenging in manuscript organization, Offer and Fischer's approach benefits by recognizing the interplay between social networks and life course processes over time. Scholars working at the intersection of life course and network perspectives typically bite off one strategy and point the causal arrow in a single direction. Future studies, however, may follow the example of Offer and Fischer to build more complicated models that allow for dynamic, reciprocal, and cumulative processes at both the individual and system level. The immense opportunities and possibilities for growth make the intersection of life course and network perspectives an exciting area for future research. Studies in this volume provide the point of the spear for such endeavors and have created a solid foundation for future research.

References

Akers, R. L. (2011). *Social learning and social structure: A general theory of crime and deviance*. New Brunswick: Transaction.

Bandura, A. (1971). *Social learning theory*. New York: General Learning Press.

Cornwell, B., Laumann, E. O., Philip Schumm, L., & Graber, J. (2009). Social networks in the NSHAP study: Rationale, measurement, and preliminary findings. *Journal of Gerontology Series B: Psychological Sciences and Social Sciences, 64*(S1), 47–55.

McPherson, M., Smith-Lovin, L., & Cook, J. M. (2001). Birds of a feather: Homophily in social networks. *Annual Review of Sociology, 27*, 415–444.

Portes, A. (1998). Social capital: Its origins and applications in modern sociology. *Annual Review of Sociology, 24*, 1–24.

Schwartz, C. R. (2013). Trends and variation in assortative mating: Causes and consequences. *Annual Review of Sociology, 39*, 451–470.

Sutherland, E. H. (1947). *Principles of criminology* (4th ed.). Philadelphia: Lippincott.

Warr, M. (1998). Life-course transitions and desistance from crime. *Criminology, 36*(2), 183–216.

Derek A. Kreager is Professor of Sociology, Criminology, and Demography at Pennsylvania State University, Research Associate in the Population Research Institute, and Director of the Justice Center for Research. His research focuses on social networks and criminal/delinquent behavior, including the connection between the experiences of incarceration and community re-entry.

Diane H. Felmlee is Professor of Sociology and Demography at Pennsylvania State University and Research Associate in the Population Research Institute. Her interests lie at the intersection of social networks and life course studies, pursuing research on aggression and friendship networks, cyberbullying, and gender inequalities.

Duane F. Alwin is the inaugural holder of the Tracy Winfree and Ted H. McCourtney Professorship in Sociology and Demography at Pennsylvania State University, where he directs the Center for Life Course and Longitudinal Studies. He is also Emeritus Research Professor at the Survey Research Center, Institute for Social Research and Emeritus Professor of Sociology, University of Michigan, Ann Arbor, where he was affiliated for 23 years. His main areas of specialization include research methods, social stratification, social psychology, family and the life course.

Index

D. F. Alwin et al. (eds.), *Social Networks and the Life Course*, Frontiers in Sociology and Social Research 2, https://doi.org/10.1007/978-3-319-71544-5

The manufacturer's authorised representative in the EU is Springer Nature Customer Service Centre GmbH, Europaplatz 3, 69115 Heidelberg, Germany. If you have any concerns regarding our products, please contact ProductSafety@springernature.com

Printed and bound by CPI Group (UK) Ltd, Croydon, CR0 4YY
01/10/2026
02225959-0010